Sanders Dewees Bruce

The Horse-Breeder's Guide and Hand Book

Sanders Dewees Bruce

The Horse-Breeder's Guide and Hand Book

ISBN/EAN: 9783337145972

Printed in Europe, USA, Canada, Australia, Japan

Cover: Foto ©Lupo / pixelio.de

More available books at **www.hansebooks.com**

THE
HORSE-BREEDER'S GUIDE

HANDBOOK.

EMBRACING ONE HUNDRED TABULATED PEDIGREES OF THE PRINCIPAL SIRES, WITH FULL PERFORMANCES OF EACH AND BEST OF THEIR GET, COVERING THE SEASON OF 1883, WITH A FEW OF THE DISTINGUISHED DEAD ONES.

By S. D. BRUCE,

Author of the American Stud Book.

PUBLISHED AT
OFFICE OF TURF, FIELD AND FARM,
39 & 41 PARK ROW.
1883.

Entered, according to Act of Congress, in the year 1883,
By S. D. BRUCE,
In the Office of the Librarian of Congress, at Washington, D. C.

INDEX

TO THE

Stallions Covering in 1883,

WHOSE PEDIGREES AND PERFORMANCES, &c., ARE GIVEN IN THIS WORK,

ALPHABETICALLY ARRANGED, PAGES 1 TO 181, INCLUSIVE.

PART SECOND.

DEAD SIRES WHOSE PEDIGREES AND PERFORMANCES, &c., ARE GIVEN IN THIS WORK, PAGES 184 TO 205, INCLUSIVE, ALPHABETICALLY ARRANGED.

Index to Sires of Stallions described and tabulated in this volume.

			PAGE.
Abd-el-Kader	Sire of	Algerine	5
Adventurer	"	Blythwood	23
Alarm	"	Himyar	75
Artillery	"	Kyrle Daly	97
Australian	"	Badeu Badeu	11
"	"	Fellowcraft	47
"	"	Harry O'Fallon	71
"	"	Spendthrift	147
"	"	Springbok	149
"	"	Wilful	177
"	"	Wildidle	179
Beadsman	"	Saxon	143
Bel Demonio	"	Feebter	45
Billet	"	Elias Lawrence	37
"	"	Volturno	171
Blair Athol	"	Glen Athol	53
"	"	Highlander	73
"	"	Stonehege	151
Bonnie Scotland	"	Bramble	25
"	"	Luke Blackburn	109
"	"	Plenipo	129
Boston	"	Lexington	199
Breadalbane	"	Ill-Used	85
Citadel	"	Glenelg	55
Compeigne	"	Mortemer	119
Diomed	"	Sir Archy	203
Drake, The	"	Muscovy	121
Duroc	"	American Eclipse	185
Eclipse	"	Alarm	3
Enquirer	"	Blue Eyes	19
"	"	Falsetto	43
Faugh-a-Ballagh	"	Learnington	197
Flageolet	"	Rayon d'Or	133
Florizel	"	Diomed	193
Gilroy	"	Grinstead	69
Gladiateur	"	Athlete	9
"	"	Matador	113
Glen Athol	"	Glenmore	59
Glencoe	"	Vandal	205
Iago	"	Bonnie Scotland	189
Jack Malone	"	Bazar	13
Kentucky	"	Bertram	15
King Afonso	"	Foxhall	49
King Alfonso	"	Grenada	63
Kingcraft	"	Royalty	141

		PAGE
Kingston	Sire of Blue Mantle	21
King Tom	" Great Tom	65
"	" King Ban	91
"	" King Ernest	93
"	" Phaeton	201
Leamington	" Aristides	7
"	" Enquirer	39
"	" Eolus	41
"	" Hyder Ali	83
"	" Iroquois	87
"	" Lelaps	101
"	" Longfellow	107
"	" Onondaga	125
"	" Powhattan	131
"	" Reform	137
"	" Sensation	145
"	" Stratford	155
Lexington	" Duke of Magenta	33
"	" Kingfisher	95
"	" Legatee	99
"	" Lever	103
"	" Monarchist	117
"	" Norfolk	123
"	" Pat Malloy	127
"	" Tom Ochiltree	159
"	" Uncas	161
"	" Wanderer	173
Macaroni	" Maccaroon	111
"	" Moccasin	113
Monarque	" Brigadier	27
Newminster	" Hurrah	81
Nutbourne	" Woodlands	181
Parmesan	" Strachino	153
Phaeton	" King Alfonso	89
"	" Lisbon	105
"	" Ten Broeck	157
Planet	" Hubbard	79
"	" Whisper	175
Rataplan	" Dalnacardoch	131
Rosicrucian	" Rossifer	139
Socks	" Rebel	135
Sultan	" Glencoe	195
Thormanby	" Glengarry	57
Timoleon	" Boston	191
War Dance	" Bullion	29
"	" Glasgow	51
Waverly	" Duke of Montrose	35
West Australian	" Australian	187
Vandal	" Ventilator	163
"	" Virgil	167
Vauxhall	" Viator	165
Virgil	" Hindoo	77
"	" Virgilian	169
Voltigeur	" Billet	17

INDEX

TO DAMS OF HORSES TABULATED.

Dam	Of	Page
Aerolite	Dam of Fellowcraft	47
Aerolite	" Spendthrift	147
Alice Carneal	" Lexington	199
Araucaria	" Rayon d'Or	133
Atlantis	" King Ban	91
Babta	" Glenelg	55
Bernice	" Bertram	15
Betty Wharton	" Rebel	135
Bistre	" Highlander	73
Bonny Bell	" Blythewood	23
Buchu	" Blue Eyes	19
Calcutta	" Billett	17
Carbine	" Glengarry	57
Carolin	" Ventilator	163
Castianira	" Sir Archy	203
Capitola	" King Alfonso	89
Coimbra	" Stonehenge	151
Colleen Rhuc	" Kyrle Daly	97
Comtesse	" Mortemer	119
Coral	" Wanderer	173
Coral	" Uncas	161
Dora	" Plenipo	129
Ellermire	" Ill-Used	85
Eltham Lass	" Kingfisher	95
Emilia	" Australian	187
Ernestine	" King Ernest	98
Fanny Holton	" Ten Broeck	157
Fanny Washington	" Eolus	41
Farfaletta	" Falsetto	43
Fenella	" Rossifer	139
Florence	" Hindoo	77
Florizel Mare	" Boston	191
Girasol	" Saxon	143
Gloriana	" Pat Malloy	127
Gold Ring	" Bullion	29
Greta	" Glen Athol	53
Heatherbell	" Viator	165
Hester	" Springbok	149
Hilda	" Fechter	45
Hira	" Himyar	75
Hymenia	" Virgil	167
Ida Dickey	" Glasgow	51
Idlewild	" Wildidle	179
Ivy Leaf	" Bazar	13
Ivy Leaf	" Bramble	25
Jamaica	" Foxhall	49
Jovial	" Hurrah	81
Katona	" Tom Ochiltree	159
Kelpie	" Duke of Montrose	35
Lady Duke	" Hyder Ali	83
Lady Love	" Lisbon	105
Lady of the Manor	" Muscovy	121
La Henderson	" Virgilian	169
Lavender	" Baden Baden	11
Levity	" Legatee	99
Levity	" Lever	103
Lida	" Enquirer	39
Lotta	" Glenmore	59
Madame Strauss	" Moccasin	115
Magenta	" Duke of Magenta	33
Maggie B. B.	" Iroquois	87
Maiden	" Powhatan	131
Mattie Gross	" Grenada	175

		PAGE.
Mattie Gross	Dam of Whisper	175
Maud	" Alarm	3
May Bell	" Strachino	153
Mayonaise	" Delacardock	31
Merry Sunshine	" Phaeton	201
Mildred	" Monarchist	117
Millers Damsel	" Eclipse	185
Minnie Mansfield	" Hubbard	79
Nantura	" Longfellow	107
Nevada	" Luke Blackburn	109
Nina	" Algerine	5
Non Pareille	" Matador	113
Novice	" Norfolk	123
Pantaloon Mare	" Leamington	197
Paradigm	" Blue Mantle	21
Pussy	" Lelaps	101
Pussy	" Wilful	177
Queen Mary	" Bonny Scotland	189
Rose	" Royalty	141
Rose of Kent	" Athlete	9
Sarong	" Aristides	7
Songstress	" Maccaroon	111
Sovereign Mare	" Grinstead	69
Spectator Mare	" Diomed	193
Sprightly	" Elias Lawrence	37
Sprightly	" Volturno	171
Stolen Kisses	" Reform	137
Sunny South	" Harry O'Fallon	71
Susan Beane	" Sensation	145
Susan Beane	" Onondaga	125
Susan Beane	" Stratford	155
Sweet Lucy	" Brigadier	27
Trampoline	" Glencoe	195
Tranby Mare	" Vandal	205
Whiteface	" Woodlands	181
Woodcraft	" Great Tom	65

INTRODUCTION.

The author in compiling the tabulated pedigrees of the sires to be found in this work has been induced to do so in hopes of their proving useful to those engaged in breeding for the turf, or who are engaged in fostering this most popular national amusement. Very many of our largest breeders seem to ignore the lessons taught in the Stud Book and Racing Calender, and we commend to all the necessity of observing what sources and what course of breeding have produced the best results in England, which may be most properly called the home of the thoroughbred horse. We have given our own views as to the best mode to successfully breed the race-horse and the best mode to select a stallion and brood mare, and the treatment of the same both in the stud and on the farm. We do not expect that all will agree with us, but the ideas expressed and plans suggested will do away with many of the chances incident to breeding. There is much uncertainty, and always will be, attending the best and most careful mode of breeding, and this opinion is strongly exemplified in the frequent occurrence of one horse being of very high form and an excellent race-horse, and a full brother or sister being only ordinary; yet we differ from a great many in the opinion that breeding depends entirely upon chance. Accidents and other unforeseen causes, some of them so unimportant and abstruse as to escape our attention or come within our knowledge, may prevent the best bred and most promising animal from arriving at its natural size and true shape, and a little difference in conformation, symmetry, and constitution may make a decided difference in goodness and speed. The foal may be weak and have a delicate constitution owing to the dam being starved and exposed to hardships while carrying it, or it may have been improperly reared. This only proves that great care and knowledge are necessary in rearing horses for the turf, as well as judgment and attention in selecting mares and stallions from which to breed. The chief points are pure blood, conformation, constitution, racing lineage, and hereditary soundness. The nearer we get to true shape with the other points combined, the more certainly we will arrive at excellence. We often find a large horse of good shape and racing symmetry; but where there is one good large one, there are a dozen small or medium sized ones. The greater the size, when combined with the good qualities, the greater the excellence and his powers, for a good little horse cannot cope with a great good one. Hence size with constitution, soundness, and symmetry constitutes the height of perfection While we advocate and commend pure blood, we are convinced that very often pedigree is the only point at which some breeders look, ignoring altogether shape and action; hence failures. The establishment of reputation by a stallion depends on his having good mares, at first, for if he has only bad and indifferent ones, the produce will be in low form and a disappointment, and the horse condemned as a failure. To prove this, it is only necessary to cite the

Godolphin Arabian and Marske; the former but for the accident of covering Roxana and getting Lath would have died unknown, while Marske who had been standing for half a guinea and was sold for twenty guineas, after siring Eclipse was sold for one thousand guineas and covered at one hundred guineas. Squirt, the sire of Marske, had been ordered shot and was saved by the intercession of his groom; he afterwards got Marske, Syphon, and the celebrated Squirt Mare the dam of Maiden Purity, Pumpkin, and other famous horses. That many good race-horses have proved failures as stallions, and many poor race-horses successful ones no one can doubt, as instance Lath, who was a famous race-horse but an indifferent stallion, whilst his full brother Cade, was an indifferent race-horse but a most excellent stallion. Flying Childers dazzled the world by the splendor of his career on the turf, yet his brother, Bartlet's Childers proved far the better stallion. According to my notions, no horse can be a good race-horse or a successful stallion, that does not possess great symmetry, by which I do not mean beauty, but a show of all those points, such as conformation, length, power and muscle justly united. Notwithstanding it is often asserted that horses run in all shapes, it cannot be denied they run better and more frequently where they are well and truly shaped, and of tried and approved conformation. A horse may appear to the eye of ordinary judges very plain and ill-shaped, and still be in high form, and to the eye of a connoisseur right in all the material points for racing purposes; the machinery properly put together is the point. Chances and accidents are closely allied to all pursuits and more particularly to breeding for the turf, and luck very frequently predominates over skill and judgment, and whilst breeding cannot be made a certainty or reduced to a science it should not be left to chance. It cannot be too minutely studied, investigated or attended to in all its branches, and the breeder who selects his mares and stallions with care, attention and judgment as to purity of pedigree, symmetry of form, temper, soundness and constitution, in fact, those possessing all those essential qualities of speed and stoutness, must be more successful than one who breeds at haphazard and pays no regard to these established rules, at the same time crossing and preserving the blood of his mares judiciously, and aiming to remedy the defects, deficient properties and inferior qualities of his mares, by the superior conformation, symmetry, admirable properties, and brilliant qualities of the stallion, or vice versa; those who do this will be more likely to produce a more symmetrical, high-typed and successful race-horse than those who pay no attention to these points. Speculative experiments may suit those of large fortunes, but the thinking and judicious breeder, aware of the great expense, constant and unremitting attention necessary for success, will confine himself to the established practise of men whose experience, judgment, attention and success in breeding are worthy of imitation. It is a matter of opinion whether the offspring partake most of the sire or dam. There is no doubt but that they partake of both, though very often more of the one than the other. Some of the mares breed more after themselves, others more after the stallion, then again one foal will partake more after the mare and the next partake most after the horse. It also occasionally happens that the foal will color and mark after the grandsire or grandam or some other more distant cross, and partake of their qualities, hence the necessity of pure blood, conformation and soundness through many generations. To appreciate what care, attention and sound judgment have done for the thoroughbred horse, it is only necessary for us to look at his origin; unquestionably the thoroughbred horse as he now exists in his great perfection originated from a cross of the Arabian Barb and Turkish horse, the representative scions being the Godolphin and Darley Arabians; the former generally conceded to be a "Barb," was the sire of Lath, Cade, Regulus, Blank, Babraham, Bajazet, Old England, etc. It is said Mr. Coke brought him from France, and that he had actually drawn a cart in the streets of Paris. Mr. Coke gave him to Mr. Williams, keeper of the St. James Coffee House, by whom he was presented to Lord Godolphin, hence his name. He was teaser to Hobgoblin in the years 1730 and 1731, and on the latter refusing to cover Roxana by the Bald Galloway, she was bred to the Arabian, and from that cover produced Lath, the first colt ever credited to him, which brought him into prominent notice. He was represented 15 hands high. The Darley Arabian was the property of Mr. Darley, of Buttercramb, near York; he was the sire of the great Flying Childers, supposed to be the fastest horse in the world, sire of Second, Snip Blacklegs, etc., Bartlet's Childers and Almanzor. Bartlet's Childers never raced, but he was famous as a stallion; he was sire of Squirt (the sire of Marske and Syphon), and the Little Hartley Mare, the dam of Janus, Blank, Old England, Slouch, etc. The Curwen Bay Barb was a present to Louis XIV. of France from the Emperor of Morocco, and was brought into England by Mr. Curwen. St. Victor Barb was the sire of the Bald Galloway, and he was the sire of Roxana that brought the Godolphin Arabian into notice. The Compton Barb was sire of Coquette and others. Hutton's Bay Barb was sire of Blacklegs. The Byerly Turk was Capt. Byerly's charger in Ireland during King William's wars in 1089. It is from this horse that the Herod blood originated. Byerly Turk got Jigg, sire of Partner, who got Tartar, sire of Herod, who got Highflyer, sire of Sir Peter (Teazle). Sir Peter got Haphazard, Stamford, Walton, sire of Phantom and Partisan, Williamson's Ditto and Sir Oliver. Herod got Fortitude, Woodpecker, the sire of Buzzard, who sired Selim, the sire of Sultan, that sired Glencoe, Bay Middleton, etc. Herod got Florizel, sire of Diomed, who got Young Giantess and Sir Archy, sire of Timoleon, who got Boston, sire of Lexington, Lecompt, etc. Godolphin Arabian got Cade, sire of Matchem, who got Conductor, sire of Imperator and Trumpator. Trumpator got Sorcerer, the sire of Comus, and Smolensko. The Darley Arabian got Bartlet's Childers, sire of Squirt, who got Marske, sire of Eclipse, who got King Fergus, Mercury, Dungannon, Meteor, Saltram and Pot-8-os. Mercury got Gohanba, King Fergus got Benningbrough, the sire of Orville, who got Emilius, the sire of Priam and Plenipotentiary, and Master Henry; Muley, the sire of Margrave, Leviathan and others; Hambletonian, the sire of Whitelock, who got Blacklock, sire of Brutandorf, Voltaire, etc.; Saltram got Whiskey, the sire of Eleanor and Cressida, the dam of Priam; Pot-8-os got Waxy, the sire of Web, Whisker, the sire of Economist, who got Echidna and Harkaway, the sire of King Tom. Whalebone, the sire of Camel, who got Touchstone, the sire of Orlando and Newminster, the sire of The Hermit; Whalebone also got Sir Hercules, the sire of Irish Birdcatcher, the sire of The Baron, who got Stockwell, Rataplan etc., and Faugh-a-Ballagh the sire of Leamington. An examination of the Stud Book and Racing Calender will show that nearly the entire family of great race-horses both in England and America, dates back to the sources mentioned, and that it is extreme folly in our day to expect to improve the present magnificent race-horse by an infusion of the blood of the modern Arabian. We commenced upon the Arab Barb and Turk with a height not exceeding 15 hands, and have, by judicious crossing, generous diet, discreet and careful handling built up the most magnificent specimens of the equine race, ranging up to 17 hands in height, with bone, muscle, length, action and all the other grand qualities in proportion. In the early days of breeding, from necessity, very many of the best horses were very much inbred, and even incestuously so, and the question of inbreeding is one which commends itself strongly to mature consideration and examination. According to the maxim that "like produces like," we ought to follow form, blood, speed and other good qualities, and if these good qualities can be maintained and improved by inbreeding, then it must be desirable to a certain extent. Some of the best English and American horses were very much inbred, and the consanguinity of blood did not work deterioration. I am not an advocate of incestuous breeding, either in the human race or the brute creation, but there is no doubt that manly beauty, graceful form and intellectual vigor have resulted from preservation of those high qualities in the human race where not carried too far, and we can see no reason why the inbreeding of the truest best bred and best shaped racers can work an injury to the equine race. Still we think an out cross of pure blood with the essential qualities of a good race-horse and then back to the superior blood and conformation likely to produce the best results. We will give a few examples of inbred modern horses, in England and the same in America, and in doing so will select those of high character which distinguished themselves on the turf, and in the stud, for instance. The Baron, not only a good race-horse, but sire of Stockwell and Rataplan was by Birdcatcher, by Sir Hercules, by Whalebone, by Waxy, by Pot-8-os, by Eclipse. The Baron's dam, Echidna, by Economist, by Whisker, own brother to Whalebone, by Waxy, by Pot-8-os, by Eclipse, Echidna's dam, Miss Pratt by Blacklock, by Whitelock, by Hambletonian, by King Fergus, by Eclipse. Touchstone, a fine race-horse, and one of the best stallions that ever lived, was by Camel, by Whalebone, by Waxy, by Pot 8-os, by Eclipse, his dam, Banter by Master Henry, by Orville, by Beningbrough, by King Fergus, by Eclipse ; 2d dam, Boadicea by Alexander, by Eclipse. The great Stockwell was much inbred on his dam's side, Pocahontas by Glencoe, dam Marpessa, by Muley, by Orville, by Beningbrough, by King Fergus, by Eclipse. Muley's dam, Eleanor by Whiskey, by Saltram, by Eclipse. Pocahontas' grandam was Clare by Marmion, by Whiskey, by Saltram, by Eclipse ; Clare's dam, Harpalice by Gohanna, by Mercury, by Eclipse. Queen Mary, the dam of Blink Bonny, Bonnie Scotland, &c., was much inbred. Gladiator, her sire, was by Partisan, by Walton, by Sir Peter, by Highflyer, by Herod ; her dam by Plenipotentiary, by Emilius, by Orville, by Beningbrough, by King Fergus, by Eclipse ; her grandam, Myrrha by Whalebone, by Waxy, by Pot-8-os, by Eclipse ; her great grandam, Gift by Y. Gohanna, by Gohanna, by Mercury, by Eclipse, out of a daughter of Sir Peter, by Highflyer, by Herod. Partisan was out of Parasol, by Pot-8-os, by Eclipse. Pocahontas' best son, Stockwell, was by an inbred horse, and Blink Bonny, Queen Mary's best daughter, was by a horse Melbourne inbred to Herod and Eclipse, so if the preservation of good blood through inbreeding in these striking cases has been a success, is it not reasonable to suppose that the same results must follow inbreeding to good blood and true shape with other desirable qualities in this country? Boston was inbred to Diomed, as also his best son, Lexington. Wanderer and Uncas are both much inbred on the dam's side, being out of a granddaughter of Glencoe, and tracing to an own sister of the Old Hero. Glenmore, one of the best race-horses recently on the turf, and whose performances are of the best at all distances, is very much inbred; his dam, Lotta, is by Hunter's Glencoe, son of Imp. Glencoe and the blue filly Fiatt by Imp. Hedgeford, she out of Lady Thompkins by American Eclipse. Glenmore's grandam Sally Lewis is by Imp. Glencoe her dam Motto by Imp. Barefoot out of Lady Thompkins by Am. Eclipse. Barefoot was by Tramp and Glencoe's dam by Tramp, so that he is, strictly speaking, incestuously bred; yet he was a first class race-horse. Norfolk, a superior race-horse, is inbred to Sir Archy and Diomed. Falsetto is inbred to Lexington; the dam of his sire is by Lexington, and his grandam by Lexington, and he has nine crosses of Diomed. Imp. Eclipse was much inbred; his dam Gaze was by Bay Middleton son of Sultan and Cobweb by Phantom son of Walton, Flycatcher, his grandam, was by Godolphin son of Partisan by Walton, and his great grandam was an own sister to Cobweb by Phantom. Then if the Lexington, Leamington and Glencoe blood is to be preserved to the country it can only be done by a judicious course of inbreeding, and so uniting the choice of both as to combine and render permanent the qualities possessed by each. Some regard inbreeding as an active cause of degenerating, as unnatural and calculated to develop hereditary diseases. These evils can only spring from abuse of the system. If proper care is taken to exclude the weak and those having hereditary tendencies to disease, from participation in reproduction it may be the means of preserving those estimable qualities so much desired in the equine race, and transmitting them unimpaired to succeeding generations. The greatest success has been achieved by breeding from the nearest affinities of blood, and one should not hesitate to breed a half-brother or sister together where they possess many points of superiority. In the selection of a stallion we want first pure blood, size, substance and conformation with symmetry, not a tall narrow-chested horse, but one inclined to be thick-set; all coarseness should be avoided especially in the head, neck, shoulders, ankles and hocks; the eye should be large, clear and bright, with no coarse hair about it, the absence of which is indicative of high breeding in all animals; the jaw bones not too massive or heavy, tapering gradually to the nose, free from beefiness; good space between the jawbones for the windpipe; a clear, full steady eye denotes good temper and enduring qualities, whilst the one showing too much white is generally found in flighty, speedy, non-staying horses. The neck of moderate length, deep and not too thick at the crest or curve, nostrils large, full and roomy. The chest moderately wide, the shoulder blade oblique and inclined backward with sufficient muscle to cover it, with arms long and muscular, cannon bones short and flat, and the pasterns moderately long not upright, knee broad and flat and rather inclined to arch or bend over than backward or calf-kneed, which causes an extra tension on the back tendons; chest deep extending down between the elbows which should be straight, inclining neither in nor out, and toes pointed straight forward, body and barrel round and not too long, muscular arched loins, with good length from point of the hip to haunch bone, a slight drooping towards the root of the tail, good length from hip to point of stifle and thence to the hock, which should be broad, finely cut and free from beefiness; the cannon bones flat, tendons detached and well defined, feet strong and hoof not too large or too small, back ribs long, round, and slightly detached from the hip joint. There should be sufficient general length not to be determined by the length of the back, but the ground the horse covers when standing in a natural position. Good blood is essential and necessary, but good form is superiority. In the selection of brood mares, form is as much a desideratum as in the stallion. First select from the most fashionable blood from running families on both sides with conformation, constitution, good temper, and speed ; some prefer large mares, others of medium height. Large mares are not preferable because they are large, but if well and truly shaped, from running blood, there is no objection to size ; as a rule, the deep-chested, large-bodied, short-legged mares with large pelvis, with wide hips and good length, from 15 to 15¼ hands high, have proved the best and most successful brood mares. The mare, above all things, should be good-tempered and free from all hereditary defects and disease. It does not follow that a mare which may be blemished from some unforseen cause, may not be as good a brood mare as one entirely sound. Mares in good health will breed until twenty-five or thirty years old, but they require attention, air and exercise, with proper shelter from storms and bad weather, with sufficient food to keep them always in good strong condition—not beefy fat, as nothing is more fatal to fruitfulness than obesity. Unless kept in good strong condition, the foals are apt to be weak and weedy at birth ; the time to make a race-horse is when the foal is in embryo ; in the vernacular to make a race-horse you must do so before he is born. Stallions, to do themselves justice, must have plenty of exercise in the open air ; if they cannot be trusted in an open paddock they should be ridden three or four hours each day. Idleness results in indigestion, loss of vigor, and flatulence, which often prove fatal. The colts, from the day they are foaled should be fed, if the dam does not afford sufficient milk to insure speedy and healthy growth, and broken at weaning time, which should be the last of September or first of October. It is a capital plan to feed the colts in pens for a month or six weeks before weaning them, and we are decidedly of the opinion that foals which come the last of March or first of April have full as much advantage as those foaled earlier before the grasses necessary to afford an ample supply of milk from the dam arrive at perfection. Those who believe in having early foals should always sow down in the early fall a patch of good rye for the use of the mares and foals. Stallions, mares, and colts all require plenty of fresh air and exercise ; air and light is life—darkness, death. Horses, and particularly colts, from their natural activity, require more exercise than any other animals, and when properly given, is productive of the most salutary effects. It is the more necessary to colts highly fed than to those stinted or fed moderately. It enables you to preserve them in a perfect state of health. The food is converted into wholesome nourishment, the circulation of the blood promoted, and all the secretions and discharges facilitated. It invigorates the whole system, gives additional flow to the spirits, adds firmness and strength to the muscles, increases the firmness, texture and growth of the bone, promotes insensible perspiration, assists digestion and prevents flatulence and prepares the system for fresh supplies of aliment. It enables the animal to endure fatigue. In fact without constant and habitual exercise no animal can enjoy perfect health. High feeding without proper exercise produces many evils, such as indigestion, flatulency, costiveness ; the circulation becomes languid, incurable diseases follow, and frequently death terminates the scene. The stallions and mares thus treated, whose blood is pure and uncontaminated, and whose conformation, strength, activity and vigor are conspicuous in every movement, must impart to their offspring not only sound constitutions, but speed, native fire and energy, which are necessary to support them under the severest exercise of their powers. With the variety of soil, perennial grasses, and favorable climate, the Americans should excel all nations in producing the most perfect and the grandest of the equine race.

THE
HORSE-BREEDERS' GUIDE
AND
HAND BOOK.

ALARM

Will be located during the season of 1883 *at the Erdenheim Stud, Chestnut Hill, Pa. He will be allowed to serve mares at* $100 *each and* $5 *to the groom. Application to Major J. R. Hubbard, Chestnut Hill, Philadelphia, Pa.*

ALARM, by imp. Eclipse, was bred by Mr. John Hunter, of the Annieswood Stud, Westchester Co., N. Y., foaled 1869, dam, imported Maud, the dam of Maudina, Magnet, Telegram, etc., by imp. Australian out of Countess of Albermarle, by Lanercost. Maudina is the dam of Galway, Piccolo, Cloverbrook, Oden, etc. Orlando, the sire of imp. Eclipse, won the Derby in 1844. Stockwell, the sire of Maud, his dam, won the 2,000 guineas and St. Leger in 1852.

Alarm made his *debut* as a two-year old at Saratoga, Aug. 10, 1871, in a match of $5,000 a side against Inverary, by imp. Leamington, one mile, which he won in 1:47½, carrying 100 lbs. Aug. 17, ran third to Sue Ryder and Joe Daniels in the Kentucky Stakes, one mile, in 1:47½, beating St. Patrick, Experience Oaks, Hubbard and three others. Jerome Park, Oct. 7, ran second to Joe Daniels in Nursery Stakes, one mile, in 1:58, track heavy, beating Woodbine, Inversnaid, Victoria and three others. Oct. 10th, was beaten in the Desert Stakes, one mile, in 1:48, by Inverary. When three years old ran 5 races, and won them all. Jerome Park, June 1, won club purse, three-quarters of a mile, in 1:18, beating Midday, Frogtown, Tubman, Platina and four others. June 6, won club purse, 1¼ miles, in 2:17½, beating Rounder, Lord Byron and five others. June 13, won club purse, one mile, in 1:46, beating Alroy, Quintard and four others. Saratoga, July 15, won club purse, three-quarters of a mile, in 1:16, beating Platina, Piedmont, Elsie, Kingfisher and four others. July 17, won club purse, one mile, in 1:42¾, beating Fadladeen and Kingfisher, the fastest mile run to that date. This closed his turf career, winning in money $12,500. Alarm made his first season at the Walnut Hill Stud Farm, the property of James A. Grinstead, Fayette County, Ky. After the appearance of Himyar, he was purchased by A. Welch, of the Chestnut Hill Stud, Pennsylvania, and made the season of 1878 at the Dixiana Stud, Major B. G. Thomas', Fayette County, Ky. He is now at the head of the Erdenheim Stud, owned by Commodore N. W. Kittson, Chestnut Hill, Pennsylvania. Alarm is a bright bay horse, stands 15 hands 3¼ inches with his shoes, has a small star, with white on his right hind leg above the pastern, white on the left fore leg nearly to pastern, and a little white around the coronet of his right fore foot. He has a neat, expressive head; great breadth between the eyes; good width of jaw; good, strong, well-set neck; broad oblique shoulders; good depth of girth; large, good barrel; strong, muscular back; broad, strong hips, with great sweep in his hind quarters; good hocks, with sound legs and feet.

Stockwell, the sire of Maud the dam of Alarm, was the emperor of stallions. He sired St. Albans, winner of the St. Leger in 1860; Caller Ou, winner of St. Leger, 1861; The Marquis, winner of 2,000 guineas and St. Leger in 1862; Blair Athol, winner of both Derby and St. Leger in 1864; Lord Lyon, winner of 2,000 guineas, Derby and St. Leger in 1866; Regalia, winner of the Oaks in 1865; Achievement, winner of the Thousand Guineas, Doncaster Cup and St. Leger in 1867; Doncaster, winner of Derby in 1873; Gang Forward, winner of the 2,000 guineas in 1873, etc., etc. Lanercost, the sire of his grandam was a superior race-horse, was third in the St. Leger, won Cambridgeshire Stakes in 1839, and Ascot Gold Cup in 1841. He was a remarkable weight-carrier and stayer over a distance of ground. He was handicapped to give the celebrated Alice Hawthorn, when 4 years old, 51 lbs. He was sire of Van Tromp, winner of the St. Leger, in 1847, and Goodwood Cup in 1848; War Eagle, winner of Doncaster Cup in 1847; Catharine Hayes, winner of the Oaks in 1853; Ellerdale, dam of Ellington, winner of the Derby in 1856, etc., etc. The pedigree is full of stout and speedy crosses; Eclipse, in addition to Alarm, sired Remorseless, Regardless, Nemesis, etc. His stock were all speedy.

Alarm sired Danger, winner of the Vestal Stakes at Baltimore, 110 lbs., one mile, in 1:42½, the Fordham Handicap, 1¼ miles, in 2:15¾, 98 lbs. Himyar, one of the best race horses ever saddled, winner of three out of five of his two-year old stakes, three-quarters of a mile in 1:16½, and a mile in 1:44½ with 95 lbs. Himyar won three out of five starts as a three-year old. The Belle Meade Stakes at Nashville, 1¼ miles, in 2:43; the Phœnix Hotel Stakes at Lexington, Ky., 1¾ miles, track very muddy, and the January Stakes at St. Louis, mile heats, in 1:42½, 1:43½, 105 lbs. As four-year old won four consecutive races, one mile and furlong in 1:56, and two miles in 3:35. He won mile heats at five years old, 115 lbs., in 1:42½, 1:44½, the Merchants and Turf Stakes at Louisville, each 1¼ miles, in 1:55½, 1:57½, and club purse, same distance, in

(*Continued on 4th page.*)

PEDIGREE OF ALARM.

ALARM.	IMP. ECLIPSE.	Touchstone.	Camel.	Whalebone.	Waxy (Pot-8-o's)—Penelope by Trumpator (Conductor)—Prunella by High-flyer (Herod)—Promise by Snap (Snip)—Julia by Blank (Godol).
				Daughter of.	Selim—Maiden by Sir Peter (Highflyer)—Dau. of Phoenomenon—Matron by Florizel (Herod)—Maiden by Matchem (Cade)—Dau. of Squirt.
		Orlando.	Banter.	Master Henry.	Orville (Beningbrough)—Miss Sophia by Stamford (Sir Peter)—Sophia by Buzzard—Huncamunca by Highflyer—Cypher by Squirrel—Fribble's dam.
				Boadicea.	Alexander (Eclipse)—Bruuette by Amaranthus (Old England)—Mayfly by Matchem—Dau. of Starling (Ancaster)—Dau. of Grasshopper (Crab).
		Vulture.	Langar.	Selim.	Buzzard—Dau. of Alexander—Dau. of Highflyer—Dau. of Alfred (Matchem)—Dau. of Engineer (Sampson)—Bay Malton's dam by Cade.
				Daughter of.	Walton (Sir Peter)—Y. Giantess by Diomed—Giantess by Matchem—Molly Longlegs by Babraham—Dau. of Cole's Foxhunter—Sis. to Cato, by Partner.
			Kite.	Bustard.	Castrel (Buzzard)—Miss Hap by Shuttle (Y. Marske)—S. to Hap-hazard by Sir Peter—M. Hervey by Eclipse—Clio by Y. Cade—D. of Old Starling (Bay Bolton)
				Olympia.	Sir Oliver (Sir Peter)—Scotilla by Anvil (Herod)—Scota by Eclipse (Marske)—Harmony by Herod (Tartar)—Rutilia by Blank (Godol.)—D. of Regulus.
		Bay Middleton.	Sultan.	Selim.	Buzzard—D. of Alexander (Ecl.)—D. of Highflyer—D. of Alfred—D. of Engineer—Bay Malton's dam by Cade (Godol.)—Lass of the Mill by Traveler.
				Bacchante.	Williamson's Ditto (Sir Peter)—Sis. to Calomel by Mercury (Eclipse)—Dau. of Herod—Folly by Marske (Squirt)—Vixen by Regulus (Godol).
		Gaze.	Cobweb.	Phantom.	Walton—Julia by Whiskey (Saltram)—Y. Giantess by Diomed—Giantess by Matchem—Molly Longlegs by Babraham (Godol).
				Filagree.	Soothsayer (Sorcerer)—Web by Waxy (Pot-8-o's)—Penelope by Trumpator—Prunella by Highflyer—Promise by Snap—Julia by Blank—Spectator's dam.
		Flycatcher.	Sister to Godolphin.	Partisan.	Walton—Parasol by Pot-8-o's—Prunella by Highflyer—Promise by Snap—Julia by Blank—Spectator's dam by Partner—Dau. of Bay Bolton.
				Ridicule.	Shuttle (Y. Marske)—Sis. to Oatland's by Dungannon (Eclipse)—Letitia by Highflyer—Dau. of Matchem—Dau. of Blank—Dau. of Babraham.
			Cobweb.	Phantom.	Walton—Julia by Whiskey—Y. Giantess by Diomed—Giantess by Matchem—Molly Longlegs by Babraham—Dau. of Cole's Foxhunter.
				Filagree.	Soothsayer—Web by Waxy—Penelope by Trumpator—Prunella by Highflyer—Promise by Snap—Julia by Blank—Spectator's dam.
	IMP. MAUD.	Stockwell.	The Baron.	Sir Hercules.	Whalebone (Waxy)—Peri by Wanderer (Gohanna)—Thalestris by Alexander—Rival by Sir Peter—Hornet by Drone (Herod)—Manilla by Goldfinder.
				Guiccioli.	Bob Booty (Chanticleer)—Flight by Irish Escape (Commodore)—Y. Heroine by Bagot (Herod)—Heroine by Hero (Cade)—D. of Snap—S. to Regulus.
			Irish Birdcatcher.	Economist.	Whisker (Waxy)—Floranthe by Octavian (Stripling)—Caprice by Anvil—Madcap by Eclipse—Dau. of Blank—Dau. of Blaze (Childers).
				Miss Pratt.	Blacklock (Whitelock)—Gadabout by Orville (Beningbrough)—Minstrel by Sir Peter—Matron by Florizel—Maiden by Matchem.
		Pocahontas.	Echidna.	Sultan.	Selim—Bacchante by Williamson's Ditto—Sis. to Calomel by Mercury—Dau. of Herod—Folly by Marske—Vixen by Regulus—Dau. of Spot.
				Trampoline.	Tramp (Dick Andrews)—Web by Waxy—Penelope by Trumpator—Prunella by Highflyer—Promise by Snap—Julia by Blank—Spectator's dam.
			Glencoe.	Muley.	Orville—Eleanor by Whiskey—Y. Giantess by Diomed—Giantess by Matchem—Molly Longlegs by Babraham—Dau. of Cole's Foxhunter.
				Clare.	Marmion (Whiskey)—Harpalice by Gohanna (Mercury)—Amazon by Driver (Trentham)—Fractions by Mercury (Eclipse)—Dau. of Woodpecker.
		Marpessa.		Tramp.	Dick Andrews (Joe Andrews)—Dau. of Gohanna—Fraxinella by Trentham (Sweepstakes)—Dau. of Woodpecker—Everlasting by Eclipse.
				Daughter of.	Whisker—Mandane by Pot-8-o's—Y. Camilla by Woodpecker (Herod)—Camilla by Trentham—Coquette by the Compton Barb.
		Liverpool.		Bustard.	Buzzard—Gipsy by Trumpator—Sis. to Postmaster by Herod—Dau. of Snap (Snip)—Dau. of Gower Stallion (Godol)—Dau. of Childers.
				Greyhurst's dam	Election (Gohanna)—Sis. to Skyscraper by Highflyer—Everlasting by Eclipse—Hyæna by Snap—Miss Belsea by Regulus—Dau. of Bartlet's Childers.
		Otis.		Blacklock.	Whitelock (Hambletonian)—Dau. of Coriander (Pot-8-o's)—Wildgoose by Highflyer (Herod)—Cobeiress by Pot-8-o's—Manilla by Goldfinder (Snap)
				Daughter of.	Juniper (Whiskey)—Dau. of Sorcerer (Trumpator)—Virgin by Sir Peter—Dau. of Pot-8-o's—Editha by Herod—Elfrida by Snap—Dau. of Regulus.
		Dau. of Velocipede.		Cerberus.	Gohauna—Dau. of Herod—Desdemona by Marske—Y. Hag by Skim (Starling)—Hag by Crab (Alcock Arabian)—Ebony by Childers—Ebony by Basto.
		Lanercost. Sis. to Hornsea. Countess of Albemarle.		Miss Cranfield.	Sir Peter—Dau. of Pegasus (Eclipse)—Dau. of Paymaster (Blank)—Pomona by Herod—Caroline by Snap—Dau. of Regulus (Godol). Dau. of Hip (Curwen Bay Barb)—Large Hartly Mare by His Blind Horse (Holderness Turk)—Flying Whig by William's Woodstock Arabian—Dau. of St. Victor Barb—Dau. of Whynot (Fenwick Barb)—Royal Mare.

ALARM.—Continued.

1:54¾. He met and defeated the best. Gabriel, another son, ran thirty-three times as a three-year old and won nine races, and thirty-seven times at four years old, winning seventeen races. Amongst them were heats of a mile and a furlong in 1:56, 1:56, with 112 lbs, he defeated many of the best horses of the year. Other creditable performers of Alarm's get are Parthenia, Bruno, Jake White, America, Aliunde, Aureolus, City Merchant, Gunnar, Africa, Startle, Judge Murray, Alley, Soubrette, Athos, Breeze, Illusion, Flight, etc. It may be truly said that Alarm has scarcely had a fair chance in the stud, those of his get are the equals of the produce of other stallions from the same mares, and in most cases the best. He traces as an examination of his pedigree will show, to Whalebone and thence to Herod and Eclipse, through the most famous of their descendents, and to imp. Diomed on both sides of sire and dam. Mares possessing the Eclipse and Stockwell blood should be bred to Alarm to perpetuate the speedy strains of his blood.

ALGERINE,

(WINNER OF THE BELMONT STAKES AT JEROME PARK IN 1876,)

Will be located in the Algeria Stud, the property of Mr. Wm. L. Scott, near Erie, Pa. Services only by private contract.

ALGERINE, by Abd-el-Kader, son of imp. Australian, was bred by Major Thos. W. Doswell, Bullfield Stud, Hanover Junction, Va.; foaled 1873, dam Nina, the dam of Planet, Exchequer, Ninette, Ecliptic, &c., by Old Boston. Algerine did not run as a two-year old; he made his bow to the public in the Preakness Stakes at Baltimore in 1876, 1¼ miles, and was third to Shirley and Rappahonnock in 2:44¾. At Jerome Park he won the Belmont Stakes, 1½ miles in 2:40¼, beating Fiddlesticks, the winner of the Withers Stakes, Barricade, brother to Bassett (Charley Howard) and Red Coat, each carrying 110 lbs. He was unplaced in the Dixie Stakes, 2 miles, at Baltimore; won by Vigil in 3:41¼, track, muddy. As a four-year old he started five times, ran second to Parole in the Maturity Stakes at Jerome Park, 3 miles, in 5:39; second to St. James, 2 miles, in 3:49¼; was unplaced in the All-Aged Sweepstake, 1¼ miles, won by Tom Ochiltree in 2:43. Won club purse, 2 mile heats, at Baltimore, in 4:02½, 3:50, 4:00; track very heavy. Barricade won the second heat; was unplaced in the Bowie Stake, 4 mile heats, won by Ten Broeck in 7:42½, 7:40. Abd-el-Kader, his sire, although badly hipped, was a fine race-horse at all distances; he won a dash of 4 miles at Saratoga in 1869, in 7:31¾, a very creditable performance. Nina, the dam of Algerine, was one of the best race-mares of her day; she was a winner at all distances, from one to four mile heats, in good time, and produced Planet, one of the best horses in the country, at all distances, and for his chances a successful sire. Algerine is a blood bay, 15¾ hands, with black points, and no white about him. He is strongly inbred to Sir Archy, and on the sire's side is a grandson of the great West Australian, winner of the tripple events, 2,000 guineas, Derby and St. Leger, in 1853. Boston, the sire of his dam, was the best horse of any day. Algerine has no colts yet upon the turf, but from good mares should get winners and stayers; he traces on both sides of sire and dam many times, to Herod and Eclipse, through the famous Waxy and Dick Andrews, with the Archy and Diomed blood in both sides, through Diomed's best sons.

PEDIGREE OF ALGERINE.

ALGERINE.	ABD-EL-KADER.	Emilia.	Imp. Australian.	Young Emilius.	Mower-ina.	West Australian.	Melbourne.
					Humphrey Clinker. Daughter of.	Comus (Sorcerer)—Clinkerina by Clinker (Sir Peter)—Pewet by Tandem (Syphou)—Termagant by Tantrum (Cripple by Goldolphin.) Cervantes (Don Quixote)—Dau. of Paynator (Trumpator)—Sis. to Zodiac by St. George (Highflyer)—Abigail by Woodpecker (Herod)—Firetail.	
					Touchstone. Emma.	Camel (Whalebone)—Banter by Master Henry (Orville)—Boadicea by Alexander (Eclipse)—Brunette by Amaranthus (Old Eng.)—Mayfly. Whisker (Waxy)—Gibside Fairy by Hermes (Mercury)—Viciessitude by Pipator (Conductor)—Beatrice by Sir Peter—Pyrrha by Matchem (Cade.)	
			Berthune.	Sidi Hamet.	Persian.	Emilius. Shoveler.	Orville (Beningbrough)—Emily by Stamford (Sir Peter)—Dau. of Whiskey (Saltram)—Gr. Dorimant by Dorimant (Otho)—Dizzy by Blank. Scud (Beningbrough)—Goosander by Hambletonian (King Fergus)—Rally by Trumpator—Fancy by Florizel—Dau. of Spectator (Crab).
						Whisker. Variety.	Waxy (Pot-8-os)—Penelope by Trumpator (Conductor)—Prunella by Highflyer—Promise by Snap—Julia by Blank (Godol.)—Spectator's dam. Selim or Soothsayer (Sorcerer)—Sprite by Bobtail (Precipitate)—Catharine by Woodpecker—Camilla by Trentham (Sweepstakes)—Coquette.
		Rescue.				Virginian. Lady Burton.	Sir Archy (Diomed)—Meretrix by Magog (Chanticleer)—Narcissa by Imp. Shark (Marske)—Rosetta by Imp. Centinel (Blank)—Diana. Sir Archy (Diomed)—Sultana by the Barb Horse Black Sultan and out of the Barb Mare presented to Prest. Jefferson by the Bey of Tunis.
			Alice Carneal.	Imp. Sarpedon.	Susette.	Aratus. Jenny Cockracy.	Director (Sir Archy)—Betsey Haxall by Imp. Sir Harry (Sir Peter)—Timoleon's Dam by Imp. Saltram (Eclipse)—Dau. of Symme's Wildair. Potomac (Imp. Diomed)—Timoleon's dam by Imp. Saltram—Dau. of Symme's Wildair (Imp. Fearnought)—Dau. of Driver (Imp. Othello.)
				Rowena.		Emilius. Icaria.	Orville—Emily by Stamford—Dau. of Whiskey—Gr. Dorimant by Dorimant—Dizzy by Blank (Godol.)—Dizzy by—Driver Dau. of Smiling Tom. The Flyer (Vandyke, Jr.)—Parma by Dick Andrews (Joe Andrews)—May by Beningbrough (King Fergus)—Primrose by Mambrino (Engineer.)
						Sumpter. Lady Grey.	Sir Archy—Flirtilla's dam by Imp. Robin Redbreast (Sir Peter)—Dau. of Imp. Obscurity (Eclipse)—Siamerkin by Imp. Wildair (Cade)—Imp. Cub Mare. Robin Grey (Imp. Royalist)—Maria by Melzar (Imp. Medley)—Dau. of Imp. Highflyer (Highflyer)—Dau. of Imp. Fearnought (Regulus).
	NINA.	Imp. Frolicksome Fanny.	Sister to Catterick.	Lottery.	Robin Brown's dam.	Imp. Diomed. Castianira.	Florizel (Herod)—Sister to Juno by Spectator (Crab)—Horatia by Blank—Dau. of F. Childers (Darley Arabian)—Miss Belvoir by Grey Grantham. Rockingham (Highflyer)—Tabitha by Trentham—Dau. of Bosphorus (Babraham)—Dau. of Wm.'s Forester (Forester)—Dau. of Coalition Colt.
			Dau. of Whisker.	Timoleon.	Boston.	Imp. Saltram. Daughter of.	Eclipse (Marske)—Virago by Snap (Snip)—Dau. of Regulus (Godol.)—Sis. to Othello by Crab (Alcock Arabian)—Miss Slamerkin by Y. True Blue. Symme's Wildair—Dau. of Old Driver (Imp. Othello)—Dau. of Imp. Fallower (Blank by Godol.)—Dau. of Imp. Vampire (Regulus).
					Ball's Florizel.	Imp. Diomed. Daughter of.	Florizel—Sister to Juno by Spectator—Horatia by Blank—Dau. of Childers—Miss Belvoir by Gr. Grantham (Brownlow Turk). Imp. Shark—Dau. of Harris' Eclipse (Partner)—Dau. of Imp. Fearnought—Dau. of Imp. Jolly Roger (Roundhead)—Dau. of Sober John.
			Mandane.	Dau. of Florizel.	Dau. of Sir Archy.	Imp. Alderman. Daughter of.	Pot-8-os (Eclipse)—Lady Bolingbroke by Squirrel (Traveler)—Cypron Herod's dam, by Blaze (Childers)—Sellma by Bethel's Arabian. Imp. Clockfast (Gimcrack)—Dau. of Symme's Wildair—Dau. of Imp. Fearnought—Imp. Kitty Fisher by Cade—Dau. of Cullen Arabian.
			Tramp.			Dick Andrews. Daughter of.	Joe Andrews—Dau. of Highflyer (Herod)—Dau. of Cardinal Puff (Babraham)—Dau. of Tatler (Blank)—Dau. of Snip (Childers)—Dau. of Godol. Gohanus (Mercury)—Fraxinella by Trentham—Dau. of Woodpecker (Herod)—Everlasting by Eclipse—Hyaena by Snap (Snip).
						Pot-8-o's. Young Camilla.	Eclipse—Sportsmistress by Warren's Sportsman (Cade)—Golden Locks by Oroonoko (Crab)—Valiant's dam by Crab—Dau. of Partner. Woodpecker—Camilla by Trentham—Coquette by Compton Barb—Sis. to Regulus by Godol. Arabian—Gr. Robinson by The Bald Galloway.
						Waxy. Penelope.	Pot-8-os—Maria by Herod (Tartar)—Lisette by Snap—Miss Windsor by Godol. Arabian—Sis. to Volunteer by Y. Belgrade—Dau. of B. Childer's Trumpator—Prunella by Highflyer—Promise by Snap—Julia by Blank—Spectator's dam by Partner—Bonny Lass by Bay Bolton.
						Bay Trophonius. Daughter of.	Beningbrough—Dau. of Phoenomenon (Herod)—Matron by Florizel—Maiden by Matchem (Cade)—Dau. of Squirt (Bartlet's Childers). Slope (Highflyer)—Lardella by Y. Marske—Dau. of Cade (Godol.)—Beaufremont's dam by Bro. to Fearnought—Miss Wyndham by Wyndham (Old Hautboy)—Dau. of Belgrade Turk—Old Scarborough Mare by Makeless (Oglethorpe Arabian)—Dau. of Brimmer (D'Arcy Yellow Turk).

ARISTIDES,

(WINNER OF THE KENTUCKY DERBY AT LOUISVILLE, THE WITHERS AND JEROME STAKES AT JEROME PARK, AND BRECKENRIDGE STAKES AT BALTIMORE, ALL IN 1875,)

Will stand the season of 1883 *at the Stud farm of Albert Hankins, near Hebron, Indiana, at* $50 *the season. Apply to A. Hankins, Hebron, Indiana.*

ARISTIDES, by imp. Leamington, was bred by the late H. P. McGrath, of McGrathiana Stud, near Lexington, Ky., foaled spring of 1872, his dam, Sarong, is by Lexington, out of the Greek Slave, by Imp. Glencoe. Aristides commenced his turf career at Lexington, Ky., by running second to Leona in a sweepstake for two-year olds, half a mile, in 49½ sec. ; was unplaced in Juvenile Stakes, half a mile, at Jerome Park ; won by Meco in 50½ ; at Monmouth Park was unplaced in the Hopeful Stakes, half a mile ; won by Caroline in 51 sec. ; was second to Sweetlips in the Thespian Stakes, same place, three-quarters of a mile in 1:18. At Saratoga was unplaced in the Saratoga Stakes, three-quarters of a mile, won by Willie Burk, in 1:23¾ ; track heavy. Same place won a handicap purse, one mile, with 96 lbs., in 1:46¼, defeating a field of five. Jerome Park, fall meeting, ran second to James A. for club purse, three-quarters of a mile, in 1 18½, four others behind him. Baltimore, Md., won club purse for two year olds, one mile, in 1·44¾, carrying 100 lbs., the best race made by a two-year old to that date. As a three-year old he started nine times, and won four races. Was unplaced in Phœnix Hotel Stakes, one mile and a furlong, won by Ten Broeck in 2:11¾, track very muddy. Louisville, Ky , won the Kentucky Derby, 1½ miles, 100 lbs. on each, in 2:37¾ ; in this race he beat Volcano, Verdigris, Bob Woolley, Ten Broeck, and ten others, including Searcher, Bill Bruce and McCreery. Jerome Park, won the Withers Stake, one mile, 110 lbs., in 1:45¾, beating Rhadamanthus, Ozark, and ten others. Same place, ran second to his stable companion, Calvin, which McGrath had backed heavy, in the Belmont Stake, 1½ miles, in 2:42¼, Milner, Ozark, Tom Ochiltree, and nine others behind him. Monmouth Park, ran second to Ozark in the Ocean Hotel Stake, 1¾ miles, in 3:10¼. Saratoga, was third to D'Artagnan and Milner in the Travers Stake, 1¾ miles, 3:06¼, each carrying 110 lbs., the fastest race run with the weights to that date. Jerome Park, Fall Meeting, won the Jerome Stakes, 2 miles, in 3:43, beating Calvin, Joe Cerns, and five others. Baltimore, was unplaced in the Dixie Stakes, 2 miles, won by Tom Ochiltree in 3:42½, with Viator second, weights 110 lbs. Same place, won the Breckenridge Stakes, 2 miles, in 3:36½. Viator second, Ochiltree third, he carrying 115 lbs. to 110 lbs. on the others. As a four-year old started in and won two races, both run at Lexington, Ky. Won a sweepstake for four-year olds, 2 miles and a furlong, in 3:45½, beating Ten Broeck, each 104 lbs. This was the fastest race ever run at the distance, and so remained until beaten by Monitor at Baltimore, October 20th, 1880, then four years old, with 110 lbs., ran the distance in 3:44½. Won club purse, 2½ miles, 104 lbs., in 4:27½, the fastest race ever run at the distance, beating Bazar, Elemi and War Jig. He ran only one other race, 1½ miles, won by Ten Broeck in 2:48¼, in which he was unplaced, having bad legs from splints. Henlopen is the only one of his get yet started in public. She won the Clabaugh Memorial Stakes, half a mile, in 51 seconds, at Baltimore, and the Juvenile Stakes, half a mile, in 50 seconds, at Jerome Park, defeating large fields in both races. $15,000 was offered and refused for her after this race. Aristides is a red chestnut, 15¾ hands high, a large star and both hind feet white ; he is a very finely-shaped horse, with plenty of bone and substance. He is one of the Leamington's, having a deep infusion of Archy and Diomed blood, with the Waxy blood through Whalebone and Web, he must be a success, as a stallion.

PEDIGREE OF ARISTIDES.

ARISTIDES							
SARONG.	IMP. LEAMINGTON.	Faugh-a-Ballagh.	Sir Hercules.	Waxy.	Pot-8-os—Maria by Herod—Lisette by Snap—Miss Windsor by Godol. Arabian—Sister to Volunteer by Y Belgrade.		
				Penelope.	Trumpator—Prunella by Highflyer—Promise by Snap—Julia by Blank—Spectator's dam by Partner—Bonny Lass.		
			Peri. Whalebone.	Wanderer.	Gohanna—Catherine by Woodpecker—Camilla by Trentham—Coquette by Compton Barb.—Sister to Regulus by Godol. Arabian.		
				Thalestris.	Alexander—Rival by Sir Peter—Hornet by Drone—Manilla by Goldfinder—Dau. of Old England—Daughter of Cullen Arabian.		
		Guiccoli.	Bob Booty.	Chanticleer.	Woodpecker—Dau. of Eclipse—Rosebud by Snap—Miss Belsea by Regulus—Dau. of Bart Childers—Dau. of Honeywood's Arabian.		
				Ierne.	Bagot—Dau. of Gamahoe—Patty by Tim—Miss Patch by Justice—Ringtail Galloway by Cur. Bay Barb—Sister to Witty Mare by Hip.		
			Flight.	Irish Escape.	Commodore—Buffer's dam by Highflyer—Shift by Sweetbriar—Black Susan by Snap—Dau. of Cade—Dau. of Belgrade—Dau. of Clif. Arabian.		
				Young Heroine.	Bagot—Heroine by Hero—Dau. of Snap—Sis. to Regulus by Godol. Arabian—Gr. Robinson by Bald Galloway—Dau. of Snake—Gray Wilkes.		
		Pantaloon.	Castrel.	Buzzard.	Woodpecker—Misfortune by Dux—Curiosity by Snap—Dau. of Regulus—Dau. of Bartlet's Childers—Dau. of Hon. Arabian—Byerly Mare.		
				Daughter of.	Alexander—Dau. of Highflyer—Dau. of Alfred—Dau. of Engineer—Bay Malton's dam by Cade—Lass of the Mill by Traveler—Miss Makeless.		
	Daughter of		Idalia.	Peruvian.	Sir Peter—Dau. of Budrow—Escape's dam by Squirrel—Dau. of Babraham—Dau. of Golden Ball—Busby Molly by Hamp. Ct. Childers.		
				Musidora.	Meteor—Maid of all Work by Highflyer—Sis. to Tandem by Syphon—Dau. of Regulus—Dau. of Sulp—Dau. of Cottingham—Warlock Galloway.		
		Daphne.	Laurel.	Blacklock.	Whitelock—Dau. of Coriander—Wildgoose by Highflyer—Coheiress by Pot-8-os—Manilla by Goldfinder—Dau. of Old Eng.—Dau. of Cul. Arabian.		
				Wagtail.	Prime Minister—Dau. of Orville—Miss Grimstone by Weasel—Dau. of Ancaster (Blank)—Daughter of Dam Arabian—Dau. of Sampson.		
			Maid of Honor.	Champion.	Selim—Podagra by Gouty—Jet by Magnet—Jewel by Squirrel—Sophia by Blank—Diana by Second—Dau. of Stanyan Arabian.		
				Etiquette.	Orville—Boadicea by Alexander—Brunette by Amaranthus—Mayfly by Matchem—Dau. of Ancaster Starling—Dau. of Grasshopper.		
	Lexington.	Boston.	Timoleon.	Sir Archy.	Diomed—Castianira by Rockingham—Tabitha by Trentham—Dau. of Bosphorus—Dau. of Wm.'s Forester—Dau. of Coalition Colt (Godol).		
				Daughter of.	Saltram—Dau. of Symme's Wildair—Dau. of Tyler's Driver—Dau. of Imp. Fallower (Blank)—Dau. of Imp. Vampire (Regulus).		
			Sis. to Tuckahoe.	Ball's Florizel.	Diomed—Dau. of Imp. Shark—Dau. of Harris' Eclipse—Dau. of Fearnought—Dau. of Jolly Roger—Dau. of Sober John (Rib).		
				Daughter of.	Imp. Alderman—Dau. of Clockfast—Dau. of Symme's Wildair—Y. Kitty Fisher by Fearnought—Imp. Kitty Fisher by Cade (Godol).		
		Alice Carneal.	Sarpedon.	Emilius.	Orville—Emily by Stamford—Dau. of Whiskey—Gr. Dorimant by Dorimant—Dizzy by Black—Dizzy by Driver—Dau. of Smiling Tom.		
				Icaria.	The Flyer—Parma by Dick Andrews—May by Benningbrough—Primrose by Mambrino—Cricket by Herod—Sophia by Blank (Godol).		
			Rowena.	Sumpter.	Sir Archy—Flirtilla's dam by Imp. Robin Redbreast—Dau. of Obscurity (Eclipse)—Slamerkin by Wildair—Imp. Cub Mare by Cub.		
				Lady Grey.	Robin Grey—Maria by Melzar—Dau of Imp. Highflyer—Dau. of Imp. Fearnought—Dau. of Ariel—Dau. of Jack of Diamonds.		
	Glencoe.	Sultan.		Selim.	Buzzard—Dau. of Alexander—Dau. of Highflyer—Dau. of Alfred—Dau. of Engineer—Bay Malton's Dam by Cade—Lass of the Mill by Traveler.		
				Bacchante.	Williamson's Ditto—Sis. to Calomel by Mercury—Dau. of Herod—Folly by Marske—Vixen by Regulus—Dau. of Hutton's Spot.		
		Trampoline.		Tramp.	Dick Andrews—Dau. of Gohanna—Fraxinella by Trentham—Dau. of Woodpecker—Everlasting by Eclipse—Hyaena by Snap (Snip).		
Greek Slave.				Web.	Waxy—Penelope by Trumpator—Prunella by Highflyer—Promise by Snap—Julia by Blank—Spectator's dam by Partner—Dau. of Bay Bolton.		
Margaret Hunter.	Margrave.			Muley.	Orville—Eleanor by Whiskey—Y Giantess by Diomed—Giantess by Matchem—Molly Longlegs by Babraham—Dau. of Cole's Foxhunter.		
Mary Hunt.				Tommy's dam.	Election—Fair Helen by Hambletonian—Helen by Delpini—Rosalind by Phoenomenon—Atalanta by Matchem—Lass of the Mill by Oroonoko.		
				Bertrand.	Sir Archy—Eliza by Imp. Bedford—Imp. Mambrina by Mambrino—Sally by Blank—Dau. of Ward (Crab)—Dau. of Merlin (Bustler).		
				Betty Coons.	Hephestion (Imp. Buzzard)—Spot by Hampton's Twigg (Jolly Friar)—Dau. of Imp. Bedford (Dungannon by Eclipse)—Dau of Harlequin (Imp. Gabriel)—Dau. of Imp. Fearnaught Regulus by Godolphin Arabian.		

ATHLETE (Imp.)

Athlete will stand the season of 1883 at Kinlock Stud farm near Columbia, Boone County, Mo., at $50 the season; dams of Winners free. Application to be made to J. Lucas Turner, Columbia, Mo. Imported by D. D. Withers, Esq:

ATHLETE, by Gladiateur, bred by Mr. W. Blenkiron, foaled 1872, dam Rose of Kent dam of Maiden's Blush, Hopbine Spartacus, Kentish Rose., etc, by Kingston out of England's Beauty by Birdcatcher. Athlete started in three races at two years old, but was unplaced in all. At three years old ran four times, won club purse at Jerome Park one mile for maiden three year olds, in 1:51; track heavy. He ran third to Leander in a handicap for all ages three-quarters of a mile in 1·21¾ and was unplaced in the other two races. Gladiateur his sire was the sensational horse of his year and accomplished what no other horse ever did—he won the two thousand guineas, Derby and St. Leger, in England, and the Grand Prix de Paris in France in 1865, and the Ascot Gold Cup in 1866. Kingston, the sire of his dam, was one of the best and most famous race-horses of his day and was truly bred to stay through his Venison and Defence blood. He was sire of Queen Bertha, winner of the Oaks, and Caractacus, winner of the Derby; Rose of Kent, the dam of Athlete, is own sister to Silverhair the dam of Garterly Bell and Silvio; the latter won both the Derby and St. Leger in 1877. Athlete is very much inbred to Whalebone through his most popular and successful sons, such as Defence, Moses, Merman, Camel and the great Sir Hercules, and is fortified by the blood of Herod and Eclipse. Athlete is a dark chesnut with a small white stripe down his face from the forehead to the nose and is full 15½ hands high. We can scarcely see how he can fail in the stud; no descendant of Old Prunella through pure strains of blood has yet failed to breed winners as evidenced by the success of Whalebone, Whisker, Web, Glencoe and others. Athlete traces six times to old Prunella, three times on side of sire and the same on his dam's side, to the blood of Herod and Eclipse from popular and successful racing sources.

PEDIGREE OF ATHLETE.

ATHLETE.	GLADIATEUR.	Monarque.	T. Baron—Sting or T. Emp'r.*	Defence.	Whalebone.	Waxy—Penelope by Trumpator—Prunella by Highflyer—Promise by Snap—Julia by Blank—Spectator's dam.
					Defiance.	Rubens—Little Folly by Highland Fling—Harriet by Volunteer—Dau. of Alfred—Magnolia by Marske—Dau. of Babraham.
				Sis. to Dang'ous.	Reveller.	Comus—Rosette by Beningbrough—Rosamond by Tandem—Tuberose by Herod—Gr. Starling by Starling—Coughing Polly.
					Design.	Tramp—Defiance by Rubens—Little Folly by Highland Fling—Harriet by Volunteer—Dau. of Alfred—Magnolia by Marske.
			Poetess.	Royal Oak.	Catton.	Golumpus—Lucy Grey by Timothy—Lucy by Florizel—Frenzy by Eclipse—Dau. of Engineer—Dau. of Blank—Lass of the Mill.
					Daughter of.	Smolensko—Lady Mary by Beningbrough—Dau. of Highflyer—Dau. of Marske—A-la-Greeque by Regulus—Dau. of Allworthy.
				Ada.	Whisker.	Waxy—Penelope by Trumpator—Prunella by Highflyer—Promise by Snap—Julia by Blank—Spectator's dam.
					Anna Bella.	Shuttle—Dau. of Drone—Contessina by Y. Marske—Tuberose by Herod—Gr. Starling by Starling—Coughing Polly.
		Miss Gladiator.	Gladiator.	Partisan.	Walton.	Sir Peter—Papillon by Snap—Miss Cleveland by Regulus—Midge by Son of Bay Bolton—Dau. of Bart. Childers—Dau. of Hon Arabian.
					Parasol.	Pot-8-os—Prunella by Highflyer—Promise by Snap—Julia by Blank—Spectator's dam by Partner—Bonny Lass by Bay Bolton.
				Pauline.	Moses.	Whalebone or Seymour—Sister Castanea by Gohanna—Grey Skim by Woodpecker—Silver's dam by Herod—Y. Hag by Skim.
					Quadrille.	Selim—Canary Bird by Whiskey or Sorcerer—Canary by Coriander—Miss Green by Highflyer—Harriet by Matchem—Flora by Regulus.
			Taffrail.	Sheet Anchor.	Lottery.	Tramp—Mandane by Pot-8-os—Y. Camilla by Woodpecker—Camilla by Trentham—Coquette by Compton Barb—Sis. to Regulus.
					Morgiana.	Muley—Miss Stephenson by Scud or Sorcerer—Sis. to Petworthby Precipitate—Sis. to Juniper by Snap—Young Marske's dam by Blank.
				Warwick Mare.	Merman.	Whalebone—Mermaid by Orville—Dau. of Sir Solomon (Sir Peter)—Miss Brim by Highflyer—Brim by Squirrel—Helen by Blank.
					Daughter of.	Ardrossan—Shepherdess by Shuttle—Dau. of Buzzard—Ann of the Forest by King Fergus—Miss West by Matchem (Cade).
	ROSE OF KENT.	Kingston.	Venison.	Partisan.	Walton.	Sir Peter—Papillon by Snap—Miss Cleveland by Regulus—Midge by Son of Bay Bolton—Dau. of Bart Childers—Dau. of Hon. Arabian.
					Parasol.	Pot-8-os—Prunella by Highflyer—Promise by Snap—Julia by Blank—Spectator's dam by Partner—Bonny Lass by Bay Bolton.
				Fawn.	Smolensko.	Sorcerer—Wowski by Mentor (Justice) Maria by Herod—Lisette by Snap—Miss Windsor by Godol. Arabian—Sis. to Volunteer.
					Jerboa.	Gohanna—Camilla by Trentham—Coquette by Compton Barb—Sis. to Regulus by Godol. Arabian—Gr. Robinson by Bald Galloway.
			Queen Anne.	Slane.	Royal Oak.	Catton—Dau. of Smolensko—Lady Mary by Beningbrough—Dau. of Highflyer—Dau. of Marske—A-la-Grecque by Regulus—Dau. of Allworthy.
					Daughter of.	Orville—Epsom Lass by Sir Peter—Alexina by King Fergus—Lardella by Y. Marske—Dau. of Cade—Beufremont's dam.
				Garcia.	Octavian.	Stripling (Phoenomenon)—Dau. of Oberon (Highflyer)—Sis. to Sharper by Ranthos (Matchem)—Dau. of Sweepstakes—Sis. to Careless.
					Daughter of.	Shuttle (Y. Cade)—Katharine by Delpini—Dau. of Paymaster (Blank)—Dau. of Le Sang (Changeling)—Dau. of Rib (Crab)—Mother Western.
		England's Beauty.	Irish Birdcatcher.	Sir Hercules.	Whalebone.	Waxy—Penelope by Trumpator—Prunella by Highflyer—Promise by Snap—Julia by Blank—Spectator's dam by Partner—Bonny Lass.
					Peri.	Wanderer—Thalestris by Alexander—Rival by Sir Peter—Hornet by Drone—Manilla by Goldfinder—Dau. of Old England (Godol).
				Guiccioli.	Bob Booty.	Chanticleer—Ierne by Bagot—Dau. of Gamahoe—Patty by Tim—Miss Patch by Justice—Ringtail Galloway by Curwen Bay Barb.
					Flight.	I. Escape—Y. Heroine by Bagot—Heroine by Hero (Cade)—Dau. of Snap—Sis. to Regulus by Godol. Arabian—Grey Robinson.
			The Prairie Bird.	Touchstone.	Camel.	Whalebone—Dau. of Selim—Maiden by Sir Peter—Dau. of Phoenomenon—Matron by Florizel—Maiden by Matchem—Dau. of Squirt.
					Banter.	Master Henry—Boadicea by Alexander—Brunette by Amaranthus (Old Eng.)—Mayfly by Matchem—Dau. of An. Starling.
				Zillah.	Reveller.	Comus—Rosette by Beningbrough—Rosamond by Tandem—Tuberose by Herod—Gr. Starling by Starling—Coughing Polly.
					Morisca.	Morisco (Muley)—Waltz by Election (Gohanna)—Penelope by Trumpator (Conductor)—Prunella by Highflyer (Herod)—Promise by Snap (Snip)—Julia by Blank (Godolphin)—Spectator's dam by Partner (Jigg)—Bonny Lass by Bay Bolton (Grey Hautboy)—Dau. of Darley Arabian—Dau. of Byerly Turk—Dau. of Taffolet Barb—Dau. of Place's White Turk—Natural Barb Mare.

*Emperor given.

BADEN-BADEN,

(WINNER OF THE YOUNG AMERICA STAKE No. I., 1376, AT NASHVILLE, TENN., AND KENTUCKY DERBY AT LOUISVILLE, KY., 1877, THE JERSEY DERBY AT LONG BRANCH AND TRAVERS STAKES AT SARATOGA, 1877.)

Will be used as private stallion in the Ferncliff Stud, the property of William Astor, Esq., near Rhinebeck, Dutchess Co., N. Y.

BADEN-BADEN, by imp. Australian, son of West Australian, bred by A. J. Alexander Woodburn Stud, Kentucky, foaled 1874, dam Lavender, the dam of Helmbold, Buchu Barricade, &c., by Wagner, son of Sir Charles, out of Alice Carneal, dam of Lexington, Waxy, Rescue, &c., by Imp Sarpedon, son of Emilius. Imp Australian, the sire of Baden Baden, can be found in this book. West Australian, his sire, was a winner of the double events in England, Derby and St. Leger. Wagner, the sire of Lavender, was the race horse of his day, and defeated the Kentucky crack, Grey Eagle, in the noted four-mile heat races run at Louisville, Kentucky, in 1839, which were the fastest to that day. Alice Carneal, his grandam, was the dam of Lexington the incomparable race horse and emperor of stallions. Baden Baden was a first-class race horse, at two years old, started five times. At Louisville, Kentucky, was second to McWhirter in the Belle Meade Stakes (three-quarters of a mile) in 117, with Lisbon and three others behind him. Ran second to Belle of the Meade in the Sanford Stake (one mile) in 144¼ (very fast), Sallie McCrea, McWhirter, Glentina, and three others behind him. Was second to Belle of the Meade in Sweepstake (one mile) in 144¼, beating McWhirter, Springbranch, and Eva Shirley. At Nashville won the Young America Stakes No. 2 (one mile) in 146¾, beating King William and three others. At three years old won the Kentucky Derby (one and a half miles) in 238, beating Leonard, King William, McWhirter, Vera Cruz, Dan K and five others. Was unplaced in the Clark Stakes (two miles), won by McWhirter in 330¼. Jerome Park, Was beaten a head for second place in Belmont Stake (one and a half miles) by Loiterer, Cleverbrook winning in 246, track heavy. Long Branch won the Jersey Derby (one and a half miles) in 240¾, beating Basil, Rifle and three others. Saratoga won the Travers Stake (one and threequarters miles) in 312¼, track heavy, beating Brademante, St. James, Cleverbrook and four others. Was unplaced in Kenner Stakes (two miles), won by Basil in 338½. Baden-Baden was sent away full a hundred yards behind, yet at the end of a mile and five furlongs he was in front, and had the race won, when he broke his ankle and was ruined for racing purposes. On his sire's side he has the Melbourne, Touchstone, Emilius and Whisker blood, and on the dam's side is much inbred to Sir Archy and Diomed, and goes back to Alice Carneal, the great fountain head of race horses and successful sires. Baden-baden is a dark chestnut, 16¼ hands high, with a star in his forehead, the only white about him. He has elegant shoulders, and is a finely-shaped horse all over. His oldest colts, now coming two years old, are promising.

PEDIGREE OF BADEN-BADEN.

BADEN-BADEN.		IMP. AUSTRALIAN.	West Australian.	Melbourne.	Touchstone.	Daughter of Humphrey Clinker.	Comus.	Sorcerer—Houghton Lass by Sir Peter—Alexina by King Fergus—Lardella by Y. Marske—Dau. of Cade—Beaufremont's dam by Bro. to Fearn'
							Clinkerina.	Clinker—Pewet by Tandem—Termagant by Tantrum—Cantatrice by Sampson—Dau. of Regulus—Marske's dam by Blackleg's Dau. of Bay Bolton.
				Mowerina.	Emilius.		Cervantes.	Don Quixote—Evelina by Highflyer—Termagant by Tantrum—Cantatrice by Sampson—Dau. of Regulus—Marske's dam by Blacklegs.
							Daughter of.	Golumpus—Dau. of Paynator—Sis. to Zodiac by St. George—Abigail by Woodpecker—Firetail by Eclipse—Dau. of Blank—Dau. of Cade.
					Shoveler.		Camel.	Whalebone—Dau. of Selim—Maiden by Sir Peter—Dau. of Phoenomenou—Matron by Florizel—Maiden by Matchem—Dau. of Squirt.
			Emilia.	Young Emilius.			Banter.	Master Henry—Boadicea by Alexander—Brunette by Amaranthus—Mayfly by Matchem—Dau. of Au. Starling—Dau. of Grasshopper.
					Whisker.		Whisker.	Waxy—Penelope by Trumpator—Prunella by Highflyer—Promise by Snap—Julia by Blank—Spectator's dam by Partner—Bonny Lass.
							Gibside Fairy.	Hermes—Vicissitude by Pipator—Beatrice by Sir Peter—Pyrrha by Matchem—Duchess by Whitenose—Miss Slamerkin by Young True Blue.
							Orville.	Beningbrough—Evelina by Highflyer—Termagant by Tantrum—Cantatrice by Sampson—Dau. of Regulus—Marske's dam by Blacklegs.
							Emily.	Stamford—Dau. of Whiskey—Gr. Dorimant by Dorimant—Dizzy by Blank—Dizzy by Driver—Dau. of Smiling Tom—Dau. of Oysterfoot.
					Pers an. Variety.		Scud.	Beningbrough—Eliza by Highflyer—Augusta by Eclipse—Hardwick's dam by Herod—Dau. of Bajazet—Dau. of Regulus—Dau. of Lon's Bay Arabian
							Goosander.	Hambletonian—Rally by Trumpator—Sis. to Diomed by Florizel—Dau. of Spectator—Horatia by Blank—Dau. of F. Childers—Miss Belvoir.
							Waxy.	Pot-8-os—Maria by Herod—Lisette by Snap—Miss Windsor by Godol Arabian—Sis. to Volunteer by Y. Belgrade—Dau. of Bartlet's Childers.
							Penelope.	Trumpator—Prunella by Highflyer—Promise by Snap—Julia by Blank—Spectator's dam by Partner—Bonny Lass by Bay Bolton.
							Selim or *Soothsayer.	Sorcerer—Golden Locks by Delpini—Violet by Shark—Dau. of Syphon—Charlotte by Blank—Dau. of Crab—Dau. of Dyer's Dimple.
							Sprite.	Bobtail—Catharine by Woodpecker—Camilla by Trentham—Coquette by Compton Barb—Sis. to Regutus by Godol. Arabian—Gr. Robinson.
	LAVENDER.	Wagner.	Sir Charles.	Sir Archy.			Diomed.	Florizel—Sis. to Juno by Spectator—Horatia by Blank—Dau. of Childers—Miss Belvoir by Gr. Granthan—Dau. of Paget Turk—Betty Percival.
							Castianira.	Rockingham—Tabitha by Trentham—Dau. of Bosphorus—Dau. of Wm's Forester—Dau. of Coalition Colt—Dau. of Bustard (Crab.)
							Imp. Citizen.	Pacolet—Princess by Turk (Regulus)—Fairy Queen by Y. Cade—Black Eyes by Crab—Warlock Galloway by Snake—Dau. of Bald Galloway.
							Daughter of.	Commutation (Symme's Wildair)—Dau. of Dare Devil (Magnet)—Sally Shark by Imp. Shark—Betsey Pringle by Imp. Fearnought—Jenny Dismal.
			Maria West.	Marion.			Sir Archy.	Diomed—Castianira by Rockingham—Tabitha by Trentham—Dau. of Bosphorus—Dau. of Wm's Forester—Dau. of Coalition Colt (Godol.).
							Daughter of.	Imp. Citizen—Dau. of Imp. Alderman—Dau. of Ashe's Roebuck (Imp. Sweeper)—Dau. of King Herod(Imp. Fearnought—Dau. of Imp. Partner.
				Ella Crump.			Imp. Citizen.	Pacolet—(Blank)—Princess by Turk—Fairy Queen by Y. Cade—Black Eyes by Crab—Warlock Galloway by Snake—Sis. to Carlisle Gelding.
							Daughter of.	Huntsman—(Moustrap by Y. Marske)—Dau. of Symme's Wildair—Dau. of Imp. Fearnought—(Regulus)—Dau. of Imp. Jauus—(Janus by Godol.)
			Sarpedon.	Emilius.			Orville.	Beningbrough—Evelina by Highflyer—Termagant by Tantrum—Cantatrice by Sampson—Dau. of Regulus—Marske's dam by Blacklegs.
							Emily.	Stamford—Dau. of Whiskey—Gr. Dorimant by Dorimant (Otho)—Dizzy by Blank—Dizzy by Driver—Dau. of Smiling Tom (Con's Arabian).
		Alice Carneal.		Icaria.			The Flyer.	Vandyke, Jr., (Walton)—Azalia by Beningbrough—Gilliflower by Highflyer—Dau. of Goldfinder—Sis. to Grasshopper by Marske—Dau. of Cul. Arabian.
							Parma.	Dick Andrews—May by Beningbrough—Primrose by Mambrino (Engineer)—Cricket by Herod—Sophia by Blank—Diana by Second.
			Rowena.	LadyGreySumpter.			Sir Archy.	Diomed—Castianira by Rockingham—Tabitha by Trentham—Dau. of Bosphorus—Dau. of Wm's Forester—Dau. of Coalition Colt (Godol.).
							Flirtilla's dam.	Robin Redbreast—(Sir Peter)—Dau. of Obscurity—Slamerkin by Imp. Wildair—Imp. Cub Mare by Cub—(Fox)—Amaranthus' dam.
							Robin Grey.	Royalist (Saltram)—Belle Mariah by Grey Diomed—(Imp. Medley)—Queen by Imp. St. George—(Highflyer)—Dau. of Cassius—Primrose by Dove.
							Maria.	Melzar (Imp. Medley)—Dau. of Imp. Highflyer—Dau. of Fearnought (Regulus)—Dau. of Ariel—(Imp. Traveler)—Dau. of Jack of Diamonds. (Cullen Arabian) Diamond (Duchess) by Cullen Arabian—Lady Thigh by Croft's Partner (Jigg)—Dau. of Greyhound (White Barb Chillaby)—Sophonisba's dam by Curwen Bay Barb—Dau. of D'Arcy Chestnut Arabian—Dau. of Whiteshirt—Old Montague Mare.

* Soothsayer given.

BAZAR (WADDLE),

(WINNER OF THE BEEFSTEAK STAKES AT CHICAGO (MILE HEATS) IN 1876,)

Will stand for mares at the stables of his owner in California by private contract. Application to W. L. Pritchard, Sacramento, Cal.

BAZAR, by Jack Malone son of Lexington, bred by Gen. W. G. Harding, Belle Meade Stud, near Nashville, Tenn., foaled 1873, dam Ivy Leaf the dam of Bramble, Brambaletta, etc., by imp. Australian, 2d dam Bayflower, by Lexington, out of Bay Leaf the dam of Baywood, Beacon, Bayswater, Preakness, etc., by imp. Yorkshire. Jack Malone, his sire, was an inbred son of Lexington to Sir Archy and imp. Diomed, the winner of the first Derby in 1780, and was a fine race-horse ; Ivy Leaf, his dam, is one of the best and most successful brood mares in the Belle Meade Stud, as his great-grandam Bay Leaf was in the Woodburn Stud. Bazar was a speedy, good race-horse and able to stay a distance ; started four times at two years old; was third to Calvin and Clemmie G. in sweepstake at Lexington, Ky., three-fourths of a mile in 1:16½, with four others behind him. Was unplaced in Alexander Stake, half a mile, at Louisville, won by Vagrant in 50¼ seconds. Was unplaced in two sweepstakes at Lexington. Ky, ¾ and one mile, both won by Vagrant in 1:18 and 1.45½. At three years old won Club purse at Lexington, 1¼ miles in 2:09½, beating Grenoble and two others. Ran second to Aristides in the Club purse, 2¼ miles, in 4:27½, the fastest race at the distance, Elemi and War Jig behind him. Chicago he was second to Preston for Club purse, 1½ miles, in 2:41¾, five others behind him. Was third in Club purse, mile heats, three best in five, won by Newbern (Council Bluffs) in 1:44, 1:45¾, 1:45¾, 1:52½ ; Jack Hardy won first heat; Bazar was second in third heat. Cleveland, O., won club purse, mile heats, in 1:43¾, 1:46½, beating War Jig and three others. Won Club purse 2 miles in 3:45¼, beating Vicksburg and War Jig. Chicago, won Beefsteak Stakes, mile heats, in 1:49¾, 1:49½, track heavy. San Francisco, Cal., ran second to Mollie McCarty in Club purse, four mile heats, in 7:43½, 7;42½, beating Bradley, Bill Bingham and Lady Amanda. Ran second to Lady Amanda for Club purse, mile heats, in 1:44¾, 1:44¾. He has covered but few mares, but has some promising colts. He is a chestnut, 15½ hands high, with all the substance and power peculiar to the Jack Malones and is one of the links to perpetuate the Archy and Diomed blood. He has nine crosses of that blood.

PEDIGREE OF BAZAR—(Waddell).

BAZAR—(Waddell).					
JACK MALONE.	Lexington.	Boston.	Sister to Timoleon.	Sir Archy. Daughter of.	Diomed—Castianira by Rockingham—Tabitha by Trentham—Dau. of Bosphorus—Dau. of Wm's Forester—Dau. of Coalition Colt (Godol). Imp. Saltram—Dau. of Symme's Wildair—Dau. of Driver (Othello)—Dau. of Imp. Fallower (Blank)—Dau. of Imp. Vampire (Regulus).
			Tuckahoe.	Ball's Florizel. Daughter of.	Diomed—Dau. of Imp.Shark—Dau. of Harris' Eclipse—Dau. of Fearnought—Dau. of Imp. Jolly Roger—Dau. of Imp. Sober John—Dau. of Shock. Imp. Alderman—Dau. of Clockfast—Dau. of Symme's Wildair—Y. Kitty Fisher by Imp. Fearnought—Imp. Kitty Fisher by Cade.
		Alice Carneal.	Sarpedon.	Emilius. Icaria.	Orville—Emily, by Stamford—Dau. of Whiskey—Gr. Dorimant by Dorimant—Dizzy by Blank—Dizzy by Driver—Dau. of Smiling Tom. The Flyer—Parma by Dick Andrews—May by Beningbrough—Primrose by Mambrino—Cricket by Herod—Sophia by Blank—Diana by Second.
			Rowena.	Sumpter. Lady Grey.	Sir Archy—Flirtilla's dam by Robin Redbreast—Dau. of Imp. Obscurity—Slamerkin by Wildair—Imp. Cub Mare by Cub—Amaranthus' dam. Robin Grey—Maria by Melzar—Dau. of Highflyer—Dau. of Fearnought—Dau. of Ariel—Dau. of Jack of Diamonds—Imp. Diamond.
	Gloriana.	Am. Eclipse.	Duroc.	Diomed. Amanda.	Florizel—Sis. to Juno by Spectator—Horatia by Blank—Dau. of Childers—Miss Belvoir by Gr. Grantham—Dau. of Paget Turk—Betty Percival. Grey Diomed—Dau. of Va Cade—Dau. of Hickman's Independence—Dolly Fine by Imp. Silvereye—Dau. of Imp. Badger—Dau. of Forester.
		Sir Charles.	Millers Damsel.	Imp. Messenger. Daughter of.	Mambrino—Dau. of Turf—Dau. of Regulus—Dau. of Starling—Snap's dam by Fox—Gipsy by Bay Bolton—Dau. of Newcastle Turk. Pot-8-os—Dau. of Gimcrack—Snap Dragon by Snap—Dau. of Regulus—Dau. of Bart. Childers—Dau. of Hon. Arabian—Dam. of True Blues.
	Trifle.			Sir Archy. Daughter of.	Diomed—Castianira by Rockingham—Tabitha by Trentham—Dau. of Bosphorus—Dau. of Wm's Forester—Dau. of Coalition Colt (Godol). Imp. Citizen—Dau. of Commutation—Dau. of Imp. Dare Devil—Sally Shark by Imp. Shark—Betsey Pringle by Imp. Fearnought.
		Dau. of		Cicero. Daughter of.	Sir Archy—Shylock's dam by Diomed—Dau. of Imp. St. George—Dau. of Imp. Fearnought—Dau. of Imp. Jolly Roger—Imp. Mary Gray. Imp. Bedford—Dau. of Bellair—Dau. of Imp.Shark—Dau. of Wildair—Dau. of Lexington (Wildair)—Dau. of Spanking Roger—Dau. of Jolly Roger.
IVY LEAF.	Imp. Australian.	West Australian.	Mowerina.	Humphrey Clinker. Daughter of.	Comus—Clinkerina by Clinker—Pewet by Tandem—Termagant by Tantrum—Cantatrice by Sampson—Dau. of Regulus—Mareke's dam. Cervantes—Dau. of Golumpus—Dau. of Paynator—Sis. to Zodiac by St. George—Abigail by Woodpecker—Firetail by Eclipse—Dau. of Blank.
		Emilia.	Y Emillus.	Touchstone. Emma.	Camel—Banter by Master Henry—Boadicea by Alexander—Brunette by Amaranthus—Mayfly by Matchem—Dau. of An Starling. Whisker—Gibside Fairy by Hermes—Vicissitude by Pipator—Beatrice by Sir Peter—Pyrrha by Matchem—Duchess by Whitenose.
				Emilius. Shoveler.	Orville—Emily by Stamford—Dau. of Whiskey—Gr. Dorimant by Dorimant—Dizzy by Blank—Dau. of Driver—Dau. of Smiling Tom. Scud—Goosander by Hambletonian—Rally by Trumpator—Fancy, Sis. to Diomed by Florizel—Sis. to Juno by Spectator—Horatia by Blank.
	Bay Flower.	Lexington.	Boston. Persian.	Whisker. Variety.	Waxy—Penelope by Trumpator—Prunella by Highflyer—Promise by Snap—Julia by Blank—Spectator's dam by Partner—Bonny Lass. Selim or Soothsayer—Sprite by Bobtail—Catbarine by Woodpecker—Camilla by Trentham—Coquette by Compton Barb—Sis. to Regulus.
				Timoleon. Robin Brown's Dam.	Sir Archy—Dau. of Imp. Saltram—Dau. of Symme's Wildair—Dau. of Driver (Imp. Othello)—Dau. of Fallower (Blank)—Dau.of Imp.Vampire. Ball's Florizel—Dau. of Alderman—Dau. of Clockfast—Dau. of Symme's Wildair—Y. Kitty Fisher by Fearnought—Imp. Kitty Fisher by Cade.
	Bay Leaf.	Alice Carneal.		Sarpedon. Rowena.	Emilius—Icaria by The Flyer—Parma by Dick Andrews—May by Beningbrough—Primrose by Mambrino—Cricket by Herod—Sophia by Blank. Sumpter—Lady Grey by Robin Grey—Maria by Melzar—Dau. of Highflyer—Dau. of Fearnought—Dau. of Ariel—Dau. of Jack of Diamonds.
		Yorkshire.		St. Nicholas. Miss Rose.	Emilius—Seamew by Scud—Goosander by Hambletonian—Rally by Trumpator—Fancy Sis. to Diomed by Florizel—Dau. of Spectator. Tramp—Dau. of Sancho—Blacklock's dam by Coriander—Wildgoose by Highflyer—Coheiress by Pot-8-os—Manilla by Goldfinder.
	Maria Black.			Filho-da-Puta. Daughter of.	Haphazard—Mrs. Barnet by Waxy—Dau. of Woodpecker—Heinel by Squirrel—Principessa by Blank—Dau. of Cul Arabian. Smolensko (Sorcerer)—Dau. of Sir Peter (Highflyer)—Dau. of Mambrino (Engineer)—Marigold by Herod (Tartar)—Whiteneck by Crab—(Alcock Arabian)—Dau. of Godolphin Arabian—Dau. of Conyer's Arabian—Dau. of CurwenBay Barb—Dau. of Marshall's Spot—Dau. of White legged Lowther Barb—Old Vintner Mare.

BERTRAM,

(WINNER OF THE JERSEY DERBY AND MONMOUTH SEQUEL STAKES AT LONG BRANCH IN 1876,

Will serve mares at Lexington, Ky., at $25 the season and $1.00 to the Groom, dams of Winners free. Application to Dr. E. M. Norwood, Lexington, Ky.

BERTRAM, by Kentucky, the best son of Lexington, bred by Hon. A. Belmont, Nursery Stud, Babylon, Long Island, foaled 1873, dam imp. Bernice by Stockwell, winner of the Two Thousand Guineas and St. Leger in 1852. Second dam, Braxy by Moss Trooper winner of the Queen's plates at Doncaster and Lincoln, out of the famous Queen Mary dam of Blink Bonny, Bonnie Scotland, etc., by Gladiator. Bertram ran only one race at two years old; was unplaced in the Champagne stakes at Jerome Park, three-quarters of a mile, won by Virginius in 1:19. At three years old started four times; was unplaced in the Wither's stake, one mile, won by his stable companion, Fiddlesticks, in 1:46¼. Some place, won Club purse, one mile and a furlong, for maiden three-year-olds, in 2:01, beating Woodland, Leamington II., Vigil and others. Long Branch, won the Jersey Derby, one and a half miles, in 2:44¼, beating Fiddlesticks, Rappahannock and Fugitive. Same place, won the Monmouth Sequel stakes, two miles in 3:45, beating Woodland and Shirley; in this race he carried 123 lbs. As a four-year-old started in twenty races, won three, was second in three and third in two. Won handicap purse, one mile, at Saratoga, with 113 lbs., in 1:46¼, track heavy. Same place, won selling purse, one mile, 111 lbs., in 1:43¼, beating Dan K. and three others. Same place, won handicap purse, one and quarter miles, 114 lbs. in 2:14¼, beating Courier and two others, track very muddy. At Baltimore, started in a race of mile heats with seven horses; won the first heat in 1:45, and was crowded through the fence in the second, falling and crippling his jockey. He could not have lost the race. This closed his turf career. Bertram has a double cross of imp. Glencoe, and traces through both dam and sire to the famous Web by Waxy, own sister to Whalebone, Whisker, etc.; his dam is by the great Stockwell, and his great grandam, Queen Mary, was the dam of Balrownie, Bonnie Scotland, Blink Bonny, the dam of Blair Athol. No descendant of Queen Mary has ever failed to reproduce itself. Bertram is a blood bay, 16¼ hands high, with small star in forehead, black points—a finely shaped horse all over, with the best of legs and feet. His immense substance and power and winning strains of blood should make him a desirable stallion. He has several crosses of Whalebone and Whisker, two of the best sons of Waxy, by Pot 8o's, son of Eclipse.

PEDIGREE OF BERTRAM.

BERTRAM

KENTUCKY (Lexington / Alice Carneal side)

Lexington — by Boston (Sister to Tuckahoe, by Timoleon) out of Alice Carneal (by Sarpedon, out of Rowena by Sumpter)

Magnolia — by Glencoe (Sultan — Trampoline) out of Myrtle (Mameluke — Miss Sophia)

Sir Archy. Daughter of.	Diomed—Castianira by Rockingham—Tabitha by Trentham—Dau. of Bosphorus—Dam of Wm's. Forester—Dau. of Coalition Colt. Imp. Saltram—Dau. of Symme's Wildair—Dau. of Driver (Othello)—Dau. of Imp. Fallower (Blank)—Dau. of Imp. Vampire (Regulus).
Ball's Florizel. Daughter of.	Diomed—Dau. of Imp. Shark—Dau. of Harris' Eclipse—Dau. of Fearnought—Dau. of Jolly Roger—Dau. of Sober John—Dau. of Shock. Alderman—Dau. of Clockfast—Dau. of Symme's Wildair—Y Kitty Fisher by Imp. Fearnought—Imp. Kitty Fisher by Cade—Dau. of Som Arabian.
Emilius. Icaria.	Orville—Emily by Stamford—Dau. of Whiskey—Gr. Dorimant by Dorimant—Dizzy by Blank—Dizzy by Driver—Dau. of Smiling Tom. The Flyer—Parma by Dick Andrews—May by Beningbrough—Primrose by Mambrino—Cricket by Herod—Sophia by Blank—Diana by Second.
Sumpter. Lady Grey.	Sir Archy—Flirtilla's dam by Robin Redbreast—Dau. of Obscurity—Slamerkin by Wildair—Imp. Cub Mare by Cub—Amaranthus' dam. Robin Grey—Maria by Melzar—Dau. of Highflyer—Dau. of Fearnought—Dau. of Ariel—Dau. of Imp. Jack of Diamonds—Imp. Diamond.
Selim. Bacchante.	Buzzard—Castrel's dam by Alexander—Dau. of Highflyer—Dau. of Alfred—Dau. of Engineer—Bay Malton's dam by Cade—Lass of the Mill. Williamson's Ditto—Sis. to Calomel by Mercury—Dau. of Herod—Folly by Maraske—Vixen by Regulus—Dau. of Hutton's Spot.
Tramp. Web.	Dick Andrews—Dau. of Gohanna—Fraxinella by Trentham—Dau. of Woodpecker—Everlasting by Eclipse—Hyaena by Snap. Waxy—Penelope by Trumpator—Prunella by Highflyer—Promise by Snap—Julia by Blank—Spectator's dam by Partner—Bonny Lass.
Partisan. Miss Sophia.	Walton—Parasol by Pot-8-os—Prunella by Highflyer—Promise by Snap—Julia by Blank—Spectator's dam by Partner—Bonny Lass. Stamford—Sophia by Buzzard—Huncamunca by Highflyer—Cypher by Squirrel—Fribble's dam by Regulus—Dau. of Bart. Childers.
Bobadil. Pythoness.	Rubens—Dau. of Skyscraper—Isabel by Woodpecker—Dau. of Squirrel—Ancaster Nancy by Blank—Phoebe by Tortoise—Dau. of Looby. Sorcerer—Princess by Sir Peter—Dau. of Dungannon—Dau. of Turf—Dau. of Herod—Golden Grove by Blank—Spinster by Partner.

BERNICE (The Baron / Pocahontas side)

Stockwell — by The Baron (Irish Birdcatcher — Echidna) out of Pocahontas (Glencoe — Marpessa)

Queen Mary — by Gladiator (out of Moss Trooper) — Sister to Liverpool. Daughter of Agreeable. Braxy.

Sir Hercules. Guiccioli.	Whalebone—Peri by Wanderer—Thalestris by Alexander—Rival by Sir Peter—Hornet by Drone—Manilla by Goldfinder. Bob Booty—Flight by I Escape—Y Heroine by Bagot—Heroine by Hero—Dau. of Snap—Sis. to Regulus by Godol. Arabian—Grey Robinson.
Economist. Miss Pratt.	Whisker—Floranthe by Octavian—Caprice by Anvil—Madcap by Eclipse—Dau. of Blank—Dau. of Blaze—Dau. of Y Greyhound. Blacklock—Gadabout by Orville—Minstrel by Sir Peter—Matron by Florizel—Maiden by Matchem—Dau. of Squirt—Lot's dam.
Sultan. Trampoline.	Selim—Bacchante by Williamson's Ditto—Sis. to Calomel by Mercury—Dau. of Herod—Folly by Maraske—Vixen by Regulus. Tramp—Web by Waxy—Penelope by Trumpator—Prunella by Highflyer—Promise by Snap—Julia by Blank—Spectator's dam.
Muley. Clare.	Orville—Eleanor by Whiskey—Y Giantess by Diomed—Giantess by Matchem—Molly Longlegs by Babraham—Dau. of Cole's Foxhunter. Marmion—Harpalice by Gohanna—Amazon by Driver—Fractions by Mercury—Dau. of Woodpecker—Everlasting by Eclipse—Hyaena.
Tramp. Daughter of.	Dick Andrews—Dau. of Gohanna—Fraxinella by Trentham—Dau. of Woodpecker—Everlasting by Eclipse—Hyaena by Snap. Whisker—Mandane by Pot-8-os—Y Camilla by Woodpecker—Camilla by Trentham—Coquette by Compton Bart—Sis. to Regulus.
Emilius. Surprise.	Orville—Emily by Stamford—Dau. of Whiskey—Gr. Dorimant by Dorimant—Dizzy by Blank—Dizzy by Driver—Dau. of Smiling Tom. Scud—Manfreda by Williamson's Ditto—Tawney by Mentor (Justice)—Jemima by Satellite (Eclipse)—Maria, Waxy's dam, by Herod.
Partisan. Pauline.	Walton—Parasol by Pot-8-os—Prunella by Highflyer—Promise by Snap—Julia by Blank—Spectator's dam by Partner—Bonny Lass. Moses—Quadrille by Selim—Canary Bird by Whiskey or Sorcerer—Canary by Coriander—Miss Green by Highflyer—Harriet by Matchem.
Plenipotentiary. Myrrha.	Emilius—Harriet by Pericles—Dau. of Selim—Pipylina by Sir Peter—Rally by Trumpator—Fancy, sis. to Diomed by Florizel. Whalebone—Gift by Y. Gohanna—Sis. to Grazier by Sir Peter—Sis. to Amaitor by Trumpator—Dau. of Herod—Dau. of Snap (Snip)—Dau. of Gower Stallion (Godolphin)—Dau. of Flying Childers (Darley Arabian).

BILLET (Imp.)

(WINNER OF THE ZETLAND STAKES AT YORK, EGHAM STAKES AT EGHAM, THE MARCHAM PARK STAKES AT ABINGDON, AND SELLING STAKES AT WORCESTER IN 1867,)

Stands at the head of the Runnymede Stud, Bourbon Co., near Paris, Ky., by private contract only, the property of Messrs. Geo. W. Bowen & Co., Post Office, Paris, Ky. Annual Sales of Yearlings in May.

BILLET, by Voltigeur, bred by Mr. James Smith, foaled in 1865, dam Calcutta, dam of Bivouac, Watchfire, Eastminster, Gen. Lee, &c., by Flatcatcher, winner of the 2,000 guineas, and son of Touchstone. Voltigeur, the sire of imp. Billet, was a superior race-horse, won the Derby, Doncaster St. Leger, and the Doncaster Cup, all in 1850, and was the only horse which ever vanquished the Flying Dutchman; his stock were all remarkable for their fine, improving, and staying qualities; imp. Billet was himself a fine race-horse. Started seventeen times as a two-year old; won five races and lost twelve; won the Zetland Stakes, five furlongs 44 yards, beating Eau de Vie, Stella, and others; won the Egham Stakes, three-quarters of a mile, beating La Sorrentina, Rally, &c., won the Marcham Park Stakes at Abingdon, three-quarters of a mile, beating Magna and Irwell. Newmarket First October Meeting, won sweepstakes for two year old, last half of the Abingdon mile, beating a field of six. At Worcester won selling sweepstakes for two year olds, five furlongs, beating Frenzy, Phantom Sail and four others. At Durham ran second to Stella for the Elsmere Stakes (he afterwards beat her); ran second to Bismarck in the Eglinton Stakes; ran second to Traviata in sweepstake at Newmarket Second October Meeting, and ran third in the Enville Plate, beating six others. As a three-year old, ran only once, unplaced. He usually ran in good company, and the severe ordeal of seventeen races as a two-year old destroyed his usefulness on the turf and caused his early retirement. He stood, for several years after his importation, in Illinois, where he served but few really good mares, but sired some remarkable race-horses, and from Sprightly, the sister of Monarchist, two excellent race-horses, Volturno, a first-class horse, and Elias Lawrence, a real good one. Volturno won in his two-year-old form four out of five races, at three years old he won six out of ten races, including the United States Hotel Stakes at Saratoga, 1¼ miles in 2:41½, beating Harold and others; a handicap sweepstake, 1¼ miles in 2:10¾; the Atlantic Handicap, 1¼ miles, at Long Branch, in 2:43, beating Bonnie Carrie, Monitor, &c.; at Brighton Beach won two handicaps, each 1¼ miles in 3:08½ each; won the Breckenridge Stakes at Baltimore, two miles in 3:35½, beating Harold, Aureolus, and Monitor, the latter carried 112 lbs., a penalty of 5 lbs.; as a four-year old won four out of six races, including the Louisville Cup. Elias Lawrence's performances in the Baden Baden Handicap when three years old was a wonderful race. With 98 lbs. he ran the distance in 5:28¼. Other winners by Billet are Kate Claxton, Mollie Lee, Billet Lee, Headlight, Frenchie Shy, Baybee, Patti, Zeta, Bedouin, Ballard, Belle of Runnymede, Bengal, Blenheim, Runnymede, winner of Clarke Stakes at Louisville, the Tidal Stakes, one mile in 1:43¼, 118 lbs., the Coney Island Derby, 1¼ miles in 2:37, beating Forester and Carley B. both at Sheepshead Bay, and the Lorillard Stakes at Monmouth Park, 1¼ miles in 2:40; Barnes, one of the best two-year old colts of the year, Miss Woodford, winner of six out of nine stakes in which she started this year, including the Ladies' Stake at Chicago, three-quarters of a mile, the Spinaway Stake at Saratoga, five furlongs in 1:03¼, the Misses Stake, three-quarters of a mile in 1:16, the Filly Stakes, three-quarters of a mile in 1:17¾, and the Colt and Filly Stake, one mile, in 1:44¼; both at Lexington, Ky. Voltigeur, the sire of Billet, sired Vedette, winner of the 2,000 guineas, and Vedette sired Galopin, winner of the Derby. The stock are remarkable for their fine, improving, and staying qualities. Billet is inbred to Waxy, the sire of Whalebone and Whisker, and traces through his collateral branches many times to Herod and Eclipse, thence to the best Oriental sources. He has also three crosses of imp. Diomed, the winner of the first Derby in 1780. His stock must be valuable.

PEDIGREE OF BILLET.

BILLET.	VOLTIGEUR.	Voltaire.	Blacklock.	Daughter of Phantom.	Dau. of Whitelock.	Hambletonian. Rosalind.	King Fergus (Eclipse)—Dau. of Highflyer—Monimia by Matchem (Cade)—Dau. of Alcides (Babraham)—Dau. of Crab—Snap's dam by Fox. Phœnomenon (Herod)—Atalanta by Matchem—Lass of the Mill by Oroonoko—Dau. of Old Traveler—Miss Makeless by Y. Grayhound.
					Catton. Dau. of	Coriander. Wildgoose.	Pot-8-os—Lavender by Herod—Dau. of Snap—Miss Roan by Cade—Madame by Bloody Buttocks—Sis. to Matchem's dam by Partner. Highflyer—Coheiress by Pot-8-os—Manilla by Goldfinder (Snap)—Dau. of Old Eng. (Godol.)—Dau. of Cul. Arabian—Miss Cade by Cade.
			Mulatto.	Desdemona.		Walton. Julia.	Sir Peter—Arethusa by Dungannon—Dau. of Prophet (Regulus)—Virago by Snap—Dau. of Regulus—Sis. to Othello by Crab—Miss Slamerkiu. Whiskey (Saltram)—Y. Giantess by Diomed—Giantess by Matchem—Molly Longlegs by Babraham—Dau. of Cole's Foxhunter—Dau. of Partner.
		Martha Lynn.				Overton. Gratitude's dam.	King Fergus—Dau. of Herod—Dau. of Snip (F. Childers)—Sis. to Regulus by Godol. Arabian—Gr. Robinson by Bald Galloway—Dau. of Snake. Walnut (Highflyer)—Dau. of Ruler (Y. Marske)—Piracantha by Matchem—Dau. of Regulus—Jenny Spinner by Partner—Dau. of Grayhound.
			Leda.	Filho-da-Puta.		Golumpus. Lucy Grey.	Gohanna—Catharine by Woodpecker—Camilla by Trentham—Coquette by Compton Barb—Sis. to Regulus by Godol. Arabian.—Gr. Robinson. Timothy (Delpini)—Lucy by Florizel (Herod)—Frenzy by Eclipse—Dau. of Engineer—Dau. of Blank—Lass of the Mill by Old Traveler.
						Orville. Fanny.	Beningbrough—Evelina by Highflyer—Tarmagant by Tantrum—Cantatrice by Sampson—Dau. of Regulus—Marske's dam by Blacklegs. Sir Peter—Dau. of Diomed—Desdemona by Marske—Y. Hag by Skim-Hag by Crab—Ebony by Childers—Ebony by Basto.
				Treasure.		Haphazard. Mrs. Barnet.	Sir Peter—Miss Hervey by Eclipse—Clio by Y. Cade—Dau. of Starling—Dau. of Bart Childers—Dau. of Bay Bolton—Dau. of Byerly Turk. Waxy—Dau. of Woodpecker—Heinel by Squirrel—Principessa by Blank—Dau. of Cullen Arabian—Lady Thigh by Partner (Jigg).
						Camillus. Daughter of.	Hambletonian—Faith by Pacolet—Atalanta by Matchem—Lass of the Mill by Oroonoko—Dau. of Old Traveler—Miss Makeless by Y. Greyhound. Hyacinthus (Coriander)—Flora by King Fergus—Atalanta by Matchem—Lass of the Mill by Oroonoko—Dau. of Old Traveler—Miss Makeless.
	CALCUTTA.	Miss Martin.	Flatcatcher.	Touchstone.	Camel	Whalebone. Daughter of.	Waxy—Penelope by Trumpator—Prunella by Highflyer—Promise by Snap—Julia by Blank—Spectator's dam by Partner—Bonny Lass. Selim—Maiden by Sir Peter—Dau. of Phœnomenon—Matron by Florizel—Maiden by Matchem—Dau. of Squirrel—Lot's dam by Mogul.
					Banter	Master Henry. Boadicea.	Orville—Miss Sophia by Stamford—Sophia by Buzzard—Huncamunca by Highflyer—Cyper by Squirrel—Fribble's dam by Regulus (Godol.). Alexander—Brunette by Amaranthus (Old Eng.)—Mayfly by Matchem—Dau. of Ancaster Starling—Dau. of Grasshopper—Dau. of Newton Arab.
				Decoy.	Filho-da-Puta.	Haphazard. Mrs. Barnet.	Sir Peter—Miss Hervey by Eclipse—Clio by Y. Cade—Dau. of Starling—Dau. of Barts Childers—Dau. of Bay Bolton—Dau. of Byerly Turk. Waxy—Dau. of Woodpecker—Heinel by Squirrel—Principessa by Blank—Dau. of Cullen Arabian—Lady Thigh by Partner—Dau. of Bloody Buttocks.
						Peruvian. Violante.	Sir Peter—Dau. of Budrow (Eclipse)—Escape's dam by Squirrel—Dau. of Babraham—Dau. of Golden Ball (Partner)—Bushy Molly by Hamp. Ct. John Bull (Fortitude)—Dau. of Highflyer—Everlasting by Eclipse—Hyaena by Snap—Miss Belsea by Regulus—Dau. of Bart Childers—Dau. of Hon Ar.
		St. Martin.	Actæon.			Send. Diana.	Beningbrough—Eliza by Highflyer—Augusta by Eclipse—Hardwick's dam by Herod—Dau. of Bajazet—Dau. of Regulus—Dau. of Lon's-Arabian. Stamford—Dau. of Whiskey—Gr. Dorimant by Dorimant—Dizzy by Blank—Dizzy by Driver—Dau. of Smiling Tom—Dau. of Oysterfoot.
						Walton. Comedy.	Sir Peter—Arethusa by Dungannon—Dau. of Prophet—Virago by Snap—Dau. of Regulus—Sis. to Othello by Crab—Miss Slamerkin. Comus—Dau. of Star (Highflyer)—Dau. of Y. Marske—Emma by Telemachus (Herod)—A-la-Grecque by Regulus—Dau. of Allworthy.
			Galena.	Finesse.		Waxy. Penelope.	Pot-8-os—Maria by Herod—Lisette by Snap—Miss Windsor by Godol. Arabian—Sis. to Volunteer by Y. Belgrade—Dau. of B. Childers. Trumpator—Prunella by Highflyer—Promise by Snap—Julia by Blank—Spectator's dam by Partner—Bonny Lass by Bay Bolton.
		Wartail.	Dau. of Whisker.			Sorcerer. Daughter of.	Trumpator—Y. Giantess by Diomed—Giantess by Matchem—Molly Longlegs by Babraham—Dau. of Cole's Foxhunter. Sir Solomon (Sir Peter)—Dau. of Y. Marske—Dau. of Phœnomenon (Herod)—Calliope by Slouch (Cade)—Lass of the Mill by Oroonoko (Crab) Dau. of Traveler (Partner)—Miss Makeless by Y. Greyhound out of Farewell—Dau. of Partner (Jigg)—Miss Doe's dam by Woodcock (Merlin)—Lusty Thornton by Croft's Bay Barb—Chestnut Thornton by Makeless (Oglethorpe Arabian)—Old Thornton by Brimmer—Dau. of Dickey Pierson (Dodsworth)—Burton Barb Mare.

BLUE EYES,

(WINNER OF THE SANFORD STAKE, 1877, AND MERCHANTS' STAKE, 1879, AT LOUISVILLE, KY., AND THE GARDEN CITY CUP AT CHICAGO, 1880,)

Will stand the Season of 1883 at the Fleetwood Stud Farm, near Frankfort, Franklin Co., Ky., at $50 the season, application to Agent of Fleetwood Stud, Frankfort, Ky.

BLUE EYES, by Enquirer, son of imp. Leamington, bred by the late Colonel J. W. H. Reynolds, Fleetwood Stud, Ky., dam Buchu, by Planet, son of Revenue, out of Lavender, by Wagner, son of Sir Charles, by Sir Archy. Blue Eyes made his *debut* at Lexington as a two-year old, running second to Himyar in the Colt Stakes, three-quarters of a mile in 1:16¾, beating Leveler and eight others. Was third to Himyar and Leveler in the Colt and Filly Stakes, one mile in 1:44½, McHenry and four others behind him. Louisville, Ky., won the Sanford Stakes, one mile in 1:45¼, beating Day Star and Himyar. Nashville, ran second to Leveler in Young America Stake No. 1, three-quarters of a mile in 1:17 McHenry and four others behind him. At three years old Louisville, ran second to Edinburg, 1¼ miles in 1:59, beating King William, &c.; won purse, 1¼ miles in 1:58, beating King Faro, Adventure, and six others. Nashville, ran second to Bergamot in Belle Meade Stakes No. 2, two miles in 3:38¾, beating Glenmore, Belle of Nelson, &c. Came in first, in dash of 1⅛ miles in 1:57¾, but was declared distanced for foul riding and race awarded to Clemmie G.; was unplaced in his other races.

At four years old started three times; won two races, and was unplaced in one. Lexington, Ky., won 1¼ miles, defeating Peru, Pomeroy, Fairy Queen, Mohur, Tom Sawyer, and Rowdy Boy in 1:58¼. Louisville, Ky., won the Merchants' Stakes, 1⅛ miles, for all ages, defeating Little Ruffin, Goodnight, Incommode, Lah-tu-nah, L'Argentine, Verdict, Glenmore, Krupp Gun, King Faro, McHenry, Bill Bass, and Essillah in 1:55¼. Saratoga, he started the third and last time during the season in two mile dash, which was won by Danicheff, Gov. Hampton second, Clara D third, Blue Eyes last; time, 3:39¾.

At five years old, Louisville, Ky., ran second to Volturno in Louisville Cup, 2¼ miles in 4:20¾, track deep in mud, with Cammie F., Irish King, Himyar, and Little Ruffin in his rear; ran second to Himyar in the Merchants' Stake, one mile and a furlong in 1:55¼ beating One Dime, Victim, Beatitude, Goodnight, and Verdict. Chicago, won the Garden City Cup, 2¼ miles, in 3:58¾, beating Long Taw, Irish King, Fortuna, Renown, Fair Count, and two others; this is one of the best races ever run at the distance.

He bursted his foot in this race, and was retired from the turf. He is a chestnut, 15¼ hands high, with star in his forehead and two white hind legs, is an evenly formed, well-shaped horse, with no lumber, and comes from a racing family. Has a large infusion of Archy and Diomed blood through both dam and sire. He possessed speed, and could stay, The Archy and Diomed blood can be perpetuated through him. He has a dozen crosses of this very desirable blood.

PEDIGREE OF BLUE EYES.

BLUE EYES.							
ENQUIRER.	Leamington.	Faugh-a-Ballagh.	Daughter of.	Guiccioli.	Sir Hercules.	Whalebone.	Waxy—Penelope by Trumpator—Prunella by Highflyer—Promise by Snap—Julia by Blank—Spectator's dam by Partner—Bonny Lass.
						Peri.	Wanderer—Thalestris by Alexander—Rival by Sir Peter—Hornet by Drone—Manilla by Goldfinder—Dau. of Old Eng—Dau. of Cul. Arabian.
			Daphne.	Pantaloon.		Bob Booty.	Chanticleer—Ierne by Bagot—Dau. of Gamahoe—Patty by Tim—Miss Patch by Justice—Ringtail Galloway by Cur Bay Barb—Sis. to Witty Mare.
						Flight.	I Escape-Y. Heroine by Bagot—Heroine by Hero—Dau. of Snap—Sis. to Regulus by G. Arabian—Gr. Robinson by Bald Galloway—Dau. of Snake.
		Boston.				Castrel.	Buzzard—Dau. of Alexander—Dau. of Highflyer—Dau. of Alfred—Dau. of Engineer—Bay Malton's dam by Cade—Lass of the Mill by Traveler.
						Idalia.	Peruvian—Musidora by Meteor—Maid of all Work by Highflyer—Sis. to Tundem by Syphon—Dau. of Regulus—Dau of Snip—Dau. of Cottingham.
						Laurel.	Blacklock—Wagtail by Prime Minister—Dau. of Orville—Miss Grimstone by Weasel—Dau. of Aucaster—Dau. of Dam Arabian—Dau. of Sampson.
						Maid of Honor.	Champion—Etiquette by Orville—Boadicea by Alexander—Brunette by Amaranthus—Mayfly by Matchem—Dau. of An. Starling.
	Lida.	Lexington.	Alice Carneal.			Timoleon.	Sir Archy—Dau. of Saltram—Dau. of Symme's Wildair—Dau. of Driver (Imp Othello)—Dau. of Fallower (Blank)—Dau. of Imp. Vampire.
						Robin Brown's Dam.	Ball's Florizel—Dau. of Alderman—Dau. of Clockfast—Dau. of Symme's Wildair—Y. Kitty Fisher by Fearnought—Imp. Kitty Fisher by Cade.
						Sarpedon.	Emilius—Icaria by the Flyer—Parma by Dick Andrews—May by Beningbrough—Primrose by Mambrino—Cricket by Herod—Sophia.
						Rowena.	Sumpter—Lady Grey by Robin Grey—Maria by Melzar—Dau. of Highflyer—Dau. of Imp. Fearnought—Dau. of Ariel—Dau. of Imp. Jack of Diamonds
		Lize.	Am. Eclipse.	Gabriella.		Duroc.	Diomed—Amanda by Grey Diomed—Dau. of Va Cade—Dau. of Hickman's Independence—Dolly Fine by Imp. Silvereye—Dau. of Imp. Badger.
						Millers Damsel.	Messenger—Dau. of Pot-8-os—Dau. of Gimcrack—Snap-Dragon by Snap—Dau. of Regulus—Dau. of Bart Childers—Dau. of Honeywood's Arabian.
						Sir Archy.	Diomed—Castianira by Rockingham—Tabitha by Trentham—Dau. of Bosphorus—Dau. of Wm's. Forrester—Dau. of Coalition Colt (Godol).
						Calypso.	Bellair—Dau. of Dare-Devil—Sallard Mare by Symme's Wildair—Piccadilla by Batte and McMacklin's Fearnought—Dau. of Baylor's Godolphin.
BUCHU.	Planet.	Revenue.	Rosalie Somers.	Trustee.		Catton.	Golumpus—Lucy Grey by Timothy—Lucy by Florizel—Frenzy by Eclipse—Dau. of Engineer—Dan. of Blank—Lass of the Mill by Traveler.
						Emma.	Whisker—Gibside Fairy by Hermes—Vicissitude by Pipator—Beatrice by Sir Peter—Pyrrha by Matchem—Duchess by Whitenose.
						Sir Charles.	Sir Archy—Dau. of Imp. Citizen—Dau. of Commutation—Dau. of Dare Devil—Sally Shark by Imp. Shark—Betsey Pringle by Fearnought.
						Mischief.	Virginian—Dau. of Imp. Bedford—Dau. of Bellair—Dau. of Imp. Shark—Dau. of Symme's Wildair. Dau. of Lexington (Wildair)—Dau. of Sp'k'g Roger.
		Nina.	Boston.			Timoleon.	Sir Archy—Dau. of Saltram—Dau. of Symme's Wildair—Dau. of Driver (Imp. Othello)—Dau. of Fallower (Blank)—Dau. of Vampire.
						Robin Brown's Dam.	Ball's Florizel—Dau. of Alderman—Dau. of Clockfast—Dau. of Symme's Wildair—Y. Kitty Fisher by Fearnought—Imp. Kitty Fisher by Cade.
			Frol's'me Fanny.			Lottery.	Tramp—Maudane by Pot-8-os—Y. Camilla by Woodpecker—Camilla by Trentham—Coquette by Compton Barb—Sis. to Regulus.
						Sis. to Catterick.	Whisker—Dau. of Bay Tropbonius—Dau. of Slope—Lardella by Y. Marske Dau. of Cade—Beaufremont's dam by Bro. to Fearnought.
	Wagner.	Sir Charles.				Sir Archy.	Diomed—Castianira by Rockingham—Tabitha by Trentham—Dau. of Bosphorus—Dau. of Wm's. Forester—Dau. of Coalition Colt (Godol).
						Daughter of.	Imp. Citizen—Dau. of Commutation—Dau. of Dare-Devil—Sally Shark by Imp. Shark—Betsey Pringle by Fearnought—Imp. Jenny Dismal by Dismal.
		Maria West.				Marion.	Sir Archy—Dau. of Citizen (Pacolet)—Dau. of Alderman—Dau. of Asche's Roebuck—Dau. of Haine's King Herod—Dau. of Imp. Partner.
						Ella Crump.	Citizen—Dau. of Huntsman—Dau. of Symme's Wildair—Dau. of Imp. Fearnought (Regulus)—Dau. of Imp. Janus (Janus by Godol).
	Lavender.	Alice Carneal.				Emilius.	Orville—Emily by Stamford—Dau. of Whiskey—Gr. Dorimant by Dorimant—Dizzy by Blank—Dizzy by Driver—Dau. of Smiling Tom.
						Icaria.	The Flyer—Parma by Dick Andrews—May by Beningbrough—Primrose by Mambrino—Cricket by Herod—Sophia by Blank (Godol).
		Sarpedon.				Sumpter.	Sir Archy—Flirtilla's dam by Robin Redbreast—Dau. of Obscurity—Slamerkin by Imp. Wildair—Imp. Cub Mare by Cub—Amaranthus' dam.
		Rowena.				Lady Grey.	Robin Grey—Maria by Melzar—Dau. of Imp. Highflyer—Dau. of Imp. Fearnought (Regulus)—Dau. of Ariel (Imp. Traveler)—Dau. of Imp. Jack of Diamonds (Cullen Arabian) imp. Diamond (Duchess) by Cullen Arabian—Lady Thigh by Croft's Partner (Jigg)—Dau. of Greyhound (White Barb Chillaby (Suphonisba's dam by Curwen Bay Barb—Dau. of D'Arcy Chestnut Arabian—Dau. of Whiteshirt—Old Montague Mare.

BLUEMANTLE,

WINNER OF THE NEW STAKES AT EPSOM IN 1862, AND THE BIENNIAL AND NEW STAKES AT ASCOT,)

Will stand the season of 1883 *at the farm of William M. Kenney, near Lexington, Ky., at* $50 *the season. Application to W. M. Kenney, Lexington, Ky.*

BLUEMANTLE, by Kingston, son of Venison, bred by Col. Pearson, foaled 1860, dam Paradigm, the dam of Lord Lyon, winner of the 2,000 guineas, Derby and St. Leger, in 1866. And Achievement, winner of the 1,000 guineas, and St. Leger, in 1867. Gardevisure etc., by Paragone, son of Touchstone, out of Ellen Horne, by Redshanks. Bluemantle made his first appearance as the property of Capt. Douglas Lane, at Northampton, in 1862, where he ran third to Biondella and Sanita for the Whittlebury Stakes, three-quarters of a mile, beating Birdhill, Brahmin, Exchequer and four others; at the same meeting, ran unplaced, to Cerintha for the Althorpe Park Stakes, half a mile; at Ascot won the fifth Ascot Biennial Stakes, five furlongs, 136 yards, beating Bateman, Tom Fool and eleven others; won the tenth Ascot Triennial Stakes, five furlongs, 136 yards, beating Cadean, Newchurch and six others; won the New Stakes, five furlongs, 136 yards, a capital good race, won by six lengths, beating Vivid, Cerintha and nine others; at Newmarket, July meeting, ran Saccharometer to a head in the July stakes, five furlongs, 136 yards, four others behind him; same meeting, was third to Saccharometer and Lady Augusta, in the Chesterfield Stakes, half a mile, fourteen others behind him. York, August meeting, was third to Tornado and Livingston, in the Convivial Stakes, five furlongs, 140 yards, eight others behind him. Newmarket, First October Meeting, won the Rutland Stakes, five furlongs, 182 yards, defeating Oscar and Newsmonger. Second October Meeting was unplaced in Criterion Stakes, won by Hospodar, and was second to Queen Bertha in a sweepstake over the Abingdon mile; as a three-year-old started nine times, was fourth in the Derby to Macoroni, Lord Clifden and Rapid Rhone; was third to Onesander and Queen Bertha in the Ascot Derby; was third to Macoroni and Queen Bertha in the Doncaster Cup; was unplaced in his other races, including the 2,000 guineas, won by Macoroni; as four-year old started sixteen times, won three races; was second in two, third in five, and unplaced in the others; won the Epsom, four-year old stakes, 1¼ miles, beating Jarnicoton; Walsall won the all-aged plate, three-quarters of a mile, defeating a field of six, carried 138 lbs; same day, won the Tradesman's Plate, 1¼ miles with 124 lbs., beating Zohrah. At five-year old, started sixteen times, won two races, was second in four, third in two, and unplaced in the others; Lichfield, won the Anson Plate (handicap), half a mile, 123 lbs., defeating a field of seven; King's Lynn won the Grand Stand Plate, defeating a field of five. At six-year old, started eight times, was second in one race, third in three, and unplaced in four. He was relegated to the stud in 1869, and up to the time of his exportation, was credited with 32 foals, two of which died as sucklings, only some twelve were trained, these won 44 races. The best of his get are Slander, Scrape, Grey Friar, Blue Beard, Blue Ruin, Sign Manual, Sapphire, Nankin and Trickett. Bluemantle is a very blood-like horse; a brown, 15 hands 2¼ inches high, with lofty carriage; he retired from the turf sound, and is a very fine bred horse, full of Herod, Matchem and Eclipse blood, tracing through the famous Prunella, to a natural Barb Mare. The descendants of Prunella are all successful stallions, as Glencoe, Whalebone, Whisker, &c. He should make an excellent cross on Lexington mares, having the Kingston and Glencoe blood.

PEDIGREE OF BLUEMANTLE.

BLUEMANTLE.	**KINGSTON.** Dau. of Octavian. Dau. of Royal Oak. Jerboa. Smolensko. Parasol. Walton.	Sir Peter.	Highflyer—Papillon by Snap—Miss Cleveland by Regulus—Midge by Son of Bay Bolton—Dau. of Bartlet's Childers—Dau. of Honeywood Arabian
		Arethusa.	Dungannon (Eclipse) Dau. of Prophet—Virago by Snap—Dau. of Regulus—Sis. to Othello by Crab—Miss Slamerkin by Young True Blue.
		Pot-8-o's.	Eclipse—Sportsmistress by Warren's Sportsman—Golden Locks by Oroonoko—Valiant's dam by Crab—Dau. of Partner—Thwait's Dun Mare.
		Prunella.	Highflyer Promise by Snap—Julia by Blank—Spectator's dam by Partner—Bonny Lass by Bay Bolton—Dau. of Darley Arabian.
		Sorcerer.	Trumpator—Y. Giantess by Diomed—Giantess by Matchem—Molly Longlegs by Babraham—Dau. of Cole's Foxhunter—Dau. of Partner.
		Wowski.	Mentor (Justice)—Maria, Waxy's dam, by Herod—Lisette by Snap—Miss Windsor by Godol. Arabian—Sis. to Volunteer by Y. Belgrade.
		Gohanna.	Mercury (Eclipse) Dau. of Herod—Maiden by Matchem—Dau. of Squirt—Dau. of Mogul (Godol.)—Camilla by Bay Bolton—Old Lady.
		Camilla.	Trentham (Sweepstakes)—Coquette by Compton Barb—Sis. to Regulus by Godol. Arabian—Gr. Robinson by Bald Galloway—Dau. of Snake.
		Catton.	Golumpus (Gohanna)—Lucy Grey by Timothy—Lucy by Florizel—Frenzy by Eclipse—Dau. of Engineer—Dau. of Blank—Lass of the Mill.
		Daughter of.	Smolensko—Lady Mary by Beningbrough—Dau. of Highflyer—Dau. of Marske—A la Grecque by Regulus—Dau. of Allworthy (Crab.)
		Orville.	Beningbrough—Evelina by Highflyer—Termagant by Tantrum—Cantatrice by Sampson—Dau. of Regulus—Marske's dam by Blacklegs.
		Epsom Lass.	Sir Peter—Alexina by King Fergus—Lardella by Y. Marske—Dau. of Cade-Beaufremont's dam by Bro. to Fearnought—Miss Windham.
		Stripling.	Phoenomenon (Herod)—Laura by Eclipse—Dau. of Locust (Crab)—Dau. of Oroonoko—Dau. of Traveler—Miss Makeless by Y. Greyhound.
		Daughter of.	Oberon (Highflyer)—Sis. to Sharper, by Ranthos (Matchem) Dau. of Sweepstakes—Sis. to Careless by Spanker—Barb. Mare.
		Shuttle.	Y. Marske—Dau. of Vauxhall Snap—(Snap)—Hip by Herod—Sis. to Mirza by Godol. Arabian—Dau. of Hobgoblin—Dau. of Whitefoot—
		Katharine.	Delpini—Dau. of Paymaster—Dau. of Le Sang (Changeling)—Dau. of Rib (Crab)—Dau. of Snake—Gr. Wilkes by Hautboy.
	PARADIGM. Ellen Horne. Redshank. Sandbeck. Paragone. Hoyden. Touchstone. Tomboy. Banter. Camel. Delhi. Picnipo, Jr. Gohanna. tentiary. Pawn.	Whalebone.	Waxy—Penelope by Trumpator—Prunella by Highflyer—Promise by Snap—Julia by Blank—Spectator's dam by Partner—Bonny Lass.
		Daughter of.	Selim—Maiden by Sir Peter—Dau. of Phoenomenon—Matron by Florizel—Maiden by Matchem—Dau. of Squirt (Syphon.)
		Master Henry.	Orville—Miss Sophia by Stamford—Sophia by Buzzard—Huncamunca by Highflyer—Cypher by Squirrel—Fribble's dam by Regulus.
		Boadicea.	Alexander—Brunette by Aramanthus—Mayfly by Matchem—Dau. of An Starling—Dau. of Grasshopper—Dau. of Newton Arabian.
		Jerry.	Smolensko—Louisa by Orville—Thomasina by Timothy—Violet by Shark—Dau. of Syphon—Charlotte by Blank—Dau. of Crab.
		Daughter of.	Ardrossan (John Bull) Lady Eliza by Whitworth—Dau. of Spadille—Sylvia by Y. Marske—Ferret by Bro. to Silvio.
		Velocipede.	Blacklock—Dau. of Juniper (Whiskey)—Dau. of Sorcerer—Virgin by Sir Peter—Dau. of Pot-8-os—Editha by Herod.
		Miss Garforth.	Walton—Dau. of Hyacinthus—Zara by Delpini—Flora by King Fergus—Atalanta by Matchem—Lass of the Mill by Oroonoko.
		Catton.	Golumpus—Lucy Grey by Timothy—Lucy by Florizel—Frenzy by Eclipse—Dau. of Engineer—Dau. of Blank—Lass of the Mill by Traveler.
		Orvillina.	Beningbrough—Evelina by Highflyer—Termagant by Tantrum—Cantatrice by Sampson—Dau. of Regulus—Marske's dam.
		Selim.	Buzzard—Dau. of Alexander—Dau. of Highflyer—Dau. of Alfred—Dau. of Engineer—Bay Malton's dam by Cade—Lass of the Mill.
		Comical's dam.	Skyscraper (Highflyer)—Dau. of Dragon (Regulus)—Bridget's dam by Matchem—Dau. of Syphon—Dau. of Shakespeare (Hobgoblin.)
		Emilius.	Orville—Emily by Stamford—Dau. of Whiskey—Gr. Dorimant by Dorimant—Dizzy by Blank—Dizzy by Driver—Dau. of Smiling Tom.
		Harriet.	Pericles (Evander)—Dau. of Selim—Pipylina by Sir Peter—Rally by Trumpator—Fancy, Sis. to Diomed by Florizel—Sis. to Juno.
		Waxy.	Pot-8-os—Maria by Herod—Lisette by Snap—Miss Windsor by Godol. Arabian—Sis. to Volunteer by Y. Belgrade—Dau. of B. Childers.
		Pawn.	Trumpator—(Conductor)—Prunella by Highflyer (Herod)—Promise by Snap (Snip)—Julia by Blank (Godolphin)—Spectator's dam by Partner (Jigg)—Bonny Lass by Bay Bolton (Grey Hautboy)—Dau. of Darley Arabian—Dau. of Byerly Turk—Dau. of Taffolett—Barb. Dau. of Place's White Turk—Natural Barb Mare.

BLYTHEWOOD (Imp.)

Blythewood will be located the season of 1883, *at the Algeria Stud Farm near Erie, Pa., the property of Mr. W. L. Scott. Services only by private contract.*

BLYTHEWOOD, by Adventurer, son of Newminster, bred by Mr. W. I'Anson, foaled 1873 ; dam Bonny Bell by Voltigeur ; the dam of Bonny Swell, Blantyre, Muscatel, Beauclerc, etc., out of Queen Mary ; the dam of Blink Bonny, Balrownie, Bonnie Scotland, etc., by Gladiator. Blythewood started in only one race ; the Colt Sapling Stakes for two-year olds, five furlongs, 44 yards at York, won by Burgie, with Humboldt second, Blythewood third. Adventurer, his sire, was a fine race-horse, although he did not start in the Derby or St. Leger; he won the Loudesborough Plate (handicap), at Doncaster ; the City and Suburban Handicap, defeating Am Umpire, Gen. Hesse, Asteroid, and a large field of others, the great Northern Handicap and Flying Dutchman handicap at York, the Craven stakes, at Epsom, and the Queen's Gold Vase, at Ascot, and was one of England's most popular sires. Blythewood is a very richly bred horse, being a grandson of the famous old Beeswing, on the side of the sire, Newminster, who won the Doncaster St. Leger, in 1851, and was the sire of Nemesis, winner of the 1,000 guineas; Lord Clifden, winner of the St. Leger; Hermit, winner of the Derby, and the most popular stallion in England. Adventurer is a very popular stallion; he is the sire of Preteuder, winner of the 2,000 guineas, and Derby in 1869 ; Apology, winner of the 1,000 guineas ; Oaks and St. Leger, in 1874, and Wheel of Fortune, winner of the 1,000 gs., and Oaks in 1879 ; he is also the sire of Mr. P. Lorillard's great two-year old Pizzarro ; Voltigeur, the sire of his dam, was one of the few horses which won both the Derby and St. Leger, which he did together with the Doncaster Cup, in 1858 ; Bonny Bell, his dam, is half sister to Blink Bonny, the dam of Blair Athol, the best son of Stockwell, and his grandam, Queen Mary, is the dam of Balrownie, Bonnie Scotland, and other famous animals. Bonnie Scotland made a reputation in this country which is as enduring as time. If there is anything in blood and racing lineage, Blythewood should make a good sire. He is a dark bay, full 15¾ hands, with black points, and a star in the forehead, he possesses substance and power commensurate with his height. The daughters of Bonnie Scotland, bred to him will do much to preserve and perpetuate a popular and successful racing strain in America. He is much inbred to Eclipse, Matchem and Herod, through Whalebone Parasol, Emilius and Highflyer.

PEDIGREE OF BLYTHWOOD (Imp.)

BLYTHWOOD (Imp.)	**ADVENTURER.** Queen Mary. Daughter of Myrtha. Plenipotentiary.	Newminster. Beeswing. Daughter of Dr. Syntax.	Touchstone. Banter. Camel. Orville. Emily. Emilius. Palmes. Francesca. Daughter of Partisan.

	Whalebone. Daughter of.	Waxy—Penelope by Trumpator—Prunella by Highflyer—Promise by Snap—Julia by Blank—Spectator's dam by Partner. Selim—Maiden by Sir Peter—Dau. of Phoenomenon—Matron by Florizel—Maiden by Matchem—Dau. of Squirt—Lot's dam.
	Master Henry. Boadicea.	Orville—Miss Sophia by Stamford—Sophia by Buzzard—Huncamunca by Highflyer—Cypher by Squirrel—Fribble's dam by Regulus. Alexander—Brunette by Amaranthus—Mayfly by Matchem—Dau. of An. Starling—Dan. of Grasshopper—Dau. of Newton Arabian.
	Paynator. Daughter of.	Trumpator—Dau. of Mark Anthony (Spectator)—Signora by Snap—Miss Windsor by Godol. Arabian—Sis. to Volunteer by Y. Belgrade. Beningbrough—Jenny Mole by Carbuncle (Babraham by Gold)—Dau. of Prince T' Quassaw (Snip)—Dau. of Regulus—Dau. of Partner.
	Ardrossan. Lady Eliza.	John Bull (Fortitude)—Miss Whip by Volunteer (Eclipse)—Wimbleton by Evergreen (Herod)—Sis. to Calash by Herod—Teresa by Matchem. Whitworth (Agonistes by Sir Peter)—Dau. of Spadille (Highflyer)—Sylvia by Y. Marske—Ferret by Bro. to Silvio—Dau. of Regulus (Godol.)
	Beningbrough. Evelina.	King Fergus—Dau. of Herod—Pyrrha by Matchem—Dutchess by Whitenose—Miss Slamerkin by Y. True Blue—Dau. of Ox Dun Arabian. Highflyer—Termagant by Tantrum—Cantatrice by Sampson—Dau. of Regulus—Marske's dam by Blacklegs—Dau. of B. Bolton.
	Stamford. Daughter of.	Sir Peter—Horatia by Eclipse—Countess, Delpini's dam by Blank—Dau. of Rib—Dau. of Wynn Arabian—Dau. of Governor. Whiskey—Gr. Dorimant by Dorimant—Dizzy by Blank—Dizzy by Driver—Dau. of Smiling Tom—Dau. of Oysterfoot.
	Walton. Parasol.	Sir Peter—Arethusa by Dungannon—Dau. of Prophet (Reg)—Virago, Saltram's dam by Snap—Dau. of Regulus (Godol.). Pot-8-os—Prunella by Highflyer—Promise by Snap—Julia by Blank—Spectator's dam by Partner—Bonny Lass.
	Orville. Daughter of.	Beningbrough—Evelina by Highflyer—Termagant by Tantrum—Cantatrice by Sampson—Dan. of Regulus—Marske's dam. Buzzard—Hornpipe by Trumpator—Luna by Herod—Proserpine, Sis. to Eclipse by Marske—Spiletta by Regulus.

BONNY BELLE. Daughter of Gladiator. Pauline. Partisan. Martha Lynn. Leda. Mulatto. Voltigeur. Voltaire. Daughter Blackluck of.	Whitelock. Daughter of.	Hambletonian—Rosalind by Phoenomenon—Atalanta by Matchem—Lass of the Mill by Oroonoko—Dau. of Traveler. Coriander—Wildgoose by Highflyer—Coheiress by Pot-8-os—Manilla by Goldfinder—Dau. of Old Eng.—Dau. of Cul. Arabian.
	Phantom. Daughter of.	Walton—Julia by Whiskey—Y. Giantess by Diomed—Giantess by Matchem—Molly Longlegs by Babraham—Dau. of Foxhunter. Overton (King Fergus)—Gratitude's dam by Walnut—Dau. of Ruler (Y. Marske) Piracautha by Matchem—Prophetess.
	Catton. Desdemona.	Golumpus—Lucy Gray by Timothy—Lucy by Florizel—Frenzy by Eclipse—Dau. of Engineer—Dau. of Blank—Lass of the Mill. Orville—Fanny by Sir Peter—Dau. of Diomed—Desdemona by Marske—Y. Hag by Skim—Hag by Crab—Ebony by F. Childers.
	Filho-da-Puta. Treasure.	Haphazard—Mrs. Barnet by Waxy—Dau. of Woodpecker—Heinel by Squirrel—Principessa by Blank—Dau. of Cul. Arabian. Camillus—Dau. of Hyacinthus—Flora by King Fergus—Atalanta by Matchem—Lass of the Mill by Oroonoko—Dau. of Traveler.
	Walton. Parasol.	Sir Peter—Arethusa by Dungannon—Dau. of Prophet—Virago by Snap—Dau. of Regulus—Sis. to Othello by Crab—Miss Slamerkin. Pot-8-os—Prunella by Highflyer—Promise by Snap—Julia by Blank—Spectator's dam by Partner—Bonny Lass by Bay Bolton.
	Moses. Quadrille.	Whalebone or Seymour—Dau. of Gohanna—Grey Skim by Woodpecker—Silver's Dam by Herod—Y. Hag by Skim—Hag by Crab. Selim—Canary Bird by Whiskey or Sorcerer—Canary by Coriander—Miss Green by Highflyer—Harriet by Matchem.
	Emilius. Harriet.	Orville—Emily by Stamford—Dau. of Whiskey—Gr. Dorimant by Dorimant—Dizzy by Blank—Dizzy by Driver—Dau. of Smiling Tom. Pericles—Dau. of Selim—Pipylina by Sir Peter—Rally by Trumpator—Fancy, Sis. to Diomed by Florizel—Dau. of Spectator.
	Whalebone. Gift.	Waxy—Penelope by Trumpator—Prunella by Highflyer—Promise by Snap—Julia by Blank—Spectator's dam by Partner. Y. Gohanna—Sis. to Grazier by Sir Peter—Sis. to Amaltor by Trumpator (Conductor), Dau. of Herod (Tartar), Dau. of Snap (Snip), Dau. of Gower Stallion (Go' Arabian)—Dau. of Flying Childers (Darley Arabian).

BRAMBLE,

(WINNER OF THE YOUNG AMERICA STAKE NO. 2 AND MAXWELL HOUSE STAKE AT NASHVILLE, SARATOGA AND CONGRESS STAKES AT SARATOGA, BALTIMORE CUP, MONMOUTH CUP, WESTCHESTER CUP, SARATOGA CUP, AND OTHER IMPORTANT RACES),

Will stand the season of 1883 *at the* ***Belle Meade Stud****, near* ***Nashville****, Tenn., at* **$100** *the season. Application to* ***Gen. W. H. Jackson****, lock box* 383 ***Nashville****, Tenn. Annual sale of yearlings about May* 1*st.*

Bramble, by imp. Bonnie Scotland, bred by Gen. W. G. Harding, Belle Meade Stud, foaled 1875, dam Ivy Leaf dam of Bazar, Brambaletta, etc., by imp. Australian, out of Bay Flower sister to Bayonet, Bayswater, Preakness, etc., by Lexington. Bramble ran seven times as a two-year old; won the Young American Stakes No. 2, at Nashville, three-quarters of a mile, in 1:20, track heavy. In this he beat Milan (who had beaten him previously, the latter taking up 5 lbs. penalty) and others. He won the Saratoga Stakes, at Saratoga, three-quarters of a mile, in 1:17¾, beating Duke of Magenta, Pride of the Village and others; ran second to Milan for the Young America Stakes No. 1, half a mile, in :50½; ran second to Pomeroy at Louisville, Ky., for the Alexander Stakes, half a mile, in :49¼; ran third to Milan and Pomeroy, for the Tennessee Stakes, three-quarters of a mile, in 1:16. At Saratoga ran third to Pride of the Village and Duke of Magenta for the Kentucky Stakes, three-quraters of a mile, in 1:18¼. Was beaten by Pique in the Special Sweepstakes at Saratoga, three-quarters of a mile, in 1:16¾. He made his *debut* in his three-year-old form in the Withers Stake at Jerome Park, one mile; was second to Duke of Magenta in 1:48, each with 118 lbs.; one of the best races ever run, the track being muddy and heavy—Danicheff and Pride of the Village were behind him; beat Simoom, Oriole, etc., one mile, in 1:48½; ran second to Duke of Magenta for the Belmont Stakes, 1½ miles, in 2:43½, Spartan, Danicheff, Bayard and others behind him. Long Branch won dash of three-quarters of a mile, beating Idalia, Egypt, etc., in 1:17; same place, was beaten a match, one and a quarter miles, by Spartan, in 2:16, evidently badly managed or out of condition. Saratoga, ran second to the Duke of Magenta in Travers Stakes, one and three-quarters miles, in 3:08, a capital race; Spartan, Danicheff and Albert were behind him. Won dash of one mile, beating Lou Lanier, Garrick and Alleveur, in 1:45; won dash of one mile, beating Idalia, Pique, &c., in 1:47½, track heavy; beat Oriole, Idalia, etc., one and a quarter miles, in 2:17; walked over for purse, one and a half miles; received half purse and entrance money; beat Pique, Pride of the Village, etc., one mile, in 1:47½, carrying 113 lbs; ran second to Duke of Magenta for Kenner stakes, two miles, in 3:41½, beating Spartan, Bonnie Wood, Kate Claxton, Bertha, etc.; won race 1⅛ miles, in 1:58, beating Bonnie Wood, Kate Claxton, etc.; ran second to Bushwhacker, 1¾ miles, in 3:18¾, beating Maumee, Kenny, etc.; he carried 109 lbs. to Bushwhacker's 105 lbs. Was beaten one mile by La Belle Helene, in 1:45¾, beating Bertha, etc. Beat Lady D'Arcy, Bonnie Wood, etc.; three-quarters of a mile, in 1:19; beat Patriot, Kate Claxton and others, one mile, in 1:45¼. He was then sent to Louisville, where he won the great American Stallion Stakes, 1¾ miles, in 3:14½, beating Cammie F., Warfield, Momentum, Day Star and five others; same place, was second to Warfield, giving him 5 lbs.—1½ miles, in 1:56—the fastest race at the distance during the year. Nashville, won the Maxwell House Stakes, mile heats, in 1:43, 1:44, beating Warfield and Bergamot Baltimore, ran second, 1½ miles, won by Bonnie Wood in 2:19½, Bertha third. He was stale from his long trip to the West. At four years old started twenty times; won fifteen races, was second in two, third in one and unplaced in two. Bramble made his first public appearance in 1879, at Baltimore, Md., won dash of 1¼ miles, defeating Gov. Hampton, Albert and Judith; time, 2:15¼; same meeting, won the Baltimore Cup, 2¼ miles, defeating Bushwbacker, Bonnie Wood, Lou Lanier and Bayard, time, 4:01¾. Jerome Park, won dash of one mile, defeating Una, Franklin, Bonnie Wood and three others; time, 145½. Same meeting, won the Westchester Cup, 2¼ miles, defeating his only opponent, Invermore; time, 4:20½. Summer Meeting, Coney Island Jockey Club, Prospect Park, Bramble, Gov. Hampton, Gen. Philips and Willful started in the Seaside Handicap, 2 miles; Willful finished first, Philips second and Bramble last; time, 3:34¾. Monmouth Park, won the Ocean Stakes, 1⅛ miles, defeating Monitor, Lancewood, Susquehanna and Belinda; time, 1:58½. Same meeting, won dash 1½ miles, defeating Una and Tom Scarlet; time, 2:37. Same meeting, won the Monmouth Cup, 2¼ miles, defeating Lou Lanier, Gen. Philips and Willful; Bramble carried 5 lbs. penalty for winning the Westchester Cup; time, 4:18½. Saratoga, ran second to Monitor in the All-Aged Stakes, 1¾ miles; time, 3:12¼. Same meeting, won the

(*Continued on page* 26.)

PEDIGREE OF BRAMBLE.

BRAMBLE.								
	IMP. BONNIE SCOTLAND.	Queen Mary, Blink Bonny's Dam.	Daughter of.	Iago.	Dau. of.	Don John.	Dick Andrews.	Joe Andrews (Eclipse)—Dau. of Highflyer (Herod)—Dau. of Cardinal Puff (Babraham)—Dau. of Tattler (Blank)—Dau. of Snip.
							Daughter of.	Gohanna (Mercury)—Fraxinella by Trentham—Dau. of Woodpecker (Herod)—Everlasting by Eclipse—Hyaena by Snap.
					Scandal.	Tramp.	Comus.	Sorcerer (Trumpator)—Houghton Lass by Sir Peter—Alexina by King Fergus (Eclipse)—Lardella by Y. Marske—Dau. of Cade.
							Marciana.	Stamford (Sir Peter)—Marcia by Coriander (Pot-8-os)—Faith by Pacolet (Blank)—Atalanta by Matchem (Cade)—Lass of the Mill.
				Gladiator.	Pauline.	Selim.	Buzzard.	Woodpecker (Herod)—Misfortune by Dux (Matchem)—Curiosity by Snap (Snip)—Dau. of Regulus (Godol.)—Dau. of Childers.
							Castrel's Dam.	Alexander (Eclipse)—Dau. of Highflyer (Herod)—Dau. of Alfred (Matchem) —Dau. of Engineer—Bay Malton's dam by Cade (Godol.)
						Dau. of.	Haphazard.	Sir Peter (Highflyer)—Miss Hervey by Eclipse (Marske)—Clio by Young Cade—Dau. of Old Starling—Dau. of Bart. Childers—Dau. of B. Bolton.
							Daughter of.	Precipitate (Mercury)—Colibri by Woodpecker—Camilla by Trentham— Coquette by the Compton Barb—Sis. to Regulus.
			Myrrha.	Plenipotentiary.	Partisan.		Walton.	Sir Peter (Highflyer)—Arethusa by Dungannon (Eclipse)—Dau. of Prophet (Regulus)—Virago by Snap—Dau. of Regulus—Sis. to Othello.
							Parasol.	Pot-8-os (Eclipse)—Prunella by Highflyer—Promise by Snap (Snip)—Julia hy Blank (Godol.)—Spectator's dam by Partner.
						Dau. of.	Moses.	Whalebone or Seymour—Dau. of Gohanna—Grey Skim by Woodpecker— Silver's dam by Herod—Y. Hag by Skim—Hag by Crab.
							Quadrille.	Selim—Canary Bird by Whiskey or Sorcerer—Canary by Coriander—Miss Green by Highflyer—Harriet by Matchem—Flora by Reg.
							Emilius.	Orville (Beningbrough)—Emily by Stamford—Dau. of Whiskey (Saltram) —Grey Dorimant by Dorimant (Otho)—Dizzy by Blank.
							Harriet.	Pericles (Evander)—Dau. of Selim—Pipylina by Sir Peter—Rally by Trumpator—Fancy by Florizel, Sister to Diomed by Florizel—Dau. of Spectator.
							Whalebone.	Waxy (Pot 8-os)—Penelope by Trumpator—Prunella by Highflyer—Promise by Snap—Julia by Blank—Spectator's dam by Partner.
							Gift.	Y. Gohanna (Gohanna)—Sister to Grazier by Sir Peter—Sis. to Amaitor by Trumpator—Dau. of Herod—Dau. of Snap—Dau. Gower Stallion.
	IVY LEAF.	Bay Flower.	Imp. Australian.	West Australian.	Mowerina.	Melbourne.	Humphrey Clinker.	Comus (Sorcerer)—Clinkerina by Clinker (Sir Peter)—Pewet by Tandem (Syphon)—Termagant by Tantrum—Cantatrice by Sampson.
							Daughter of.	Cervantes (Don Quixote)—Dau. of Golumpus (Gohanna)—Dau. of Paynator (Trumpator)—Sis. to Zodiac by St. George—Abigail by Woodpecker
						Young Emilius.	Touchstone.	Camel (Whalebone)—Banter by Master Henry (Orville)—Boadicea by Alexander (Eclipse)—Brunette by Amaranthus—Mayfly by Matchem.
							Emma.	Whisker (Waxy)—Gibside Fairy by Hermes (Mercury)—Vicissitude by Pipator (Conductor)—Beatrice by Sir Peter—Pyrrha by Matchem.
			Emilia.	Imp. Emilius.	Persian.		Emilius.	Orville—Emily by Stamford—Dau. of Whiskey (Saltram)—Grey Dorimant by Dorimant—Dizzy by Blank—Dau. of Driver—Dau. of Smiling Tom.
							Shoveler.	Scud (Beningbrough) Goosander by Hambletonian—Rally by Trumpator —Fancy by Florizel—Dau. of Spectator (Crab)—Horatia by Blank.
							Whisker.	Waxy—Penelope by Trumpator—Prunella by Highflyer—Promise by Snap —Julia by Blank—Spectator's dam by Partner.
		Bay Leaf.	Lexington.	Boston.			Variety.	Selim or Soothsayer (Sorcerer)—Sprite by Bobtail (Precipitate)—Catharine by Woodpecker—Camilla by Trentham.
					Alice Carneal.		Timoleon.	Sir Archy (Diomed)—Dau. of Saltram (Eclipse)—Dau. of Wildair (Fearnought)—Dau. of Driver (Imp. Othello)—Dau. of Fallower (Blank.)
							Sister to Tuckahoe.	Ball's Florizel (Diomed)—Dau. of Alderman (Pot-8-os)—Dau. of Clockfast (Gimcrack)—Dau. of Symme's Wildair—Y. Kitty Fisher.
		Maria Black.	Imp. Yorkshire.				Imp. Sarpedon.	Emilius (Orville)—Icaria The Flyer (Vandyke, Jr.)—Parma by Dick Andrews—May by Beningbrough—Primrose.
							Rowena.	Sumpter (Sir Archy)—Lady Grey by Robin Grey (Royalist)—Maria by Melzar (Imp. Medley)—Dau. of Imp. Highflyer—Dau. of Ariel.
							St. Nicholas.	Emilius—Seamew by Scud—Goosander by Hambletonian (King Fergus)— Rally by Trumpator—Fancy by Florizel—Sis. to Juno.
							Miss Rose.	Tramp (Dick Andrews)—Dau. of Sancho (Don Quixote)—Blacklock's dam by Coriander—Wildgoose by Highflyer—Coheiress by Pot-8-os.
							Filho-da-Puta.	Haphazard (Sir Peter)—Mrs. Barnet by Waxy—Dau. of Woodpecker— Heinel by Squirrel—Principessa by Blank—Dau. of Cul Arabian.
							Daughter of.	Smolensko (Sorcerer)—Dau. of Sir Peter—Dau. of Mambrino—Marigold by Herod—Toy by Blank—Whiteneck by Crab—Dau. of Go' Arabian—Dau. of Conyer's Arabian—Dau. of Curwen Bay Barb—Dau. of Marshall's Spot—Dau. of White-legged Chestnut Lowther Barb—Old Vintner Mare.

BRAMBLE—Continued.

Saratoga Cup, 2¼ miles, defeating Willful, Lou Lanier, Belle and Dauicheff; time, 4:11¼. Same place, won dash of 1⅛ miles, defeating Mintzer, Dan Sparling and Dairy Maid time, 2·00. Same place, won dash 1 mile, defeating Bennett; time, 1:49. Same place, won three-quarters of a mile, defeating Annie Augusta, Oriole, Bonnie Wood, Lottery and Gabriel, time, 1:17¼. Same place, won dash of 1 mile, defeating Oriole and Gabriel time, 1:44¼. Same place, started in the Summer Handicap, 1¼ miles, won by Franklin in 2:39½; Bramble carried 126 lbs., and failed to secure a place. Same place won dash 1⅛ miles, defeating Gabriel, Dan Sparling and Eunice; time, 1:58. Same place, won the Congress Hall Stakes, heats of three-quarters of a mile, defeating Shylock, Lady Middleton and Lady D'Arcy; time, 1:19, 1:18. Brighton Beach Fair Grounds, N. Y., ran second to Fortuna in sweepstakes for all ages, 2¼ miles; time, 4:02¼. Same place, won the Brighton Cup, 2¼ miles, defeating Franklin by a head; time, 4:16½; Fortuna and Mintzer also ran; Monmouth Park ran third in the Champion Stakes, 1½ miles, won by Spendthrift, Report second; time, 2:41½; at 5 years won the Centennial Stakes at Nashville Tenn., 1⅛ miles, in 1:58, beating Beatitude and others; at 6 years, starting only once; ran second to Ferida; at Baltimore, mile heats in 1:44½, 1:44½, 1:48¾, Bramble won the first heat. This was his last race. Ivy Leaf the dam of Bramble was never trained, Bay Flower his grandam was a good race mare at all distances, she beat the famoms Rhynodyne three and four mile heats at St. Louis; four miles, in 7:45½, 7:45. Bramble is a rich red bay with large star in forehead, 15 hands 2½ inches high, girths 70 inches, length of shoulder 28 inches, around the arm 20 inches, below the knee 8¼ inches, from hip to point of hock 36¾ inches, around gaskins 16½ inches, from point of shoulder to point of buttocks 64 inches. He is full of substance and power, and greatly resembles his sire. He is strongly inbred to Herod and Eclipse through the best sources with the Archy and Diomed blood through Lexington, he was speedy, could stay and pack weight. He should prove a success upon the matrons at Belle Meade.

BRIGADIER (Imp.)

Brigadier will be located the season of 1883 at the stables of Col. A. R. Wynn, Castalian, Springs, Tenn., and will serve mares at $25 the season.

Brigadier, by Monarque, bred in France, foaled 1869, imported by Mr. J. A. Smith, dam Sweet Lucy, by Sweetmeat. Brigadier ran but once in public in a plate at Newmarket Second October Meeting won by Nudel, he was unplaced. His sire, Monarque, was a fine race-horse, won the Goodwood Cup in 1857, and sired Gladiateur, who not only won the 2,000 guineas, Derby and St. Leger in 1865, but the Grand Prix de Paris same year, and he is the only horse which ever accomplished the feat. Gladiateur also won the Ascot Gold Cup in 1866, and many other important events. Sweetmeat, the sire of his dam, Sweet Lucy, was sire of Macaroni, winner of the 2,000 guineas and Derby in 1863, and of Mincepie winner of the Oaks in 1856, and Mincemeat winner of the Oaks in 1854. Macheath, the crack two year old, of England, for this year 1882, is by Macaroni. The pedigree is full of stout and speedy crosses; the horse served no thorough-bred mares until 1880, and his colts are pronounced very promising. His blood is one of the links through which the Sweetmeat and Whalebone blood can be perpetuated in this country, he is strongly inbred to Waxy, through both Whisker and Whalebone, and to Eclipse through these two stout crosses and through Orville, and Blacklock. Beningbrough, the sire of Orville, won the St. Leger in 1794, and Hambletonian, the grandsire of Blacklock, won it in 1795, both were grandsons of the great Eclipse, both being by King Fergus, the famous son of that horse, and he traces through his dam to Proserpine, an own sister of Eclipse. Brigadier is a brown 16½ hands, with little white on one heel behind, is a fine tempered, well shaped horse.

PEDIGREE OF BRIGADIER.

BRIGADIER.	MONARQUE.	The Baron Sting, or The Emperor.*	Defence. Daughter of.	Whalebone. Reveller. Defiance. Design. Catton. Dau. of Royal Oak. Whisker. Ada. Anna Bella.	Waxy. Penelope.	Pot-8-os—Maria by Herod—Lisette by Snap—Miss Windsor by Godol Arabian—Sis. to Volunteer by Y. Belgrade—Dau. of Bart Childers. Trumpator—Prunella by Highflyer—Promise by Snap—Julia by Blank—Spectator's dam by Partner—Bonny Lass by Bay Bolton.
					Rubens. Little Folly.	Buzzard—Selim's dam by Alexander—Dau. of Highflyer—Dau. of Alfred—Dau. of Engineer—Bay Malton's dam by Cade (Godol). Highland Fling—Harriet by Volunteer—Lady Sarah's dam by Alfred—Magnolia by Marske—Dau. of Babraham—Dau. of Sedbury.
					Comus. Rosette.	Sorcerer—Houghtou Lass by Sir Peter—Alexina by King Fergus—Lardella by Y. Marske—Dau. of Cade—Beaufremont's dain. Beningbrough—Rosamond by Tandem—Tuberose by Herod—Gr. Starling by Starling—Coughing Polly by Bartlet's Childers.
					Tramp. Defiance.	Dick Andrews—Dau. of Gohanna—Fraxinella by Trentham—Dau. of Woodpecker—Everlasting by Eclipse—Hyaena. Rubens—Little Folly by Highland Fling—Harriet by Volunteer—Dau. of Alfred—Magnolia by Marske—Dau. of Babraham—Dau. of Sedbury.
		Poetess.			Golumpus. Lucy Grey.	Gohanna—Catharine by Woodpecker—Camilla by Trentham—Coquette by Compton Barb—Sis. to Regulus by Godol Arabian. Timothy (Whisker or Prime Minister)—Lucy by Florizel—Frenzy by Eclipse—Dau. of Engineer—Dau. of Blank—Lass of the Mill by Traveler.
					Smolensko. Lady Mary.	Sorcerer—Wowski by Mentor (Justice)—Maria Waxy's dam by Herod—Lisette by Suap—Miss Windsor by Godol Arabian—Sis. to Volunteer—Beningbrough—Dau. of Highflyer—Dau. of Marske (Squirt)—A la Grecque by Regulus—Dau. of Allworthy (Crab)—Dau. of Bol Starling.
					Waxy. Penelope.	Pot-8-os—Maria by Herod—Lisette by Suap—Miss Windsor by Godol Arabian—Sis. to Volunteer by Y. Belgrader—Dau. of Bart Childers. Trumpator—Prunella by Highflyer—Promise by Snap—Julia by Blank—Spectator's dam by Partner—Bonny Lass by Bay Bolton.
					Shuttle. Daughter of.	Y. Marske—Dau. of Vauxhall-Snap—Hip by Herod—Sister to Mirza by Godol Arabian—Dau. of Hobgoblin—Dau. of Whitefoot. Drone (Herod)—Contessina by Y. Marske—Tuberose by Herod—Gr. Starling by Starling—Coughing Polly by Bart Childers.
	SWEET LUCY.	Sweetmeat.	Gladiator. Lollypop. Launcelot.	Partisan. Pauline. Starch, or Voltaire * Bellnda. Camel. Banter. Sheet Anchor. Lady Emeline.	Walton. Parasol.	Sir Peter—Arethusa by Dungannon—Dau. of Prophet—Virago by Snap—Dau. of Regulus—Sis. to Othello by Crab—Miss Slamerkin. Pot-8-os—Pruuella by Highflyer—Promise by Suap—Julia by Blank—Spectator's dam by Partner—Bonny Lass.
					Moses. Quadrille.	Whalebone or Seymour (Delpini)—Sis. to Castania by Gohanna—Gr. Skim by Woodpecker—Silver's dam by Herod—Y. Hag. Selim—Canary Bird by Whiskey or Sorcerer—Canary by Coriander—Miss Green by Highflyer—Harriet by Matchem.
					Blacklock. Daughter of.	Whitelock—Dau. of Coriander—Wildgoose by Highflyer—Coheiress by Pot-8-os—Manilla by Goldfinder—Dau. of Old Eng. Phantom—Dau. of Overton (King Fergus)—Gratitude's dam by Walnut—Dau. of Ruler (Y. Marske)—Piracantha by Matchem.
					Blacklock. Wagtail.	Whitelock—Dau. of Coriander—Wildgoose by Highflyer—Coheiress by Pot-8-os—Manilla by Goldfinder—Dau. of Old Eng. Whisker—Dau. of Sorcerer—Dau. of Sir Solomon (Sir Peter)—Dau. of Y. Marske—Dau. of Phoenomenon—Calliope by Slouch.
		Coquette.			Whalebone. Daughter of.	Waxy—Penelope by Trumpator—Prunella by Highflyer—Promise by Snap—Julia by Blank—Spectator's dam by Partner—Bonny Lass. Selim—Maiden by Sir Peter—Dau. of Phoenomenon—Matron by Florizel—Maideu by Matchem—Dau. of Squirt—Lot's dam.
					Master Henry. Boadicea.	Orville—Miss Sophia by Stamford—Sophia by Buzzard—Huncamunca by Highflyer—Cypher by Squirrel—Dau. of Regulus. Alexander—Brunette by Amaranthus—Mayfly by Matchem—Dau. of An. Starling—Dau. of Grasshopper—Dau. of Newton Arabian.
					Lottery. Morgiana.	Tramp—Mandane by Pot-8-os—Y. Camilla by Woodpecker—Camilla by Trentham—Coquette by Compton Barb—Sis. to Regulus. Muley—Miss Stephenson by Scud or Sorcerer—Sis. to Petworth by Precipitate—Dau. of Woodpecker—Sis. to Juniper by Snap.
					Young Phantom Daughter of.	Phantom—Emmeline by Waxy—Sorcery by Sorcerer—Cobbea by Skyscraper—Dau. of Woodpecker—Heinel by Squirrel. Orville—Goldenleg's dam by Buzzard—Hornpipe by Trumpator (Conductor)—Luna by Herod (Tartar)—Proserpine Sis. to Eclipse by Marske (Squirt)—Spiletta by Regulus (Godol)—Mother Western by Smith's Son of Snake—Dau. of Old Montagu—Dau. of Hautboy—Dau. of Brimmer.

*The Emperor and Voltaire given.

BULLION

Will stand the season of 1883 *at the Minnehaha Stud, Samuel Y. Keene, proprietor, near Georgetown, Scott Co., Ky., and will serve mares at* $25 *the season. Application to S. Y. Keene, Georgetown, Ky.*

BULLION, by War Dance, son of Lexington, bred by the late A. Keene Richards, Blue Grass Stud, Ky, foaled 1873, dam Gold Ring by Ringgold, son of Boston, out of Ann Percy, by imp. Albion; Ringgold, the sire of Bullion's dam, was a fine race-horse, and a winner of some good races, he covered but few mares, but got those fine race-horses, Delaware and Onward, both speedy and capable of staying a distance. Albion, the sire of Bullion's grandam, was imported at a yearling, and was a winner in Virginia at all distances, and in good company, and became noted as a sire of winners and successful brood mares. Bullion was one of the unfortunate race-horses, he was cut down when a two-year old in one of his races, and was thought to have been ruined, but he recovered so far that he was trained, and in the Kentucky Derby at Louisville won by Vagrant, he was again cut down when looking dangerous and close up. This ruined him for racing purposes. Bullion started in one race as two years old, and was cut down in the race. He came out as three years old, and won a Sweepstake at Lexington mile heats in 1:46¼, 1:45¼ beating Eaglet, Dailgasian, L'Argentine and others, was unplaced in the Citizen Stake, two miles won by Red Coat in 3:34¼. Bullion carried 111 lbs., and Red Coat, 105 lbs., the other starters, 100 lbs each. Started in the Kentucky Derby 1½ miles won by Vagrant in 2:38¼. Bullion was cut down when running third, and ruined for racing purposes. Bullion has covered only a few mares, those of his owners. The following creditable winners are by him: Fairfield, winner of the Criterion Stake at Long Branch, three-quarters of a mile in 1:17¾. Golden Era, Gold Basis, the latter, a good one, Wendover a winner, Rufus L. Bullington, Coinage and Free Gold, who defeated Aella and Hilarity. Bullion is inbred to Old Boston, having the cross through War Dance and Ringgold, he has a Glencoe cross through famous Reel, dam of Lecompte, Starke Prioress, etc., and seven direct crosses of Sir Archy and Diomed, and any number to Herod and Eclipse through his collateral branches. Bullion is a rich chestnut, 16¼ hands, with one white heel behind, and is a horse of fine temper with great substance and power, and transmits his qualities to his progeny.

PEDIGREE OF BULLION.

BULLION.	WAR DANCE.	Lexington.	Alice Carneal.	Boston.	Sister to Tuckahoe.	Timoleon.	Sir Archy.	Diomed—Castianira by Rockingham—Tabitha by Trentham—Dau. of Bosphorus—Dau. of Wm's Forester.
							Daughter of.	Saltram (Eclipse)—Dau. of Symme's Wildair—Dau. of Driver (Imp. Othello)—Dau. of Fallower (Blank)—Dau. of Vampire.
				Sarpedon.			Ball's Florizel.	Diomed—Dau. of Imp. Shark—Dau. of Harris' Eclipse—Dau. of Imp. Fearnought—Dau. of Jolly Roger—Dau. of Sober John.
							Daughter of.	Alderman—Dau. of Clockfast—Dau. of Symme's Wildair—Y. Kitty Fisher by Fearnought—Imp. Kitty Fisher.
			Rowena.				Emilius.	Orville—Emily by Stamford—Dau. of Whiskey—Gr. Dorimant by Dorimant—Dizzy by Blank—Dizzy by Driver.
							Icaria.	The Flyer—Parma by Dick Andrews—May by Beningbrough—Primrose by Mambrino—Cricket by Herod.
		Reel.		Sultan.			Sumpter.	Sir Archy—Robin Mare by Robin Redbreast—Dau. of Obscurity—Slamerkin by Imp. Wildair—Imp. Cub Mare by Cub.
							Lady Grey.	Robin Grey—Maria by Melzar—Dau. of Highflyer—Dau. of Fearnought—Dau. of Ariel—Dau. of Jack of Diamonds.
			Glencoe.				Selim.	Buzzard—Dau. of Alexander—Dau. of Highflyer—Dau. of Alfred—Dau. of Engineer—Bay Malton's dam by Cade.
				Trampoline.			Bacchante.	Williamson's Ditto—Sis. to Calomel by Mercury—Dau. of Herod—Folly by Marske—Vixen by Regulus—Dau. of Hutton's Spot.
		Gallopade.					Tramp.	Dick Andrews—Dau. of Gohanna—Fraxinella by Trentham—Dau. of Woodpecker—Everlasting by Eclipse—Hyaena by Snap.
							Web.	Waxy—Penelope by Trumpator—Prunella by Highflyer—Promise by Snap—Julia by Blank—Spectator's dam by Partner.
			Camillina.	Catton.			Golumpus.	Gohanna—Catharine by Woodpecker—Camilla by Trentham—Coquette by Comp. Barb—Sis. to Regulus by Godol. Arabian.
							Lucy Grey.	Timothy—Lucy by Florizel—Frenzy by Eclipse—Dau. of Engineer—Dau. of Blank—Lass of the Mill by Traveler.
							Camillus.	Hambletonian—Faith by Pacolet—Atalanta by Matchem—Lass of the Mill by Oroonoko—Dau. of Traveler.
							Daughter of.	Smolensko—Miss Cannon by Orville—Dau. of Weathercock—Cora by Matchem—Dau. of Turk—Dau. of Cub—Dau. of Allworthy.
	GOLD RING.	Ann Percy.	Albion.	Ringgold.	Boston.	Timoleon.	Sir Archy.	Diomed—Castianira by Rockingham—Tabitha by Trentham—Dau. of Bosphorus—Dau. of Wm's Forester.
							Daughter of.	Saltram—Dau. of Symme's Wildair—Dau. of Driver (Imp. Othello)—Dau. of Fallower (Blank)—Dau. of Vampire.
					Sister to Tuckahoe.		Ball's Florizel.	Diomed—Dau. of Imp. Shark—Dau. of Harris' Eclipse—Dau. of Fearnought—Dau. of Jolly Roger—Dau. of Sober John.
							Daughter of.	Alderman—Dau. of Clockfast—Dau. of Symme's Wildair—Y. Kitty Fisher by Fearnought—Imp. Kitty Fisher by Cade.
				Flirtilla, Jr.	Sir Archy.		Diomed.	Florizel—Sis. to Juno by Spectator—Horatia by Blank—Dau. of F. Childers—Miss Belvoir by Gr. Grantham—Dau. of Paget Turk.
							Castianira.	Rockingham—Tabitha by Trentham—Dau. of Bosphorus—Dau. of Wm's Forester—Dau. of Coalition Colt—Dau. of Bustard.
					Flirtilla.		Sir Archy.	Diomed—Castianira by Rockingham—Tabitha by Trentham—Dau. of Bosphorus—Dau. of Wm's Forester—Dau. of Coalition Colt.
							Sumpter's dam.	Robin Redbreast—Dau. of Obscurity—Slamerkin by Wildair (Regulus)—Imp. Cub Mare by Cub—Amaranthus' dam.
		Fanny Percy.	Ambassador.	Cain or *Actaeon.			Scud.	Beningbrough—Eliza by Highflyer—Augusta by Eclipse—Hardwick's dam by Herod—Dau. of Bajazet—Dau. of Regulus.
							Diana.	Stamford—Dau. of Whiskey—Gr. Dorimant by Dorimant—Dizzy by Blank—Dizzy by Driver—Dau. of Smiling Tom.
				Panthea.			Comus or *Blacklocke.	Whitelock—Dau. of Coriander—Wildgoose by Highflyer—Coheiress by Pot-8-os—Manilla by Goldfinder—Dau. of Old Eng.
							Manuella.	Dick Andrews—Mandane by Pot-8-os—Y. Camilla by Woodpecker—Camilla by Trentham—Coquette by Comp. Barb.
			Celerity.				Plenipotentiary.	Emilius—Harriet by Pericles—Dau. of Selim—Pipylina by Sir Peter—Rally by Trumpator—Fancy, Sis. to Diomed.
							Jenny Mills.	Whisker—Hornsea's dam by Cerberus—Miss Cranfield by Sir Peter—Dau. of Pegasus—Dau. of Paymaster—Pomona by Herod.
							Leviathan.	Muley—The Dandy's dam by Windle—Dau. of Anvil (Herod)—Virago by Snap—Dau. of Regulus—Sis. to Othello by Crab.
							Patty Puff.	Pacolet (Imp. Citizen)—Rosy Clack by Saltram (Eclipse)—Camilla by Melzar (Imp. Medley)—Jet by Haine's Flimnap (Imp. Flimnap)—Diana by Clodius (Imp. Janus)—Sally Painter by Imp. Sterling—Imp. Silver by Belsize Arabian—Dau. of Croft's Partner (Jigg)—Sis. to Roxana by Bald Galloway (St. Victor Barb)—Sis. to Chanter by Akaster Turk—Dau. of Leede's Arabian—Dau. of Spanker.

* Blacklock and Actaeon given.

DALNACARDOCH (Imp.)

(WINNER OF THE ST. JAMES' PALACE STAKES AT ASCOT, THE GRATWICKE STAKES AT GOODWOOD IN 1871, AND GREAT YORKSHIRE HANDICAP AT NEWMARKET IN 1882,)

Will make the season of 1883 *at the Stud Farm of Messrs. Chinn and Morgan, near Harrodsburg, Mercer Co., Ky., at* $50 *the season. Application to be made to Messrs. Chinn and Morgan, Harrodsburg, Ky.*

DALNACARDOCK, by Rataplan, own brother to Stockwell, bred by Mr. W. S. Crawfurd, foaled 1868, dam Mayonnaise dam of Carine Garbrock, etc., by Teddington, winner of the Derby in 1851, out of Pic Nic by Glancus. Dalnacardock did not run as a two-years old. He made his first appearance at Newmarket in the 2,000 guineas, but was unplaced in the race, won by Bothwell, by Stockwell. At Ascot he won the St. James' Palace Stakes, one mile, beating Field Marshall and Cheesewring. At Goodwood, he won the Gratwicke Stakes 1½ miles defeating The Pearle Toucques, etc. At Doncaster ran second to Field Marshall in the Doncaster stakes, beating Ringwood, the favorite. He was unplaced in the Newmarket Derby, won by Henry, by Monarque, in this race he beat Bothwell, the winner of the 2,000 guineas. At Newmarket Houghton Meeting won a handicap sweepstake across the flat one mile, 2 furlongs, 73 yards, beating Roquefort, Aeronaut and three others, at Shrewsbury was unplaced in the Wilton Welter handicap won by Conspiritor. At four years old started six times, won one race, was second in four, and unplaced in one. At Ascot ran second to Khedive (3) 98 lbs. by Macaroni in the Ascot Plate handicap, 1¼ miles, Dalnacardock (4) 108 lbs., Tynemouth Alaric and nine others behind him. At Brighton ran second to Proto-Martyr by St. Albans (3) 97, Daluacardock (4) 124 lbs., Uhlan-Munille and four others behind him. At Doncaster September Meeting won the great Yorkshire handicap, St. Leger course carrying 124 lbs., defeating Napolitain, Silvester, Field Marshall, Proto-Martyr and seven others. At Newmarket ran second to the great Hannah, winner of the 1,000 guineas and St. Leger, in the Twenty-third Triennial Produce Stakes for four-year olds Hannah, 119 lbs.; Dalnacardock, 122 lbs., beating Toucques. Newmarket Houghton Meeting was unplaced in a handicap Plate, Cambridgeshire Course, won by Manille. Same course ran second to Uhlan (3) 92 lbs., Dalnacardock (4) 124 lbs. for a handicap sweepstake across the flat, Houghton and Falkland behind him. At five years old ran second in one race, and unplaced in three. At Newmarket First October Meeting was second to Tourbillon by Cape Flyaway, in the trial stakes across the flat Cedric the Saxon, behind him. This closed his turf career, he always ran in good company, and carried the top weights. Dalnacardock's pedigree is full of speedy and staying crosses, he covered no thorough-bred mares in England, but from his confirmation and high breeding should get race-horses. He is a dark bay, with black points, full 15½ hands high, with good substance and sound legs and feet. He is very much inbred to Eclipse on both sides through Whalebone, Whisker, Whiskey, Parasol, Mandane, Web, Gohanna, etc., and to Herod through Highflyer, Sir Peter, and direct crosses to the Byerly Mare, dam, of the famous two True Blues.

PEDIGREE OF DALNACARDOCH.

DALNACARDOCH.	RATAPLAN.	The Baron.	Echidna.	Irish Birdcatcher.	Sir Hercules.	Whalebone.	Waxy (Pot-8-os)—Penelope by Trumpator (Conductor)—Prunella by Highflyer (Herod)—Promise by Snap (Snip)—Julia by Blank (Godol.)
						Peri.	Wanderer (Gohauna)—Thalestris by Alexander (Eclipse)—Rival by Sir Peter (Highflyer)—Hornet by Drone (Herod)—Manilla by Goldfinder.
					Guiccioli.	Bob Booty.	Chanticleer (Woodpecker)—Ierne by Bagot (Herod)—Dau. of Gamahoe (Bustard by Crab)—Patty by Tim (Squirt)—Miss Patch by Justice.
					Economist.	Flight.	Irish Escape (Commodore)—Young Heroine by Bagot—Heroine by Hero (Cade)—Dau. of Snap—Sis. to Regulus by Godol. Arabian—Gr. Robinson.
				Miss Pratt.		Whisker.	Waxy—Penelope by Trumpator—Prunella by Highflyer—Promise by Snap—Julia by Blank—Spectator's dam by Partner—Dau. of Bay Bolton.
						Floranthe.	Octavian—Caprice by Anvil—Madcap by Eclipse—Dau. of Blank—Dau. of Blaze—Dau. of Y. Greyhound.
					Sultan.	Blacklock.	Whitelock (Hambletonian)—Dau. of Coriander (Pot-8-os)—Wildgoose by Highflyer—Coheiress by Pot-8-os (Eclipse)—Manilla by Goldfinder.
						Gadabout.	Orville (Beningbrough)—Minstrel by Sir Peter—Matron by Florizel—Maiden by Matchem (Cade)—Dau. of Squirt—Lot's dam.
			Glencoe.			Selim.	Buzzard (Woodpecker)—Castrel's dam by Alexander (Eclipse)—Dau. of Highflyer—Sis. to Dr. by Alfred (Matchem)—Dau. of Engineer.
						Bacchante.	Williamson's Ditto (Sir Peter)—Sis. to Calomel by Mercury (Eclipse)—Dau. of Herod—Folly by Marske—Vixen by Regulus—Dau. of Hutton's Spot.
		Pocahontas.		Trampoline.		Tramp.	Dick Andrews—Daughter of Gohanna—Fraxinella by Trentham—Dau. of Woodpecker—Everlasting by Eclipse—Hyaena by Snap (Snip.)
						Web.	Waxy—Penelope by Trumpator—Prunella by Highflyer—Promise by Snap—Julia by Blank—Spectator's dam by Partner (Jigg.)
			Marpessa.	Muley.		Orville.	Beningbrough (King Fergus)—Evelina by Highflyer—Termagant by Tantrum—Dau. of Sampson (Blaze)—Daughter of Regulus (Godol.)
						Eleanor.	Whiskey (Saltram)—Y. Giantess by Diomed—Giantess by Matchem (Cade)—Molly Longlegs by Babraham (Godol)—Dau. of Cole's Foxhunter.
				Clare.		Marmion.	Whiskey—Y. Noisette by Diomed—Noisette by Squirrel (Traveler)—Carina by Marske—Thunder's dam by Blank—Dizzy by Driver (Snake.)
						Harpalice.	Gohanna—Amazon by Driver (Trentham) Fractions by Mercury—Dau. of Woodpecker—Everlasting by Eclipse—Hyaena by Snap—Miss Belsea.
	MAYONAISE.	Teddington.	Orlando.	Vulture.	Touchstone.	Camel.	Whalebone—Dau. of Selim—Maiden by Sir Peter—Dau. of Phoenomenon (Herod)—Matron by Florizel (Herod)—Maiden by Matchem.
						Banter.	Master Henry—Boadicea by Alexander—Brunette by Amaranthus—Mayfly by Matchem—Dau. of Au. Starling—Dau. of Grasshopper.
					Rockingham.	Laugar.	Selim—Dau. of Walton—Y. Giantess by Diomed—Giantess by Matchem—Molly Longlegs by Babraham—Dau. of Cole's Foxhunter (Brisk.)
						Kite.	Bustard (Castrel)—Miss Hap by Shuttle (Y. Marske)—Sis. to Haphazard by Sir Peter—Miss Hervey by Eclipse—Clio by Y. Cade—D. of Old Starling.
			Miss Twickenham.	Electress.		Humphrey Clinker.	Comus (Sorcerer)—Clinkerina by Clinker (Sir Peter)—Pewet by Tandem (Syphon)—Termagant by Tantrum (Cripple)—Cantatrice by Sampson.
						Medora.	Swordsman (Prizefighter)—Dau. of Trumpator—Sis. to Prunella by Highflyer—Promise by Snap—Julia by Blank—Spectator's dam by Partner.
				Partisan.		Election.	Gohanna—Ch. Skim by Woodpecker—Silver's dam by Herod—Y. Hag by Skim (Starling)—Hag by Crab—Ebony by Childers—Ebony by Basto.
						Daughter of.	Stamford—Miss Judy by Alfred (Matchem)—Manilla by Goldfinder (Snap)—Dau. of Old England (Godol.)—Dau. of Cul. Arabian—Miss Cade.
		Pic-Nic.	Glaucus.			Walton.	Sir Peter—Arethusa by Dungannon (Eclipse)—Dau. of Prophet (Regulus)—Virago by Snap—Dau. of Regulus—Sis. to Othello by Crab.
						Parasol.	Pot-8-os—Prunella by Highflyer—Promise by Snap—Julia by Blank—Spectator's dam by Partner—Dau. of Bay Bolton—Dau. of D. Arabian.
				Nopine.		Selim.	Buzzard—Castrel's dam by Alexander—Dau. of Highflyer—Sis to Dr. by Alfred—Dau. of Engineer—Bay Malton's dam Cade.
						Bizarre.	Peruvian (Sir Peter)—Violante. by John Bull (Fortitude by Herod)—Dau. of Highflyer—Everlasting by Eclipse—Hyaena by Snap (Snip.)
		Estelle.	Brutandorf.			Blacklock.	Whitelock (Hambletonian)—Dau. of Coriander—Wildgoose by Highflyer—Coheiress by Pot-8-os—Manilla by Goldfinder—D. of Old England.
						Mandane.	Pot-8-os—Y. Camilla by Woodpecker—Camilla by Trentham—Coquette by the Compton Barb—Sis. to Regulus by Godol. Arabian.
			Dau. of			Juniper.	Whiskey—Jenny Spinner by Dragon (Woodpecker)—Sis. to Soldier by Eclipse—Miss Spindleshanks by Omar (Godol.)—Dau. of Starling.
						Daughter of.	Sorcerer (Trumpator)—Virgin by Sir Peter—Dau. of Pot-8-os (Eclipse)—Editha by Herod (Tartar)—Elfrida by Snap (Snip)—Miss Belsea by Regulus (Godol)—Dau. of Bartlet's Childers (Darley Arabian)—Dau. of Honeywood's Arabian—Byerly Mare, dam of the Two True Blues.

DUKE OF MAGENTA,

(WINNER OF THE WITHERS ANNUAL AND BELMONT STAKES AT JEROME PARK; TRAVERS, SEQUEL, AND KENNER STAKES AT SARATOGA; PREAKNESS, DIXIE, AND BRECKENRIDGE STAKES AT BALTIMORE, AND OTHER RACES,)

Will be used as private Stallion in the Rancocas Stud, Mr. P. Lorillard, proprietor, Jobstown, Burlington County, N. J. Surplus sold annually.

Duke of Magenta, by Lexington, son of Boston, bred at the Woodburn Stud, A. J. Alexander, proprietor, foaled 1875, dam Magenta by imp. Yorkshire, out of Miriam by Imp. Glencoe.

The Duke's pedigree, although not a long or fashionable one, has some strong elements, and the family have been quite famous as racers. Magenta, his dam, produced Larkin and Queen Victoria, by Lexington, the latter the dam of Albert, Blenkiron, by imp. Bonnie Scotland, Mademoiselle, by Red Eye, the Duke of Magenta, by Lexington, and Duke of Montalban, by King Alfonso. None of them were very noted before the Duke. Miriam, by imp. Glencoe, his grandam, produced Magenta, quite a famous race-mare and winner at all distances from one to four mile heats; Mamona, by imp. Sovereign, a superior race-mare and winner of the fastest mile run to that date, 1861—1:44½, and since a dam of winners, Merrill and Marion, both by Lexington. Merrill won the Jersey Derby, at Paterson, in 1866, and the Travers Stake, at Saratoga, the same year. Marion was also a fine race-horse. She produced in succeeding years Grecian Bend, Hollywood, Miranda, and Neecy Hale, all by Lexington. Both Hollywood and Neecy Hale were superior race-mares. Hollywood won both the three-quarter and mile stakes at Lexington, Fall of 1870, then two years old, in 1:18¾ and 1:45¾. She later won at two mile heats in 3:38¾, 3:40½. Neecy Hale, three years old, won the sweepstakes, 1¾ miles, at Lexington, in 3:07¾, beating Creedmoor and others. Duke of Magenta started seven times as a two-year old, lost three, won three and ran a dead heat for the seventh one, carrying 115 lbs. to Spartan's 110. In the three races he lost, he was barely beaten a scant head. He won half a mile in :49½, ran dead heat three-quarters, in 1:16¾, and won the same distance in 1:17½. The Duke opened his three-year old campaign at Baltimore, May 27, by winning the Preakness Stakes, 1½ miles, in 2:41¾, beating Bayard and Albert. His second appearance was in the Withers Stakes, one mile, at Jerome Park, and, notwithstanding the track was very heavy and muddy, he won with 118 lbs. up, in 1:48. Eight days after he won the Belmont Stakes, 1½ miles, in 2:43½. He next appeared at Long Branch, June 29, and, being out of condition, was beaten for the Jersey-Derby, 1½ miles, by both Spartan and Danicheff.

Traveling to Saratoga on July 20, he won the Travers Stake, 1¾ miles, in 3:08, beating Spartan, Bramble and others. This race with the weight, 118 lbs., was about the best race of the year at the distance. On the 3d of August, penalized 5 lbs. 123 lbs. up, he won the Sequel Stakes, 1¾ miles, in 3.15, track heavy. On the 13th of the same month he won the Kenner Stakes, 2 miles, in 3:41½. He finished his season at Saratoga by winning in hollow style the Harding Stakes, 1½ miles, in 2:50½. He opened the Fall campaign at Jerome Park by winning the Jerome Stakes, 1¾ miles, in 3:11½. A few days after he captured the Annual Stakes, two miles, in 3:43, running the first mile in 1:45. Going to Baltimore, he easily won the Dixie Stakes, 110 lbs. up, in 3:41. Three days after he closed his three-year old campaign and turf career by winning the Breckenridge Stakes, 2 miles, with 115 lbs., in 3·43, the first mile being run in 1:46½. His gross winnings during the year amounted to $36,550. Thus starting in twelve races, winning eleven, and defeating all the best colts of the year, and striking his colors only once during the season, being then notoriously out of condition.

Duke of Magenta is a bay, 16½ hands, with star and long narrow white stripe down the face over his nose, both hind legs white half way to his hocks, and two black spots on coronet of each hind foot; he measures 75 inches around the girth. He is much like his famous sire Lexington, but much larger model. His oldest colts are now two years old and resemble the sire very much, and are very promising. Few such race-horses as the Duke ever face the starter in America. He has Diomed blood on both sides.

PEDIGREE OF DUKE OF MAGENTA.

DUKE OF MAGENTA.							
LEXINGTON.	Boston.	Timoleon.	Sir Archy.	Diomed.	Florizel—Sister to Juno Spectator—Horatia by Blank—Dau. of F. Childers—Miss Belvoir by Gr. Grantham—Dau. of Paget Turk.
				Castianira.	Rockingham—Tabitha by Trentham—Dau. of Bosphorus—Dau. of Wm's Forester—Dau. of Coalition Colt—Dau. of Bustard (Crab.)
			Ball's Florizel.	Saltram.	Eclipse—Virago by Snap—Dau. of Regulus—Sis. to Othello by Crab—Miss Slamerkin by Y. True Blue—Dau. of Ox Dun Arabian—D'Arcy Royal Mare.
				Daughter of.	Symme's Wildair—Dau. of Driver (Imp. Othello)—Dau. of Imp. Fallower (Blank by Godol.)—Dau. of Imp. Vampire (Regulus.)
		Robin Brown's dam.	Diomed.	Florizel—Sister to Juno by Spectator—Horatia by Blank—Dau. of F. Childers—Miss Belvoir by Gr. Grantham—Dau. of Paget Turk.
				Daughter of.	Imp. Shark—Dau. of Harris' Eclipse—Dau. of Imp. Fearnought—Dau. of Imp. Jolly Roger—Dau. of Imp. Sober John (Rib).
	Sarpedon.	Emilius.	Dau. of	Imp. Alderman.	Pot-8-os—Lady Bolingbroke by Squirrel—Cypron by Blaze—Selima by Bethel's Arabian—Dau. of Gra. Champion—Dau. of Dar. Arabian.
				Daughter of.	Imp. Clockfast—Dau. of Symme's Wildair—Y Kitty Fisher by Fearnought—Imp. Kitty Fisher by Cade—Dau. of Som. Arabian.
		Icaria.	Orville.	Beningbrough—Evelina by Highflyer—Termagant by Tantrum—Cantatrice by Sampson—Dau. of Regulus—Marske's dam.
				Emily.	Stamford—Dau. of Whiskey—Gr. Dorimant by Dorimant—Dizzy by Blank—Dizzy by Driver—Dau. of Smiling Tom.
Alice Carneal.	Rowena.	Sumpter.	The Flyer.	Vandyke Jr.—Azalia by Beningbrough—Gillyflower by Highflyer—Dau. of Goldfinder—Sister to Grasshopper by Marske.
				Parma.	Dick Andrews—May by Beningbrough—Primrose by Mambrino—Cricket by Herod—Sophia by Blank—Diana.
	Lady Grey.		Sir Archy.	Diomed—Castianira by Rockingham—Tabitha by Trentham—Dau. of Bosphorus—Dau. of Wm's Forester—Dau. of Coalition Colt.
				Flirtilla's dam.	Robin Redbreast—Dau. of Obscurity—Slamerkin by Wildair—Imp. Cub Mare by Cub—Amaranthus' dam.
			Robin Grey.	Royalist—Belle Mariah by Grey Diomed—Queen by Imp. St. George—Dau. of Cassius—Primrose by Imp. Dove.
				Maria.	Melzar—Dau. of Highflyer—Dau. of Fearnought—Dau. of Ariel—Dau. of Imp. Jack of Diamonds—Imp. Diamond.
MAGENTA.	Miss Rose.	Imp. Yorkshire.	St. Nicholas.	Emilius.	Orville.	Beningbrough—Evelina by Highflyer—Termagant by Tantrum—Cantatrice by Sampson—Dau. of Regulus—Marske's dam.
					Emily.	Stamford—Dau. of Whiskey—Gr. Dorimant by Dorimant—Dizzy by Blank—Dizzy By Driver—Dau. of Smiling Tom.
				Seamew.	Scud.	Beningbrough—Eliza by Highflyer—Augusta by Eclipse—Hardwick's dam by Herod—Dau. of Bajazet—Dau. of Regulus.
					Goosander.	Hambletonian—Rally by Trumpator—Fancy, Sis. to Diomed by Florizel—Dau. of Spectator—Dau. of Blank—Dau. of F. Childers.
			Tramp.		Dick Andrews.	Joe Andrews—Dau. of Highflyer—Dau. of Cardinal Puff—Dau. of Tattler—Dan. of Snip—Dau. of Godol. Arabian—Dau. of Whiteneck.
					Daughter of.	Gohanna—Fraxinella by Trentham—Dau. of Woodpecker—Everlasting by Eclipse—Hyaena by Snap—Miss Belsea.
		Dau. of	Saucho.	Herod—Dau. of Cade—Dau. of Bolton Little John—Durham's Favorite by son of Bald Galloway—Daffodil's dam by Gascoigne's Foreign Horse.
				Blacklock's dam	Coriander—Wildgoose by Highflyer—Coheiress by Pot-8-os—Manilla by Goldfinder—Dau. of Old Eng.—Dau. of Cullen Arabian.
	Glencoe.	Sultan.		Selim.	Buzzard—Castrel's dam by Alexander—Dau. of Highflyer—Dau. of Alfred—Dau. of Engineer—Bay Malton's dam by Cade.
				Bacchante.	Williamson's Ditto—Sis. to Calomel by Mercury—Dau. of Herod—Folly by Marske—Vixen by Regulus—Dau. of Hutton's Spot.
		Trampoline.	Tramp.	Dick Andrews—Dau. of Gohanna—Fraxinella by Trentham—Dau. of Woodpecker—Everlasting by Eclipse—Hyaena.
			Web.	Waxy—Penelope by Trumpator—Prunella by Highflyer—Promise by Snap—Julia by Blank—Spectator's dam by Partner.
Minerva Anderson.	Imp. Luzborough.	Dau. of	Williamson's Ditto.	Sir Peter—Arethusa by Dungannon—Dau. of Prophet—Virago by Snap—Dau. of Regulus—Sis. to Othello by Crab—Miss Slamerkin.
			Daughter of	Dick Andrews—Eleanor by Whiskey—Y. Giantess by Diomed—Giantess by Matchem—Molly Longlegs by Babraham (Godol.)
	Dau. of Imp. Luzborough.		Sir Charles.	Sir Archy—Dau. of Citizen—Dau. of Commutation—Dau. of Dare Devil—Sally Shark by Imp. Shark—Betsy Pringle.
			Daughter of.	Bess' Brimmer—Son of Blue Beard, Dam by Mendoza (Imp. Medley)—Grandam by imp. Medley.

DUKE OF MONTROSE

Will be located at McGrathiana Stud, near Lexington, Ky., as a private stallion. Milton Young, proprietor, Lexington, Ky. Yearlings Sold Annually.

DUKE OF MONTROSE, by Waverley, son of imp. Australian, bred by Jas A. Grinstead, Walnut Hill Stud, near Lexington, Ky., dam Kelpie—the dam of Janet, four miles in 7:25—by imp Bonnie Scotland, out of sister to Ruric dam of Grinstead by imp. Sovereign, son of Emilius, the winner of the Derby in 1823, and sire of the two famous Derby winners, Priam and Plenipotentiary, Oxygen winner of the Oaks, and Mango winner of the St. Leger. Sovereign's dam, Fleur-de-Lis by Bourbon, was one of the best mares of her day. In addition to other races she won the Goodwood Cup in 1829 and '30. Duke of Montrose made his *debut* as a three-year old, and started in five races and won one race at Gravesend, a dash of 1¼ miles in 2:12; at Jerome Park was second in the Lorillard Stakes for three-year-olds, one mile and three furlongs, won by Grenada, no time taken. At Gravesend was second in the Coney Island Handicap, one mile and three furlongs, won by Luke Blackburn in 2:24¼; Monmouth Park, was second in the Ocean Stakes, one mile and a furlong, won by Luke Blackburn in 2:03½; was second in a Sweepstakes, 1¼ miles, won by Luke Blackburn in 2:11½

Four years old, started in thirteen races of which he won five; Saratoga won a dash in one mile in 1:42½, beating Knight Templar and eight others; Monmouth Park, won a dash of one mile in 1:45¾, beating Jack of Hearts and two others ; won a selling race, one mile, in 1:44; Jerome Park, won dash of three-quarters of a mile in 1:19¼, beating Clarendon, Valparaiso and nine others; won a dash of one mile in 1:50¼, beating Marathon and others. In this race, to a false start the horses ran the distance, and Montrose finished first in 1:45¾. At Saratoga, was second in a dash of one mile, won by Fireman in 1:44; Monmouth Park, was second in a dash of one mile won by Sir Hugh in 1:44¾; was second in a Selling Race, one mile, won by Viola in 1:44¼ ; Saratoga was third in a dash of one mile and a furlong, welter weights, won by Boulevard in 1:59¾. Jerome Park was third in a dash of one mile, won by Marathon in 1:45¾. Was unplaced in his other races. It will be observed he ran good seconds to such horses as Grenada and the great Luke Blackburn.

This closes his racing career, having given away in his fore legs. Duke of Montrose is a blood bay, full 16 hands high with black points; is a large, fine, well developed horse, and possessed a wonderful turn of speed. He is inbred to Waxy through his famous sons, Whalebone and Whisker, and traces through the dams of Vandal and Ruric to the famous old Lady Grey, the grandam of Lexington, from whom so many successful sires and brood mares have descended.

PEDIGREE OF DUKE OF MONTROSE.

DUKE OF MONTROSE.	KELPIE.	Sister to Rurie. Levity. Vandal's dam.	Sovereign. Fleur-de Lis. Trustee.	Bonnie Scotland. Queen Mary. Daughter of Emilius.	Iago. Scandal. Don John. Gladiator.	Humphrey Clinker. Daughter of.	Comus—Clinkerina by Clinker—Pewet by Tandem—Termagant by Tantrum—Cantatrice by Sampson—Dau. of Regulus—Marske's dam. Cervantes—Dau. of Golumpus—Dau. of Paynator—Sister to Zodiac by St. George—Abigail by Woodpecker—Fivetail by Eclipse—Dau. of Blank.
						Touchstone. Emma.	Camel—Banter by Master Henry—Boadicea by Alexander—Brunette by Amaranthus—Mayfly by Matchem—Dau. of An. Starling. Whisker—Gibside Fairy by Hermes—Vicissitude by Pipator—Beatrice by Sir Peter—Pyrrha by Matchem—Duchess by Whitenose.
						Emilius. Shoveler.	Orville—Emily by Stamford—Dau. of Whiskey—Gr. Dorimant by Dorimant—Dizzy by Blank—Dizzy by Driver—Dau. of Smiling Tom. Scud—Goosander by Hambletonian—Rally by Trumpator—Fancy, Sis. to Diomed by Florizel—Dau. of Spectator—Horatia by Blank (Godol.)
		WAVERLY.	Imp. Australian. West Australian. Mowerina. Melbourne.	Emilia. Persian. Y Emilius.	Sheet Anchor. Weatherbit.	Whisker. Variety.	Waxy—Penelope by Trumpator—Prunella by Highflyer—Promise by Snap—Julia by Blank—Spectator's dam by Partner—Bonny Lass. Selim or Soothsayer—Sprite by Bobtail—Catharine by Woodpecker—Camilla by Trentham—Coquette by Compton Barb—Sis. to Regulus.
						Lottery. Morgiana.	Tramp—Mandane by Pot-8-os—Y Camilla by Woodpecker—Camilla by Trentham—Coquette by Compton Barb—Sis. to Regulus. Muley—Miss Stephenson by Scud or Sorcerer—Sis. to Petworth by Precipitate—Dau. of Woodpecker—Sis. to Juniper by Snap—Dau. of Blank.
			Cicily Jopson.	Miss Letty.		Priam. Daughter of.	Emilius—Cressida by Whiskey—Y Giantess by Diomed—Giantess by Matchem—Molly Longlegs by Babraham—Dau. of Cole's Foxhunter. Orville—Dau. of Buzzard—Hornpipe by Trumpator—Luna by Herod—Proserpine, Sis. to Eclipse by Marske—Spiletta by Regulus.
				Cestra. Daughter of Faugh-a-Ballagh.		Sir Hercules. Guicciolli.	Whalebone—Peri by Wanderer—Thalestris by Alexander—Rival by Sir Peter—Hornet by Drone—Manilla by Goldfinder—Dau. of Old Eng. Bob Booty—Flight by I Escape—Y Heroine by Bagot—Heroine by Hero—Dau. of Snap—Sister to Regulus by Godol. Arabian.
						Liverpool. Rachel.	Tramp—Dau. of Whisker—Mandane by Pot-8-os—Y Camilla by Woodpecker—Camilla by Trentham—Coquette by Compton Barb. Muley—Dau. of Comus—Margrave's dam by Election—Fair Helen by Hambletonian—Helen by Delpini—Rosalind by Phoenomenon.
						Tramp. Daughter of.	Dick Andrews—Dau. of Gohanna—Fraxinella by Trentham—Dau. of Woodpecker—Everlasting by Eclipse—Hyaena by Snap—Miss Belsea. Comus—Marciana by Stamford—Marcia by Coriander—Faith by Pacolet—Atalanta by Matchem—Lass of the Mill by Oroonoko.
						Selim. Daughter of.	Buzzard—Castrel's dam by Alexander—Dau. of Highflyer—Dau. of Alfred—Dau. of Engineer—Bay Malton's dam by Cade—Lass of the Mill. Haphazard—Dau. of Precipitate—Colibri by Woodpecker—Camilla by Trentham—Coquette by Compton Barb.—Sis. to Regulus by Go. Arabian.
						Partisan. Pauline.	Walton—Parasol by Pot-8-os—Prunella by Highflyer—Promise by Snap—Julia by Blank—Spectator's dam by Partner—Bonny Lass. Moses—Quadrille by Selim—Canary Bird by Whiskey or Sorcerer—Canary by Coriander—Miss Green by Highflyer—Harriet by Matchem.
						Plenipotentiary. Myrrha.	Emilius—Harriet by Pericles—Dau. of Selim—Pipylina by Sir Peter—Rally by Trumpator—Fancy, sis. to Diomed by Florizel. Whalebone—Gift by Y. Gohanna—Sis. to Grazier by Sir Peter—Sis. to Amaitor by Trumpator—Dau. of Herod—Dau. of Snap
						Orville. Emily.	Beningbrough—Evelina by Highflyer—Termagant by Tantrum—Cantatrice by Sampson—Dau. of Regulus—Marske's dam. Stamford—Dau. of Whiskey—Gr. Dorimant by Dorimant—Dizzy by Blank—Dizzy by Driver—Dau. of Smiling Tom—Dau. of Oysterfoot.
						Bourbon. Lady Rachel.	Sorcerer—Dau. of Precipitate—Dau. of Highflyer—Tiffany by Eclipse—Y Hag by Skim—Hag by Crab—Ebony by F. Childers—Ebony by Basto. Stamford—Y Rachel by Volunteer—Rachel by Highflyer—Sis. to Tandem by Syphon—Dau. of Regulus—Dau. of Snip.
						Catton. Emma.	Golumpus—Lucy Grey by Timothy—Lucy by Florizel—Frenzy by Eclipse—Dau. of Engineer—Dau. of Blank—Lass of the Mill by Traveler. Whisker—Gibside Fairy by Hermes—Vicissitude by Pipator—Beatrice by Sir Peter—Pyrrha by Matchem—Duchess by Whitenose.
						Tranby. Lucilla.	Blacklock—Dau. of Orville—Miss Grimstone by Weasel—Dau. of Ancaster—Dau. of Dam Arabian—Dau. of Sampson—Dau. of Oroonoko. Trumpator—Lucy by Orphan—Lady Gray by Robin Grey—Maria by Melzar—Dau. of Highflyer—Dau. of Fearnought—Dau. of Ariel—Dau. of Jack of Diamonds—Imp. Diamond by Cullen Arabian—Lady Thigh by Croft's Partner—Dau. of Greyhound—Dau. of Curwen Bay Barb—Dau. of D'Arcy Chestnut Arabian—Dau. of Whiteshirt—Old Montague Mare.

ELIAS LAWRENCE,

(WINNER OF THE PEOPLE'S LINE STAKES AND BADEN BADEN
HANDICAP AT SARATOGA, 1880.)

Will stand the season of 1883 at the Kaskaskia Stud Farm of Messrs. McCulloughs and Savage near Urbana, Ill. Application to J. S. McCullough, Urbana, Ill.

ELIAS LAWRENCE (first called Bilozi then Bilstein) by imp. Billet, son of Voltigeur, bred by Samuel Powers, Decatur, Ill., foaled 1877, dam Sprightly, dam of Volturno by Lexington, son of Boston out of Lightsome by imp. Glencoe. See Billet in this book, Sprightly, his dam, was never trained, and her first thoroughbred foal was Volturno one of the best race horses ever on the turf. Lexington, her sire, is referred to in this book. Lightsome, the grandam was the dam of Nevada, dam of Luke Blackburn, Salina and Crucifix all by Lexington, and first-class mares and dams of winners. Elias Lawrence ran two races at two years old, was third to Luke Blackburn, and Quito in Ocean Stakes, ¾ of a mile, at Long Branch, in 1:18¼, with three others behind him, was unplaced in his other race. At three years old started 18 times, won six races, was second in six, third in three, and unplaced in three. Saratoga, ran second to Ferncliff, in Sequel Stakes, 1¾ miles, in 3:09¼, beating Dawn and Clarendon, won club purse, one mile and a furlong, for three-year olds, in 2:01½, beating Turfman and four others, won People's Line Stakes, a handicap for all ages, 89 lbs., two miles, in 3:37¼, beating Jericho (4), 98 lbs.; Cammie F. (5), 98 lbs., and three others; won club purse, one mile and five furlongs, in 2:55, carrying 99 lbs., beating Gabriel (4), 110 lbs., and two others; won handicap purse, 100 lbs., one mile and five furlongs in 2:58, beating Checkmate (5), 121 lbs., Oriole (6), 113 lbs., and two others: won Baden Baden Handicap, for all ages, three miles, in 5:28¼, carrying 98 lbs , beating Irish King (4). 108 lbs., and five others; this is the fastest three miles ever run by a three-year-old. He was second to Luke Blackburn in Long Island St. Leger; second to Oden in a dash of 1¼ miles, in 2:15, with two others behind him; second to Ferida, 2 mile heats, in 3:39½, 3:42½, beating Clyde Hampton; all run at Gravesend. Brighton Beach, was second to Bye-and-Bye in Autumn Stakes, 1⅝ miles, in 3:15, beating Buster. Jerome Park, won club purse, mile heats, in 1:47, 1:48, 1:50¼, beating Ingomar, who won first heat, Bowstring and Harold. He closed his season by a defeat at the hands of Monitor in Jerome Park Cup, three miles, in 5:52.

At four years old started nine times, won one race, was second in two, third in two, unplaced in the others. Baltimore ran third to Grenada, and Oden in the Peyton Handicap, mile heats, in 1:43½, 1:43½, 1:47½, Oden won second heat, ran second to Monitor in in Baltimore Cup, 2¼ miles, in 4:02, beating Grenada. Sheepshead Bay, won the Handicap Sweepstake heats of 1¼ miles in 2:11, 2:11¼, 2:20, beating One Dime, who won first heat, Ferida and Oden. Ran second to Glenmore in the Great Long Island Stakes, four mile heats, in 8:18, 7:40, Lawrence won the first heat, but pulling up lame in the second was withdrawn, being by Billet with Blacklock Waxy, and Touchstone blood on the side of his sire with the Archy, and Diomed blood through Lexington and Boston, and out of the family which produced Ruric, Vandal, Lexington, and a host of other good ones, with size, substance, power and conformation he should get racehorses. In color Lawrence is a dark bay, 16¼ hands high, with two white pasterns behind, measures 73 inches around the girth, and weighs 1,100 lbs.

PEDIGREE OF ELIAS LAWRENCE.

ELIAS LAWRENCE.	**IMP. BILLET.**	Voltigeur.	Martha Lynn.	Voltaire.	Dau. of.	Black-lock.	Whitelock.	Hambletonian—Rosalind by Phoenomenon—Atalanta by Matchem—Lass of the Mill by Oroonoko—Dau. of Old Traveler.	
						Mulatto.	Daughter of.	Coriander—Wildgoose by Highflyer—Coheiress by Pot-8-os—Manilla by Goldfinder—Dau. of Old Eng.—Dau. of Cul. Arabian.	
				Leda.	Touch-stone.		Phantom.	Walton—Julia by Whiskey—Y. Giantess by Diomed—Giantess by Matchem—Molly Longlegs by Babraham—Dau. of C. Foxhunter.	
							Daughter of.	Overton—Gratitude's dam by Walnut—Dau. of Ruler—Piracantha by Matchem—Dau. of Regulus—Jenny Spinner.	
							Catton.	Golumpus—Lucy Grey by Timothy—Lucy by Florizel—Frenzy by Eclipse—Dau. of Engineer—Dau. of Blank—Lass of the Mill by Old Traveler.	
							Desdemona.	Orville—Faouy by Sir Peter—Dan. of Diomed—Desdemona by Marske—Y. Hag by Skim—Hag by Crab—Ebony by F. Childers—Ebony by Basto.	
			Fleatcatcher.		Decoy.		Filho-da-Puta.	Haphazard—Mrs. Barnet by Waxy—Dau. of Woodpecker—Heinel by Squirrel—Principessa by Blank—Dau. of Cul. Arabian—Lady Thigh.	
							Treasure.	Camillus—Dau. of Hyacinthus—Flora by King Fergus—Atalanta by Matchem—Lass of the Mill by Oroonoko—Dau. of Old Traveler.	
							Camel.	Whalebone—Dau. of Selim—Maiden by Sir Peter—Dau. of Phoenomenon—Matron by Florizel—Maiden by Matchem—Dau. of Squirt.	
							Banter.	Master Henry—Boadicea by Alexander—Brunette by Amaranthus—Mayfly by Matchem—Dau. of An. Starling—Dau. of Grasshopper.	
		Calcutta.					Filho-da-Puta.	Haphazard—Mrs. Barnet by Waxy—Dau. of Woodpecker—Heinel by Squirrel—Principessa by Blank—Dau. of Cul. Arabian.	
			Miss Martin.	St. Martin.	Wagtail.		Finesse.	Peruvian—Violante by John Bull—Dau. of Highflyer—Everlasting by Eclipse—Hyaena by Snap—Miss Belsea by Regulus—Dau. of Bart. Childers.	
							Actaeon.	Scud—Diana by Stamford—Dau. of Whiskey—Gr. Dorimant by Dorimant—Dizzy by Blank—Dizzy by Driver—Dau. of Smiling Tom.	
							Galena.	Walton—Comedy by Comus—Dau. of Star—Dan. of Y. Marske—Emma by Telemachus—A-la-Greeque by Regulus—Dau. of Allworthy.	
							Whisker.	Waxy—Penelope by Trumpator—Prunella by Highflyer—Promise by Snap—Julia by Blank—Spectator's dam by Partner.	
							Daughter of.	Sorcerer—Dau. of Sir Solomon—Dau. of Y. Marske—Dau. of Phoenomenon—Calliope by Slouch—Lass of the Mill by Oroonoko.	
	SPRIGHTLY.	Lexington.	Boston.	Sister to Tuckahoe.	Timo-leon.		Sir Archy.	Diomed—Castianira by Rockingham—Tabitha by Trentham—Dau. of Bosphorus—Dau. of William's Forrester—Dau. of Coalition Colt.	
							Daughter of.	Saltram—Dau. of Symme's Wildair—Dau. of Driver (Imp Othello)—Dau. of Fallower (Blank)—Dau. of Vampire (Regulus).	
							Ball's Florizel.	Diomed—Dau. of Imp Shark—Dau. of Harris' Eclipse—Dau. of Fearnought—Dau. of Jolly Roger—Dau. of Sober John—Dau. of Shock.	
							Daughter of.	Alderman—Dau. of Clockfast—Dau. of Symme's Wildair—Y. Kity Fisher by Fearnought—Imp. Kitty Fisher by Cade (Godol).	
			Alice Carneal.	Sarpedon.			Emilius.	Orville—Emily by Stamford—Dau. of Whiskey—Gr. Dorimant by Dorimant—Dizzy by Blank—Dizzy by Driver—Dau. of Smiling Tom.	
							Icaria.	The Flyer—Parma by Dick Andrews—May by Benningbrough—Primrose by Mambrino—Cricket by Herod—Sophia by Blank—Diana.	
		Glencoe.	Sultan.	Rowena.			Sumpter.	Sir Archy—Flirtilla's dam by Robin Redbreast—Dau. of Obscurity—Slamerkin by Wildair—Imp. Cub Mare by Cub—Amaranthus' dam.	
							Lady Grey.	Robin Grey—Maria by Melzar—Dau. of Highflyer—Dau. of Fearnought—Dau. of Ariel—Dau. of Jack of Diamonds—Imp. Diamond by Cul. Arabian.	
							Selim.	Buzzard—Castrel's dam by Alexander—Dau. of Highflyer—Dau. of Alfred—Dau. of Engineer—Bay Malton's dam by Cade.	
							Bacchante.	Williamson's Ditto—Sis. to Calomel by Mercury—Dau. of Herod—Folly by Marske—Vixen by Regulus—Dau. of Hut's Spot—Dau. of Bay Bolton.	
		Trampoline.					Tramp.	Dick Andrews—Dau. of Gohanna—Fraxinella by Trentham—Dau. of Woodpecker—Everlasting by Eclipse—Hyanea by Snap—Miss Belsea.	
							Web.	Waxy—Penelope by Trumpator—Prunella by Highflyer—Promise by Snap—Julia by Blank—Spectator's dam by Partner—Bonny Lass.	
	Lightsome.						Catton.	Golumpus—Lucy Grey by Timothy—Lucy by Florizel—Frenzy by Eclipse—Dau. of Engineer—Dau. of Blank—Lass of the Mill by Old Traveler.	
							Emma.	Whisker—Gibside Fairy by Hermes—Vicissitude by Pipator—Beatrice by Sir Peter—Pyrrha by Matchem—Duchess by Whitenose—Miss Slamerkin.	
		Levity.	Vandal's Trustee. Dam.				Tranby.	Blacklock—Dau. of Orville—Miss Grimstone by Weasel—Dau. of Ancaster—Dau. of Dam Arabian—Dau. of Sampson—Dau. of Oroonoko.	
							Lucilla.	Trumpator (Sir Solomon)—Lucy by Orphan (Ball's Florizel)—Lady Grey by Robin Grey (Royalist)—Maria by Melzar—Dau. of Highflyer—Dau. of Fearnought—Dau. of Ariel—Dau. of Jack of Diamonds—Imp. Diamond by Cullen Arabian—Lady Thigh by Croft's Partner—Dau. of Greyhound—Dau. of Curwen Bay Barb—Dau. of D'Arcy Ch. Arabian—Dau. of Whiteshirt—Old Montague Mare.	

ENQUIRER,

(WINNER OF THE PHŒNIX HOTEL AND CITIZEN STAKES AT LEXINGTON; CONTINENTAL HOTEL AND ROBINS STAKES AT LONG BRANCH, AND THE KENNER STAKES AT SARATOGA ALL IN 1870,)

Will stand for mares the Season of 1883, at the Belle Meade Stud, Gen. W. G. Harding, Proprietor, near Nashville, Tenn. Season full October 1st, 1882. Application to Gen. W. H. Jackson, lock box 383, Nashville, Tenn. Yearling sales annually about May 1st.

ENQUIRER, by imp Leamington, son of Faugh-a-Ballagh, bred by H. F. Vissman, Louisville, Kentucky; dam Lida, by Lexington, son of Boston, 2d dam Lize, by Am. Eclipse, out of Gabriella, dam of George Martin, by Garrison's Zinganee, son of Sir Archy. As a race-horse Enquirer ranks as the best son of Leamington both as race-horse and sire: he started three times as a two-year-old in 1869; was unplaced in sweepstake at Cincinnati (one mile) won by Hamburg, in 1:45; ran unplaced in Willard Hotel Stakes at Louisville (one mile) in 1:48, won by his stable companion, Lynchburg. Won George Elliot Stake for two-year olds at Memphis (one mile), beating Hamburg, Lynchburg, Mundane, and Kildare, in 1:48. In 1870, when three years old, ran six races and won them all. Lexington won the Phœnix Hotel Stakes (mile heats) in 1:44¾, 1:44¼, beating Catina and distancing Longfellow in the second heat; same place won Citizens' Stake (two-mile heats) in 3:35¾, 3:44½, beating Lyttleton; the first mile in the first heat was run in 1:43½. Cincinnati won sweepstake for three-year olds (two-mile heats) in 3:50½, 3:39½, beating Conductor and Restless. Long Branch won the Continental Hotel Stakes (mile heats) in 1:47, 1:49, 1:51¾, beating Lynchburg (who won the first heat and broke his shoulder at the start of the second), Maggie B. B., dam of Iroquois, Haric, Susan Ann, dam of Thora, &c. Same place won the Bobbins' Stake (two mile heats), beating Kingfisher, who won the first heat, and the Major, in 3:56½, 3:54, 4:00; track muddy. Saratoga won the Kenner Stakes (two miles), in 3:48½, beating Hamburg, Telegram and Remorseless; value $10,250, the most valuable Kenner ever run. Value of winnings at three years old, $20,800; his leg gave way in his four-year old form, and he was put into the stud, but trained again at seven years old, when he started in one race (two miles) but was unplaced. The family from which he descends is a good racing one. His dam, Lida, and grandam, Lize, were not trained. Eclipse, the sire of his grandam, was the race-horse of his day; he beat all the best horses of his time, and won the great sectional match, the North against the South, run over the Union Course, L. I., May 27, 1823, for $20,000 a side, Eclipse beating Henry, who won the first heat, in 7:37½, 7:49, 8:24. Gabrielle, his great grandam, was by the renowned Sir Archy; was a fine race-mare, and dam of the noted Geo. Martin, which beat Reel and Hannah Harris (four-mile heats) in 7;33, 7:43. Enquirer has not had a fair chance in the stud; he was virtually retired for several years, there being five living foals reported by him in 1878, four in 1879, and three in 1880. Yet he has always held a high position as a winning sire. Amongst the best of his get, all winners, are Leander (Searcher), mile in 1:41¾; McWhirter, 2 miles, 3:30½; the fastest race was run by a three-year old, Lizzie Whipps (two mile heats), in 3:36½, 3:39; Harkaway (mile heats) in 1:43, 1:42½ (two mile heats), in 3:39, 3:35½; Solicitor, two miles in 3:34½; Bill Bruce, three-quarters of mile in 1:15½, mile heats 1:43¾, 1:44, 2 miles in 3:36½; McHenry, Blue Eyes, 2⅛ miles in 1:55¼, and 2¼ miles in 3:58¾; Goodnight, seven-eighth of mile in 1:28¾, mile 1:42½, and 1⅛ miles, 120 lbs., in 1:55½; Getaway, 1¼ miles in 2:07¾, fastest on record 2-mile heats in 3:36½, 3:35½; Falsetto, 1¼ miles in 2:08¾, 2 miles in 3:35½ with 118 lbs.: Pinafore, one mile five hundred yards in 2:11. Other reputable winners in good time are Fortuna, Ascot, Enlight, Mannie Grey, Yelton, Clandeboy, Fairy Queen, Lizzie D, Enterprise, Miss Ella, Enquiress, Caligula, Clarissima, Ed. Turner, Carrie M, Bailey (now Revenge), Responso, Bosque Belle, Gen. Jackson, Rambeau, Mascotte. He had but four or five representatives on the turf in 1882, and they won a fair share of the races in about the fastest time. Enquirer is a dark bay with an irregular-shaped star in his forehead and a narrow streak of grey hair running down his face and left hind leg, white above the pastern and three white splotches in left flank. He has a neat head and ear, good width of jaw, well-set neck, running into an oblique, strong, broad shoulder; good depth of girth, well-shaped, round barrel, though rather light near the standing ribs; good, strong hips, though inclined to be angular; good length from point of hip to whirlbone, and thence to stifle; good hocks, good sound legs and feet, with the exception of

Continued on page 40.

PEDIGREE OF ENQUIRER.

ENQUIRER.	**IMP. LEAMINGTON.**	Faugh-a-Ballagh.	Sir Hercules.	Whalebone.	Waxy.	Pot-8-os—Maria by Herod—Lizette by Snap—Miss Windsor by Godol. Arabian—Sis. to Volunteer by Y. Belgrade.
					Penelope.	Trumpator—Prunella by Highflyer—Promise by Snap—Julia by Blank—Spectator's dam by Partner—Bonny Lass.
				Peri.	Wanderer.	Gohanna—Catharine by Woodpecker—Camilla by Trentham—Coquette by Compton Barb—Sis. to Regulus—Gr. Robinson.
					Thalestris.	Alexander—Rival by Sir Peter—Hornet by Drone—Manilla by Goldfinder—Dau. of Old Eng.—Dau. of Cullen Arabian.
		Guiccioli.	Bob Booty.		Chanticleer.	Woodpecker—Dau. of Eclipse—Rosebud by Soap—Miss Belsca by Regulus—Dau. of Bart. Childers—Dau. of Hon. Arabian.
					Ierne.	Bagot—Dau. of Gamahoe—Patty by Tim—Miss Patch by Justice—Ringtail Galloway by Cur Bay Barb—Sis. to Witty Man by Pelham's Hip.
			Flight.		Irish Escape.	Commodore—Buffer's dam by Highflyer—Shift by Sweetbriar—Black Susan by Snap—Dau. of Cade—Dau. of Belgrade—Dau. of Clif. Arabian.
					Young Heroine.	Bagot—Heroine by Hero—Dau. of Snap—Sis. to Regulus by Godol. Arabian—Gr. Robinson by Bald Galloway—Dau. of Snake—Gr. Wilkes.
		Daughter.	Pantaloon.	Castrel.	Buzzard.	Woodpecker—Misfortune by Dux—Curiosity by Snap—Dau. of Regulus—Dau. of Bart. Childers—Dau. of Hon. Arabian.
					Selim's dam.	Alexander—Dau. of Highflyer—Dau. of Alfred—Dau. of Engineer—Bay Malton's dam by Cade—Lass of the Mill by Traveler—Miss Makeless.
				Idalia.	Peruvian.	Sir Peter—Dau. of Budrow—Escape's dam by Squirrel—Dau. of Babraham—Dau. of Goldeu Ball—Busby Molly by Hamp Ct. Childers.
					Musidora.	Meteor—Maid of All Work by Highflyer—Sis. to Tandem by Syphon—Dau. of Regulus—Dau. of Soip—Dau. of Cottingham—Warl. Galloway.
			Daphne.	Laurel.	Blacklock.	Whitelock—Dau. of Coriander—Wildgoose by Highflyer—Coheiress by Pot-8-os—Manilla by Goldfinder—Dau. of Old Eng.
					Wagtail.	Prime Minister—Dau. of Orville—Miss Grimstone by Weasel—Dau. of Ancaster—Dau. of Dam. Arabian—Dau. of Sampson—Dau. of Oroonoko.
				Maid of Honor.	Champion.	Selim—Podagra by Gouty—Jet by Magnet—Jewel by Squirrel—Sophia by Blank—Diana by Second—Hanger's Br. Mare by Stan. Arabian.
					Etiquette.	Orville—Boadicea by Alexander—Brunette by Amaranthus—Mayfly by Matchem—Dau. of An. Starling—Dau. of Grasshopper.
	LIDA.	Lexington.	Boston.	Timoleon.	Sir Archy.	Diomed—Castianira by Rockingham—Tabitha by Trentham—Dau. of Bosphorus—Dau. of Wm's Forester—Dau. of Coalition Colt (Godol.)
					Daughter of.	Imp. Saltram—Dau. of Symme's Wildair—Dau. of Driver (Othello)—Dau. of Fallower (Blank)—Dau. of Imp. Vampire (Regulus.)
				Sis. to Tuckahoe.	Ball's Florizel.	Diomed—Dau. of Shark—Dau. of Harris' Eclipse—Dau. of Fearnought—Dau. of Jolly Roger (Rouodhead)—Dau. of Imp. Sober John (Rib.)
					Daughter of.	Alderman—Dau. of Clockfast—Dau. of Symme's Wildair—Y Kitty Fisher by Fearnought—Imp. Kitty Fisher by Cade—Dau. of Som. Arabian.
			Alice Carneal.	Sarpedon.	Emilius.	Orville—Emily by Stamford—Dau. of Whiskey—Gr. Dorimant by Dorimant—Dizzy by Blank—Dizzy by Driver—Dau. of Smiling Tom.
					Icaria.	The Flyer—Parma by Dick Andrews—May by Beningbrough—Primrose by Mambrino—Cricket by Herod—Sophia by Blank—Diana.
				Rowena.	Sumpter.	Sir Archy—Flirtilla's dam by Robin Redbreast—Dau. of Obscurity—Slamerkin by Wildair—Imp. Cub Mare by Cub—Amaranthus' dam.
					Lady Grey.	Robin Grey—Maria by Melzar—Dau. of Highflyer—Dau. of Fearnought—Dau. of Ariel—Dau. of Jack of Diamonds—Imp. Diamond.
		Am. Eclipse.	Duroc.		Diomed.	Florizel—Sis. to Juno by Spectator—Horatia by Blank—Dau. of F. Childers—Miss Belvoir by Gr. Grantham—Dau. of Paget Turk.
					Amanda.	Grey Diomed—Dau. of Va Cade (Partuer)—Dau. of Independence (Fearnought)—Dolly Fice by Imp. Silvereye (Cul. Arabian.)
			Miller's Damsel.		Imp. Messenger.	Mambrino (Engineer)—Dau. of Turf (Matchem)—Dau. of Regulus—Dau. of Starling—Snap's dam by Fox—Gipsy by Bay Bolton.
					Daughter of.	Pot-8-os—Dau. of Gimcrack (Cripple)—Snap Dragon by Snap—Dau. of Regulus—Dau. of Bart. Childers—Dau. of Hon. Arabian.
		Gabriella.	Sir Archy.		Diomed.	Florizel—Sis. to Juno by Spectator—Horatia by Blank—Dau. of F. Childers—Miss Belvoir by Gr. Grantham—Dau. of Paget Turk.
					Castianira.	Rockingham—Tabitha by Trentham—Dau. of Bosphorus—Dau. of Wm's Forester—Dau. of Coalition Colt—Dau. of Bustard (Crab.)
		Calypso.			Bellair.	Imp. Medley (Gimcrack)—Y. Selima by Yorick (Bellair)—Bl. Selima by Fearnought—Imp. Selima by Godol. Arabian—Large Hartley Mare.
					Daughter of.	Imp. Dare Devil (Magnet by Herod)—Sallard Mare by Imp. Fearnought (Regulus)—Piccadilla by Batt & Macklin's Imp. Fearnought—Dau. of Baylor's Godolphin (Fearnought)—Dau. of Imp. Hob or Nob (Goliah by Fox)—Dau. of Imp. Jolly Roger (Roundhead by F. Childers)—Dau. of Imp. Valiant (Dormouse by Godolphin)—Dau. of Tryall (Imp. Traveler by Partner.)

ENQUIRER—Continued.

the injury to his ankle, which caused his retirement from the turf. Enquirer traces through several crosses of Sir Archy to the great imp. Diomed, winner of the first English Derby, and a horse in which the best stock of America can be traced through uncontaminated sources. There is no better line through which to perpetuate and retain this blood, with the Whalebone and Pantaloon blood inherited through his sire. He is 16¼ hands high girth 73 in., length of shoulder 29¾ in., circumference of arm 22 in., around the leg below the knee 9 in., from point of shoulder to turn of the buttocks 69 in., from point of hip to point of hock 38½ in., around the gaskins 18 in., and weighs 1,200 lbs.

EOLUS,

(WINNER OF THE CITY HOTEL STAKES AT BALTIMORE, AND OTHER GOOD RACES.)

Will stand the season of 1883 *at the Ellerslie Stud near Charlottsville, Albermarle County, Va., at* $100 *the season. Application to R. J. Hancock, proprietor, Overton, P. O., Va. Yearlings will be sold annually.*

Eolus, by imp. Leamington, son of Faugh-a-Ballagh, bred by Major Thomas W. Doswell, Bullfield Stud, Hanover Junction, Va., foaled 1868, dam Fanny Washington, dam of Rappahannock, etc., by Revenue, son of imp. Trustee, out of Sarah Washington the dam of Oratrix. Inspector, etc., by Garrison's Zinganee, son of Sir Archy. Leamington, his sire, can be found in this book. Fanny Washington, his dam, was one of the best mares of her day; was winner at all distances, 2 mile heats in 3:47¾, 3:40½, 3 mile heats in 5:48, 5:44½, defeating Tar River, and in 5:43¼, 5:33¾, she won 4 mile heats in 7:37, 8:02, defeating La Variete, Endorser and others, and beat the best ones on all the tracks; her full sister, Sue Washington, was also noted as winner at all distances. Revenue, her sire, won at all distances, and was the sire of the great Planet, Exchequer and other good race-horses. Sarah Washington, his grandam, was one of the best mares of her day, winner at all distances; 3 mile heats in 5:42, 5:39½, and beat the famous Lady Clifden 4 mile heats. She produced Inspector, one of the best race-horses of his day, and Oratrix that beat the noted Bostona. Eolus did not start as a two-year old, but won three out of the six races in which he started as a three-year old, a club purse, 2 miles, at Saratoga, in 3:38¾; a purse, 1¾ miles, in 3:14½, beating such horses as Tubman, Frogtown and others, and the City Hotel Stakes at Baltimore, 1½ miles, in the mud, in 2:55 He did not start as a four-year-old, and only won three races at five years old; 1½ miles at Baltimore, in 2:43¾; 1¾ miles at Saratoga, in 3:15, and one of 1¼ miles in 2:02½. He was close up in several races in first-class company. When six years old he ran three races, won two, one of 2½ miles at Baltimore, in 4:39, and one of two mile heats, in 3:40, 3:39¼, 3:36¾, Mart Jordan winning the second heat. This third heat is the fastest and best third heat ever run, and stamped him as a race-horse of the first water, possessing both speed and stamina. He had but one representative on the turf in 1881, Eole, and although much out of condition during the year, he ran creditably in all his races and won some of great merit, notably his 1¾ miles in 3:07½, one mile and five furlongs in 2:49¾, one mile and a furlong, with 116 lbs., in 1:58¾, one mile and three furlongs in 2:24, 1½ miles in 2:11½, 1¼ miles in 2:39¼. In 1882, Eole, although saddled with the top weights, won the great Metropolitan Stakes at Jerome Park, 1½ miles, in 2:41, defeating General Monroe, Monitor, Parole, etc., and the Jockey Club Handicap, 2 miles, in 3:38¼, carrying 123 lbs. to Monitor's 122, he being second. In the Coney Island Cup he forced Hindoo to run the first 2 miles in 3:29¾, and the 2¼ miles in 3:58, the fastest race at the distance during the year. Eole won the Monmouth Cup, 2¼ miles, in 4:07¾, beating Girofle and Monitor. He won theC hampion Stakes, the Morrissey Stakes at Saratoga, and the Autumn Cup at Coney Island, 3 miles, in 5:26½, in which he defeated Lida Stanhope, Thora, Glenmore and four others. In this race he carried 120 lbs., and conceded all lumps of weight. When beaten he was out of condition or over loaded by the handicappers. Eolist is the only other colt by him which has been trained. Eolus is a dark bay horse, with star in his forehead and two white hind heels, full 15¾ hands, and weighs 1,100 lbs. He is a large, fine horse, of great substance and power, and in addition to his Waxy blood through Whalebone and Whisker, he has four distinct crosses of Sir Archy on his dam's side, and traces to Eclipse and Herod through his collateral branches. The stock all possess symmetry, constitution and staying powers. He should command the patronage of the public.

PEDIGREE OF EOLUS.

EOLUS.	IMP. LEAMINGTON.	Faugh-a-Ballagh.	Sir Hercules.	Whalebone.	Waxy.	Penelope.	Pot-8-os—Maria by Herod—Lisette by Snap—Miss Windsor by Godol. Arabian—Sis. to Volunteer by Y. Belgrade—Dau. of Bart. Childers. Trumpator—Prunella by Highflyer—Promise by Snap—Julia by Blank—Spectator's dam by Partner—Bonny Lass by Bay Bolton.
				Peri.	Wanderer.	Thalestria.	Gohanna—Catharine by Woodpecker—Camilla by Trentham—Coquette by Comp. Barb—Sis. to Regulus by Godol. Arabian. Alexander—Rival by Sir Peter—Hornet by Drone—Manilla by Goldfinder—Dau. of old Eng.—Dau. of Cullen Arabian—Miss Cade.
		Guiccioli.	Bob Booty.		Chanticleer.	Ierne.	Woodpecker—Dan. of Eclipse—Rosebud by Snap—Miss Belsea by Regulus—Dau. of Bart. Childers—Dau. of Hon. Arabian, dam of True Blues. Bagot—Dau. of Gamahoe—Patty by Tim—Miss Patch by Justice—Ringtail Galloway by Cur Bay Barb—Sis. to Witty Mare by Hip.
			Flight.		Irish Escape.	Young Heroine.	Commodore—Buffer's dam by Highflyer—Shift by Sweetbriar—Black Susan by Snap—Dau. of Cade—Dau. of Belgrade. Bagot—Heroine by Hero—Dau. of Snap—Sis. to Regulus by Godol. Arabian—Gr. Robinson by the Bald Galloway—Dau. of Snake—Gr. Wilkes.
		Daughter of.	Pantaloon.	Castrel.	Buzzard.	Selim's dam.	Woodpecker—Misfortune by Dux—Curiosity by Snap—Dau. of Regulus—Dau. of Bart. Childers—Dau. of Hou. Arabian—Dam of True Blues. Alexander—Dau. of Highflyer—Dau. of Alfred—Dau. of Engineer—Bay Malton's dam by Cade—Lass af the Mill by Traveler.
			Idalia.		Peruvian.	Musidora.	Sir Peter—Dau. of Budrow—Escape's dam by Squirrel—Dau. of Babraham—Dau. of Golden Ball—Bushy Molly by Hamp. Ct. Childers. Meteor—Maid of all Work by Highflyer—Sis. to Tandem by Syphon—Dau. of Regulus—Dau. of Snip—Dau. of Cottingham—War. Galloway.
		Daphne.	Laurel.		Blacklock.	Wagtail.	Whitelock—Dau. of Coriander—Wildgoose by Highflyer—Coheiress by Pot-8-os—Manilla by Goldfinder—Dau. of Old Eng.—Dau. of Cul. Arabian. Prime Minister—Dau. of Orville—Miss Grimstone by Weasel—Dau. of Ancaster—Dau. of Dam Arabian—Dau. of Sampson—Dau. of Oroonoko.
			Maid of Honor.		Champion.	Etiquette.	Selim—Podagra by Gouty—Jet by Magnet—Jewel by Squirrel—Sophia by Blank—Diana by Second—Dau. of Stanyan Arabian. Orville—Boadicea by Alexander—Brunette by Amaranthus—Mayfly by Matchem—Dau. of An. Starling—Dau. of Grasshopper (Crab.)
	FANNY WASHINGTON.	Sarah Washington.	Trustee.	Catton.	Golumpus.	Lucy Grey.	Gobanna—Catharine by Woodpecker—Camilla by Trentham—Coquette by Comp. Barb—Sis. to Regulus by Godol. Arabian—Gr. Robinson. Timothy—Lucy by Florizel—Frenzy by Eclipse—Dau. of Engineer—Dau. of Blank—Lass of the Mill by Traveler—Miss Makeless.
				Emma.	Whisker.	Gibside Fairy.	Waxy—Penelope by Trumpator—Prunella by Highflyer—Promise by Snap—Julia by Blank—Spectator's dam by Partner. Hermes—Vicissitude by Pipator—Beatrice by Sir Peter—Pyrrha by Matchem—Duchess by Whitenose—Miss Slamerkin by Y. True Blue.
		Stella.	Revenue.	Sir Charles.	Sir Archy.	Daughter of.	Diomed—Castianira by Rockingham—Tabitha by Trentham—Dau. of Bosphorus—Dau. of Wm's Forester—Dau. of Coalition Colt (Godol.) Commutation—Dau. of Dare Devil—Sally Shark by Imp. Shark—Betsey Pringle by Fearnought—Imp. Jenny Dismal by Dismal,
			Rosalie Somers.	Mischief.	Virginian.	Grandam of Trifle.	Sir Archy—Meretrix by Magog—Narcissa by Imp. Shark—Rosetta by Imp. Centinel—Diana by Clodius—Sally Painter. Bedford—Dau. of Bellair—Dau. of Imp. Shark—Dau. of Wildair—Dau. of Lexington (Wildair)—Dan. of Spanking Roger.
		Miss Chance.	Garrison's Zinganee.	Sir Archy.	Diomed.	Castianira.	Florizel—Sis. to Juno by Spectator—Horatia by Blank Dau. of F. Childers—Miss Belvoir by Gr. Grantham—Dau. of Paget Turk. Rockingham—Tabitha by Trentham—Dau. of Bosphorus—Dau. of Wm's Forester—Dau. of Coalition Colt—Dau. of Bustard.
			Contention.	Chance.	Imp. Chance.	Daughter of.	Lurcher (Dungannon)—Recovery by Hyder Ally (Blank)—Perdita by Herod—Fair Forester by Sloe—Dau. of Forester. Imp. Eagle (Volunteer)—Maria by Bay Yankee (President)—Dau. of Meade's Celer—Dau. of Partner—Dau. of Apollo—Dau. of Valiant.
		Dau. of.			Sir Archy. Reapbook's dam.		Diomed—Castianira by Rockingham—Tabitha by Trentham—Dau. of Bosphorus—Dau. of Wm's Forester—Dau. of Coalition Colt. Dare Devil—Dau. of Symme's Wildair—Picadilla by Batte's Fearnought—Dau. of Godolphin (Fearnought)—Dau. of Hob or Nob.
					Imp. Speculator.		Dragon (Woodpecker) Sis. to Stiug by Herod—Florizel's dam by Cygnet—Dau. of Cartouch—Ebony by Childers—Ebony by Basto.
					Pompadour.		Valiant (Dormouse by Godol. Arabian)—Imp. Jeuny Cameron by Cuddy (Fox)—Miss Belvoir by Gr. Grantham—Dau. of Paget Turk—Betty Percival by Leede's Arabian—Dau. of Spanker (D'Arcy Yellow Turk.)

FALSETTO,

(WINNER OF THE PHŒNIX HOTEL STAKE AT LEXINGTON, CLARK STAKE AT LOUISVILLE, TRAVERS AND KENNER STAKES AT SARATOGA, N. Y., ALL IN 1879).

Will stand the season of 1883 at the Woodburn Stud, A. J. Alexander proprietor, near Spring Station, Ky., at $50 the season. Application to L. Brodhead, Spring Station. Annual sales of yearlings in May.

FALSETTO, by Enquirer, son of imp. Leamington, bred by the late Col. J. W. Hunt Reynolds, Fleetwood Stud, Ky., foaled 1876, dam Farfaletta, dam of Felicia, Fortuna, etc., by imp. Australian, out ot Elkhorna, dam of Elkhorn Arcturus, etc., by Lexington. Leamington, Enquirer, Australian and Lexington, all noted horses covering the first four crosses of the blood of Falsetto, are to be found in this book. His dam, Farfaletta, has never produced any thing but good ones. Felicia and Fortuna were both good race mares and creditable performers. Falsetto made his maiden effort at Lexington, Ky., May 10, first day of the Spring meeting, in Phœnix Hotel Stakes, 1¼ miles. Falsetto, never having started before, was ignored in the betting. Trinidad, Ada Glenn and Lilly R., were the three favorites. Ten horses started, Falsetto won, defeating Ada Glenn by a neck, Scully a good third, Trinidad, Lily R., Hamadan, Wissahickon, Bucktie, Bailey and Black Hills unplaced; time, 2:08¼. Falsetto's second appearance was at Louisville, Ky., May 20, in the Kentucky Derby, 1½ miles; he ran second to Lord Murphy, suffering his first and only defeat. Strathmore, Trinidad, Ada Glenn, One Dime, Gen. Pike, Bucktie and Wissahickon also started; time of race, 2:37. Same place, May 27, won the Clark Stakes, 2 miles, defeating Bucktie, Trinidad, Mary Ann, Gen. Pike, Borak and Wissahickon; time, 3:40¼. Falsetto, with his stable companions, was sent to Saratoga at the conclusion of the Louisville meeting, and had nearly two months in which to rest and prepare for their engagements at that point. Saratoga, July 19, he met the hitherto invincible Spendthrift, also Harold, Jericho and Dan Sparling, in the Travers Stakes, 1¾ miles. The history of the race is too well known to require repetition here. Falsetto won; Spendthrift was second, Harold third; time, 3:09¼, a very fast race for the track. While not detracting in the least from Falsetto's magnificent performance, it is safe to say that Spendthrift was not himself, as his wonderful race for the Lorillard Stakes, at Jerome Park, June 10, amply proved. Saratoga, Aug. 12, won the Kenner Stakes, 2 miles, defeating Spendthrift, Jericho, Monitor and Harold; time, 3:35¼. Total winnings in his three-year old year form, $18,275. Falsetto was then purchased and sent to England by Mr. P. Lorillard, he paying $18,000 for him; giving away in one of his legs in his preparation, he was returned to America and sold to the Woodburn Stud. Falsetto is from one of the great racing families of America, his dam, grandam and great grandam were handled but little, but all have produced winners; Mary Morris, his fifth dam, was a fine race-mare at all distances, and was the dam of the two fine race-horses, Wild Irishman and Prankfort; her dam was the great grandam of Parole, and from the same blood in a direct line sprang Rattler, Childers and Sumpter, all good race-horses and stallions. Flirtilla, by Sir Archy, was out of the same family, and from her came Ringgold, the sire of Onward and Delaware. The imported Cub Mare, from which all this stock emanated, was out of Amaranthus, dam by Second, and they trace through popular racing families of England to the Layton Barb Mare. Falsetto, has four of the best racing strains in this country to begin with, and his blood is pure through a long line of distinguished horses; if racing lineage is worth anything, Falsetto must make a successful sire. He is inbred to Lexington, and has the Waxy blood on both sides, from Whalebone, winner of the Derby in 1810, to Whisker, winner in 1815, and his son Memnon, sire of Envoy, won the St. Leger in 1825. He is also very strongly inbred to Diomed through Lexington, Am. Eclipse and Gabriella. Falsetto is a brown, stands 16 hands ⅜ of an inch high, with a blaze in his face and snip on the nose, and four white ankles. He is a grand-looking horse, without any surplus lumber, and can scarcely fail in the stud. If he is bred to Lexington mares or the daughters of Lexington mares through racing strains he will not fail,

PEDIGREE OF FALSETTO.

FALSETTO.	**ENQUIRER.**	Leamington.	Daughter of Daphne.	Faugh-a-Ballagh. / Guiccioli.	Pantaloon. / Sir Hercules.	Whalebone. / Peri.	Waxy—Penelope by Trumpator—Prunella by Highflyer—Promise by Snap—Julia by Blank—Spectator's dam by Partner. Wanderer—Thalestris by Alexander—Rival by Sir Peter—Hornet by Drone Manilla by Goldfinder—Dau. of Old England (Godol.)
						Bob Booty. / Flight.	Chanticleer—Ierne by Bagot—Dau. of Gamahoe—Patty by Tim—Miss Patch by Justice—Ringtail Galloway by Cur. Bay Barb. Irish Escape—Y. Heroine by Bagot—Heroine by Hero—Dau. of Snap—Sis. to Regulus by Godol. Arabian—Gr. Robinson by Bald. Galloway.
						Castrel. / Idalia.	Buzzard—Dau. of Alexander—Dau. of Highflyer—Dau. of Alfred—Dau. of Engineer—Bay Malton's dam by Cade—Lass of the Mill. Peruvian—Musidora by Meteor—Maid of all Work by Highflyer—Sis. to Tandem by Syphon—Dau. of Regulus—Dau. of Snip (Childers.)
						Laurel. / Maid of Honor.	Blacklock—Wagtail by Prime Minister—Dau. of Orville—Miss Grimstone by Weasel—Dau. of Ancaster—Dau. of Damascus Arabian. Champion—Etiquette by Orville—Boadicea by Alexander—Brunette by Amaranthus—Mayfly by Matchem—Dau. of Ancaster Starling.
		Lda.	Lexington.	Alice Carneal.	Boston.	Timoleon. / Robin Brown's dam.	Sir Archy—Dau. of Saltram—Dau. of Symme's Wildair—Dau. of Driver (Imp. Othello)—Dau. of Fallower (Blank)—Dau. of Imp. Vampire. Ball's Florizel—Dau. of Alderman—Dau. of Clockfast—Dau. of Symme's Wildair—Y. Kitty Fisher by Fearnought—Imp. Kitty Fisher by Cade.
						Sarpedon. / Rowena.	Emilius—Icaria by The Flyer—Parma by Dick Andrews—May by Beningbrough—Primrose by Mambrino—Cricket by Herod—Sophia. Sumpter—Lady Grey by Robin Grey—Maria by Melzar—Dau. of Highflyer—Dau. of Fearnought—Dau. of Ariel—Dau. of Jack of Diamonds.
		Lize.	Am. Eclipse.	Gabriella.		Duroc. / Miller's Damsel.	Diomed—Amanda by Grey Diomed—Dau. of Va. Cade—Dau. of Hickman's Independence—Dolly Fine by Imp. Silvereye. Messenger—Imp. Mare by Pot-8-os—Dau. of Gimcrack—Snapdragon by Snap—Dau. of Regulus—Dau. of Bartlet's Childers—Dau. of Hon. Arabian.
						Sir Archy. / Calypso.	Diomed—Castianira by Rockingham—Tabitha by Trentham—Dau. of Bospborus—Dau. of Wm's Forester—Dau. of Coalition Colt (Godol.) Bellair (Imp. Medley)—Dau. of Imp. Dare Devil (Magnet)—Dau. of Symme's Wildair—Picadilla by B. & M's. Fearnought—Dau. of Godol.
	FARFALETTA.	Australian.	Emilia.	West Australian.	Melbourne.	Humphrey Clinker. / Daughter of.	Comus—Clinkerina by Clinker—Pewet by Tandem—Termagant by Tantrum—Cantatrice by Sampson—Dau. of Regulus—Marske's dam. Cervantes—Dau. of Golumpus—Dau. of Paynator—Sis. to Zodiac by St. George—Abigail by Woodpecker—Firetail by Eclipse.
					Mowerina.	Touchstone. / Emma.	Camel—Banter by Master Henry—Boadicea by Alexander—Brunette by Amaranthus—Mayfly by Matchem—Dau. of An. Starling. Whisker—Gibside Fairy by Hermes—Vicissitude by Pipator—Beatrice by Sir Peter—Pyrrha by Matchem—Duchess by Whitenose.
				Young Emilius.	Persian.	Emilius. / Shoveler.	Orville—Emily by Stamford—Dau. of Whiskey—Gr. Dorimant by Dorimant—Dizzy by Blank—Dizzy by Driver—Dau. of Smiling Tom. Scud—Goosander by Hambletonian—Rally by Trumpator—Fancy Sis. to Diomed by Florizel—Dau of Spectator—Horatia by Blank (Godol.)
						Whisker. / Variety.	Waxy—Penelope by Trumpator—Prunella by Highflyer—Promise by Snap—Julia by Blank—Spectator's dam by Partner—Bonny Lass. Selim or Sootbsayer—Sprite by Bobtail—Catharine by Woodpecker—Camilla by Trentham—Coquette by Compton Barb—Sis. to Regulus.
		Elkhorna.	Lexington.	Alice Carneal.	Boston.	Timoleon. / Robin Brown's dam.	Sir Archy—Dau. of Saltram—Dau. of Symme's Wildair—Dau. of Driver (Othello)—Dau. of Fallower (Blank)—Dau. of Imp. Vampire. Ball's Florizel—Dau. of Alderman—Dau. of Clockfast—Dau. of Symme's Wildair—Dau. of Highflyer—Dau. of Fearnought—Dau. of Ariel.
						Sarpedon. / Rowena.	Emilius—Icaria by The Flyer—Parma by Dick Andrews—May by Beningbrough—Primrose by Mambrino—Cricket by Herod—Sophia. Sumpter—Lady Grey by Robin Grey—Maria by Melzar—Dau. of Highflyer Daughter of Fearnought—Dau. of Ariel—Dau. of Jack of Diamonds.
		Glencona.	Glencoe.	Daughter of.		Sultan. / Trampoline.	Selim—Bacchante by Williamson's Ditto—Sis. to Calomel by Mercury—Dau. of Herod—Folly by Marske—Vixen by Regulus—Dau. of Hut. Spot. Tramp—Web by Waxy—Penelope by Trumpator—Prunella by Highflyer—Promise by Snap—Julia by Blank—Spectator's dam by Partner.
						Imp. Envoy. / Mary Morris.	Memnon (Whisker)—Zarius by Morisco (Muley)—Ina by Smolensko—Morgiana by Coriander—Fairy by Highflyer—Fairy Queen by Y. Cade. Medoc (Am. Eclipse)—Miss Obstinate by Sumpter—Jenny Slamerkin by Tiger (Cook's Whip)—Hannah Harris by Imp. Buzzard (Woodpecker)—Indiana by Columbus (Imp. Pantaloon)—Jane Hunt by Paragon (Imp. Flimnap)—Moll by Imp. Figure (Grey Figure)—Slamerkin by Imp. Wildair (Cade by Godolphin—Imp. Cub Mare by Cub (Fox)—Dau. of Second (F. Childers)—Dau. of Starling (Bay Bolton)—Sis. to Vane's Partner by Partner (Jigg)—Sis. to Guy by Greyhound (White Bab Chillaby)—Br. Farewell by Makeless (Oglethorpe Arabian)—Dau. of Brimmer (Yellow Turk)—Dau. of Place's White Turk—Dau. of Dodsworth (Nat. Barb)

FECHTER (Imp.)

Will be located at the Fairview Stud Farm, near Gallatin, Sumner Co., Tenn., and will be permitted to serve mares at $50 each, for the season, and $5 to the Groom. Application to Charles Reed, Gallatin, Tenn. Annual Sales of Yearlings at Saratoga in July.

FECHTER, by Bel Demonio, son of Weatherbit, bred by Mr. W. Blenkiron, foaled 1873; dam Hilda, dam of Ursula, Ersilia, Cherry, etc., by Prime Minister, son of Melbourne, out of Ethel by Ethelbert. Fechter never ran in public, but is descended on both sire's and dam's sides from a long line of distinguished racers. Bel Demonio started in two races as a three-year-old, and won both; the Easby Triennial Produce Stakes at Catterich Bridge, beating War Dance and Revival, and a sweepstake of 50 sovs. each for three-year-olds, over the Rowley mile at the Newmarket Craven Meeting. Prime Minister, the sire of his dam, was highly esteemed and thoroughly tried previous to the Derby, and was so well liked that he was backed to win a large sum of money; he was sire of Farfalla, Lord Burleigh, Lustre, Pastime, Sporting Life, Knight of the Garter, and other reputable runners. Ethelbert, the sire of his grandam, was by Faugh-a-Ballagh, the sire of Leamington, was a good race-horse, won the City and Suburban Handicap in 1858, after a dead heat with Pancake; he was sire of Big Ben that beat the great Dundee. Ethelbert was the best produce of his dam. Fechter, in addition to his many crosses to Highflyer, Herod and Eclipse, has a double cross of Whalebone, through his best son, Sir Hercules, each through the noted stallions, Irish Birdcatcher and Faugh-a-Ballagh, in addition to his cross of Priam through Miss Letty, an Oaks winner, one of Pantaloon and several of Orville through Emilius and Muley, and the hard bottom crosses of Buzzard and Trumpator. With such a combination of speedy and stout crosses, with size, substance and pure blood, he can scarcely fail to get racehorses. Fechter is a blood-bay, 16¼ hands high, with a star in his forehead. He has an excellent shoulder, fine through the heart, and an extra fine hip, back and loin. Taking him altogether, he is a remarkably fine horse.

PEDIGREE OF FECHTER—(Imp.).

FECHTER (Imp.)—Bay Horse foaled 1873; bred by Mr. W. Blenkiron.

Sire/Dam lines							
Ethel	Idyl	Ecologue.	Prime Minister.	Pantalouair.	Melbourne.	Humphrey Clinker.	Tramp.
		Ithuriel.		Castrel.	Dau. of Cervantes.	Clinkerina.	Mandane.
	Ethelbert	Espoir.		Faugh-a-Ballagh.	Sir Hercules.		Comus.
		Italia.			Guiccioli.		Clinkerina.
HILDA.							Muley.
							Miss Stepheson.
							Emilius.
							Cressida.
	Augusta.	Memento.	Annulet.	Giuiccioli.	Sir Hercules.		Orville.
							Golden Legs. Dam.
				Voltaire.	Dau. of Herules.		Whalebone.
							Peri.
							Bob Booty.
							Flight.
		Irish Birdcatcher.	Sir Hercules.				Blacklock.
							Daughter of.
			Guiccioli.				Jerry.
	BEL DEMONIO.						Emilla.
	Miss Letty.	Priam.					Cervantes.
							Daughter.
							Buzzard.
							Selim's Dam.
		Morgiana.					Peruvian.
							Musidora.
							Sir Hercules.
							Guiccioli.
	Sheet Anchor.	Lottery.					Tramp.
	Weatherbit.						Mandane.
							Sir Hercules.
							Guiccioli.

Breeding notes:

Tramp—Mandane.
Dick Andrews—Dau. of Gohanna—Fraxinella by Trentham—Dau. of Woodpecker—Everlasting by Eclipse—Hyacua by Snap—Miss Belsea.
Pot-8-os—Y. Camilla by Woodpecker—Camilla by Trentham—Coquette by Compton Barb—Sis. to Regulus by Godol. Arabian—Grey Robinson.

Muley—Miss Stepheson.
Orville—Eleanor by Whiskey—Y. Giantess by Diomed—Giantess by Matchem—Molly Longlegs by Babraham—Dau. of Cole's Foxhunter.
Scud or Sorcerer—Sis. to Petworth by Precipitate—Dau. of Woodpecker—Sis. to Juniper by Snap—Y. Marske's dam by Blank.

Emilius—Cressida.
Orville—Emily by Stamford—Dau. of Whiskey—Gr. Dorimant by Dorimant—Dizzy by Blank—Dizzy by Driver—Dau. of Smiling Tom (Con. Arabian.)
Whiskey—Y. Giantess by Diomed—Giantess by Matchem—Molly Longlegs by Babraham—Dau. of Cole's Foxhunter—Sis. to Cato by Partner (Jigg).

Orville—Golden Legs. Dam.
Beningbrough—Evelina by Highflyer—Termagant by Tautrum—Cantatrice by Sampson—Dau. of Regulus—Marske's dam by Blacklegs.
Buzzard—Hornpipe by Trumpator—Luna by Herod—Proserpine, Sis. to Eclipse by Marske—Mother Western by Smith's Son of Snake.

Whalebone—Peri.
Waxy—Penelope by Trumpator—Prunella by Highflyer—Promise by Snap—Julia by Blank—Spectator's dam by Partner—Bonny Lass by Bay Bolton.
Wanderer—Thalestris by Alexander—Rival by Sir Peter—Hornet by Drone—Manilla by Goldfinder—Dau. of Old Eng.—Dau. of Cullen Arabian.

Bob Booty—Flight.
Chanticleer—Ierne by Bagot—Dau. of Gamahoe—Patty by Tim—Miss Patch by Justice—Rlugtail Galloway by Cur Bay Barb—Sis. to Witty Mare.
I Escape—Y. Heroine by Bagot—Heroine by Hero (Cade)—Dau. of Snap—Sis. to Regulus by Godol. Arabian—Gr. Robinsou by Bald Galloway.

Blacklock—Daughter of.
Whitelock—Dau. of Coriander—Wildgoose by Highflyer—Coheiress by Pot-8-os—Manilla by Goldfinder—Dau. of Old Eng. (Godol.).
Phantom—Dau. of Overton—Dau. of Walnut—Dau. of Ruler—Piracantha by Matchem—Dau. of Regulus—Jenny Spinner by Partner.

Jerry—Emilla.
Smolensko—Louisa by Orville—Thomasina by Timothy—Violet by Shark—Dau. of Syphon—Charlotte by Blank—Dau. of Crab—Dau. of Dy's Dimple.
Abjer (Truffle)—Emily of Stamford—Dau. of Whiskey—Gr. Dorimant by Dorimant—Dizzy by Blank—Dizzy by Driver—Dau. of Smiling Tom.

Comus—Clinkerina.
Sorcerer—Houghton Lass by Sir Peter—Alexina by King Fergus—Lardella by Y. Marske—Dau. of Cade—Beaufremont's dam by Bro. to Fearnought.
Clinker—Pewet by Tandem—Termagant by Tantrum—Cantatrice by Sampson—Dau. of Regulus—Marske's dam by Blacklegs (By Turk).

Cervantes—Daughter.
Don Quixote—Evelina by Highflyer—Termagant by Tantrum—Cantatrice by Sampson—Dau. of Regulus—Marske's dam by Blacklegs.
Golumpus—Dau. of Paynator—Sis. to Zodiac by St. George—Abigail by Woodpecker—Firetail by Eclipse—Dau. of Blank—Naylor by Cade.

Buzzard—Selim's Dam.
Woodpecker—Misfortune by Dux—Curiosity by Snap—Dau. of Regulus—Dau. of Bart's Childers—Dau. of Hon. Arabian—True Blue's dam.
Alexander—Dau. of Highflyer—Dau. of Alfred—Dau. of Engineer—Bay Malton's dam by Cade—Lass of the Mill by Traveler.

Peruvian—Musidora.
Sir Peter—Dau. of Budrow—Escape's dam by Squirrel—Dau. of Babraham—Dau. of Golden Ball—Bushy Molly by Hamp. Ct. Childers.
Meteor—Maid of all Work by Highflyer—Sis. to Tandem by Syphon—Dau. of Regulus—Dau. of Snip—Dau. of Cottingham—War Galloway.

Sir Hercules—Guiccioli.
Whalebone—Peri by Wanderer—Thalestris by Alexander—Rival by Sir Peter—Hornet by Drone—Manilla by Goldfinder—Dau. of Old Eng.
Bob Booty—Flight by I Escape—Y. Heroine by Bagot—Heroine by Hero—Dau. of Snap—Sis. to Regulus by Godol. Arabian—Gr. Robinson.

Liverpool—Esperance.
Tramp—Dau. of Whisker—Mandane by Pot-8-os—Y. Camilla by Woodpecker—Camilla by Trentham—Coquette by Compton Barb.
Lap-dog—Grisette by Merlin—Coquette by Dick Andrews—Vanity by Buzzard—Dabchick by Pot-8-os—Drab by Highflyer—Hebe by Chrysolite.

Touchstone—Verbena.
Camel—Banter by Master Henry—Boadicea by Alexander—Brunette by Amarantbus—Mayfly by Matchem—Dau. of An. Starling.
Velocipede—Rosalba by Milo—Sis. to Rubens by Buzzard—Dau. of Alexander—Dau. of Highflyer—Dau. of Alfred—Dau. of Engineer.

Emilius—Apollonia.
Orville—Emily by Stamford—Dau. of Whiskey—Gr. Dorimant by Dorimant—Dizzy by Blank—Dizzy by Driver.
Whisker—My Lady by Comus—The Colonel's dam by Delpini (Highflyer)—Tipple Cyder by King Fergus (Eclipse)—9th dam Sylvia by Y. Marske (Mareke)—10th dam Ferret by Bro. to Silvio (Cade)—11th dam by Regulus (Godol.)—12th dam by Ld. Moreton's Arabian—13th dam by Mixbury—14th dam by Muleo Bay Turk—15th dam by Bay Bolton—16th dam by Coneyskins—17th dam by Hutton's Gr. Barb—18th dam by Byerly Turk—19th dam by Bustler.

FELLOWCRAFT,

(THE FIRST HORSE TO BEAT LEXINGTON'S FOUR MILE TIME, 7:19¾, WHICH HE DID AT SARATOGA, AUG, 20TH, 1874, RUNNING IN 7:19½.)

Will stand the season of* 1883 *at the Dixiana Stud (if not sold), by private contract. Application to Maj. B. G. Thomas, proprietor, Lexington, Ky.

FELLOWCRAFT, by imp. Australian, son of West Australian, bred by A. J. Alexander, Woodburn Stud, Ky.; foaled 1870, dam Aerolite the dam of Mozart, Rutherford, Spendthrift, etc., by Lexington 2d, dam Florine, the dam of Idlewild, by imp. Glencoe, out of Melody by Medoc, son of Am. Eclipse. As a two-year-old Fellowcraft started five times and won one race. At Long Branch was unplaced in Hopeful Stakes, one-half mile; unplaced in a dash of three-quarters of a mile; won a dash of three-quarters of a mile in 1:20, beating Marsyas and three others. At Saratoga was unplaced in the Flash Stakes and in the Saratoga Stakes, same place. As a three-year old he started nine times and won one race. Jerome Park, was unplaced in the Belmont Stakes; was second to Survivor in a dash of 1¼ miles, run in 2:15¾; was unplaced in the Weatherby Stakes, 1⅛ miles; same place, was third to Tom Bowling and Springbok in the Jerome Stakes, 2 miles; was third in the Grand National Handicap 2¼ miles, won by Preakness in 4:08¾, with Harry Basset second, At Saratoga was unplaced in the Travers Stakes, 1¾ miles, won by Tom Bowling in 3:09¾. Same place, was second in the Sequel Stakes, won by imp. Ill Used in 3:40½; same place, walked over for a sweepstakes for three year-olds, 2 miles. When four years old he started twelve times and won three races. At Jerome Park was unplaced in the Fordham Handicap; also in the Jockey Club Handicap; unplaced in a race of mile heats won by Kitty Pease in 1:43¾, 1:44; was third in purse race, 1¾ miles; third in Handicap Sweepstakes, 2½ miles, won by Kitty Pease in 4:35½. At Long Branch, was unplaced in a race of two-mile heats. Same place, won purse, $1,000, 4 miles, in 7:43. Again, same place, was second in a race of two-mile heats, won by Vandslite n 3:49, 3:;7. At Saratoga, August 4, was third in a dash of three miles, won by iSpringbok in 5:42¼, with Preakness second. Same place, won dash of 1½ miles in 2:42½, beating Katie Pease, The Governess and Wanderer. Same place, was second in a dash of 2¼ miles, won by Wanderer in 4:00¼. Same place won dash of 4 miles in 7:19½, beating Wanderer and Katie Pease. This was the best race, at the distance, ever run up to that date. The first mile was run in 1:47¼, two miles in 3:38, three miles in 5:29½, and the four miles as stated. This closed the turf career of Fellowcraft, and since his retirement, while he has had a limited advantage as a sire, still he has sired some fast horses. Knight Templar won three-quarters of a mile in 1:14, three-quarter mile heats, in 1:16¼. 1:16¼, and one mile in 1:42, all of which are very creditable, 1:14 being the fastest time on record for three-quarters of a mile. Blue Lodge won heats of three-quarters of a mile in 1:20, 1:19¼, beating Brambaletta, Pilgrimage, Maggie C. and others. She ran dead heat and divided Citizen's Plate with Long Taw, at St. Louis, 1⅛ miles, in 155¼. Blue Lodge won some good races in in 1882. Fellowcraft is only credited with ten foals, three of which are rising two years old. Nearly all that have been trained have won. Fellowcraft is a rich chestnut, with star and two white hind feet, is well formed and a fine blood-like specimen of a horse, 16 hands high. He is handsomely bred, and was a race-horse with great speed and the capacity to stay over a distance of ground, He is strongly inbred to Diomed and imp. Medley, son of Gimcrack by Cripple, son of Godolphin Arabian; he possesses the Waxy blood through Whisker and Whalebone, and numerous crosses to Herod and Eclipse, the pedigree terminating in the blood of Medley by Gimcrack. With a chance he will make a real good sire.

PEDIGREE OF FELLOWCRAFT.

FELLOWCRAFT.	**IMP. AUSTRALIAN.**	West Australian.	Melbourne.	Daugh- ter of. Humphrey Clinker.	Comus. Clinkerina.	Sorcerer—Houghton Lass by Sir Peter—Alexina by King Fergus—Lardella by Young Marske.—Dau. of Cade—Beaufremont's dam. Clinker—Pewet by Tandem—Termagant by Tantrum—Cautatrice by Sampson—Dau. of Regulus—Marske's dam by Blacklegs.
					Cervantes. Daughter.	Don Quixote—Evelina by Highflyer—Termagant by Tantrum—Cantatrice by Sampson—Dau. of Regulus—Marske's dam by Blacklegs. Golumpus—Dau. of Paynator—Sis. to Zodiac by St. George—Abigail by Woodpecker—Firetail by Eclipse—Dau. of Blank—Naylor by Cade.
		Mowerina.	Touchstone.	Emma.	Camel. Banter.	Whalebone—Dau. of Selim—Maiden by Sir Peter—Dau. of Phoenomenon.—Matron by Florizel—Maiden by Matchem—Dau. of Squirt. Master Henry—Roadicea by Alexander—Brunette by Amaranthus—Mayfly by Matchem—Dau. of An. Starling—Dau. of Grasshopper.
					Whisker. Gibside Fairy.	Waxy—Penelope by Trumpator—Prunella by Highflyer—Promise by Snap Spectator's dam by Partner—Bonny Lass by Bay Bolton (G. Hautboy.) Hermes—Vicissitude by Pipator—Beatrice by Sir Peter—Pyrrha by Matchem—Duchess by Whitenose—Miss Slamerkin by Y. True Blue.
		Emilia.	Young Emilius.	Emilius.	Orville. Emily.	Beningbrough—Evelina by Highflyer—Termagant by Tantrum—Cantatrice by Sampson—Dau. of Regulus—Marske's dam by Blacklegs. Stamford—Dau. of Whiskey—Gr. Dorimant by Dorimant—Dizzy by Blank—Dizzy by Driver—Dau. of Smiling Tom—Dau. of Oysterfoot.
				Shoveler.	Scud. Goosander.	Beningbrough—Eliza by Highflyer—Augusta by Eclipse—Hardwick's dam by Herod—Dau. of Bajazet—Dau. of Regulus (Godol). Hambletonian—Rally by Trumpator—Sis. to Diomed by Florizel—Dau. of Spectator—Horatia by Blank—Dau. of F. Childers—Miss Belvoir.
			Persian.	Whisker.	Waxy. Penelope.	Pot-8-os—Maria by Herod—Lisette by Snap—Miss Windsor by Godol. Arabian—Dau. of Y. Belgrade—Dau. of Bartlet's Childers. Trumpator—Prunella by Highflyer—Promise by Snap—Julia by Blank—Spectator's dam by Partner—Bonny Lass by Bay Bolton.
				Variety.	Selim or Soothsayer.* Sprite.	Sorcerer—Golden Locks by Delpini—Violet by Shark—Dau. of Syphon—Charlotte by Blank—Dau. of Crab—Dau. of Dyer's Dimple. Bobtail—Catharine by Woodpecker—Camilla by Treutham—Coquette by Compton Barb—Sis. to Regulus by Godol. Arabian.
	AEROLITE.	Florine.	Lexington.	Boston.	Sir Archy. Daughter of.	Diomed—Castianira by Rockingham—Tabitha by Trentham—Dau. of Bosphorus—Dau. of Wm's Forester—Dau. of Coalition Colt. Saltram—Dau. of Symme's Wildair—Dau. of Driver (Othello)—Dau. of Fallower (Blank)—Dau. of Vampire (Regulus.)
				Sister to Tuckahoe.	Ball's Florizel. Daughter of.	Diomed—Dau. of Imp. Shark—Dau. of Harris' Eclipse—Dau. of Imp. Fearnought—Dau. of Jolly Roger—Dau. of Sober John—Dau. of Shock. Imp. Aldermau—Dau. of Clockfast—Dau. of Symme's Wildair—Y. Kitty Fisher by Imp. Fearnought—Imp. Kitty Fisher by Cade (Godol.)
			Alice Carneal.	Sarpedon.	Emilius. Icaria.	Orville—Emily by Stamford—Dau. of Whiskey—Gr. Dorimant by Dorimant—Dizzy by Blank—Dizzy by Driver—Dau. of Smiling Tom. The Flyer—Parma by Dick Andrews—May by Beningbrough—Primrose by Mambrino—Cricket by Herod—Sophia by Blank.
				Rowena.	Sumpter. Lady Grey.	Sir Archy—Flirtilla's dam by Robin Redbreast—Dau. of Obscurity—Slamerkin by Wildair—Imp. Cub Mare by Cub Amaranthus' dau. Robin Gray—Maria by Melzar—Dau. of Imp. Highflyer—Dau. of Imp. Fearnought—Dau. of Ariel—Dau. of Imp. Jack of Diamonds.
		Glencoe.	Trampoline.	Sultan.	Selim. Bacchante.	Buzzard—Dau. of Alexander—Dau. of Highflyer—Dau. of Alfred—Dau. of Engineer—Bay Multon's dam by Cade—Lass of the Mill. Williamson's Ditto—Sis. to Calomel by Mercury—Dau. of Herod—Folly by Marske—Vixen by Regulus—Dau. of Hutton's Spot.
				Trampoline.	Tramp. Web.	Dick Andrews—Dau. of Gohanna—Fraxinella by Trentham—Dau. of —Woodpecker—Everlasting by Eclipse—Hyaena by Snap—Miss Belsea. Waxy—Penelope by Trumpator—Prunella by Highflyer—Promise by Snap—Julia by Blank—Spectator's dam by Partner—Bonny Lass.
		Melody.	Rodolph's Dam.	Medoc.	Am. Eclipse. Young Maid of the Oaks.	Duroc—Miller's Damsel by Messenger—Dau. of Pot-8-os—Dau. of Gimcrack—Snap Dragon by Snap—Fribble's dam by Regulus. Expedition—Maid of the Oaks by Spread Eagle—Annette by Shark—Dau. of Rockingham—Dau. of Gallant—Dau. of True Whig.
					Haxall's Moses. Daughter.	Sir Harry—Mermaid by Waxy—Promise by Buzzard—Dau. of Precipitate—Lady Harriet by Mark Anthony—Georgiana by Matchem. Blackburn's Whip—Maria by Craig's Alfred (Imp. Medley)—Dau. of Taylor's Bellair (Imp. Medley)—Dau. of Imp. Medley (Gimcrack).

* Soothsayer given.

FOXHALL,

(WINNER OF THE BEDFORD STAKES AND THE BRETBY NURSERY HANDICAP PLATE AT NEWMARKET, IN 1880; THE GRAND DUKE MICHAEL STAKES, THE CESAREWITCH STAKE (HANDICAP), THE SELECT STAKES, THE CAMBRIDGESHIRE STAKES HANDICAP AND GRAND PRIX DE PARIS, ALL IN 1881.)

FOXHALL, by King Alfonso, son of imp. Phaeton, bred by A. J. Alexander, Woodburn Stud, Ky., foaled 1878, dam Jamaica by Lexington, son of Boston, out of Fanny Ludlow by imp. Eclipse, son of Orlando. Foxhall was selected and purchased for James R. Keene, Esq., by S. D. Bruce, when a yearling, and has only raced in England and France. King Alfonso, his sire, can be found in this book; also Lexington the sire of his dam. Jamaica, his dam, was never trained, but his grandam, Fanny Ludlow, was a good race-mare; she won a dash of 1¼ miles at Saratoga in 1869, in 1:56¼, the fastest race ever run at the distance to that day. Mollie Jackson, his great grandam, was Vandal's best daughter; she was winner from one to four mile heats, won 3-mile heats in 5:35½, 5:34¼, 5:28¼, the fastest three heats ever run, and the third heat unequaled to this day; she ran the ninth mile in 1:48¼. Foxhall made his début at the Newmarket Second October Meeting in the Bedford Stakes, five furlongs, defeating Myra, who was favorite at 3 to 1 on her, Ishmael and Mynheer. Same meeting, was second to Savoyard in the Ashley Sweepstakes, five furlongs, beating Simnel, Lamprey and Montgomerie, Newmarket Houghton Meeting, won the Bretby Nursery Handicap Plate, five furlongs, defeating Heyday, the favorite, to whom he gave 24 lbs., Accelerato and fifteen others. Heydey was the favorite; this stamped him as a first-class colt. At three years old was second to the great Bend Or in the City and Surburban Handicap, with Post Obit, Peter, Prestonpans, Petronel and seventeen others behind him. He then crossed the Channel and won the Grand Prix de Paris, one mile and seven furlongs, defeating Tristan, Albion, Fiddler and six others. The race was run in 3:17. He was returned to England, and without a gallop started in the Ascot Cup but was unplaced. Newmarket First October Meeting, won the Grand Duke Michael Stakes across the flat, 1 mile, 2 furlongs, 73 yards, beating Don Fulano, Ishmael and Maskelyne. Second October Meeting, won the Cesarewitch Stakes (handicap), 2 miles, 2 furlongs, 28 yards, carrying 110 lbs., defeating Chippendale, Fiddler, Petronel and fifteen others; won the Select Stakes for three-year olds, Rowley mile, beating Tristan and Maskelyne. Houghton Meeting, won the Cambridgeshire Stakes, (handicap), 1¼ miles, carrying 126 lbs., defeating Lucy Glitters (3), 91 lbs., Tristan (3), 107 lbs., lbs., Peter (5), 140 lbs., Bend Or (4), 134 lbs., and 27 others. This is the only time in the history of the turf that the two great handicaps were ever won by one and the same horse, except when Rosebery, a four-year old, won the Cesarewitch in 1876, with 103 lbs., 7 less than Foxhall carried, and the Cambridgeshire with 117 lbs., 9 less than Foxhall carried, he only three-years old. No horse has ever won this race with the weight carried by Foxhall. He won the Ascot Gold Cup in 1882, and was defeated when out of condition, by Fiddler, whom he had beaten in several races. It is hoped that when he retires he will be returned to America.

PEDIGREE OF FOXHALL.

FOXHALL.	KING ALFONSO.	Daughter of.	Mistletoe. Margrave.	Alaric's dam.	Capitola.	Economist.	Whisker—Floranthe by Octavian—Caprice by Anvil—Madcap by Eclipse—Dau. of Blank—Dau. of Blaze—Dau. of Y. Greyhound.

Rendering this complex nested pedigree as a linear outline:

FOXHALL.

- **KING ALFONSO.**
  - **Capitola.**
    - **Daughter of.**
      - **Mistletoe. Margrave.** (Alaric's dam.)
        - **Economist.** | Fanny Dawson.
          - Whisker—Floranthe by Octavian—Caprice by Anvil—Madcap by Eclipse—Dau. of Blank—Dau. of Blaze—Dau. of Y. Greyhound.
          - Nabocklish—Miss Tooley by Teddy the Grinder—Lady Jane by Sir Peter—Paulina by Florizel—Captive by Matchem—Calliope.
        - **Glencoe.** | Marpessa.
          - Sultan—Trampoline by Tramp—Web by Waxy-Penelope by Trumpator—Prunella by Highflyer—Promise by Snap—Julia.
          - Muley—Clare by Marmion—Harpalice by Gohanna—Amazon by Driver—Fractions by Mercury—Dau. of Woodpecker.
        - **Touchstone.** | Ghuznee.
          - Camel—Banter by Master Henry—Boadicea by Alexander—Brunette by Amaranthus—Mayfly by Matchem—Dau. of An. Starling.
          - Pantaloon—Languish by Cain—Lydia by Poultou—Variety by Hyacinthus—Sis. to Swordsman by Weazel—Dau. of Turk.
      - **Vandal.** (Merry Sunshine. Dau. of Storm.)
        - **Falstaff.** | Sis. to Pompey.
          - Touchstone—Decoy by Filho-da-Puta—Finesse by Peruvian—Violante by John Bull—Dau. of Highflyer—Everlasting by Eclipse.
          - Emilius—Variation by Bustard—Johannah Southcote by Beningbrough—Lavinia by Pipator—Dau. of Highflyer—Dau. of Car Puff.
        - **Sultan.** | Trampoline.
          - Selim—Bacchante by Williamson's Ditto—Sis. to Calomel by Mercury—Dau. of Herod—Folly by Marske—Vixen by Regulus.
          - Tramp—Web by Waxy—Penelope by Trumpator—Prunella by Highflyer—Promise by Snap—Julia by Blank—Spectator's dam.
    - **Glencoe.** (Phaeton. King Tom. Pocahontas. Harkaway.)
      - **Tranby.** | Lucilla.
        - Blacklock—Dau. of Orville—Miss Grimstone by Weasel—Dau. of Ancaster—Dau. of Dam Arabarian—Dau. of Sampson.
        - Trumpator—Lucy by Orphan—Lady Grey by Robin Grey—Maria by Melzar—Dau. of Highflyer—Dau. of Fearnought.
      - **Muley.** | Chatham's dam.
        - Orville—Eleanor by Whiskey—Y. Giantess by Diomed—Giantess by Matchem—Molly Longlegs by Babraham—Dau. of Cole's Foxhunter.
        - Election—Fair Helen by Hambletonian—Helen by Delpini—Rosalind by Phoenomenon—Atalanta by Matchem—Lass of the Mill.
      - **Cherokee.** | Black-eyed Susan.
        - Sir Archy—Roxana by Hephestion (Buzzard)—Roxana by Imp. Marplot—Juliet by Imp. Mexican—Dau. of Imp. Friar (South).
        - Tiger—Dau. of Albert—Dau. of Algerine—Dau. of Grey Alfred—Dau. of Imp. Medley—Dau. of Imp. Shark—Dau. of Imp. Fearnought.

- **JAMAICA.**
  - **Alice Carneal.** (Lexington. Boston. Timoleon.)
    - **Sir Archy.** | Daughter of.
      - Diomed—Castianira by Rockingham—Tabitha by Trentham—Dau. of Bosphorus—Dau. of Wm.'s Forester—Dau. of Coalition Colt.
      - Imp. Saltram—Dau. of Symme's Wildair—Dau. of Driver (Imp. Othello)—Dau. of Imp. Fallower (Blank)—Dau. of Imp. Vampire.
    - **Ball's Florizel.** | Daughter of.
      - Diomed—Dau. of Imp. Shark—Dau. of Harris' Eclipse—Dau. of Fearnought—Dau. of Imp. Jolly Roger—Dau. of Imp. Sober John.
      - Imp. Alderman—Dau. of Clockfast—Dau. of Symme's Wildair—Y Kitty Fisher by Imp. Fearnought—Imp. Kitty Fisher by Cade.
  - **Sis. to Tuckahoe.** (Rowena. Sarpedon.)
    - **Emilius.** | Icaria.
      - Orville—Emily by Stamford—Dau. of Whiskey—Gr. Dorimant by Dorimant—Dizzy by Blank—Dizzy by Driver—Dau. of Smiling Tom.
      - The Flyer—Parma by Dick Andrews—May by Beningbrough—Primrose by Mambrino—Cricket by Herod—Sophia by Blank—Diana.
    - **Sumpter.** | Lady Grey.
      - Sir Archy—Flirtilla's dam by Robin Redbreast—Dau. of Imp. Obscurity—Slamerkin by Wildair—Imp. Cub Mare.
      - Robin Gray—Maria by Melzar—Dan. of Highflyer—Dau. of Fearnought—Dau. of Ariel—Dau. of Imp. Jack of Diamonds.
  - **Imp. Eclipse.** (Gaze. Orlando.)
    - **Touchstone.** | Vulture.
      - Camel—Banter by Master Henry—Boadicea by Alexander—Brunette by Amaranthus—Mayfly by Matchem.
      - Langar—Kite by Bustard—Olympia by Sir Oliver—Scotilla by Anvil—Scota by Eclipse—Harmony by Herod.
    - **Bay Middleton.** | Flycatcher.
      - Sultan—Cobweb by Phantom—Filagree by Soothsayer—Web by Waxy—Penelope by Trumpator—Prunella by Highflyer.
      - Godolphin—Sis. to Cobweb by Phantom—Filagree by Soothsayer—Web by Waxy—Penelope by Trumpator—Prunella by Highflyer.
  - **Vandal.** (Fanny Ludlow. Mollie Jackson. Emma Wright.)
    - **Glencoe.** | Alaric's dam.
      - Sultan—Trampoline by Tramp—Web by Waxy—Penelope by Trumpator—Prunella by Highflyer—Promise by Snap.
      - Tranby—Lucilla by Trumpator—Lucy by Orphan—Lady Gray by Robin Gray—Maria by Melzar—Dau. of Highflyer.
    - **Margrave.** | Fanny Wright.
      - Muley—Dau. of Election—Fair Helen by Hambletonian—Helen by Delpini—Rosalind by Phoenomenon—Atalanta by Matchem.
      - Silverheels (Oscar by Gabriel)—Aurora by Vingt'un (Imp. Diomed)—Pandora by Grey Diomed (Imp. Medley) dam of Floretta by Hall's Union (Imp. Slim)—Dau. of Leonidas (Lloyd's Traveler)—Dau. of Imp. Othello (Crab)—Dau. of Imp. Juniper (Babraham)—Dau. of Imp. Traveler (Partner)—Imp. Selima by Godol. Arabian—Large Hartley Mare by Hartley's Blind Horse (Holderness Turk)—Flying Whig by Wm.'s Woodstock Arabian—Dau. of St. Victor Barb—Dau. of Whynot (Fenwick Barb.)—Royal Mare.

GLASGOW.

Glasgow will stand the season of 1883 at the Stud Farm of his owner, J. P. Dawes, Lachine, Canada, at $25 the season. Application to J. P. Dawes, Lachine, Canada.

GLASGOW by War Dance, son of Lexington, bred by Redding & Bros., Barren Co., Ky., near Glasgow, foaled 1873, dam Ida Dickey, by Joe Stoner, son of Wagner, out of a daughter of imp Glencoe. Glasgow at two years old, started three times and was unplaced. As a three-year old, started in four races. At Louisville, Ky., was third in the Louisville Hotel Stakes for three-year olds, 1¼ miles, won by Grit in 2:12¼, and was unplaced in the others. As a four-year old, started twelve times, and won four races. Nashville, Tenn., won mile heats in 1:52½, 1:53, beating Highland Vintage, the only other starter; track muddy. Cincinnati, won two mile heats in 3:58, 4:10, beating three others, track heavy. Columbus, Ohio, won a dash of 1½ miles in 2:39¾, beating Verdigris and six others. Cleveland, Ohio, won a dash of 1¼ miles in 2:10¾, beating Courier and five others. Nashville, Tenn., was second in a race of mile heats, won by Courier in 1:46, 1:45. Louisville, Ky., was third in a dash of 2 miles, won by Whisper in 3:36¾, was second in a dash of 2 miles, won by Courier in 3:31¾, Saratoga was third in a dash of 1½ miles won by Parole in 2:36¾, and was unplaced in the balance of his races. As a six-year old, started in five races. Montgomery, Ala., was second in a dash of one mile, won by Aspasia in 1:50½. Same place was third in a race of mile heats, won by Capt. Fred. Rice in 1:49, 1:47¾; was second to Aspasia, two mile heats, in 3:50, 3:46¾. Eight years old, started in thirteen races, and won eight. Louisville, Ky. won a race of 1¼ miles, over five hurdles, in 2:19, beating Duke of Kent and two others. St. Louis, won hurdle race, 1¼ miles, over five hurdles, in 2:20, beating Woodcock and Turin. Won hurdle race, 2 miles, over eight hurdles, in 3:57½. Saratoga, won hurdle race, ran 1¼ miles, over five hurdles, in 2:21¾, carrying 148 lbs., and beating Disturbance and Rosella. Won a handicap hurdle race, 1½ miles, over six hurdles, in 2:58½, carrying 156 lbs., and beating Faustina (5), 132 lbs., only two starters. Won hurdle race, one mile and a furlong, over five hurdles, in 2:07, carrying 160 lbs., and beating Postguard (aged), 148 lbs., Faustina (5), 128 lbs., and Terror (6), 130 lbs. Won a handicap hurdle, 1¼ miles, over five hurdles, in 2:28½, carrying 165 lbs., and beating Capt. Franklin (6), 130 lbs., Disturbance (aged), 154 lbs., and Postguard (aged), 154 lbs. Monmouth Park, won handicap steeplechase over the short course in 3:16¼, carrying 160 lbs., and beating Lizzie D, Joe Hunt, and four others. Monmouth Park, was second in a handicap steeplechase over the short course, won by Strychnine in 3:13¼. Was third in a handicap hurdle, 1¼ miles, over five hurdles, won by Ingomar in 2:19¼; Glasgow carried 165 lbs.; was unplaced in his other races.

Nine years old, started in seven races, of which he won one. New Orleans, La., won a hurdle, 1¼ miles, in 2:32, track heavy. Louisville, Ky., was third in steeplechase, 2 miles and a furlong, won by Miss Malloy, in 4:10½. Was third in a steeplechase, about 1½ miles, won by Guy, in 3:03½. Saratoga, was third in a handicap hurdle, 1¼ miles, over five hurdles, won by Judge Burnett in 2:29, was third in a handicap hurdle race, 1½ miles, over six hurdles, won by Revenge in 2:48½, was third in a handicap hurdle race, 1¼ miles, over five hurdles, won by Revenge in 2:19. Did not run in his 5 or 7 year old form. Glasgow was in poor hands during his racing career, but was a speedy and game horse. He is much inbred to Glencoe, having three crosses of that desirable blood; he has nine crosses of Sir Archy through his distinguished sons, and traces to Web the own sister to Whalebone and Whisker, and thence through an own sister of Diomed to a daughter of Spanker. Glasgow is a bright chestnut, full 15¾ hands high, with a star in his forehead, near fore foot white to ankle, and near hind foot white to fetlock, and dark spot on his left hind quarter, he is full of substance and quality, with plenty of bone. Should breed both hunters and racers.

PEDIGREE OF GLASGOW.

GLASGOW.								
WAR DANCE.	Lexington.	Alice Carneal.	Boston.	Sir Archy. Daughter of.	Diomed—Castianira by Rockingham—Tabitha by Trentham—Dau. of Bosphorus—Dau. of Wm.'s Forester—Dau of Coalition Colt. Saltram—Dau of Symme's Wildair—Dau. of Driver (Imp. Othello)—Dau. of Imp. Fallower—(Blank)—Dau. of Imp. Vampire (Regulus.)
			Sis. to Tuckahoe.	Ball's Florizel. Daughter of.	Diomed—Dau. of Imp. Shark—Dau. of Harris Eclipse—Dau. of Fearnought—Dau. of Jolly Roger—Dau. of Sober John—Dau. of Shock. Alderman—Dau. of Clockfast—Dau. of Symme's Wildair—Kitty Fisher by Fearnought—Imp. Kitty Fisher by Cade—Dau. of Somer. Arabian.
		Rowena.	Sarpedon.	Emilius. Icaria.	Orville—Emily by Stamford—Dau. of Whiskey—Gr. Dorimant by Dorimant—Dizzy by Blank—Dizzy by Driver—Dau. of Smiling Tom. The Flyer—Parma by Dick Andrews—May by Beningbrough—Primrose by Mambrino—Cricket by Herod—Sophia by Blank—Diana by Second.
			Timoleon.	Sumpter. Lady Grey.	Sir Archy—Flirtilla's dam by Robin Redbreast—Dau. of Obscurity—Old Slamerkin by Wildair—Imp. Cub Mare by Cub—Amaranthus' dam. Robin Grey—Maria by Melzar—Dau. of Highflyer—Dau. of Fearnought—Dau. of Ariel—Dau. of Jack of Diamonds—Imp. Diamond by Cul. Arabian.
	Glencoe.	Trampoline.	Sultan.	Selim. Bacchante.	Buzzard—Dau. of Alexander—Dau. of Highflyer—Dau. of Alfred—Dau. of Engineer—Bay Malton's dam by Cade—Lass of the Mill by Traveler. Williamson's Ditto—Sis. to Calomel by Mercury—Dau. of Herod—Folly by Marske—Vixen by Regulus—Dau. of Hutton's Spot.
			Reel.	Tramp. Web.	Dick Andrews—Dau. of Gohanna—Fraxinella by Trentham—Dau. of Woodpecker—Everlasting by Eclipse—Hyaena by Suap (Snip). Waxy—Penelope by Trumpator—Prunella by Highflyer—Promise by Snap—Julia by Blank—Spectator's dam by Partner—Bonny Lass by B. Bolton.
		Camillina.	Gallopade.	Golumpus. Lucy Gray.	Gohanna—Catharine by Woodpecker—Camilla by Trentham—Coquette by Compton Barb—Sis. to Regulus by Godol. Arabian—(Gr. Robinson. Timothy—Lucy by Florizel—Frenzy by Eclipse—Dau. of Engineer—Dau. of Blank—Lass of the Mill by Traveler—Miss Makeless.
			Catton.	Camillus. Daughter of.	Hambletoulan—Faith by Pacolet—Atalanta by Matchem—Lass of the Mill by Oroonoko—Dau. of Traveler—Miss Makeless by Y. Greyhound. Smolensko—Miss Cannon by Orville—Dau. of Weathercock—Cora by Matchem—Dau. of Turk—Dau. of Cub—Dau. of Allworthy.
IDA DICKEY.	Joe Stoner.	Mollie Campbell.	Wagner.	Sir Archy. Daughter of.	Diomed—Castianira by Rockingham—Tabitha by Trentham—Dau. of Bosphorus—Dau. of Wm.'s Forester—Dau of Coalition Colt. Citizen—Dau. of Commutation—Dau. of Dare Devil—Sally Shark by Imp. Shark—Betsey Prinkle by Fearnought (Regulus).
			Maria West.	Marion. Ella Crump.	Sir Archy—Dau. of Citizen—Dau of Alderman—Dau. of Asche's Roebuck—Dau. of Haine's King Herod—Dau. of Imp. Partner. Citizen—Dau. of Huntsman—Dau. of Symme's Wildair—Dau. of Imp. Fearnought (Regulus)—Dau. of Imp. Janus.
		Medina.	Glencoe.	Sultan. Trampoline.	Selim—Bacchante by Williamson's Ditto—Sis. to Calomel by Mercury—Dau. of Herod—Folly by Marske—Vixen by Regulus—Dau. of Spot. Tramp—Web by Waxy—Penelope by Trumpator—Prunella by Highflyer—Promise by Snap—Julia by Blank—Spectator's dam by Partner.
			Sir Charles.	Bertrand. Directress.	Sir Archy—Eliza by Bedford—Imp. Mambrina by Mambrino—Sis. to Naylor's Sally by Blank—Dau. of Ward—Dau. of Merlin. Director (Sir Archy)—Dau. of Potomac (Diomed)—Dau. of Gimcrack Randolph's Roan (Imp. Medley)—Dau. of Imp. Flimnap.
	Daughter of.	Mirth.	Glencoe.	Selim. Bacchante.	Buzzard—Dau. of Alexander—Dau. of Highflyer—Dau. of Alfred—Dau. of Engineer—Bay Malton's dam by Cade—Lass of the Mill. Williamson's Ditto—Sis. to Calomel by Mercury—Dau. of Herod—Folly by Marske—Vixen by Regulus—Dau. of Hutton's Spot.
			Trampoline.	Tramp. Web.	Dick Andrews—Dau. of Gohanna—Fraxinella by Trentham—Dau. of Woodpecker—Everlasting by Eclipse—Hyaena by Suap (Snip.) Waxy—Penelope by Trumpator—Prunella by Highflyer—Promise by Snap—Julia by Blank—Spectator's dam by Partner—Bonny Lass.
		Cheap.	Wagner.	Sir Charles. Maria West.	Sir Archy—Dau. of Citizen—Dau. of Commutation—Dau. of Dare Devil—Sally Shark by Shark—Betsey Pringle by Fearnought. Marion—Ella Crump by Citizen—Dau. of Huntman—Dau. of Symme's Wildair—Dau. of Fearnought—Dau. of Imp. Janus.
			Trampoline.	Glaucus. Christobel.	Partisan—Nanine by Selim—Bizarre by Peruvian—Violante by John Bull—Dau. of Highflyer—Everlasting by Eclipse—Hyaena by Snap. Woful (Waxy)—Harriet by Pericles—Dau. of Selim—Pypilina by Sir Peter—Rally by Trumpator (Conductor)—Fancy, Sis. to Diomed by Florizel (Herod)—Dau. of Spectator (Crab)—Dau. of Blank (Godol.)—Dau.of Childers (Darley Arabian)—Miss Belvoir by Gr. Grantham (Brownlow Turk)—Dau. of Paget Turk—Betty Percival by Leede's Arabian—Dau. of Spanker (D'Arcy Yellow Turk.)

GLEN ATHOL (Imp.)

Glen Athol will be located the season of 1883 at the Woodburn Stud, Spring Station, Woodford Co., Kentucky, and will be permitted to serve mares at $50 each. Application to be made to L. Brodhead, Spring Station, Kentucky. Annual sales of yearlings in May.

GLEN ATHOL, by Blair Athol, son of Stockwell, bred by Mr. J. Johnstone, foaled 1869, "called in the *English Stud Book* The Reaper," dam Greta, the dam of Heather Bloom, Harvester, Maid of Tyne, by Voltigeur, out of Mountain Flower, dam of Richochet, Heather, Alpenstock, etc., by Ithuriel. Glen Athol was imported by Mr. R. W. Cameron when two years old ; he was so badly injured on the voyage that he was never trained ; Blair Athol, his sire, is well known as the best son of Stockwell ; the latter won the 2,000 guineas and the St. Leger in 1852, and sired more winners of the great turf events in England than any other horse which ever lived, such as The Marquis, winner of the 2,000 guineas and St. Leger ; Bothwell and Gang Forward, winners of the 2,000 guineas ; Lady Augusta and Repulse, winners of the 1,000 guineas ; Achievement, winner of the 1,000 guineas and St. Leger ; Lord Lyon, winner of the 2,000 guineas, Derby and St. Leger ; Doncaster, winner of the Derby and sire of Bend Or ; St. Albans, winner of the St. Leger ; Caller On, winner of St. Leger and other good races. Voltigeur, the sire of his dam, was one of the few horses that won the "double event," Derby and St. Leger ; is a fine improving strain of blood and noted for stoutness. Ithuriel, the sire of his great grandam. was by Touchstone, who was one of the great horses of England, and who defeated in the St. Leger, Plenipotentiary, surnamed The Lion of Doncaster, and also won the Doncaster Cup in 1835-36, and the Ascot Cup in 1836-37. The blood is as good as it can be made ; in addition to the speedy crosses of Touchstone and Melbourne, his blood is fortified by that of Blacklock and Waxy through his best sons Whalebone and Whisker, Glen Athol has only covered a limited number of mares and has gotten some first-class race horses. There has not been upon the American turf for years two such aged horses as Checkmate and Glenmore, which not only possess great speed, but wonderful staying powers with ability to carry weight. Checkmate ran during the season of 1881 a series of the most remarkable races ever run by any horse in the annals of racing ; he won one mile and a furlong in 1:56¼, carrying 131 lbs. ; 1¼ miles in 2:09, carrying 117 lbs. ; 1½ miles in 2:35½, with 119 lbs. ; and 1¾ miles in 3:01¼, with 124 lbs. ; the history of the turf furnishes no parallel to these grand performances. Glenmore accomplished nearly as much ; he won at mile heats in 1:43½, 1:42½, 1:46½ ; 1¼ miles in 2:10 ; 1¾ miles 3:10¼, and 2¼ miles in 3:58¾, the fastest at the distance during the year 1881.

Checkmate in 1882 won the Dixiana Stakes one mile 110 yards in 1:50½, beating Hindoo, Fellowplay and six others, won the Swigert Stake, one mile, 118 lbs., in 1:42, beating Runnymede, etc ; won the Brewer's Cup, St. Louis, 2¼ miles, in 4:01, beating John Davis.

Glenmore's heats of 1¼ miles in 2:09, 2:10, 2:14, have never been equaled. His great race in the Bowie Stakes, four-mile, heats in 7:29¼, 7:30¼, 7:31 ; the average has never been equaled in the world. Other reputable winners by him are Nannie H., Mamie H., Sagamore (Glen Ogle), Frank Short, Athol, Mattie Moore, Alec Grant, Tolima, Macedonicus, Mattie Glenn, Voltague, etc. Glen Athol is a dark chestnut, 16¼ hands high, with a blaze face and two white stockings behind ; he is fine through the heart and shoulders and, for his chances, one of the successful sires of the day. He is by the best son of Stockwell and he traces through the blood of Waxy, Eclipse and Herod to a Royal mare.

PEDIGREE OF GLEN ATHOL.

GLEN ATHOL.							
	BLAIR ATHOL.	Stockwell.	The Baron.	Birdcatcher.	Sir Hercules.	Whalebone—Perl by Wanderer—Thalestris by Alexander—Rival by Sir Peter—Hornet by Drone—Manilla by Goldfinder.	
					Guiccioli.	Bob Booty—Flight by Irish Escape—Y. Heroine by Bagot—Heroine by Hero—Dau. of Snap—Sis. to Regulus by Godol. Arabian.	
				Echidna.	Economist.	Whisker—Floranthe by Octavian—Caprice by Anvil—Madcap by Eclipse—Dau. of Blank—Dau. of Blaze—Dau. of Y. Greyhound.	
					Miss Pratt.	Blacklock—Gadabout by Orville—Minstrel by Sir Peter—Matron by Florizel—Maiden by Matchem—Dau. of Squirt.	
		Pocahontas.	Glencoe.		Sultan.	Selim—Bacchante by Williamson's Ditto—Sis. to Calomel by Mercury—Dau. of Herod—Folly by Marske—Vixen by Regulus.	
				Marpessa.	Trampoline.	Tramp—Web by Waxy—Penelope by Trumpator—Prunella by Highflyer—Promise by Snap—Julia by Blank—Spectator's dam.	
		Blink Bonny.	Melbourne.	Humphrey Clinker.	Muley.	Orville—Eleanor by Whisker—Y. Giantess by Diomed—Giantess by Matchem—Molly Longlegs by Babraham (Godol).	
					Clare.	Marmion—Harpalice by Gohanna—Amazon by Driver—Fractious by Mercury—Dau. of Woodpecker—Everlasting by Eclipse.	
					Comus.	Sorcerer—Houghton Lass by Sir Peter—Alexina by King Fergus—Lardella by Y. Marske—Dau. of Cade—Beaufremont's dam.	
				Dau. of	Clinkerina.	Clinker—Pewet by Tandem—Termagant by Tantrum—Cantatrice by Sampson—Dau. of Regulus—Marske's dam by Blacklegs.	
		Queen Mary.	Gladiator.		Cervantes.	Don Quixote—Evelina by Highflyer—Termagant by Tantrum—Cantatrice by Sampson—Dau. of Regulus—Marske's dam.	
				Dau. of	Daughter of.	Golumpus—Dau. of Paynator—Sis. to Zodiac by St. George—Abigail by Woodpecker—Firetail by Eclipse—Dau. of Blank.	
					Partisan.	Walton—Parasol by Pot-8-os—Prunella by Highflyer—Promise by Snap—Julia by Blank—Spectator's dam by Partner—Bonny Lass.	
					Pauline.	Moses—Quadrille by Selim—Canary Bird by Whiskey or Sorcerer—Canary by Coriander—Miss Green by Highflyer—Harriet by Matchem.	
					Plenipotentiary.	Emilius—Harriet by Pericles—Dau. of Selim—Pipylina by Sir Peter—Rally by Trumpator—Fancy, Sis. to Diomed by Florizel.	
					Myrrha.	Whalebone—Gift by Young Gohanna—Sis. to Grazier by Sir Peter—Sis. to Amaitor by Trumpator—Dau. of Herod—Dau. of Snap (Snip).	
	GRETA.	Voltigeur.	Voltaire.	Blacklock.	Whitelock.	Hambletonian—Rosalind by Phœnomenon—Atalanta by Matchem—Lass of the Mill by Oroonoko—Daughter of Old Traveler—Miss Makeless.	
					Daughter of.	Coriander—Wildgoose by Highflyer—Coheiress by Pot-8-os—Manilla by Goldfinder—Dau. of Old Eng—Dau. of Cullen Arabian.	
				Dau. of	Phantom.	Walton—Julia by Whiskey—Y. Giantess by Diomed—Giantess by Matchem—Molly Longlegs by Babraham—Dau. of Cole's Foxhunter.	
					Daughter of.	Overton—Gratitude's dam by Walnut—Dau. of Ruler—Piracartha by Matchem—Dau. of Regulus—Jenny Spinner by Partner.	
		Martha Lynn.	Mulatto.		Catton.	Golumpus—Lucy Gray by Timothy—Lucy by Florizel—Frenzy by Eclipse—Dau. of Engineer—Dau. of Blank—Lass of the Mill.	
				Leda.	Desdemona.	Orville—Fanny by Sir Peter—Dau. of Diomed—Desdemona by Marske—Y. Hag by Skim—Hag by Crab—Ebony by F. Childers.	
					Filho-da-Puta.	Haphazard—Mrs. Barnet by Waxy—Dau. of Woodpecker—Heinel by Squirrel—Principessa by Blank—Dau. of Cul Arabian.	
					Treasure.	Camillus—Dau. of Hyacinthus—Flora by King Fergus—Atalanta by Matchem—Lass of the Mill by Oroonoko—Dau. of Traveler.	
	Mountain Flower.	Ithuriel.	Touchstone.		Camel.	Whalebone—Dau. of Selim—Maiden by Sir Peter—Dau. of Phœnomenon—Matron by Florizel—Maiden by Matchem.	
					Banter.	Master Henry—Boadicea by Alexander—Brunette by Amaranthus—Mayfly by Matchem—Dau. of An. Starling—Dau. of Grasshopper.	
			Verbena.		Velocipede.	Blacklock—Dau. of Juniper (Whiskey)—Dau. of Sorcerer—Virgin by Sir Peter—Dau. of Pot-8-os—Editha by Herod.	
					Rosalba.	Milo (Sir Peter)—Sis. to Rubens by Buzzard—Dau. of Alexander—Dau. of Highflyer—Dau. of Alfred—Dau. of Engineer—Bay Malton's dam.	
		Heatherbell.	Bay Middleton.		Sultan.	Selim—Bacchante by Williamson's Ditto—Sis. to Calomel by Mercury—Dau. of Herod—Folly by Marske—Vixen by Regulus.	
					Cobweb.	Phantom—Filagree by Soothsayer—Web by Waxy—Penelope by Trumpator—Prunella by Highflyer—Promise by Snap—Julia.	
			Maid of Lune.		Whisker.	Waxy—Penelope by Trumpator—Prunella by Highflyer—Promise by Snap—Julia by Blank—Spectator's dam.	
					Gibside Fairy.	Hermes—Vicissitude by Pipator (Imperator)—Beatrice by Sir Peter (Highflyer)—Pyrrha by Matchem (Cade by Godol.)—Duchess by Whitenose (Godol)—Miss Slamerkin by Y. True Blue (William's Turk—Dau. of Ld. Oxford's Dun Arabian—D'Arcy Black-legged Royal Mare.	

GLENELG (Imp.)

(WINNER OF THE TRAVERS STAKE AT SARATOGA, 1869; THE CHAMPION STAKES AT JEROME PARK SAME YEAR; THE MATURITY STAKES AT JEROME PARK, 1870; AND THE BOWIE STAKES AT BALTIMORE (FOUR MILE HEATS) SAME YEAR,)

Will stand for mares at the Elmendorf Stud (North Elkhorn), near Lexington, Fayette County, Ky., at $100 the season. Application to D. Swigert, Muirs P. O., Ky. Annual sale of yearlings in May.

GLENELG, by Citadel, son of Stockwell, bred by R. W. Cameron, Clifton Stud, Staten Island, N. Y., foaled 1866, dam Babta, imp. when in foal to Citadel by Kingston, son of Venison, out of Alice Lowe, by Defence, son of Whalebone. Glenelg was purchased by Hon. A. Belmont, in whose colors he ran all his races. Glenelg was a first class race-horse; did not run at two years old. He made his *début* in the Belmont Stakes in 1869, running second to his stable companion, Fenian, one mile and five furlongs, in 3:04½. Saratoga, 1869, won the Travers Stakes, 1¾ miles in 3:14. Same year won the Champion Stakes at Jerome Park (mile heats), beating Vespucius, who won the first heat, and five others, in 1:48½, 1:48½, 1:49. Same meeting ran second to Vespucius in the Annual Stakes, 2 miles, in 3:54, Invercauld, Niagara, Blarney Stone, etc., behind him; 1870, June 7, was unplaced in Westchester Cup, won by Helmbold, 2¼ miles, in 4:11. Same meeting won purse 1¾ miles, beating Vespucius, in 3:16¾. October 8, won the Maturity Stakes, for four-year olds, 3 miles, in 5:42½, beating Helmbold. October 11, ran third to Niagara and Mozart, in Grand National Handicap, 2¼ miles, in 4:09½—Glenelg carried 119 lbs. to Niagara's 104, both four years old. Saratoga, July 14, Glenelg won the Sweepstake for All Ages, 1¼ miles, in 2:18¼, beating Maggie B. B., Niagara and others. July 15, ran third to Helmbold and Hamburg in Saratoga Cup, 2¼ miles, in 4:08¾. August 16, ran third to Judge Curtis and General Yorke, 1¼ miles in 2:40½. August 18, won purse, 1¾ miles, in 3:12½, beating Alta Vela, &c. Long Branch, July 30, ran second to Helmbold, in Monmouth Cup, 2¼ miles, in 4:33½. August 2, won dash, 1¼ miles, in 2:37¾, beating Legatee and others. Baltimore, October 29, won the Bowie Stakes, 4 mile heats, in 7:47, 7:44, beating Niagara and distancing Abd-el-Kader, Nannie Douglas, Plantagenet and Carrie Atherton in the second heat; 1871, Jerome Park, June 13, ran second to Preakness in Westchester Cup, 2¼ miles, in 4:15½, beating Helmbold. This closed his turf career. While on the turf he met the best horses and at all distances, and won a large majority of his races with the top weights. He lost one or two races which he would have won but for an ugly habit of turning the wrong way as the flag fell. Citadel, the sire of Glenelg, was a good race-horse. In 1863 he won the Prince of Wales Stakes, at Newmarket, Cesarewich Course, 2 miles two furlongs 28 yards. Same meeting won Free Handicap Sweepstakes, 2 middle miles of Beacon Course—1 mile 7 furlongs 158 yards, and ran reputably in others. Kingston, the sire of Babta, was one of the best race-horses which ever started in England; was a winner at all distances, from two years old up to five, carrying the heaviest weights and against the best horses of his day, from one to four miles. He was by Venison (son of Partisan and Fawn, by Smolensko), dam Queen Anne, by Slane. The late Mr. Wm. Blenkiron thought the Kingston cross superior to all others, and very many of his daughters were in Middle Park Stud. Glenelg is much inbred to Waxy, through his sons Whalebone, Whisker and daughter Web, and the collateral branches are full of the blood of Eclipse, Herod, Regulus and the Godolphin Barb. Glenelg is a blood bay full 16½ hands high, of grand presence, having a beautiful head and neck, running into well-set, oblique shoulders, well covered with muscle; deep, roomy chest, with good breadth through the heart; most excellent body, strong back, the ribs running close up to the hips, which are broad and well rounded, with good length, long well-muscled quarters, and great length from the point of the hip to stifle and thence to the hock, which is well shaped, tapering gradually into the shank, with most excellent legs and sound, good feet. Taking him altogether, there is not a handsomer, better-formed and more blood-like stallion in the world, with most excellent temper. There are few (if any) of his colts which are not handsome and well-shaped, and generally good feeders, with immense speed. As he could stay a distance with weight, most of his colts possess these qualities in an eminent degree. The best of his get are Ferida, the equal of any mare which ever started in America. She has won at all distances; from one to four mile heats, has met and defeated the best, her four-mile heat race in 7:33½, 7:41, is not

Continued on page 56.

PEDIGREE OF GLENELG.

GLENELG.	CITADEL.	Stockwell.	The Baron.	Birdcatcher.	Irish	Sir Hercules.	Whalebone—Peri by Wanderer—Thalestris by Alexander—Rival by Sir Peter—Hornet by Drone—Manilla by Goldfinder.
						Guiccioli.	Bob Booty—Flight by I. Escape—Y. Heroine by Bagot—Heroine by Hero—Dau. of Snap—Sis. to Regulus by Godol. Arabian—Gr. Robinson.
				Echidna		Economist.	Whisker—Floranthe by Octavian—Caprice by Anvil—Madcap by Eclipse—Dau. of Blank—Dau. of Blaze—Dau. of Young Greyhound.
						Miss Pratt.	Blacklock—Gadabout by Orville—Minstrel by Sir Peter—Matron by Florizel—Maiden by Matchem—Dau. of Squirt.
		Pocahontas.	Glencoe.			Sultan.	Selim—Bacchante by Williamson's Ditto—Sis. to Calomel by Mercury—Dau. of Herod—Folly by Marske—Vixen by Regulus.
						Trampoline.	Tramp—Web by Waxy—Penelope by Trumpator—Prunella by Highflyer—Promise by Snap—Julia by Blank—Spectator's dam by Partner.
			Marpessa.			Muley.	Orville—Eleanor by Whiskey—Y. Giantess by Diomed—Giantess by Matchem—Molly Longlegs by Babraham—Dau. of Cole's Foxhunter.
						Clare.	Marmion—Harpalice by Gohanna—Amazon by Driver—Fractious by Mercury—Dau. of Woodpecker—Everlasting by Eclipse—Hyaena.
		Sortie.	Melbourne.	Humphr'y Clinker.		Comus.	Sorcerer—Houghton Lass by Sir Peter—Alexina by King Fergus—Lardella by Y. Marske—Dau. of Cade—Beaufremont's dam.
						Clinkerina.	Clinker—Pewet by Tandem—Termagant by Tantrum—Cantatrice by Sampson—Dau. of Regulus—Marske's dam by Blacklegs.
			Touchstone.	Daughter of.		Cervantes.	Don Quixote—Evelina by Highflyer—Termagant by Tantrum—Cantatrice by Sampson—Dau. of Regulus—Marske's dam.
						Daughter of.	Golumpus—Dau. of Paynator—Sis. to Zodiac by St. George—Abigail by Woodpecker—Firetail by Eclipse—Dau. of Blank—Dau. of Cade.
		Escapade.		Ghuznee.		Camel.	Whalebone—Dau. of Selim—Maiden by Sir Peter—Dau. of Phoenomenon—Matron by Florizel—Maiden by Matchem—Dau. of Squirt.
						Banter.	Master Henry—Boadicea by Alexander—Brunette by Amaranthus—Mayfly by Matchem—Dau. of An. Starling—Dau. of Grasshopper.
						Pantaloon.	Castrel—Idalia by Peruvian—Musidora by Meteor—Maid of All Work by Highflyer—Sis. to Tandem by Syphon—Dau. of Regulus.
						Languish.	Cain—Lydia by Poulton—Variety by Hyacinthus—Dau. of Weasel—Dau. of Turk—Dau. of Locust—Dau. of Changeling.
	BABTA.	Kingston.	Venison.	The Fawn.	Partisan.	Walton.	Sir Peter—Arethusa by Dungannon—Dau. of Prophet—Virago by Snap—Dau. of Regulus—Sis. to Othello by Crab—Miss Slamerkin.
						Parasol.	Pot-8-os—Prunella by Highflyer—Promise by Snap—Julia by Blank—Spectator's dam by Partner—Bonny Lass by Bay Bolton.
						Smolensko.	Sorcerer—Wowski by Mentor—Maria Waxy's dam, by Herod—Lizette by Snap—Miss Windsor by Godol. Arabian.
						Jerboa.	Gohanna—Camilla by Trentham—Coquette by Compton Barb—Sis. to Regulus by Godol. Arabian—Gr. Robinson by Bald Galloway.
		Queen Ann.	Slane.	Garcia.		Royal Oak.	Catton—Dau. of Smolensko—Lady Mary by Beningbrough—Dau. of Highflyer—Dau. of Marske—A la Grecque by Regulus.
						Daughter of.	Orville—Epsom Lass by Sir Peter—Alexina by King Fergus—Lardella by Y. Marske—Dau. of Cade—Beaufremont's dam.
						Octavian.	Stripling (Phoenomenon)—Dau. of Oberon—Sis. to Sharper by Ranthos (Matchem)—Dau. of Sweepstakes—Sis. to Hutton's Careless.
						Daughter of.	Shuttle—Katharine by Delpini—Dau. of Paymaster—Dau. of Le Sang—Dau. of Rib—Eclipse's dam Spiletta by Regulus.
		Defence.	Whalebone.	Defiance.		Waxy.	Pot-8-os—Maria by Herod—Lisette by Snap—Miss Windsor by Godol. Arabian—Sis. to Volunteer by Young Belgrade—Dau. of B. Childers.
						Penelope.	Trumpator—Prunella by Highflyer—Promise by Snap—Julia by Blank—Spectator's dam by Partner—Bonny Lass by Bay Bolton.
						Rubens.	Buzzard—Dau. of Alexander—Dau. of Highflyer—Dau. of Alfred—Dau. of Engineer—Bay Malton's dam by Cade.
						Little Folly.	Highland Fling—Harriet by Volunteer—Dau. of Alfred—Magnolia by Marske—Dau. of Babraham—Dau. of Sedbury—Ebony.
		Alice Low.	Pet.	Gaiusborough.		Rubens.	Buzzard—Dau. of Alexander—Dau. of Highflyer—Dau. of Alfred—Dau. of Engineer—Bay Malton's dam by Cade—Lass of the Mill.
						Tiny Sis. to Agonistes.	Sir Peter—Wren by Woodpecker—Papillon, Sir Peter's dam, by Snap—Miss Cleveland by Regulus—Midge by Son of Bay Bolton.
			Daughter of.			Topsy-Turvy.	St. George (Highflyer)—Dau. of Beningbrough—Dau. of Phlegon (Mat)—Dau. of Turk (Regulus)—Dau. of Bosphorus—Dau. of Rib—Dau. of Hip.
						Agnes.	Shuttle (Y. Marske)—Dau. of Highflyer—Dau. of Goldfinder (Snap)—Lady Bolingbroke by Squirrel (Traveler)—Cypron, Herod's dam, by Blaze (F. Childers)—Selima by Bethel's Arabian—Dau. of Graham's Champion (Harpun Arabian)—Dau. of Darley Arabian—Dau. of Merlin (Bustler by Helmsley Turk).

GLENELG (Imp.)—Continued.

only the fastest race ever run by a mare, but the average of the two heats is better than Lecompte's when he beat Lexington, and better than Fashion's when she beat Boston. Monitor, a winner at all distances, Westchester, Baltimore and Coney Island cups—1¾ miles, in 3:02¾; 2¼ miles, in 4:36½; 2¼ miles, in 3:44½; the fastest ever run at the distance. Other good ones by him are Ada Glenn, Dan Sparling, Aella, Clara D, Bertha, the best mare over timber in America, Judith, Edenderry, Gladstone, Harry Gow, Jennie B, Kitty Clark, Lillie R, Mintzer, Post Guard (Gen. Philips), Strathspey, Danicheff, Cammie F, Glenita, Minnock, Harlequin, Vender, Mirth in England, Diana, Orion, Sally Polk, Start in England, Faustina, Vanderdecken, Glencairne, Lotta C, Glen Dudley, Glen Jorsa in England, Glendolin, Susquehanna and Saratoga in England, Alta B., Herbert (Tom Plunket), Magnate, Little Minch, Corsair, Arsenic, Heel and Toe and many others. Glenelg is very handsomely and fashionably bred, running back to Eclipse, King Herod, Highflyer blood and many times to the hard-bottomed and stout Whalebone blood. He also has, through his sire, Citadel, a cross of Glencoe through Pocahontas, the dam of Stockwell. This blood is highly prized in England, and in America it is invaluable, and will ultimately prove itself. Glenelg's stock are all handsome, blood-like, speedy and stout; but, like all the other stallions in the country, the best of his get are from Lexington mares, bred from daughters of Glencoe. Glenelg has always stood high as a sire, his stock have invariably good legs and feet, and his daughters will be of inestimable value in the stud.

—

GLENGARRY (Imp.)

Glengarry will be located for the season of 1883 at the Kennesaw Stud, near Gallatin, Tenn., and will be permitted to serve mares at $50 each, with the privilege of returning next season if not in foal. Application to be made to Capt. James Franklin, Gallatin, Tenn.

Glengarry, by Thormanby, son of Melbourne or Windhound, was bred by Capt. Lane, foaled 1866, dam Carbine by Rifleman, son of Touchstone out of Troica, dam of Comfit by Lanercost. Glengarry was imported in the fatal lot on the Helvetia in December, 1866—thirty-five out of thirty-nine head were lost on the passage, and those which survived were so badly used up that they were unfit to race. Glengarry was trained, after he seemingly recovered from his injuries, and started in the Hopeful Stakes, 1868, at Jerome Park, five furlongs, 1:06½, and a sweepstake, half a mile, in .54¾, and was unplaced, both won by Bonny Lass. At Jerome Park, 1869, was fourth in the Belmont Stakes to Fenian, Glenelg and Invercauld, one mile and five furlongs, in 3:04½, with Viola and three others behind him. Ran third in Club Purse to Vespucius and Belmont, one mile and a furlong, in 2:08½, track muddy. At four years old ran second to Cottrill, in Fordham Handicap, 1¼ miles, in 2:12½, beating R. B. Connolly, Nannie Douglas, Corsican, Metarie and three others. Was unplaced in Club Purse, heats of 1¾ miles, won by Sanford in 3:15¾, 3:17½, track heavy. Thormanby, his sire, although credited with a double paternity, was unquestionably by Windhound, the son of Pantaloon, by Castrel; he won the Derby, defeating, amongst others, The Wizard, winner of the 2,000 guineas; he also won the Ascot Gold Cup in 1861; he was sire of Atlantic and Charibert, winners of the 2,000 guineas. Alice Hawthorne, Thormanby's dam, was the best mare of her day in England, won the Goodwood Cup in 1844 and the Doncaster Cup in 1843 and 1844. Glengarry is bred from speedy blood on the sire's side and well fortified on the dam's side by the stout crosses of Waxy, Herod and Eclipse. For his chances he has sired some good colts. Kennesaw is the best produce of his dam; Matagorda is also a fast and good mare and winner of seven races in one year; Peru was also a good performer and the best produce of her dam; Greenland, although an uncertain horse, ran, when fit, some most excellent races; he won the Great Metropolitan Stakes at Jerome Park, 1½ miles, in 2:40½, beating Geo. McCullough, Parole and others. The Cash Handicap at Saratoga, 1⅛ miles, in 1:54¼, defeating a good field, mile heats, in 1:45, 1:45. He is also sire of Capt. Franklin, Gladiola, Emma Cooper, Glenarm, Kingsland, Martinique (London), all winners. He is a brown, 16½ hands high; a well shaped, robust and fine horse, with a broad white stripe down his face—no other white. We expect to see some good ones from his loins.

PEDIGREE OF GLENGARRY—(Imp.)

GLENGARRY (Imp.)								Ancestor	Pedigree
THORMANBY	Melbourne or Windbound.*	Humphrey	Phyrne.	Decoy.				Buzzard.	Woodpecker—Misfortune by Dux—Curiosity by Snap—Dau. of Regulus—Dau. of Bart Childers—Dau. of Hon. Arabian—Dam of True Blues.
								Selim's Dam.	Alexander—Dau. of Highflyer—Dau. of Alfred—Dau. of Engineer—Bay Malton's dam by Cade—Lass of the Mill by Traveler—Miss Makeless.
		Pantaloon.	Idalia.					Peruvian.	Sir Peter—Dau. of Budrow (Eclipse)—Escape's dam by Squirrel—Sis. to Bahraham by Babraham—Dau. of Godleu Ball—Busby Molly.
			Castrel.					Musidora.	Meteor (Eclipse)—Maid of all Work by Highflyer—Sis. to Tandem by Syphon—Dau. of Regulus—Dau. of Snip—Dau. of Cottingham—Warlock Galloway.
	Alice Hawthorn.	Muley Moloch.	Muley.					Camel.	Whalebone—Dau. of Selim—Maiden by Sir Peter—Dau. of Phoenomenon Matron by Florizel—Maiden by Matchem—Dau. of Squirt.
								Banter.	Master Henry—Boadicea by Alexander—Brunette by Amaranthus—Mayfly by Matchem—Dau of An. Starling—Dau. of Grasshopper.
			Nancy.					Filho-da-Puta.	Haphazard—Mrs. Barnet by Waxy—Dau. of Woodpecker—Heinel by Squirrel—Principessa by Blank—Dau. of Cul. Arabian—Gris. Lady Thigh.
		Rebecca.						Finesse.	Peruvian—Violante by John Bull—Sis. to Skyscraper by Highflyer—Everlasting by Eclipse—Hyaena by Snap—Miss Belsea by Regulus.
			Dau. of Lottery.					Orville.	Beningbrough—Evelina by Highflyer—Termagant by Tantrum—Cantatrice by Sampson—Dau. of Regulus—Marske's dam by Blacklegs.
								Eleanor.	Whiskey—Y. Giantess by Diomed—Giantess by Matchem—Molly Longlegs by Babraham—Dau. of Cole's Foxhunter—Dau. of Partner.
								Dick Andrews.	Joe Andrews—Dau. of Highflyer—Dau. of Car. Puff (Babraham)—Dau. of Tatler (Blank)—Dau. of Snap—Dau. of Godol. Arabian—Dau. of Whiteneck.
								Spitfire.	Beningbrough—Dau. of Y. Sir Peter—Dau. of Engineer—Dau. of Wilson Arabian—Dau. of Hutton's Spot—Dau. of Mogul—Dau. of Crab.
								Tramp.	Dick Andrews—Dau. of Gohanna—Fraxinella by Trentham—Dau. of Woodpecker—Everlasting by Eclipse—Hyaena by Snap.
								Mandane.	Pot-8-os—Y. Camilla by Woodpecker—Camilla by Trentham—Coquette by Compton Barb—Sis. to Regulus by Godol. Arabian—Gr. Robinson.
								Cervantes.	Don Quixote—Evelina by Highflyer—Termagant by Tantrum—Cantatrice by Sampson—Dau. of Regulus—Marske's dam by Blacklegs.
								Anticipaton.	Beningbrough—Expectation by Herod—Dau. of Skim—Dau. of Janus (Godol.)—Spinster by Crab—Spinster by Partner (Jigg).
CARBINE.	Riflleman.	Touchstone.	Banter.	Camel.				Whalebone.	Waxy—Penelope by Trumpator—Prunella by Highflyer—Promise by Snap—Julia by Blank—Spectator's dam by Partner.
								Daughter of.	Selim—Maiden by Sir Peter—Dau. of Phoenomenon—Matron by Florizel—Maiden by Matchem—Dau. of Squirt—Lot's dam.
								Master Henry.	Orville—Miss Sophia by Stamford—Sophia by Buzzard—Huncamunca by Highflyer—Cypher by Squirrel—Fribble's dam.
								Boadicea.	Alexander—Brunette by Amaranthus—Mayfly by Matchem—Dau. of An Starling—Dau. of Grasshopper—Dau. of New. Arabian.
		Camp Follower.	The Colonel.					Whisker.	Waxy—Penelope by Trumpator—Prunella by Highflyer—Promise by Snap—Julia by Blank—Spectator's dam by Partner—Bonny Lass.
								Daughter of.	Delpini—Tapple Cyder by King Fergus—Sylvia by Y. Marske—Ferret by Bro. to Silvio—Dau. of Regulus—Dau. of Ld. Moreton's Arabian.
			Galatea.					Amadis.	Don Quixote—Fanny by Sir Peter—Dau. of Diomed—Desdemona by Marske—Y. Hag by Skim—Hag by Crab—Ebony by F. Childers.
								Paulina.	Sir Peter—Pewet by Tandem—Termagant by Tantrum—Cantatrice by Sampson—Dau. of Regulus—Marske's dam.
		Lanercost.	Liverpool.					Tramp.	Dick Andrews—Dau. of Gohanna—Fraxinella by Trentham—Dau. of Woodpecker—Everlasting by Eclipse—Hyaena by Snap.
	Troica.							Daughter of.	Whisker—Mandane by Pot-8-os—Y. Camilla by Woodpecker—Camilla by Trentham—Coquette by Compton Barb—Sis. to Regulus.
			Otis.					Bustard.	Buzzard—Gipsy Sis. to Amaitor by Trumpator—Sis. to Postmaster by Herod—Dau. of Snap—Dau. of Gower Stallion—Dau. of F. Childers.
								Gayhurst's Dam.	Election—Sis. to Skysweeper by Highflyer—Dau. of Eclipse—Rosebud by Snap—Miss Belsea by Regulus—Dau. of Bartlet's Childers.
	Siberia.		Brutandorf.					Blacklock.	Whitelock—Dau. of Coriander—Wildgoose by Highflyer—Coheiress by Pot-8-os—Manilla by Goldfinder—Dau. of Old Eng.—Dau. Cul. Arabian.
								Mandane.	Pot-8-os—Y. Camilla by Woodpecker—Camilla by Trentham—Coquette by Compton Barb—Sis. to Regulus by Godol. Arabian—Grey Robinson.
		Dau. of						Blucher.	Waxy—Platina by Buzzard—Dau. of Trentham—Sis. to Drone by Herod—Lily by Blank—Peggy by Cade—Sis. to Widdrington Mare.
								Opal.	Sir Peter (Highflyer)—Olivia by Justice (Herod)—Cyper by Squirrel (Traveler)—Fribble's dam by Regulus (Godolphin)—Dau. of Bartlet's Childers (Darley Arabian)—Dau. of Honeywood Arabian—Byerly Mare, dam of the Two True Blues.

* Windbound given.

GLENMORE,

(WINNER OF THE GATE CITY CUP AT ATLANTA, 1878; BOWIE STAKES, FOUR MILE HEATS, AT BALTIMORE, 1879; AND THE GREAT LONG ISLAND SWEEPSTAKES, FOUR MILE HEATS, AND CONEY ISLAND CUP, 1881)

Will stand the season of 1883 *at Glengar Stud, the property of Wm. Jennings, at* $50 *the season. Application to Wm. Jennings, Mount Washington, Baltimore Co., Md.*

GLENMORE by imp. Glen Athol, son of Blair Athol, bred by A. J. Alexander, Woodburn Stud, Kentucky, foaled 1875, dam Lotta, by Hunter's Glencoe, son of imp. Glencoe, out of Sally Lewis, dam of Acrobat, John Morgan, Susan Beane, etc., by imp. Glencoe. Glenmore made his bow to the public as a three-year old, starting 14 times, won six races, was second in one, third in one, and unplaced in the others. Louisville, Ky., September 27, won Galt House Purse, mile heats, defeating Fortuna, Tom Sawyer and Vril, in 1:50, 1:47½. Same place, October 1, won Sweepstakes for three-year olds, mile heats, in 1:46½, 1:45½, defeating Fortuna and three others. Nashville, Tenn., October 11, ran dead heat with Essillah for first place in first heat, mile heats, in 1:46½. King Faro won second heat in 1:50, distancing Col. Hull and Essillah. Glenmore was ruled out for a foul. Same place, October 14, won 1¼ miles in 2:00, beating Henry Owens and Bonnie Itaska. Atlanta, Ga., October 22, ran second to Bergamot, 1½ miles; time, 2:43½. Same meeting, October 23, won the Gate City Cup, 2½ miles in 4:43, defeating Bergamot and Clemmie G. Macon, Ga., October 30, beat Bill Dillon and Scar-Faced Charley, 2½ miles, in 4:41½. Same place, November 1, won mile dash for three-year olds and under, in 1:46¾, defeating Mary Walton, Silver Maid and Bonnie Itaska. At four years old Glenmore started twenty-three times; won ten races, ran dead heat for one with Fortuna (sister of Falsetto), and divided purse and stakes, was second in three, third in one, and unplaced in eight. Louisville, Ky., May 20, Glenmore and Fortuna made their first appearance in 1879, and ran a dead heat in a 1¼-mile dash, defeating an excellent field, consisting of Keene Richards, Jr., Mollie McGinley, Mary R, Signal, Dunkirk, Douglass, Conn and Essillah; time, 2:10½. St. Louis, Mo., June 14, ran second to Goodnight in 1¼ miles, defeating Bill Bass, who finished first, but was placed last for fouling Goodnight, and seven others; time, 2:10½. Chicago, Ill., June 30, won dash of two miles, defeating Checkmate, Blossom, Edinburg and Aunt Winnie; time, 3:37¾. Detroit, Mich., July 3, ran second to Checkmate in 1½ miles—the first mile was run in 1:43½; time 2:43; Edwin A. and King George also ran. Same place, July 4, won one mile, defeating Virgilian, Eli, Mollie McGinley and Lady D'Arcy; time, 1:42¾. Same day, won 2 mile dash, defeating L'Argentine, Claudia and Enterprise; time, 3:33½. Brighton Beach Fair Grounds, Coney Island, N. Y., July 19, won sweepstakes, 2 miles, defeating Virginian and Pilot; time, 3:51½. Same place, July 22, won dash 1⅛ miles, defeating Shylock, Hattie F, Baton Rouge, Loiterer and Farley; time, 2:02. Same place, July 28, won one mile, defeating Farley and Albert; time, 1:52. Same place, August 7, ran dead heat with Claudia for sweepstakes, 1¾ miles; times, 3:25; divided. Monmouth Park, August 26, ran second to Danicheff in the Elberon Handicap; 2 miles; time, 3:51½; Lou Lanier and Tom Scarlet also ran. Same place, August 30, finished second in handicap, 1¾ miles, won by Ferida in 3:10, but was disqualified for fouling Jericho; Pilot, Lou Lanier, Gov. Hampton and Gen. Philips, also ran. Autumn

Continued on page 60.

PEDIGREE OF GLENMORE.

GLENMORE.	IMP. GLEN ATHOL.	Blair Athol.	Stockwell.	The Baron.	Irish Birdcatcher.	Sir Hercules—Guicciolli by Bob Booty—Flight by Irish Escape—Young Heroine by Bagot—Heroine by Hero—Dau. of Snap—Sis. to Regulus.
				Pocahontas.	Echidna.	Economist—Miss Pratt by Blacklock—Gadabout by Orville—Minstrel by Sir Peter—Matron by Florizel—Maiden by Matchem.
			Blink Bonny.	Melbourne.	Glencoe.	Sultan—Trampoline by Tramp—Web by Waxy—Penelope by Trumpator—Prunella by Highflyer—Promise by Snap—Julia by Blank.
				Queen Mary.	Marpessa.	Muley—Clare by Marmion—Harpalice by Gohanna—Amazon by Driver—Fractious by Mercury—Dau. of Woodpecker—Everlasting.
		Greta.	Voltigeur.		Humphrey Clinker.	Comus—Clinkerina by Clinker—Pewet by Tandem—Termagant by Tantrum—Cantatrice by Sampson—Dau. of Regulus—Marske's dam.
					Daughter of.	Cervantes—Dau. of Golumpus—Dau. of Paynator—Sis. to Zodiac by St. George—Abigail by Woodpecker—Firetail by Eclipse—Dau. of Blank.
			Martha Lynn.		Gladiator.	Partizan—Pauline by Moses—Quadrille by Selim—Canary Bird by Whiskey or Sorcerer—Canary by Coriander—Miss Green by Highflyer.
					Daughter of.	Plenipotentiary—Myrrha by Whalebone—Gift by Y Gohanna—Sis. to Grazier by St. Peter—Sis. to Amaitor by Trumpator—Dau. of Herod (Tartar).
		Mountain Flower.	Ithuriel.		Blacklock.	Whitelock—Dau. of Coriander—Wildgoose by Highflyer—Coheiress by Pot-8-o's—Manilla by Goldfinder—Dau. of Old Eng—Dau. of Cul Arabian.
					Daughter of.	Phantom—Dau. of Overton—Gratitude's dam by Walnut—Dau. of Ruler—Piracantha by Matchem—Dau. of Regulus—Jenny Spinner.
			Heatherbell.	Voltaire.	Mulatto.	Catton—Desdemona by Orville—Fannyby Sir Peter—Dau. of Diomed—Desdemona by Marske—Y. Hag by Skim—Hag by Crab—Ebony by Childers.
					Leda.	Filho-da-Puta—Treasure by Camillus—Dau. of Hyacinthus—Flora by King Fergus—Atalanta by Matchem—Lass of the Mill by Croonoko.
					Touchstone.	Camel—Banter by Master Henry—Boadicea by Alexander—Brunette by Amaranthus—Mayfly by Matchem—Dau. of An. Starling.
					Verbena.	Velocipede—Rosalba by Milo—Sis. to Rubens by Buzzard—Dau. of Alexander—Dau. of Highflyer—Dau. of Alfred—Dau. of Engineer.
					Bay Middleton.	Sultan—Cobweb by Phantom—Filagree by Soothsayer—Web by Waxy—Penelope by Trumpator—Prunella by Highflyer—Promise by Snap.
					Maid of Lune.	Whisker—Gibside Fairy by Hermes—Vicissitude by Pipator—Beatrice by Sir Peter—Pyrrha by Matchem—Duchess by Whitenose.
	LOTTA.	Hunter's Glencoe.	Blue Filly Flatt.	Glencoe.	Selim.	Buzzard—Castrel's dam by Alexander—Dau. of Highflyer—Dau. of Alfred—Dau. of Engineer—Bay Malton's dam by Cade (Godol.)
				Sultan.	Bacchante.	Williamson's Ditto—Sis. to Calomel by Mercury—Dau. of Herod—Folly by Marske—Vixen by Regulus—Dau. of Hutton's Spot.
				Trampoline.	Tramp.	Dick Andrews—Dau. of Gohanna—Fraxinella by Trentham—Dau. of Woodpecker—Everlasting by Eclipse—Hyaena by Snap.
			Lady Thompkins.		Web.	Waxy—Penelope by Trumpator—Prunella by Highflyer—Promise by Snap—Julia by Blank—Spectator's dam by Partner.
			Hedgeford.		Filho-da-Puta.	Haphazard—Mrs. Barnet by Waxy—Dau. of Woodpecker—Heinel by Squirrel—Principessa by Blank—Dau. of Cul. Arabian.
					Miss Craigie.	Orville—Marchioness by Lurcher (Dungannon by Eclipse)—Miss Cogden by Phoenomenon. Dau. of Y. Marske—Dau. of Silvio—Daphne.
					Am. Eclipse.	Duroc—Millers Damsel by Messenger—Dau. of Pot-8-os—Dau. of Gimcrack—Snap Dragon by Snap—Dau. of Regulus—Dau. of Bart's Childers.
					Katy Ann.	Ogle's Oscar—(Imp. Gabriel)—Y. Maid of the Oaks by Expedition—Maid of the Oaks by Spread Eagle—Annette by Imp. Shark.
		Sally Lewis.	Glencoe.	Sultan.	Selim.	Buzzard—Castrel's dam by Alexander—Dau. of Highflyer—Dau. of Alfred—Dau. of Engineer—Bay Malton's dam by Cade.
					Bacchante.	Williamson's Ditto—Sis. to Calomel by Mercury—Dau. of Herod—Folly by Marske—Vixen by Regulus—Dau. of Hutton's Spot—Dau. of Bay Bolton
				Trampoline.	Tramp.	Dick Andrews—Dau. of Gohanna—Fraxinella by Trentham—Dau. of Woodpecker—Everlasting by Eclipse—Hyaena by Snap (Snip).
					Web.	Waxy—Penelope by Trumpator—Prunella by Highflyer—Promise by Snap—Julia by Blank—Spectator's dam by Partner—Bonny Lass.
		Motto.	Barefoot.	Tramp.	Tramp.	Dick Andrews—Dau. of Gohanna—Fraxinella by Trentham—Dau. of Woodpecker—Everlasting by Eclipse—Hyaena by Snap (Snip).
					Rosamond.	Buzzard—Roseberry by Phoenomenon—Miss West by Matchem—Dau. of Regulus—Dau. of Crab—Dau. of Flying Childers—Dau. of Basto.
		Lady Thompkins.			Am. Eclipse.	Duroc—Millers Damsel by Messenger—Dau. of Pot-8-o's—Dau. of Gimcrack—Snap-Dragon by Snap—Dau. of Regulus—Dau. of Bart. Childers.
					Katy Ann.	Ogle's Oscar—Y. Maid of the Oaks, Medoc's dam by Expedition—Maid of the Oaks by Spread Eagle (Volunteer)—Annette by Imp. Shark (Marske)—Dau. of Rockingham (Partner)—Dau. of Gallant (Fearnought)—Dau. of True Whig (Fitzhugh's Regulus)—Dau. of Imp. Regulus (Regulus)—Imp. Diamond by Cullen Arabian—Lady Thigh by Croft's Partner (Jigg)—Dau. of Greyhound—Dau. of Curwen Bay Barb—Dau. of D'Arcy Chestnut Arabian—Dau. of Whiteshirt—Old Montague Mare.

GLENMORE—Continued.

Meeting Coney Island Jockey Club, Prospect Park, L. I., September 6, won Fog Handicap Sweepstakes, heats of 1⅛ miles, defeating Chiquita, Virgilian, Mark L, Zoo Zoo, Skylark and Gabriel; time, 1:58¾, 2:00, 2:02¾; Chiquita won the first heat. Jerome Park, October 11, won handicap sweepstakes, 2¼ miles, defeating Ferida, Fortuna, Willie D, Invermore, Gen. Philips and Day Star; time, 3:51. Baltimore, Md., October 25, Glenmore won the Bowie Stakes, 4-mile heats, defeating Willie D, Lou Lanier and Charley Bush; time, 7:29½, 7:30½, 7:31; Willie D. won the first heat, Lou Lanier and Charley Bush were distanced in the second. This is the best and fastest three heats ever run in the world. At five years old started thirteen times, won six races, was second in five, and third in two. Glenmore commenced the season at Washington by running second to Checkmate in the Willard's Hotel Cup, 2 miles, in 3:36½, beating Ben Hill and Werter. Baltimore, May 25, won Club Purse, 1¼ miles, in 2:15½, beating Scotilla, Werter, and five others; May 28, ran second to Monitor in Baltimore Cup, 2¼ miles, in 4:02½, beating Harold. Gravesend, June 25, won the Club Purse, 1⅝ miles, in 3:04, beating Report, Ferida and St. Martin. This was the fastest race ever run at the distance to that date. June 26, won the Stirrup Cup, 2 miles and a furlong, in 3:48½, carrying 114 lbs., beating Uncas (4), 111 lbs., and Jim Beck (4) 95 lbs.; this was a capital race. Saratoga, August 7, ran third to Luke Blackburn (3), 116 lbs., and One Dime (4), 110 lbs.; Glenmore (5), 118 lbs., in the Grand Union Prize, 1⅝ miles, in 3:07, beating Cammie F, Gen. Philips and Chimney Sweep. Brighton Beach, August 18, ran second to Virgilian in Club Purse, one mile and a furlong, in 1:55, beating Baby, Virginius and three others, 100 lbs. on each. Gravesend, September 7, won Club Purse, 1⅝ miles in 3:09, Glenmore, 107 lbs., beating Uncas (4), 107; Monitor (4), 109, and two others. September 16, was third to Checkmate and Monitor, one mile and 5 furlongs in 2:50, Uncas, One Dime and Krupp Gun behind him; September18, ran second to Ferida in the great Long Island stakes, 4-mile heats, in 7:23½, 7:41, beating Irish King; September 25, won handicap sweepstakes, heats of one mile and a furlong, in 2:09, 2:10, 2:14, he carrying 114 lbs., beating Mary Anderson (3), 88 lbs., who won first heat, Dan Sparling (4), 107 lbs., and four others, an excellent race. Baltimore, October 19, won Club Purse, 2-mile heats in 3:46, 3:40½, beating Surge, Mintzer and Cammie F. His last race of the season was in the Bowie Stakes, 4-mile heats, won by Monitor in 7:41, 7:42, only the two starting. Six years old started sixteen times and won eleven races. Brighton Beach, won a dash of one mile, in 1:47, beating Startle, Scotilla and six others, track heavy. Sheepshead Bay, won mile heats, in 1:42½, 1:42½, 1:46½, beating Dan Sparling, Ferida and others; Dan Sparling won the first heat and Glenmore was fifth. Won Coney Island Cup, 2¼ miles, in 3:58¾, beating Monitor, Parole, Luke Blackburn and Uncas. Won a dash of 1⅝ miles, in 3.01½, the fastest on record, beating Geo. McCullough and 3 others. Brighton Beach, won the Kings County Cup, 2 miles, no time taken, Gouverneur the only other starter; Glenmore carried 123 lbs., Gouverneur (3), carried 94 lbs. Won the Engeman Handicap, 1½ miles, in 2:40, beating Ingomar, Scotilla and Jury. Monmouth Park, won a dash of 1¼ miles, in 2:10; Parole the only other starter. Brighton Beach, won a dash of one mile, in 1:43¾, beating Rosalie and two others. Sheepshead Bay, walked over for a purse of $500, 1⅝ miles. Won a dash of 1⅝ miles, in 3:08½, beating Monitor and Irish King. Won the Great Long Island Stakes, 4-mile heats, in 8:18, 7:40; Elias Lawrence the only other starter; Lawrence won the first heat, and was drawn in the third. Baltimore, was second in a dash of one mile and a furlong, won by Oden, in 1:59. Was second in a dash of one mile and a furlong, won by Monitor, in 1:57. Brighton Beach, was second in a dash of one mile and a furlong, won by Victim, in 1:58½. Baltimore, was second in a race of 2-mile heats, won by Ferida, in 3:39, 3:37, 3:41; Glenmore won second heat; only two starters. Seven years old started eighteen times, and won six races. Washington, D. C., won the National Handicap, one mile and a furlong, in 2:00, carrying 120 lbs., and beating Blue Lodge and six others. Won the Diplomatic Stakes, 1½ miles, in 2:57¾. Brighton Beach, won the Kings County Cup, 2 miles, in 3:36¾. Monmouth Park, won the Shrewsbury Handicap, 1⅝ miles, in 3:08½, beating Glidelia, Girofle, Monitor and Aella. Won a handicap sweepstakes, 1½ miles, in 2:38½, beating Mary Anderson, Priam and

Macbeth. Sheepshead Bay, won a handicap sweepstakes, heats of one mile and a furlong, in 1:57¼, 1:57½, 2:00; Haledon won the first heat and Glenmore was fourth. Washington, D. C., was second in a dash of 1¼ miles, won by Col. Sprague, in 2:11¼. Baltimore, was second in a dash of one mile and a furlong, won by Crickmore, in 1:56¾; was second in the Baltimore Cup, 2¼ miles, won by Thora, in 4:00. Brighton Beach, was second in a dash of one mile and a furlong, won by Barney Lyon, in 1:57. Sheepshead Bay, was second in a race of mile heats, won by Dan K, in 1:43, 1:42¾; was second in a handicap sweepstakes, heats of one mile and a furling, won by Keno, in 1:56, 1:58, 1:59¾, Glenmore won the first heat, carrying 115 lbs. Keno (aged), carried only 90 lbs. Brighton Beach, was second in the Engeman Handicap, 1¼ miles, won by Gov. Hampton, in 2:39. Monmouth Park, was third in a handicap sweepstakes, 1¼ miles, won by Monitor, in 3:07¼. Sheepshead Bay, was second in the Great Long Island Stakes, 4-mile heats, won by Bushwhacker, in 8:01¼, 8:10; track very muddy and wet. Glenmore is much inbred to Glencoe having three crosses of that desirable strain of blood, and a double cross of Am. Eclipse, and another cross of Sultan through Bay Middleton.

Glenmore is chestnut, 15 hands 2½ inches high, with large star and snip, both fore feet white below ankle and little white on one hind foot. He is one of the most symmetrical horses in the world.

GRENADA,

(WINNER OF WINDSOR HOTEL STAKES, SARATOGA, BELMONT, JEROME AND LORILLARD STAKES, AT JEROME PARK, TRAVERS STAKES AT SARATOGA, CONEY ISLAND DERBY, AT SHEEPSHEAD BAY, POTOMAC AND DIXIE STAKES, AT BALTIMORE, AND OTHER IMPORTANT RACES,)

Will stand for mares the season of 1883, *at the stables of Irvine & Noyes, Marion, Ohio, at* $30 *the season. Application to Irvine & Noyes, Marion, Ohio.*

GRENADA, by King Alfonso, son of imp. Phaeton, bred in Woodburn Stud, Ky., foaled 1877, dam Mattie Gross, dam of Mate, by Lexington, out of Dick Doty's dam, by American Eclipse. Grenada, as a two-gear-old started eleven times, won Club Purse at Long Branch, half a mile, in 49¾ sec., beating Canaan, Maggie C, and three others. Ran second to his stable companion, Sensation, in the July Stakes, 5 furlongs, in 1:07, track heavy, Rosalie, Ferncliff and nine others behind him. Saratoga, ran second to Sensation, in Flash Stakes, half a mile, in 49¾ sec., Rosalie, Luke Blackburn and four others behind him. Ran second to Sensation in Saratoga Stakes, three-quarters of a mile in 1:18, Beata, Glidelia, Girofle, and Bye-and-Bye behind him. Won Windsor Hotel Stakes, 5 furlongs, in 1:03½, beating Luke Blackburn, Glidelia and four others. Long Branch, ran second to Sensation in August Stakes, three-quarters of a mile, in 1:18½, seven others behind him Ran second to Sensation in Criterion Stakes, three-quarters of a mile, in 1:22, track muddy, five others behind him. Was third at Jerome Park, in Nursery Stakes, to Sensation and Ferncliff, three-quarters of a mile, in 1:18, Girofle and three others behind him. Baltimore, Md., second to Sensation in Central Stakes, one mile in 1:50½, beating Oden, track muddy. Was unplaced in two races. At three years old, started in nineteen races, of which he won ten, was second in four, third in three, and unplaced in two, placing to his credit $31,112.50. Baltimore, May 19, won the Potomac Stakes for three-year-olds, 1¼ miles, in 2:39½, beating Colonel Sprague, Oden, and four others. May 28, won Preakness Stakes, 1¼ miles, in 2:40½, beating Oden and theee others. Jerome Park, June 3, was beaten a head for the Withers Stakes, one mile, in 1:49, by Ferncliff, Oden and three others behind him. June 8, won the Belmont Stakes, 1½ miles, in 2:47, beating Ferncliff and two others. June 12, won the Lorillard Stakes, one mile and 3 furlongs, in 2:28½ (unofficial time), beating Duke of Montrose, Ferncliff and 3 others. Sheepshead Bay, June 24, won the Coney Island Derby, 1½ miles, in 2:40½, beating Quito and Kimball. Saratoga, July 17, won the Travers Stakes, 1¾ miles, in 3:12½, beating Oden, Turfman, Ferncliff and two others. Monmouth Park, Aug. 21, won Atlantic Handicap, 1½ miles, in 2:48½, with 118 lbs. up, beating Edelweiss, 100 lbs., Nancy, 100 lbs. and Diana, 95 lbs. Jerome Park, Oct. 2, won Jerome Stakes, 1¾ miles, in 3:12¾, beating Oden, Ferncliff, etc. Oct. 7, ran second to his stable companion, Monitor, 1¾ miles, in 3:13½. Baltimore, Oct. 19, won the Dixie Stakes, 2 miles, in 3:38, beating Oden and Ferncliff, and wound up the season by running a dead heat and dividing the Breckenridge Stakes, 2 miles, in 3:43½, with Glidelia. He was defeated in the Jersey Derby by Ferncliff when amiss, but in the St. Leger, Ferncliff defeated him in the capital time of 3:09 for 1¾ miles. Grenada did not run up to his form in several of his races. As a four-year-old, won four out of six races. Baltimore, won the Peyton Handicap, mile heats, in 1:43½, 1.43½, 1:47½, beating Oden, who won the first heat, Elias Lawrence and four others, was third to Monitor, his stable companion in Baltimore Cup, 2¼ miles in 4:02. Jerome Park, won Handicap Sweepstakes, 1¾ miles, in 3:15½, beating Ventriloquist and two others, track heavy. Won the Jockey Club Handicap, 2 miles, in 3:43, beating McCullough, Monitor, Uncas, and three others. Won Handicap Sweepstakes, with 112 lbs., 1¾ miles, in 3:26, beating Girofle and Sly Dance, track very heavy. Was unplaced in Club Purse, 1¾ miles, won by Glenmore in 3:01½. Grenada bursted his foot in this race, and was never himself afterwards, At five years old, ran second to Vampire, in Welter Cup, one mile, in 1:51, ran second to Thora, in Westchester Cup, 2¼ miles, in 4:12, and was unplaced in Members Cup, 1⅛ miles, won by Woodcock, in 2:06½. Grenada was a first class race-horse. In his two-year-old year he ran second to his stable companion, Sensation, in most all of the great Stakes, and had the best colts of the year behind him. As a three-year-old, he demonstrated his quality by winning a majority of the great three-year-old stakes, and at four years old, won four out of six good races before injuring his foot, which virtually destroyed him for racing purposes. Grenada is from a racing family. Mattie Gross, his dam, produced Mate and Whisper, both good horses, and his grandam produced Dick Doty, a good race-horce, won four-mile heats in 7:37½ and 7:46½, the fastest race run in that State, Kentucky, to that date, 1858. Creath, another famous race-horse, is also from this family. Grenada, in addition to being by King Alfonso, sire of Foxhall, Fonso, and other good ones, is much inbred to Sir Archy and Diomed, and to the Godolphin Arabian, on the dam's side. We commend Grenada to the breeders of Ohio.

PEDIGREE OF GRENADA.

									Name	Pedigree
GRENADA.	KING ALFONSO.	Phaeton.	Merry Sunshine.	Dau. of Storm.	King Tom.	Pocahontas.	Harkaway.		Economist.	Whisker—Floranthe by Octavian—Caprice by Anvil—Madcap by Eclipse—Dau. of Blank—Dau. of Blaze (Childers).
									Fanny Dawson.	Nabocklish—Miss Tooley by Teddy the Grinder—Lady Jane by Sir Peter—Paulina by Florizel—Captive by Matchem—Calliope.
									Glencoe.	Sultan—Trampoline by Tramp—Web by Waxy—Penelope by Trumpator—Prunella by Highflyer—Promise by Snap—Julia.
									Marpessa.	Muley—Clare by Marmion—Harpalice by Gohanna—Amazon by Driver—Fractious by Mercury—Dau. of Woodpecker.
				Vandal.		Alaric's dam.	tilencoe.		Touchstone.	Camel—Bauter by Master Henry—Boadicea by Alexander—Brunette by Amaranthus—Mayfly by Matchem—Dau. of An. Starling.
									Ghuzuee,	Pantaloon—Langush by Cain—Lydia by Poulton—Variety by Hyacinthus—Sis. to Swordsman by Weasel—Dau. of Turk—Dau. of Locust.
									Falstaff.	Touchstone—Decoy by Filho-da-Puta—Finesse by Peruvian—Violante by John Bull—Dau. of Highflyer—Everlasting by Eclipse—Hyaena.
									Sis. to Pompey.	Emilius—Variation by Bustard—Johanna Southcote by Beningbrough—Lavinia by Pipator—Dau. of Highflyer—Dau. of Car. Puff.
			Capitola.						Sultan.	Selim—Bacchante by Williamson's Ditto—Sis. to Calomel by Mercury—Dau. of Herod—Folly by Marske—Vixen by Regulus.
									Trampoline.	Tramp—Web by Waxy—Penelope by Trumpator—Prunella by Highflyer—Promise by Snap—Julia by Blank—Spectator's dam.
									Tranby.	Blacklock—Dau. of Orville—Miss Grimstone by Weasel—Dau. of Ancaster—Dau. of Dam Arabian—Dau. of Sampson—Dau. of Oroonoko.
									Lucilla.	Trumpator—Lucy by Orphan—Lady Grey by Robin Grey—Maria by Melzar—Dau. of Highflyer—Dau. of Fearnought—Dau. of Ariel.
				Margravine.		Mar-grave.	Mistletoe.		Muley.	Orville—Eleanor by Whiskey—Y. Giantess by Diomed—Giantess by Matchem—Molly Longlegs by Babraham—Dau. of Cole's Foxhunter.
									Daughter of.	Election—Fair Helen by Hambletonian—Helen by Delpini—Rosalind by Phoenomenon—Atalanta by Matchem—Lass of the Mill by Oroonoko.
									Cherokee.	Sir Archy—Roxana by Hephestion—Roxana by Marplot—Juliet by Imp. Mexican—Dau. of Imp. Friar (South by Regulus).
									Black-eyed Susan.	Tiger—Dau. of Albert—Dau. of Algerine—Dau. of Grey Alfred—Dau. of Americus—Dau. of Imp. Medley—Dau. of Imp. Shark.
	MATTIE GROSS.		Lexington.	Boston.		Sis. to Tuckahoe.	Timoleon.		Sir Archy.	Diomed—Castianira by Rockingham—Tabitha by Trentham—Dau. of Bosphorus—Dau. of Wm's Forester—Dau. of Co. Colt—Dau. of Bustard.
									Daughter of.	Imp. Saltram—Dau. of Symme's Wildair—Dau. of Driver (Imp. Othello)—Dau. of Fallower (Blank)—Dan. of Imp. Vampire.
									Ball's Florizel.	Diomed—Dau. of Imp. Shark—Dau. of Harris' Eclipse—Dau. of Fearnought—Dau. of Jolly Roger—Dau. of Sober John—Dau. of Shock.
									Daughter of.	Alderman—Dau. of Clockfast—Dau. of Symme's Wildair—Y. Kitty Fisher by Fearnought—Kitty Fisher by Cade—Dau. of Som. Arabian.
				Alice Carneal.		Sarpedon.			Emilius.	Orville—Emily by Stamford—Dau. of Whiskey—Gr. Dorimant by Dorimant—Dizzy by Blank—Dizzy by Driver—Dau. of Smiling Tom.
									Icaria.	The Flyer—Parma by Dick Andrews—May by Beningbrough—Primrose by Mambrino—Cricket by Herod—Sophia by Blank.
							Rowena.		Sumpter.	Sir Archy—Flirtilla's dam by Robin Redbreast—Dau. of Obscurity—Slamerkin by Wildair—Imp. Cub Mare by Cub—Amaranthus' dam.
									Lady Grey.	Robin Grey—Maria by Melzar—Dau. of Highflyer—Dau. of Fearnought—Dau. of Ariel—Dau. of Imp. Jack of Diamonds.
		Dick Doty's dam.	Am. Eclipse.	Duroc.					Diomed.	Florizel—Sis. to Juno by Spectator—Horatia by Blank—Dau. of Childers Miss Belvoir by Gr. Grantham—Dau. of Paget Turk.
									Amanda.	Grey Diomed—Dau. of Va Cade—Dau. of Hickman's Independence—Dolly Fine by Silvereye—Dau. of Imp. Badger—Dau. of Forester.
				Miller's Damsel.					Messenger.	Mambrino—Dau. of Turf—Dau. of Regulus—Dau. of Starling—Snap's dam by Fox—Gipsy by Bay Bolton—Dau. of Newcastle Turk.
									Daughter of.	Pot-8-os—Dau. of Gimcrack—Snap Dragon by Snap—Dau. of Regulus—Dau. of Bart. Childers—Dau. of Hon. Arabian—Dam of True Blues.
		Nell.	Dau. of Orphan.						Ball's Florizel.	Diomed—Dau. of Imp. Shark—Dau. of Harris' Eclipse—Dau. of Fearnought—Dau. of Jolly Roger—Dau. of Sober John—Dau. of Shock.
									Fair Rachel.	Diomed (Florizel)—Susan Jones by Imp. Shark (Marske)—Dau. of Thornton's Wildair (Symme's Wildair by Fearnought).
									Buzzard.	Woodpecker—Misfortune by Dux—Curiosity by Snap—Dau. of Regulus—Dau. of Bart. Childers—Dau. of Hon. Arabian—Dam of True Blues.
									Daughter of.	Silvertail (Imp. Fearnought, son of Regulus by Godolphin Arabian)—Dau. of Imp. Dove (Young Cade, son of Cade by Godolphin Arabian).

GREAT TOM (Imp.)

(WINNER OF ST. JAMES PALACE STAKES AT ASCOT, AND DONCASTER STAKES AT DONCASTER, IN 1876,)

Will stand the season of 1883 *at the Belle Meade Stud near Nashville, Tenn., at* $100 *the season. Application to Gen. W. H. Jackson, lock box* 383, *Nashville, Tenn. Annual sale of Yearlings about May* 1st.

GREAT TOM, by King Tom, son of Harkaway, bred by Lord Falmouth, foaled 1873, dam Woodcraft, the dam of Kingcraft, Andred and Anderida, by Voltigeur, winner of the Derby, St. Leger and Doncaster Cup, out of Falcon and Ostreger's dam by Venison.

Great Tom started once at two years old ; at Newmarket First October Meeting, for the Boscawen Post Stakes of 100 sovereigns each, for two-year olds, three-quarters of a mile (six subs.) ; won by Twine the Plaiden, 119 lbs. ; bay filly by Macaroni, out of Fairminster, 116 lbs., second ; Camembert, 119 lbs., third ; Great Tom, 122 lbs., fourth ; Morning Star, 119 lbs., fifth.

At three years old, started nine times ; won two, was second three times, third twice and unplaced in two. Newmarket Craven Meeting for Post Sweepstakes of 100 sovereigns each, half forfeit, for three-year olds, Ditch Mile, 7 furlongs 220 yards, Wild Tommy, 122 lbs., was first ; Great Tom, 122 lbs., second ; Coltness, 118 lbs., third ; Camembert, 117 lbs., fourth ; won by a head, a length and a half between second and third. At Newmarket, for Two Thousand Guineas Stakes, Rowley Mile, one mile and 17 yards, won by Petrarch, Julius Cæsar second, Kaleidoscope third ; in a field of fourteen Great Tom was unplaced. At Epsom, for the Derby, $1\frac{1}{2}$ miles, won by Kisber, Forerunner second, Julius Cæsar third, Great Tom was unplaced. Fifteen started. At Ascot, for the Prince of Wales Stakes of 50 sovereigns each, with 1,000 sovereigns added, for three-year olds, second to have 300 sovereigns, a mile and five furlongs, Petrarch, 127 lbs., first ; Great Tom, 115 lbs., second ; Julius Cæsar, 122 lbs., third ; Glacis, 115 lbs., fourth ; Zee, 117 lbs., fifth ; Marquesas, 115 lbs., sixth ; won by a length ; a bad third. Same meeting, for the St. James' Palace Stakes of 100 sovereigns each, half forfeit, for three-year olds ; old mile (12 subs.), Great Tom, 115 lbs., and Glacis, 115 lbs., ran a dead heat. Great Tom afterwards walked over, and the stakes were divided. At Doncaster, for the Doncaster Stakes of 10 sovereigns each, with 100 added, for three-year olds ; mile and a half (36 subs.), Great Tom, 122 lbs., was first ; Coltness, 127 lbs., second ; Morning Star, 122 lbs.. third ; won by two lengths, three lengths between second and third. At Newmarket, for the Triennial Produce Stakes of 10 sovereigns each, for three-year olds, colts 122 lbs., fillies 119 lbs., A. F., 1 mile 2 furlongs, 73 yards, won by Camembert, Twine the Plaiden second, Great Tom third, Villafranca, Timballo and Murrumbidgee unplaced. Same place, for the Beaufort Post Stakes of 100 sovereigns each, half forfeit, for three-year olds, colts 122 lbs., fillies 118 lbs., Rowley mile (5 subs.), won by Twine the Plaiden, Great Tom second, Wild Tommy third, Camembert fourth. Same meeting, for the Newmarket Derby of 25 sovereigns each, 10 forfeit, with 100 added, for three-year olds, $1\frac{1}{2}$ miles, Lord Falmouth's Skylark, 123 lbs., first ; Moulin, 123 lbs., second ; Great Tom, 123 lbs., third ; Hellenest, 123 lbs., fourth ; Sailor, 123 lbs., fifth ; won by a length, two lengths between the second and third.

At four years old, he started six times and won once, second once, third twice, and unplaced twice. At Newmarket First October Meeting for the Triennial Produce

Continued on page 66.

PEDIGREE OF GREAT TOM.

GREAT TOM.									
KING TOM.	Harkaway.	Economist.	Whisker	Waxy.	Pot-8-os (Eclipse)—Maria by Herod (Tartar)—Lisette by Snap (Snip)—Miss Windsor by Godolphin Arabian.—Sis. to Volunteer.
			Floranthe.	Penelope.	Trumpator (Conductor)—Prunella by Highflyer (Herod)—Promise by Snap (Snip)—Julia by Blank—Spectator's dam.
		Fanny Dawson.	Nabocklish.	Octavian.	Stripling (Phoenomenon)—Dau. of Oberon (Highflyer)—Sis. to Sharper by Ranthos (Matchem)—Dau. of Sweepstakes.
			Miss Tooley.	Caprice.	Anvil (Herod)—Madcap by Eclipse (Marske)—Dau. of Blank—Dau. of Blaze—Dau. of Y. Greyhound—Dau. of Cur B. Barb.
	Pocahontas.	Imp. Glencoe.	Sultan.	Rugantino.	Commodore (Tug)—Dau. of Highflyer—Shift by Sweetbriar (Syphon)—Bl. Susan by Snap—Dau. of Cade—Dau. of Belgrade.
			Trampoline.	Butterfly.	Master Bagot (Bagot)—Dau. of Bagot (Herod)—Mother Brown by Trunnion (Cade)—Dau. of Old England—Dau. of Bolton Starling.
		Marpessa.	Muley.	Teddy the Grinder.	Asparagus (Pot-8-os)—Stargazer by Highflyer (Herod)—Miss West by Matchem (Cade)—Dau. of Regulus (Godol.)—Dau. of Crab—Dau. of Childers.
			Clare.	Lady Jane.	Sir Peter (Highflyer)—Paulina by Florizel (Herod)—Captive by Matchem (Cade)—Calliope by Slouch—Lass of the Mill by Oroonoko.
				Selim.	Buzzard (Woodpecker)—Dau. of Alexander (Eclipse)—Dau. of Highflyer (Herod)—Dau. of Alfred (Matchem)—Dau. of Engineer.
				Bacchante.	Williamson's Ditto (Sir Peter)—Sis. to Calomel by Mercury (Eclipse)—Dau. of Herod (Tartar)—Folly by Marske—Vixen by Regulus.
				Tramp.	Dick Andrews (Joe Andrews)—Dau. of Gohanna (Mercury)—Fraxinella by Trentham (Sweepstakes)—Dau. of Woodpecker—Everlasting by Eclipse.
				Web.	Waxy (Pot-8-os)—Penelope by Trumpator (Conductor)—Prunella by Highflyer (Herod)—Promise by Snap (Snip)—Julia by Blank.
				Orville.	Beningbrough (King Fergus)—Evelina by Highflyer—Termagaut by Tantrum (Cripple) Cantatrice by Sampson—Dau. of Regulus.
				Eleanor.	Whiskey (Saltram)—Y. Giantess by Diomed (Florizel)—Giantess by Matchem (Cade)—Molly Longlegs by Babraham—Dau. of Foxhunter.
				Marmion.	Whiskey (Saltram)—Y. Noisette by Diomed—Noisette by Squirrel (Traveler)—Carina by Marske (Squirt)—Dau. of Blank.
				Harpalice.	Gohanna (Mercury)—Amazon by Driver (Trentham)—Fractious by Mercury (Eclipse)—Dau. of Woodpecker—Everlasting by Eclipse.
WOODCRAFT.	Daughter of.	Voltigeur.	Voltaire.	Whitelock.	Hambletonian (King Fergus)—Rosalind by Phoenomenon (Herod)—Atalanta by Matchem—Lass of the Mill by Oroonoko.
			Blacklock.	Daughter of.	Coriander (Pot-8-os)—Wildgoose by Highflyer—Coheiress by Pot-8-os (Eclipse)—Manilla by Goldfinder (Snap)—Dau. of Old England.
		Martha Lynn.	Mulatto.	Phantom.	Walton (Sir Peter)—Julia by Whiskey—Y. Giantess by Diomed—Giantess by Matchem—Molly Longlegs by Babraham—Dau. of Foxhunter.
			Dau. of Leda.	Daughter of.	Overton (King Fergus)—Dau. of Walnut (Highflyer)—Dau. of Ruler (Young Marske)—Piracantha by Matchem—Prophetess by Regulus.
	Wedding Day.	Venison.	Partisan.	Catton.	Golumpus (Gohanna)—Lucy Gray by Timothy (Delpini)—Lucy by Florizel (Herod)—Giantess by Matchem—Molly Longlegs by Babraham.
				Desdemona.	Orville (Beningbrough)—Fanny by Sir Peter (Highflyer)—Dau. of Diomed—Desdemona by Marske—Y. Hag by Skim—Hag by Crab—Ebony.
			Fawn.	Filho-da-Puta.	Haphazard (Sir Peter)—Mrs. Barnet by Waxy—Dau. of Woodpecker (Herod)—Heinel by Squirrel—Principessa by Blank.
				Treasure.	Camillus (Hambletonian)—Dau. of Hyacinthus (Coriander)—Flora by King Fergus (Eclipse)—Atalanta by Matchem—Lass of the Mill.
		Margelina.	Camel.	Walton.	Sir Peter (Highflyer)—Arethusa by Dugannon (Eclipse)—Dau. of Prophet (Regulus)—Virago by Snap—Dau. of Regulus—Sis. to Othello.
				Parasol.	Pot-8-os (Eclipse)—Prunella by Highflyer—Promise by Snap—Julia by Blank (Godolphin)—Dau. of Partner—Dau. of Bay Bolton.
				Smolensko.	Sorcerer (Trumpator)—Wowski by Mentor (Justice)—Maria by Herod—Lisette by Snap—Miss Windsor by Godol. Arabian.—Sis. to Volunteer.
				Jerboa.	Gohanna—Camilla by Trentham—Coquette by the Compton Barb—Sis. to Regulus by Godolphin Arabian—Grey Robinson.
				Whalebone.	Waxy—Penelope by Trumpator—Prunella by Highflyer—Promise by Snap Julia by Blank—Spectator's dam by Partner—Dau. of Bay Bolton.
				Daughter of.	Selim—Maiden by Sir Peter—Dau. of Phoenomenon—Matron by Florizel—Maiden by Matchem (Cade)—Dau. of Squirt—Lot's dam.
				Whisker.	Waxy—Penelope by Trumpator—Prunella by Highflyer—Promise by Snap Julia by Blank—Spectator's dam by Partner—Dau. of Bay Bolton.
				Manuella.	Dick Andrews—Mandane by Pot-8-os—Y. Camilla by Woodpecker—Camilla by Trentham—Coquette by Compton Barb—Sis. to Regulus by Go. Arabian—Grey Robinson by the Bald Galloway (St. Victor Barb.)—Dau. of Snake (Lister Turk)—Grey Wilkes by Old Hautboy—Miss D'Arcy's Pet Mare dau. of a Sedbury Royal Mare.

GREAT TOM—Continued.

Stakes, 10 sovereigns each, for four-year olds, colts 122 lbs., fillies 119 lbs., Ditch In, 2 miles, 105 yards, Augusta was first, Great Tom second, Footstep third. For the Cesarewitch Handicap Stakes, 2¼ miles, 28 yards, won by Hilarious, 3 years, 88 lbs.; Great Tom, 4 years, 111 lbs., was unplaced. Same place, for the Champion Stakes of 20 sovereigns each, half forfeit, with 1,000 added, Across the Flat, 1¼ miles, 73 yards, second to have ten per cent. and thirty-five per cent. of the stakes (225 subs.), Springfield, 4 years, 130 lbs., first ; Silvio, 3 years, 118 lbs., second ; Great Tom, 4 years, 130 lbs., third ; Hesper, 4 years, 130 lbs.; Duchess of Cambridge, 3 years, 115 lbs.; Zucchero, 3 years, 118 lbs., and Midlothian, 3 years, 118 lbs., unplaced. Same place, for the Winding-up Handicap of 10 sovereigns each, with 100 added, Rowley mile, 1 mile 17 yards, Great Tom, 3 years, 117 lbs., was first ; Augusta, 4 years, 105 lbs., second ; Sheldrake, 3 years, 91 lbs., third ; Chevron, 3 years, and Buridan, 86 lbs., unplaced. Won by three lengths, a head between the second and third. At Shrewsbury, for the Queen's Plate of 200 guineas, about 2¼ miles, Sheldrake, 3 years old, 117 lbs., was first ; Redoubt, 3 years old, 117 lbs,, second ; Great Tom, 4 years old, 133 lbs., third ; Little Beware, 5 years old, 135 lbs., and Drumhead, 4 years old, 133 lbs., unplaced. Same meeting, was unplaced for the Hawkstone Welter Cup, New mile, won by Speculation, 3 years old, 134 lbs.; Plaisante, 3 years old, 139 lbs., second ; Skatka, 5 years old 139 lbs., third ; Great Tom, 4 years old, 176 lbs.; Hippias, aged, 152 lbs., and Trommel, 3 years old, 124 lbs., unplaced. Great Tom, as will be seen, conceded lumps of weight to every horse in the race.

King Tom, the sire of Great Tom, started three times as a two-year old ; won two races, and was third in one ; ran third to Marsyas, 122 lbs., and Scythian, 119 lbs., King Tom, 119 lbs.; 174 subscribers, 12 starters, for the great North and South of England Biennial Stakes, at Goodwood, T. Y. C.; three-quarters of a mile, won by three-quarters of a length, a head between the second and third. Brighton, won the Brighton Biennial Stakes, T. Y. C., beating Student, Bracken, and four others, each carrying 119 lbs. Newmarket First October Meeting, won the Triennial Produce Stakes, T. Y. C., three-quarters of a mile, 87 subscribers, beating Champagne, Miranda and six others. 1854, King Tom, 3 years old, ran only once ; was second to Andover for the Derby Stakes at Epsom, 217 subscribers, 27 starters ; Hermit third, each 119 lbs. At 4 years old King Tom made a season at Mentmore, limited to twenty mares. He, however, ran two races, Newmarket First October Meeting won the Triennial Produce Stakes, Ditch In, 2 miles and 119 yards, beating Boer. Alembic and six others. Newmarket Second October Meeting, broke down and was unplaced in the Cesarewitch Stakes, handicap, won by Mr. Sykes. As a sire, King Tom, styled the Monarch of Mentmore, was a grand success, although not so popular or successful as his half-brother, Stockwell. The most noted of his get are Mainstone ; Wingrave, sire of Lillian ; old Calabar ; Tomato, winner of the 1,000 guineas in 1864 ; Zephyr, dam of Favonius, winner of the Derby in 1871 ; Tormentor, winner of the Oaks in 1866 : Hippia, winner of the Oaks in 1867 ; King Alfred ; Restitution, winner of the Alexander Plate at Ascot and the Goodwood and Brighton cups in 1869 ; Kingcraft, winner of the Derby in 1870 ; King Lud ; Corisande, winner of Cesarewitch in 1871 ; Hannah, winner of the 1,000 guineas ; Oaks and Doncaster St. Leger in 1871, a feat never accomplished by a filly, except by Formosa in 1868, and Apology in 1874 ; Lady Golightly, King Death, King Ban, Phaeton, so famous in this country as the sire of Ten Broeck : King Alfonso, Tolons, King Faro, etc.; Regina, dam of Scamp, winner of the Goodwood Stakes in 1874 ; Mogador, Peeping Tom, Reginella, Coltness, Columbus, Blue Blood, and many others.

Harkaway, sire of Great Tom, was the best and most successful race-horse of his day. He was not in either the Derby or St. Leger, but he won 21 out of the 28 races in which he started up to the end of his four-year old year, including eight King's Plates, the Goodwood Cup and the Royal Whip, beating all the best horses on the Irish and English turf, carrying the top weights. He also won the Goodwood Cup when five years old with 130 lbs.

Kingcraft, own brother to Great Tom, won the Derby in 1870, and was second to

Hawthornden for the St. Leger. Kingcraft has been quite successful in the stud ; he sired King Shepherd, Strathblane, King Pippin, King Lear, Queen Pippin, Royal, Distel, Chevalier d'Este, Apollo, Cabul, Leap Year, King Cob, Swift, and Witchcraft, one of the greatest two-year-olds of 1882, and now one of the favorites for the Oaks, 1883. Kingcraft stands well on the list of sires in 1882, the Hermit being first, Macaroni second.

Great Tom is a rich, golden chestnut, with a white stripe down his face, running down between his nostrils, and two white feet behind, half way to the hock ; he has a very neat head, fine ear, with good breadth of forehead and width of jaw ; good-shaped, arched neck, running into most excellent oblique shoulders, with great depth of girth, good-shaped, round body, well-ribbed home to strong, good hips and arched loin, indicative of ability to carry weight ; great length from point of the hip to whirl-bone, and thence to the stifle joint and point of the hock ; has good, sound legs and feet. He measures 16 hands 2 inches high ; around the girth, 77 inches ; length of shoulder, 32 inches ; around the arm, 22 inches ; below the knee, 9 inches ; from point of hip to point of hock, 40 inches ; circumference of gaskin, 19 inches ; from point of shoulder to point of buttocks, 69 inches, and weighs 1305 lbs. In 1880, 24 foals were dropped by Great Tom. Ella won four out of eight starts. The following are his best : Tangent, Talleyrand, Tullahoma, Tocsin, Tom Boy, Tea Rose, and Tennyson. His colts have size, power and substance, and he bids fair to be a success.

GRINSTEAD,

(WINNER OF THE CHAMPAGNE STAKES AT JEROME PARK, MANSION HOUSE STAKES AT LONG BRANCH, ALL-AGED SWEEPSTAKES AND SUMMER HANDICAP AT SARATOGA).

Will stand the season of 1883 *at the Ranche of E. J. Baldwin, Savannah, Los Angelos Co., California, at* $100 *the season. Application to L. R. Martin, San Francisco.*

GRINSTEAD, by Gilroy, son of Lexington, bred by Jas. A. Grinstead, Walnut Hill Stud, Ky., foaled 1871, dam sister to Ruric, by imp. Sovereign, son of Emilius, out of Levity, dam of Lever, Mildred, Legatee, etc., by imp. Trustee. Grinstead, as a two-year old, started in two races, of which he won one. At Jerome Park, the Champagne Stakes for two-year olds, three-quarters of a mile, in 1:17¾, beating Dublin, Weathercock, and seven others. At Saratoga, was second in the Kentucky Stakes for two-year olds, one mile, won by Battle-Axe in 1:45½. Three years old, started twelve times, and won three races. Jerome Park, won a dash of 1½ miles in 2:40¾, beating Kadi and seven others, among which were Harry Bassett, Whisper and Spindrift. Won a dash of 1¾ miles in 3:10, beating Shylock, Lyttleton, Wildidle, Kadi and others. Baltimore, Md., won a compensation purse, mile heats, in 1:45¼, 1:45½, beating six others, among which were Aaron Pennington and Survivor. Jerome Park, was second in the Belmont Stakes, 1½ miles, won by imp. Saxon, in 2:39½. Among the starters were Aaron Pennington, Elkhorn, Rutherford, Brigand and Reform. Saratoga, was second in the Sequel Stakes for three-year olds, 2 miles, won by Vandalite in 3:40¾. Was third in a dash of one mile and a furlong, won by Madge in 1:57½. Was third in a dash of 2 miles, won by Culpepper in 3:40½. Jerome Park, was second in a handicap, 1½ miles, won by Shylock in 2:38. Four-years old, started in eleven races, of which he won seven. Jerome Park, won a race of heats of one mile and a furlong, in 1:59¾, 2:01¾, beating Rhadamanthus and Fadladeen. Monmouth Park, won a race of mile heats, in 1:45½; 1:45, 1:47. D'Artagnan won first heat, and Grinstead was fifth. Won Mansion House Stakes for four-year olds, 2½ miles, in 4:40½, beating Rutherford, Stampede, and two others. Saratoga, won Sweepstakes for all ages, 1¼ miles, 2:08¾, beating Springbok, Olitipa and Mate. Won the Summer Handicap, 2 miles, in 3:37½, beating Wildidle and Mattie W. Won a dash of 1½ miles in 2:40, beating Aaron Pennington, Scratch, and two others. Jerome Park, was third in the Jockey Club Handicap, two miles, in 3:38½, won by Wildidle. Was third in the Woodburn Stakes for four-year olds, 2½ miles, won by Aaron Pennington, in 4:36½. Saratoga, was third in the Saratoga Cup, 2¼ miles, Springbok and Preakness running a dead heat for first place, in 3:56¼, which still stands the fastest time on record at the distance. Reno, Nevada, won race, mile heats, three in five, in 1:47, 1:46½, 1:46½. Bay District Course, Cal., was second in the Wise Plate, a post stake, four miles, won by Wildidle, in 7:25½. As a five-year old started once, and was unplaced. Grinstead is a blood bay horse, full 16 hands, of great substance and power, with excellent shoulders, good body, and strong, well placed back, hips and loin. He was a good, honest race-horse and comes from a running family, Ruric, Alaric, Vandal, Lexington, Monitor, Luke Blackburn, and a host of other good ones descended from it. Grinstead has covered only a few mares ; he sired Gano, winner of the Connor Stake, three-quarters of a mile, in 1:15, and other good races, and Grismer, also a winner. He will make a successful sire.

PEDIGREE OF GRINSTEAD.

GRINSTEAD.	GILROY.	Lexington.	Alice Carneal.	Boston.	Sarpedon.	Sister to Tuckahoe.	Timoleon.	Sir Archy.	Diomed—Castianira by Rockingham—Tabitha by Trentham—Dau. of Bosphorus—Dau. of Wm's Forester—Dau. of Coalition Colt.
								Daughter of.	Saltram—Dau. of Symme's Wildair—Dau. of Driver (Imp. Othello)—Dau. of Fallower (Blank)—Dau. of Imp. Vampire.
							Ball's Florizel.	Diomed—Dau. of Imp. Shark—Dau. of Harris' Eclipse—Dau. of Fearnought—Dau. of Jolly Roger—Dau. of Sober John—Dau. of Shock.
							Daughter of.	Alderman—Dau. of Clockfast—Dau. of Symme's Wildair—Kitty Fisher by Fearnought—Imp. Kitty Fisher by Cade.
				Magnolia.	Glencoe.	Rowena.	Sultan.	Emilius.	Orville—Emily by Stamford—Dau. of Whiskey—Gr. Dorimant by Dorimant—Dizzy by Blank—Dizzy by Driver—Dau. of Smiling Tom.
								Icaria.	The Flyer—Parma by Dick Andrews—May by Beningbrough—Primrose by Mambrino—Cricket by Herod—Sophia by Blank—Diana.
								Sumpter.	Sir Archy—Flirtilla's dam by Robin Redbreast—Dau. of Obscurity—Slamerkin by Wildair—Imp. Cub mare by Cub—Amaranthus' dam.
								Lady Grey.	Robin Grey—Maria by Melzar—Dau. of Highflyer—Dau. of Fearnought—Dau. of Ariel—Dau. of Jack of Diamonds.
							Trampoline.	Selim.	Buzzard—Castrel's dam by Alexander—Dau. of Highflyer—Dau. of Alfred—Dau. of Engineer—Bay Malton's dam by Cade (Godol.)
								Bacchante.	Williamson's Ditto—Sis. to Calomel by Mercury—Dau. of Herod—Folly by Marske—Vixen by Regulus—Dau. of Hutton's Spot.
					Myrtle.	Mameluke.		Tramp.	Dick Andrews—Dau. of Gohanna—Fraxinella by Trentham—Dau. of Woodpecker—Everlasting by Eclipse—Hyaena by Snap.
								Web.	Waxy—Penelope by Trumpator—Prunella by Highflyer—Promise by Snap—Julia by Blank—Spectator's dam by Partner—Bonny Lass.
						Bobadilla.		Partisan.	Walton—Parsol by Pot-8-os—Prunella by Highflyer—Promise by Snap—Julia by Blank—Spectator's dam by Partner—Bonny Lass.
								Miss Sophia.	Stamford—Sophia by Buzzard—Huncamunca by Highflyer—Cypher by Squirrel—Fribble's dam by Regulus—Dau. of Bart. Childers.
								Bobadil.	Rubens—Dau. of Skyscraper—Isabel by Woodpecker—Dau. of Squirrel—Ancaster Nancy by Blank—Phoebe by Tortoise—Dau. of Looby.
								Pythoness.	Sorcerer—Princess by Sir Peter—Dau. of Dungannon—Dau. of Turf—Dau. of Herod—Golden Grove by Blank—Spinster by Partner (Jigg).
	SISTER TO RUBIC.	Imp. Sovereign.	Emilius.	Orville.				Beningbrough.	King Fergus—Dau. of Herod—Pyrrha by Matchem—Duchess by Whitenose—Miss Slamerkin by Y. True Blue—Dau. of Ox. Dun Arabian.
								Evelina.	Highflyer—Termagant by Tantrum—Cantatrice by Sampson—Dau. of Regulus—Marske's dam by Blacklegs—Dau. of Bay Bolton.
								Stamford.	Haphazard—Bess by Waxy—Vixen by Pot-8-os—Cypher by Squirrel—Fribble's dam by Regulus—Dau. of Bart. Childers.
								Daughter of.	Whiskey—Gr. Dorimant by Dorimant—Dizzy by Blank—Dizzy by Driver—Dau. of Smiling Tom—Dau. of Oysterfoot.
								Sorcerer.	Trumpator—Y. Giantess by Diomed—Giantess by Matchem—Molly Longlegs by Babraham—Dau. of Cole's Foxhunter.
								Daughter of.	Precipitate—Dau. of Highflyer—Tiffany by Eclipse—Y. Hag by Skim—Hag by Crab—Ebony by Childers—Ebony by Basto.
				Fleur de Lis.	Lady Rachel.	Bourbon.		Stamford.	Haphazard—Bess by Waxy—Vixen by Pot-8-os—Cypher by Squirrel—Fribble's dam by Regulus—Dau. of Bart. Childers.
								Young Rachel.	Volunteer (Eclipse)—Rachel by Highflyer—Sis. to Tandem by Syphon—Dau. of Snip—Dau. of Cottingham—War. Galloway.
						Catton.		Golumpus.	Gohanna—Catharine by Woodpecker—Camilla by Trentham—Coquette by Compton Barb—Sis. to Regulus by God. Arabian—Gr. Robinson.
								Lucy Grey.	Timothy—Lucy by Florizel—Frenzy by Eclipse—Dau. of Engineer—Dau. of Blank—Lass of the Mill by Traveler—Miss Makeless.
		Levity.	Trustee.	Emma.				Whisker.	Waxy—Penelope by Trumpator—Prunella by Highflyer—Promise by Snap—Julia by Blank—Spectator's dam by Partner.
								Gibside Fairy.	Hermes—Vicissitude by Pipator—Beatrice by Sir Peter—Pyrrha by Matchem—Duchess by Whitenose—Miss Slamerkin by Y. True Blue.
				Tranby.				Blacklock.	Whitelock—Dau. of Coriander—Wildgoose by Highflyer—Coheiress by Pot-8-os—Manilla by Goldfinder—Dau. of Old Eng.—Dau. of Cul. Ara.
								Daughter of.	Orville—Miss Grimstone by Weasel—Dau. of Ancaster—Dau. of Dam Arabian—Dau. of Sampson—Dau. of Oronooko—Sophia.
		Vandal's dam.	Lucilla.					Trumpator.	Sir Solomon—Dau. of Hickory—Imp. Trumpetta by Trumpator—Sis. to Lambinos by Highflyer—Dau. of Eclipse—Vauxhall's dam by Cade.
								Lucy.	Orphan (Ball's Florizel)—Lady Grey by Robin Grey—Maria by Melzar (Imp. Medley)—Dau. of Imp. Highflyer (Highflyer)—Dau. of Imp. Fearnought (Regulus)—Dau. of Ariel (Moreton's Imp. Traveler)—Dau. of Imp. Jack of Diamonds (Cullen Arabian)—Imp. Diamond (Duchess) by Cullen Arabian—Lady Thigh by Croft's Partner (Jigg)—Dau. of Greyhound (White Barb. Chillaby)—Dau. of Curwin's Bay Barbe—Dau. of D'Arcy's Chestnut Arabian—Dau. of Whiteshirt—Old Montague mare.

HARRY O'FALLON

Will stand the season of 1883 near Danville, Ky., limited to twenty approved mares by private contract. Application to L. B. Fields, Danville, Ky.

HARRY O. FALLON, by imp. Australian, bred by James O. Fallon, St. Louis, Mo., foaled 1869, dam imp. Sunny South, dam of Ozark, by Irish Birdcatcher, son of Sir Hercules, 2d dam Equal, by The Cure, out of Equation, the dam of Diophantus, Archimedes, Artesian, etc., by Emilius. Australian is in this volume. Sunny South, Harry's dam, was the dam of the good race-horse Ozark, and others, she by the great Birdcatcher, sire of The Baron, who got Stockwell and Rataplan, Birdcatcher sired Habena and Manganese, winners of the 1,000 guineas, Songstress, winner of the Oaks, Daniel O'Rourk, winner of the Derby, The Baron, Knight of St. George and Warlock, winners of the St. Leger, Chanticleer, Early Bird, Saunterer, Exact, and other good race-horses. The Cure, sire of his grandam, was a fine race-horse; he won the Champagne Stakes, at Doncaster, the Dee Stakes, at Chester, the Suffolk Stakes at Newmarket, the North Derby Stakes, and was second to Faugh-a-Ballagh in the St Leger, 1844. He sired Little Agnes, Dictator, and others. Harry's great-grandam was the dam of Exact, Diophantus, winner of the 2,000 guineas, and others. Maria, his 4th dam, was the dam of Euclid who was third in the Derby, and ran a dead heat with Charles XII., for the St. Leger, Extempore, winner of the the 1,000 guineas, and other good ones. Harry O. Fallon ran only two races, when out of condition, and was unplaced. There is no more stoutly-bred horse in America than Harry O. Fallon. He has double crosses of Whalebone and Whisker, the famous sons of Waxy, and double crosses of the speedy Emilius, and a cross of Touchstone, with any number to Eclipse and Herod through his collateral branches. Harry has only sired some six or eight horses which have been trained, and they have all run creditably; amongst them, Krupp Gun, Sam Ecker, Expectation, Harry Doswell, Jack of Spades, and John Davis, the latter a winner of the Citizens' Plate, 1¼ miles, at St. Louis, 104 lbs., in 3:06¼, 1¼ miles in 2:11, the Garden City Cup, at Chicago, 2¼ miles, in 4:30¼, track very muddy, one mile and 500 yards, 112 lbs., in 2:13¼, NorthwesternStakes at Chicago, 117 lbs., in 3:06½, and the October Handicap, 111 lbs., in 2:09. Harry is inbred to Waxy through Whalebone and Whisker, both Derby winners, and has many crosses to Eclipse, Herod and Matchem. With a chance he will get race-horses.

PEDIGREE OF HARRY O'FALLON.

							Name	Pedigree
HARRY O'FALLON	AUSTRALIAN	West Australian	Mowerina	Touchstone	Emma	Daugh-ter of Clinker	Humphrey Clinker	Comus	Sorcerer—Houghton Lass by Sir Peter—Alexina by King Fergus—Lardella by Y Marske—Dau. of Cade—Beaufremont's dam.
							Clinkerina	Clinker—Pewet by Tandem—Termagant by Tantrum—Cantatrice by Sampson—Dau. of Regulus—Maraske's dam by Blacklegs.
						Melbourne.	Cervantes.	Don Quixote—Evelina by Highflyer—Termagant by Tantrum—Cantatrice by Sampson—Dau. of Regulus (Godol.)—Marske's dam by Blacklegs.
							Daughter of.	Golumpus—Dau. of Paynator—Sis. to Zodiac by St. George—Abigail by Woodpecker—Firetail by Eclipse—Dau. of Blank—Dau. of Cade.
							Camel.	Whalebone—Dau. of Selim—Maiden by Sir Peter—Dau. of Phoenomenon—Matron by Florizel—Maiden by Matchem—Dau. of Squirt.
							Banter.	Master Henry—Boadicea by Alexander—Brunette by Amaranthus—Mayfly by Matchem—Dau. of An. Starling—Dau. of Grasshopper.
							Whisker.	Waxy—Penelope by Trumpator—Prunella by Highflyer—Promise by Snap—Julia by Blank—Spectator's dam by Partner—Bonny Lass.
							Gibside Fairy.	Hermes—Vicissitude by Pipator—Beatrice by Sir Peter—Pyrrha by Matchem—Duchess by Whitenose—Miss Slamerkin by Y True Blue.
		Emilia.	Young Emilius.	Emilius.	Shoveler.		Orville.	Beningbrough—Evelina by Highflyer—Termagant by Tantrum—Cantatrice by Sampson—Dau. of Regulus—Marske's dam by Blacklegs.
							Emily.	Stamford—Dau. of Whiskey—Gr. Dorimant by Dorimant—Dizzy by Blank—Dizzy by Driver—Dau. of Smiling Tom—Dau. of Oysterfoot.
							Scud.	Beningbrough—Eliza by Highflyer—Augusta by Eclipse—Hardwick's dam by Herod—Dau. of Bajazet—Dau. of Regulus.
							Goosander.	Hambletonian—Rally by Trumpator—Fancy, sis. to Diomed by Florizel—Dau. of Spectator—Horatia by Blank—Dau. of F. Childers.
			Persian.	Whisker.	Variety.		Waxy.	Pot-8-os—Maria by Herod—Lisette by Snap—Miss Windsor by Godol. Arabian—Sister to Volunteer by Y Belgrade.
							Penelope.	Trumpator—Prunella by Highflyer—Promise by Snap—Julia by Blank—Spectator's dam by Partner—Bonny Lass by Bay Bolton.
							Selim or Soothsayer.*	Sorcerer—Golden Locks by Delpini—Violet by Shark—Dau. of Syphon—Charlotte by Blank—Dau. of Crab—Dau. of Dyer's Dimple.
							Sprite.	Bobtail—Catherine by Woodpecker—Camilla by Trentham—Coquette by Compton Barb.—Sis. to Regulus by Godol. Arabian—Gr. Robinson.
	SUNNY SOUTH.	Irish Birdcatcher.	Sir Hercules.	Whalebone.	Peri.		Waxy.	Pot-8-os—Maria by Herod—Lisette by Snap—Miss Windsor by Godol. Arabian—Sister to Volunteer by Y Belgrade—Dau. of Bartlet's Childers.
							Penelope.	Trumpator—Prunella by Highflyer—Promise by Snap—Julia by Blank—Spectator's dam by Partner—Bonny Lass by Bay Bolton.
							Wanderer.	Gohanna—Catherine by Woodpecker—Camilla by Trentham—Coquette by Compton Barb.—Sis. to Regulus by Godol. Arabian—Gr. Robinson.
							Thalestris.	Alexander—Rival of Sir Peter—Hornet by Drone—Manilla by Goldfinder—Dau. of Old Eng. (Godol.)—Dau. of Cul. Arabian—Miss Cade.
			Guiccioli.	Bob Booty.			Chanticleer.	Woodpecker—Dau. of Eclipse—Rosebud by Snap—Miss Belsea by Regulus—Dau. of Bart. Childers—Dau. of Hon. Arabian.
							Ierne.	Bagot—Dau. of Gamahoe—Patty by Tim—Miss Patch by Justice—Ringtail Galloway by Cur. Bay Barb—Sis. to Witty Mare by Hip.
				Flight.			Irish Escape.	Commodore—Buffer's dam by Highflyer—Shift by Sweetbriar—Black Susan by Snap—Ld. Bruce's Mare by Cade—Dau. of Belgrade.
							Young Heroine.	Bagot—Heroine by Hero (Cade)—Dau. of Snap—Sister to Regulus by Godol. Arabian—Gr. Robinson by Bald Galloway—Dau. of Snake.
		Equation.	The Cure.	Physician.	Morsel.		Brutandorf.	Blacklock—Mandane by Pot-8-os—Y Camilla by Woodpecker—Camilla by Trentham—Coquette by Compton Barb—Sis. to Regulus.
							Primette.	Prime Minister (Sancho)—Miss Paul by Sir Paul (Sir Peter)—Miss Dunnington by Shuttle—Miss Grimstone by Weasel—Dau. of Ancaster.
							Mulatto.	Catton—Desdemona by Orville—Fanny by Sir Peter—Dau. of Diomed—Desdemona by Marske—Y Hag by Skim—Hag by Crab—Ebony.
							Linda.	Waterloo (Walton)—Cressida by Whiskey—Y Glantess by Diomed—Giantess by Matchem—Molly Longlegs by Babraham.
		Equal.	Maria.	Emilius.			Orville.	Beningbrough—Evelina by Highflyer—Termagant by Tantrum—Cantatrice by Sampson—Dau. of Regulus—Marske's dam.
							Emily.	Stamford—Dau. of Whiskey—Gr. Dorimant by Dorimant—Dizzy by Blank—Dizzy by Driver—Dau. of Smiling Tom.
							Whisker.	Waxy—Penelope by Trumpator—Prunella by Highflyer—Promise by Snap—Julia by Blank—Spectator's dam by Partner.
							Gibside Fairy.	Hermes (Mercury)—Vicissitude by Pipator—(Imperator by Conductor)—Beatrice by Sir Peter (Highflyer)—Pyrrha by Matchem (Cade by Godol.)—Duchess by Whitenose (Godol.)—Miss Slamerkin by Y True Blue (William's Turk)—Dau. of Ld. Oxford's Dun Arabian—D'Arcy's Blacklegged Royal Mare.

* Soothsayer given.

HIGHLANDER (Imp.)

Will be located at the Fairview Stud Farm, near Gallatin, Sumner Co., Tenn., and will be permitted to serve mares at $50 each, for the season, and $5 to the groom. Application to be made to Charles Reed, Gallatin, Tenn. Annual Sales in July, at Saratoga.

HIGHLANDER, by Blair Athol, son of Stockwell, bred by Mr. Gulliver, foaled 1868, dam Bistre, the dam of Verbena, by West Australian, out of Blister, dam of Maidstone and Cheddington by Bay Middleton. Highlander, from an accident, never raced, but he is bred as fashionably and truly as it is possible to breed a horse for racing purposes. His sire, Blair Athol, was the best son of the great Stockwell. Blair Athol won both the Epson Derby and the Doncaster St. Leger, and was the sire of Prince Charlie, winner of the 2,000 guineas, Scottish Queen and Cecilia, winners of the 1,000 guineas, Silvio, winner of both Derby and St. Leger, and Craig Miller, winner of the St. Leger. West Australian, the sire of his dam, won the triple events, 2,000 guineas, Derby and St. Leger, and was sire of The Wizard, winner of the 2,000 guineas, and Summerside, winner of the Oaks. He was also the sire of imp. Australian, which was so successful in America. Bay Middleton, the sire of his grandam, was half-brother to Glencoe on the sire's side, won the 2000 guineas, and Derby, in 1836, and was the sire of Hermit, winner of the 2,000 guineas, Aphrodite, winner of the 1,000 guineas, and of the great Flying Dutchman, winner of the Derby and St. Leger, in 1849, Ellington and Andover, winners of the Derby. He also sired Brown Dutchess, an Oaks winner, Amsterdam, Autocrat, Fly-by-Night, Ellen Middleton, dam of Wild Dayrell, Eunice, the dam of Saunterer, Bridal, dam of Special License, and others. Touchstone, the sire of his great grandam, Hope, was one of the best race horses of his day, won the St. Leger, the Doncaster Cup, in 1835 and '36, the Ascot Gold Cup in 1836 and '37, and was the sire of Flatcatcher and Nunnykirk, winners of the 2,000 guineas, Cotherstone, winner of the 2,000 guineas, and Derby, Orlando, winner of the Derby, and Surplice, winner of the Derby and St. Leger, Mendicant, winner of the 1,000 guineas, and Oaks, Blue Bonnet, winner of St. Leger, and the great Newminster, winner of the St. Leger, whose son, The Hermit, stands at the head of winning sires in England. In addition to his crosses of Glencoe and Priam, both grand ones, he has the Whalebone and Whisker, one of which won the Derby in 1810, and the other in 1815. Highlander has three crosses of Imp. Diomed through his best daughter, Young Giantess, and crosses of Matchem through Maiden, and traces through an own sister of Eclipse to a daughter of Brimmer. The pedigree is rich in blood of the noted winners of the classic events. Highlander covered a few mares in England, prior to his importation, and Buz, one of his get, has been a winner. None of his colts have started in this country, but, from conformation and constitution, should make their mark. Highlander is a rich brown, 16 hands high, with white blaze in his face. He measures 78 inches around the heart, and below the knee 8 inches. He is a very fine horse through his heart and shoulders, with good body and wide strong hip, and with good mares should get race-horses, or blood from the highest racing sources is a failure.

PEDIGREE OF HIGHLANDER—(Imp.)

HIGHLANDER (Imp.)					Ancestor	Details
BLAIR ATHOL (Imp.)	Stockwell	The Baron	Irish Birdcatcher		Sir Hercules.	Whalebone—Peri by Wanderer—Thalestris by Alexander—Rival by St. Peter—Hornet by Drone—Manilla by Goldfinder—Dau. of Old. Eng.
					Guiccioli.	Bob Booty—Flight by I. Eclipse—Y. Heroine by Bagot—Heroine by Hero—Dau. of Snap—Sis. to Regulus by Godol. Arabian—Grey Robinson.
			Echidna		Economist.	Whiskey—Floranthe by Octavian—Caprice by Anvil—Madcap by Eclipse—Dau. of Blank—Dau. of Blaze—Dau. of Y. Greyhound.
					Miss Pratt.	Blacklock—Gadabout by Orville—Minstrel by Sir Peter—Matron by Florizel—Maiden by Matchem—Dau. of Squirt—Lot's dam.
		Pocahontas	Glencoe		Sultan.	Selim—Bacchante by Williamson's Ditto—Sis. to Calomel by Mercury—Dau. of Herod—Folly by Marske—Vixen by Regulus.
					Trampoline.	Tramp—Web by Waxy—Penelope by Trumpator—Pruuella by Highflyer—Promise by Snap—Julia by Blank—Spectator's dam.
			Marpessa		Muley.	Orville—Eleanor by Whiskey—Y. Giantess by Diomed—Giantess by Matchem—Molly Longlegs by Babraham—Dau. of Cole's Foxhunter.
					Clare.	Marmion—Harpalice by Gohanna—Amazon by Driver—Fractious by Mercury—Dau. of Woodpecker—Everlasting by Eclipse.
	Blink Bonny	Melbourne	Humphrey Clinker		Comus.	Sorcerer—Houghton Lass by Sir Peter—Alexina by King Fergus—Lardella by Y. Marske—Dau. of Cade—Beaufremont' dam.
					Clinkerina.	Clinker—Pewet by Tamdeu—Termagant by Tantrum—Cautatrice by Sampson—Dau. of Regulus—Marske's dam by Blacklegs.
			Dau. of Cervantes		Cervantes.	Don Quixote—Evelina by Highflyer—Termagant by Tantrum—Cantatrice by Sampson—Dau. of Regulus—Marske's dam by Blacklegs.
					Daughter of.	Golumpus—Dau. of Paynator—Sis. to Zodiac by St. George—Abigail by Woodpecker—Firetail by Eclipse—Dau. of Blank (Godol.)
		Queen Mary	Dau. of Gladiator		Partisan.	Walton—Parasol by Pot-8-os—Prunella by Highflyer—Promise by Snap—Julia by Blank—Spectator's dam by Partner.
					Pauline.	Moses—Quadrille by Selim—Canary Bird by Whiskey or Sorcerer—Canary by Coriander—Miss Green by Highflyer.
			Dau. of Plenipotentiary		Plenipotentiary.	Emilius—Harriet by Pericles—Dau. of Selim—Pipylina by Sir Peter—Rally by Trumpator—Fancy, Sis. to Diomed by Florizel.
					Myrrha.	Whalebone—Gift by Y. Gohanna, Sis. to Grazier by Sir Peter—Dau. of Trumpator—Dau. of Herod—Dau. of Snap—Dau. of Gower Stallion.
BISTRE.	Mowerina.	West Australian.	Melbourne	Humphrey Clinker	Comus.	Sorcerer—Houghton Lass by Sir Peter—Alexina by King Fergus—Lardella by Y. Marske—Dau. of Cade—Beaufremont's dam.
					Clinkerina.	Clinker—Pewet by Tandem—Termagant by Tantrum—Cantatrice by Sampson—Dau. of Regulus—Marske's dam.
				Daughter of Cervantes	Cervantes.	Don Quixote—Evelina by Highflyer—Termagant by Tantrum—Cantatrice by Sampson—Dau. of Regulus—Marske's dam.
					Daughter of.	Golumpus—Dau. of Paynator—Sis. to Zodiac by St. George—Abigail by Woodpecker—Firetail by Eclipse—Dau. of Blank.
			Emma.	Touchstone.	Camel.	Whalebone—Dau. of Selim—Maiden by Sir Peter—Dau. of Phoenomenon—Matron by Florizel—Maiden by Matchem (Cade).
					Banter.	Master Henry—Boadicea by Alexander—Brunette by Amaranthus—Mayfly by Matchem—Dau. of An. Starling—Dau. of Grasshopper.
					Whisker.	Waxy—Penlope by Trumpator—Prunella by Highflyer—Promise by Snap—Julia by Blank—Spectator' dam by Partner.
					Gibside Fairy.	Hermes—Vicissitude by Pipator—Beatrice by Sir Peter—Pyrrha by Matchem—Duchess by Whitenose—Miss Slamerkin.
	Miss Letty.	Bay Middleton.	Sultan.	Cobweb.	Selim.	Buzzard—Castrel's dam by Alexander—Dau. of Highflyer—Dau. of Alfred Dau. of Engineer—Bay Maltom's dam by Cade (Godol.)
					Bacchante.	Williamson's Ditto—Sis. to Calomel by Mercury—Dau. of Herod—Folly by Marske—Vixen by Regulus—Dau. of Hutton's Spot.
					Phantom.	Walton—Julia by Whiskey—Y. Giantess by Diomed—Giantess by Matchem Molly Longlegs by Babraham—Dau. of Cole's Foxhunter.
					Filagree.	Soothsayer—Web by Waxy—Penlope by Trumpator—Prunella by Highflyer—Promise by Snap—Julia by Blank—Spectator's dam.
		Hope.	Touchstone.	Blister.	Camel.	Whalebone—Dau. of Selim—Maiden of Sir Peter—Dau. of Phoenomenon—Matron by Florizel—Maiden by Matchem—Dau of Squirt.
					Banter.	Master Henry—Boadicea by Alexander—Brunette by Amaranthus—Mayfly by Matchem—Dau. of An. Starling—Dau. of Grasshopper.
					Priam.	Emilius—Cressida by Whiskey—Y. Giantess by Diomed—Giantess by Matchem—Molly Longlegs by Babraham—Dau. of Cole's Foxhunter.
					Daughter of.	Orville—Golden Legs' dam by Buzzard—Hornpipe by Trumpator—Luna by Herod (Tartar)—Proserpine, Sis. to Eclipse by Marske—10th dam Spiletta by Regulus (Godol)—11th dam—Mother Western by Smith's son of Snake—12th dam by Old Montague—13th dam by Hautboy 14th dam by Brimmer.

HIMYAR,

(WINNER OF THE BELLE MEADE STAKES FOR TWO-YEAR OLDS AT LOUISVILLE; BELLE MEADE STAKES, NO 1, AT NASHVILLE; PHŒNIX HOTEL STAKES, AT LEXINGTON; THE MERCHANTS AND TURF STAKES, AT LOUISVILLE, KY., AND JANUARY STAKES AT ST. LOUIS,)

Will stand for mares at the Dixiana Stud, Maj. B. G. Thomas, proprietor, near Lexington, Ky., by private contract. Application to Maj. B. G. Thomas, Lexington, Ky.

HIMYAR, by Alarm, son of imp. Eclipse, bred and owned by Maj. B. G. Thomas, Dixiana Stud, Lexington, Ky., foaled, 1875, dam Hira by Lexington, out of Hegira by imp. Ambassador. Himyar made his *debut* as a two-year old at Lexington, Ky., in the Colt and Filly Stakes, five furlongs, running third to Pomeroy, in 1:04½. Won the Colt Stakes, three-quarters of a mile, in 1:16¾, beating Blue Eyes, Leveler, etc. Fall, won the Colt and Filly Stakes, one mile, in 1:44½, beating Leveler, Blue Eyes, and five others. Louisville, won the Belle Meade Stakes, three-quarters of a mile in 1:16½, beating Leveler and four others. Was third in the Sanford Stakes to Blue Eyes and Day Star, one mile in 1:45. Himyar, 3 years old, started in five races; won three and was second in two. Nashville, May 4, won Belle Meade Stake No. 1, 1¼ miles in 2:43, track heavy, beating Bergamot, Artful and Glenmore. Lexington, Ky., May 10, won Phœnix Hotel Stakes, 1¾ miles, in 3:22½, track deep in mud, beating McHenry, J. R. Swinney and Solicitor. Louisville, Ky., May 21, ran second to Day Star, in Kentucky Derby 1½ miles, in 2:37½, the fastest Derby ever run in that State, beating Leveler, Solicitor, McHenry and four others. St. Louis, June 4, won January Stakes, mile heats, in 1:42½, 1:43½, beating Leveler, Kate Claxton and McHenry. Lexington, Sept. 13, was second in Elkhorn Stakes, 2 miles, in 4:04½; won by Cammie F.; track very muddy. Four years old started four times, won all of his races. Lexington, won a dash of one mile in 1:51¾, track muddy, defeating a field of four. Walked over for Club Purse two miles. Louisville, won a sweepstake for all ages, 1½ miles, beating Goodnight, Long Taw and four others, in 1:56. Won Club Purse 2 miles in 3:35, beating Long Taw and two others. At five years old started twelve times. Lexington, Ky., was third to Mendlessohn and Verdict in sweepstake for all ages 1¾ miles in 2:08. Won Club Purse, mile heats, in 1:42½, 1:44½ beating Warfield, Victim and four others. Louisville, was unplaced in Louisville Cup, 2¼ miles in 4:20½, won by Volturno, track very muddy. Won the Merchants' Stake, 1⅛ miles in 1:55½, beating Blue Eyes, One Dime and four others. St. Louis, was second to L'Argentine, 1¼ miles in 2:10½. Was unplaced in Citizens Plate, 1⅛ miles, dead heat and stakes divided between Long Taw and Blue Lodge, in 1:55½. Lexington Fall Meeting, was third to Renown and Montreal, one mile in 1:49¾, track heavy. Was second to Renown in Club Purse, 1⅛ miles, no time, five others behind him. Louisville, won Turf Stakes, 1⅛ miles, in 1:57½, beating Renown and three others. Was second to Bowling Green in Club Purse, 1½ miles, in 2:42½, three others behind him. Won Club Purse 1⅛ miles in 1:54¾, defeating Montreal and Mattie Walker. Nashville, was beaten by Jim Malone in Citizens' Stake, mile heats, in 1:46¾, 1:47½, 1:53¾. Himyar won first heat. Six years old, Lexington, Ky., was unplaced in Club Purse, one mile, won by Patti in 1:44½. The family is a distinguished racing one. Hira, his dam, was a fine race-mare, Hegira, his grandam, had no equal for speed in her day. She ran two miles at New Orleans in 1850, in 3:34½, the fastest time made to that day. Mecca, her full sister, was also a fine race-mare. Flight, his great-grandam, was a superior race-mare and dam of Oliver, a very distinguished race-horse, by Wagner, winner of three-mile heats, in 5:38½, 5:38½. Shylock, Cicero, Pedlar, etc., all distinguished in their day, descended from the family. Himyar is a light bay with a long star and both hind feet white, he has a neat, bony head, broad between the eyes; good neck; splendid well-set, oblique shoulders, with abundance of muscle over the shoulder blade; great depth of girth; good body, but rather short back ribs, which makes his flank look light; with broad, strong hips, immense stifle and second thigh, and the muscle running tapering to excellent hocks; with sound feet and legs. Taking him altogether, he is a very fine, well-shaped horse, with most wonderful muscular power behind. If racing lineage and speed is worth anything, Himyar should be a success in the stud; his breeding is unexceptional.

PEDIGREE OF HIMYAR.

	Whalebone—Dau. of Selim—Maiden by Sir Peter—Dau. of Phoenomenon—Matron by Florizel—Maiden by Matchem. Master Henry—Boadicea by Alexander—Brunette by Amaranthus—Mayfly by Matchem—Dau. of Ancaster Starling.
	Selim—Dau. of Walton—Y. Giantess by Diomed—Giantess by Matchem—Molly Longlegs by Babraham—Dau. of Foxhunter. Bustard (Castrel)—Olympia by Sir Oliver—Scotilla by Anvil—Scota by Eclipse—Harmony by Herod—Rutilia by Blank.
	Selim—Bacchante by Williamson's Ditto—Sis. to Calomel by Mercury—Dau. of Herod—Folly by Marske—Vixen by Regulus. Phantom—Filagree by Soothsayer—Web by Waxy—Penelope by Trumpator—Prunella by Highflyer—Promise by Snap.
b.	Partisan—Ridicule by Shuttle—Sis. to Oatlands by Dungannon—Letitia by Highflyer—Dau. of Matchem—Dau. of Blank—Dau. of Babraham. Phantom—Filagree by Soothsayer—Web by Waxy—Penelope by Trumpator—Prunella by Highflyer—Promise by Snap—Julia.
	Sir Hercules—Guiccioli by Bob Booty—Flight by I. Escape—Y. Heroine by Bagot—Heroine by Hero—Dau. of Snap—Sis. to Regulus. Economist—Miss Pratt by Blacklock—Gadabout by Orville—Minstrel by Sir Peter—Maiden by Matchem—Dau. of Squirt—Dau. of Mogul.
	Sultan—Trampoline by Tramp—Web by Waxy—Penelope by Trumpator—Prunella by Highflyer—Promise by Snap. Muley—Clare by Marmion—Harpalice by Gohanna—Amazon by Driver—Fractious by Mercury—Dau. of Woodpecker.
	Tramp—Dau. of Whisker—Mandane by Pot-8-os—Y. Camilla by Woodpecker—Camilla by Trentham—Coquette by Compton Barb. Bustard (Buzzard)—Greyhurst's dam by Election—Sis. to Skyscraper by Highflyer—Everlasting by Eclipse—Hyaena by Snap.
t.	Blacklock—Dau. of Juniper—Dau. of Sorcerer—Virgin by Sir Peter—Dau. of Pot-8-o's—Editha by Herod—Elfrida by Snap. Cerberus—Miss Cranfield by Sir Peter—Dau. of Pegasus—Dau. of Paymaster—Pomona by Herod—Caroline by Snap (Snip).
f.	Diomed—Castianira by Rockingham—Tabitha by Trentham—Dau. of Bosphorus—Dau. of Wm's Forester—Dau. of Coalition Colt. Saltram—Dau. of Symme's Wildair—Dau. of Driver (Imp. Othello)—Dau. of Fallower (Blank)—Dau. of Vampire (Regulus).
el. f.	Diomed—Dau. of Imp. Shark—Dau. of Harris' Eclipse—Dau. of Fearnought—Dau. of Jolly Roger—Dau. of Sober John (Rib). Alderman—Dau. of Clockfast—Dau. of Symme's Wildair—Y, Kitty Fisher by Fearnought—Imp. Kitty Fisher by Cade (Godol).
	Orville—Emily by Stamford—Dau. of Whiskey—Gr. Dorimant by Dorimant—Dizzy by Blank—Dizzy by Driver—Dau. of Smiling Tom. The Flyer—Parma by Dick Andrews—May by Beningbrough—Primrose by Mambrino—Cricket by Herod—Sophia by Blank.
	Sir Archy—Flirtilla's dam by Robin Redbreast—Dau. of Obscurity—Slamerkin by Wildair—Cub Mare by Cub—Amaranthus' dam. Robin Grey—Maria by Melzar—Dau. of Highflyer—Dau. of Fearnought—Dau. of Ariel—Dau. of Jack of Diamonds—Imp. Diamond.
	Orville—Emily by Stamford—Dau. of Whiskey—Gr. Dorimant by Dorimant—Dizzy by Blank—Dizzy by Driver—Dau. of Smiling Tom. Pericles—Dau. of Selim—Pipylina by Sir Peter—Rally by Trumpator—Fancy, sis. to Diomed by Florizel—Dau. of Spectator—Horatia.
m.	Waxy—Penelope by Trumpator—Prunella by Highflyer—Promise by Snap—Julia by Blank—Spectator's dam by Partner. Cerberus—Miss Cranfield by Sir Peter—Dau. of Pegasus—Sis. to Sir Sidney by Paymaster—Pomona by Herod—Caroline by Snap.
's	Orville—Eleanor by Whiskey—Y. Giantess by Diomed—Giantess by Matchem—Mollie Longlegs by Babraham. Windle—Dau. of Anvil (Herod)—Virago by Snap—Dau. of Regulus—Sis. to Othello by Crab—Miss Slamerkin by Y. True Blue.
e	Sir Archy—Dau. of Citizen—Dau. of Commutation—Dau. of Dare Devil, Sally Shark by Imp. Shark—Betsy Pringle by Fearnought—Jenny Dismal.
	Imp. Sir Harry (Sir Peter)—Dau. of Diomed—Dau. of Imp. St. George (Dragon)—Dau. of Fearnought (Regulus)—Dau. of Jolly Roger (Roundhead by F. Childers)—Imp. Mary Grey by Roundhead—Ringbone by Partner (Jigg)—Dau. of Croft's Bay Barb—Dau. of Makeless (Oglethorpe Arabian)—Dau. of Brimmer (Yellow Turk)—Dau. of Dicky Pierson (Dodwsorth)—Burton Barb Mare.

HINDOO,

(WINNER OF SEVEN OUT OF NINE STAKES AT 2 YEARS OLD, WINNER OF THE KENTUCKY DERBY, AND CLARK STAKES AT LOUSVILLE, BLUE RIBBON STAKES AT LEXINGTON, TIDAL STAKES AND CONEY ISLAND DERBY AT SHEEPSHEAD BAY, OCEAN STAKES, JERSEY DERBY AND LORILLARD STAKES AT LONG BRANCH, THE TRAVERS AND KENNER STAKES AT SARATOGA ALL IN 1881; LOUISVILLE CUP AND TURF STAKES AND CONEY ISLAND CUP, 1882,)

Will stand the season of 1883 *at the Runnymede Stud, near Paris, Ky., at* $100 *the season. Application to Geo. W. Bowen & Co., Paris, Ky. Annual sales of yearlings in May.*

HINDOO, by Virgil, son of Vandal, bred by D. Swigert, Elemendorf Stud, Ky., foaled 1878; dam Florence by Lexington, son of Boston, out of imp. Weatherwitch, dam of Little Mack and Mollie Cad by Weatherbit, son of Sheet Anchor. Hindoo was the sensational two-year old of his year; started in nine races, won seven, was second in one, third in one. Hindoo made his first appearance at Lexington, Ky., May 13, in the Colt and Filly Stakes for two-year olds, three-quarters of a mile, winning in 1:17¼, beating Alfambra, Brambaletta, Lizzie S., Edison and five others. Louisville, Ky., May 19, won Alexander Stakes, half a mile, in 50 seconds, beating Banter, Maretzek and eight others; May 24, won the Tennessee Stakes for two-year olds, three-quarters of a mile, in 1:16, beating Brambaletta, Ripple, Bootjack and five others. St. Louis, June 9, won the Juvenile Stakes, for two-year olds, three-quarters of a mile, in 1:17¼, beating Voltague, Story, Sligo and four others; June 12, won the Jockey Club Stakes, for two-year olds, one mile, in 1:44, beating Lelex, Voltague and Enniskillen—a fast and good race. Chicago, June 21, won the Criterion Stakes, for two-year-olds, three-quarters of a mile, in 1:15, beating Ripple, Greenland and three others. This was the fastest three-quarters ever run by a two-year-old to that date; June 26, won the Tremont Hotel Stakes, for two-year-olds, one mile, in 1:48, beating Lizzie S., Ripple and Moses. In all these races, except the Tennessee Stakes, he carried 100 lbs.; in the Tennessee, 105 lbs. Saratoga, Aug. 14, ran third to Crickmore and Bonnie Lizzie in the Windsor Hotel Stakes, for two-year olds, five furlongs, in 1:05, track heavy, beating Thora and four others; Aug. 19, ran second to Thora in the Day Boat Line Stakes, three-quarters of a mile, in 1:17¼, beating Bonnie Lizzie and three others. In these races he carried 110 lbs. In justice to the colt it must be stated, that he had changed hands and did not run up to his previous form.

Three years old, started in twenty races, of which he won eighteen. Lexington, Ky., won the Blue Ribbon Stakes, for three-year olds, 1½ miles, in 2:38, beating Getaway, Bend Or, Creosote and four others. At Louisville, Ky., won the Kentucky Derby for three-year olds, 1½ miles, in 2:40, beating Lelex, Alfambra and three others; won the Clark Stakes, for three-year olds, 1¼ miles, in 2:10¾, beating Alfambra, Bootjack, Bend Or and Sligo.

Jerome Park, won a dash of one mile and a furlong, in 2:02¼, beating Sir Hugh, Jack of Hearts and Rob Roy; won a dash of one mile and three furlongs, in 2:34, track heavy. Sheepshead Bay, won the Tidal Stakes for three-year-olds, one mile, in 1:43¼, beating Crickmore and Saunterer; won the Coney Island Derby for three-year olds, 1½ mile, in 2:47¼, Baltic the only other starter. Monmouth Park, won the Ocean Stakes for all ages, one mile and a furlong, in 1:57, beating Monitor, Glidelia and Valentino; won the Lorillard Stakes for three-year olds, 1¼ miles, in 2:39¼, beating Crickmore and Saunterer; walked over for a sweepstakes of one thousand dollars each with $2,000 added. Saratoga, won the Travers Stakes, for three-year olds, 1¾ miles, in 3:07½, beating a field of good horses, amongst which were Eole, Getaway and Compensation; won the Sequel Stakes for three-year olds, 1¾ miles, in 3:21; track heavy. In this race Hindoo carried 123 lbs., including a penalty of five pounds, and beat Greenland and Valentino; won the United States Hotel Stakes, 1½ miles, in 2:36, beating Crickmore, Bonfire and Gladiola; won the Kenner Stakes for three-year olds, 2 miles, in 3:32—a fast race. Monmouth Park, won the Champion Stakes for all ages, 1¼ miles, in 2:39, beating Monitor and Parole; won the Jersey St. Leger for three-year olds, 1½ miles, in 3:18, carrying 123 lbs., Bona Fide the only other starter. Sheepshead Bay, won race of mile heats, in 1:42¾, 1:45¼, Sir Hugh the only other starter; won a dash of one mile in 1:43, beating Sir Hugh and Edendary; was second in the Brighton Beach Purse, 1¼ miles, won by Crickmore

Continued on page 76.

PEDIGREE OF HINDOO.

HINDOO.	VIRGIL.	Vandal.	Glencoe.	Sultan.	Selim.	Buzzard—Dau. of Alexander—Dau. of Highflyer—Dau. of Alfred—Dau. of Engineer—Bay Malton's dam by Cade—Lass of the Mill.
					Bacchante.	Williamson's Ditto—Sis. to Calomel by Mercury—Dau. of Herod—Folly by Marske—Vixen by Regulus—Dau. of Hutton's Spot.
			Alaric's dam.	Tramp-oline.	Tramp.	Dick Andrews—Dau. of Gohanna—Fraxinella by Trentham—Dau. of Woodpecker—Everlasting by Eclipse—Hyaena by Snap.
					Web.	Waxy—Penelope by Trumpator—Prunella by Highflyer—Promise by Snap —Julia by Blank—Spectator's dam by Partner—Bonny Lass.
		Hymenia.	Luellla.	Tranby.	Blacklock.	Whitelock—Dau. of Coriander—Wildgoose by Highflyer—Coheiress by Pot-8-os—Manilla by Goldfinder—Dau. of Old England.
					Daughter of.	Orville—Miss Grimstone by Weasel—Dau. of Ancaster—Dau. of Dam Arabian—Dau. of Sampson—Dau. of Oroonoko—Sis. to Mirza.
				St. Nicholas.	Trumpator.	Sir Solomon—Dau. of Hickory—Imp. Trumpetta by Trumpator—Sis. to Lambinos by Highflyer—Dau. of Eclipse—Vauxball Snap's dam by Cade.
					Lucy.	Orphan—Lady Grey by Robin Grey—Maria by Melzar—Dau. of Imp. Highflyer—Dau. of Im. Fearnought—Dau. of Ariel—Dau. of Jack of Diamonds.
				Miss Rose.	Emilius.	Orville—Emily by Stamford—Dau. of Whiskey—Gr. Dorimant by Dorimant—Dizzy by Blank—Dizzy by Driver—Dau. of Smiling Tom.
			Yorkshire.		Seamew.	Scud—Goosander by Hambletonian—Rally by Trumpator—Fancy, Sis. to Diomed by Florizel—Dau. of Spectator—Horatia by Blank.
		Little Peggy.	Peggy Stewart.	Cripple.	Tramp.	Dick Andrews—Dau. of Gohanna—Fraxinella by Trentham—Dau. of Woodpecker—Everlasting by Eclipse—Hyaena by Snap—Miss Belsea.
					Daughter of.	Sancho—Blacklock's dam by Coriander—Wildgoose by Highflyer—Coheiress by Pot-8-os—Manilla by Goldfinder—Dau. of Old Eng.
				Grecian Princess	Medoc.	Am. Eclipse—Y. Maid of the Oaks by Imp. Expedition—Miad of the Oaks by Spread Eagle—Annette by Imp. Shark—Dau. of Rockingham.
					Cook's Whip (same as Blackburn's Whip)—Jane Hunt by Hampton's Paragon—Moll by Imp. Figure—Old Slamerkin by Imp. Wildair.
				Mary Bedford.	Blackburn's Whip.	Imp. Whip—Speckleback by Randolph's Celer (Meade's Celer dam by Sloe)—Speckleback by Meade's Celer—Dau. of Imp. Sober John (Rib).
						Duke of Bedford—Dau. of Speculator (Dragon)—Dau. of Dare Devil (Magnet)—Imp. Trumpetta by Trumpator—Sis. to Lambinos by Highflyer.
	FLORENCE.	Lexington.	Boston.	Sister to Timoleon.	Sir Archy.	Diomed—Castianira by Rockingham—Tabitha by Trentham—Dau. of Bosphorus—Dau. of Wm.'s Forester—Dau. of Coalition Colt.
					Daughter of.	Imp. Saltram (Eclipse)—Dau. of Symme's Wildair—Dau. of Driver (Imp. Othello)—Dau. of Fallower (Blank)—Dam of Vampire (Regulus).
				Tu'kahoe.	Ball's Florizel.	Diomed—Dau. of Imp. Shark—Dau. of Harris' Eclipse—Dau. of Fearnought—Dau. of Jolly Roger—Dau. of Sober John—Dau. of Imp. Shock.
					Daughter of.	Alderman—Dau. of Clockfast—Dau. of Symme's Wildair—Kitty Fisher by Fearnought—Imp. Kitty Fisher by Cade—Dau. of Cullen Arabian.
			Alice Carneal.	Sarpedon	Emilius.	Orville—Emily by Stamford—Dau. of Whiskey—Gr. Dorimant by Dorimant—Dizzy by Blank—Dizzy by Driver—Dau. of Smiling Tom.
					Icaria.	The Flyer—Parma by Dick Andrews—May by Beningbrough—Primrose by Mambrino—Cricket by Herod—Sophia by Blank.
				Rowena.	Sumpter.	Sir Archy—Flirtilla's dam by Robin Redbreast—Dau. of Obscurity—Old Slamerkin by Wildair—Imp. Cub Mare by Cub—Amaranthus' dam.
					Lady Grey.	Robin Gray—Maria by Melzar—Dau. of Imp. Highflyer—Dau. of Imp. Fearnought—Dau. of Ariel—Dau. of Imp. Jack of Diamonds.
		Weatherbit.	Sheet Anchor.		Lottery.	Tramp—Mandane by Pot-8-os—Y. Camilla by Woodpecker—Camilla by Trentham—Coquette by Compton Rarb—Sis. to Regulus.
					Morgiana.	Muley—Miss Stephenson by Scud or Sorcerer—Sis. to Petworth by Precipitate—Dau. of Woodpecker—Sis. to Juniper by Snap—Y. Marske's dam.
			Miss Letty.		Priam.	Emilius—Cressida by Whiskey—Y. Giantess by Diomed—Giantess by Matchem—Molly Longlegs by Babraham—Dau. of Cole's Foxhunter.
					Daughter of:	Orville—Dau. of Buzzard—Hornpipe by Trumpator—Luna by Herod—Proserpine Sis. to Eclipse by Marske—Spiletta by Regulus.
		Weather-Witch.	Daughter of.	Irish Birdcatcher.	Sir Hercules.	Whalebone—Peri by Wanderer—Thalestris by Alexander—Rival by Sir Peter—Hornet by Drone—Manilla by Goldfinder.
					Guiccioli.	Bob Booty—Flight by I. Escape—Y. Heroine by Bagot—Heroine by Hero —Dau. of Snap—Sis. to Regulus by G. Arabian—Gr. Robinson.
				Colocynth.	Physician.	Brutandorf, (Blacklock)—Primette by Prime Minister—Miss Paul By Sir Paul (Sir Peter)—Miss Dunnington by Shuttle—Miss Grimstone.
					Camelina.	Whalebone (Waxy)—Dau. of Selim (Buzzard)—Maiden by Sir Peter—Dau. of Phoenomenon (Herod)—Matron by Florizel—Maiden by Matchem (Cade)—Dau. of Squirt (Syphon)—Lot's dam by Mogul (Godolphin)—Camilla by Boy Bolton (Grey Hautboy)—Old Lady, Starling's dam by Pullein's Chestnut Arabian—Dau. of Rockwood—Dau. of Bustler.

HINDOO—Continued.

in 2:36½; was third in the September handicap, 1¾ miles, won by Crickmore, in 3:03, Hindoo carrying 123 lbs.

As a four-year-old, started six times and won five races. Louisville, Ky., won the Louisville Cup, 2¼ miles, in 3:57¾, beating Checkmate, Glidelia, Lida Stanhope and Blazes.

Won the Merchants' Stakes for all ages, one mile and a furlong, in 1:59½, beating Checkmate, Runnymede and Creosote. Won the Turf Stakes, 1¼ miles, in 2:08½, carrying 122 lbs, beating Checkmate (aged), 123 lbs., and Creosote (4), 114 lbs. Sheepshead won the Coney Island Stakes, for three-year-olds and upwards, one mile and a furlong, in 1:57¾, Barrett being the only other starter; won the Coney Island Cup, 2¼ miles, in 3:58, beating Eole and Parole. This was the best race run at the distance during the year, and compares favorably with similar races. There is no question but that Hindoo was the best race-horse which has appeared in this country for more than a decade. It is doubtful if any horse in England could have beaten him in the great classic events. Hindoo is a nicely bred horse, his blood combining all the best strains in England and America, his sire is by the best son of Glencoe, and he has a large infusion of Diomed blood through both sides, together with a double cross of imp. Buzzard, fortified by the stout crosses Whalebone, Herod and Eclipse on the dam's side. We shall expect to see him a great success in the stud. Hindoo is a dark bay, 15 hands 3¼ inches high, with large star in his forehead, right hind foot white to pastern; he is symmetrically shaped all over or he could not have done what he did.

HUBBARD,

(WINNER OF JULY STAKES AND GRAND SWEEPSTAKES, FOUR MILE HEATS, AT LONG BRANCH.)

Will stand for mares at the stables of his owner in California, by private contract. Application to Jas. B. Chase, San Francisco, Cal.

Hubbard by Planet, son of Revenue, bred at Woodburn Stud, Ky., foaled 1868, dam Minnie Mansfield, by imp. Glencoe, out of Argentile, by Old Bertrand, son of Sir Archy. Hubbard, as a two-year old, started four times, and won one race, Monmouth Park, won the July Stakes, three-quarters of a mile in 1:22, beating Experience, Oaks, and two others; was third in the Thespian Stakes for two-year olds, three-quarters of a mile, won by Malita, in 1:19¼, and unplaced in the other two races. Three years old, started in six races, winning two. Baltimore, Md., won the Dixie Stakes for three-year olds, 2 miles, in 3:36½, beating Joe Daniels's True Blue and six others. Saratoga, won a sweepstake for three-year olds, 2 miles, in 3:53, beating imp. Buckden, Nevada, and Gorlitza. Jerome Park, was second in the Annual Sweepstakes for three-year olds, won by Joe Daniels, in 3:45¾. Saratoga, was second in the Summer Handicap, 2¼ miles, won by Defender, in 4:24½, and was unplaced in his other races. As a four-year old, started in eight races, of which he won three. Monmouth Park, won the Grand Sweepstakes for all ages, four-mile heats, distancing Wheatly and Bessie Lee in the first heat, run in 7:37½. Saratoga won a dash of three miles, in 5:34, beating Wanderer, Harry Bassett, and King Henry. Won dash of 2¾ miles in 4:58¾, the fastest on record, beating Boss Tweed and Katy Pease, the only other starters. Monmouth Park, was third in the Mammoth Cup, 2½ miles, won by Wanderer, in 4:34½. Jerome Park, was third in the Jockey Club Handicap, 2 miles, won by Preakness, in 3:38½. Was second in a dash of 1¾ miles, won by Mate in 3:09¼. Saratoga, was third in a dash of 2 miles won by True Blue, in 3:32½, Mate was second. Was unplaced in his other races.

Hubbard has covered only a few thoroughbred mares. Is the sire of some few winners—viz., Warwick, Jim Farley, and Rebecca. He is inbred to Sir Archy and Diomed, in addition to his cross of Glencoe and Trustee. The family is a racing one, and capable of staying a distance. In addition to his crosses of Sir Archy, he traces through a long line of distinguished ancestry to the Old Vintner mare.

PEDIGREE OF HUBBARD.

HUBBARD.	PLANET.	Revenue.	Trustee.	Emma. Catton.	Golumpus.	Gohanna—Catharine by Woodpecker—Camilla by Trentham—Coquette by Compton Barb—Sis. to Regulus by Godol. Arabian—Gr. Robinson.
					Lucy Grey.	Timothy—Lucy by Florizel—Frenzy by Eclipse—Dau. of Engineer—Dau. of Blauk—Lass of the Mill by Traveler—Miss Makeless.
			Rosalie Somers.	Sir Charles. Mischief.	Whisker.	Waxy—Penelope by Trumpator—Prunella by Highflyer—Promise by Snap—Julia by Blank—Spectator's dam by Partner—Bonny Lass.
					Gibside Fairy.	Hermes—Vicissitude by Pipator—Beatrice by Sir Peter—Pyrrha by Matehem—Duchess by Whitenose—Miss Slamerkin.
					Sir Archy.	Diomed—Castianira by Rockingham—Tabitha by Trentham—Dau. of Bosphorus—Dau. of Wm.'s Forester—Dau. of Coalition Colt.
					Daughter of.	Citizen—Dau. of Commutation—Dau. of Dare Devil—Sally Shark by Imp. Shark—Betsey Pringle by Fearnought—Jenny Dismal.
					Virginian.	Sir Archy—Meretrix by Magog—Narcissa by Imp. Shark—Rosetta by Imp. Centinel—Diana by Clodius—Sally Painter.
					Daughter of.	Imp. Bedford—Dau. of Bellair—Dau. of Imp. Shark—Dau. of Symme's Wildair—Dau. of Lexington (Wildair)—Dau. of Spanking Roger.
		Nina.	Boston.	Sister to Tuckahoe. Timoleon.	Sir Archy.	Diomed—Castianira by Rockingham—Tabitha by Trentham—Dau. of Bosphorus—Dau. of Wm.'s Forester—Dau. of Coalition Colt,
					Daughter of.	Imp. Saltram—Dau. of Symme's Wildair—Dau. of Driver (Imp. Othello)—Dau. of Fallower (Blank)—Dan. of Vampire (Regulus).
					Ball's Florizel.	Diomed—Dau. of Imp. Shark—Dau. of Harris' Eclipse—Dau. of Fearnought—Dau. of Jolly Roger—Dau. of Sober John (Rib)—Dau. of Imp. Shock.
					Daughter of.	Alderman—Dau. of Clockfast—Dau. of Symme's Wildair—Kitty Fisher by Fearnought—Imp. Kitty Fisher by Cade—Dau. of Som. Arabian.
			Frolicksome Fanny.	Sister to Lottery. Catterick.	Tramp.	Dick Andrews—Dau. of Gohanna—Fraxinella by Trentham—Dau. of Woodpecker—Everlasting by Eclipse—Hyaena by Snap.
					Mandane.	Pot-8-os—Y. Camilla by Woodpecker—Camilla by Trentham—Coquette by Compton Barb—Sis. to Regulus by G. Arabian—Gr. Robinson.
					Whisker.	Waxy—Penelope by Trumpator—Prunella by Highflyer—Promise by Snap—Julia by Blank—Spectator's dam by Partner.
					Daughter of.	Bay Trophonius—Dau. of Slope (Highflyer)—Lardella by Y. Marske—Dau. of Cade—Beaufremont's dam by Bro. to Fearnought.
	MINNIE MANSFIELD.	Glencoe.	Sultan.	Selim.	Buzzard.	Woodpecker—Misfortune by Dux—Curiosity by Snap—Dau. of Regulus—Dau. of Bart. Childers—Dau of Hon. Arabian.
					Castrel's Dam.	Alexander—Dau. of Highflyer—Dau. of Alfred—Dau. of Engineer—Bay Malton's dam by Cade—Lass of the Mill by Traveler.
				Bacchante.	Williamson Ditto.	Sir Peter—Arethusa by Dungannon—Dau. of Prophet—Virago by Snap—Dau. of Regulus—Sis. to Othello by Crab—Miss Slamerkin.
					Sis. to Calomel.	Mercury—Dau. of Herod—Folly by Marske—Vixen by Regulus—Dau. of Hutton's Spot—Dau. of Bay Bolton—Dau. of Fox Cub.
			Trampolige.	Tramp.	Dick Andrews.	Joe Andrews—Dau. of Highflyer—Dau. of Cardinal Puff—Dau. of Tatler—Dau. of Snip—Dau. of G. Arabian—Dan. of Whiteneck.
					Daughter of.	Gohanna—Fraxinella by Trentham—Dau. of Woodpecker—Everlasting by Eclipse—Hyaena by Snap—Miss Belsea.
				Web.	Waxy.	Pot-8-os (Eclipse)—Maria by Herod—Lisette by Snap—Miss Windsor by G. Arabian—Sis. to Volunter by Y. Belgrade—Dau. of B. Childers.
					Penelope.	Trumpator—Prunella by Highflyer—Promise by Snap—Julia by Blank—Spectator's dam by Partner—Bonny Lass by Bay Bolton.
		Bertrand.	Sir Archy.		Diomed.	Florizel—Sis. to Juno by Spectator—Horatia by Blank—Dau. of F. Childers—Miss Belvoir by Gr. Grantham—Dau. of Paget Turk.
					Castianira.	Rockingham—Tabitha by Trentham—Dau. of Bosphorus—Dau. of Wm.'s Forester—Dau. of Coalition Colt, (Godol.)—Dau. of Bustard (Crab).
			Eliza.		Imp. Bedford.	Dungannon (Eclipse)—Fairy by Highflyer—Fairy Queen by Y. Cade—Routh's Blackeyes by Crab—Warlock Galloway by Snake (Lister Turk).
					Imp. Mambrina.	Mambrino—Sis. to Naylor's Sally by Blank (Godol.)—Dau. of Ward (Crab)—Dau. of Merlin (Bustler)—Dau. of Pert (Ely Turk)—Dau. of St. Martins.
		Alegrante.	Young Truffle.		Truffle.	Sorcerer—Hornby Lass by Buzzard—Puzzle by Matchem—Princess by Herod—Dau. of Blank—Spectator's dam by Partner.
					Helen.	Whiskey—Br. Justice by Justice—Xenia by Challenger (Herod)—Xantippe by Eclipse—Grecian Princess by Wm.'s Forester—Dau. of Coal. Colt.
		Argentile.	Phantomia.		Phantom.	Walton—Julia by Whiskey—Y. Giantess by Diomed—Giantess by Matchem—Molly Longlegs by Babraham—Dau. of Cole's Foxhunter.
					Daughter of.	Walton—Alegrante by Pegasus (Eclipse)—Orange Squeezer by Highflyer—Mop-Squeezer by Matchem (Cade)—Lady by Turner's Sweepstakes (Old Sweepstakes)—Shuttle's dam by Patriot (Bay Bolton)—Dau. of Crab (Alcock Arabian)—Sis. to Sloven by Bay Bolton (Grey Hautboy)—Dau. of Curwen Bay Barb—Dau. of Snot (Selaby Turk)—Dau. of Whitelegged Lowther Barb—Old Vintner Mare.

HURRAH (Imp.)

Will stand the season of 1883 *at the Stud Farm of his owner, John Reber, near Lancaster, Ohio, at* $30 *the season. Mares not proving in foal can be returned next season. Application to John Reber, Lancaster, Ohio.*

HURRAH by Newminster, son of Touchstone, bred by the Rawcliff Stud Co., foaled 1862, dam Jovial by Bay Middleton, son of Sultan, out of sis. to Grey Momus by Comus. Newminster, his sire, won the St. Leger in 1851, was son of Touchstone (winner of the St. Leger, in 1834), and the celebrated Beeswing, by Dr. Syntax, who won the Doncaster Cup in 1837 and also in 1840, 1841, and 1842, the only time any animal ever accomplished the feat, carrying in 1840 and 1841 126 lbs. Bay Middleton, sire of his dam, was winner of the Derby in 1836.

Hurrah, as a two-year old, started eleven times, won two races, was second in three, and unplaced in the others. Newmarket, won plate for two-years-olds, 5 furlongs 140 yards, beating Zephyr and six others; ran second to Tragedy in sweepstake, 5 furlongs 182 yards, beating Bessy. Shrewsbury, ran second to Peignoir in the Racing Plate, one mile, beating Procella and Teddy. Ran second to Antoinette in the Acton Burnel Stakes, three-quarters of a mile, defeating Princess Dagmar; won a Handicap plate, three-quarters of a mile, beating Usher; was unplaced in his other races. At three-year old, started twelve times, won one race, was third in one, and unplaced in the others. Won Selling Race, three-quarters of a mile, at West Drayton, defeating Little Pickles and Linus. At four years old, ran ten races, was second in one, third in two, and unplaced in the others.

Hurrah is one of the most fashionable bred sires of the present day. Independent of his good looks and soundness, he is one of the stoutest bred animals living. He is a rich bay, without white, over 16 hands high, has capital legs and feet, straight, grand action; is also sound in every respect, being free from curbs, spavin, roaring, or any other hereditary disease. He cannot be said to have had a fair chance in the stud, as he has only covered a few good fashionable mares, being located in a section where there are not many breeders of thoroughbreds. The best of his get are Chaquita, winner of a mile in 1:44¼, 2 miles in 3:37, the Fordham Handicap at Jerome Park, 1¼ miles, in 2:11¼, Dill Wiggins, mile in 1:45; 2 miles, 3:36; Huckleberry, Burgoo, a winner of many races; Lady Amanda, Lady Mack, Waller, a winner with high weights; Bonnie Lizzie, three-quarters of a mile heats in 1:15¼ and 1:14¼, 5 furlongs in 1:02¼, and other good races; Ohio Boy, Lady Middleton, Hermit, Dispute, Bonnie Ford, Reber, Louise Gwynne, Little Buttercup, Hippogriff, Lady Blandy, George IV., Nightcap, Nellie Peyton, Red Fox, Tramway, Fanny Cook, Medusa, Wauculla, Brad (Stand Off), Referee, Monk, Hostage, Maniac, and others that were winners. He has a combination of speedy and stout blood, and his daughters should prove valuable in the stud. He traces on both sides to Eclipse and Herod, through reputable horses, to the Burton Barb mare.

PEDIGREE OF HURRAH (Imp.)

HURRAH. (Imp.)									
NEWMINSTER.	Touchstone.	Camel.	Whalebone.	Waxy.	Pot-8-o's—Maria by Herod—Lisette by Snap—Miss Windsor by Godol. Arabian—Sis. to Volunteer by Y. Belgrade—Dau. of Bart. Childers.
				Penelope.	Trumpator—Prunella by Highflyer—Promise by Snap—Julia by Blank—Spectator's dam by Partner—Bonny Lass by Bay Bolton.
			Master Henry.	Selim.	Buzzard—Castrel's dam by Alexander—Dau. of Highflyer—Dau. of Alfred Dau. of Engineer—Bay Malton's dam by Cade—Lass of the Mill.
			Dau. of	Maiden.	Sir Peter—Dau. of Phoenomonon—Matron by Florizel—Maiden by Matchem—Dau. of Squirt—Lot's dam by Mogul—Camilla by Bay Bolton.
		Banter.		Orville.	Beningbrough—Evelina by Highflyer—Termagant by Tantrum—Cantatrice by Sampson—Dau. Regulus—Marske's dam by Blacklegs.
				Miss Sophia.	Stamford—Sophia by Buzzard—Huncamunca by Highflyer—Cypher by Squirrel—Fribble's dam by Regulus—Dau. of Bart. Childers.
	Beeswing.	Dr. Syntax.	Paynator.	Alexander.	Eclipse—Grecian Princess by Wm.'s Forester—Dau. of Coalition Colt—Dan. of Bustard (Crab)—Charming Molly by Second—Dau. of Stan Arabian.
				Brunette.	Amaranthus (Old Eng.)—Mayfly by Matchem—Dau. of An. Starling—Dau. of Grasshopper—Dau. of Newton Arabian—Dau. of Pert
			Boadicea.	Trumpator.	Conductor (Matchem)—Brunette by Squirrel—Dove by Matchless—Dau. of An. Starling—Dau. of Grasshopper—Dau. of New. Arabian.
			Dau. of	Daughter of.	Mark Anthony (Spectator)—Signora by Snap—Miss Windsor by Gold. Arabian—Sis. to Volunteer by Y. Belgrade—Dau. of Bart. Childers.
		Daughter of.	Androssan.	Beningbrough.	King Fergus (Eclipse)—Dau. of Herod—Pyrrha by Matchem—Duchess by Whitenose—Miss Slamerkin by Y. True Blue.
			Lady Eliza.	Jenny Mole.	Carbuncle—(Babraham)—Dau. of Prince T. Quassaw (Snip)—Dau. of Regulus (Godol.)—Dau. of Partner (Jigg).
				John Bull.	Fortitude (Herod) Zantippe by Eclipse—Grecian Princess by Wm.'s Forester—Dau. of Coalition colt—Dau. of Bustard (Crab)—Charming Molly.
				Miss Whip.	Volunteer (Eclipse) Wimbleton by Evergreen (Herod)—Sis. to Calash by Herod—Teresa by Matchem—Dau. of Regulus—Sis. to An. Starling.
				Whitworth.	Agonistes (Sir Peter)—Dau. of Jupiter (Eclipse)—Dau. of Highflyer—Dau. of Matchem—Sis. to Pioneer by Old Eng—Dau. of Traveler.
				Daughter of,	Spadille (Highflyer)—Sylvia by Y. Marske—Ferret by Bro. to Silvio.—Dau. Regulus—Dau. of Morton Arabian—Dau. of Mixbury.
JOVIAL.	Sister to Grey Momus.	Bay Middleton.	Sultan.	Buzzard.	Woodpecker—Misfortune by Dux—Curiosity by Snap—Dau. of Regulus—Dau. of Bart. Childers—Dau. of Honeywood Arabian.
				Castrel's dam.	Alexander—Dau. of Highflyer—Dau. of Alfred—Dau. of Engineer—Bay Malton's dam by Cade—Lass of the Mill by Traveler.
			Cobweb.	Williamson's Do	Sir Peter—Arethusa by Dungannon—Dau. of Prophet (Regulus)—Virago by Snap—Dau. of Regulus—Sis. to Othello by Crab.
				Sister to Calomel	Mercury (Eclipse)—Dau. of Herod—Folly by Marske—Vixen by Regulus—Dau. of Hutton's Spot—Dau. of Bay Bolton.
			Phantom.	Walton.	Sir Peter—Arethusa by Dungannon—Dau. of Prophet—Virago by Snap—Dau. of Regulus—Sis. to Othello by Crab.
			Filagree.	Julia.	Whiskey—Y. Giantess by Diomed—Giantess by Matchem—Molly Longlegs by Babraham—Dau. of Cole's Foxhunter.
		Comus.	Sorcerer.	Soothsayer.	Sorcerer—Goldenlocks by Delpini—Violet by Shark—Dau. of Syphon—Quick's Charlotte by Blank—Dau. of Crab—Dau. of Dyer's Dimple.
				Web.	Waxy—Penelope by Trumpator—Prunella by Highflyer—Promise by Snap Julia by Blank—Spectator's dam by Partner.
	Daughter of.	Houghton Lass.	Bacchante.	Trumpator.	Conductor—Brunette by Squirrel—Dove by Matchless (Godol.)—Dau. of An. Starling—Dau. of Grasshopper—Dau. of New. Arabian.
				Young Giantess.	Diomed—Giantess by Matchem—Molly Longlegs by Babraham—Dau. of Cole's Foxhunter—Sis. to Cato by Partner—Sis. to Roxana.
			Selim.	Sir Peter.	Highflyer—Papillon by Snap—Miss Cleveland by Regulus—Midge, by Son of Bay Bolton—Dau. of Bart. Childers—Dau. of Hon. Arabian.
				Alexina.	King Fergus—Lardella by Y. Marske—Dau. of Cade—Beaufremont's dam by Bro. to Fearnought—Miss Windham by Windham.
		Emma.	Cervantes.	Don Quixote.	Eclipse—Grecian Princess by Wm's Forester—Dau. of Coalition colt—Dau. of Bustard (Crab)—Charming Molly by Second—Hanger's Br. Mare
				Evelina.	Highflyer—Termagant by Tantrum—Cantatrice by Sampson—Dau. of Regulus—Marske's dam by Blacklegs—Dau. of Bay Bolton.
				Don Cossack.	Haphazard—Alderney by Skyscraper—Caelia by Volunteer—Sis. to Pharamond by Highflyer—Giantess by Matchem—Molly Longlegs.
				Vesta.	Delpini (Highflyer)—Faith by Pacolet (Blank)—Atalanta by Matchem (Cade)—Lass of the Mill by Oroonoko (Crab)—Dau. of Traveler (Partner)—Miss Makeless by Young Greyhound (Greyhound by Chillaby Barb)—Dau. of Partner (Jigg)—Miss Doe's dam by Woodcock (Merlin)—Dau. of Croft's Bay Barb—Desdemona's dam by Makeless (Oglethorpe's Arabian)—Old Thornton by Brimmer (D'Arcy Y. Turk)—Dau. of Dicky Pierson (Dodsworth)—Burton Barb Mare.

HYDER ALI,

(WINNER OF THE CHAMPAGNE STAKES AT JEROME PARK,)

Will stand the season of 1883 *at the Meadows Stud, near Carlinville, Ill., at* $50 *the Season. Application to Gen. Rich, Rowett, Carlinville, Ill. Annual Sales at Chicago, in June.*

HYDER ALI by imp. Leamington, son of Faugh-a-Ballagh, bred by A. Welch Erdenheim Stud, Pa., foaled 1872, dam Lady Duke, by Lexington, out of Magdalen, dam of Bonnie Lassie, Bonnie Laddie, etc., by Medoc, son of American Eclipse. Hyder Ali as a three-year old started in three races, of which he won one. Jerome Park, won the Champagne Stakes for two-year olds, three-quarters of a mile in 1:20, beating James, A, Finework, and six others; was beaten in a match race of $2,500 each, three-quarters of a mile, won by James A, in 1:19; was third in a dash of three-quarters of a mile, won by James A, in 1:18½. He was injured in the spring of his three-year old year, and did not run again. His dam, Lady Duke, was not trained, and had only a few foals, amongst them Mary Buckley, a good mare and dam of Buckstone. Magdalen his grandam was a good race-mare, and the dam of the great race-mare Bonnie Lassie, and the horse Bonnie Laddie which had great reputation in their day. Bonnie Lassie won the Association Stakes, mile heats, and the Citizen's Stake, 2 mile heats, at Lexington, Ky., in 1857. She won many important races in the South. Gossamer, another sister to Bonnie Lassie was dam of Leather Lungs, La Rose and Gossip, the latter dam of Lida Gaines. The Sumpter Mare dam of Magdalen was the dam of Keph, and Leda both successful racers. Hyder Ali is a large, well developed horse, full 16 hands high, with great substance and power. In addition to his being a son of Leamington, he is strongly inbred on the dam's side to Sir Archy and Diomed, having six crosses of that inestimable blood upon a large infusion of Medley blood, and thence to the noted Gimcrack by Cripple, son of Godolphin Arabian (Barb). Upon the matrons of the Meadows Stud we expect to record his success.

PEDIGREE OF HYDER ALI.

HYDER ALI.	IMP. LEAMINGTON.	Daughter of Pantaloon.	Faugh-a-Ballagh.	Sir Hercules.	Waxy.	Pot-8-os—Maria by Herod—Lisette by Snap—Miss Windsor by Godol. Arabian—Sis. to Volunteer by Y. Belgrade—Dau. of Bart. Childers.
				Whalebone.	Penelope.	Trumpator—Prunella by Highflyer—Promise by Suap—Julia by Blank—Spectator's dam by Partner—Bonny Lass by Bay Bolton.
			Guiccioli.	Bob Booty.	Wanderer.	Gohanna—Catharine by Woodpecker—Camilla by Trentham—Coquette by Compton Barb—Sis. to Regulus by Godol. Arabian—Gr. Robinson.
				Perl.	Thalestris.	Alexander—Rival by Sir Peter—Hornet by Drone—Manilla by Goldfinder—Dau. of Old Eng.—Dau. of Cullen Arabian.
			Flight.	Castrel.	Chanticleer.	Woodpecker—Dau. of Eclipse—Rosebud by Snap—Miss Belsca by Regulus—Dau. of Bart. Childers—Dau. of Honeywood's Arabian.
					Ierne.	Bagot—Heroine by Hero—Dau. of Snap—Sis. to Regulus by Godol. Arabian—Dau. of Gamahoe—Patty by Tim—Miss Patch by Justice—Ringtail Galloway by Cur. Bay Barb—Sis. to Witty Mare by Pelham's Hip.
		Daughter of.	Idalia.		Irish Escape.	Commodore—Buffer's dam by Highflyer—Shift by Sweetbriar—Bl. Susan by Snap—Dau. of Cade—Dau. of Belgrade—Dau. of Clif. Arabian.
					Young Heroine.	Bagot—Heroine by Hero—Dau. of Snap—Sis. to Regulus by Godol. Arabian—Gr. Robinson by Bald Galloway—Dau. of Snake.
			Laurel.		Buzzard.	Woodpecker—Misfortune by Dux—Curiosity by Snap—Dau. of Regulus—Dau. of Bart. Childers—Dau. of Hon. Arabian.
					Selim's dam.	Alexander—Dau. of Highflyer—Dau. of Alfred—Dau. of Engineer—Bay Malton's dam by Cade—Lass of the Mill by Traveler—Miss Makeless.
		Daphne.	Maid of Honor.		Peruvian.	Sir Peter—Dau. of Budrow—Escape's dam by Squirrel—Dau. of Babraham—Dau. of Golden Ball—Bushy Molly by Hamp. Court Childers.
					Musidora.	Meteor—Maid of All Work by Highflyer—Sis. to Tandem by Syphon—Dau. of Regulus—Dau. of Snip—Dau. of Cottingham—Warlock Galloway.
					Blacklock.	Whitelock—Dau. of Coriander—Wildgoose by Highflyer—Coheiress by Pot-8-os—Manilla by Goldfinder—Dau. of Old Eng.
					Wagtail.	Prime Minister—Dau. of Orville—Miss Grimstone by Weasel—Dau. of Ancaster—Dau. of Dam Arabian—Dau. of Sampson—Dau. of Oroonoko.
					Champion.	Selim—Podagra by Gouty—Jet by Magnet—Jewel by Squirrel—Sophia by Blank—Diana by Second—Han. Br. Mare by Stanyan Arabian.
					Etiquette.	Orville—Boadicea by Alexander—Brunette by Amaranthus—Mayfly by Matchem—Dau. of An. Starling—Dau. of Grasshopper.
	LADY DUKE.	Magdalen.	Lexington.	Boston.	Sir Archy.	Diomed—Castianira by Rockingham—Tabitha by Trentham—Dau. of Bosphorus—Dau. of Wm's Forester—Dau. of Coalition Colt (Godol.)
				Timoleon.	Daughter.	Imp. Saltram (Eclipse)—Dau. of Symme's Wildair—Dau. of Driver (Imp. Othello)—Dau. of Fallower (Blank)—Dau. of Vampire (Regulus).
			Alice Carneal.	Sister to Tuckahoe.	Ball's Florizel.	Diomed—Dau. of Shark—Dau. of Harris' Eclipse—Dau. of Imp. Fearnought—Dau. of Jolly Roger—Dau. of Sober John—Dau. of Shock.
				Sarpedon.	Daughter of.	Alderman—Dau. of Clockfast—Dau. of Symme's Wildair—Y. Kitty Fisher by Fearnought—Imp. Kitty Fisher by Cade—Dau. of Som. Arabian.
		Keph's dam.	Medoc.	Am. Eclipse.	Emilius.	Orville—Emily by Stamford—Dau. of Whiskey—Gr. Dorimant by Dorimant—Dizzy by Blank—Dizzy by Driver—Dau. of Smiling Tom.
					Icaria.	The Flyer—Parma by Dick Andrews—May by Beningbrough—Primrose by Mambrino—Cricket by Herod—Sophia by Blank—Diana.
			Sump-ter.	Rowena.	Sumpter.	Sir Archy—Flirtilla's dam by Robin Redbreast—Dau. of Obscurity—Slamerkin by Wildair—Imp. Cub Mare by Cub—Amaranthus' dam.
					Lady Grey.	Robin Grey—Maria by Melzar—Dau. of Highflyer—Dau. of Fearnought—Dau. of Ariel—Dau. of Jack of Diamonds.
		Dau. of.	Y. Maid of the Oaks.		Duroc.	Diomed—Amanda by Grey Diomed—Dau. of Va. Cade—Dau. of Hickman's Independence—Dolly Fine by Imp. Silvereye—Dau. of Imp. Badger.
					Millers Damsel.	Messenger—Dau. of Pot-8-os—Dau. of Gimcrack—Snap Dragon by Snap—Dau. of Regulus—Dau. of Bart. Childers.
					Imp. Expedition	Pegasus (Eclipse)—Active by Woodpecker—Laura by Whistle Jacket (Mogul)—Pretty Polly by Starling—Sis. to Diana by Second (Childers).
					Maid of the Oaks.	Spread Eagle (Volunteer)—Annette by Shark—Dau. of Rockingham—Dau. of Gallant—Dau. of True Whig—Dau. of Imp. Regulus.
					Sir Archy.	Diomed—Castianira by Rockingham—Tabitha by Trentham—Dau. of Bosphorus—Dau. of Wm's Forester—Dau. of Coalition Colt (Godol.)
					Flirtilla's dam.	Robin Redbreast—Dau. of Imp. Obscurity—Slamerkin by Wildair—Imp. Cub Mare by Cub—Amaranthus' dam by Second—Dau. of Starling.
					Lewis' Eclipse.	Diomed—Bellona by Harris' Eclipse (Partner)—Nettle by Granby (Blank)—Nell Gwynn by Imp. Janus—Poll Flaxen by Imp. Jolly Roger.
					Maria.	Craig's Alfred (Imp. Medley)—Dau. of Tayloe's Bellair (Imp. Medley)—Dau. of Imp. Medley (Gimcrack by Cripple by Godol.)

ILL-USED (Imp.)

(WINNER OF THE SEQUEL AND KENNER STAKES, AT SARATOGA, 1873,)

Will be used as private stallion in the Nursery Stud, Hon. A. Belmont, proprietor, near Babylon, L. I., N. Y. Yearlings sold annually in June.

ILL-USED by Breadalbane, own brother to Blair Athol, son of Stockwell, bred by Col. Townley, foaled 1870, dam Ellermire, dam of Elland, by Chanticleer, 2d dam Ellerdale, dam of Formosa, winner of the One Thousand Guineas, Oaks and St. Leger in 1868, by Lanercost, out of the dam of Colsterdale, by Tomboy. Ill-Used made his first appearance on the turf as a three-year old in the Belmont Stakes, won by Springbok, but getting a bad start was unplaced. He won two races out of three starts. At Saratoga won the Sequel Stakes, 2 miles in 3:40¼, beating Fellowcraft and four others. Same place won the Kenner Stakes, 2 miles, in 3:39, beating imp. Strachino, Springbok, Waverly, Whisper, Catesby and other good horses. This closed his turf career. Breadalbane his sire is own brother to Blair Athol, and although he did not win any of the great events, the Derby or Leger, he won the Prince of Wales Stakes at Ascot, the Gratwicke Produce Stakes, 1¼ miles at Goodwood, and other good races. Ellermire his dam won eight races, at three-years old, including two Queen's Plates for mares. Ellerdale, his grandam, was also a winner of several important events, including the Great Yorkshire Stakes. Lanercost her sire was third in the St. Leger to Don John, and won the Ascot Gold Cup, and Cambridgeshire Handicap. He has covered only one or two mares outside of those in the nursery, and has gotten some very reputable performers. Forester won as two-years old, and in 1882 won the Withers Stake, one mile, in 1:46¼, Belmont Stakes 1½ miles, in 2:43, the Barnegat Stakes, 1⅜ miles at Long Branch in 2:54, carrying 123 lbs. ; and Jersey Derby, 1¼ miles. Jack of Hearts, the Mid-summer Handicap at Long Branch, one mile in 1:48¼, the Harvest Handicap, 1¼ miles in 2:11, and a Club Purse, 1¼ mile in 1:56¼, beating Clara D and Parole. Other winners by him are Bellona (Jessie D), 1¼ miles in 2:11, 1¼ miles in 1:58 ; Olivia five furlongs in 1:01¾, Mosquito, Topsy, Woodcraft, Woodflower, winner of two out of three races ; Jacobus, Felicia, Gertie M, Florimel, Delilah, Clara, Carnation, Camillus, and others, It would be difficult to find in the Stud Book, a higher bred horse than Ill-Used. He has a double cross of Whalebone through the famous Irish Birdcatcher, and five other Waxy crosses through Whisker, Web, Pyrrha, Kiss, etc., in addition to a Glencoe cross through Pocahontas and Melbourne through Blink Bonny. Ill-Used is a blood bay 15 hands 2¼ inches high, with a half moon star in his forehead, near fore and hind legs white to the ankle, off hind foot white around the coronet, and white hairs at the root of his tail showing his Birdcatcher descent. He is full of substance and symmetry all over, and is destined to make his mark in the stud.

PEDIGREE OF ILL-USED (Imp.)

								Ancestor	Pedigree
ILL-USED. (Imp.)	BREADALBANE.	Blink Bonny.	Melbourne.	Humphrey Clinker.	Gladiator.	Stockwell.	The Baron.	Sir Hercules.	Whalebone—Peri by Wanderer—Thalestris by Alexander—Rival by Sir Peter—Hornet by Drone—Manilla by Goldfinder—Dau. of Old Eng.
								Guicciolli.	Bob Booty—Flight by I. Escape—Y. Heroine by Bagot—Heroine by Hero —Dau. of Snap—Sis. to Regulus by Godol. Arabian.
							Echidna.	Economist.	Whisker—Floranthe by Octavian—Caprice by Anvil—Madcap by Eclipse —Dau. of Blank—Dau. of Blaze—Dau. of Y. Greyhound.
								Miss Pratt.	Blacklock—Gadabout by Orville—Minstrel by Sir Peter—Matron by Florizel—Maiden by Matchem—Dau. of Squirt.
						Pocahontas.	Irish Birdcatcher.	Sultan.	Selim—Bacchante by Williamson's Ditto—Sis. to Calomel by Mercury— Dau. of Herod—Folly by Marske—Vixen by Regulus.
								Trampoline.	Tramp—Web by Waxy—Penelope by Trumpator—Prunella by Highflyer— Promise by Snap—Julia by Blank—Spectator's dam by Partner.
							Glencoe.	Muley.	Orville—Eleanor by Whiskey—Y Giantess by Diomed—Giantess by Matchem—Molly Longlegs by Babraham—Dau. of Cole's Foxhunter.
								Clare.	Marmion—Harpalice by Gohanna—Amazon by Driver—Fractious by Mercury—Dau. of Woodpecker—Everlasting by Eclipse—Hyaena by Snap.
			Queen Mary.	Dau. of			Marpessa.	Comus.	Sorcerer—Houghton Lass by Sir Peter—Alexina by King Fergus—Lardella by. Y Marske—Dau. of Cade—Beaufremont's dam by Bro. to Fearnought.
								Clinkerina.	Clinker—Pewet by Tandem—Termagant by Tantrum—Cantatrice by Sampson—Dau. of Regulus—Marske's dam by Blacklegs.
								Cervantes.	Don Quixote—Evelina by Highflyer—Termagant by Tantrum—Cantatrice by Sampson—Dau. of Regulus—Marske's dam by Blacklegs.
								Daughter of.	Golumpus—Dau. of Paynator—Sis. to Zodiac by St. George—Abigail by Woodpecker—Firetail by Eclipse—Dau. of Blank—Naylor by Cade.
								Partisan.	Walton—Parasol by Pot-8-os—Pruuella by Highflyer—Promise by Snap— Julia by Blank—Spectator's dam by Partner—Bonny Lass.
								Pauline.	Moses—Quadrille by Selim—Canary Bird by Whiskey or Sorcerer—Canary by Coriander—Miss Green by Highflyer—Harriet by Matchem.
								Plenipotentiary.	Emilius—Harriet by Pericles—Dau. of Selim—Pipylina by Sir Peter—Rally by Trumpator—Fancy, Sis. to Diomed by Florizel—Sis. to Juno.
								Myrrha.	Whalebone—Gift by Y. Gohanna, to Grazier by Sir Peter—Sis. to Amaitor by Trumpator—Dau. of Herod—Dau. of Snap.
	ELLERMIRE.	Chanticleer.	Whim.	Irish Birdcatcher.	Sir (Guicciolli.)	Irish Drone.	Sir Hercules.	Whalebone.	Waxy—Penelope by Trumpator—Prunella by Highflyer—Promise by Snap—Julia by Blank—Spectator's dam by Partner—Bonny Lass.
								Peri.	Wanderer—Thalestris by Alexander—Rival by Sir Peter—Hornet by Drone—Manilla by Goldfinder—Dau. of Old Eng.
								Bob Booty.	Chanticleer—Irene by Bagot—Dau. of Gamahoe—Patty by Tim (Squirt)— Miss Patch by Justice—Ringtail Galloway by Curwen Bay Barb.
								Flight.	I. Escape—Y. Heroine by Bagot—Heroine by Hero (Cade)—Dau. of Snap —Sis. to Regulus by Godol. Arabian—Gr. Robinson by Bald Galloway.
								Master Robert.	Buffer (Prizefighter)—Spinster by Shuttle—Dau. of Sir Peter—Bab by Bordeaux (Herod)—Speranza by Eclipse—Virago by Snap.
								Daughter of.	Sir Walter Raleigh (Waxy)—Miss Tooley by Teddy the Grinder—Lady Jane by Sir Peter—Paulina by Florizel—Captive by Matchem.
		Ellerdale.	Lanercost.	Liverpool.	Otis.			Waxy.	Pot-8-os—Maria by Herod—Lisette by Snap—Miss Windsor by Godol. Arabian—Sis. to Volunteer by Y. Belgrade—Dau. of Bart. Childers.
								Miss Stavely.	Shuttle—Dau. of Drone (Herod)—Dau. of Matchem—Jocasta by Cornforth's Forester—Sis. to Y. Cade by Cade—Dau. of Chanter.
								Tramp.	Dick Andrews—Dau. of Gohanna—Fraxinella by Trentham—Dau. of Woodpecker—Everlasting by Eclipse—Hyaena by Snap (Snip).
								Daughter of.	Whisker—Mandane by Pot-8-os—Y. Camille by Woodpecker—Camilla by Trentham—Coquette by Compton Barb—Sis. to Regulus.
					Kiss.			Bustard.	Buzzard—Gipsy by Trumpator—Sis. to Postmaster by Herod—Dau. of Gower Stallion (Godol.)—Dau. of F. Childers.
								Gayhurst's dam.	Election—Sis. to Skysweeper by Highflyer—Dau. of Eclipse—Rosebud by Snap—Miss Belsea by Regulus—Dau. of Bartlet's Childers.
		Daughter of.	Tesane.	Tomboy.				Jerry.	Smolensko—Louisa by Orville—Thomasina by Timothy (Delpini)—Violet by Shark—Dau. of Syphon—Charlotte by Blank.
								Beeswing's dam.	Ardrossan (Jn Bull)—Lady Eliza by Whitworth (Agonistes)—Dau. of Spadille—Sylvia by Y. Marske—Ferret by Bro. to Silvio—Dau. of Regulus.
								Whisker.	Waxy—Penelope by Trumpator—Prunella by Highflyer—Promise by Snap —Julia by Blank—Spectator's dam by Partner—Bonny Lass.
								Lady of the Tees.	Octavian—Dau. of Sancho (Herod)—Miss Fury by Trumpator (Conductor)—Dau. of Mark Anthony (Spectator)—Signora by Snap (Snip)— Miss Windsor by Godolphin Arabian—Sister to Volunteer by Young Belgrade (Belgrade Turk)—Dau. of Bartlet's Childers (Dar. Arabian)—Dau. of Dov. Ch. Arabian—Sis. to Westbury by Curwen Bay Barb—Dau. of Old Spot (Selaby Turk)—Dau. of Woodcock (Old Merlin).

IROQUOIS,

(WINNER OF THE CHESTERFIELD STAKES AT NEWARKET AND LEVANT STAKES AT GOODWOOD, 1880 ; THE BURWELL STAKES, DERBY AT EPSOM, PRINCE OF WALES STAKES, DONCASTER ST. LEGER, NEWMARKET DERBY, AND OTHER IMPORTANT EVENTS IN ENGLAND,)

Will be located upon his return from England in the Rancocas Stud, Mr P. Lorillard, proprietor, near Jobstown, Burlington Co., N. J., as private stallion.

IROQUOIS by imp. Leamington, son of Faugh-a-Ballagh, bred by Mr. A. Welch, Erdenheim Stud, foaled 1878, dam Maggie B. B., dam of Harold, by imp. Australian; 2d dam Madeline, by Old Boston, out of Magnolia dam of Kentucky, by imp. Glencoe. As a two-year-old Iroquois started 12 times, won four races, was second in two and unplaced in six. He made his bow to the public by winning the Newmarket two-year-old Plate 5 furlongs, defeating Herman, Kuhleborn and three others; his second success was winning the two-year-old stakes at Epsom 5 furlongs, beating Eliacin. At the Newmarket July Meeting ran Bal Gal to a head for the July stakes, 5 furlongs 136 yards, having Neophite, Thebais and seven others behind him; same meeting won the Chesterfield Stakes 5 furlongs, beating Panique, Voluptuary and seven others ; at Goodwood won the Levant Stakes, 5 furlongs, defeating Isola Madre, Canace and three others ; same meeting ran second to Wandering Nun in the Findon Stakes three-quarters of a mile, with Albion, Ishmael and Worthing behind him ; he was unplaced in his other races. As a three-year-old made his first appearance by running second to Peregrine in the 2000 guineas, having Don Fulano, Camiliard, Scobel and nine others behind him; won the Newmarket Stakes, Ditch mile, beating Lennoxlove; Newmarket Second Spring Meeting walked over for the Burwell Stakes, Abingdon mile ; Epsom Summer Meeting won the 102d renewal of the Derby Stakes 1½ miles, defeating Peregrine, Town Moor, Scobel, Geologist, St. Louis, Don Fulano, Tristan and seven others. Ascot won the Prince of Wales Stakes, 1⅜ miles, defeating Geologist, Great Carle and four others ; same place won the St. James Place Stakes Old mile, beating Leon his only opponent. Doncaster September Meeting won the Doncaster St. Leger Stakes, one mile six furlongs, 132 yards, defeating Geologist, Lucy Glitters, St. Louis, Falkirk, Bal Gal and nine others. Newmarket Second October Meeting was third to Bend'Or, and Scobel in Champion Stakes across the flat one mile two furlongs and 73 yards ; Buckhannon, Falkirk, Muriel and Fiddler behind him ; won the Newmarket Derby 1¼ miles, beating Ishmael, Lennoxlove and Ld. Clemsford. Thus starting in nine races running second for the 2,000 guineas, third in the Champion Stakes, and winning the Derby and St. Leger, a feat only accomplished nine times in the one hundred and three years it has been run. Surplace in 1848, Flying Dutchman in 1849, Voltigeur in 1850, West Australian 1853, Blair Athol in 1864, Gladiateur in 1865, Lord Lyon in 1866, Silvio in 1877, and Iroquois in 1881; not one of all these won so many good races in the same year. Iroquois is a brown, 16 hands high with white stripe down the face and white around the coronet of the left fore foot; he has a well placed oblique shoulder, good barrel, fine hip and loin and sound good legs and feet. We shall expect to see him a grand success in the stud.

PEDIGREE OF IROQUOISE.

IROQUOISE.							Ancestry
IMP. LEAMINGTON.	Faugh-a-Ballagh.	Sir Hercules.	Whalebone.	Waxy.		Pot-8-os—Maria by Herod—Lisette by Snap—Miss Windsor by Godol. Arabian—Sis. to Volunteer by Y. Belgrade—Dau. of Bart. Childers.
				Penelope.		Trumpator—Prunella by Highflyer—Promise by Snap—Julia by Blank—Spectator's dam by Partner—Bonny Lass by Bay Bolton.
		Guiccioli.	Bob Booty.	Wanderer.		Gohanna—Catharine by Woodpecker—Camilla by Trentham—Coquette by Compton Barb.—Sis. to Regulus by Godol. Arabian—Gr. Robinson.
				Thalestris.		Alexander—Rival by Sir Peter—Hornet by Drone—Manilla by Goldfinder—Dau. of Old Eng.—Dau. at Cul Arabian—Miss Cade by Cade.
				Chanticleer.		Woodpecker—Dau. of Eclipse—Rosebud by Snap—Miss Belsea by Regulus—Dau. of Bart. Childers—Dau. of Hon. Arabian—Dam of True Blues.
				Ierne.		Bagot—Dau. of Gamahoe—Patty by Tim—Miss Patch by Justice—Ringtail Galloway by Cur. Bay Barb—Sis. to Witty Mare by Pelham's Hip.
				Irish Escape.		Commodore—Dau. of Highflyer—Shift by Sweetbriar—Bl. Susan by Snap—Dau. of Cade—Dau. of Belgrade—Dau. of Clif. Arabian.
				Young Heroine.		Bagot—Heroine by Hero—Dan. of Snap—Sis. to Regulus by Godol. Arabian—Grey Robinson by Bald Galloway—Dau. of Snake—Gr. Wilkes.
	Daughter of.	Pantaloon.	Castrel.	Buzzard.		Woodpecker—Misfortune by Dux—Curiosity by Snap—Dau. of Regulus—Dau. of Bart. Childers—Dau. of Hon. Arabian—Dam of True Blues.
				Daughter of.		Alexander—Dau. of Highflyer—Dau. of Alfred—Dau. of Engineer—Bay Malton's dam by Cade—Lass of the Mill by Traveler—Miss Mekeless.
				Peruvian.		Sir Peter—Dau. of Boudrow—Escape's dam by Squirrel—Dau. of Babraham—Dau. of Golden Ball—Busby Molly by Ham. Ct. Childers.
			Idalia.	Musidora.		Meteor—Maid of all Work by Highflyer—Sis. to Tandem by Syphon—Dau. of Regulus—Dau. of Snip—Dau. of Cottingham—War Galloway.
		Daphne.	Laurel.	Blacklock.		Whitelock—Dau. of Coriander—Wildgoose by Highflyer—Coheiress by Pot-8-os—Manilla by Goldfinder—Dau. of Old Eng.—Dau. of Cul. Arabian.
				Wagtail.		Prime Minister—Dau. of Orville—Miss Grimstone by Weasel—Dau. of Ancaster—Dau. of Dam Arabian—Dau. of Sampson—Dau. of Oroonoko.
			Maid of Honor.	Champion.		Selim—Podagra by Gouty—Jet by Magnet—Jewel by Squirrel—Sophia by Blank—Diana by Second—Hanger's Br. Marc.
				Etiquette.		Orville—Boadicea by Alexander—Brunette by Amaranthus—Mayfly by Matchem—Dau. of An. Starling—Dau. of Grasshopper.
MAGGIE B. B.	Madeline.	Imp. Australian.	West Australian.	Melbourne.	Humphrey Clinker.		Comus—Clinkerina by Clinker—Pewet by Tandom—Termagant by Tantrum—Cantatrice by Sampson—Dau. of Regulus—Marske's dam.
					Daughter of.		Cervantes—Dau. of Golumpus—Dau. of Paynator—Sis. to Zodiac by St. George—Abigail by Woodpecker—Firetail by Eclipse—Dau. of Blank.
				Mowerina.	Touchstone.		Camel—Banter by Master Henry—Boadicea by Alexander—Brunette by Amaranthus—Mayfly by Matchem—Dau. of An. Starling.
					Emma.		Whisker—Gibside Fairy by Hermes—Vicissitude by Pipator—Beatrice by Sir Peter—Pyrrha by Matchem—Duchess by Whitenose.
		Emilia.	Young Emilius.	Emilius.			Orville—Emily by Stamford—Dau. of Whiskey—Gr. Dorimant by Dorimant—Dizzy by Blank—Dizzy by Driver—Dau. of Smiling Tom.
				Shoveler.			Scud—Goosander by Hamiltonian—Rally by Trumpator—Fancy, Sis. to Diomed by Florizel—Dau. of Spectator—Horatia by Blank.
			Persian.	Whisker.			Waxy—Penelope by Trumpator—Prunella by Highflyer—Promise by Snap—Julia by Blank—Spectator's dam by Partner—Bonny Lass.
				Variety.			Selim or Soothsayer—Sprite by Bobtail—Catharine by Woodpecker—Camilla by Trentham—Coquette by Compton Barb—Sis. to Regulus.
	Boston.	Sister to Tuckahoe.	Timoleon.	Sir Archy.			Diomed—Castianira by Rockingham—Tabitha by Trentham—Dau. of Bosphorus—Dau. of Wm.'s Forester—Dau. of Coalition Colt.
				Daughter of.			Imp. Saltram—Dau. of Symme's Wildair—Dau. of Driver (Othello)—Dau. of Imp. Fallower (Blank)—Dau. of Imp. Vampire (Regulus).
				Ball's Florizel.			Diomed—Dau. of Imp. Shark—Dau. of Harris' Eclipse—Dau. of Imp. Fearnought—Dau. of Imp. Jolly Roger—Dau. of Imp. Sober John (Rib).
				Daughter of.			Alderman—Dau. of Imp. Clockfast—Dau. of Symme's Wildair—Kitty Fisher by Fearnought—Imp. Kitty Fisher by Cade.
	Magnolia.	Glencoe.	Sultan.				Selim—Bacchante by Williamson's Ditto—Sis. to Calomel by Mercury—Dau. of Herod—Folly by Marske—Vixen by Regulus—Dau. of Spot.
			Trampoline.				Tramp—Web by Waxy—Penelope by Trumpator—Prunella by Highflyer—Promise by Snap—Julia by Blank—Spectator's dam by Partner.
		Myrtle.	Mameluke.				Partisan—Miss Sophia by Stamford—Sophia by Buzzard—Huncamunca by Highflyer—Cypher by Squirrel—Fribble's dam by Regulus.
			Bobadilla.				Bobadil (Rubens)—Pythoness by Sorcerer (Trumpator)—Princess by Sir Peter (Highflyer)—Dau. of Dungannon (Eclipse)—Dau. of Herod (Tartar)—Golden Grove by Blank (Godol.)—Spinster by Partner (Jigg)—Bay Bloody Buttocks by Bloody Buttock's Arabian—Sis. to Guy by Greyhound (White Barb Chillaby)—Brown Farewell by Makeless (Oglethorpe Arabian)—Dau. of Brimmer (D'Arcy Yellow Turk)—Dau. of Place's White Turk—Dau. of Dodsworth—Layton Barb Mare.

KING ALFONSO,

(WINNER OF THE KENTUCKY ST. LEGER, TOBACCO STAKES AND GALT HOUSE STAKE AT LOUISVILLE, KY., AND THE LINCK'S HOTEL STAKE AT NASHVILLE, TENN., ALL IN 1875,)

Will stand the season of 1883 at the Woodburn Stud, near Spring Station, Ky., A. J. Alexander, proprietor, at $100 the season. Application to L. Brodhead, Spring, Ky. Annual sales of yearlings in May.

KING ALFONSO by imp. Phaeton, son of King Tom, bred by Warren Viley, Esq., Stonewall Stud, near Midway, Ky., foaled 1872, dam Capitola, dam of Belle Barclay, and Hospodar by Vandal, son of Glencoe out of Margravine, Versaille's dam by imp. Margrave.

King Alfonso's turf career was short but brilliant; he made his *debut* at Lexington, Ky., Sept. 6, 1875, in a sweepstake for three-year olds, one mile and a furlong, 90 lbs. on each. Bob Woolley won in 1:54, the fastest race ever run at the distance; King Alfonso was a close second, with Katie Pearce, Ten Broeck, Elemi and Redman behind him. Sept. 9, was unplaced in sweepstakes for three- ear olds, one mile and 5 furlongs; won by Ten Broeck in 2:49¼, the fastest race ever run at that distance to that date, Bob Woolley being second. Louisville, Ky., Sept. 20, won the Kentucky St. Leger, two miles, in 3:34½, beating Ten Broeck, second; Verdegris, third; Geo. Graham, Voltigeur and five others. Same place, Sept. 24, won the Tobacco Stakes, mile heats, for three-year olds, in 1:44½, 1:45¼, beating Gyptis, Misdeal and three others. The next day, Sept. 25, won the Galt House Stakes, two mile heats, in 3:34, 3:40½, 3:49, beating George Graham, who won the first heat by a head from King Alfonso, the last quarter of the heat being run in 24 seconds, Emma C., Add, and two others. This stamped him not only as a fast, but game horse. He closed the season and his turf career by winning the Linck's Hotel Stakes, at Nashville, mile heats, in 1:45, 1:47¾, beating Misdeal, Asterlite, and three others. He was trained the spring of 1876, when four years old, and showed himself a better horse than ever, but in a very fast trial struck his leg and was thrown out of training, and sold to A. J. Alexander and placed in the Woodburn Stud.

The family has always, as a racing one, ranked one of the best in America. The Albert Mare produced the famous Tiger Gelding and Black-eyed Susan, a superior racemare, dam of Dick Singleton, Plato, Mistletoe, Dick Johnson, Catharine, etc. Dick Singletoe defeated the great Collier, four mile heats; Mistletoe won the match between Kentucky and Tennessee. Mistletoe was the dam of Evergreen, by imp. Glencoe, who produced Goodwood, Maggiore, Verbena, Glendower and others, and Margravine, the dam of Mary Churchill, Tourist, Capitola, The Grand Dutch S., Versailles, etc. Mary Churchill was the dam of Hamburg, Wade Hampton, winner of the Sequel Stakes at Long Branch and Saratoga in 1872, by Asteroid, and Nettie Viley, she the dam of Conductor, Mirah, etc. The Grand Dutch S. was the dam of Yandell and Lizzie Whips, both fine race nags.

King Alfonso is sire of Fonso, winner of the Phoenix Hotel Stakes, 1¼ miles, in 2:10¾, beating Kinkead, Luke Blackburn and others, and Kentucky Derby, 1½ miles, in 2:37½, the fastest it was ever run, with 105 lbs. Grenada, the winner of the Potomac Stakes, 1¼ miles, in 2:39¼, and Preakness Stakes, both at Baltimore, Belmont, Jerome and Lorillard Stakes at Jerome Park, Coney Island Derby, at Sheepshead Bay, and Dixie Stakes at Baltimore, 2 miles, in 3:38, winning $32,000, as three-year old. At 4 years old, won 4 out of 6 starts. Peyton Handicap at Baltimore, mile heats, in 1:43¼, 1:43¼, 1:47½; Oden won second heat. Other winners by him are Quito Lavacca. Dodette, Ladies' Stake, at Chicago. Telemachus, 1¾ miles, in 2:09¼, Go Forth, Alfambra, May Wilson, Mollie Brown, 5 furlongs in 1:02, Edison, Duke of Montalban, Mary S., Lost Cause, Windrush, 2 miles in 3:33½, and again in 3:36¼, Bayadere, Bob Johnson, Infanta, winner of Elizabeth Stakes at Long Branch, Issie, winner of Ashland Oaks, Lexington, Ky., Katie Creel, winner of the Kentucky Oaks at Louisville, 1½ miles, 2:39, and Illinois Oaks, Chicago. Arno, Lady Prewitt, The Judge (Cordova), Lorca, Mary S., Olivette, Vera, Don Fulana and Golden Gate, raced creditably in England, and Foxhall won two out of three stakes in which he started at two years old, beating the best colts of the year, and giving weight. He won the Grand Prix de Paris in 1881, and is the second horse that ever won the Cesarewitch and Cambridge Handicaps in England in one and the same year. The first was Rosebery, a four-year old, carrying in the Cesarewitch, 103 lbs., and in Cambridgeshire 117 lbs. Foxhall, a three-year old, carried in the first 110, and in the latter 126 lbs., beating

Continued on page 90.

PEDIGREE OF KING ALFONSO.

KING ALFONSO.							
IMP. PHÆTON.	King Tom.	Harkaway.	Fanny Economist.	Whisker.	Waxy—Penelope by Trumpator—Prunella by Highflyer—Promise by Snap—Julia by Blank—Spectator's dam.
				Floranthe.	Octavian—Caprice by Anvil—Madcap by Eclipse—Dau. of Blank—Dau. of Blaze—Dau. of Y. Greyhound—Dau. of Curwen Bay Barb.
		Pocahontas.	Glencoe.	Nabocklish.	Rugantino—Butterfly by Master Bagot—Dau. of Bagot (Herod)—Mother Brown by Trunnion—Dau. of Old Eng.—Dau. of Bol. Starling.
				Miss Tooley.	Teddy the Grinder—Lady Jane by Sir Peter—Paulina by Florizel—Captive by Matchem—Calliope by Slouch—Lass of the Mill by Oroonoko.
	Merry Sunshine.	Marpessa.		Sultan.	Selim—Bacchante by Williamson's Ditto—Sis. to Calomel by Mercury—Dau. of Herod—Folly by Marske—Vixen by Regulus.
				Trampoline.	Tramp—Web by Waxy—Penelope by Trumpator—Prunella by Highflyer—Promise by Snap—Julia by Blank—Spectator's dam by Partner.
			Touchstone.	Muley.	Orville—Eleanor by Whiskey—Y. Giantess by Diomed—Giantess by Matchem—Molly Longlegs by Babraham—Dau. of Cole's Foxhunter.
				Clare.	Marmion—Harpalice by Gohanna—Amazon by Driver—Fractious by Mercury—Dau. of Woodpecker—Everlasting by Eclipse—Hyaena.
		Storm.		Camel.	Whalebone—Dau. of Selim—Maiden by Sir Peter—Dau. of Phoenomenon—Matron by Florizel—Maiden by Matchem—Dau. of Squirt—Lot's dam.
				Banter.	Master Henry—Boadicea by Alexander—Brunette by Amaranthus—Mayfly by Matchem—Dau. of An. Starling—Dau. of Grasshopper (Crab).
	Sis. to Pompey.	Ghuznee.	Falstaff.	Pantaloon.	Castrel—Idalia by Peruvian—Musidora by Meteor—Maid of All Work by Highflyer—Sis. to Tandem by Syphon—Dau. of Regulus—Dau. of Snip.
				Languish.	Cain—Lydia by Poulton—Variety by Hyacinthus—Sis. to Swordsman by Weasel—Dau. of Turk—Dau. of Locust—Dau. of Changeling.
	Daughter of.			Touchstone.	Camel—Banter by Master Henry—Boadicea by Alexander—Brunette by Amaranthus—Mayfly by Matchem—Dau. of An. Starling.
				Decoy.	Filho-da-Puta—Finesse by Peruvian—Violante by John Bull—Dau. of Highflyer—Everlasting by Eclipse—Hyaena by Snap—Miss Belsea.
				Emilius.	Orville—Emily by Stamford—Dau. of Whiskey—Gr. Dorimant by Dorimant—Dizzy by Blank—Dizzy by Driver—Dau. of Smiling Tom.
				Variation.	Bustard—Johaunab Southcote by Beningbrough—Lavinia by Pipator—Dick Andrews' dam by Highflyer—Dau. of Cardinal Puff.
CAPITOLA.	Vandal.	Glencoe.	Sultan.	Selim.	Buzzard—Castrel's dam by Alexander—Dau. of Highflyer—Dau. of Alfred—Dau. of Engineer—Bay Malton's dam hy Cade (Godolphin).
				Bacchante.	Williamson's Ditto—Sis. to Calomel by Mercury—Dau. of Herod—Folly by Marske—Vixen by Regulus—Dau. of Hutton's Spot.
			Trampoline.	Tramp.	Dick Andrews—Dau. of Gohanna—Fraxinella by Trentham—Dau. of Woodpecker—Everlasting by Eclipse—Hyaena by Snap—Miss Belsea.
				Web.	Waxy—Penelope by Trumpator—Prunella by Highflyer—Promise by Snap—Julia by Blank—Spectator's dam by Partner—Bonny Lass.
		Alaric's dam.	Tranby.	Blacklock.	Whitelock—Dau. of Coriander—Wildgoose by Highflyer—Coheiress by Pot-8-os—Manilla by Goldfinder—Dau. of Old Eng.
				Daughter of.	Orville—Miss Grimstone by Weasel—Dau. of Ancaster—Dau. of Dam Arabian—Dau. of Sampson—Dau. of Oroonoko.
	Imp. Margrave.		Lucilla.	Trumpator.	Sir Solomon—Dau. of Hickory—Imp. Trumpetta by Trumpator—Sis. to Lambinos by Highflyer—Dau. of Eclipse—Dau. of Cade.
				Lucy.	Orphan—Lady Grey by Robin Grey—Maria by Melzar—Dau. of Imp. Highflyer—Dau. of Imp. Fearnought—Dau. of Ariel.
		Dau. of Muley.		Orville.	Beningbrough—Evelina by Highflyer—Termagant by Tantrum—Cantatrice by Sampson—Dau. of Regulus—Marske's dam by Blacklegs.
				Eleanor.	Whiskey—Y. Giantess by Diomed—Giantess by Matchem—Molly Longlegs by Babraham—Dau. of Cole's Foxhunter—Dau. of Partner.
	Mistletoe.			Election.	Gohanna—Ch. Skim by Woodpecker—Silver's dam by Herod—Y. Hag by Skim—Hag by Crab—Ebony by F. Childers—Ebony by Basto.
				Fair Helen.	Hambletonian—Helen by Delpini—Rosalind by Phoenomenon—Atalanta by Matchem—Lass of the Mill by Oroonoko—Dau. of Traveler.
		Black-eyed Cherokee.		Sir Archy.	Diomed—Castianira by Rockingham—Tabitha by Trentham—Dau. of Bosphorus—Dau. of Wm's Forester—Dau. of Coalition Colt (Godol.)
				Roxana.	Hepheston (Buzzard)—Roxana by Imp. Marplot (Highflyer)—Juliet by Imp. Mexican (Snap)—Dau. of Imp. Friar (South by Regulus).
		Black-eyed Susan.		Tiger.	Blackburn's Whip (Imp. Whip)—Jane Hunt by Paragon (Flimnap)—Moll by Imp. Figure—Slamerkin by Imp. Wildair—Imp. Cub Mare by Cub.
				Daughter of.	Albert (Americus by Shark)—Dau. of Algerine (Dey of Algiers)—Dau. of Grey Alfred (Lindsay's Arabian)—Dau. of Imp. Medley (Gimcrack by Cripple by Godolphin)—Dau. of Imp. Shark (by Marske, sire of O'Kelly's Eclipse)—Dau. of Imp. Fearnought by Regulus (Godolphin).

KING ALFONSO—Continued.

with the top weight Lucy Glitters (3), 91. Tristan (3), 107, Mistake (4), 102, Wallenstein (4), 97, and twenty-seven others. He won the Ascot Gold Cup in 1882, but has been amiss since.

King Alfonso is a red bay, 16 hands, with a star in his forehead, and is one of the truest and best shaped horses in the world; his head is plain but well shaped, and set upon a good, strong, muscular neck, with wide, deep throttle, the shoulders oblique, broad and well placed, and covered with suitable muscle; the chest is well shaped and full, with great depth of girth, the body full and round, with the finest back, hip and loin ever put on a horse, being broad, well rounded and slightly curved. He has great length from the point of the hip to the whirlbone, thence to the point of stifle and hocks, being full of strength and muscle, which run into broad, powerful hocks, the legs and feet being sound and good. His temper is of the best. In addition to his double cross of Glencoe, he has the Waxy blood through Web, Whisker and Whalebone, and is inbred to Sir Archy and imp. Shark, with many crosses of Herod and Eclipse in the collateral branches.

KING BAN (Imp.)

King Ban will be located at the Dixiana Stud Farm, near Lexington, Fayette Co., Ky., and will be permitted to serve 15 mares, at $150 the season. Application to be made to Maj. B. G. Thomas, Lexington, Ky.

KING BAN, son of King Tom, son of Harkaway, bred by Lord Falmouth, foaled 1875, dam Atlantis, dam of Happy-go-Lucky, Bower of Bliss, etc., by Thormanby, out of Hurricane, dam of Atlantic, Cataclysm, etc., by Wild Dayrell. King Ban only ran once as a two-year old; was second to Mourle, by Ruy Blas, in the Granby Stakes, three-quarters of a mile, run at Newmarket First October Meeting. At three years old, ran two races, Newmarket Craven Meeting, was unplaced in the Craven Stakes, Ancaster Mile, one mile 18 yards, won by Thurio with Sefton second; Newmarket First Meeting, ran second to Mida, by Parmesan, in the Coffee Room Stakes, across the flat, 1 mile 2 furlongs and 73 yards, Miss Rovel and King o' Scots behind him. Atlantis, his dam, started nine times as a two-year-old, won five races, was second in one, third in one, and unplaced in two. Newmarket Craven Meeting, won Sweepstakes for two-year-olds, last half mile of the Beacon Course, beating Violet and Canoe. Newmarker, First Spring Meeting, won Sweepstakes for two-year-olds, Rowley mile, beating Tit-Bit and Violet. Same meeting, walked over for a Sweepstakes, last half mile of the Two-year-old Course. Newmarket Second October Meeting, won the Clearwell Stakes, 5 furlongs, 140 yards, beating Sunlight and six others. Same meeting, won the Prendergast Stakes, same distance, defeating Atlas, Hawthornden and five others. King Tom, his sire, was by the great Harkaway, and although he is not credited with any of the great events of the turf, yet, he sired Tomato, winner of the 1,000 guineas, Tormentor and Hippia, winner of the Oaks, Hannah, winner of the 1,000 guineas, Oaks, and St. Leger, Kingcraft, winner of the Derby, Great Tom, Phæton, etc. Phæton sired Ten Broeck, King Alfonso, and other good ones. He also sired Old Calabar, Wingrave, Mainstone, Breeze, Prince Plausible, and others. Wild Dayrell, the sire of his grandam, won the Derby in 1855. Soothsayer, the sire of his great grandam, won the St. Leger in 1811, and Waxy, the Derby in 1793. The pedigree of King Ban is a happy combination of stout and speedy crosses, and he traces through first-class horses many times to Eclipse and Herod. The oldest of his get are two years old, and they have made a very creditable showing. Punster is one of the most promising two-year olds of the year. He has started nine times, and won five races. Won the St. Nicholas Hotel Stake, half a mile in .50¼, a Sweepstake for two-year-olds, half a mile, in .50½, both at Lexington. In these races he beat such good ones as Clipsetta, Vera, Wandering and others. Won the Alexander Stakes, at Louisville, 5 furlongs, in 1:03¼, beating Ascender, Bondholder, and eight others, and the Test Stakes, three-quarters of a mile in 1:15¾, defeating Bondholder, Clipsetta, Barnes, and Geo. Kenney. Won purse for two-year-olds, at Saratoga, 5 furlongs, in 1:03¼, defeating a field of seven. Queen Ban won three out of five races. The Blue Grass Stakes at Lexington, three-quarters of a mile, in 1:16, defeating Bellona, Miss Woodford and others, the West Va. Stakes, three-quarters of a mile, in 1:20, and a purse one mile in 1:58; both at White Sulphur, Va. Violator won three out of nine starts. The Selling Purse, half a mile, at Lexington, Ky., in .52, a purse, 5 furlongs, in 1:07, at St. Louis, and a purse, three-quarters of a mile, at Louisville, in 1:20. Ada Ban, another daughter was also a winner. King Ban is a rich chestnut, 16¼ hands high, with a star in his forehead. He is a horse of good shape and muscular development, which he imparts to his progeny in a remarkable degree. He traces through a long line of speedy and stout crosses to the Bryerly Mare, dam of the famous Two True Blues.

PEDIGREE OF KING BAN.

KING BAN.	KING TOM.	Harkaway.	Economist.		Waxy.	Pot-8-os—Maria by Herod—Lisette by Snap—Miss Windsor by Godol. Arabian—Sis. to Volunteer by Y. Belgrade.
					Penelope.	Trumpator—Prunella by Highflyer—Promise by Snap—Julia by Blank—Spectator's dam by Partner—Bonny Lass by Bay Bolton.
			Nabock-lish.	Florinthe.	Octavian.	Stripling (Phoenomenon)—Dau. of Oberon (Highflyer)—Sis. to Sharper by Ranthos (Matchem)—Dau. of Sweepstakes—Sis. to Careless by Spanker.
				Whisker.	Caprice.	Anvil (Herod)—Madcap by Eclipse—Dau. of Blank—Dau. of Blaze—Dau. of Y. Greyhound—Dau. of Cur. Bay Barb.
		Fanny Dawson.	Miss Tooley.		Rugantino.	Commodore (Tug)—Dau. of Highflyer—Shift by Sweetbriar (Syphon)—Black Susan by Snap (Snip)—Dau. of Cade—Dau. of Belgrade.
					Butterfly.	Master Bagot (Bagot)—Dau. of Bagot (Herod)—Mother Brown by Trunnion (Cade)—Dau. of Old England (Godolphin)—Dau. of Bay Bolton.
				Sultan.	Teddy the Grinder.	Asparagus (Pot-8-os)—Stargazer by Highflyer—Miss West by Matchem—Dau. of Regulus (Godol.)—Dau. of Crab—Dau. of F. Childers.
		Glencoe.			Lady Jane.	Sir Peter—Paulina by Florizel (Herod)—Captive by Matchem (Cade)—Calliope by Slouch (Cade)—Lass of the Mill by Oroonoko (Crab).
					Selim.	Buzzard—Dau. of Alexander (Eclipse)—Dau. of Highflyer—Dau of Alfred—Dau. of Engineer—Bay Malton's dam by Cade (Godol.)
					Bacchante.	Williamson's Ditto—Sis. to Calomel by Mercury—Dau. of Herod—Folly by Marske—Vixen by Regulus—Dau. of Hutton's Spot.
		Pocahontas.	Marpessa.	Trampoline.	Tramp.	Dick Andrews—Dau. of Gohanna—Fraxinella by Trentham—Dau. of Woodpecker—Everlasting by Eclipse—Hyaena by Snap.
					Web.	Waxy—Penelope by Trumpator—Prunella by Highflyer—Promise by Snap—Julia by Blank—Spectator's dam by Partner.
				Muley.	Orville.	Beningbrough—Evelina by Highflighr—Termagant by Tantrum—Cantatrice by Sampson—Dau. of Regulus—Marske's dam by Blacklegs.
					Eleanor.	Whiskey—Y. Giantess by Diomed—Giantess by Matchem—Molly Longlegs by Babraham—Dau. of Cole's Foxhunter—Dau. of Partner.
				Clare.	Marmion.	Whiskey—Y. Noisette by Diomed—Noisette by Squirrel—Carina by Marske—Dau. of Blank—Dizzy by Driver (Wynn Arabian).
					Harpalice.	Gohanna—Amazon by Driver (Trentham)—Fractious by Mercury—Dau. of Woodpecker—Everlasting by Eclipse—Hyaena by Snap.
	ATLANTIS.	Thormanby.	Alice Hawthorn.	Muley Moloch.	Castrel.	Buzzard—Dau. of Alexander—Dau. of Highflyer—Dau. of Alfred—Dau. of Engineer—Bay Malton's dam by Cade—Lass of the Mill.
				Melb. or Wind'hd.*	Idalia.	Peruvian (Sir Peter)—Musidora by Meteor (Eclipse)—Maid of all Work by Highflyer—Sis. to Tandem by Syphon—Dau. of Regulus.
				Phyrne Pantaloon.	Touchstone.	Camel—Banter by Master Henry—Boadicea by Alexander—Brunette by Amarauthus—Mayfly by Matchem—Dau. of Au. Starling.
					Decoy.	Filho-da-Puta—Finesse by Peruvian—Violante by John Bull—Dau. of Highflyer—Everlasting by Eclipse—Hyaena by Snap.
		Wild Dayrell.	Ion.		Muley.	Orville—Eleanor by Whiskey—Y. Giantess by Diomed—Giantess by Matchem—Molly Longlegs by Babraham—Dau. of Cole's Foxhunter.
					Nancy.	Dick Andrews—Spitfire by Beningbrough—Dau. of Y. Sir Peter (Doge)—Dau. of Engineer—Dau. of Wilson's Arabian—Dau. of Hutton's Spot.
					Lottery.	Tramp—Mandane by Pot-8-os—Y. Camilla by Woodpecker—Camilla by Trentham—Coquette by Compton Barb—Sis. to Regulus.
			Ellen Middleton.	Rebecca.	Daughter of.	Cervantes—Anticipation by Beningbrough—Expectation by Herod—Dau. of Skim (Starling)—Dau. of Janus (Godol.)—Spinster by Crab.
					Cain.	Panlowitz (Sir Paul)—Dau. of Paynator (Trumpator)—Dau. of Delpini—Dau. of Y. Marske—Gentle Kitty by Silvio—Dau. of Dorimond.
		Hurricane.			Margaret.	Edmund (Orville)—Medora by Selim—Dau. of Sir Harry (Sir Peter)—Dau. of Volunteer—Dau. of Herod—Golden Grove by Blank.
					Bay Middleton.	Sultan—Cobweb by Phantom—Filagree by Soothsayer—Web by Waxy—Penelope by Trumpator—Prunella by Highflyer.
		Midia.	Marinella.	Scutari.	Myrrha.	Malek (Blacklock)—Bessy by Y. Gouty—Grandiflora by Sir Harry Dimsdale (Sir Peter)—Dau of Pipator (Imperator)—Dau. of Phoenomenon.
					Sultan.	Selim—Bacchante by Williamson's Ditto—Sis. to Calomel by Mercury—Dan. of Herod—Folly by Marske—Vixen by Regulus.
					Velvet.	Oiseau (Camillus)—Wire by Waxy—Penelope by Trumpator—Prunella by Highflyer—Promise by Snap—Julia by Blank.
					Soothsayer.	Sorcerer—Goldenlocks by Delpini—Violet by Shark—Dau. of Syphon—Quick's Charlotte by Blank—Dau. of Crab—Dau. of Dyer's Dimple.
					Bess.	Waxy(Pot-8-os)—Vixen by Pot-8-os (Eclipse)—Cypher by Squirrel(Traveler) Fribble's dam by Regulus (Godolphin)—Dau. of Bartlet's Childers (Darley Arabian)—Dau. of Honeywood's Arabian—Byerly Mare, dam of the Two True Blues.

* Windhound given.

KING ERNEST (Imp.)

King Ernest is a private Stallion in the Brookdale Stud, situated in Monmouth Co., near Holmdel, N. J., the property of D. D. Withers, Esq.

KING ERNEST by King Tom, son of the great Irish horse Harkaway, bred by Sir L. Newman, foaled 1869, dam Ernestine dam of Stockhausen, Mamhead Lass, Chilton Lass etc., by Touchstone, winner of the St. Leger in 1834, son of Camel-by Whalebone, out of Lady Geraldine by the Colonel, winner of the St. Leger in 1828, son of Whisker winner of the Derby in 1815, by Waxy winner of the Derby in 1793. King Ernest never ran in public from an injury to one of his knees by falling on the pavement, but his private trials were of the best, and he was regarded as a very fast race-horse, his pedigree traces through a long line of distinguished winners, having a cross of Whalebone and a double cross of Whisker the own brother to Whalebone upon a strong foundation of the blood of Herod and Eclipse to the Byerly Mare dam of the Two True Blues. King Ernest has only covered a few mares, except those of his owners, and only a few altogether, yet he has sired some real good horses, their forte being speed. Amongst the best of his get are Jersey Lass winner of the Maryland Stakes at Jerome Park and dam of that most excellent three-year-old, Macduff ; Report, the winner of the Jockey Club Handicap at Jerome Park, two miles, in 3:36¼ ; four years old, carrying 108 lbs., one of the best races ever run on this slow course, defeating McCullough St. Martin, Harold, Ferida and others. At Long Branch, won the Long Branch Handicap, 1¼ miles, in 2:19¼ ; carrying 110 lbs., beating Ferida (4) 107 lbs. and two others. Same place won the Shrewsbury Handicap 1¾ miles, 108 lbs. defeating Uncas (4) 114 lbs., Ferida (4) 105 lbs., and Danicheff (5) 100 lbs., in 3:12½, and won the Monmouth Cup 115 lbs., 2¼ miles, in 4:07, defeating Monitor (4) 120 lbs., and Uncas (4) 121 lbs., Reporter a winner, Marathon also a winner, Gov. Shevlin, Maggie C, Kingcraft, a fast good horse, all winners. Ninus, Regicide, King Fan, Duplex, Retort. King Ernest is a blood bay; stands over 16 hands high, with small blaze in his face and snip on his nose; has broad forehead, with intelligent countenance, indicative of his amiable disposition and good temper ; neat, well-shaped head ; fine ear; jaws a little inclined to be massive; arched and rangy neck, running into a good-shaped, but rather upright shoulder ; good depth of girth, with round, well-shaped barrel ; good back and loin ; strong, wide hips, with good length from point of hip to whirlbone, and thence to the hock, which is bony and strong ; good, sound feet and legs. His daughters from his high breeding should prove valuable in the stud, and he will yet distinguish himself as a sire. To perpetuate the King Tom cross he should be bred to the daughters of Phaeton, King Ban, Great Tom, or to the daughters of King Alfonso and Ten Broeck.

PEDIGREE OF KING ERNEST.

KING ERNEST.	KING TOM.	Harkaway.	Economist.	Whisker.	Waxy.	Pot-8-os—Maria by Herod—Lissette by Snap—Miss Windsor by Godol. Arablan—Sis. to Volunteer by Y. Belgrade—Dau. of Bart. Childers.
					Penelope.	Trumpator—Prunella by Highflyer—Promise by Snap—Julia by Blank—Spectator's dam by Partner—Bonny Lass.
				Floranthe.	Octavian.	Stripling (Phonom)—Dau. of Oberon (Highflyer)—Sis. to Sharper by Ranthos (Matchem)—Dau. of Sweepstakes—Sis. to Hutton's Careless.
					Caprice.	Anvil (Herod)—Madcap by Eclipse—Dau. of Blank—Dau. of Blaze—Dau. of Greyhound—Dau. of Curwen Bay Barb.
			Fanny Dawson.	Nabocklish.	Rugantino.	Commodore (Tug) (Rover) by Herod—Buffer's dam by Highflyer—Shift by Sweetbriar—(Syphon)—Black Susan by Snap—Ld. Bruce's Cade Mare.
					Butterfly.	Master Bagot—Dau. of Bagot (Herod)—Mother Brown by Trunnion (Cade)—Dau. of Old Eng (Godol.)—Dau. of Bolton Starling.
				Miss Tooley.	Teddy the Grinder.	Asparagus (Pot-8-os)—Stargazer by Highflyer—Miss West by Matchem—Dau. of Regulus—Dau. of Crab—Dau. of F. Childers.
					Lady Jane.	Sir Peter—Pauline by Florizel—Captive by Matchem—Calliope by Slouch—Lass of the Mill by Oroonoko—Dau. of Traveler.
		Pocahontas.	Glencoe.	Sultan.	Selim.	Buzzard—Castrel's dam by Alexander—Dau. of Highflyer—Dau. of Alfred—Dau. of Engineer—Bay Malton's dam by Cade.
					Bacchante.	Williamson's Ditto—Sis. to Calomel by Mercury—Dau. of Herod—Folly by Marske—Vixen by Regulus—Dau. of Hutton's Spot.
				Trampoline.	Tramp.	Dick Andrews—Dau. of Gohanna—Fraxinella by Trentham—Dau. of Woodpecker—Everlasting by Eclipse—Hyaena by Snap.
					Web.	Waxy—Penelope by Trumpator—Prunella by Highflyer—Promise by Snap—Julia by Blank—Spectator's dam by Partner.
		Marpessa.	Muley.		Orville.	Beningbrough—Evelina by Highflyer—Termagant by Tantrum—Cantatrice by Sampson—Dau. of Regulus—Marske's dam.
					Eleanor.	Whiskey—Y. Giantess by Diomed—Giantess by Matchem—Molly Longlegs by Babraham—Dau. of Cole's Foxhunter—Dau. of Partner.
			Clare.		Marmion.	Whiskey—Y. Noisette by Diomed—Noisette by Squirrel—Carina by Marske—Dau. of Blank—An. Dizzy by Driver.
					Harpalice.	Gohanna—Amazon by Driver—Fractious by Mercury—Dau. of Woodpecker—Everlasting by Eclipse—Hyaena by Snap.
	ERNESTINE.	Touchstone.	Camel.	Whalebone.	Waxy.	Pot-8-os—Maria by Herod—Lisette by Snap—Miss Windsor by Godol. Arabian—Sis. to Volunteer by Y. Belgrade—Dau. of Bart. Childers.
					Penelope.	Trumpator—Prunella by Highflyer—Promise by Snap—Julia by Blank—Spectator's dam by Partner—Bonny Lass by Bay Bolton.
				Dau. of Selim.	Selim.	Buzzard—Castrel's dam by Alexander—Dau. of Highflyer—Dau. of Alfred—Dau. of Engineer—Bay Malton's dam by Cade.
					Maiden.	Sir Peter—Dau. of Phoenomenon—Matron by Florizel—Maiden by Matchem—Dau. of Squirt—Lot's dam by Mogul—Camilla by Bay Bolton.
			Banter.	Master Henry.	Orville.	Beningbrough—Evelina by Highflyer—Termagant by Tantrum—Cantatrice by Sampson—Dau. of Regulus—Marske's dam by Blacklegs.
					Miss Sophia.	Stamford—Sophia by Buzzard—Huncamunca by Highflyer—Cypher by Squirrel—Dau. of Regulus—Dau. of Bartlet's Childers.
				Boadicea.	Alexander.	Eclipse—Grecian Princess by Wm.'s Forester—Dau. of Coalition Colt—Dau.of Bustard(Crab)—CharmingMolly bySecond—Dau.of Stan.Arabian.
					Brunette.	Amaranthus (Old Eng.)—Mayfly by Matchem—Dau. of An. Starling—Dau. of Grasshopper—(Crab)—Dau. of New. Arabian—Dau. of Pert.
		Lady Geraldine.	The Colonel.	Whisker.	Waxy.	Pot-8-os—Maria by Herod—Lisette by Snap—Miss Windsor by Godol. Arabian—Sis. to Volunteer by Y. Belgrade—Dau. of Bart. Childers. Trumpator—Prunella by Highflyer—Promise by Snap—Julia by Blank—Spectator's dam by Partner—Bonny Lass by Bay Bolton.
					Penelope.	
				Dau. of Whisker.	Delpini.	Highflyer—Countess by Blank—Dau. of Rib (Crab)—Dau. of Wynn Arabian—Dau. of Governor—Dau. of Alcock Arabian.
					Tipple Cyder.	King Fergus—Sylvia by Y. Marske—Ferret by Bro. to Silvio—Dau. of Regulus—Dau. of Moreton Arabian—Dau. of Mixbury.
		Nurse.	Neptune.		Tiresias.	Soothsayer—Pledge by Waxy—Prunella by Highflyer—Promise by Snap—Julia by Blank—Spectator's dam by Partner.
					Rivulet.	Rubens—Sis. to Champion by Pot-8-os—Dau. of Highflyer—Cypher by Squirrel—Fribble's dam by Regulus—Dau. of Bart. Childers.
			Otis.		Bustard.	Buzzard—Gipsy, Sis. to Amaitor by Trumpator—Sis. to Postmaster by Herod—Dau. of Snap—Dau. of Gower Stallion (Godol.)
					Gayhurst's dam.	Election (Gohanna)—Sis. to Skysweeper by Highflyer (Herod)—Dau. of Eclipse (Marske)—Rosebud by Snap (Snip)—Miss Belsea by Regulus (Godol.)—Dau. of Bartlet's Childers (Darley Arabian)—Dau. of Honeywood's Arabian—Byerly Mare, dam of Two True Blues.

KINGFISHER,

(WINNER OF THE BELMONT AND CHAMPION STAKES AT JEROME PARK, AND TRAVERS STAKES OF SARATOGA.)

Kingfisher is a private stallion in the Nursery Stud located near Babylon, Long Island, N. Y., the property of Hon. A. Belmont, New York City. Annual sales of Yearlings in June.

KINGFISHER by Lexington, son of Boston, bred by A. J. Alexander, Woodburn Stud, Spring Station, Ky., foaled spring of 1867, dam imp. Eltham Lass, dam of Kingbolt, Kingpin, etc., by Kingston son of Venison by Partisan, second dam by Pyrrhus the First winner of the Derby in 1846. Kingston the sire of his dam was a superior race-horse, and won the Goodwood Cup, Venison was a noted stayer and the blood is remarkable for stoutness. Kingfisher was purchased at the Woodburn sale in 1868 by Mr. D. Swigert, for $490. He entered him in the most prominent events at Jerome Park, Saratoga and Long Branch. He did not start in the West, but was brought to Jerome Park and won the Belmont Stakes, 1½ miles, in 2:59¼, beating Foster, Midday, imp. Nellie James, Stamps and others. Going to Saratoga, he won the Travers Stake, 1¾ miles, in 3:15½, beating Telegram, Foster, Chillicothe and others; Hon. A. Belmont then purchased Kingfisher for $15,000, and he was transferred to the Nursery Stables. At Long Branch, was second to Enquirer in the Robins Stake, 2 mile heats, in 3:56½, 3:54½, 4:00; Kingfisher won first heat; track muddy. Jerome Park Fall Meeting, won the Champion Stakes, mile heats, in 1:49, 1:49, beating Haric, Midday and others. Same meeting, walked over for Annual Stakes, 2 miles. Same fall, won a sweepstake at Baltimore, two miles, in 3:46¼, beating Midday, winning in his three-year-old form $28,200. Kingfisher started only twice as a four-year old. Saratoga, July 14, 1871, was beaten for the Cup by Longfellow, 2¼ miles, in 4:02¾. They ran the first mile lapped, in 1:40. July 18, walked over for purse of $1,000, three miles. He started in a four-mile dash at the Branch, but broke down in the first mile and was stopped. Kingfisher's blood is of the hard bottom stout kind, being much inbred on his sire's side to Diomed who won the first Derby in 1780, and a cross of the great imp. Shark, with many to Eclipse and Herod, he traces through the same blood on the dam's side with a double cross of the famous Whalebone. Kingfisher has covered a few mares outside of the Nursery Stud and has sired some good horses, such as Oriole, Emily F, Kingston, Pirate, Turenne; Ada, half-mile at two-years old, in 50 sec. 5 furlongs 1:03¾, three-quarters of a mile, in 1.15½. Lady Roseberry 5 furlongs in muddy track, 1:03¼, and the Champagne Stakes, at Jerome Park, three-quarters of a mile, in 1:18¼; Rica, two-years old, Breeders Stake, three-quarters of a mile, in 1:16, and Home Bred Produce Stake, three-quarters of a mile, in 1:15¼; Edelweiss (4) 147 lbs. three-quarters of a mile, in 1:17¼, one mile, in 1:43¾, one mile and 1 furlong, in 1:56¼, and was capable of running a distance; Fillette, Turco, winner of the Raritan Stakes, 1¾ miles at Long Branch, in 2:29; Statesman and others, also good winners. Kingfisher is a beautiful bay, with a star and small blaze in his face; stands 15¾ hands high, with very neat head and neck, broad, oblique shoulders, great depth of heart, large, well-shaped body, good back, arched loins, with broad strong hips, great length from point of hip to whirlbone, thence to stifle and hocks; with most excellent legs and feet. He possessed wonderful speed and good staying qualities. His blood should be preserved through both sons and daughters

PEDIGREE OF KINGFISHER.

KINGFISHER.								
LEXINGTON.	Boston.	Timoleon.	Sir Archy.	Diomed.	Florizel—Sis. to Juno by Spectator—Horatia by Blank—Dau. of F. Childers—Miss Belvoir by Gr. Grantham—Dau. of Paget Turk.
				Castianira.	Rockingham—Tabitha by Trentham—Dau. of Bosphorus—Dau. of Wm's Forester—Dau. of Coalition Colt—Dau. of Bustard (Crab).
		Robin Brown's dam.	Ball's Florizel.	Imp. Saltram.	Eclipse—Virago by Snap—Dau. of Regulus—Sis. to Othello by Crab—Mias Slamerkin by Y. True Blue—Dau. of Ox. Dun. Arabian—Royal Mare.
			Dau. of	Daughter of.	Symme's Wildair (Fearnought)—Dau. of Driver (Imp. Othello)—Dau. of Fallower (Blank)—Dau. of Imp. Vampire (Regulus).
				Diomed.	Florizel—Sis. to Juno by Spectator—Horatia by Blank—Dau. of F. Childers—Miss Belvoir by Gr. Grantham—Dau. of Paget Turk.
				Daughter.	Imp. Shark—Dau. of Harris' Eclipse—Dau. of Imp. Fearnought—Dau. of Imp. Jolly Roger—Dau. of Imp. Sober John (Rib)—Dau. of Imp. Shock.
	Alice Carneal.	Sarpedon.	Emilius.	Alderman.	Pot-8-os—Lady Bolingbroke by Squirrel—Cypron by Blaze—Selima by Bethel's Arabian—Dau. of Graham's Champion—Dau. of Dar. Arabian.
			Dau. of	Daughter of.	Imp. Clockfast—Dau. of Symme's Wildair—Y. Kitty Fisher by Fearnought—Imp. Kitty Fisher by Cade—Dau. of Somerset Arabian.
			Icaria.	Orville.	Beningbrough—Evelina by Highflyer—Termagant by Tantrum—Cantatrice by Sampson—Dau. of Regulus—Marske's dam by Blacklegs.
				Emily.	Stamford—Dau. of Whiskey—Gr. Dorimant by Dorimant—Dizzy by Blank—Dizzy by Driver—Dau. of Smiling Tom—Dau. of Oysterfoot.
		Rowena.	Sumpter.	The Flyer.	Vandyke, Jr.—Azalia by Beningbrough—Gillyflower by Highflyer—Dau. of Goldfinder—Sis. to Grasshopper by Murske—Dau. of Cul. Arabian.
				Parma.	Dick Andrews—May by Beningbrough—Primrose by Mambrino—Cricket by Herod—Sophia by Blank—Ld. Leigh's Diana by Second.
		Lady Grey.		Sir Archy.	Diomed—Castianira by Rockingham—Tabitha by Trentham—Dau. of Bosphorus—Dau. of Wm's Forester—Dau. of Coalition Colt.
				Flirtilla's dam.	Robin Redbreast—Dau. of Imp. Obscurity—Slamerkin by Wildair—Imp. Cub Mare by Cub—Amaranthus' dam by Second—Dau. of Starling.
				Robin Grey.	Royalist—Belle Mariah by Grey Diomed—Queen by Imp. St. George—Dau. of Cassius—Primrose by Imp. Dove—Stella by Othello.
				Maria.	Melzar—Dau. of Highflyer—Dau. of Fearnought—Dau. of Ariel—Dau. of Jack of Diamonds—Imp. Diamond (Duchess) by Cul. Arabian.
IMP. ELTHAM LASS.	Kingston.	Venison.	Partisan.	Walton.	Sir Peter—Arethusa by Dungannon—Dau. of Prophet—Virago by Snap—Dau. of Regulus—Sis. to Othello by Crab—Miss Slamerkin.
				Parasol.	Pot-8-os—Prunella by Highflyer—Promise by Snap—Julia by Blank—Spectator's dam by Partner—Bonny Lass by Bay Bolton.
			Fawn.	Smolensko.	Sorcerer—Wowski by Mentor—Maria, Waxy's dam by Herod—Lisette by Snap—Miss Windsor by Godol. Arabian—Sis. to Volunteer.
				Jerboa.	Gohanna—Camilla by Trentham—Coquette by Compton Barb—Sis. to Regulus by Godol. Arabian—Gr. Robinson by Bald Galloway.
		Queen Ann.	Slane.	Royal Oak.	Catton—Dau. of Smolensko—Lady Mary by Beningbrough—Dau. of Highflyer—Dau. of Marske—A la Greeque by Regulus—Dau. of Allworthy.
				Daughter of.	Orville—Epsom Lass by Sir Peter—Alexina by King Fergus—Lardella by Y. Marske—Dau. of Cade—Beaufremont's dam.
			Garcia.	Octavian.	Stripling (Phoenomenon)—Dau. of Oberon—Sis. to Sharper by Ranthos (Matchem)—Dau. of Sweepstakes—Sis. to Hutton's Careless.
				Daughter of.	Shuttle—Katharine by Delpini—Dau. of Paymaster—Dau. of Le Sang—Dau. of Rib—Mother Western.
	Daughter of.	Pyrrhus the First.	Epirus.	Langar.	Selim—Dau. of Walton—Y. Giantess by Diomed—Giantess by Matchem—Molly Longlegs by Babraham—Dau. of Cole's Foxhunter.
				Olympia.	Sir Oliver (Sir Peter)—Scotilla by Anvil—Scota by Eclipse—Harmony by Herod—Rutilla by Blank—Dau. of Regulus—Dau. of Sorebeels.
		Fortress.		Defence.	Whalebone—Defiance by Rubens—Little Folly by Highland Fling—Harriet by Volunteer—Dau. of Alfred—Magnolia by Marske.
	Palmyra.			Jewess.	Moses—Calendulae by Camerton (Hambletonian)—Snowdrop by Highland Fling—Daisy by Buzzard—Tulip by Damper.
		Sultan.		Selim.	Buzzard—Castrel's dam by Alexander—Dau. of Highflyer—Dau. of Alfred—Dau. of Engineer—Bay Malton's dam by Cade (Godol).
				Bacchante.	Williamson's Ditto—Sis. to Colomel by Mercury—Dau. of Herod—Folly by Marske—Vixen by Regulus—Dau. of Hutton's Spot.
	Hester.			Camel.	Whalebone—Dau. of Selim—Maiden by Sir Peter—Dau. of Phoenomenon—Matron by Florizel—Maiden by Matchem.
				Monimia.	Muley (Orville)—Sis. to Petworth by Precipitate (Mercury)—Dau. of Woodpecker (Herod)—Sis. to Juniper by Snap (Snip)—Young Marske's dam by Blank (Godol.)—Bay Starling by Bolton Starling (Bay Bolton)—Miss Meynell by Partner (Jigg)—Dau. of Greyhound (White Barb Chillaby)—Dau. of Curwen Bay Barb—Dau. of Ld. D'Arcy's chestnut Arabian—Dau. of Whiteshirt—Old Montague Mare.

KYRLE DALY (Imp.)

(WINNER OF THE IRISH DERBY STAKES, 1½ MILES, CURRAGH MEETING, JUNE, 1873, THE CURRAGH PLATE, 7 FURLONGS, THE STEWARDS' PLATE (HANDICAP), ONE MILE, AND THE DARDISTOWN PLATE (HANDICAP), AT BELLEWSTOWN IN 1874.)

Will stand the season of 1883 *at the stables of his owner, John Reber, near Lancaster, Ohio, at* $30 *the season. Mares not proving in foal can be returned if the horse is alive and at Lancaster, Ohio.*

KYRLE DALY, by Artillery, son of Touchstone, bred by Mr. Jos. Lyons, foaled 1870, dam Colleen Rhue, dam of Maid of Athens, Zuleika, etc., by Gemma di Vergy, son of Sir Hercules. Kyrle Daly started but once as a two-year old and was unplaced. At three years old started nine times, won one race, was second in four, third in one, and unplaced in three. At Curragh, won the Irish Derby, 1½ miles, defeating Angela, Evora, Hooton, etc. Ran second to Evora in the Second Class Madfid Stakes, 1½ miles, each carring 106 lbs., five others behind him. At Down Royal, was beaten in her Majesty's Plate three miles, by Night Thought. Currah, September Meeting, was second to Royal Arms (5), 118 lbs. Kyrle Daly (3), 107 lbs., in the Stewards Plate Handicap, Condore, Eagle Hill, and eight others behind him. Curragh October Meeting, was second to Bedouin for the Royal Whip, with 100 guineas added, four miles, each 140 lbs., beating Speculation. At four years old started 16 times, won three races, ran a dead heat for one and won the deciding heat, but was disqualified by his jockey weighing in with his whip; was second in three, third in two, and unplaced in the others. Curragh June Meeting, won the Stewards' Plate (handicap), one mile, 97 lbs., defeating Saracen, Eagle Hill, and three others. Same day, won the Curragh Plate, 7 furlongs of the Queen's Plate Course, carrying 128 lbs., beating Hilarity, Bunbeg, and three others. Bellewstown, won the Dardistown Plate (handicap), 118 lbs., 1½ miles, beating Niochi, Cutty Sark, and Prophecy. Ran a dead heat with Old Tom (4), 140 lbs., for Her Majesty's Plate, three miles. Kyrle Daly, 133 lbs., he beat Old Tom the deciding heat, but was disqualified. Curragh June Meeting, was second to Chancellor (3), 131 lbs., for the Welter Handicap, 7 furlongs. Kyrle Daly (4), 152 lbs., four others behind him. Londonderry was second to Niochi (5), 138 lbs., for Her Majesty's Plate, two miles, Kyrle Daly (4), 133 lbs., two others behind him. Same day, was second to Niochi, 129 lbs., for the Stewards' Plate (handicap), Kyrle Daly 124 lbs., two miles, two others behind him.

Kyrle Daly is blood bay, 16¼ hands high, black points with star in his forehead. He has a neat head, fine width of jaws and large throttle. The setting of head and neck is magnificent, the neck rangy, full-crested, and masculine, running smoothly into the shoulders and chest, middle-piece unusually fine in the roundness of the ribs and powerful development of muscles along the spine and over the loins. The back ribs are out fully even with the hips, idicating a good feeder and a hardy constitution; quarters full, and well-developed stifles. His limbs, both in front and behind, are admirable in their flinty look of quality, with powerful knees and finely-turned hocks, and a rather straight hind leg for an English type of thoroughbred. He is much inbred to Waxy through his sons Whalebone and Whisker, having double crosses of both on side of sire and dam, and is also inbred to Eclipse and Herod. Only a few of his get have yet appeared. They are reputed speedy.

PEDIGREE OF KYRLE DALY.

KYRLE DALY.	ARTILLERY.	Touchstone.	Camel.	Whalebone.	Waxy. Penelope.	Pot-8-os—Maria by Herod—Lisette by Snap—Miss Windsor by Godol. Arabian—Sis. to Volunteer by Y. Belgrade—Dau. of Bartlet's Childers. Trumpator—Prunella by Highflyer—Promise by Snap—Julia by Blank—Spectator's dam by Partner—Bonny Lass by Bay Bolton.
				Banter. Master Henry.	Selim. Maiden.	Buzzard—Castrel's dam by Alexander—Dau. of Highflyer—Dau. of Alfred—Dau. of Engineer—Bay Malton's dam by Cade—Lass of the Mill. Sir Peter—Dau. of Phœnomenon—Matron by Florizel—Maiden by Matchem—Dau. of Squirt—Lot's dam by Mogul.
			Boadicea.	Sir Hercules.	Orville. Miss Sophia.	Beningbrough—Evelina by Highflyer—Termagant by Tantrum—Cantatrice by Sampson—Dau. of Regulus—Marske's dam by Blacklegs. Stamford—Sophia by Buzzard—Huncamunca by Highflyer—Cypher by Squirrel—Dau. of Regulus—Dau. of Bart. Childers.
		Irish Birdcatcher.	Guiccoli.		Alexander. Brunette.	Eclipse—Grecian Princess by Wm's Forester—Dau. of Coalition Colt (Godol.)—Dau. of Bustard (Crab)—Charming Molly by Second. Amaranthus—Mayfly by Matchem—Dau. of An. Starling—Dau. of Grasshopper (Crab)—Dau. of New. Arabian—Dau. of Pert (Ely Turk).
		Jeanette.	Langar.		Whalebone. Perl.	Waxy—Penelope by Trumpator—Prunella by Highflyer—Promise by Snap—Julia by Blank—Spectator's dam by Partner—Bonny Lass. Wanderer—Thalestris by Alexander—Rival by Sir Peter—Hornet by Drone—Manilla by Goldfinder—Dau. of Old Eng.—Dau. of Cul. Arabian.
		Perdita.	Delenda.		Bob Booty. Flight.	Chanticleer—Ierne by Bagot—Dau. of Gamahoe—Patty by Tim—Miss Patch by Justice—Ringtail Galloway by Cur. Bay Barb. I. Escape—Y. Heroine by Bagot—Heroine by Hero (Cade)—Dau. of Snap—Sis. to Regulus by Godol. Arabian—Gr. Robinson.
					Selim. Daughter of.	Buzzard—Castrel's dam by Alexander—Dau. of Highflyer—Dau. of Alfred—Dau. of Engineer—Bay Malton's dam by Cade. Walton—Y. Giantess by Diomed—Giantess by Matchem—Molly Longlegs by Babraham—Dau. of Cole's Foxhunter (Brisk)—Dau. of Partner.
					Gohanna. Carthage.	Mercury—Dau. of Herod—Maiden by Matchem—Dau. of Squirt—Lot's dam by Mogul—Dau. of Bay Bolton. Driver—Fractious by Mercury—Dau. of Woodpecker—Everlasting by Eclipse—Hyæna by Snap—Miss Belsea by Regulus.
	COLLEEN RHUE.	Gemma di Vergy.	Sir Hercules.	Whalebone.	Waxy. Penelope.	Pot-8-os—Maria by Herod—Lisette by Snap—Miss Windsor by Godol. Arabian—Sis. to Volunteer by Y. Belgrade—Dau. of Bart. Childers. Trumpator—Prunella by Highflyer—Promise by Snap—Julia by Blank—Spectator's dam by Partner—Bonny Lass by Bay Bolton.
			Snowdrop.	Perl.	Wanderer. Thalestris.	Gohanna—Catherine by Woodpecker—Camilla by Trentham—Coquette by Compton Barb—Sis to Regulus by Godolphin Arabian—Gr. Robinson. Alexander—Rival by Sir Peter—Hornet by Drone (Herod)—Manilla by Goldfinder—Dau. of Old Eng.—Dau. of Cul. Arabian—Miss Cade.
		Princess.	Fairy.	Heron.	Bustard. Daughter of.	Castrel—Miss Hap by Shuttle—Sis. to Haphazard by Sir Peter—Miss Hervey by Eclipse—Clio by Y. Cade—Dau. of Starling. Orville—Rosanne by Dick Andrews—Rosette by Beningbrough—Rosamond by Tandem—Tuberose by Herod—Gr. Starling by Starling.
		Retriever.	Recovery.		Filho-da-Puta. Britannia.	Haphazard—Mrs. Barnet by Waxy—Dau. of Woodpecker—Heinel by Squirrel—Principessa by Blank—Dau. of Cul. Arabian. Orville—Rovedino's dam by Coriander—Sis. to Fauny by Weasel—Dau. of Turk (Regulus)—Dau. of Locust—Dau. of Changeling.
		Echidna.	Taglioni.		Emilius. Daughter of.	Orville—Emily by Stamford—Dau. of Whiskey—Gr. Dorimant by Dorimant—Dizzy by Blank—Dizzy by Driver—Dau. of Smiling Tom. Rubens—Tippitywitchet by Waxy—Hare by Sweetbriar—Dau. of Justice—Dau. of Chymist (Matchem)—Dau. of South (Regulus).
			Economist.		Whisker. Daughter of.	Waxy—Penelope by Trumpator—Prunella by Highflyer—Promise by Snap—Julia by Blank—Spectator's dam by Partner. Catton—Dau. of Paynator—Violet by Shark—Dau. of Syphon.—Charlotte by Blank—Dau. of Crab—Dau. of Dyer's Dimple.
		Miss Pratt.			Whisker. Floranthe.	Waxy—Penelope by Trumpator—Prunella by Highflyer—Promise by Snap—Julia by Blank—Spectator's dam by Partner—Bonny Lass. Octavian—Caprice by Anvil—Madcap by Eclipse—Dau. of Blank—Dau. of Blaze—Dau. of Y. Greyhound—Dau. of Curwen Bay Barb.
					Blacklock. Gadabout.	Whitelock—Dau. of Coriander—Wildgoose by Highflyer—Coheiress by Pot-8-os—Manilla by Goldfinder—Dau. of Old Eng. (Godol.) Orville—Minstrel by Sir Peter—Matron by Florizel (Herod)—Maiden by Matchem (Cade)—Dau. of Squirt (Syphon)—Lot's dam by Mogul (Godol)—Camilla by Bay Bolton (Gr. Hautboy) Old Lady, Starling's dam by Pullein's Ch. Arabian—Dau. of Rockwood—Dau. of Bustler (Helmsley Turk).

LEGATEE,

(WINNER OF THE RESTORATION STAKES, FOUR MILE HEATS AT LONG BRANCH, 1870,)

Will stand the season of 1883 *at the Fairview Stud, Prince George Co., Md., by private contract. Application to Hon. Oden Bowie, Baltimore, Md.*

LEGATEE by Lexington, son of Boston, bred in the Woodburn Stud, Ky., foaled 1866, dam Levity, dam of Ruric, Lever, etc., by imp Trustee, son of Catton, out of Alaric's and Vandal's dam by imp Tranby. Legatee made his appearance as a three-year old, starting in five races. Jerome Park was second in a race of 2 mile heats, won by Abd-el-Kader, in 3:54, 3:54¾, track muddy. Was third in the Grand National Handicap, 2¼ miles, won by La Polka in 4:18¼. At Saratoga was third in a dash of three-quarters of a mile, won by Fanny Ludlow, in 1:19, and was unplaced in his other races. As a four-year old started six times, and won one race. Monmouth Park won the Restoration Stakes, four mile heats, in 7:45½, 7:52½, beating Carrie Atherton and Abd-el-Kader, the only other starters. Was second in a dash of 1¼ miles, won by imp. Glenelg, in 2:37¾. Saratoga was second in a dash of 2 miles, won by the Banshee in 3:35½. Was second in a dash of 1¾ miles, won by Haric, in 3.10. Jerome Park was third in the Jockey Club Handicap, 2 miles, won by Helmbold, in 3:44. Saratoga was third in a dash of 1¾ miles, won by Gen. Duke, in 3:10¼. This closed his turf career. He stood near Willmington, Del., but covered no thoroughbred mare until 1879, Mirth and Fairview are the only ones by him trained, the latter won three-quarters of a mile, in 1:18½, five furlongs in 1:02¾, and again in 1:04. He is a solid bay with black points, and a compact highly shaped horse all over. He possesses the stoutest and speediest of our native cross from Sir Archy and Diomed, decends from the family of Blacknose, Alaric, Ruric, Vandal and Lexington, all famous as race-horses and sires. His brother, Lever, has been a great success, and he only needs a chance to show his quality. Legatee is much inbred to Herod and Eclipse, thence to the Cullen Arabian, Darley and Godolphin Arabians.

PEDIGREE OF LEGATEE.

LEGATEE.	**LEXINGTON.** (Boston / Alice Carneal)	**Boston** — Timoleon / Robin Brown's dam (Dau. of Sir Archy / Ball's Florizel)	Diomed Castianira.	Florizel—Sis. to Juno by Spectator—Horatia by Blank—Dau. of F. Childers—Miss Belvoir by Gr. Grantham—Dau. of Puget Turk—Betty Percival. Rockingham—Tabitha by Trentham—Dau. of Bosphorus—Dau. of Wm's Forester—Dau. of CoalitionColt.—Dau. of Bustard(Crab)—Charm'g Molly.
			Imp. Saltram. Daughter of.	Eclipse—Virago by Snap—Dau. of Regulus—Sis. to Othello by Crab (Alcock Arabian)—Miss Slamerkin by Y. True Blue. Symme's Wildair (Imp. Fearnought)—Dau. of Driver (Imp. Othello)—Dau. of Imp. Fallower (Blank)—Dau. of Imp. Vampire (Regulus).
			Diomed. Daughter of.	Florizel—Sis. to Juno by Spectator—Horatia by Blank—Dau. of F. Childers—Miss Belvoir by Gr. Grantham—Dau. of Paget Turk. Imp. Shark—Dau. of Harris' Eclipse—Dau. of Fearnought—Dau. of Jolly Roger—Dau. of Sober John—Dau. of Imp. Shock (Old Shock).
		Sarpedon / Icaria Emilina. Dan. of	Imp. Alderman. Daughter of.	Pot-8-os—Lady Bolingbroke by Squirrel—Cypron, Herod's dam by Blaze—Selima by Bethel's Arabian—Dau. of Grabam's Champion. Imp. Clockfast—Dau. of Symme's Wildair—Y. Kitty Fisher by Fearnought—Imp. Kitty Fisher by Cade—Dau. of Som. Arabian—Bald Charlotte.
			Orville. Emily.	Beningbrough—Evelina by Highflyer—Termagant by Tantrum—Cantatrice by Sampson—Dau. of Regulus—Marske's dam by Blacklegs. Stainford—Dau. of Whiskey—Gr. Dorimant by Dorimant—Dizzy by Blank—Dizzy by Driver—Dau. of Smiling Tom—Dau. of Oysterfoot.
		Rowena / Lady Grey. Sumpter.	The Flyer. Parma.	Vandyke Jr.—Azalia by Beningbrough—Gillyflower by Highflyer—Dau. of Goldfinder—Sis. to Grasshopper by Marske—Dau. of Cullen Arabian. Dick Andrews—May by Beningbrough—Primrose by Mambrino—Cricket by Herod—Sophia by Blank—Diana by Second—Dau. of Stan. Arabian.
			Sir Archy. Flirtilla's dam.	Diomed Castianira by Rockingham—Tabitha by Trentham—Dau. of Bosphorus—Dau. of Wm.'s Forester—Dau. of Coalition Colt.—Dau. of Bustard Robin Redbreast—Dau. of Obscurity—Slamerkin by Imp. Wildair—Imp. Cub Mare by Cub—Amarauthus' dam by Second—Dau. of Starling.
			Robin Grey. Maria.	Royalist (Saltram)—Belle Mariab by Grey Diomed—Queen by Imp. St. George—Dau. of Cassius—Primerose by Imp. Dove—Stella. Melzar—Dau. of Imp. Highflyer—Dau. of Fearnought—Dau. of Ariel—D. of Imp. Jack of Diamonds—Imp. Diamond (Duchess) by Cul. Arabian.
LEVITY. (Imp. Trustee / Emma / Vandal's dam Lucilla. Imp. Tranby. Lucy. Trumpator. Dan. of Blackbock.)	Catton / Gibside Fairy. Lucy Golumpus. Grey. Whisker.		Gohanna. Catharine.	Mercury—Dau. of Herod—Maiden by Matchem—Dau. of Squirt—Lot's dam by Mogul—Dau. of Bay Bolton—Dau. of Pullein's Ch. Arabian. Woodpecker—Camilla by Trentham—Coquette by Compton Barb—Sis. to Regulus by Godol. Arabian—Gr. Robinson by Bald Galloway.
			Timothy. Lucy.	Delpini (Highflyer)—Cora by Matchem—Dau. of Turk—Dau. of Allworthy—Dau. of Starling—Dau. of Bloody Buttocks—Dau. of Greyhound. Florizel (Herod)—Frenzy by Eclipse—Dau. of Engineer—Dau. of Blank—Lass of the Mill by Traveler—Miss Makeless by Y. Greyhound.
			Waxy. Penelope.	Pot-8-os—Maria by Herod—Lisette by Snap—Miss Windsor by Godol. Arabian—Sis. to Volunteer by Y. Belgrade—Da. of Bart Childers (D. Arabian). Trumpator—Prunella by Highflyer—Promise by Snap—Julia by Blank—Spectator's dam by Partner—Bonny Lass by Bay Bolton—Dau. of D. Arabian.
			Hermes. Vicissitude.	Mercury—Rosina by Woodpecker—Petworth by Herod—Golden Grove by Blank—Spinster by Partner—Dau. of Bloody Buttocks—Dau. of Greyhound. Pipator—Beatrice by Sir Peter—Pyrrha by Matchem—Duchess by Whitenose—Miss Slamerkin by Y. True Blue—Dau. of Ox Dun Arabian.
			Whitelock. Daughter of.	Hambletonian—Rosalind by Phoenomenon—Atalanta by Matchem—Lass of the Mill by Oroonoko—Dau. of Traveler—Miss Makeless. Coriander—Wildgoose by Highflyer—Coheiress by Pot-8-os—Manilla by Goldfinder—Dau. of Old England—Dau. of Cullen Arabian.
			Orville. Miss Grimstone.	Beningbrough—Evelina by Highflyer—Termagant by Tantrum—Cantatrice by Sampson—Dau. of Regulus—Marske's dam. Weasel (Herod)—Dau. of Ancaster—Dau. of Dam. Arabian—Dau. of Sampson—Dau. of Oroonoko—Sophia, Sis. to Mirza by G. Arabian.
			Sir Solomon. Daughter of.	Imp. Tickle Toby (Alfred)—Vesta by Dreadnought (Celer)—Bandy by Imp. Clockfast—Dau. of Americus (Imp. Shark)—Dau. of Imp. Fearnought. Hickory (Imp. Whip)—Imp. Trumpetta by Trumpator—Sis. to Lambinos by Highflyer—Dau. of Eclipse—Vauxhall's dam by Cade.
			Orphan. Lady Grey.	Ball's Florizel (Diomed)—Fair Rachel by Diomed—Susan Jones by Imp. Shark (Marske)—Dau. of Thornton's Wildair by Symme's Wildair. Robin Grey—Maria by Melzar (Imp. Medley)—Dau. of Imp. Highflyer (Highflyer)—Dau. of Imp. Fearnought (Regulus)—Dau. of Ariel (Mor. Imp. Traveler)—Dau. of Imp. Jack of Diamonds (Cul. Arabian)—Imp. Diamond (Duchess) by Cullen Arabian—Lady Thigh by Croft's Partner (Jigg)—Dau. of Greyhound—Sophonisba's dam by Curwen Bay Barb—Dau. of D'Arcy Chestnut Arabian—Dau. of Whiteshirt—Old Montague Mare.

LELAPS

Will stand the season of 1883, *at the Dixiana Stud, near Lexington, Ky., (if not sold)* $50 *the season. Application to Maj. B. G. Thomas, Lexington, Ky.*

LELAPS, by imp. Leamington, son of Faugh-a-Ballagh, bred by R. W. Cameron, Clifton Stud, N. Y., foaled 1872, dam imp. Pussy, by Diophantus, son of Orlando-out of Agapemone, by Bay Middleton. Lelaps did not run as a two-year old, but made his first appearance as a three-year old at Jerome Park, running unplaced in Fordham Handicap, won by Wildidle in 2:12; Monmouth Park, was third in a dash of one mile, won by Searcher in 1:44¾. Won a dash of 1½ miles, for beaten horses, in 2:45¾. Jerome Park Fall Meeting, unplaced in a Selling Race, 1½ miles, won by Picolo in 2:45¾. Was second in a Selling Race, 1¾ miles, won by Josie B., in 3:20½, was third in a Handicap Sweepstakes, 1¾ miles, won by Madge in 3:15¾, was unplaced in a Handicap Sweepstakes, 1½ miles, won by Weatherby in 2:51½. (4.) At Jerome Park, was second in a Selling Race, 1¼ miles, won by Spendthrift in 2:16½; unplaced in the Westchester Cup, won by Viator, in 4:10½, unplaced in the, Jockey Club Handicap, 2 miles, won by Tom Ochiltree in 3:41¾. Saratoga, was unplaced in a Selling Race, 1 mile and a furlong, won by Meco in 1:58½, unplaced in a Selling Race, 1¼ miles, won by Arcturus in 2:13½, was third in a dash of 1¾ miles, won by Vigil in 3:08. Lelaps is from a racing family, his dam's sire, Diophantus, won the 2,000 guineas. Orlando, his grandsire, won the Derby, and was the sire of Teddington, a Derby winner, and Imperieuse, winner of the St. Leger Bay Middleton, the sire of his grandam, won the Derby, and was sire of the Flying Dutchman, that won both the Derby and St. Leger. Lelaps has only covered a very few mares. He is sire of Lelex, winner of the Sanford Stakes for two-year-olds, at Louisville, one mile in 1:45, Green Stake at Nashville, and the Young America Stake, No. 2, one mile, in 1:45¼, both for two-year-olds. At three years old, won the Merchants' Stake at Louisville, 1⅛ miles, in 1:56. In this race he defeated Gabriel, Bancroft, Checkmate, and six others. Others which promised well, were Tom Bush, Elexor, Hassan, Hatef, Thesis and Juliet M, and last though not least, Pearl Jennings, winner of the Hotel Stakes at St. Louis, 1¼ miles, in 2:12¾. Lelaps is a blood bay, with a star in his forehead, and black legs, stands 16 hands and ½ an inch high, is well and truly shaped. His blood is a combination of speedy and stout crosses, tracing to Whalebone on both sides, through Sir Hercules and Camel. He has also a cross of Whisker, and a strong foundation of the blood of Eclipse and Herod, through the best sources.

The Horse-Breders' Guide and Hand Book. 101

PEDIGREE OF LELAPS.

LELAPS.								
IMP. LEAMINGTON.	Daughter of.	Pantaloon.	Idalia.	Castrel.	Flight.	Bob Booty.	Peri.	Sir Hercules.	Fangh-a-ballagh.	Whalebone.			

IMP. LEAMINGTON.

Waxy.	Pot-8-os—Maria by Herod—Lisette by Snap—Miss Windsor by Godol. Arabian—Sis. to Volunteer by Y. Belgrade—Dam of Bart. Childers.
Penelope.	Trumpator—Prunella by Highflyer—Promise by Snap—Julia by Blank—Spectator's dam by Partuer—Bonny Lass by Bay Bolten.
Wanderer.	Gohanna—Catharine by Woodpecker—Camilla by Trentham—Coquette by Compton Barb—Sis. to Regulus by Godol. Arabian—Gr. Robinson.
Thalestris.	Alexander—Rival by Sir Peter—Hornet by Drone (Herod)—Manilla by Goldfinder—Dau. of Old. Eng.—Dau. of Cul. Arabian—Miss Cade.
Chanticleer.	Woodpecker—Dau. of Eclipse—Rosebud by Snap—Miss Belsea by Regulus—Dau. of Bart Childers—Dau. of Hon. Arabian—Dam of True Blues.
Ierne.	Bagot—Dau of Gamahoe—Patty by Tim—Miss Patch by Justice—Ringtail Galloway by Cur. Bay Barb—Sis. to Witty Mare by Pelham's Hip.
Irish Escape.	Commodore—Dau. of Highflyer—Shift by Sweetbriar—Bl. Susan by Snap—Ld. Bruce's Cade Mare by Cade—Dau. of Belgrade.
Young Heroine.	Bagot—Heroine by Hero—Dau. of Snap—Sis. to Regulus by Godol. Arabian—Gr. Robinson by Bald Galloway—Dau. of Snake (Lis. Turk).
Buzzard.	Woodpecker—Misfortune by Dux—Curiosity by Snap—Dau. of Regulus—Dau. of Bart. Childers—Dau. of Hon. Arabian—Dam of True Blues.
Selim's dam.	Alexander—Dau. of Highflyer—Dau. of Alfred—Dau. of Engineer—Bay Malton's dam by Cade—Lass of the Mill by Traveler—Miss Makeless.
Peruvian.	Sir Peter—Dau. of Budrow—Escape's dam by Squirrel—Dau. of Babraham—Dau. of Golden Ball—Busby Molly by Hamp. Ct. Childers.
Musidora.	Meteor—Maid of All Work by Highflyer—Sis. to Tamdem by Syphon—Dau. of Regulus—Dau. of Snip—Dau. of Cottingham—War. Galloway.
Blacklock.	Whitelock—Dau. of Corinder—Wildgoose by Highflyer—Coheiress by Pot-8-os—Manilla by Goldfinder—Dau. of Old Eng.—Dau. of Cul. Arabian.
Wagtail.	Prime Minister—Dau. of Orville—Miss Grimstone by Weasel—Dau. of Ancaster—Dau. of Dam Arabian—Dau. of Sampson—Dau. of Oroonoko.
Champion.	Selim—Podagra by Gouty—Jet by Magnet—Jewel by Squirrel—Sophia by Blank—Diana by Second—Hauger's Br. Marc by Stan. Arabian.
Etiquette.	Orville—Boadicea by Alexander—Brunette by Amaranthus—Mayfly by Matchem—Dau. of An. Starling—Dau. of Grasshopper.

IMP. PUSSY.

Camel.	Whalebone—Dau. of Selim—Maiden by Sir Peter—Dau. of Phoenomenon—Matron by Florizel—Maiden by Matchem—Dau. of Squirt.
Banter.	Master Henry—Boadicea by Alexander—Brunette by Amaranthus—Mayfly by Matchem—Dau. of An. Starling—Dau. of Grasshopper.
Langar.	Selim—Dau. of Walton—Y. Giantess by Diomed—Giantess by Matchem—Molly Longlegs by Babraham—Dau. of C. Foxhunter.
Kite.	Bustard (Castrel)—Olympia by Sir Oliver—Scotilla by Anvil—Scota by Eclipse—Harmony by Herod—Rutilla by Blank.
Orville.	Beningbrough—Evelina by Highflyer—Termagant by Tantrum—Cantatrice by Sampson—Dau. of Regulus—Marske's dam.
Emily.	Stamford—Dau. of Whiskey—Gr. Dorimant by Dorimant—Dizzy by Blank—Dizzy by Driver—Dau. of Smiling Tom.
Whisker.	Waxy—Penelope by Trumpator—Prunella by Highflyer—Promise by Snap—Julia by Blank—Spectator's dam by Partner.
Gibside Fairy.	Hermes—Vicissitude by Pipator—Beatrice by Sir Peter—Pyrrha by Matchem—Duchess by Whitenose—Miss Slamerkin.
Selim.	Buzzard—Castrel's dam by Alexander—Dau. of Highflyer—Dau. of Alfred Dau. of Engineer—Bay Malton's dam by Cade.
Bacchante.	Williamson's Ditto—Sis. to Calomel by Mercury—Dau. of Herod—Folly by Marske—Vixen by Regulus—Dau. of Hutton's Spot.
Phantom.	Walton—Julia by Whiskey—Y. Giantess by Diomed—Giantess by Matchem Molly Longlegs by Babraham—Dau. of Cole's Foxhunter.
Filagree.	Soothsayer—Web by Waxy—Penelope by Trumpator—Prunella by Highflyer—Promise by Snap—Julia by Blank.
Whalebone.	Waxy—Penelope by Trumpator—Prunella by Highflyer—Promise by Snap—Julia by Blank—Spectator's dam by Partuer.
Peri.	Wanderer—Thalestris by Alexander—Rival by Sir Peter—Hornet by Drone—Manilla by Goldfinder—Dau. of Old Eng.
Emilius.	Orville—Emily by Stamford—Dau. of Whiskey—Gr. Dorimant by Dorimant—Dizzy by Blank—Dizzy by Driver—Dau. of Smiling Tom.
Daughter of.	Scud or Pioneer (Whiskey)—Canary Bird by Whiskey or Sorcerer—Canary by Coriander (Pot-8-os)—Miss Green by Highflyer (Herod)—Harriet by Matchem (Cade)—Flora by Regulus (Godol.)—Dau. of Bartlet's Childers (Darley Arabian)—Dau. of Bay Bolton (Grey Hautboy)—Dau of Belgrade Turk.

Left column ancestor names (IMP. LEAMINGTON side): Daughter of — Pantaloon — Idalia — Castrel — Flight — Bob Booty — Peri — Sir Hercules — Fangh-a-ballagh — Whalebone — Daphne — Maid of Honor — Laurel — Guicoli.

Left column ancestor names (IMP. PUSSY side): Agapemone — Diophantus — Orlando — Touchstone — Vulture — Emilius — Maria — Sultan — Cobweb — Bay Middleton — Sir Hercules — Echo — Venus.

LEVER

Will stand the season of 1883 at the Elmendorf Stud, D. Swigert, proprietor, near Lexington, Ky., (if not sold) at the season. Application to D. Swigert, Muir's Post Office, Fayette Co., Ky. Annual sales of yearlings in May.

LEVER by Lexington, son of Boston, bred in the Woodburn Stud, Kentucky, foaled 1863, dam Levity, dam of Ruric, Legatee, &c., by imp. Trustee, son of Catton out of Alaric's and Vandal's dam by imp. Tranby. Lever was never trained, having been injured in one of his hocks when a yearling, but from his high breeding and the racing qualities of the family, he would doubtless have been a superior race-horse. He is by the emperor of stallions, Lexington (admitted to have been not only the best race-horse this country has ever produced, but its most successful stallion); dam Levity (dam of Ruric, Lightsome, Mildred, Legatee, &c.), by imp. Trustee, who was a good third for the Derby in 1832, won by St. Giles, beating Margrave, who won the Doncaster St. Leger the same year, in which Trustee was again third ; Trustee by Catton (son of Golumpus), dam Emma, by Whisker (own brother to Whalebone), Web, Woeful, &c., by Waxy). Trustee was a most successful sire, having gotten the renowned Fashion, who distanced Boston and afterward beat him in the great sectional match, the North against the South, for $20,000 a side, run on the Union Course, Long Island, May 10, 1842, in 7:32½, 7:45, which was the fastest and best race run to that day Reube, Revenue and other good ones. 2d dam Vandal's dam by imp. Tranby (son of Blacklock, by Whitelock). Blacklock was a distinguished race-horse in his day, starting in twenty-three races and winning seventeen. He was equally as famous in the stud, having sired such horses as Brutandorf, Buzzard, Brownlock, Belzoni, Laurel, Malek, Velocipede, Voltaire, Belshazzar and Tranby. Tranby's dam was by Orville, winner of the Doncaster St. Leger in 1802. He started in no less than thirty-nine races, winning twenty-two, the most of them at four miles and over. He was also one of the most distinguished stallions of his day, being the sire of the great Emilius, Master Henry, Bizarre, Souvenir, &c. For many years, Lever was in an obscure neighborhood in Scott County, Ky., and covered no thoroughbred mares. Finally, by mere accident, Sally of the Valley was bred to him, and produced Essilah, who won twelve races in one season. He sired Leveler, a capital race-horse, winner of the Clark Stake, at Louisville, 2 miles in 3:37, Merchants Stake, at St. Louis, mile heats, in 1:45, 1:45 1:51, Milon won first heat, and the Viley Stake, at Lexington, 1¾ miles in 3:07½, and the Kentucky St. Leger Stake, two miles at Louisville in 3:42¼, Lou Lauler a fine race-mare and good winner in fast time, Mahlstick, winner of Louisville Cup, 2¼ miles in 4:07½, Greely Stakes, St. Louis, three miles in 5:40, one mile and furlong in 1:56½, and three miles in 5:33. Other good ones, all winners, by him, are Sweetheart, Petrel, La Gloria, Lamartine, Okolona, Louise, Harry Mann (Punch), Palanca, Maj. Hughes, and a few others. The colts by him are about the best the mares ever produce, and the few good mares he served, produced good race-horses. A careful analysis of Lever's pedigree, will show that he not only possesses the stoutest and speediest blood of our native stock, but traces through the collateral branches on the dam and sire side to that grand old mare, Lady Grey, from which so many distinguished race-horses, stallions and brood mares have descended. He has also a large infusion of the blood of Diomed, Highflyer, Herod and Eclipse. He stands 15 hands 2½ inches high ; has a neat, well-shaped head, fine ears, good, strong neck running into most excellent, well-set shoulders ; great depth of girth ; good, strong, well-muscled back, with round, well-ribbed body ; strong hips, with good length of whirlbone, stifle and thence to the hock ; he has Tranby legs, which look as hard and firm as whalebone with good, sound feet.

PEDIGREE OF LEVER.

LEVER.	**LEXINGTON.**	Boston.	Robin Brown's dam.	Timoleon.	Diomed.	Florizel—Sis. to Juno by Spectator—Horatia by Blank—Dau. of F. Childers—Miss Belvoir by Gr. Grantham—Dau. of Paget Turk.
					Castianira.	Rockingham—Tabitha by Trentham—Dau. of Bosphorus—Dau. of Wm.'s Forester—Dau. of Coalition Colt—Dau. of Bustard (Crab).
				Ball's Florizel.	Imp. Saltram.	Eclipse—Virago by Snap—Dau. of Regulus—Sis. to Othello by Crab—Miss Slamerkin by Y. True Blue—Dau. of Ox Dun Arabian—Royal Mare.
					Daughter of.	Symme's Wildair (Imp. Fearnought)—Dau. of Driver (Imp. Othello)—Dau. of Imp. Fallower (Blank)—Dau. of Imp. Vampire (Regulus).
				Dau. of Sir Archy.	Diomed.	Florizel—Sis. to Juno by Spectator—Horatia by Blank—Dau. of F. Childers—Miss Belvoir by Gr. Grantham—Dau. of Paget Turk.
					Daughter of.	Imp. Shark—Dau. of Harris' Eclipse (Partner)—Dau. of Fearnought—Dau. of Jolly Roger—Dau. of Sober John (Rib)—Dau. of Imp. Shock (Old Shock).
			Sarpedon.	Emilius.	Imp. Alderman.	Pot-8-os—Lady Bolingbroke by Squirrel—Cypron, Herod's dam by Blaze—Selima by Beth. Arabian—Dau. of Graham's Champion.
					Daughter of.	Imp. Clockfast—Dau. of Symme's Wildair—Y. Kitty Fisher by Fearnought—Imp. Kitty Fisher by Cade—Dau. of Som. Arabian—Bald Charlotte.
		Alice Carneal.		Icaria.	Orville.	Beningbrough—Evelina by Highflyer—Termagant by Tantrum—Cantatrice by Sampson—Dau. of Regulus—Marske's dam by Blacklegs.
					Emily.	Stamford—Dau. of Whiskey—Gr. Dorimant by Dorimant—Dizzy by Blank—Dizzy by Driver—Dau. of Smiling Tom—Dau. of Oysterfoot.
			Rowena.	Sumpter.	The Flyer.	Vandyke, Jr.—Azalia by Beoingbrough—Gillyflower by Highflyer—Dau. of Goldfinder—Sis. to Grasshopper by Marske—Dau. of Cul. Arabian.
					Parma.	Dick Andrews—May by Beningbrough—Primrose by Mambrino—Cricket by Herod—Sophia by Blank—Diana by Second—Dau. of Stan. Arabian.
				Lady Grey.	Sir Archy.	Diomed—Castianira by Rockingham—Tabitha by Trentham—Dau. of Bosphorus—Dau. of Wm.'s Forester—Dau. of Coalition Colt.
					Flirtilla's dam.	Robin Redbreast—Dau. of Obscurity—Slamerkin by Imp. Wildair—Imp. Cub Mare by Cub—Amaranthus' dam Second—Dau. of Starling.
					Robin Grey.	Royalist—Belle Mariah by Grey Diomed (Imp. Medley)—Queen by Imp. St. George (Highflyer)—Dau. of Cassius—Primrose by Imp. Dove.
					Maria.	Melzar (Imp. Medley)—Dau. of Highflyer—Dau. of Fearnought—Dau. of Ariel—Dau. of Imp. Jack of Diamonds—Imp. Diamond.
	LEVITY.	Trustee.	Catton.	Lucy Golumpus.	Gohanna.	Mercury—Dau. of Herod—Maiden by Matchem—Dau. of Squirt—Lot's dam by Mogul—Camilla by Bay Bolton—Old Lady.
					Catharine.	Woodpecker—Camilla by Trentham—Coquette by Compton Barb—Sis. to Regulus by Godol. Arabian—Gr. Robinson by Bald Galloway.
				Grey.	Timothy.	Delpini—Cora by Matchem—Dau. of Turk—Dau. of Allworthy—Dau. of Starling—Dau. of Bloody Buttocks—Dau. of Greyhound.
					Lucy.	Florizel—Frenzy by Eclipse—Dau. of Engineer—Dau. of Blank—Lass of the Mill by Traveler—Miss Makeless by Y. Greyhound.
			Emma.	Whisker.	Waxy.	Pot-8-os—Maria by Herod—Lisette by Snap—Miss Windsor by Godol. Arabian—Sis. to Volunteer by Y. Belgrade—Dau. of Bart. Childers.
					Penelope.	Trumpator—Prunella by Highflyer—Promise by Snap—Julia by Blank—Spectator's dam by Partner—Bonny Lass by Bay Bolton.
				Gibside Fairy.	Hermes.	Mercury—Rosina by Woodpecker—Petworth by Herod—Golden Grove by Blank—Spinster by Partner—Dau. of Bloody Buttocks.
					Vicissitude.	Pipator (Conductor)—Beatatrice by Sir Peter—Pyrrha by Matchem—Duchess by Whitenose—Miss Slamerkin by Y. True Blue.
		Vandal's Dam.	Imp. Tranby.	Blacklock.	Whitelock.	Hambletonian—Rosalind by Phoenomenon—Atalanta by Matchem—Lass of the Mill by Oroonoko—Dau. of Traveler—Miss Makeless.
					Daughter of.	Coriander—Wildgoose by Highflyer—Coheiress by Pot-8-os—Manilla by Goldfinder—Dau. of Old Eng.—Dau. of Cul. Arabian.
				Dau. of Trumpator.	Orville.	Beningbrough—Evelina by Highflyer—Termagant by Tantrum—Cantatrice by Sampsom—Dau. of Regulus—Marske's dam.
					Miss Grimstone.	Weasel (Herod)—Dau. of Ancaster—Dau. of Dam. Arabian—Dau. of Sampson—Dau. of Oroonoko—Sophia, Sis. to Mirza by G. Arabian.
			Lucilla.	Lucy.	Sir Solomon.	Tickle Toby (Alfred)—Vesta by Dreadnought (Celer)—Bandy by Imp. Clockfast—Dau. of Americus (Shark)—Dau. of Imp. Fearnought.
					Daughter of.	Hickory (Imp. Whip)—Imp. Trumpetta by Trumpator—Sis. to Lambinos by Highflyer—Dau. of Eclipse—Vauxhall's dam by Cade.
					Orphan.	Ball's Florizel (Diomed)—Fair Rachel by Imp. Diomed—Susan Jones by Imp. Shark—Dau. of Thornton's Wildair by Symme's Wildair.
					Lady Grey.	Robin Gray—Maria by Melzar (Imp. Medley)—Dau. of Imp. Highflyer (Highflyer)—Dau. of Imp. Fearnought (Regulus)—Dau. of Ariel (Mor. Imp. Traveler)—Dau. of Imp. Jack of Diamonds (Cullen Arabian)—Imp. Diamond (Duchess) by Cullen Arabian—Lady Thigh by Croft's Partner (Jigg)—Dau. of Greyhound—Sophonisba's dam by Curwen Bay Barb—Dau. of D'Arcy Chestnut Arabian—Dau. of Whiteshirt—Old Montague Mare.

LISBON,

(WINNER OF THE ALEXANDER STAKE AT LOUISVILLE, KENTUCKY, 1876.)

Will stand the season of 1883 at the Woodburn Stud Farm, near Spring, Ky. at $50 the season. Application to L. Brodhead, Spring, Ky., Annual sales of yearlings in May.

LISBON by imp. Phaeton son of King Tom, bred by Richard Ten Broeck, foaled 1874, dam imp. Lady Love by Stockwell or Caterer, son of Stockwell, second dam Chere Amie by Sweetmeat, out of Blame by Touchstone. Phaeton will be found in this volume, his dam Lady Love was a winner in England at two-years old, and won the Stewards Cup at Chester at four-years old, Chere Amie her grandam was also a race-mare and winner. Caterer the reputed sire of Lady Love was a good race-horse, he won the Findon Stakes at Goodwood when two-years old, defeating Wingrave, Alvediston, Kaiser and others, and was second to the Marquis in the 2000 guineas with Alvediston, Wingrave and thirteen others behind him. Sweetmeat the sire of his grandam, was a superior race-horse, won the Queen's Vase at Ascot, and the Doncaster Cup in 1845, he was the sire of Mincepie and Mincemeat, both Oaks winners, and Macoroni winner of the Derby and 2000 guineas, and second in the list of winning sires in 1882. Touchstone the sire of his great grandam Blame, won the St. Leger, the Ascot Gold Cup in 1836-37, and the Doncaster Cup in 1835-36, and was second to no sire of his day. Lisbon started three times as a two-year old and won one race. At Louisville, Ky., won the Alexander Stakes, half mile, in :49¾, beating McWhirter and seven others. Was third in the Colt Stakes at Lexington, Ky., three-quarters of a mile, King Faro and McWhirter running dead heat for first place, in 1:18¼. In this race Lisbon beat Allen Pinkerton, Headlight, Planetarian and Edingburg. Was third in the Belle Meade Stakes at Louisville, three-quarters of a mile, in 1:17, won by McWhirter, Baden-Baden second. As a three-year old he started only twice, and was unplaced in both of his races. Only a few of Lisbon's get have appeared on the turf, but the performances of Ripple alone have made him conspicuous as a sire. Ripple, the season of 1881, won seven of his eleven starts. He won the Long Branch Handicap, 1¼ miles, in 2:10¼, beating Checkmate, Parole and Sir Hugh; also the Shrewsbury Handicap, 1¾ miles, in 3:09¾. In this race he carried a penalty of 5 lbs. and 3 lbs. overweight. He unfortunately died that winter. Lisbon is a red bay, full 15¼ hands high, with a blaze face and four white ankles, he is a horse of immense substance and power, and in conformation second to none, is very muscular like all of Phaeton's sons, and great constitution. In addition to his double cross of Glencoe through King Tom and Stockwell, he has a double cross of Touchstone on each side, four or five crosses of Waxy through Economist and Emma by Whisker and Camel and Sir Herculus by Whalebone, fortified by the blood of Herod through the famous Highflyer, and Eclipse through Pot-8-os and King Fergus. The blood is worth preserving through the grandaughters of Phaeton and daughters of Great Tom, King Ban and King Ernest.

PEDIGREE OF LISBON.

Waxy—Penelope by Trumpator—Prunella by Highflyer—Promise by Snap
—Julia by Blank—Spectator's dam by Partner—Bonny Lass.
Octavian—Caprice by Anvil—Madcap by Eclipse—Dau. of Blank—Dau. of
Blaze—Dau. of Y. Greyhound—Dau. of Cur. Bay Barb.

Rugantino—Butterfly by Master Bagot—Dau. of Bagot (Herod)—Mother
Brown by Trunnion (Cade)—Dau. of Old England (Godol.)
Teddy the Ginder—Lady Jane by Sir Peter—Paulina by Florizel—Captive
by Matchem—Calliope by Slouch—Lass of the Mill by Oroonoko.

Selim—Bacchante by Williamson's Ditto—Sis. to Calomel by Mercury—
Dau. of Herod—Folly by Marske—Vixen by Regulus (Godol.)
Tramp—Web by Waxy—Penelope by Trumpator—Prunella by Highflyer—
Promise by Snap—Julia by Blank—Spectator's dam by Partner.

Orville—Eleanor by Whiskey—Y. Giantess by Diomed—Giantess by
Matchem—Molly Longlegs by Babraham—Dau. of Cole's Foxhunter.
Marmion—Harpalice by Gohanna—Amazon by Driver—Fractious by Mer-
cury—Dau. of Woodpecker—Everlasting by Eclipse—Hyaena.

Whalebone—Dau. of Selim—Maiden by Sir Peter—Dau. of Phoenomenon
—Matron by Florizel—Maiden by Matchem—Dau. of Squirt.
Master Henry—Boadicea by Alexander—Brunette by Amaranthus—Mayfly
by Matchem—Dau. of An. Starling—Dau. of Grasshopper.

Castrel—Idalia by Peruvian—Musidora by Meteor—Maid of All Work by
Highflyer—Sis. to Tandem by Syphon—Dau. of Regulus—Dau. of Snip.
Cain—Lydia by Poulton—Variety by Hyacinthus—Sis. to Swordsman by
Weasel—Dau. of Turk—Dau. of Locust—Dau. of Changeling.

Camel—Banter by Master Henry—Boadicea by Alexander—Brunette
by Amaranthus—Mayfly by Matchem—Dau. of An. Starling.
Filho-da-Puta—Finesse by Peruvian—Violante by John Bull—Dau. of
Highflyer—Everlasting by Eclipse—Hyaena by Snap—Miss Belsea.

Orville—Emily by Stamford—Dau. of Whiskey—Gr. Dorimant by Dori-
mant—Dizzy by Blank—Dizzy by Driver—Dau. of Smiling Tom.
Bustard (Castrel)—Johannah Southcote by Beningbrough—Lavinia by
Pipator—Dick Andrews' dam by Highflyer—Dau. of Cardinal Puff.

Sir Hercules—Guicciolli by Bob Booty—Flight by I. Escape—Y. Heroine
by Bagot—Heroine by Hero—Dau. of Snap.
Economist—Miss Pratt by Blacklock-Gadabout by Orville-Minstrel by Sir
Peter-Matron by Florizel-Maiden by Matchem-Dau. of Squirt-Lot'sdam.

Sultan—Trampoline by Tramp—Web by Waxy—Penelope by Trumpator—
Prunella by Highflyer—Promise by Snap—Julia by Blank.
Muley—Clare by Marmion—Harpalice by Gohanna—Amazon by Driver—
Fractious by Mercury—Dau. of Woodpecker—Everlasting.

Camel—Banter by Master Henry—Boadicea by Alexander—Brunette by
Amaranthus—Mayfly by Matchem—Dau. of An. Starling.
Langar—Kite by Bustard (Castrel)—Miss Hap by Shuttle—Sis. to Haphaz-
ard by Sir Peter—Miss Hervey by Eclipse—Clio by Y. Cade.

Blacklock—Dau. of Juniper—Dau. of Sorcerer—Virgin by Sir Peter—Dau.
of Pot-8-os—Editha by Herod—Elfrida by Snap—Dau. of Regulus.
Whisker—Gibside Fairy by Hermes—Vicissitude by Pipator—Beatrice by
Sir Peter—Pyrrha by Matchem—Duchess by Whitenose.

Walton—Parasol by Pot-8-os—Prunella by Highflyer—Promise by Snap—
Julia by Blank—Spectator's dam by Partner—Bonny Lass.
Moses—Quadrille by Selim—Canary Bird by Whiskey or Sorcerer—Canary
by Coriander—Miss Green by Highflyer—Harriet by Matchem.

Blacklock—Dau. of Phantom—Dau. of Overton—Gratitude's dam by Walnut—Dau. of Ruler—Piracantha by Matchem—Prophetess.
Blacklock—Wagtail by Prime Minister—Dau. of Orville—Miss Grimstone
by Weasel—Dau. of Ancaster—Dau. of dam Arabian.

Whalebone—Dau. of Selim—Maiden by Sir Peter—Dau. of Phoenomenon
—Matron by Florizel—Maiden by Matchem—Dau. of Squirt.
Master Henry—Boadicea by Alexander—Brunette by Amaranthus—Mayfly
by Matchem—Dau. of An. Starling—Dau. of Grasshopper.

Jerry—Beeswings' dam by Ardrossan—Lady Eliza by Whitworth—Dau.
of Spadille—Sylvia by Y. Marske—Ferret by Bro. to Silvio.

Bustard (Castrel)—Dau. of Muley (Orville)—Rosanne by Dick Andrews
(Joe Andrews by Eclipse)—Rosette by Beningbrough (King Fergus)—
Rosamond by Tandem (Syphon)—Tuberose by Herod (Tartar)—Grey
Starling by Starling (Bay Bolton)—Coughing Polly by Bartlet's Childers
(Darley Arabian)—Sis. to Thunderbolt by Counsellor—Dau. of Lugge—
Dau. of Davill's Old Woodcock.

LONGFELLOW,

(WINNER OF THE PRODUCE STAKES AT LEXINGTON, KY., OHIO STAKES AT CINCINNATI, AND CITIZENS' STAKE AT NASHVILLE, 1873, MONMOUTH CUP AT LONG BRANCH, 1871 AND 1872, SARATOGA CUP IN 1871.)

Longfellow will stand the season of 1883 *at the Nantura Stud Farm, near Midway, Woodford Co., Ky., at* $100 *the season. Application to F. B. Harper, Midway, Ky.*

LONGFELLOW, by imp. Leamington, son of Faugh-a-Ballagh, bred by John Harper, foaled 1870, dam Nantura, dam of Extra, Fanny Holton, &c., by Brawner's Eclipse, son of Am. Eclipse, out of Queen Mary, by Bertrand, son of Sir Archy. Longfellow was a fast, good race-horse, made his *debut* at Lexington, Ky., May 16, 1870, in Phœnix Stakes, mile heats, for three-year olds, won by Enquirer in 1:44¾, 1:44½, Catina second, and Longfellow third and distanced. Same place, Sept. 16, won Produce Stake for three-year olds, 2 mile heats, in 3:43¼, 3:44, beating Twinkle, etc. Cincinnati, Ohio, Sept. 30, won Ohio Stake, for three-year olds, 2 mile heats, in 3:37½, 3:55½, beating Pilgrim. Memphis, Tenn, October 25, won Post Stake, 2 mile heats in 3:40¼, 3:40, beating Defender, Morgan Scout, etc. Nashville, Oct. 12, won Citizens' Stake, 2 mille heats, in 3.41¾, 3:41, beating and distancing Morgan Scout, etc. Lexington, Ky., May 24, 1871, walked over for purse $400, 2 mile heats. Long Branch, July 5, won Monmouth Cup, 2½ miles, in 4:41½, beating Helmbold, Regards, and Preakness. Saratoga, July 14, won Saratoga Cup, 2¼ miles, in 4:02¾, beating Kingfisher; the first mile was run in 1:40. Aug. 19, walked over for purse of $800, 2¾ miles. Aug. 23, was beaten by Helmbold, 4 miles, in 7:49¼. Lexington, Ky., Sept. 12, won club purse, 2 mile heats, in 3:38¾, 3:41½. Lexington, Ky., May 15, 1872, won purse, 1½ miles, in 2;41¼, beating Metella and Aureola. May 18, won Woolley Stake, 3 miles, in 6:00¾, beating Metella, Talaria, etc. Loug Branch, July 2, won Monmouth Cup, 2½ miles, in 4:34. July 4, won purse, mile heats, three best in five, in 1:56¼, 1:54, 1:43¾, beating Susan Ann, Metella aud Arizona. Saratoga, July 16, was beaten by Harry Bassett for the Cup, 2¼ miles, in 3:59, the fastest race to that date. The first mile was run in 1:44, the first two miles in 3:30. Longfellow pulled up lame, and with this race closed his turf career, starting in sixteen races, won fourteen, lost two, and won $15,000 in money. Leamington, his sire, will be found in this vol. Nantura, his dam, was a very superior mare and good winner, Brawner's Eclipse, her sire, was a fine race-horse, and much inbred to imp. Diomed, Queen Mary his grandam was a fine race-mare, Bertrand her sire, son of Sir Archy, was one of the best race-horses and stallions of his day.

Longfellow stands nearly 17 hands high, with white stripe down his face, with left hind foot white above the ankle, and a little white on the coronet of the right hind foot. He has a neat ear, broad forehead, with Roman nose, long well-shaped neck, running into strong, well-shaped shoulders, great depth of girth, rather light flank, good strong hips, with good length of whirlbone and stifle, and thence to the hock; good legs and feet. The following are the best of his get: Thora, a first-class mare, her 3 miles at Saratoga when three years old, with 99 lbs., in 5:25½, was a remarkable race; also her Pimlico Stake, 2⅛ miles, in 3:47½, beating Checkmate and Monitor. Other good ones are Edinburg, Irish King, Jils Johnson, Leonard, Lilly R, Long Taw (Dave Moore), Mollie Merrill, Gen. Pike, John Harper, Georgia A, Odd Fellow, Tom Montague, Bell Boy, Coquena (Miss Nailer), Longitude, Long Girl, Wildmoor, Wildfellow, Freeland, Hospodar, Fellowplay, Minnie D, Lucy Long, Mary Corbett, King Dutchman, Long Girl, Annie G, and some others. In addition to his being a son of Leamington, he is much inbred on the dam's side to Sir Archy and Diomed, well fortified with the blood of Herod and Eclipse, upon that of Partner and Regulus, son of the Godolphin Arabian.

PEDIGREE OF LONGFELLOW.

LONGFELLOW.	LEAMINGTON.	Daughter of.	Sir Hercules.	Whalebone.	Waxy.	Pot-8-os—Maria by Herod—Lisette by Snap—Miss Windsor by Godol. Arabian—Sis. to Volunteer by Y. Belgrade—Dau. of B. Childers.
					Penelope.	Trumpator—Prunella by Highflyer—Promise by Snap—Julia by Blank—Spectator's dam by Partner—Bonny Lass by B. Bolton.
				Peri.	Wanderer.	Gohanna—Catharine by Woodpecker—Camilla by Trentham—Coquette by Compton Barb—Sis. to Regulus by Godol. Arabian.
			Fangh-a-Ballagh.		Thalestris.	Alexander—Rival by Sir Peter—Hornet by Drone—Manilla by Goldfinder—Dau. of Old Eng.—Dau. of Cul. Arabian—Miss Cade.
				Bob Booty.	Chanticleer.	Woodpecker—Dau. of Eclipse—Rosebud by Snap—Miss Belsea by Regulus—Dau. of Bart. Childers—Dau. of Hon. Arabian.
			Guiccioli.		Ierne.	Bagot—Dau. of Gamahoe—Patty by Tim—Miss Patch by Justice—Ringtail Galloway by Cur. Bay Barb—Sis. to Witty Mare.
		Daphne.		Flight.	I. Escape.	Commodore—Dau. of Highflyer—Shift by Sweetbriar—Bl. Susan by Snap—Ld. Bruce's Cade Mare by Cade—Dau. of Belgrade.
			Pantaloon.		Young Heroine.	Bagot—Heroine by Hero—Dan. of Snap—Sis. to Regulus by Godol. Arabian—Gr. Robinson by Bald Galloway—Dau. of Snake.
				Castrel.	Buzzard.	Woodpecker—Misfortune by Dux—Curiosity by Snap—Dau. of Regulus—Dau. of Bart. Childers—Dau. of Honeywood Arabian.
					Selim's dam.	Alexander—Dau. of Highflyer—Dau. of Alfred—Dau. of Engineer—Bay Malton's dam by Cade—Lass of the Mill by Traveler.
			Idalia.	Laurel.	Peruvian.	Sir Peter—Dau. of Budrow—Escape's dam by Squirrel—Dau. of Babraham—Dau. of Golden Ball—Bushy Molly by Hamp. Ct. Childers.
		Maid of Honor.			Musidora.	Meteor—Maid of All Work by Highflyer—Sis. to Tandem by Syphon—Dau. of Regulus—Dau. of Snip—Dau. of Cottingham.
					Blacklock.	Whitelock—Dau. of Coriander—Wildgoose by Highflyer—Coheiress by Pot-8-os—Manilla by Goldfinder—Dau. of Old Eng.
					Wagtail.	Prime Minister—Dau. of Orville—Miss Grimstone by Weasel—Dau. of Ancaster—Dau. of Dam Arabian—Dau. of Sampson—Dau. of Oroonoko.
					Champion.	Selim—Podagra by Gouty—Jet by Magnet—Jewel by Squirrel—Sophia by Blank—Diana by Second—Han. Br. Mare by Stan. Arabian.
					Etiquette.	Orville—Boadicea by Alexander—Brunette by Amaranthus—Mayfly by Matchem—Dau. of An. Starling—Dau. of Grasshopper (Crab).
	NANTURA.	Queen Mary.	Brawner's Eclipse.	Am. Eclipse. Duroc.	Diomed.	Florizel—Sis. to Juno by Spectator—Horatia by Blank—Dau. of F. Childers—Miss Belvoir by Gr. Grantham—Dau. of Paget Turk.
					Amanda.	Grey Diomed—Dau. of Va. Cade—Dau. of Hick's Independence—Dolly Fine by Imp. Silvereye—Dau. of Imp. Badger.—Dau. of Forester.
				Miller's Damsel.	Messenger.	Mambrino—Dau. of Turf—Sis. to Figurante by Regulus—Dau. of Starling—Snap's dam by Fox—Gipsy by Bay Bolton.
			Daughter of.		Daughter of.	Pot-8-os—Dau. of Gimcrack—Snap-Dragon by Snap—Dau. of Regulus—Dau. of Bart. Childers—Dau. of Hon. Arabian—True Blue's dam.
				Henry.	Sir Archy.	Diomed—Castianira by Rockingham—Tabitha by Trentham—Dau. of Bosphorus—Dau. of Wm's Forester—Dau. of Coalition Colt (Godol.)
		Bertrand.	Sir Archy.		Daughter of.	Diomed—Bellona by Bellair—Indian Queen by Meade's Pilgrim—Dau. of Imp. Janus—Dau. of Imp. Jolly Roger—Dau. of Imp. Valliant.
			Y. Romp.		Duroc.	Diomed—Amanda by Gr. Diomed—Dau. of Va. Cade—Dau. of Independence—Dolly Fine by Imp. Silvereye—Dau. of Imp. Badger.
					Romp.	Duroc—Dau. of Pot-8-os—Dau. of Gimcrack—Snap-Dragon by Snap—Dau. of Regulus—Dau. of Bart. Childers—Dau. of Hon. Arabian.
		Lady Fortune.	Eliza.		Diomed.	Florizel—Sis. to Juno by Spectator—Horatia by Blank—Dau. of F. Childers—Miss Belvoir by Gr. Grantham—Dau. of Paget Turk.
					Castianira.	Rockingham—Tabitha by Trentham—Dau. of Bosphorus—Dau. of Wm's Forester—Dau. of Coalition Colt—Dau. of Bustard (Crab).
					Bedford.	Dungannon (Eclipse)—Fairy by Highflyer—Fairy Queen by Young Cade—Black Eyes by Crab—Warlock Galloway by Snake.
					Mambrina.	Mambrino—Sis. to Naylor's Sally by Blank—Dau. of Ward—Dau. of Merlin (Bustler)—Dau. of Pert (Ely Turk)—Dau. of St. Martin.
			Woodpeck-Brim or er's dam. Bl. Beard.		*Brimmer.	Blue Beard (Imp. Sterling)—Dau. of Mendosa (Imp. Medley)—Arminda by Imp. Medley—Dau. of Imp. Bolton—Sally Wright.
					Daughter of.	Lamplighter (Imp. Medley)—Dau. of Imp. Medley (Gimcrack)—Dau. of Imp. Fearnought (Regulus)—Dau. of Imp. Janus (Janus by Godol.)
					Buzzard.	Woodpecker—Misfortune by Dux—Curiosity by Snap—Dau. of Regulus—Dau. of Bart. of Childers—Dau. of Hon. Arabian.
					The Fawn.	Craig's Alfred (Imp. Medley)—Shepherdess by Wornesley's King Herod (Imp. Fearnought)—Dau. of Morton's Imp. Traveler (Partner)—Dau. of Imp. Whittington (Whitenose)—Dau. of Imp. Childers (Blaze)—Dau. of Babraham (Godol.)—Dau. of Bethel's Arabian—Dau. of Graham's Champion—Dau. of Darley Arabian—Dau. of Old Merlin—[As believed.]

Blue Beard by Imp. Sterling dam Brilliant by Imp. Matchem—2d dam Imp. by Brilliant—as the author believes.
* Brimmer given.

LUKE BLACKBURN

(WINNER OF THE TIDAL, LONG ISLAND, ST. LEGER AND GREAT CHALLENGE STAKES AT SHEEPSHEAD BAY, OCEAN AND CHAMPION STAKES AT LONG BRANCH, UNITED STATES HOTEL STAKES, AND GRAND UNION PRIZE AT SARATOGA, KENTUCKY ST. LEGER AND GREAT AMERICAN STALLION STAKES AT LOUISVILLE, KY.)

Will stand the season of 1883 *at Belle Meade Stud., Gen. W. G. Harding, proprietor, near Nashville, Tenn., at* $100 *the season. Application to Gen. W. H. Jackson, lock box* 383, *Nashville, Tenn. Annual sale of yearlings about May* 1st.

LUKE BLACKBURN by imp. Bonnie Scotland, bred by Messrs. J. and A. C. Franklin, Sumner Co., Tenn., foaled 1877, dam Nevada by Lexington out of Lightsome, dam of Salina, Sprightly and Crucifix by imp. Glencoe. In 1879, as a two-year old, Blackburn ran with indifferent success. He started thirteen times; won two races, was second in six, third in one and unplaced in four. Lexington, May 12, ran second to Knight Templar in the Colt Stakes, half-mile; time :50; Moscow, Wargentine, Fonso, Amazon and Hamerfest also ran. Louisville, Ky., May 21, ran second to Kimball, in the Alexander Stakes, half-mile; time :49¾; eight started. St. Louis, Mo., June 13, again finished second to Kimball, in the Hotel Stakes, three-quarters of a mile; time, 1:16¼; Amazon, Chris. Doyle, Victory and Slicer also started. Chicago, Ill., June 23, ran second to Kimball (third time) in Grand Pacific Hotel Stakes, three-quarters of a mile; time, 1:18¼; Wargentine finished third, Vapor, Victory and Mistake unplaced. Saratoga, Aug. 2, ran second to Lucy George, five-eights of a mile; time, 1:04½; Giroflé and Cassatt also started. Same place, Aug. 12, ran second to Grenada in the Windsor Hotel Stakes, five-eights of a mile; time, 1:03¼; seven started. Autumn Meeting, Coney Island Jockey Club, Prospect Park, Sept. 6, won his maiden race, the Breeze Purse, three-quarters of a mile, defeating Giroflé, Queen's Own and four others; time, 1:17¼. Brighton Beach Fair Grounds, N. Y., Sept 18, won the Ocean Stakes, three-quarters of a mile, defeating Elias Lawrence (Late Bilstein), Quito and three others; time, 1:18¼. After this race Luke Blackburn was retired for the season, and became the property of Dwyer Bros., Brooklyn, N. Y., who gave $2,500 for him.

In the year 1880, Luke Blackburn entered in twenty-four races, lost two and won twenty-two; his first race was at Lexington, Ky., when he ran third to Fonso and Kinkead in the Phœnix Hotel Stakes, 1¼ miles, won by Fonso in 2:08¾. Blackburn had been sick and was unfit to run. He was then sent East, and won a dash of three-quarters of a mile at Jerome Park in 1:18, defeating Checkmate and three others. Two days after he won a dash of 1¼ mile in 1:58, beating Scotilla, Checkmate and two others. Three days after won a race of one mile and three furlongs in 2.28¼, beating Scotilla and two others. Two days after defeated Monitor, 1⅛ miles, in 2:39½, and two days afterward won the handicap sweepstakes, 1¼ miles, in 2:13.

All these races were run at Jerome Park during the Spring meeting. Sheepshead Bay, June 19, won the Tidal Stake, one mile, in 1:45, defeating Kimball, Kitty J., and Grenada. June 22, won the Coney Island Handicap, one mile and 3 furlongs, in 2:24½, beating Duke of Montrose and Vagrant. June 26, was beaten in purse race, 1¼ miles, in 2:12, by Duke of Montrose. Blackburn fell after running the first quarter and unseated his jockey. Long Branch, July 3, won the Ocean Stakes, one mile and a furlong, in 2:03¼, beating Duke of Montrose and Harold. July 10, won sweepstakes, 1⅛ miles, in 2:11¼, beating, with 110 lbs. up, Duke of Montrose, 105 lbs., and Grenada, 110 lbs. Saratoga, July 16, won the All-aged sweepstakes, 1¼ miles, in 2:11¾, beating Checkmate and Volturno. July 24, won mile and a furlong, in 1:58, beating Gabriel and Giroflé. July 27, won dash of a mile, in 1:43¼, beating Turfman. July 31, won Summer Handicap, 1⅛ miles, in 2:39, carrying 110 lbs., beating Juanita, 102 lbs.; Gen. Philips, 112 lbs.; and Ada Glenn, 105 lbs., conceding Juanita 20, Gen. Philips 23, and Ada Glenn 17 lbs. Saratoga, Aug. 5, won United States Hotel Stakes, for three-year olds, 1¼ miles, in 2:41, beating Ferncliff, Oden, &c. Aug. 7, won the Grand Union Hotel Prize, handicap, 110 lbs. up, 1⅜ miles, in 3:07, beating One Dime, 110 lbs., Gleumore, 118 lbs., and three others. In this race he conceded Glenmore, 20; One Dime 32; Cammie F 24, and Gen. Philip 35 lbs. Aug. 12, won the Kenner Stakes, two miles, in 3:35¼, beating Glidelia and Oden. Long Branch, Aug. 17th, won the Champion Stakes, 1½ miles, in 2:34, beating Monitor, Uncas, Grenada and Report, in the fastest and best race ever run at the distance. Sheepshead Bay, Sept. 4, won the Great Challenge Stakes, for all ages, 1¼ miles, in 2:38, beating Monitor, Uncas and One Dime. Sept. 9, won the Long Island St. Leger, 1⅝ miles, in 4:07¼. Sept. 14, won a match race for $5,000, beating Uncas, each carrying 103 lbs., 1¼ miles, in 2:42½. Louisville, Ky., Sept. 27, won the Kentucky St. Leger, two miles, in 3:42, beating Kinkead. Sept. 30, won the Great American Stallion Stakes, 1⅞ miles, in 3:04, beating Kimball and Big Medicine. In this race he injured the quarter of one of his fore-feet badly and was stopped in his work.

Continued on page 110.

The Horse-Breeders' Guide and Hand Book. 109

PEDIGREE OF LUKE BLACKBURN.

LUKE BLACKBURN.	NEVADA.	Lightsome.	Levity.	Vandal's dam.			Whalebone.	Waxy—Penelope by Trumpator—Prunella by Highflyer—Promise by Snap—Julia by Blank—Spectator's dam by Partner.
							Margretta.	Sir Peter—Sis. to Cracker by Highflyer—Nutcracker by Matchem—Miss Starling by Starling—Dau. of Partner—Dau. of Croft's Bay Barb.
				Trustee.	Hetman Platoff's d.	Tramp or Waverly.*	Comus.	Sorcerer—Houghton Lass by Sir Peter—Alexina by King Fergus—Lardella by Y. Marske—Dau. of Cade—Beaufremont's dam.
						Don John.	Marciana.	Stamford—Marcia by Coriander—Faith by Pacolet—Atalanta by Matchem—Lass of the Mill by Oroonoko—Dau. of Old Traveler.
		Glencoe.	Trampo-line.			Iago.	Buzzard.	Woodpecker—Misfortune by Dux—Curiosity by Snap—Dau. of Regulus—Dau. of Bart. Childers—Dau. of Hon Arabian—Dam of True Blues.
				Sultan.	Dau. of Selim.		Castrel's dam.	Alexander—Dau. of Highflyer—Dau. of Alfred—Dau. of Engineer—Bay Malton's dam by Cade—Lass of the Mill by Traveler.
					Partisan.	Scandal.	Haphazard.	Sir Peter—Miss Hervey by Eclipse—Clio by Y. Cade—Dau. of Old Starling Dau. of Bart. Childers—Dau. of Bay Bolton—Dau. of By. Turk.
				Rowena.	Gladiator.		Daughter.	Precipitate—Colibri by Woodpecker—Camilla by Trentham—Coquette by Compton Barb—Sis. to Regulus by Godol. Arabian—Gr. Robinson.
		Alice Carneal.		Sarpedon.		Queen Mary.	Walton.	Sir Peter—Arethusa by Dungannon—Dau. of Prophet—Virago by Snap—Dau. of Regulus—Sis. to Othello by Crab—Miss Slamerkin.
					Pauline.		Parasol.	Pot-8-os—Prunella by Highflyer—Promise by Snap—Julia by Blank—Spectator's dam by Partner—Bonny Lass by Bay Bolton.
				Sister to Tuckahoe.		Daughter of.	Moses.	Whalebone or Seymour—Dau. of Gobanna—Gr. Skim by Woodpecker—Silver's dam by Herod—Y. Hag by Skim—Hag by Crab—Ebony.
					Pleanipo-tentiary.		Quadrille.	Selim—Canary Bird by Whiskey or Sorcerer—Canary by Coriander—Miss Green by Highflyer—Harriet by Matchem—Flora by Regulus.
		Boston.				Myrrha.	Emilius.	Orville—Emily by Stamford—Dau. of Whiskey—Gr. Dorimant by Dorimant—Dizzy by Blank—Dizzy by Driver—Dau. of Smiling Tom.
				Timo-leon.			Harriet.	Pericles—Dau. of Selim—Pipylina by Sir Peter—Rally by Trumpator—Fancy, Sis. to Diomed by Florizel—Dau. of Spectator—Horatia by Blank.
						BONNIE SCOTLAND.	Whalebone.	Waxy—Penelope by Trumpator—Prunella by Highflyer—Promise by Snap—Julia by Blank—Spectator's dam by Partner.
		Lexington.					Gift.	Y. Gohanna—Sis. to Grazier by Sir Peter—Sis. to Amaitor by Trumpator—Dau. of Herod—Dau. of Snap—Dau. of Gower Stallion—Dau. of Childers.
							Sir Archy.	Diomed—Castianira by Rockingham—Tabitha by Trentham—Dau. of Bosphorus—Dau. of Wm.'s Forester—Dau. of Coalition Colt. (Godol).
							Daughter.	Imp. Saltram (Eclipse)—Dau. of Symme's Wildair—Dau. of Driver (Imp. Othello)—Dau. of Fallower (Blank)—Dau. of Vampire (Regulus).
							Ball's Florizel.	Diomed—Dau. of Imp. Shark—Dau. of Harris' Eclipse—Dau. of Imp. Fearnought—Dau. of Jolly Roger—Dau. of Sober John—Dau. of Shock.
							Daughter of.	Alderman—Dau. of Clockfast—Dau. of Symme's Wildair—Y. Kitty Fisher by Fearnought—Imp. Kitty Fisher by Cade—Dau. of Som. Arabian.
							Emilius.	Orville—Emily by Stamford—Dau. of Whiskey—Gr. Dorimant by Dorimant—Dizzy by Blank—Dizzy by Driver—Dau. of Smiling Tom.
							Icaria.	The Flyer—Parma by Dick Andrews—May by Beningbrough—Primrose by Mambrino—Cricket by Herod—Sophia by Blank.
							Sumpter.	Sir Archy—Flirtilla's dam by Robin Redbreast—Dau. of Obscurity—Slamerkin by Wildair—Imp. Cub Mare by Cub—Amaranthus dam.
							Lady Grey.	Robin Grey—Maria by Melzar—Dau. of Highflyer—Dau. of Fearnought—Dau. of Ariel—Dau. of Jack of Diamonds—Imp. Diamond by Cul. Arabian.
							Selim.	Buzzard—Castrel's dam by Alexander—Dau. of Highflyer—Dau. of Alfred—Dau. of Engineer—Bay Malton's dam by Cade—Lass of the Mill.
							Bacchante.	Williamson's Ditto—Sis. to Calomel by Mercury—Dau. of Herod—Folly by Marske—Vixen by Regulus—Dau. of Hut. Spot—Dau. of Fox Cub.
							Tramp.	Dick Andrews—Dau. of Gohanna—Fraxinella by Trentham—Dau. of Woodpecker—Everlasting by Eclipse—Hyaena by Snap.
							Web.	Waxy—Penelope by Trumpator—Prunella by Highflyer—Promise by Snap—Julia by Blank—Spectator's dam by Partner—Bonny Lass.
							Catton.	Golumpus—Lucy Grey by Timothy—Lucy by Florizel—Frenzy by Eclipse—Dau. of Engineer—Dau. of Blank—Lass of the Mill by Traveler.
							Emma.	Whisker—Gibside Fairy by Hermes—Vicissitude by Pipator—Beatrice by Sir Peter—Pyrrha by Matchem—Duchess by Whitenose.
							Tranby.	Blacklock—Dau. of Orville—Miss Grimstone by Weasel—Dau. of Ancaster Dau. of Dam. Arabian—Dau. of Sampson—Dau. of Oroonoko.
							Lucilla.	Trumpator (Sir Solomon)—Lucy by Orphan (Ball's Florizel)—Lady Grey by Robin Grey (Imp. Royalist)—Maria by Melzar (Imp. Medley)—Dau. of Imp. Highflyer (Highflyer)—Dau. of Fearnought (Regulus)—Dau. of Ariel (Mor. Imp. Traveler)—Dau. of Jack of Diamonds (Cul. Arabian)—Imp. Diamond (Duchess) by Cul. Arabian—Lady Thigh by Croft's Partner (Jigg)—Dau. of Greyhound (White Barb Chillaby)—Dau. of Cur. Bay Barb—Dau. of D'Arcy's Ch. Arabian—Dau. of Whiteshirt—Old Montague Mare.

* Waverly given.

LUKE BLACKBURN—Continued.

At 4 years old started in two races. Jerome Park, won club purse, one mile, in 1:45, beating Topsy and Potomac. Was unplaced in Coney Island Cup won by Glenmore in 3:58½. This closed his racing career.

Nevada, the dam of Blackburn, won the West End Hotel Stakes at Long Branch in 1872; she is own sister to Salina, winner of the Monmouth Oaks, Jersey St. Leger and Robins Stakes at Long Branch in 1871, and of Sprightly, the dam of the great race-horse Volturno, by imp. Billet, winner of the Breckenridge Stakes at Baltimore in 1879, two miles, in 3:35¼; 1¾ miles in 3:08½, and the Louisville Cup the year 1880, and of Elias Lawrence who won the Baden-Baden Handicap, three miles, at Saratoga same year, in 5:28½, the fastest race ever run by a three-year old at the distance. Crucifix, another sister, is the dam of Fairplay and Quito. Levity, the great grandam of Blackburn, was the dam of Lever, Legatee, Brenna (the dam of the fine race-mare Bradamante), and of Ruric, by imp. Sovereign, who won two prominent stakes at Lexington, Ky., when three years old, and was sold for $5,000, a high price in those days. The Tranby mare, his fourth dam, was the dam of the great race-horse and superior stallion Vandal, (who won three-mile heats in 5:36, 5:33), Alaric (who was the first horse that ever ran two miles in the thirties in America; this he did at Lexington, in 1845, winning a second heat in 3:39), Atala and Volga, etc.

Blackburn is a light bay, with large star and two white ankles behind; he stands, fairly measured, 15 hands and 2¼ inches high, has a fine, well-shaped head, with great breadth of forehead, indicating much brain power, well-set on a good-shaped neck with very wide throttle; his shoulders are well-set and oblique, the shoulder blade being very broad, with great depth of girt, and his body is large, well-ribbed home to very broad, strong and muscular hips, with great length from point of hip to whirlbone, and thence to stifle and hock he has good bone, broad knees and excellent hocks; measures 69½ in. around the girth; length of shoulder, 27½ in.; around the arm, 19 in.; below the knee, 8 in.; from point of shoulder to point of buttocks, 64 in.; from hip to point of hock, 38 in.; around gaskins, 17 inches

His pedigree is a happy combination of speedy and stout crosses, being much inbred to Diomed through his best son Sir Archy, and from the family which produced Lexington and Vandal. If high form and racing ability, with faultless action coupled with high breeding and racing descent are tokens of excellence, Luke Blackburn is the peer of any horse living, and must prove an invaluable stallion.

MACCAROON (Imp.)

Maccaroon is a private stallion in the Brookdale Stud, Mr. D. D. Withers, proprietor, Monmouth Co., near Holmdel, N. J.

MACCAROON by Macaroni, son of Sweetmeat, bred by Mr. T. T. Parker, foaled 1871; dam Songstress by Chanticleer, son of Irish Birdcatcher, out of Mrs. Carter by Humphrey, son of Sandbeck by Catton. Maccaroon made his first appearance as two-year-old in the Champaign Stakes, one mile, won by Rutherford, in 1:47½, and was unplaced, same meeting ran second to the Asteroid, Sue Washington Colt, three-quarters of a mile in 1:18¾, beating Atilla, Lava and Weathercock. Won a club purse for maiden two-year olds, three-quarters of a mile, in 1:17¼, beating Weathercock, Mattie W, Mary Buckley and Juliana. As three-year old started four times. Was unplaced in Withers Stakes, one mile, won by Dublin in 1:50, track heavy. Was unplaced in club purse, one mile, won by Atilla in 1:44½. Long Branch, was unplaced in Jersey Derby 1½ miles, won by Brigand in 2:44¾. Was third in Robins Stake, two miles, won by Acrobat in 3:42, beating Bannerette. Macaroni, his sire, won the 2,000 guineas, and the Derby, and is the sire of Spinaway, the winner of 1,000 guineas and Oaks, Camelia, winner of the 1,000 guineas, sire also of Lamphrey, Ramsbury, Vermicilli, Gloucester, Bonny Jean, and Macheath, the best two-year old in England in 1882, winner of eight out of eleven prominent events in which he started. Macoroni is second to Hermit on the list of winning sires in 1882. Chanticleer, the sire of his dam, was son of Birdcatcher, own brother to Faugh-a-Ballagh, and sired Habena and Manganese, winner of the 1,000 guineas, Songstress winner of the Oaks, Daniel O'Rourke winner of the Derby, Knight of St. George, Warlock and The Baron, all St. Leger winners. The Baron was sire of the great Stockwell and Rataplan. Maccaroon has not sired a dozen colts which have been trained. Nancy, at two-year old, won Homebred Stakes at Jerome Park, three-quarters of a mile, in 1:19, beating Oden, Juanita and others. She also won Monmouth Oaks, beating Glidelia, Bye-and Bye and others. Macbeth and Macduff both winners at two years old, Macduff won Champagne Stakes at Jerome Park, and in 1882 won a handicap purse at Jerome 1¼ miles, in 1:59, defeating a field of eight and the free handicap 1½ miles in 2:41, 107 pounds, beating Gen. Monroe (4) 1:05 and four others. He has the speedy crosses of Sweetmeat, Pantaloon and the stout ones of Whalebone and Margrave, and goes through the Herod blood and Sister of Diomed to the D'Arcy Royal Mare. Maccaroon is a red chestnut, 16 hands and ½ of an inch high, has a small star and snip and weighs 1,180 lbs. He is a fine formed horse, of good temper, and only needs a chance to distinguish himself in the stud.

PEDIGREE OF MACCAROON (Imp.)

MACCAROON (Imp.)	**MACARONI**	Sweetmeat. {Gladiator. / Partisan.}	Walton. / Parasol.		Sir Peter—Arethusa by Dungannon—Dau. of Prophet—Virago by Snap—Dau. of Regulus—Sis. to Othello by Crab—Miss Slamerkin. Pot-8-os—Prunella by Highflyer—Promise by Snap—Julia by Blank—Spectator's dam by Partner—Bonny Lass by Bay Bolton—Dau. of D. Arabian.
		Lollypop. {Pau- / line.}	Moses. / Quadrille.		Whalebone or Seymour—Sis. to Castanea by Gohanna—Grey Skim by Woodpecker—Silver's dam by Herod—Y. Hag by Skim—Hag by Crab. Selim—Canary Bird by Whiskey or Sorcerer—Canary by Coriander—Miss Green by Highflyer—Harriet by Matchem—Flora by Regulus.
		Starch or Voltaire.*	Blacklock. / Daughter of.		Whitelock—Dau. of Coriander—Wildgoose by Highflyer—Coheiress by Pot-8-os—Manilla by Goldfinder—Dau. of Old Eng.—Dau. of Cul. Arabian. Phantom—Dau. of Overton—Gratitude's dam by Walnut—Dau. of Ruler—Piracantha by Matchem—Prophetess by Regulus.
		Belinda.	Blacklock. / Wagtail.		Whitelock—Dau. of Coriander—Wildgoose by Highflyer—Coheiress by Pot-8-os—Manilla by Goldfinder—Dau. of Old Eng.—Dau. of Cul. Arabian. Prime Minister—Dau. of Orville—Miss Grimstone by Weasel—Dau. of Ancaster—Dau. of Dam. Arabian—Dau. of Sampson.
		Joocse. {Pantaloon. / Castrel.}	Buzzard. / Selim's dam.		Woodpecker—Misfortune by Dux—Curiosity by Snap—Dau. of Regulus—Dau. of Bart. Childers—Dau. of Hon. Arabian—True Blue's dam. Alexander—Dau. of Highflyer—Dau. of Alfred—Dau. of Engineer—Bay Malton's dam by Cade—Lass of the Mill by Traveler.
		Idalia.	Peruvian. / Musidora.		Sir Peter—Dau. of Budrow—Escape's dam by Squirrel—Sis. to Babraham by Babraham—Dau. of Golden Ball—Bushy Molly. Meteor—Maid of all Work by Highflyer—Sis. to Tandem by Syphon—Dau. of Regulus—Dau. of Snip—Dau. of Cottingham—War Galloway.
		Banter. {Master Henry.}	Orville. / Miss Sophia.		Beningbrough—Evelina by Highflyer—Termagant by Tantrum—Cantatrice by Sampson—Dau. of Regulus—Marske's dam. Stamford—Sophia by Buzzard—Huncamunca by Highflyer—Cypher by Squirrel—Dau. of Regulus—Dau. of B. Childers.
		Boadicea.	Alexander. / Brunette.		Eclipse—Grecian Princess by Wm.'s Forester—Dau. of Coalition Colt—Dau. of Bustard (Crab)—Charming Molly by Second. Amaranthus—Mayfly by Matchem—Dau. of An. Starling—Dau. of Grasshopper—Dau. of New. Arabian—Dau. of Pert (Ely Turk).
	SONGSTRESS.	Chanticleer. {Irish Birdcatcher.}	Whalebone. / Peri.		Waxy—Penelope by Trumpator—Prunella by Highflyer—Promise by Snap—Julia by Blank—Spectator's dam by Partner. Wanderer—Thalestris by Alexander—Rival by Sir Peter—Hornet by Drone—Manilla by Goldfinder—Dau. of Old Eng.
		Sir Hercules.	Bob Booty. / Flight.		Chanticleer—Ierne by Bagot—Dau. of Gamahoe—Patty by Tim—Miss Patch by Justice—Ringtail Galloway by C. Bay Barb. I. Escape—Y. Heroine by Bagot—Heroine by Hero—Dau. of Snap—Sis. to Regulus by Godol. Arabian—Gr. Robinson.
		Whim. {Drone.}	Master Robert. / Daughter of.		Buffer—Spinster by Shuttle—Dau. of Sir Peter—Bab by Bordeaux—Speranza by Eclipse—Virago by Snap—Sis. to Othello by Crab. Sir Walter Raleigh (Waxy)—Miss Tooley by Teddy the Grinder—Lady Jane by Sir Peter—Paulina by Florizel—Captive.
		Kiss.	Waxy Pope. / Daughter of.		Waxy—Prunella by Highflyer—Promise by Snap—Julia by Blank—Spectator's dam by Partner—Bonny Lass by Bay Bolton. Champion (Pot-8-os)—Brown Fanny by Maximin—Dau. of Highflyer—Dau. of Matchem—Gimcrack's dam by Gries' Partner.
		Humphrey. {Saudbeck.}	Catton. / Orvillina.		Golumpus—Lucy Grey by Timothy—Lucy by Florizel—Frenzy by Eclipse—Dau. of Engineer—Dau. of Blank—Lass of the Mill by Traveler. Beningbrough—Evelina by Highflyer—Termagant by Tantrum—Cantatrice by Sampson—Dau. of Regulus—Marske's dam.
		Oceana.	Cerberus. / Dr. Syntax's dam.		Gohanna—Dau. of Herod—Desdemona by Marske—Y. Hag by Skim—Hag Crab—Ebony by F. Childers—Ebony by Basto. Beningbrough—Jenny Mole by Carbuncle (Babraham Blank)—Dau. of Prince T. Quassaw (Snip)—Dau. of Regulus—Dau. of Partner (Jigg).
	Mrs. Carter. {Daughter of Mar- / grave.}		Muley. / Chatham's dam.		Orville — Eleanor by Whiskey—Y. Giantess by Diomed — Giantess by Matchem—Molly Longlegs by Babraham—Dau. of Cole's Foxhunter. Election—Fair Helen by Hambletonian—Helen by Delpini—Rosalind by Phoenomenon—Atalanta by Matchem—Lass of the Mill.
	Daughter of Elastic dam.		Thunderbolt. / Daughter of.		Sorcerer—Wowski by Mentor—Maria Waxy's dam by Herod—Lisette by Snap—Miss Windsor by Godol. Arabian. Sanebo (Herod)—Miss Teazle by Sir Peter (Highflyer)—Fanny by Diomed—Ambrosia by Woodpecker (Herod)—Ruth by Blank (Godol.)—Dau. of Regulus (Godol.)—Dau. of Soreheels (Basto)—Dau. of Makeless (Oglethorpe Arabian)—Christopher D'Arcy's Royal Mare.

* Voltaire given.

MATADOR (Imp.)

Will be located the season of 1883 *at the Nursery Stud, Hon. A. Belmont, proprietor, as private stallion. Annual sale of yearlings in June.*

MATADOR, by Gladiateur, son of Monarque bred by Hon. A. Belmont, Nursery Stud, near Babylon, L. I., foaled 1872, dam imp. Non Parielle, own sister to Silverhair, by Kingston out of England's Beauty by Irish Birdcatcher, son of Sir Hercules. Matador made his debut as a two-year old, started twice and was unplaced in both races. As a three-year old, started in four races and won one. Jerome Park, won a dash of one mile and a furlong in 2:02, beating Consignee, Lord Zetland and four others. Was unplaced in the other three races. As a four-year old he started twice and was unplaced in both races. Gladiatuer, ranked as a race-horse second to none, he won the 2,000 guineas, Derby, St. Leger and Grand Prix de Paris, in 1865, and is the only horse which ever accomplished this wonderful feat. Monarque, his sire, won the Newmarket Handicap, and the Goodwood Cup, and was sire of Reine, winner of the 1,000 guineas, and many notable winners in France. Kingston, the sire of his dam, was one of the noted horses of England, and Non Parielle, his dam, is own sister to Silverhair, the dam of Silvio; which won both the Derby and St. Leger in 1877. His grandam was by Irish Birdcatcher, one of the best and most popular horses that has ever graced the English harem, he proved his quality in The Baron who got Stockwell and Rataplan. England's beauty was the dam of The Rake that the late Joseph Dawson thought one of the best horses he ever trained, not excepting Peter or Prince Charlie. He has a double cross of Whalebone, with Whisker, Venison and Touchstone, and his pedigree runs through old Penelope the dam of Web, Whalebone, Whisker and other famous horses and successful stallions. Only one or two of his colts have been trained ; he will be a success with a fair chance. Matador is a dark bay with a few white hairs in his forehead, black legs, and is 16 hands high, and a strong, well shaped horse all over, and of excellent temper.

PEDIGREE OF MATADOR (Imp.)

MATADOR (Imp.)							
GLADIATEUR	Monarque	The Bar. Stg. or The Emp.*	Royal Oak	Whalebone. Defiance.	Waxy—Penelope by Trumpator—Prunella by Highflyer—Promise by Snap—Julia by Blank—Spectator's dam by Partner—Bonny Lass. Rubens—Littly Folly by Highland Fling—Harriet by Volunteer—Dau. of Alfred—Magnolia by Marske—Dau. of Babraham.		
			Daughter of.	Reveller. Design.	Comus—Rosette by Beningbrough—Rosamond by Tandem—Tuberose by Herod—Grey Starling by Starling—Coughing Polly by Bart. Childers. Tramp—Defiance by Rubens—Little Folly by Highland Fling—Harriet by Volunteer—Dau. of Alfred—Magnolia by Marske—Dau. of Babraham.		
		Poetess.	Ada.	Catton. Daughter of.	Golumpus—Lucy Gray by Timothy—Lucy by Florizel—Frenzy by Eclipse—Dau. of Engineer—Dau. of Blank—Lass of the Mill by Traveler. Smolensko—Lady Mary by Beningbrough—Dau. of Highflyer—Dau. of Marske—A la Grecque by Regulus—Dau. of Allworthy.		
				Whisker. Anna Bella.	Waxy—Penelope by Trumpator—Prunella by Highflyer—Promise by Snap—Julia by Blank—Spectator's dam by Partner. Shuttle—Dau. of Drone—Contessina by Y. Marske—Tuberose by Herod—Gr. Starling by Starling—Coughing Polly by Bart. Childers.		
	Miss Gladiator.	Gladiator.	Pauline. Partisan.	Walton. Parasol.	Sir Peter—Arethusa by Dungannon—Dau. of Prophet—Virago by Snap—Dau. of Regulus—Sis. to Othello by Crab—Miss Slamerkin. Pot-8-os—Prunella by Highflyer—Promise by Snap—Julia by Blank—Spectator's dam by Partner—Bonny Lass by Bay Bolton.		
				Moses. Quadrille.	Whalebone or Seymour—Dau. of Gohanna—Grey Skim by Woodpecker—Silver's dam by Herod—Y. Hag by Skim—Hag by Crab—Ebony. Selim—Canary Bird by Whiskey or Sorcerer—Canary by Coriander—Miss Green by Highflyer—Harriet by Matchem—Flora by Regulus.		
		Taffrail.	Sheet Anchor.	Lottery. Morgiana.	Tramp—Mandane by Pot-8-os—Y. Camilla by Woodpecker—Camilla by Trentham—Coquette by Compton Barb—Sis. to Regulus. Muley—Miss Stephenson by Scud or Sorcerer—Sis. to Petworth by Precipitate—Dau. of Woodpecker—Sis. to Juniper by Snap.		
			Warwick Mare.	Merman. Daughter of.	Whalebone—Mermaid by Orville—Dau. of Sir Solomon—Miss Brim by Highflyer—Brim by Squirrel—Helen by Blank—Dau. of Crab. Ardrossan—Sherpherdess by Shuttle—Dau. of Buzzard—Ann of the Forest by King Fergus—Miss West by Matchem (Cade).		
NON PAREILLE	England's Beauty.	Kingston.	Venison.	Walton. Parasol.	Sir Peter—Arethesa by Dungannon—Dau. of Prophet—Virago by Snap—Dau. of Regulus—Sis. to Othello by Crab—Miss Slamerkin. Pot-8-os—Prunella by Highflyer—Promise by Snap—Julia by Blank—Spectator's dam by Partner—Bonny Lass by Bay Bolton—Dau. Dar. Arabian.		
			Fawn.	Smolensko. Jerboa.	Sorcerer—Wowski by Mentor—Waxy's dam by Herod—Lisette by Snap—Miss Windsor by Godol. Arabian—Sis. to Volunteer. Gohanna—Camilla by Trentham—Coquette by Compton Barb—Sis. to Regulus by Godol. Arabian—Gr. Robinson by B. Galloway.		
		Queen Ann.	Partisan.	Royal Oak. Daughter of.	Catton—Dau. of Smolensko—Lady Mary by Beningbrough—Dau. of Highflyer—Dau. of Marske—A la Grecque by Regulus. Orville—Epsom Lass by Sir Peter—Alexina by King Furgus—Lardella by Y. Marske—Dau. of Cade—Beaufremont's dam.		
			Garcia.	Octavian. Daughter of.	Stripling—Dau. of Oberon (Highflyer)—Sis. to Sharper by Ranthos (Matchem)—Dau. of Sweepstakes (Old Sweepstakes)—Sis. to Careless. Shuttle—Catharine by Delpini—Dau. of Paymaster (Herod)—Dau. of Le Sang—Dau. of Rib—Eclipse's gr. dam Mother Western.		
	Prairie Bird.	Sir Hercules.	Slane.	Whalebone. Peri.	Waxy—Penelope by Trumpator—Prunella by Highflyer—Promise by Snap—Julia by Blank—Spectator's dam by Partner. Wanderer—Thalestris by Alexander—Rival by Sir Peter—Hornet by Drone (Herod)—Manilla by Goldfinder—Dau. of Old Eng.		
				Bob Booby. Flight.	Chanticleer—Ierne by Bagot—Dau of Gamahoe—Patty by Tim—Miss Patch by Justice—Ringtail Galloway by Cur. Bay Barb. I. Escape—Y. Heroine by Bagot—Heroine By Hero—Sis. to Regulus by Godol. Arabian—Gr. Robinson by Bald Galloway—Dau. of Snake.		
	Zillah.	Irish Birdcatcher. Touchstone.	Guicciolli.	Camel. Banter.	Whalebone—Dau. of Selim—Maiden by Sir Peter—Dau. of Phoenomenon—Matron by Florizel—Maiden by Matchem—Dau. of Squirt. Master Henry—Boadicea by Alexander—Brunette by Amaranthus—Mayfly by Matchem—Dau. of An. Starling—Dau. of Grasshopper.		
				Reveller. Morisca.	Comus—Rosette by Beningbrough—Rosamond by Tandem—Tuberose by Herod—Gr. Starling by Starling—Coughing Polly by Bart. Childers. Morisco (Muley)—Waltz by Election (Gohanna)—Penelope by Trumpator (Conductor)—Prunella by Highflyer (Herod)—Promise by Snap (Snip)—Julia by Blank (Godol.)—Spectator's dam by Partner (Jigg)—Bonny Lass by Bay Bolton (Gray Hautboy)—Dau. of Darley Arabian—Dau. of Byerly Turk—Dau. of Taffolet Barb—Dau. of Place's White Turk—Natural Barb Mare.		

The Baron Sting or The Emperor, given.*

MOCCASIN (Imp.)

(MOCCASIN, IS OWNED BY MR. P. LORILLARD OF THE RANCOCUS STUD, NEAR JOBSTOWN, BURLINGTON CO., N. J., AND HAS ONLY SERVED A FEW MARES OF THE OWNERS WHICH WERE UNCERTAIN BREEDERS, HE IS FOR SALE AND CAN BE PURCHASED ON APPLICATION TO COL. S. D. BRUCE, "TURF, FIELD AND FARM," N. Y.)

MOCCASIN, by Macaroni, son of Sweetmeat by Gladiateur, bred by Mr. H. W. Deacon, foaled 1874 and imported by Mr. Lorillard when a yearling ; dam Madame Strauss, dam of Rawcliff and Ormelie, by King Tom, son of Harkaway, out of Jetty Treffz, by Melbourne, son of Humphrey Clinker, by Comus. Macaroni the sire of Moccasin, won the 2,000 guineas and the Derby in 1863 and is the sire of Spinaway, winner of the 1,000 guineas and Oaks, Camelia winner of the 1,000 guineas, and of Macheath the best two-year-old in England this year, 1882, and now favorite for the Derby. Sweetmeat, Macaroni's sire, was by Gladiateur second to Bay Middleton in the Derby. Sweetmeat was a noted race-horse, ran twenty-four times as a two and three-year-old, and met hut one defeat, he won the Doncaster Cup and other important events. Moccasin has a double cross of that popular blood Pantaloon, which is famous for speed and staying qualities, and is a true racing strain. Pantaloon's son Van Amberg was second to Coronation in the Derby, and Sitirist, another son, won the St. Leger, beating Coronation; he is sire of Ghuznee winner of the Oaks and of Cardinal Puff, Elthiron, Hobbie Noble, The Riever, second to West Australian in the St. Leger, Hernandez, winner of the 2,000 guineas, and of Windhound, the sire of Thormanby. Leamington was out of a daughter of Pantaloon. King Tom the sire of his dam is too well known to need comment, snfficient to say he was by Harkaway out of Pochahontas. the dam of Stockwell and Rataplan, by Glencoe. His grandam is by Melbourne, sire of West Australian, winner of the double events, Derby and St. Leger, Blink Bonny winner of the Oaks and Derby, and the dam of Blair Athol winner of the Derby and St. Leger. Sir Tatton Sykes winner of the St. Leger, Cymba and Marchioness winner of the Oaks. The Melbourns are remarkble for size, substance and soundness, large bone and racing shape. Moccasin never raced, but from his colts, all out of mares the refuse of his owner, has sired some very reputable performers. Vampire and Faith won six races out of twenty-four starts in 1881. Vampire three, carried 140 lbs., and ran a mile 1:46¼. The two-year-old P. Lorillard, has won four races out of seven starts this year, 1882. Amazon and Disdain are both creditable performers, Disdain won Optional stakes. He is a dark bay or brown with great substance and power, fine temper and full 16 hands high. He should be invaluable to perpetuate the King Tom strain of blood through the descendents of Phaeton, King Ban and Great Tom.

PEDIGREE OF MOCCASIN (Imp.)

MOCCASIN (Imp.)									
MADAME STRAUS.	Jetty Treffz.	Ellen Loraine.	Melbourne.	Humphrey Clinker.	Pocahontas.	Marpessa.	King Tom.	Harkaway.	Walton.
		Lady Mary.	The Lord Mayor.	Dau. of Dau. of	Glencoe.	Fanny Dawson.		Economist.	Parasol.

		Sire/Dam details
	Walton.	Sir Peter—Arethusa by Dungannon—Dau. of Prophet—Virago by Snap—Dau. of Regulus—Sis. to Othello by Crab—Miss Slamerkin.
	Parasol.	Pot-8-os—Prunella by Highflyer—Promise by Snap—Julia by Blank—Spectator's dam by Partner—Bonny Lass by Bay Bolton.
	Moses.	Whalebone or Seymour—Dau. of Gohanna—Gr. Skim by Woodpecker—Silver's dam by Herod—Y. Hag by Skim—Hag by Crab.
	Quadrille.	Selim—Canary Bird by Whiskey or Sorcerer—Canary by Coriander—Miss Green by Highflyer—Harriet by Matchem.
	Blacklock.	Whitelock—Dau. of Coriander—Wildgoose by Highflyer—Coheiress by Pot-8-os—Manilla by Goldfinder—Dau. of Old Eng. (Godol.)
	Daughter of.	Phantom—Dau. of Overton—Gratitude's dam by Walnut—Dau. of Ruler—Piracantha by Matchem—Prophetess by Regulus.
	Blacklock.	Whitelock—Dau. of Coriander—Wildgoose by Highflyer—Coheiress by Pot-8-os—Manilla by Goldfinder—Dau. of Old Eng.
	Wagtail.	Prime Minister—Dau. of Orville—Miss Grimstone by Weasel—Dau. of Ancaster—Dau. of Dam Arabian—Dau. of Sampson.
	Buzzard.	Woodpecker—Misfortune by Dux—Curiosity by Snap—Dau. of Regulus—Dau. of Bart. Childers—Dau. of Hon. Arabian—Dam of True Blues.
	Selim's dam.	Alexander—Dau. of Highflyer—Dau. of Alfred—Dau. of Engineer—Bay Malton's dam by Cade—Lass of the Mill by Traveler.
	Peruvian.	Sir Peter—Dau. of Budrow (Eclipse)—Escape's dam by Squirrel—Dau. of Babraham—Dau. of Golden Ball—Busby Molly.
	Musidora.	Meteor—Maid of All Work by Highflyer—Sis. to Tandem by Syphon—Dau. of Regulus—Dau. of Snip—Dau. of Cottingham.
	Orville.	Beningbrough—Evelina by Highflyer—Termagant by Tantrum—Cantatrice by Sampson—Dau. of Regulus—Marske's dam.
	Miss Sophia.	Stamford—Sophia by Buzzard—Huncamunca by Highflyer—Cypher by Squirrel—Dau. of Regulus—Dau. of Bart. Childers.
	Alexander.	Eclipse—Grecian Princess by Wm's Forester—Dau. of Coalition Colt—Dau. of Bustard (Crab)—Ld. Leigh's Charming Molly.
	Brunette.	Amaranthus—Mayfly by Matchem—Dau. of An. Starling—Dau. of Grasshopper (Marske)—Dau. of Newton Arabian—Dau. of Pert.
	Whisker.	Waxy—Penelope by Trumpator—Prunella by Highflyer—Promise by Snap—Julia by Blank—Spectator's dam by Partner—Bonny Lass.
	Floranthe.	Octavian—Caprice by Anvil—Madcap by Eclipse—Dau. of Blank—Dau. of Blaze—Dau. of Y. Greyhound—Dau. of Cur. Bay Barb.
	Nabocklish.	Rugantino—Butterfly by Master Bagot—Dau. of Bagot—Mother Brown by Trunnion—Dau. of Old Eng.—Dau. of Bolton Starling.
	Miss Tooley.	Teddy the Grinder—Lady Jane by Sir Peter—Paulina by Florizel—Captive by Matchem—Calliope by Slouch.
	Sultan.	Selim—Bacchante by Williamson's Ditto—Sis. to Calomel by Mercury—Dau. of Herod—Folly by Marske—Vixen by Regulus.
	Trampoline.	Tramp—Web by Waxy—Penelope by Trumpator—Prunella by Highflyer—Promise by Snap—Julia by Blank—Spectator's dam.
	Muley.	Orville—Eleanor by Whiskey—Y. Giantess by Diomed—Giantess by Matchem—Molly Longlegs by Babraham (Godol.)
	Clare.	Marmion—Harpalice by Gohanna—Amazon by Driver—Fractious by Mercury—Dau. of Woodpecker—Everlasting by Eclipse.
	Comus.	Sorcerer—Houghton Lass by Sir Peter—Alexina by King Fergus—Lardella by Y. Marske—Beaufremont's dam by Bro. to Fearnought.
	Clinkerina.	Clinker—Pewet by Tandem—Termagant by Tantrum—Cantatrice by Sampson—Dau. of Regulus—Marske's dam.
	Cervantes.	Don Quixote—Evelina by Highflyer—Termagant by Tantrum—Cantatrice by Sampson—Dau. of Regulus—Marske's dam.
	Daughter of.	Golumpus—Dau. of Paynator—Sis. to Zodiac by St. George—Abigail by Woodpecker—Firetail by Eclipse—Dau. of Blank (Godol.)
	Pantaloon.	Castrel—Idalia by Peruvian—Musidora by Meteor—Maid of All Work by Highflyer—Sis. to Tandem by Syphon (Squirt).
	Honeymoon.	Filho-da-Puta—Hybla by Rubens—Larissa by Trafalgar (Sir Peter)—Meteora by Meteor—Maid of All Work by Highflyer.
	Voltaire.	Balcklock—Dau. of Phantom—Dau. of Overton—Gratitude's dam by Walnut (High.)—Dau. of Ruler—Piracantha by Matchem.
	Lady Moore Carew.	Tramp—Kite by Bustard (Castrel)—Olympia by Sir Oliver (Sir Peter)—Scotilla by Anvil (Herod)—Scota by Eclipse—Harmony Herod (Tartar)—Rutilia, Sis. to dam of Highflyer by Blank (Godolphin)—Dau. of Regulus (Godolphin)—Dau. of Soreheels (Basto by Byerly Turk)—Dau. of Makeless (Oglethorpe Arabian)—C. D'Arcy's Royal Mare.

* Voltaire given.

MONARCHIST,

(WINNER OF THE ANNUAL STAKE, 1871, MATURITY STAKE, 1872, AT JEROME PARK, AND METIARIE CUP, AT NEW ORLEANS,)

Will be located the season of 1883, *at the Elmendorf Stud (North Elkhorn), near Lexington, Ky., and will serve mares at the season. Application to D. Swigert, Muir's Post Office, Ky.*

MONARCHIST by Lexington, son of Boston, bred by A. J. Alexander, Woodburn Stud, Spring Station, Ky., dam Mildred, dam of Minx, Stamps, Sultana, etc., by imp. Glencoe, son of Sultan, out of Levity, Ruric's dam by imp. Trustee, son of Catton. Monarchist is bred to the mark, having in his veins the blood of the best-known racing families. Through Lexington, his sire, he is descended through the best racing strains of this country, from imp. Diomed, the winner of the first English Derby, in 1780. Out of his grandam Levity, came Ruric, Lightsome, Brenna, Lever and Legatee—all horses of note. Lightsome is the dam of Sprightly (Volturno's dam), by Lexington, and of Nevada, the dam of Luke Blackburn and other good ones. His third dam was the dam of Vandal, a race-horse himself and sire of the great Virgil, first on the list of winning sires in America in 1881, and sire of Hindoo. Monarchist was himself a good race-horse, as would be expected from such a combination of blood, and has performances to his credit worthy of the best. He made his first appearance in public as a three-year-old, when he started eight times, and won four races. At Jerome Park, Oct. 14, 1871, he won the Annual Sweepstakes, 2 miles, in 3:53¼. Same place, won the Grand National Handicap, 2¼ miles, in 4:09. Won the Post Stake at New Orleans, two mile heats, in 3:52¼, 3:49¼, beating Foster and Sentinel. As a four-year-old he started nine times and won eight races. At New Orleans, April 13, won the Grand Inaugural Post Stake, two mile heats, in 3:39, 3:44, beating Frank Hampton, Nellie Ransom and three others. Same place, April 16, won Louisiana Stakes, 2 mile heats, in 3:44¼, 3:40. Same place, won the Metairie Cup 2 miles and a quarter, in 4:12, beating Barney Williams, Nellie Ransom and Wanderer. At Baltimore, Oct. 22, won dash of three miles in 6:01¾. Jerome Park, Oct. 2, won Maturity Stakes, three miles, in 5:34¼, defeating the great Bassett. Oct. 12, won dash of 4 miles in 7:33¼, beating Harry Bassett and King Henry. This closed the turf career of Monarchist. He was relegated to the stud, and has covered only a very limited number of mares. The best of his get are Little Ruffin, winner of the Tobacco Stakes, at Louisville, Ky., mile heats in 1:44¼, 1:44⅔. Fireman (Montreal), Marchioness, a mile in 1:41, Mate, ch. f. Miss. Hardaway, Experiment, Storey, winner of Chicago Stakes, 1¼ miles, Una B, Josie H (Louise d'Or), Frankie B, winner of nine races out of fifteen starts as two-year-old, a mile in 1:45, and winner of the U. S. Hotel Stake at Saratoga, 1¼ miles in 2:40¼, beating Apollo Boatman, etc., Ida B, John Sullivan (Darley), Monte, Monarch, three-quarters of a mile in 1:14, mile 1:44 ; Green Stakes at Louisville, and Dixie Stakes at Baltimore, 2 miles 3:44 ; track heavy. Aristocrat, a winner in England. The family is one of the great racing ones of America. The horses have been large winners on the turf, and successful sires, and the mares have almost uniformly been successful and paying investments as brood mares. So if a racing strain is worth anything. Monarchist must be a successful sire with the strong infusion of Archy blood on both sides, and he is much inbred to the great English Eclipse. Monarchist is a beautiful bay, 16 hands, with a large star in his forehead and snip on his nose, both fore and near hind pasterns white, and is almost a finished model of a race-horse, no extra lumber, but clean-cut and highly finished. A little inbreeding from him will serve to perpetuate one of the best racing families in the world.

PEDIGREE OF MONARCHIST.

MONARCHIST (sire: **LEXINGTON** — Boston × Alice Carneal; dam: **MILDRED** — Glencoe × Levity)

LEXINGTON side

Boston — by Timoleon, out of Robin Brown's dam (by Ball's Florizel, Dau. of Sir Archy)

- **Timoleon** — by Sir Archy
  - **Diomed**
    - Florizel—Sister to Juno by Spectator—Horatia by Blank—Dau. of Childers—Miss Belvoir by Gr. Grantham—Dau. of Paget Turk.
  - **Castianira**
    - Rockingham—Tabitha by Trentham—Dau. of Bosphorus—Dau. of Wm's Forester—Dau. of Coalition Colt—Dau. of Bustard (Crab).
- **Ball's Florizel** (Dau. of Sir Archy)
  - **Imp. Saltram**
    - Eclipse—Virago by Snap—Dau. of Regulus—Sis. to Othello by Crab—Miss Slamerkin by Y. True Blue—Dau. of Oxford Dnn. Arabian.
  - **Daughter of**
    - Symme's Wildair (Imp. Fearnought)—Dau. of Driver (Imp. Othello)—Dau. of Imp. Fallower (Blank)—Dau. of Imp. Vampire (Regulus).

Robin Brown's dam — (Sarpedon × Lady Grey)

- **Sarpedon / Sumpter**
  - **Diomed**
    - Florizel—Sis. Juno by Spectator—Horatia by Blank—Dau. of F.Childers—Miss Belvoir by Gr. Grantham—Dau. of Paget Turk—Betty Percival.
  - **Daughter of**
    - Imp. Shark—Dau. of Harris' Eclipse—Dau. of Fearnought—Dau. of Jolly Roger (Roundhead)—Dau. of Sober John (Rib)—Dau. of Shock.
- **Emilius / Icaria**
  - **Imp. Alderman**
    - Pot-8-os—Lady Bolingbroke by Squirrel—Cypron, Herod's dam by Blaze—Selima by Bethel's Arabian—Dau. of Gra. Champion.
  - **Daughter of**
    - Clockfast—Dau. of Symme's Wildair—Y. Kitty Fisher by Fearnought—Imp. Kitty Fisher by Cade—Dau. of Somerset Arabian.

Alice Carneal — (Rowena × Lady Grey)

- **Rowena**
  - **Orville**
    - Beningbrough—Evelina by Highflyer—Termagant by Tantrum—Cantatrice by Sampson—Dau. of Regulus—Marske's dam by Blacklegs.
  - **Emily**
    - Stamford—Dau. of Whiskey—Gr. Dorimant by Dorimant—Dizzy by Blank—Dizzy by Driver—Dau. of Smiling Tom—Dau. of Oysterfoot.
- **Selim / Bacchante**
  - **The Flyer**
    - Vandyke, Jr.—Azalia by Beningbrough—Gillyflower by Highflyer—Dau. of Goldfinder—Sis. to Grasshopper by Marske—Dau. of Cul. Arabian.
  - **Parma**
    - Dick Andrews—May by Beningbrough—Primrose by Mambrino—Cricket by Herod—Sophia by Blank—Ld. Leigh's Diana by Second.

Lady Grey

- **Sir Archy**
  - Diomed—Castianira by Rockingham—Tabitha by Trentham—Dau. of Bosphorus—Dau. of Wm's Forester—Dau. of Coalition Colt (Godol).
- **Flirtilla's dam**
  - Robin Redbreast—Dau. of Imp. Obscurity—Slamerkin by Wildair—Imp. Cub Mare by Cub—Amaranthus dam by Second—Dau. of Starling.
- **Robin Grey**
  - Royalist—Belle Mariah by Gray Diomed—Queen by Imp. St. George—Dau. of Cassius—Primrose by Imp. Dove—Stella by Othello.
- **Maria**
  - Melzar—Dau. of Highflyer—Dau. of Fearnought—Dau. of Ariel—Dau. of Jack of Diamonds—Imp. Diamond (Duchess) by Cul. Arabian.

MILDRED side

Glencoe — (Trampoline × Sultan)

- **Trampoline / Web. Tramp.**
  - **Buzzard**
    - Woodpecker—Misfortune by Dux—Curiosity by Soap—Dau. of Regulus—Dau. of Bart. Childers—Dau. of Hon. Arabian—True Blue's dam.
  - **Castrel's dam**
    - Alexander—Dan. of Highflyer—Dau. of Alfred—Dau. of Engineer—Bay Malton's dam by Cade—Lass of the Mill by Traveler—Miss Makeless.
- **Sultan / Bacchante**
  - **Williamson's Ditto**
    - Sir Peter—Arethusa by Dungannon—Dau. of Prophet—Virago by Snap—Dau. of Regulus—Sis. to Othello by Crab—Miss Slamerkin.
  - **Sis. to Calomel**
    - Mercury—Dau. of Herod—Folly by Marske—Vixen by Regulus—Dau. of Hnt. Spot—Dau. of Bay Bolton—Dau. of Fox Cub—Dau. of Coneyskins.

Trustee / Emma / Cotton

- **Dick Andrews**
  - Joe Andrews—Dau. of Highflyer—Dau. of Car. Puff—Dau. of Tatler—Dau. of Snip—Dau. of Godol. Arabian—Dau. of Whiteneck—Dan. of Pel. Barb.
- **Daughter of**
  - Gohanna—Fraxinella by Trentham—Dau. of Woodpecker—Everlasting by Eclipse—Hyaena by Snap—Miss Belsea by Regulus.
- **Waxy**
  - Pot-8-os—Maria by Herod—Lisette by Snap—Miss Windsor by Godol. Arabian—Sis. to Volunteer by Y. Belgrave—Dau. of Bart. Childers.
- **Penelope**
  - Trumpator—Prunella by Highflyer—Promise by Snap—Julia by Blank—Spectator's dam by Partner—Bonny Lass by Bay Bolton.

Levity / Vandal's dam — (Lucilla × Tranby)

- **Emma / Cotton**
  - **Golumpus**
    - Gohanna—Catharine by Woodpecker—Camilla by Trentham—Coquette by Compton Barb—Sis. to Regulus by Godol. Arabian—Gr. Robinson.
  - **Lucy Grey**
    - Timothy—Lucy by Florizel—Frenzy by Eclipse—Dau. of Engineer—Dau. of Blank—Lass of the Mill by Traveler—Miss Makeless by Y. Greyhound.
- **Whisker**
  - Waxy—Penelope by Trumpator—Prunella by Highflyer—Promise by Snap—Julia by Blank—Spectator's dam by Partner—Bonny Lass.
- **Gibside Fairy**
  - Hermes—Vicissitude by Pipator—Beatrice by Sir Peter—Pyrrha by Matchem—Duchess by Whitnose—Miss Slamerkin by Y. True Blue.
- **Blacklock**
  - Whitelock—Dau. of Coriander—Wildgoose by Highflyer—Coheiress by Pat-8-os—Manilla by Goldfinder—Dau. of Old Eng.—Dau. of Cul. Arabian.
- **Daughter of**
  - Orville—Miss Grimstone by Wessel—Dau. of Ancaster—Dau. of Dam. Arabian—Dau. of Sampson—Dau. of Oroonoko—Sis. to Mirza by G. Arabian.
- **Trumpator**
  - Sir Solomon—Dau. of Hickory—Imp. Trumpetta by Trumpator—Sis. to Lambinos by Highflyer—Dau. of Eclipse—Vauxhall's dam by Cade.
- **Lucy**
  - Orphan (Ball's Florizel)—Lady Grey by Robin Grey—Maria by Melzar (Imp. Medley)—Dau. of Highflyer (Highflyer)—Dau. of Fearnought (Regulus)—Dau. of Ariel (Mor. Imp. Traveler)—Dau. of Jack of Diamonds (Cul. Arabian)—Imp. Diamond (Duchess) by Cul. Arabian—Lady Thigh by Croft's Partner (Jigg)—Dau. of Greyhound (White Barb Chillaby)—Dau. of Cur. Bay Barb—Dau. of D'Arcy's Chestnut Arabian—Dau. of Whiteshirt—Old Montague Mare.

MORTEMER (Imp.)

Mortemer is located at the head of the Rancocas Stud, near Jobstown, Burlington Co., N. J., owned by Mr. P. Lorillard, and is exclusively for private use.

MORTEMER, by Compiegne, son of Fitz Gladiator, bred in France, foaled 1865, dam Comtesse by The Baron or Nuncio, son of Plenipotentiary, winner of the Derby, out of Eusebia by Emilius, winner of the Derby. Mortemer was a very superior race-horse, winner of many important events on the Continent and in England. In 1867, as a two-year-old, he started eight times, won two races, viz., Prix Jacques Cœur, half a mile, at Bourges, beating a good field; the Omnium, nearly a mile, with 123 lbs., defeating a good field; ran second to Nuage for the Prix de Morny, three-quarters of a mile; ran second to Météore for the Grand Prix de la Société des Courses, one mile; ran second to Cesar in the Criterium, one mile, at Bordeaux; was unplaced in the other three races. He was unplaced in his only race in England that year. In 1868, when three years old, he ran eight times on the Continent, winning four races, viz., the Prix de la Seine, 1½ miles; the Eleventh Biennial Stakes, 1½ miles, and the Prix des Acacias, 1½ miles, all at Paris; won Prix Principal, one mile and 7 furlongs, at Moulins; ran second to Le Petit Caporal in Prix de Lutére, one mile and 3 furlongs; was second to Sedan in the Great St. Leger de France, one mile and 7 furlongs; was second in the Grand St. Leger International, one mile and 7 furlongs, and third in Prix du Volga, about one mile, at Baden-Baden. Same year ran four times in England. Was third in the Ninth Biennial Stakes at Stockbridge, 1½ miles, won by See-Saw; was second to Athena in the Grand Duke Michael Stakes, one mile one quarter and 73 yards, at Newmarket First October Meeting, and was unplaced in two others. In 1869, when four years old, ran eighteen times on the Continent, winning nine races, including the Prix de la Seine, 1½ miles, 134 lbs.; the Eleventh Biennial Stakes, two miles, 132 lbs.; Prix du Printemps, 1¾ miles, 132 lbs.; Prix de Satory, 2¼ miles, 142 lbs.; Prix de la Porte-Maillot, one mile; Prix de L'Empereur, one mile and a furlong, 153 lbs.; the Coupe de Deauville, 1¼ miles, 121 lbs.; Prix de Bois Roussel, 2½ miles, 121 lbs., and the Grand Prix de la Ville, two miles, 134 lbs. He ran second to really good horses in seven and third in one race and was unplaced in one. In 1870, then five years old, ran six times on the Continent; won five races, including Prix de la Seine, 1½ miles, 145 lbs.; The Cup un objet d'Art, about two miles, 144 lbs.; Prix la Moscowa, 2½ miles, 139 lbs.; Prix de L'Empereur, two miles, 133 lbs.; and the Prix des Pavillons, two miles, 151 lbs.—in this race he beat Dutch Skater, then four years old, 128 lbs. and others. Ran one race in England; won Stockbridge Cup. In 1871, six years old, ran four races in England; won Sweepstake at Newmarket First Spring Meeting, three-quarters of a mile. Ran second to Glenlivat in Tradesman's Plate, 2¼ miles, at Chester, beating a large field; won the Gold Cup at Ascot, 2½ miles, 131 lbs.; ran third to Shannon and Favonius in the Goodwood Cup at Goodwood, beating Dutch Skater and others.

An analysis of his pedigree will show that Mortemer is finely bred, and traces to some of the best race and hardest bottomed horses in England, being inbred to such famous horses as Whalebone, Orville, Sir Peter Teazle, Eclipse and Highflyer. Emilius, the sire of his grandam Eusebia, not only won the Derby in 1823, but sired Plenipotentiary and Priam, both Derby winners, and a host of other good ones; in his collateral branches he traces through a host of Derby and St. Leger winners, to the family of Diomed, the winner of the first Derby ever run. Derby winners in pedigree—Diomed; 1780; Sir Peter Teazle, 1787; Waxy, 1793; Whalebone, 1810; Whisker, 1815; Moses, 1822; Emilius, 1823; Plenitopentiary, 1834; St. Leger winners—Beninghbrough, 1794; Hambletonian, 1795; Filho-da-Puta, 1815; Reveler, 1818.

He is the sire of Augusta, Clementine, Champion, Douceereuse, Hallate, La Buzardiere, Oeillet, Pagnotte, Visite, Miss Rovel, Ambassade, St. Christophe, Vernueil, Reveur, Boyanmont, Chantilly, Isaure, Chamant—the latter winner of the 2,000 guineas in 1877. St. Christophe won the grand Prix de Paris, 1877, and other races. Vernueil was winner both in England and on the Continent; he won the Gold Vase, Gold Cup and the Alexandra Plate at Ascot in 1878. The only time it was ever done by one and the same horse. Clementine won ten races in 1880 and '81, many of them importants events with top weights. The others mentioned were all winners on the Continent.

Mortemer is a large, fine chestnut horse, standing 16¼ hands, with a large star and short white stripe in his face, and one white hind foot to the ankle. His head is plain, but well shaped and bony, with good ears, and wide, capacious throttle; his neck strong, deep, and broad, running into well placed, oblique shoulders, with ample muscle to work the same; great depth of chest, good, strong, short, muscular back, with broad and strong, hips, and great length from the point of hip to whirlbone, thence to stifle and hocks, which are clean cut and well shaped. His legs and feet are good and sound, except the foot which was injured during his turf career. His temper is of the best. The colts by him in America now only yearlings are very fine and promising.

PEDIGREE OF MORTEMER.

MORTEMER.	COMPIEGNE.	Fitz Gladiator.	Gladiator.	Pauline. Partisan.	Walton. Parasol.	Sir Peter—Arethusa by Dungannou—Dau. of Prophet—Virago by Snap—Dau. of Regulus—Sis. to Othello by Crab—Miss Slamerkin. Pot-8-os—Prunella by Highflyer—Promise by Snap—Julia by Blank—Spectator's dam by Partner—Bonny Lass by Bay Bolton.
					Moses. Quadrille.	Whalebone or Seymour—Dau. of Gohauna—Gr. Skim by Woodpecker—Silver's dam by Herod—Y. Hag by Skim—Hag by Crab. Selim—Canary Bird by Whiskey or Sorcerer—Canary by Coriander—Miss Green by Highflyer—Harriet by Matchem—Flora by Regulus.
			Zarah.	Reveller. Sis. to Wou vermans.	Comus. Rosette.	Sorcerer—Houghton Lass by Sir Peter—Alexina by King Fergus—Lardella by Y. Marske—Dau. of Cade—Beaufremont's dam by Bro. to Fearnought. Beningbrough—Rosamond by Tandem—Tuberose by Herod—Gr. Starling by Starling—Coughing Polly by Bart. Childers.
				The Saddler.	Rubens. Brightonia.	Buzzard—Selim's dam by Alexander—Dau. of Highflyer—Dau. of Alfred—Dau. of Engineer—Bay Malton's dam by Cade—Lass of the Mill. Gobanna—Nutmeg by Sir Peter—Nimble by Florizel—Rantipole by Blank—Sis. to Careless by Regulus—Silvertail by Whitenose.
		Maid of Hart.	The Provost.	Mulatto.	Waverly. Castrellina.	Whalebone—Margretta by Sir Peter—Sis. to Cracker by Highflyer—Nutcracker by Matchem—Miss Starling by An. Starling—Dau. of Partner. Castrel—Dau. of Waxy—Bizarre by Peruvian—Violante by John Bull—Sis. to Skyscraper by Highflyer—Everlasting by Eclipse—Hyaena by Snap
				Rebecca.	Lottery. Daughter of.	Tramp—Mandane by Pot-8-os—Y. Camilla by Woodpecker—Camilla by Trentham—Coquette by Compton Barb. Cervantes—Anticipation by Beningbrough—Expectation by Herod—Dau. of Skim (Starling)—Dau. of Janus (Godol.)—Spiuster by Crab.
			Martha Lynn.		Catton. Desdemona.	Golumpus—Lucy Grey by Timothy—Lucy by Florizel—Frenzy by Eclipse Dau. of Engineer—Dau. of Blank—Lass of the Mill by Traveler. Orville—by Sir Peter—Dau. of Diomed—Desdemona by Marske—Y. Hag by Skim—Hag by Crag—Ebony by Childers—Ebony by Basto.
				Leda.	Filho-da-Puta. Treasure.	Haphazard—Mrs. Barnet by Waxy—Dau. of Woodpecker—Heinel by Squirrel—Principessa by Blank—Dau. of Cul. Arabian—Lady Thigh. Camillus (Hambletonian)—Dau. of Hyacinthus (Coriander)—Flora by King Fergus—Atalanta by Matchem—Lass of the Mill by Oroonoko.
	COMTESSE.	The Baron, or Nuncio.*	Plenipotentiary. Ally.	Harriet. Partisan. Emilius.	Orville. Emily.	Beningbrough—Evelina by Highflyer—Termagant by Tantrum—Cantatrice by Sampson—Dau. of Regulus—Marske's dam by Blacklegs. Stamford—Dau. of Whiskey—Gr. Dorimant by Dorimaut—Dizzy by Blank—Dizzy by Driver—Dau. of Smiling Tom—Dau. of Oysterfoot.
					Pericles. Daughter of.	Evander (Highflyer)—Dau. of Precipitate—Ospray by Highflyer—Dau. of Snap—Dau. of Ld. Orford's Barb—Dau. of Bartlet's Childers. Selim—Pipylina by Sir Peter—Rally by Trumpator—Fancy, Sis. to Diomed by Florizel—Sis. to Juno by Spectator—Horatio by Blank.
				Jest.	Walton. Parasol.	Sir Peter—Arethusa by Dungannon—Dau. of Prophet (Regulus)—Virago by Snap—Dau. of Regulus—Sis. to Othello by Crab—Miss Slamerkin. Pot-8-os—Prunella by Highflyer—Promise by Snap—Julia by Blank—Spectator's dam by Partner—Bonny Lass by Bay Bolton.
					Waxy. Scotia.	Pot-8-os—Penelope by Trumpator—Prunella by Highflyer—Promise by Snap—Julia by Blank—Spectator's dam by Partner—Bonny Lass. Delpini—Dau. of King Fergus—Caelia by Herod—Proserpine, Sis. to Eclipse by Marske—Spilletta by Regulus—Mother Western.
		Emilius.	Orville.	Emily.	Beningbrough. Evelina.	King Fergus—Dau. of Herod—Pyrrha by Matchem—Duchess by Whitenose—Miss Slamerkin by Y. True Blue—Dau. of Ox. Dun. Arabian. Highflyer—Termagant by Tantrum—Cantatrice by Sampson—Dau. of Regulus—Marske's dam by Blacklegs—Dau. of Bay Bolton—Dau. of Fox Cub.
					Stamford. Daughter of.	Sir Peter—Horatia by Eclipse—Countess, Delpini's dam by Blank—Dau. of Rib (Crab)—Dau. of Wynn Arabian—Dau. of Governor. Dau. of Whiskey—Gr. Dorimant by Dorimant—Dizzy by Blank—Dizzy by Diver—Dau. of Smiling Tom (Con. Arabian)—Dau. of Oysterfoot.
		Eusebia.	Merlin.	Emily.	Castrel. Miss Newton.	Buzzard—Selim's dam by Alexander—Dau. of Highflyer—Dau. of Alfred—Dau. of Engineer—Bay Malton's dam by Cade (Godol.) Delpini—Tipple Cyder by King Fergus—Sylvia by Y. Marske—Ferret by Bro. to Sylvio—(Cade)—Dau. of Regulus—Dau. of Mor. Arabian.
			Mangel Wurzel.	Morel.	Sorcerer.	Trumpator—Y. Giantess by Diomed—Giantess by Matchem—Molly Longlegs by Babraham—Dau. of Cole's Foxhunter—Dau. of Partner.
					Hornby Lass.	Buzzard (Woodpecker)—Puzzle by Matchem (Cade)—Princess by Herod (Tartar)—Julia by Blank (Godol.)—Spectator's dam by Partner (Jigg)—Bonny Lass by Bay Bolton (Gray Hautboy)—Dau. of Darley Arabian—Dau. of Byerly Turk—Dau. of Taffolet Barb—Dau. of Place's White Turk—Natural Barb Mare.

* Nuncio given.

MUSCOVY (Imp.)

Muscovy will be located at the Fairview Stud Farm near Gallatin, Sumner Co., Tenn., and will be permitted to serve mares at $50 each and $5 to the groom. Application to be made to Charles Reed, proprietor, Gallatin, Tenn. Annual sale of yearlings at Saratoga, in July.

MUSCOVY by The Drake, son of the great Stockwell, bred by Her Majesty the Queen; foaled spring of 1873, dam Lady of the Manor, the dam of Athbania, Bluestone, etc., by Voltigeur, winner of the double events, Derby and St. Leger; 2d dam Hersey, the dam of Bay Celia, Desdemona, etc., by Glaucus, winner of the Gold Cup at Ascot and Goodwood Stakes and sire of Refraction, winner of the Oaks Stakes at Epsom, out of Hester dam of Palmyra, Chatham, The Nabob, etc., by Camel son of Whalebone and sire of the great Touchstone, Launcelot, etc. The Drake, sire of Muscovy, was a winner in his two and three-year-old form and is a stoutly bred horse, being a son of the Emperor of stallions, Stockwell, and out of a daughter of Pyrrhus the First, a Derby winner, and his great grandam a daughter of Jerry, a St. Leger winner. The Provost, the sire of his grandam, ran a dead heat for second place in the St. Leger won by Charles XII. He has a double cross of Waxy through the brothers Woful, Whisker and Whalebone. Muscovy is bred for speed and stoutness, the pedigree on both sire and dam's side tracing through a long line of distinguished performers in the great Classic events, and is full of Eclipse and Herod blood through their most famous sons, Pot-8o-s and Highflyer, upon the favorite Oriental sources, Godolphin Barb and Darley Arabian. Muscovy never raced; but some of the best sires, for causes, made no reputation on the turf. Muscovy is a very dark brown horse, full 16 hands high, with black points. He is truly shaped all over and full of substance and quality.

PEDIGREE OF MUSCOVY.

MUSCOVY.	THE DRAKE.	Stockwell.	The Baron.	Sir Hercules.	Whalebone—Peri by Wanderer—Thalestris by Alexander—Rival by Sir Peter—Hornet by Drone—Manilla by Goldfinder—Dau. of Old Eng.		
				Guicciolli.	Bob Booty—Flight by I. Escape—Y. Heroine by Bagot—Heroine by Hero—Dau. of Snap—Sis. to Regulus by Godol. Arabian.		
			Echid. Irish Bird-catcher. na.	Economist.	Whisker—Floranthe by Octavian—Caprice by Anvil—Madcap by Eclipse—Dau. of Blank—Dau. of Blaze—Dau. of Young Greyhound.		
				Miss Pratt.	Blacklock—Gadabout by Orville—Minstrel by Sir Peter—Matron of Florizel—Maiden by Matchem—Dau. of Squirt—Lot's dam.		
		Pocahontas.	Marpessa. Glencoe.	Sultan.	Selim—Bacchante by Williamson's Ditto—Sis. to Calomel by Mercury—Dau. of Herod—Folly by Marske—Vixen by Regulus.		
				Trampoline.	Tramp—Web by Waxy—Penelope by Trumpator—Prunella by Highflyer—Promise by Snap—Julia by Blank—Spectator's dam by Partner.		
				Muley.	Orville—Eleanor by Whiskey—Y. Giantess by Diomed—Giantess by Matchem—Molly Longlegs by Babraham—Dau. of Cole's Foxhunter.		
				Clare.	Marmion—Harpalice by Gohanna—Amazon by Driver—Fractious by Mercury—Dau. of Woodpecker—Everlasting by Eclipse.		
		Pyrrha the First.	Epirus.	Langar.	Selim—Dau. of Walton—Y. Giantess by Diomed—Giantess by Matchem—Molly Longlegs by Babraham—Dau. of Cole's Foxhunter.		
				Olympia.	Sir Oliver (Sir Peter)—Scotilla by Anvil (Herod)—Scota by Eclipse—Harmony by Herod—Rutilia by Blank—Dau. of Regulus (Godol.)		
		Daughter of.	Fortress.	Defence.	Whalebone—Defiance by Rubens—Little Folly by Highland Fling—Harriet by Volunteer—Dau. of Alfred—Magnolia by Marske (Godol).		
				Jewess.	Moses—Calendulae by Camerton (Hamb.)—Snowdrop by Highland Fling—Daisy by Buzzard—Tulip by Damper (Spectator).		
		Miss Whip.	The Provost.	The Saddler.	Waverly—Castrellina by Castrel—Dau. of Waxy—Bizarre by Peruvian—Violante by John Bull—Sis. to Skyscraper by Highflyer.		
				Rebecca.	Lottery—Dau. of Cervantes—Anticipation by Beningbrough—Expectation by Herod—Dau. of Skim—Dau. of Janus (Godol.)		
		Miss Whip.		Jerry.	Smolensko—Louisa by Orville—Thomasina by Timothy—Violet by Shark—Dau. of Syphon—Charlotte by Blank (Godol.)		
				Georgiana.	Woful—Shepherdess by Shuttle—Dau. of Buzzard—Ann of the Forest by King Fergus—Miss West by Matchem—Dau. of Regulus.		
	LADY OF THE MANOR.	Voltigeur.	Voltaire.	Whitelock.	Hambletonian—Rosalind by Phoenomenon—Atalanta by Matchem—Lass of the Mill by Oroonoko—Dau. of Old Traveler.		
				Daughter of.	Coriander—Wildgoose by Highflyer—Coheiress by Pot-8-os—Manilla by Goldfinder—Dau. of Old Eng.—Dau. of Cul. Arabian.		
			Blacklock.	Phantom.	Walton—Julia by Whiskey—Y. Giantess by Diomed—Giantess by Matchem—Molly Longlegs by Babraham—Dau. of Cole's Foxhunter.		
				Daughter of.	Overton—Gratitude's dam by Walnut—Dau. of Ruler—Piracantha by Matchem—Prophetess by Regulus—Jenny Spinner.		
		Martha Lynn.	Mulatto. Dau. of	Catton.	Golumpus—Lucy Grey by Timothy—Lucy by Florizel—Frenzy by Eclipse—Dau. of Engineer—Dau. of Blank—Lass of the Mill by Traveler.		
				Desdemona.	Orville—Fanny by Sir Peter—Dau. of Diomed—Desdemona by Marske—Y. Hag by Skim—Hag by Crab—Ebony by Childers—Ebony by Basto.		
			Leda.	Filho-da Puta.	Haphazard—Mrs. Barnet by Waxy—Dau. of Woodpecker—Heinel by Squirrel—Principessa by Blank—Dau. of Cul. Arabian—Lady Thigh.		
				Treasure.	Camillus—Dau. of Hyacinthus—Flora by King Fergus—Atalanta by Matchem—Lass of the Mill by Oroonoko—Dau. of Old Traveler.		
		Glaucus.	Partisan.	Walton.	Sir Peter—Arethusa by Dungannon—Dau. of Prophet—Virago by Snap—Dau. of Regulus—Sis. to Othello by Crab—Miss Slamerkin.		
				Parasol.	Pot-8-os—Pruneila by Highflyer—Promise by Snap—Julia by Blank—Spectator's dam by Partner—Bonny Lass by Bay Bolton.		
			Nanine.	Selim.	Buzzard—Castrel's dam by Alexander—Dau. of Highflyer—Dau. of Alfred—Dan. of Engineer—Bay Malton's dam by Cade.		
				Bizarre.	Peruvian—Violante by John Bull—Sis. to Skyscraper by Highflyer—Everlasting by Eclipse—Hyaena by Snap—Miss Belsea by Regulus.		
		Hersey.	Camel.	Whalebone.	Waxy—Penelope by Trumpator—Prunella by Highflyer—Promise by Snap—Julia by Blank—Spectator's dam by Partner—Bonny Lass.		
				Daughter of.	Selim—Maiden by Sir Peter—Dau. of Phoenomenon—Matron by Florizel—Maiden by Matchem—Dau. of Squirt—Lot's dam by Mogul.		
		Hester.	Monimia.	Muley.	Orville—Eleanor by Whiskey—Y. Giantess by Diomed—Giantess by Matchem—Molly Longlegs by Babraham—Dau. of Cole's Foxhunter.		
				Sis. to Petworth.	Precipitate—Dau. of Woodpecker (Herod)—Sis. to Juniper by Snap (Snip)—Y. Marske's dam by Blank (Godol.)—Bay Starling by Bolton Starling (Bay Bolton)—Miss Meynell by Partner (Jigg)—Dau. of Greyhound (White Barb Chillaby)—Dau. of Cur. Bay Barb—Dau. of Ld. D'Arcy's Chestnut Arabian—Dau. of Whiteshirt—Old Montague Mare.		

NORFOLK,

(WINNER OF THE JERSEY DERBY AT PATERSON, 1854.)

Norfolk will stand the season of 1883 at the El Aroyo Stud Farm, Winters, Yolo Co., California, only by private contract. Theodore Winters, proprietor, Winters, Yolo Co., California.

NORFOLK by Lexington son of Boston, bred by the late R. A. Alexander, Woodburn Stud, foaled 1861, dam Novice by imp. Glencoe out of Chloe Anderson by Rodolph, son of Sir Archy Montorio, by Sir Archy. Norfolk did not run at two-years old, but made his debut at St. Louis, May 16th, 1864 in the sweepstake for three-year olds, mile heats which he won in 1:46¼, 1:47, beating Tipperary and four others. June 7th, 1864, won the Jersey Derby at Paterson, N. J., 1¼ miles, in 2:46¼, defeating Tipperary and ten others. May 23d, 1865, won two mile heats at San Francisco, California, beating Lodi, in 3:43¼, 3:42¾, 3:51¾. September 18th, 1865, Sacramento, California, won two mile heats, beating Lodi in 3:37½, 3:38½. Same place September 23d, 1865, won match three mile heats, beating Lodi in 5:27½, 5:29½, the fastest and best two heats ever run. Lexington the sire of Norfolk was the best race-horse and stallion ever bred in America. Norfolk is the peer of his best son if not the best one. His dam Novice was a fine race-mare and daughter of the great Glencoe, his grandam Chloe Anderson was by Rodolph the best race-horse of his day ; he met and defeated all comers ; beat Angora in the great match between Kentucky and Tennessee, four mile heats and won a second beat of three miles, in 5:40, the fastest ever run at the distance to that day 1886. Norfolk in addition to being a son of the great Lexington and a Glencoe mare, is full of Archy and Diomed blood being very much inbred to those famous horses. Boston the sire of Lexington was by Timoleon by Sir Archy by Diomed. Boston's dam by Ball's Florizel son of Diomed, Lexington's grandam was by Sumpter son of Sir Archy by Diomed, Novice, Norfolk's dam by Glencoe, his grandam Chloe Anderson by Rodolph, by Sir Archy Montorio by Sir Archy by Diomed, Sir Archy Montorio's dam Transport by Virginius by Diomed, Belle Anderson his great grandam was by Sir Archy of Transport by Sir Archy by Diomed, dam Transport by Virginius, by Diomed, and her dam Butterfly was by Sumpter, by Sir Archy, by Diomed. Much of his excellence comes from this hard bottomed blood. Norfolk is a bay, truly shaped all over, and for his chances an excellent sire, the following of his get have been winners : Bill Hazel, Emma Skaggs, Winters, Maid of the Mist, Scamperdown, Boston, Dice Box, Ballot Box, Snap, Twilight, Vanderbilt, Bradley, Morphine, Connor, Trade Dollar, Flood, Ralston, Duke of Norfolk, Lonesome, and Duchess of Norfolk, one of the best three-year olds of the year. Won, 1¾ miles, in 3:04. The blood from the large infusion of Diomed in it should be valuable. He never lost a race.

PEDIGREE OF NORFOLK.

NORFOLK.	**LEXINGTON.**	Boston.	Timoleon.	Sir Archy.	Diomed.	Florizel—Sis. to Juno by Spectator—Horatia by Blank—Dau. of F. Childers—Miss Belvoir by Gr. Grantham—Dau. of Paget Turk.
				Dau. of Florizel.	Castianira.	Rockingham—Tabitha by Trentham—Dau. of Bosphorus—Dau. of Wm's Forester—Dau. of Coalition Colt—Dan. of Bustard (Crab).
				Ball's Florizel.	Saltram.	Eclipse—Virago by Snap—Dau. of Regulus—Sis. to Othello by Crab—Miss Slamerkin by Y. True Blue—Dau. of Ox Dun Arabian.
			Robin Brown's dam.	Dau. of	Daughter of.	Symme's Wildair (Fearnought)—Dau. of Driver (Imp. Othello)—Dau. of Fallower (Blank)—Dau. of Vampire (Regulus).
		Alice Carneal.	Sarpedon.	Emilius. Dau. of.	Diomed.	Florizel—Sis. to Juno by Spectator—Horatia by Blank—Dau. of F. Childers—Miss Belvoir by Gr. Grantham—Dau. of Paget Turk.
					Daughter of.	Imp. Shark—Dau. of Harris' Eclipse—Dau. of Fearnought—Dau. of Jolly Roger—Dau. of Sober John (Rib)—Dau. of Shock.
				Icaria.	Alderman.	Pot-8-os—Lady Bolingbroke by Squirrel—Cypron by Blaze—Selima by Bethel's Arabian—Dau. of Graham's Champion.
					Daughter of.	Clockfast—Dau. of Symme's Wildair—Y. Kitty Fisher by Fearnought—Imp. Kitty Fisher by Cade—Dau. of Som. Arabian.
				Sumpter.	Orville.	Beningbrough—Evelina by Highflyer—Termagant by Tantrum—Cantatrice by Sampson—Dau. of Regulus—Marske's dam.
		Rowena.			Emily.	Stamford—Dau. of Whiskey—Gr. Dorimant by Dorimant—Dizzy by Blank—Dizzy by Driver—Dau. of Smiling Tom—Dau. of Oysterfoot.
				Lady Grey.	The Flyer.	Vandyke, Jr.—Azalia by Beningbrough—Gillyflower by Highflyer—Dau. of Goldfinder—Sis. to Grasshopper by Marske—Dau. of Cul. Arabian.
					Parma.	Dick Andrews—May by Beningbrough—Primrose by Mambrino—Cricket by Herod—Sophia by Blank—Ld. Leigh's Diana by Second.
					Sir Archy.	Diomed—Castianira by Rockingham—Tabitha by Trentham—Dau. of Bosphorus—Dau. of Wm's Forester—Dau. of Coalition Colt.
					Flirtilla's dam.	Robin Redbreast—Dau. of Obscurity—Slamerkin by Wildair—Imp. Cub Mare by Cub—Amarantbus' dam by Second.
					Robin Grey.	Royalist—Belle Mariah by Gr. Diomed—Queen by Imp. St. George—Dau. of Cassius—Primrose by Imp. Dove—Stella by Othello.
					Maria.	Melzar—Dau. of Highflyer—Dau. of Fearnought—Dau. of Ariel—Dau. of Jack of Diamonds—Imp. Diamond by Cul. Arabian.
	NOVICE.	Chloe Anderson.	Trampoline.	Selim.	Buzzard.	Woodpecker—Misfortune by Dux—Curiosity by Snap—Dau. of Regulus—Dau. of Bart. Childers—Dau. of Honeywood's Arabian.
					Castrel's dam.	Alexander—Dau. of Highflyer—Dau. of Alfred—Dau. of Engineer—Bay Malton's dam by Cade—Lass of the Mill by Traveler.
				Bacchante.	Williamson's Ditto.	Sir Peter—Arethusa by Dungannon—Dau. of Prophet—Virago by Snap—Dau. of Regulus—Sis. to Othello by Crab.
		Belle Anderson.			Sis. to Calomel.	Mercury—Dau. of Herod—Folly by Marske—Vixen by Regulus—Dau. of Hutton's Spot—Dau. of Bay Bolton.
			Rodolph.	Sultan.	Dick Andrews.	Joe Andrews—Dau. of Highflyer—Dau. of Cardinal Puff—Dau. of Tatler—Dau. of Snip—Dau. of Godol. Arabian—Dau. of Whiteneck.
					Daughter of.	Gohanna—Fraxinella by Trentham—Dau. of Woodpecker—Everlasting by Eclipse—Hyaena by Snap—Miss Belsea by Regulus.
				Tramp.	Waxy.	Pot-8-os—Maria by Herod—Lisette by Snap—Miss Windsor by Godol. Arabian—Sis. to Volunteer by Belgrade—Dau. of Bart. Childers.
					Penelope.	Trumpator—Prunella by Highflyer—Promise by Snap—Julia by Blank—Spectator's dam by Partner—Bonny Lass by Bay Bolton.
		Butterfly.	Sir Wm. of Transport.	Web.	Sir Archy.	Diomed—Castianira by Rockingham—Tabitha by Trentham—Dau. of Bosphorus—Dau. of Wm's Forester—Dau. of Coalition Colt.
					Transport.	Virginius (Diomed)—Nancy Air by Imp. Bedford—Annette by Imp. Shark—Dau. of Rockingham—Dau. of Gallant.
				Sir Archy.	Haxall's Moses.	Imp. Sir Harry—Imp. Mermaid by Waxy—Promise by Buzzard—Dau. of Precipitate—Lady Harriet by Mark Anthony—Georgiana.
					Daughter of.	Cook's Whip—Maria by Craig's Alfred (Imp. Medley)—Dau. of Taylor's Bellair (Imp. Medley)—Dau. of Medley (Gimcrack).
			Dau. of Montorio.	Dau. of Transport.	Sir Archy.	Diomed—Castianira by Rockingham—Tabitha by Trentham—Dau. of Bosphorus—Dau. of Wm's Forester—Dau. of Coalition Colt.
					Transport.	Virginius—Nancy Air by Bedford—Annette by Imp. Shark—Dau. of Rockingham—Dau. of Gallant—Dau. of True Whig.
					Sumpter.	Sir Archy—Flirtilla's dam by Robin Redbreast—Dau. of Obscurity—Slamerkin by Wildair—Imp. Cub Mare by Cub.
					Daughter of.	Imp. Buzzard (Woodpecker)—Dau. of Dandridge's Fearnought (Imp. Fearnaught dam Imp. Calista)—Dau. of Imp. Janus (Janus).

ONONDAGA,

(WINNER OF THE JUVENILE STAKES AT JEROME PARK, JULY STAKES AT LONG BRANCH, AND KENTUCKY STAKES AT SARATOGA, 1881.)

Will be used as private stallion in the McGrathiana Stud, near Lexington, Fayette County, Ky., Milton Young, proprietor. Annual sales of yearlings in May.

ONONDAGA by imp. Leamington, son of Faugh-a-Ballagh, bred by Mr. A. Welsh, Erdenheim Stud, Pa., foaled 1879, dam Susan Beane, dam of Stratford, Sensation, &c. by Lexington out of Sally Lewis, dam of John Morgan, Hunter's Lexington, Acrobat, &c., by imp. Glencoe. Onondaga as a two-year old started in nine races, of which he won four; Jerome Park, won the Juvenile Stakes, half a mile in 50¼, beating Gerald, Memento and twelve others ; Sheepshead Bay, won match three-quarters of a mile in 1:15¼, beating Sachem ; Monmouth Park, won the July Stakes for two-year olds, five furlongs in 1:02¼, beating Gerald, Memento and three others ; Saratoga, won the Kentucky Stakes for two-year olds, three-quarters of a mile in 1:16, beating Nightcap and Glenarm ; Sheepshead Bay was second in the Surf Stakes for two-year olds, five furlongs, won by Stonehenge Julietta Colt, in 1:08¼ ; at Monmouth Park, was third in the August Stakes for two-year olds, three-quarters of a mile, won by Stonehenge Julietta Colt, in 1:16, and was unplaced in his other races. Onondaga complaining in his legs was retired ; he is from one of the great racing families of America, is own brother to Sensation, the invincible horse of his year, his dam is own sister to Acrobat and Hunter's Lexington, and half-sister to John Morgan ; all were good race-horses, and for their chances, successful sires. The pedigree is well-fortified with Archy and Diomed blood, upon the Eclipse and Herod, and traces through the dam of Medoc to the family which gave Lexington and other famous horses to the country. Onondaga is a chestnut, 15¾ hands, large star in his forehead, and snip on the nose, with white hairs in his flanks, left hind foot white above the ankle ; he is a good shaped horse, and was quite speedy ; the family is a racing one, and upon good mares should reproduce itself.

PEDIGREE OF ONONDAGA.

ONONDAGA.			Waxy.	Pot-8-os—Maria by Herod—Lisette by Snap—Miss Windsor by Godol. Arabian—Sis. to Volunteer by Y. Belgrade.
	IMP. LEAMINGTON.	Faugh-a-Ballagh. Sir Hercules. Whalebone.	Penelope.	Trumpator—Prunella by Highflyer—Promise by Snap—Julia by Blank—Spectator's dam by Partner—Bonny Lass by Bay Bolton.
		Gulcciolli. Bob Booty. Perl.	Wanderer.	Gohanna—Catharine by Woodpecker—Camilla by Trentham—Coquette by Comp. Barb—Sis. to Regulus by Godol. Arabian—Gr. Robinson.
			Thalestris.	Alexander—Rival by Sir Peter—Horaet by Drone—Manilla by Goldfinder—Dau. of Old Eng.—Dau. of Cullen Arabian.
		Pantaloon. Castrel. Flight.	Chanticleer.	Woodpecker—Dau. of Eclipse—Rosebud by Snap—Miss Belsea by Regulus—Dau. of Bart. Childers—Dau. of Hon. Arabian.
			Ierne.	Bagot—Dau. of Gamahoe—Patty by Tim—Miss Patch by Justice—Ringtail Galloway by Cur. Bay Barb—Sis. to Witty Mare.
			Irish Escape.	Commodore—Buffer's dam by Highflyer—Shift by Sweetbriar—Bl. Susan by Snap—Ld. Bruce's Cade Mare by Cade—Dau. of Belgrade.
			Young Heroine.	Bagot—Heroine by Hero—Dau. of Snap—Sis. to Regulus by Godol. Arabian—Gr. Robinson by Bald Galloway—Dau. of Snake—Grey Wilkes.
			Buzzard.	Woodpecker—Misfortune by Dux—Curiosity by Snap—Dau. of Regulus—Dau. of Bart. Childers—Dau. of Hon. Arabian—Dam of True Blues.
			Selim's dam.	Alexander—Dau. of Highflyer—Dau. of Alfred—Dau. of Engineer—Bay Malton's dam by Cade—Lass of the Mill by Traveler.
	Daughter of. Daphne. Laurel. Idalia.		Peruvian.	Sir Peter—Dau. of Budrow—Escape's dam by Squirrel—Dau. of Babraham—Dau. of Golden Ball—Bushey Molly by Hamp. Ct. Childers.
			Musidora.	Meteor—Maid of all Work by Highflyer—Sis. to Tandem by Syphon—Dau. of Regulus—Dau. of Snip—Dau. of Cottiogham—Warlock Galloway.
		Maid of Honor.	Blacklock.	Whitelock—Dau. of Coriander—Wildgoose by Highflyer—Coheiress by Pot-8-os—Manilla by Goldfinder—Dau. of Old Eng.
			Wagtail.	Prime Minister—Dau. of Orville—Miss Grimstone by Weasel—Dau. of Ancaster—Dau. of Dam Arabian—Dau. of Sampson.
			Champion.	Selim—Podagra by Gouty—Jet by Magnet—Jewel by Squirrel—Sophia by Blank—Diana by Second—Dau. of Stan. Arabian.
			Etiquette.	Orville—Boadicea by Alexander—Brunette by Amaranthus—Mayfly by Matchem—Dau. of An. Starling—Dau. of Grasshopper.
	SUSAN BEANE.	Lexington. Boston. Sister to Tuckahoe Timoleon	Sir Archy.	Diomed—Castianira by Rockingham—Tibatha by Trentham—Dau. of Bosphorus—Dau. of Wm.'s Forester—Dau. of Coalition Colt.
			Daughter of.	Saltram—Dau. of Symme's Wildair—Dau. of Driver (Imp. Othello)—Dau. of Fallower (Blank)—Dau. of Vampire (Regulus).
			Ball's Florizel.	Diomed—Dau. of Imp. Shark—Dau. of Harris' Eclipse—Dau. of Fearnought—Dau. of Jolly Roger—Dau. of Sober John—Dau. of Shock.
			Daughter of.	Alderman—Dau. of Clockfast—Dau. of Synme's Wildair—Y. Kitty Fisher by Fearnought—Imp. Kitty Fisher by Cade—Dau. of Som. Arabian.
		Alice Carneal. Rowena. Sarpedon.	Emilius.	Orville—Emily by Stamford—Dau. of Whiskey—Gr. Doriniant by Dorimant—Dizzy by Blank—Dizzy by Driver—Dau. of Smiling Tom.
			Icaria.	The Flyer—Parma by Dick Andrews—May by Beningbrough—Primrose by Mambrino—Cricket by Herod—Sophia by Blank—Diana.
			Sumpter.	Sir Archy—Flirtilla's dam by Robin Redbreast—Dau. of Obscurity—Slamerkin by Wildair—Imp. Cub Mare by Cub—Aramanthus' dam.
			Lady Grey.	Robin Grey—Maria by Melzar—Dau. of Highflyer—Dau. of Fearnought—Dau. of Ariel—Dau. of Jack of Diamonds—Imp. Diamond.
		Glencoe. Sultan.	Selim.	Buzzard—Castrel's dam by Alexander—Dau. of Highflyer—Dau. of Alfred—Dau. of Engineer—Bay Malton's dam by Cade—Lass of the Mill.
			Bacchante.	Williamson's Ditto—Sis. to Calomel by Mercury—Dau. of Herod—Folly by Marske—Vixen by Regulus—Dau. of Hut. Spot—Dau. of Bay Bolton.
		Trampoline.	Tramp.	Dick Andrews—Dau. of Gohanna—Fraxinella by Trentham—Dau. of Woodpecker—Everlasting by Eclipse—Hyaena by Snap—Miss Belsea.
			Web.	Waxy—Penelope by Trumpator—Prunella by Highflyer—Promise by Snap—Julia by Blank—Spectator's dam by Partner—Bonny Lass.
		Barefoot.	Tramp.	Dick Andrews—Dau. of Gohanna—Fraxinella by Trentham—Dau. of Woodpecker—Everlasting by Eclipse—Hyaena by Snap—Miss Belsea.
			Rosamond.	Buzzard—Roseberry by Phoenomenon—Miss West by Matchem—Dau. of Regulus—Dau. of Crab—Dau. of F. Childers—Dau. of Basto.
	Sally Lewis. Lady Thompkins.		Am. Eclipse.	Duroc—Millers Damsel by Messenger—Dau. of Pot-8-os—Dau. of Gimcrack—Soap-Dragon by Snap—Dau. of Regulus—Dau. of Bart. Childers.
	Motto.		Katy Ann.	Ogle's Oscar (Imp. Gabriel)—Y. Maid of the Oaks, Medoc's dam by Imp. Expedition (Pegasus by Eclipse)—Maid of the Oaks by Spread Eagle (Volunteer)—Annette by Imp. Shark (Marske)—Dau. of Rockingham (Partner)—Dau. of Gallant (Fearnought)—Dau. of True Whig (Fitzhugh's Regulus)—Dau. of Imp. Regulus (Regulus by Godol.)—Imp. Diamond by Cul. Arabian—Lady Thigh by Partner (Jigg)—Sis. to Guy by Greyhound (White Barb Chillaby)—Dau. of Cur. Bay Barb—Dau. of D'Arcy Ch. Arabian—Dau. of Whiteshirt—Old Montague Mare.

PAT MALLOY,

(WINNER OF THE CUMBERLAND STAKES, NOS. 1 AND 2, AT NASHVILLE, SENATE STAKES, AT MEMPHIS, AND SOUTHERN HOTEL STAKES, AT ST. LOUIS, MO.)

Pat Malloy will be located for the season of 1883 *at the Woodburn Stud, near Spring Station, Ky., the property of A. J. Alexander, and will be permitted to serve mares at* $50 *the season. Application to be made to L. Brodhead, Spring Station, Ky. Aunual sale of yearlings in May.*

PAT MALLOY. own brother to Jack Malone, by the great Lexington, son of Boston, bred by the late R. A. Alexander, Woodburn Stud, foaled 1665, dam Gloriana, by American Eclipse, son of Duroc, by imp. Diomed, winner of the first Derby ever run, in 1780, out of the famous Trifle, by Sir Charles, son of Sir Archy, by imp. Diomed. Pat Malloy made his *debut* on the turf at Louisville, Ky., in the fall of 1867, as a two-year-old, running second to Spinola in the two-year-old stakes, one mile, run in 1:46½, beating Jessamine Porter, Biddy Malone, Hazard, etc. Nashville Fall Meeting, 1867, Pat Malloy won the Cumberland Stakes, No. 2, for two-year olds, one mile, in 1:50. Memphis, April 27, 1868, won Jockey Club Purse, mile heats, three best in five, in 1:59, 2:01, 2:02, 2:04, 2:06½; Transit won the second heat and Nell Gwynn the third. Memphis, April 29, won the Senate Stakes for three-year-olds, 2 miles, in 4:08½; the track in both these races was muddy and heavy. Nashville, May 7, 1868, walked over for the Cumberland Stakes, No. 1, mile heats, for three-year olds. May 8, won Club Purse, 1½ miles, for all ages, in 2:18½. May 9, walked over for the Cumberland Stakes, No. 2, for three-year-olds, 2 miles. St. Louis, May 18, 1868, ran second to The Banshee, in Sweepstakes for three-year olds, mile heats, in 1:48½, 1:48¼. May 20, won the Southern Hotel Stakes, for three-year-olds, 2-mile heats, in 3:44¼, 3:43¾, 3:50¾; The Banshee won the second heat. Chicago, July 8, 1868, won the Union Stock-Yard Purse, 2½ miles, for all ages, in 4:45½. Complaining in one of his legs, he was not trained in 1869. Springfield, Ill., June 9, 1870, ran second to Barney Williams in Club Purse, 2 miles, in 4:05½. June 10, ran second to his stable companion, The Banshee, three miles, in 6:02. Saratoga, July 20, ran third to Helmbold and Vespucius, 3 miles, in 5:50. August 15, ran third to Haric (3), 86 lbs., Legatee (4), 105 lbs. Pat Malloy (5), 114 lbs., in a Handicap Purse, 1¾ miles, in 3:10. Aug. 18, ran second to Helmbold in Club Purse, 4 miles, in 7:32½, beating Carrie Atherton. His leg gave way in this race and he was retired from the turf. Pat Malloy was a speedy and very game horse, could pack his weight and stay any distance. With his limited chances in the stud, he has sired some real good race-horses. Ozark and Lord Murphy were probably his best sons. Ozark was third in the Withers Stake to Aristides, ran a dead heat with Milner, for, and divided, the Kenner Stakes, 2 miles in 3:43½ Won the Jersey Derby, 1¾ miles in 3:10¾, defeating Aristides and others. At Washington, D.C., won 1¼ miles in the mud, in 2:08½, and won the 4 mile purse in 7:40, defeating Nettie Norton and five others, Lord Murphy won the Belle Meade Stakes, at Nashville, 1½ miles, in 2:43¾, won the Kentucky Derby at Louisville, 1½ miles in 2:37, defeating the great Falsetto and seven others. Won the January Stakes at St. Louis, mile heats, in 1:43½, 1:45, 1:50¼, defeating Goodnight, winner of the first heat, and four others. Won the Kentucky St. Leger, at Louisville, 2 miles, in 3:34, defeating Aureolus, Ada Glenn, and others. Other winners by Pat Malloy are Gen. Harney, Osage, Patrol, Charlemagne, Omega, Mollie Seabrook, Athlone, W. I. Higgins, Alpha, Joe Shelby, Chariton (Osseo), Miss Malloy, Caleb, Pat's Boy, Mary B, Volusia, Rambler, Little Pat, Lenore, Joe Thompson, Lillie Belle, and others. Pat Malloy is a bright bay, with blaze face, and right hind foot white, and stands 15 hands 1½ inches high, is own brother to Jack Malone, a superior race-horse, and is marked very much like his sire, Lexington, with immense muscular development in his back, hips and loins. He evinces great constitution, and his colts are almost invariably fine feeders, with great turn of speed. As Jack Malone's daughters have proved a grand success in the stud, we see no reason why Pat Malloy's daughters should not prove excellent. You get more of the Archy and Diomed blood than is possible from any other source.

PEDIGREE OF PAT MALLOY.

PAT MALLOY.	**LEXINGTON.**	Boston.	Timoleon.	Sir Archy.	Diomed.	Florizel—Sis. to Juno by Spectator—Horatia by Blank—Dau. of F. Childers—Miss Belvoir by Gr. Grantham—Dau. of Paget Turk.
				Dau. of Ball's Florizel.	Castianira.	Rockingham—Tabitha by Trentham—Dau. of Bosphorus—Dau. of Wm's Forester—Dau. of Coalition Colt—Dau. of Bustard (Crab).
			Robin Brown's Dam.		Imp. Saltram.	Eclipse—Virago by Snap—Dau. of Regulus—Sis. to Othello by Crab—Miss Slammerkin by Y True Blue—Dau of Ox. Dun. Arabian.
					Daughter of.	Symme's Wildair—Dau. of Driver (Imp. Othello)—Dau. of Imp. Fallower (Blank)—Dau. of Imp. Vampire (Regulus).
		Alice Carneal.	Sarpedon.	Emilius.	Diomed.	Florizel—Sis. to Juno by Spectator—Horatia by Blank—Dau. of F. Childers—Miss Belvoir by Gr. Grantham—Dau. of Paget Turk.
					Daughter of.	Imp. Shark—Dau. of Harris' Eclipse—Dau. of Fearnought—Dau. of Jolly Roger—Dau. of Sober John (Rib)—Dau. of Shock.
				Icaria.	Alderman.	Pot-8-os—Lady Bolingbroke by Squirrel—Cypron Herod's dam by Blaze—Selima by Beth. Arabian—Dau. of Graham's Champion.
					Daughter of.	Clockfast—Dau. of Symme's Wildair—Y Kitty Fisher by Fearnought—Imp. Kitty Fisher by Cade—Dau. of Som. Arabian—Bald Charlotte.
			Rowena.	Sumpter.	Orville.	Beningbrough—Evelina by Highflyer—Termagant by Tantrum—Cantatrice by Sampson—Dau. of Regulus—Marske's dam by Blacklegs.
					Emily.	Stamford—Dau. of Whiskey—Gr. Dorimant by Dorimant—Dizzy by Blank Dizzy by Driver—Dau. of Smiling Tom.
				Lady Grey.	The Flyer.	Vandyke, Jr.—Azalia by Beningbrough—Gillyflower by Highflyer—Dau. of Goldfinder—Sis. to Grasshopper by Marske—Dau. of Cul. Arabian.
					Parma.	Dick Andrews—May by Beningbrough—Primrose by Mambrino—Cricket by Herod—Sophia by Blank—Diana by Second.
					Sir Archy.	Diomed—Castianira by Rockingham—Tabitha by Trentham—Dau. of Bosphorus—Dau. of Wm's Forester—Dau. of Coalition Colt.
					Flirtilla's Dam.	Robin Redbreast—Dau. of Obscurity—Slamerkin by Wildair—Imp. Cub Mare by Cub—Amaranthus' dam by Second—Dau. of Starling.
					Robin Grey.	Royalist—Belle Mariah by Grey Diomed—Queen by Imp. St. George—Dau. of Cassius—Primrose by Imp. Dove—Stella by Othello.
					Maria.	Melzar—Dau. of Highflyer—Dau. of Fearnought—Dau. of Ariel—Dau. of Jack of Diamonds—Imp. Diamond by Cul. Arabian—Ld. Thigh.
	GLORIANA.	Trifle.	Am. Eclipse.	Duroc.	Florizel.	Herod—Dau. of Cygnet (Godol.)—Dau. of Cartouche (Bald Galloway)—Ebony by F. Childers—Ebony by Basto—Massey Mare.
					Sister to Juno.	Spectator—Horatia by Blank—Dau. of F. Childers—Miss Belvoir by Gr. Grantham—Dau. of Paget Turk—Betty Percival by L. Arabian.
					Grey Diomed.	Imp. Medley (Gimcrack)—Dau. of Sloe (Partner)—Dau. of Vampire—Imp. Calista by Forester—Dau. of Crab—Dau. of Hobgoblin.
					Daughter of.	Va. Cade—Dau. of Hickman's Independence—Dolly Fine by Imp. Silvereye—Dau. of Imp. Badger—Dau. of Forester—Dau. of Silvereye.
			Miller's Damsel.	Imp. Messenger.	Mambrino.	Engineer (Sampson)—Dau. of Cade—Dau. of Bol. Little John (Partner)—Durham's Favorite by Son of Bald Galloway.
					Daughter of.	Turf (Matchem)—Sis. to Figurante by Regulus—Dau. of Starling—Snap's dam by Fox—Gipsey by Bay Bolton—Dau. of Newcastle Turk.
				Amanda.	Pot-8o's.	Eclipse—Sportsmistress by War Sportsman—Golden Locks by Oroonoko—Valiant's dam by Crab—Dau. of Partner—Thwait's Dun Mare.
					Daughter.	Gimcrack—Snap Dragon by Snap—Dau. of Regulus—Dau. of Bartlet's—Dau. of Hon. Arabian—Byerly Mare dam of Two True Blues.
		Daughter of.	Sir Charles.	Diomed.	Diomed.	Florizel—Sis. to Juno by Spectator—Horatia by Blank—Dau. of F. Childers—Miss Belvoir by Gr. Grantham—Dau. of Paget Turk.
					Castianira.	Rockingham—Tabitha by Trentham—Dau. of Bosphorus—Dau. of Wm's Forester—Dau. of Coalition Colt—Dau. of Bustard (Crab).
				Dau. of Sir Archy.	Imp. Citizen.	Pacolet—Princess by Turk—Fairy Queen by Y Cade—Black Eyes by Crab—Warlock Galloway by Snake—Dau. of Bald Galloway.
					Daughter of.	Commutation—Dau. of Imp. Dare Devil—Sally Shark by Imp. Shark—Betsey Pringle by Imp. Fearnought—Imp. Jenny Dismal.
			Dau. of Cicero.	Dau. of	Sir Archy.	Diomed—Castianira by Rockingham—Tabitha by Trentham—Dau. of Bosphorus—Dau. of Wm's Forester—Dau. of Coalition Colt.
					Daughter of.	Diomed—Dau. of Imp. St. George (Dragon)—Dau. of Imp. Fearnought—Dau. of Imp. Jolly Roger—Imp. Mary Gray by Roundhead.
					Imp. Bedford.	Dungannon (Eclipse)—Fairy by Highflyer—Fairy Queen by Y. Cade—Black Eyes by Crab—Warlock Galloway by Snake—Sis. to Car. Gelding.
					Daughter of.	Bellair (Imp. Medley)—Dau. of Imp. Shark (Maraske)—Dau. of Wildair—Dau. of Lexington (Symme's Wildair)—Dau. of Spanking Roger (Jolly Roger)—Dau. of Imp. Jolly Roger (Roundhead)—Imp. Miss Belle by An. Starling—Dau. of Cade (Godol.)—Dau. of Counsellor (Shaftsbury Turk)—Dau. of Snake (Lister Turk)—Dau. of Luggs (D'Arcy White Turk)—Dau. of Davill's Old Woodcock.

PLENIPO

Will stand the season of 1883 at the Richland Stud, near Nashville, Tenn., at $25 the season. Application to B. F. Cockrill, proprietor, Nashville, Tenn.

PLENIPO by imp. Bonnie Scotland, son of Iago, bred by B. F. Cockrill, Richland stud, Tenn., foaled 1874, dam Dora by imp. Australian, son of West Australian, out of Lindora by Lexington, son of Boston. Plenipo was one of the most promising colts in Tennessee, but like many others, his trainer was not satisfied with good work and great speed, so he fell a victim to too many trials, the fate of very many good horses. At three-year old ran second to Melvern in Commercial Hotel Stake, at Nashville, 1¼ miles in 2:14, track heavy ; in this race, Felicia, Joe Burt, Alice Murphy and two others were behind him. Complaining he was laid up and started in one race, when six years old, and was unplaced. Plenipo was named from his striking resemblance to the famous Lion of Doncaster, Eng., Plenipotentiary, and is from one of the racing families of America, from it came Picayune, the great grandam of Plenipo, she was a fine race-mare, and the dam of the famous race-horses Doubloon, Florin, Louis D'or, she was also the grandam of Quartermaster, the great grandam of Madge, Ventilator, and the great grandam of Vagrant, Bounce, Ella and other good ones. He has an infusion of the blood of Tramp, Buzzard, Plenipotentiary and Whalebone, through Bonnie Scotland, and the Melbourne, Emilius and Whisker blood through Australian, which is well fortified through his dam with Archy and Diomed, and doubled on that of the Godolphin Arabian (Barb). Plenipo is a chestnut, with white stripe in his face, and very much resembles the pictures of the great English horse, Plenipotentiary, hence his name. He is full of substance and quality, with good legs and feet, and taking him all over it would be difficult to find a finer specimen of a race-horse.

PEDIGREE OF PLENIPO.

PLENIPO.	IMP. BONNIE SCOTLAND.	Queen Mary, Blink Bonny's dam.	Daughter of Plenipotentiary.	Myrrha.	Dick Andrews. / Daughter of.	Joe Andrews—Dau. of Highflyer—Dau. of Cardinal Puff—Dau. of Tatler—Dau. of Snip—Dau. of Godol. Arabian—Dau. of Framp. Whiteneck. / Gohanna—Fraxinella by Trentham—Dau. of Woodpecker—Everlasting by Eclipse—Hyaena by Snap—Miss Belsea by Regulus—Dau. of B. Childers.	Don John. / Daughter Tramp. of. / Iago.
					Comus. / Marciana.	Sorcerer—Houghton Lass by Sir Peter—Alexina by King Fergus—Lardella by Y. Marske—Dau. of Cade—Beaufremont's dam. / Stamford—Macia by Coriander—Faith by Pacolet—Atalanta by Matchem—Lass of the Mill by Oroonoko—Dau. of Traveler.	
					Buzzard. / Castrel's dam.	Woodpecker—Misfortune by Dux—Curiosity by Snap—Dau. of Regulus—Dau. of Bart. Childers—Dau. of Hon. Arabian—Dam of True Blues. / Alexander—Dau. of Highflyer—Dau. of Alfred—Dau. of Engineer—Bay Malton's dam by Cade—Lass of the Mill by Traveler—Miss Makeless.	Scandal. / Gladiator. / Pauline. Partisan. / Daughter Selim. of.
					Haphazard. / Daughter of.	Sir Peter—Miss Hervey by Eclipse—Clio by Y. Cade—Dau. of Old Starling—Dau. of Bart. Childers—Dau. of Bay Bolton—Dau of Byerly Turk. / Precipitate—Colibri by Woodpecker—Camilla by Trentham—Coquette by Compton Barb—Sis. to Regulus by Godol. Arabian—Gr. Robinson.	
					Walton. / Parasol.	Sir Peter—Arethusa by Dungannon—Dau. of Prophet—Virago by Snap—Dau. of Regulus—Sis. to Othello by Crab—Miss Slamerkin. / Pot-8-os—Prunella by Highflyer—Promise by Snap—Julia by Blank—Spectator's dam by Partner—Bonny Lass by Bay Bolton.	
					Moses. / Quadrille.	Whalbone or Seymour—Dau. of Gohanna—Grey Skim by Woodpecker—Silver's dam by Herod—Y. Hag by Skim—Hag by Crab. / Selim—Canary Bird by Whiskey or Sorcerer—Canary by Coriander—Miss Green by Highflyer—Harriet by Matchem—Flora by Regulus (Godol.)	
					Emilius. / Harriet.	Orville—Emily by Stamford—Dau. of Whiskey—Gr. Dorimant by Dorimant—Dizzy by Blank—Dizzy by Driver—Dau. of Smiling Tom. / Pericles—Dau. of Selim—Pipylina by Sir Peter—Rally by Trumpator—Fancy, Sis. to Diomed by Florizel—Sis. to Juno by Spectator.	
					Whalebone. / Gift.	Waxy—Penelope by Trumpator—Prunella by Highflyer—Promise by Snap—Julia by Blank—Spectator's dam by Partner—Bonny Lass. / Y. Gohanna—Sis. to Grazier by Sir Peter—Sis to Amaltor by Trumpator—Dau. of Herod—Dau. of Snap—Dau. of Gower Stallion—Dau. of Childers.	
	DORA.	Imp. Australian.	Emilia. / West Australian. / Emilius. Y.Emilius.	Mel-Mower-bourne. ina.	Humphrey Clinker. / Daughter of.	Comus—Clinkerina by Clinker—Pewet by Tandem—Termagant by Tantrum—Cantatrice by Sampson—Dau. of Regulus—Marske's dam. / Cervantes—Dau. of Golumpus—Dau. of Paynator—Sis. to Zodiac by St. George—Abigail by Woodpecker—Firetail by Eclipse—Dau. of Blank.	
					Touchstone. / Emma.	Camel—Banter by Master Henry—Boadicea by Alexander—Brunette by Amaranthus—Mayfly by Matchem—Dau. of An. Starling. / Whisker—Gibside Fairy by Hermes—Vicissitude by Pipator—Beatrice by Sir Peter—Pyrrha by Matchem—Duchess by Whitenose.	
					Emilius. / Shoveler.	Orville—Emily by Stamford—Dau. of Whiskey—Gr. Dorimant by Dorimant—Dizzy by Blank—Dizzy by Driver—Dau. of Smiling Tom. / Scud—Gossander by Hambletonian—Rally by Trumpator—Fancy by Florizel—Sis. to Juno by Spectator—Horatia by Blank (Godol.)	
					Whisker. / Variety.	Waxy—Penelope by Trumpator—Prunella by Highflyer—Promise by Snap—Julia by Blank—Spectator's dam by Partner—Bonny Lass. / Selim or Soothsayer—Sprite by Bobtail—Catharine by Woodpecker—Camilla by Trentham—Coquette by Compton Barb.—Sis. to Regulus.	
		Lindora. / Picayune. / Sally Howe.	Lexington. / Medoc.	Alice Boston. Persian. Y.Emilius. Carneal.	Timoleon. / Robin Brown's dam.	Sir Archy—Dau. of Saltram—Dau. of Symme's Wildair—Dau. of Driver (Imp. Othello)—Dau. of Fallower (Blank)—Dau. of Vampire. / Ball's Florizel—Dau. of Alderman—Dau. of Clockfast—Dau. of Symme's Wildair—Y. Kitty Fisher by Fearnought—Imp. Kitty Fisher by Cade.	
					Sarpedon. / Rowena.	Emilius—Icaria by the Flyer—Parma by Dick Andrews—May by Beningbrough—Primrose be Mambrino—Cricket by Herod—Sophia. / Sumpter—Lady Grey by Robin Grey—Maria by Melzar—Dau. of Highflyer Dau. of Fearnought—Dau. of Ariel—Dau. of Jack of Diamonds.	
					Am. Eclipse. / Y. Maid of the Oaks.	Duroc—Millers Damsel by Imp. Messenger—Dau. of Pot-8-os—Dau. of Gimcrack—Snap-Dragon by Snap—Dau. of Regulus—Dau. of Bart. Childers. / Expedition—Maid of the Oaks by Spread Eagle—Annette by Imp. Shark—Dau. of Rockingham—Dau. of Gallant—Dau. of True Whig—Dau. of Regulus.	
					Sir Wm. of Transport. / Lady Robin.	Sir Archy—Transport by Virginius (Diomed)—Nancy Air by Imp. Bedford—Annette by Imp. Shark—Dau. of Rockingham. / Robin Grey (Imp. Royolist by Saltram)—Dau. of Quicksilver (Imp. Medley by Gimcrack)—Dau. of Mede's Celer (Janus by Janus by Godol.)	

POWHATTAN,

(OWN BROTHER TO PAROLE),

Will stand the season of 1883 at the Woodburn Stud, A. J. Alexander, proprietor, near Spring, Woodford County, Ky., at $50 the season. Application to L. Brodhead, Spring, Ky. Annual sales of yearlings in May.

POWHATTAN by imp. Leamington, son of Faugh-a-Ballagh, bred by Mr. A. Welch, Erdenheim Stud, Pa., foaled 1879, dam Maiden, dam of Parole by Lexington, son of Boston, out of Kitty, Clark by imp. Glencoe. Powhattan started in only one public race, that at Long Branch, meeting with an accident he was unplaced. He was considered quite promising, and ran a very fast trial at Jerome Park, in the spring. Leamington, his sire, can be found in this Vol. Parole, his own brother, has been one of the noted popular favorites of the Turf. After racing in his three, four and five-year old form in this country, he was sent to England, and won the Newmarket Handicap, last 1¼ miles of the Beacon Course, beating the great Isonomy, Lina and three others. He won the City and Suburban handicap, 1¼ miles, 119 lbs., beating Rdiotto, Cradle and fifteen others, and the great Metropolitan Stakes (handicap), 2¼ miles, 124 lbs., beating Castlereagh ; the Great Cheshire Handicap Stakes, 1¼ miles, carrying 134 lbs., defeating Reefer, Sir Joseph, Ridotto and four others, and also won the Epsom Gold Cup, 1¼ miles, 125 lbs., beating Alchemist and Primrose. The family has always been a successful racing one. Maiden, his dam, won the Travers Stakes at Saratoga ; the grandam and great grandam were all winners, and from the stock have come such horses as Mary Morris, Wild Irishman, Frankfort, Falsetto, Felicia, Fortuna, Sumpter, Childers, Rattler, Ringgold, Flirtilla, Mary Wynn, Tom Kimball, Cassandra, The Countess, Turco, John Bascomb, Helen Mar, Ann Merry, Tiger, Ann Innis, Hebron, Meteor, George Kinney, and in the early days of racing, Old Slamerkin. Then on the score of blood and racing lineage, Powhattan should commend himself to the public. Powhattan is a solid bay, with large star, left fore and right hind ankles white, his head is bony and expressive, with large, full eyes, high at the withers like his noted brother, good barrel, great depth of girth, with good loin and fine coupling, and has the Lexington hind leg ; he is 16½ hands high : whilst he has not the racing record of his great brother, he is a Leamington from a racing family on both sides, and as all the Leamington's are successes in the stud, he should be. Flying Childers electrified the world by his brilliant racing career, but his brother, Bartlet's Childers, excelled him in the stud, as also did Cade, his famous racing brother, Lath. Powhattan is much inbred to Sir Archy and Diomed, and traces back without a flaw, through Amaranthus dam to the Layton Barb Mare.

PEDIGREE OF POWHATTAN.

POWHATTAN.							
IMP. LEAMINGTON.	Faugh-a-Ballagh.	Sir Hercules.	Peri.	Whalebone	Waxy.	Pot-8-os—Maria by Herod—Lisette by Snap—Miss Windsor by Godol. Arabian—Sis. to Volunteer by Y. Belgrade—Dau. of Bart. Childers.
					Penelope.	Trumpator—Prunella by Highflyer—Promise by Snap—Julia by Blank—Spectator's dam by Partner—Bonny Lass by Bay Bolton.
			Bob Booty.		Wanderer.	Gohanna—Catharine by Woodpecker—Camilla by Trentham—Coquette by Compton's Barb—Sis. to Regulus by Godol, Arabian—Gr. Robinson.
					Thalestris.	Alexander—Rival by Sir Peter—Hornet by Drone—Manilla by Goldfinder Dau. of Old Eng.—Dau. of Cul. Arabian—Miss Cade.
		Guiccioli.			Chanticleer.	Woodpecker—Dau. of Eclipse—Rosebud by Snap—Miss Belsea by Regulus—Dau. of Bart. Childers—Dau. of Hon. Arabian.
					Ierne.	Bagot—Dau. of Gamahoe—Patty by Tim—Miss Patch by Justice—Ringtail Galloway by Cur. Bay Barb—Sis. to Witty Mare by Pelham's Hip.
			Flight.		Irish Escape.	Commodore—Dau. of Highflyer—Shift by Sweetbriar—Bl. Susan by Snap—Ld. Bruce's Mare by Cade—Dau. of Belgrade—Dau. of Clif. Arabian.
					Young Heroine.	Bagot—Heroine by Hero—Dau. of Snap—Sis. to Regulus by Godol. Arabian—Gr. Robinson by Bald Galloway—Dau. of Snake.
	Daughter of.	Pantaloon.	Castrel.		Buzzard.	Woodpecker—Misfortune by Dux—Curiosity by Snap—Dau. of Regulus—Dau. of Bart. Childers—Dau. of Hon. Arabian.
					Selim's dam.	Alexander—Dau. of Highflyer—Dau. of Alfred—Dau. of Engineer—Bay Maltou's dam by Cade—Lass of the Mill by Traveler—Miss Makeless.
			Idalia.		Peruvian.	Sir Peter—Dau. of Budrow—Escape's dam by Squirrel—Dau. of Babraham—Dau. of Golden Ball—Bushy Molly by Hamp. Ct. Childers.
					Musidora.	Meteor—Maid of All Work by Highflyer—Sis. to Tandem by Syphon—Dau. of Regulus—Dau. of Snip—Dau. of Cottingham—War. Galloway.
	Daphne.	Maid of Honor.	Laurel.		Blacklock.	Whitelock—Dau. of Coriander—Wildgoose by Highflyer—Coheiress by Pot-8-os—Manilla by Goldfinder—Dau. of Old Eng.
					Wagtail.	Prime Minister—Dau. of Orville—Miss Grimstone by Weasel—Dau. of Ancaster—Dau. of Dam Arabian—Daughter of Sampson.
					Champion.	Selim—Podagra by Gouty—Jet by Magnet—Jewel by Squirrel—Sophia by Blank—Diana by Second—Hang Br. Mare by Stan. Arabian.
					Etiquette.	Orville—Boadicea by Alexander—Brunette by Amaranthus—Mayfly by Matchem—Dau. of An. Starling—Dau. of Grashopper.
MAIDEN.	Lexington.	Boston.	Sis. to Tuckahoe.	Timoleon.	Sir Archy.	Diomed—Castianira by Rockingham—Tabitha by Trentham—Dau. of Bosphorus—Dau. of Wm.'s Forester—Dau. of Coalition Colt.
					Daughter of.	Imp. Saltram—Dau. of Symme's Wildair—Dau. of Driver (Imp. Othello)—Dau. Fallower (Blank)—Dau. of Vampire (Regulus).
					Ball's Florizel.	Diomed—Dau. of Imp. Shark—Dau. of Harris's Eclipse—Dau. of Fearnought—Dau. of Jolly Roger—Dau. of Sober John—Dau. of Imp. Shock
					Daughter of.	Alderman—Dau. of Clockfast—Dau. of Symme's Wildair—Y. Kitty Fisher —by Fearnought—Imp. Kitty Fisher by Cade—Dau. of Som. Arabian.
		Alice Carneal.	Rowena.	Sarpedon	Emilius.	Orville—Emily by Stamford—Dau. of Whiskey—Gr. Dorimant by Dorimant—Dizzy by Blank—Dizzy by Driver—Dau. of Smiling Tom.
					Icaria.	The Flyer—Parma by Dick Andrews—May by Beninbrough—Primrose by Mambrino—Cricket by Herod—Sophia by Blank.
					Sumpter.	Sir Archy—Flirtilla's dam by Robin Redbreast—Dau. of Obscurity—Slamerkin by Wildair—Imp. Cub Mare by Cub—Amaranthus' dam.
					Lady Grey.	Robin Grey—Maria by Melzar—Dau. of Highflyer—Dau. of Fearnought—Dau. of Ariel—Dau. of Jack of Diamonds—Imp. Diamond.
	Glencoe.	Trampoline.	Saltan.		Selim.	Buzzard—Castrel's dam by Alexander—Dau. of Highflyer—Dau. of Alfred Dau. of Engineer—Bay Malton's dam by Cade—Lass of the Mill.
					Bacchante.	Williamson's Ditto—Sis. to Calomel by Mercury—Dau. of Herod—Folly by Marske—Vixen by Regulus—Dau. of Hut. Spot—Dau. of Bolton.
					Tramp.	Dick Andrews—Dau. of Gohanna—Fraxinella by Trentham—Dau. of Woodpecker—Everlasting by Eclipse—Hyaena by Snap—Miss Belsea.
					Web.	Waxy—Penelope by Trumpator—Prunella by Highflyer—Promise by Snap Julia nk—Spectator's dam by Partner—Bonny Lass.
	Kitty Clark.	Sumpter.	Trampoline.		Sir Archy.	Diomed—Castianira by Rockingham—Tabitha by Trentham—Dau. of Bosphorus—Dau. of Wm.'s Forester—Dau. of Coalition Colt (Godol.)
					Flirtilla's dam.	Robin Redbreast—Dau. of Obscurity—Slamerkin by Wildair—Imp. Cub Mare by Cub—Amaranthus' dam by Second—Dau. of Starling.
	Miss Obstinale.	Jenny Slamerkin.	Sis. to Slamerkin.		Tiger.	Cook's Whip—Jane Hunt by Hamptons's Paragon—Moll by Imp. Figure —Slamerkin by Wildair—Imp. Cub Mare by Cub—Amaranthus' dam.
					Paragon.	Imp. Buzzard—Indians by Columbus (Imp. Pantaloon)—Jane Huntby Paragon (Imp. Fliimnap)—Moll by Imp. Figure (Gr. Figure)—Slamerkin by Imp. Wildair (Cade)—Imp. Cub Mare by Cub (Fox)—Amaranthus' dam by Second (F. Childers)—Dam of Leed's Flash and Fop by Starling (Bay Bolton)—Sis. to Vane's Partner by Croft's Partner (Jigg)—Sis. to Guy by Greyhound (White Barb Chillaby)—Brown Farewell by Makeless (Oglethorpe Arabian) — Dau. of Brimmer (Yellow Turk) -- Dau. of Place's White Turk—Dau. of Dodsworth—Layton BarbMare.

RAYON D'OR (Imp.)

(WINNER OF THE CLEARWELL AND LEVANT STAKES IN 1878; ST. JAMES' PALACE STAKES, THE GREAT CHALLENGE STAKES, CHAMPION STAKES AND DONCASTER ST. LEGER, IN 1879,)

Will stand the season of 1883 *at the Algeria Stud, near Erie, Pa., the property of Mr. W. L. Scott, as private stallion.*

RAYON D'OR (Ray of Gold), by Flageolet, son of Plutus, bred in Dangu Stud, France, foaled 1876, dam Araucaria, dam of Chamant, Camelia, etc., by Ambrose, son of Touchstone, out of Pocahontas, dam of Stockwell, Rataplan, King Tom, etc., by imp. Glencoe. Rayon d'Or made his debut in England as a two-year old by winning the Levant Stakes, half a mile, at Goodwood, carrying 122 pounds, beating Flavius, Galantha and two others. At Doncaster, in September, he won a sweepstake, at at three-quarters of a mile, with 129 pounds, beating Charibert and Reconciliation At the Newmarket Second October Meeting won the Clearwell Stakes, carrying 131 pounds, with such horses as Ringleader and Bay Archer, 122 pounds each, second and third, and three others; the Glasgow Stakes, at the Newmarket Houghton Meeting, three-quarters of a mile, beating Ringleader and Glencairn. During the winter and spring which followed, Rayon d'Or was much fancied both for the 2,000 guineas and Derby, but his running was a disappointment. He was third to Charibert and Cadogan for the 2,000 guineas, and was unplaced for the Derby, won by Sir Bevys. At Ascot, on the first day, he was third for the Prince of Wales Stakes, to Wheel of Fortune and Adventure, but on the third day he won the St. James Palace Stakes with 122 pounds, over the severe "Old Mile," beating Charibert, Ruperra and seven others. At Goodwood Rayon d'Or won the Sussex Stakes, one mile, beating Ruperra, Leap Year and Exeter, and won the great Doncaster St. Leger, Ruperra second and Exeter third, and fourteen others unplaced, including the winner of the Derby, Sir Bevys. The next day Rayon d'Or "walked over" for the Zetland Stakes, Mr. Crawfurd's Pell Mell Colt saving his stake. At the Newmarket First October Meeting won the Great Foal Stakes with 131 pounds, beating Discord, Palmbearer and three others, but at the same meeting was beaten by Bay Archer for the Newmarket St. Leger, he yielding 7 pounds, after which Rayon d'Or won the Select Stakes, Rowley Mile, beating Discord and three others; the Champion Stakes, across the flat, one mile 2 furlongs 73 yards, beating Placida, the Oaks winner, Exeter and five others, and the Grea Challenge Stakes, Bretby Course, six furlongs, beating Lollypop, Placida, Parole and others. He ended his three-year-old career by running third for a handicap "Across the Flat" to Out of Bounds, who carried 110 pounds to Rayon d'Or's 126 pounds. His earnings for the year amounted to $87,735. As a four-year-old Rayon d'Or began by winning the Prix du Cadran, 2 miles and 5 furlongs, beating Zut, Salteador and others, and the Prix Rainbow, 3 miles and a furlong, beating Zut and Clocher at the Paris Spring Meeting in March. He was immediately afterward sent to England, where, on the 16th of April, at Newmarket, he "walked over" for the Post Stakes (the two middle miles). At the Newmarket First Spring Meeting—two weeks later—he walked over for the Prince of Wales Stakes (the Cesarewitch Course). At Ascot he won the Rous Memorial Stakes over the New Mile, carrying 132 pounds; but in running for the Hardwicke Stakes at the same meeting over the Swinley course (mile and a half) he was beaten a head by Exeter, to whom he was giving 10 pounds. This race closed his turf career.

Flageolet, his sire, was a superior race-horse. He won his first race in France at two years old, defeating a large field. Won the Hopeful Stakes, one-half mile, at Newmarket, 128 pounds; won the Rutland Stakes, three quarters of a mile, 129 pounds, beating His Grace and two others; won the Forlorn Stakes, Rowley mile, 128 pounds, beating Lord Mayo, 122 pounds; won Burwell Stakes, 5 furlongs, 128 pounds, defeating Amulle Von Edelreich, 122 pounds, was unplaced in Middle Park Plate, won by Surinam. Ran second to Andred in the Prendergast Stakes, Surinam and three others behind him. Won the Criterion Stakes, three-quarters of a mile defeating Paladin, Kaiser and four others. As three-year old ran second to Boiard in the Prix du Jockey Club (French Derby), and second to him in the Grand Prix de Paris in 1873. He was also second to Apollon in the Prix du Cêdre, same year. Crossing the channel, he was unplaced in the 2,000 guineas, won by Gang Forward; ran second to Cremorne in the Gold Cup at Ascot; won the Goodwood Cup, in which he bent both Favonius and

Continued on page 134.

PEDIGREE OF RAYON D'OR (Imp.)

RAYON D'OR. (Bay of Gold.) Chesnut horse foaled 1876. Bred at Dangu, France. Imported and owned by W. L. Scott, Erie, Pa.							
Marpessa.	Pocahontas.	ARAUCARIA.	Ambrose.	Touchstone.	Camel.	Touchstone.	Camel—Banter by Master Heury—Boadicca by Alexander—Brunette by Amaranthus—Mayfly by Matchem—Dau. of An. Starling.
						Vulture.	Langar—Kite by Bustard—Miss Hap by Shuttle—Dau. of Sir Peter—Miss Hervey by Eclipse—Clio by Y. Cade—Dau. of Old Starling.
				Annette.	Priam.	Redshank.	Sandbeck—Johanna by Selim—Comical's dam by Skyscraper—Dau. of Dragon—Fidget's dam by Matchem—Dau. of Syphon.
						Oxygen.	Emilius—Whizgig by Rubens—Penelope by Trumpator—Prunella by Highflyer—Promise by Snap—Julia by Blank—Spectator's dam.
				Potentate's dam.	Sultan.	Bay Middleton.	Sultan—Cobweb by Phantom—Filagree by Soothsayer—Web by Waxy—Penelope by Trumpator—Prunella by Highflyer—Julia.
						Pleuary.	Emilius—Harriet by Pericles—Dau. of Selim—Pipylina by Sir Peter—Rally by Trumpator—Fancy, Sis. to Diomed, by Florizel.
					Trampoline.	Venison.	Partisan—Fawn by Smolensko—Jerboa by Gohanna—Camilla by Trentham—Coquette by Compton Barb—Sis. to Regulus.
		Glencoe.				Darkness.	Glencoe—Fanny by Whisker—Dau. of Camillus—Dau. of Precipitate—Mendoza's dam by Paymaster—Pomona by Herod.
						Defence.	Whalebone—Defiance by Rubens—Little Folly by Highland Fling—Harriet by Volunteer—Dau. of Alfred—Magnolia by Marske.
				Gladiator.	The Ba. St., or The Emp.*	Daughter of.	Reveler—Design by Tramp—Defiance by Rubens—Little Folly by Highland Fling—Harriet by Voluuteer—Dau. of Alfred—Magnolia.
						Royal Oak.	Catton—Dau. of Smolensko—Lady Mary by Beningbrough—Dau. of Highflyer—Dau.of Marske—A-la-Grecque by Regulus—Dau.of Allworthy
	Muley.		La Favorite.	Poetess.	Bray.	Ada.	Whisker—Anna Bella by Shuttle—Dau. of Drone—Contessina by Young Marske—Tuberose by Herod—Gr. Starling by Starling.
Clare.						Partisan.	Walton—Parasol by Pot-8-os—Prunella by Highflyer—Promise by Snap—Julia by Blank—Spectator's dam by Partner—Bonny Lass.
					Alice Planet.	Pauline.	Moses—Quadrille by Selim—Canary Bird by Whiskey or Sorcerer—Canary by Coriander—Miss Green by Highflyer—Harriet by Matchem.
			Constance.	Lanterne.		Hercule.	Rainbow—Amable by Election—Aladdin's dam by Walnut—Dau. of Javelin—Sis. to Spadille by Highflyer—Flora by Squirrel.
					Cavetina.	Elvira.	Eryx—Sis. to Bos.by Buzzard—Bennington's dam by Percy Arabian—Dau. of Herod—Dau. of Snap—Chalkstone's dam by Shepherd's Crab.
		FLAGEOLET.		Monarque.	Orlando.	Whalebone.	Waxy—Penelope by Trumpator—Prunella by Highflyer—Promise by Snap—Julia by Blank—Spectator's dam by Partner.
						Daughter of.	Selim—Maiden by Sir Peter—Dan. of Phoenomenon—Matron by Florizel—Maiden by Matchem—Dau. of Squirt—Lot's dam.
					Trumpeter.	Master Henry.	Orville—Miss Sophia by Stamford—Sophia by Buzzard—Huncamunca by Highflyer—Cypher by Squirrel—Fribble's dam.
			Daughter of.			Boadicea.	Alexander—Brunette by Amaranthus—Mayfly by Matchem—Dau. of Ancaster Starling—Dau. of Grasshopper—Dau. of New Arabian.
						Emilius.	Orville—Emily by Stamford—Dau. of Whiskey—Gr. Dorimant by Dorimant—Dizzy by Blank—Dizzy by Driver—Dau. of Smiling Tom.
						Cressida.	Whiskey—Y. Giantess by Diomed—Giantess by Matchem—Molly Longlegs by Babraham—Dau. of Cole's Foxhunter—Dau. of Partner.
						Don Juan.	Sorcerer—Dau. of Highflyer—Toucer's dam by Marske—A-la-Grecque by Regulus—Dau. of Allworthy—Dau. of Bolton Starling.
				Plutus.		Moll in the Wad.	Hambletonian—Spitfire by Pipator—Farewell by Slope—Dau. of Y. Marske Dau. of Bro. to Silvio—Sis. to Stripling by Hutton's Spot.
						Selim.	Buzzard—Dau. of Alexander—Dau. of Highflyer—Dau. of Alfred—Dau. of Engineer—Bay Malton's dam by Cade—Lass of the Mill.
						Bacchante.	Williamson's Ditto—Sis. to Calomel by Mercury—Dau. of Herod—Folly by Marske—Vixen by Regulus—Dau. of Hutton's Spot.
						Tramp.	Dick Andrews—Dau. of Gohanna—Fraxinella by Trentham—Dau. of Woodpecker—Everlasting by Eclipse—Hyaena by Snap.
						Web.	Waxy—Penelope by Trumpator—Prunella by Highflyer—Promise by Snap—Julia by Blank—Spectator's dam by Partner—Bonny Lass.
						Orville.	Beningbrough—Evelina by Highflyer—Termagant by Tantrum—Cantatrice by Sampson—Dau. of Regulus—Marske's dam.
						Eleanor.	Whiskey—Y. Giantess by Diomed—Giantess by Matchem—Molly Longlegs by Babraham—Dau. of Cole's Foxhunter—Dau. of Partner.
						Marmion.	Whiskey—Y. Noisette by Diomed—Noisette by Squirrel—Carina by Marske—Thunder's dam by Blank—Dizzy by Driver.
						Harpalice.	Gohanna—Amazon by Driver—Fractious by Mercury—Dau. of Woodpecker—Everlasting by Eclipse—Hyaena by Snap—Miss Belsea by Regulus (Godol.)—Dau. of Bartlet's Childers (Darley Arabian)—Dau. of Honeywood's Arabian—Byerly Marc dam of the Two True Blues.

* Emperor given.

RAYON D'OR (Imp.)—Continued.

Cremorne, the Derby winners of 1871 and 1872. He ran second to Uhlan in Brighton Cup; won the Grand Duke Michael Stakes at Newmarket First October Meeting; won a free handicap sweepstakes across the flat, and the Jockey Club Cup at the Newmarket Houghton Meeting. As a four-year-old he ran second to Boiard twice in France; won the Claret Stakes at Newmarket, England; was second to Boiard in the Gold Cup, and third to King Lud and Boiard in the Alexandra Plate, both at Ascot. This closed his turf career. Plutus, his sire, was unplaced in the Derby of 1866, but won some races and ran creditably in others.

Araucaria, Rayon d'Or's dam, was the dam of Camelia, winner of the 1,000 guineas, and ran a dead heat and divided the Oaks Stakes with Enguerrande. Chamant, by Mr. Lorillard's Mortemer, out of Araucaria, won the Middle Park Plate and the Dewhurst Plate in England at two years old, and at three won the 2,000 guineas. The blood on the sire side is a combination of Touchstone through Orlando, a Derby winner, Bay Middleton, son of Sultan, a Derby winner, Venison and Glencoe, through Darkness, a winner of the Ascot Stakes. On the dam's side Touchstone, St. Leger winner, Priam, Derby winner, and Glencoe, through Pocahontas, dam of Stockwell, Rataplan, King Tom, etc. An analysis of the tabulated pedigree will show that he is richly and fashionably bred; he has a double cross of Glencoe, a triple cross of Diomed, a double cross of Touchstone, fortified by the blood of Whalebone, doubled in upon the Herod and Eclipse blood on both sides to the Byerly Mare, dam of the Two True Blues. Rayon d'Or is probably the most magnificent specimen of his race ever imported. He is the highest-priced horse ever shipped across the Atlantic. His cost delivered at his home is little short of $40,000. In color he is a rich true chestnut, with a large, rather faint, star in his forehead, standing 16 hands, 3½ inches in height. He has a beautiful head, very broad between the eyes, with a very fine, clean and tapering ear; neck long, but broad where it enters the head; shoulders well set and broad, with great depth of girth; good, round barrel, with splendid back, hip and loin. His hips will be found broad, with great length from the point of the hip to whirlbone, and thence to stifle and hocks, the latter clean cut and well placed, and the finest, soundest and best set of legs ever seen under a horse; in fact, it is one of his great excellent points, and certainly nothing is more essential to a good race-horse. Rayon d'Or (Ray of Gold) deserves his name. Bred to the daughters or granddaughters of Lexington possessing the Australian or Glencoe blood, or to the daughters of Bonnie Scotland with the Lexington Glencoe and Archy blood, he must and will be a grand success in the stud.

REBEL

Will stand for the season of 1883 at the stables of Capt. W. Cottrill, near Mobile, Ala. Services only by private contract.

REBEL, by Socks, son of imp. Albion, bred by John L. Connally, Haze Co., Texas, foaled 1861, dam Betty Wharton, by Othello, son of imp. Leviathan, out of a daughter of imp. Consol, by Lottery, she out of Lady Huntsville, own sister to John Bascomb, by Bertrand. Rebel may have been a first-class horse as a racer, but we have no record of his performances. Socks, the sire of Rebel, was a fine race-horse; he beat Planet in the Hutchison Stakes, mile heats, at Charleston, S. C., in 1859, in 1:48¼, 1:47¾, and the following week won the Hutchison Stakes, same place, 2-mile heats, in 3:41, 3:48½, beating Fanny Washington and Hennie Farrow. Albion, the sire of Socks, was imported as a yearling. Was a winner at from one to three-mile heats, and famous as a stallion. On the dam's side, Rebel is exceptionally well bred, and is descended from one of the oldest and most noted racing families in America. Othello, sire of his dam, out of Sally Burton, by Sir Archy, was a very fine race-horse at all distances. Imp. Consol, the sire of his grandam, was a successful sire, having gotten the prodigy, Miss Foot; she won a second heat of four miles in 7:35, and in the fall of 1842, beat Argentile and Alice Carneal, Lexington's dam, four-mile heats, at Lexington, Ky., in 7:42, 7:40, the best and fastest race run in the state to that date. His great grandam, Lady Huntsville, was own sister to the great race-horse, John Bascomb, the conquerer of Post Boy in the great match over the Union Course, L. I., by the celebrated Old Bertrand. The family has always been a racing one, Ratler, Childers, Sumpter, Wild Irishman, Frankfort, Parole, Falsetto, and a host of others, trace back to the imp. Cub Mare, through Old Slamerkin by imp. Wildair. The best of Rebel's get are Sam Harper, Ella Harper, Little Reb, Capt. Fred. Rice, Judith C, Bessie Davis, Tunic, Col. Sellers (*alias* Tug Wilson, *alias* Little Dan), Texan and others, all of which have been winners. Rebel is a dark brown horse, full 16 hands high, with gray or silvered legs. He is a well shaped horse, possessing great constitution which he imparts to his progeny.

PEDIGREE OF REBEL.

REBEL.	SOCKS.	Imp. Albion.	Panthea.	Cain or Actæon.*	Beningbrough.	King Fergus—Dau. of Herod—Pyrrha by Matchem—Duchess by Whitenose—Miss Slamerkin by Y. True Blue.
					Eliza.	Highflyer—Augusta by Eclipse—Hardwick's dam by Herod—Dau. of Bajazet—Dau. of Regulus—Dau. of Lons' Bay Arabian—Dau. of Bay Bolton.
				Diana. Scud.	Stamford.	Sir Peter—Horatia by Eclipse—Countess by Blank—Dau. of Rib—Dau. of Wynn. Arabian—Dau. of Governor—Dau. of Alcock Arabian.
					Daughter of.	Whiskey—Gr. Doimant by Dorimant—Dizzy by Blank—Dizzy by Driver—Dau. of Smiling Tom—Dau. of Oysterfoot—Dau. of Merlin.
				Mama-ella. Comus or †Blacklock.	Whitelock.	Hambletonian—Rosalind by Phoenomenon—Atalauta by Matchem—Lass of the Mill by Oroonoko—Dau. of Traveler—Miss Makeless.
					Daughter of.	Coriander—Wildgoose by Highflyer—Coheiress by Pot-8-os—Manilla by Goldfinder—Dau. of Old Eng.—Dau. of Cul. Arabian.
			Ainderby.	Volocipede.	Dick Andrews.	Joe Andrews—Dau. of Highflyer—Dau. of Cardinal Puff—Dau. of Tatler—Dau. of Snip—Dau. of Go. Arabian—Dau. of Frampton's Whiteneck.
					Mandane.	Pot-8-o's—Y. Camilla by Woodpecker—Camilla by Trentham—Coquette by Comp. Barb—Sis. to Regulus by Go. Arabian—Gr. Robinson.
		Daughter of.			Blacklock.	Whitelock—Dau. of Coriander—Wildgoose by Highflyer—Coheiress by Pot-8-os—Manilla by Goldfinder—Dau. of Old. Eng.—Dau. of Cul. Arabian.
				Kate.	Daughter of.	Juniper (Whiskey)—Dau. of Sorcerer—Virgin by Sir Peter—Dau. of Pot-8-os—Editha by Herod—Elfrida by Snap—Dau. of Regulus.
					Catton.	Golumpus—Lucy Gray by Timothy—Lucy by Florizel—Frenzy by Eclipse Dau. of Engineer—Dau. of Blank—Lass of the Mill by Traveler.
					Miss Garforth.	Walton—Dau. of Hyacinthus—Zara by Delpini—Flora by Regulus—Dau. of Bart. Childers—Dau. of Bay Bolton—Dau. of Belgrade Turk.
			Prima.	Corsica.	John Richards.	Sir Archy—Dau. of Rattle (Imp. Shark)—Dau. of Imp. Medley—Dau. of Symme's Wildair—Dau. of Nonpariel (Imp. Fearnought).
					Sellma.	Top. Gallant—John Bull by Imp. Gabriel—Active by Chatham (Regulus)—Shepherdess by Imp. Slim—Shrewsbury by Imp. Figure.
				Lady Arabiana.	Sir Archy.	Diomed—Castianira by Rockingham—Tabitha by Trentham—Dau. of Bosphorus—Dau. of Wm's. Forester—Dau. of Colition Colt.
					Pandora 2d.	Silverheels (Ogle's Oscar)—Equa by Imp. Chance—Dau. of Republican President (Imp. Highflyer)—Dau. of Imp. Ranger—Dau. of Lind. Arabian.
	BETTY WHARTON.	Othello.	Sally Burton.	Leviathan.	Orville.	Beningbrough—Evelina by Highflyer—Termagant by Tantrum—Cantatrice by Sampson—Dau. of Regulus—Marske's dam.
					Daughter of.	Windle (Beningbrough)—Dau. of Anvil (Herod)—Virago by Snap—Dau. of Regulus—Sis. to Othello by Crab—Miss Slamerkin by Y. True Blue.
				Muley.	Windle.	Beningbrough—Mary Anu by Sir Peter—Dau. of Y. Marske—Dau. of Matchem—Dau. of Tarquin—Sis. to Antelope by Y. Belgrade.
					Daughter of.	Anvil (Herod)—Virago by Snap—Dau. of Regulus—Sis. to Othello by Crab—Miss Slamerkin by Y. True Blue—Dau. of Ox Dun Arabian.
			Sir Archy.	The Dandy's Dam.	Diomed.	Florizel—Sis. to Juno by Spectator—Horatia by Blank—Dau. of F. Childers—Miss Belvoir by Gr. Grantham.
					Castianira.	Rockingham—Tabitha by Trentham—Dau. of Bosphorus—Dau. of Wm's. Forester—Dau. of Coalition Colt—Dau. of Bustard.
					Junius.	Imp. Buzzard (Woodpecker)—Dau. of Imp. Pantaloon (Herod by Tartar)—Francis Steger's Imported Mare.
					Daughter.	Imp. Citizen (Pacolet by Blank)—The Imp. Barb. Mare sent to his Excellency Prest. Jefferson in 1806 by the Bey of Tunis.
		Daughter of.	Imp. Consol.	Dau. of Lottery.	Tramp.	Dick Andrews—Dau. of Gobanna—Fraxinella by Trentham—Dau. of Woodpecker—Everlasting by Eclipse—Hyanea by Snap.
					Mandane.	Pot-8-o's—Y. Camilla by Woodpecker—Camilla by Trentham—Coquette by Compton Barb—Sis. to Regulus by Godol. Arabian.
					Cerberus.	Gohanna—Dau. of Herod—Desdemona by Marske—Y. Hag by Skim—Hag by Crab—Ebony by F. Childers—Ebony by Basto.
					Merlin's dam.	Delpini—Tripple Cyder by King Fergus—Sylvia by Y. Marske—Ferret by Bro. to Silvio—Dau. to Regulus—Dau. of Mor. Arabian.
			Lady Huntsville.	Grey Bertrand.	Sir Archy.	Diomed—Castianira by Rockingham—Tabitha by Trentham—Dau. of Bosphorus—Dau. of Wm's. Forester—Dau. of Coalition Colt.
					Eliza.	Imp. Bedford—Mambrina by Mambrino—Sis. to Naylor's Sally by Blank—Dau. of Ward—Dau. of Merlin—Dau. of Pert.
				Grey Goose.	Pacolet.	Imp. Citizen—Mary Gray by Tippoo Saib— (True Whig)—Dau. of Goode's Brimmer (Harris' Eclipse)—Dau. of Imp. Silvereye.
					Sally Sneed.	Imp. Buzzard—Jane Hunt by Hampton's Paragon (Flimnap)—Moll by Imp. Figure (Gr. Figure)—Slamerkin by Imp. Wildair (Code)—Imp. Cub Mare by Cub (Fox)—Amaranthus' dam by Second (F. Childers)—Dau. of Starling (Bay Bolton)—Dau. of Croft's Partner (Jigg)—Sis. to Guy by Greyhound (White Barb. Chillaby)—Brown Farewell by Makeless—Dau. of Brimmer, Dau. of Place's White Turk—Dau. of Dodsworth—Layton Barb. Mare.

*Actæon given, see Royalty for Cain
†Blacklock given.

REFORM,

(WINNER OF THE SEQUEL STAKES, AT MONMOUTH PARK, 1874,)

Will stand the season of 1883 *at the Erdenheim Stud, Chestnut Hill, Pa., at* $100 *the season, and* $5 *to the groom. Application to Maj. J. R. Hubbard, Chestnut Hill, Philadelphia, Pa.*

REFORM, by imp. Leamington, son of Faugh-a-Ballagh, bred by Mr. R. W. Cameron, Clifton Stud, N. Y., foaled 1871, dam imp. Stolen Kisses, by the Knight of Kars, son of Nutwith, out of Defamation, by Iago. Defamation, his grandam, was the dam of Saccharometer, winner of the Newmarket two year-old Plate, the July Stakes, and Chesterfield Stakes, and was second to Macaroni for the 2,000 guineas. As a two-year-old, started in six races. At Jerome Park, was second in the Nursery Stakes for two-year olds, one mile, won by Rutherford in 1:47¾, Atilla, Saxon, and others behind him, and was unplaced in all his other races. As a three-year-old, started in nine races, of which he won two. Monmouth Park, won the Sequel Stakes for three-year-olds, 2 miles, in 3:37½, beating Dublin, Vandalite, and five others. Saratoga, won a dash of 1¾ miles, 83 lbs., in 3:05¾, beating Dublin, London, and one other. This was the fastest race to that date at the distance. At Jerome Park, was third to Dublin and Vandalite, in the Withers Stakes, one mile, in 1:50, track muddy, Grinstead, Maccaroon, and nine others behind him. Saratoga was third to Vandalite and Grinstead in the Sequel Stakes, 2 miles, in 3:40¾, Madge and three others behind him. Was third to Stampede and Acrobat, in the Kenner Stake, 2 miles, in 3:42, Rutherford behind him. At four years old, was second to Ballinkeel, in Westchester Cup, 2¼ miles, with Botany Bay and Shylock behind him. Was second to Aaron Pennington in the Woodburn Stakes, 2¼ miles, in 4:36¼, beating Grinstead and Rutherford. At six years old, was second to Frederick the Great, in a race of mile heats, the first heat in 1:47, was then withdrawn. Frederick won second heat in 1:47. Was unplaced in a Club Purse, 1¼ miles, won by Hattie F, in 2:01¾. Aged, won a race of three-quarters of a mile heats, in 1:24, 1:24, defeating a field of four, and one of mile heats in 1:55, 2:00, beating Gasconade and Odd Fellow, both run at Ambler Park, Pa. Reform has only a few colts on the turf, and they have run creditably. Little Fred (Yorkshire) won a mile in 1:43 and in 1:44; 1¼ miles in 2:13¼. Tonawanda, three-quarters of a mile in 1:16¾, one mile in 1:43¼, five furlongs in 1:02¾. Miss Lumley by Leamington, or Reform by the later, mile in 1:48, and won the Hunter Stake at Jerome Park, 1¾ miles, in 3:20, track muddy, beating Amazon and six others. Tuscaloosa, by Leamington, or Reform evidently by the latter, won the Army and Navy Stakes at Washington, 1¼ miles, in 2:40¾, beating Free Gold, La Gloria, and three others, and the Delight filly a winner. Reform is a brown, 15 hands 3¾ inches high, white face, wide expanding nostrils, large prominent eyes, clean cut, with no superfluous lumber, and possesses much quality, but has the Melbourn ear, having a double Pantaloon cross, with the Glencoe Whalebone, and traces through a long line of Herod blood to the dam of the Two True Blues. He will be a success.

PEDIGREE OF REFORM.

REFORM.	IMP. LEAMINGTON.	Daughter of.	Daphne.	Maid of Honor.	Pantaloon.	Laurel.	Idalia.	Castrel.	Flight.	Guiccioli.	Bob Booty.	Faugh-a-Ballagh.	Sir Hercules.	Peri.	Whalebone.	Waxy. Penelope.	Pot-8-o's (Eclipse)—Maria by Herod (Tartar)—Lisette by Snap(Snip)—Miss Windsor by Godol. Arabian—Sis. to Volunteer by Y. Belgrade (Belgrade). Trumpator (Conductor)—Prunella by Highflyer—Promise by Snap—Julia by Blank—Spectator's dam by Partner (Jigg)—Dau. of Bay Bolton.
										Wanderer. Thalestris.	Gohanna (Mercury)—Catharine by Woodpecker—Camilla by Trentham—Coquette by the Compton Barb—Sis. to Regulus by Godol. Arabian. Alexander—Rival by Sir Peter—Hornet by Drone—Manilla by Goldfinder—Dau. of Old Eng. (Godol.)—Dau. of Cullen Arabian—Miss Cade by Cade
										Chanticleer. Ierne.	Woodpecker—Dau. of Eclipse—Rosebud by Snap—Miss Belsea by Regulus—Dau. of Bartlet's Childers—Dau of Hon. Arabian. Bagot—Dau. of Gamahoe—Patty by Tim—Miss Patch by Justice—Ringtail Galloway by Cur. Bay Barb.
										Irish Escape. Young Heroine.	Commodore—Buffer's dam by Highflyer—Shift by Sweetbriar—Bl. Susan by Snap—Lord Bruce's Mare by Cade—Dau. of Belgrade. Bagot—Heroine by Hero—Dau. of Snap—Sis. to Regulus by Godol. Arabian—Grey Robinson by Bald Galloway.
										Buzzard. Daughter of.	Woodpecker—Misfortune by Dux—Curiosity by Snap—Dau. of Regulus—Dau. of Bartlet's Childers—Dau. of Hon. Arabian. Alexander—Dau. of Highflyer—Dau. of Alfred—Dau. of Engineer—Bay Malton's dam by Cade—Lass of the Mill by Traveler—Miss Makeless.
										Peruvian. Musidora.	Sir Peter—Dau. of Budrow—Escape's dam by Squirrel—Dau. of Babraham—Dau. of Golden Ball—Busby Molly. Meteor—Maid of all Work by Highflyer—Sis. to Tandem by Syphon—Dau. of Regulus—Dau. of Snip—Dau. of Cottingham.
										Blacklock. Wagtail.	Whitelock—Dau. of Coriander—Wildgoose by Highflyer—Coheiress by Pot-8-os—Manilla by Goldfinder—Dau. of Old Eng.—Dau. of Cul. Arabian. Prime Minister—Dau. of Orville—Miss Grimstone by Weasel—Dau. of Ancaster—Dau. of Damascus Arabian—Dau. of Sampson.
										Champion. Etiquette.	Selim—Podagra by Gouty—Jet by Magnet—Jewel by Squirrel—Sophia by Blank—Diana by Second—Hanger's Br. Mare by Stan. Arabian. Orville—Boadicea by Alexander—Brunette by Amaranthus—Mayfly by Matchem—Dau. of An. Starling—Dau. of Grasshopper.
IMP. STOLEN KISSES.	Defamation.	Caricature.	Pasquinade.	Pantaloon.	Iago.	Scandal.	Don John.	Marpessa.	Glencoe.	The Knight of Kars. Nutwith.	Pocahontas. Dau. of Tomboy.	Jerry. Daughter of.	Smolensko (Sorcerer)—Louisa by Orville—Thomasina by Timothy (Delpini)—Violet by Shark (Marske)—Dau. of Syphon—Charlotte by Blank. Ardrossan (John Bull)—Lady Eliza by Whitworth (Agonistes by Sir Peter)—Dau. of Spadille (Highflyer)—Sylvia by Y. Marske.
										Comus. Plumper's dam.	Sorcerer (Trumpator)—Houghton Lass by Sir Peter—Alexina by King Fergus—Lardella by Y. Marske—Dau. of Cade. Delpini (Highflyer)—Miss Maston by King Fergus (Eclipse)—Columbine by Esperaykes—Dau. of Babraham Blank—Tipsy by Starling.
										Sultan. Trampoline.	Selim—Bacchante by Williamson's Ditto—Sis. to Calomel by Mercury—Dau. of Herod—Folly by Marske—Vixen by Regulus. Tramp—Web by Waxy—Penelope by Trumpator—Prunella by Highflyer Promise by Snap—Julia by Blank—Spectator's dam by Partner.
										Muley. Clare.	Orville—Eleanor by Whiskey—Y. Giantess by Diomed—Giantess by Matchem—Molly Longlegs by Babraham—Dau. of Cole's Foxhunter. Marmion (Whiskey)—Harpalice by Gohanna—Amazon by Driver—Fractious by Mercury—Dau. of Woodpecker—Everlasting by Eclipse.
										Tramp or *Waverley. Daughter of.	Whalebone—Margretta by Sir Peter—Sis. to Cracker by Highflyer—Nutcracker by Matchem—Miss Starling by Starling—Dau. of Partner. Comus—Marciana by Stamford—Marcia by Coriander—Faith by Pacolet—Atalanta by Matchem—Lass of the Mill by Oroonoko.
										Selim. Daughter of.	Buzzard—Castrel's dam by Alexander—Dau. of Highflyer—Dau. of Alfred—Dau. of Engineer—Bay Malton's dam by Cade—Lass of the Mill. Haphazard (Sir Peter)—Dau. of Precipitate—Colibri by Woodpecker—Camilla by Trentham—Coquette By Compton Barb.
										Castrel. Idalia.	Buzzard—Dau. of Alexander—Dau. of Highflyer—Dau. of Alfred—Dau. of Engineer—Bay Malton's dam by Cade—Lass of the Mill by Old Traveler. Peruvian—Musidora by Meteor—Maid of all Work by Highflyer—Dau. of Syphon—Dau. of Regulus—Dau. of Snip—Dau. of Cottingham.
										Camel. Banter.	Whalebone—Dau. of Selim—Maiden by Sir Peter—Dau. of Phoenomenon Matron by Florizel—Maiden by Matchem—Dau. of Squirt. Master Henry—Miss Sophia by Stamford (Sir Peter)—Sophia by Buzzard (Woodpecker)—Huncamunca by Highflyer (Herod)—Cypher by Squirrel (Traveler)—Fribble's dam by Regulus (Godolphin)—Dau. of Bartlet's Childers (Darley Arabian)—Dau. of Honeywood's Arabian—Byerly Mare dam of the Two True Blues.

* Waverley given.

ROSSIFER (Imp.)

Rossifer will be located the season of 1883 at the Fairview Stud, near Gallatin, Sumner County, Tenn., and will serve mares at $50 the season, and $5 to the groom. Application to Mr. Charles Reed, proprietor, Gallatin, Tenn.

ROSSIFER by Rosicrucian, son of Beadsman, bred by Mr. W. Blenkiron, Middle Park Stud, dam Fenella, dam of Candahar, Cleveland, &c., by Cambuscan, son of Newminster, out of La Favorita by Monarque. Rossifer, from an injury to one of his ankles, was never trained. Rosicrucian, his sire, own brother to the Palmer, won three out of his four races at two-years old, such as the Criterion Stakes at Newmarket Houghton Meeting, defeating a field of seven, including Leonie and King Alfred, at three-years old was unplaced in the 2,000 guineas, won by Moslem, and in the Derby, won by his half brother, Blue Gown ; when four years old, won the All-aged Stakes at Newmarket Houghton Meeting, defeating Formosa and Heather Bell ; at five years old, won six out of thirteen races ; the Craven Stakes at Goodwood, defeating Vespasian and others ; the York Cup and the All-aged Stakes at Newmarket, beating Normanby. Kingcraft, &c. ; Beadsman, the sire of Rosicrucian, won the Derby in 1858, and is sire of Blue Gown, winner of the Derby, Pero Gomez, winner of the St. Leger and other good horses ; Cambuscan, the sire of Rossifer's dam, won the July Stakes and Croome Stakes at Newmarket, his only two races as a two-year old. He was unplaced in the Derby, won by Blair Athol, and was third to Blair Athol and Gen. Peel in the St. Leger, he won five races that year and defeated Gen. Peel, the sire of Camballo, winner of the 2,000 guineas ; Monarque, the sire of his grandam, won the Goodwood Cup and French Derby, and was sire of Gladiateur, winner of the 2,000 guineas, Derby, St. Leger and Grand Prix de Paris. The pedigree is a racing one throughout, he has a double cross of Touchstone, two crosses of imp. Priam, through his famous daughters, Crucifix and Miss Letty, both Oaks winners, his gransire, Newminster, on the dam's side, was out of the famous Beeswing, who won the Ascot Cup and the Doncaster Cup in 1837, and again in 1840, 1841 and 1842, and a thribble cross of Whalebone through his great son, Defence, and a double one through Camel, the sire of Touchstone, so that if one wishes to breed to a horse of racing descent, possessing both speed and bottom, the blood of Rossifer cannot be excelled. Rossifer is a bay horse, full 15½ hands high, without white, is truly shaped, and should get race horses.

PEDIGREE OF ROSSIFER (Imp.)

ROSSIFER (Imp.)								
ROSSICRUCIAN	Beadsman	Weatherbit	Sheet Anchor	Lottery	Tramp—Mandane by Pot-8-os—Y. Camilla by Woodpecker—Camilla by Trentham—Coquette by Compton Barb.		
				Morgiana	Muley—Miss Stephenson by Scud or Sorcerer—Sis. to Petworth by Precipitate—Dau. of Woodpecker—Sis. to Juniper by Snap—Dau. of Blank.		
			Miss Letty	Priam	Emilius—Cressida by Whiskey—Y. Giantess by Diomed—Giantess by Matchem—Molly Longlegs by Babraham—Dau. of Cole's Foxhunter.		
				Daughter of	Orville—Dau. of Buzzard—Hornpipe by Trumpator—Luna by Herod—Proserpine, Sis. to Eclipse by Marske—Spiletta by Regulus.		
		Mendicant	Touchstone	Camel	Whalebone—Dau. of Selim—Maiden by Sir Peter—Dau. of Phoenomenon—Matron by Florizel—Maiden by Matchem—Dau. of Squirt.		
				Banter	Master Henry—Boadicea by Alexander—Brunette by Amaranthus—Mayfly by Matchem—Dau. of An. Starling—Dau. of Grasshopper.		
			Bay Mid-dleton.	Tramp	Dick Andrews—Dau. of Gohanna—Fraxinella by Trentham—Dau. of Woodpecker—Everlasting by Eclipse—Hyaena by Snap.		
			L'y Moore Carew	Kite	Bustard (Castrel)—Olympia by Sir Oliver—Scotilla by Anvil (Herod)—Harmony by Herod—Rutilla by Blank (Godol.).		
	Madame Eglantine	Cowl	Crucifix	Sultan	Selim—Bacchante by Williamson's Ditto—Sis. to Calomel by Mercury—Dau. of Herod—Folly by Marske—Vixen by Regulus.		
				Cobweb	Phantom—Filagree by Soothsayer—Web by Waxy—Penelope by Trumpator—Prunella by Highflyer—Promise by Snap—Julia.		
			Defence	Priam	Emilius—Cressida by Diomed—Giantess by Matchem—Molly Longlegs by Babraham—Dau. of Cole's Foxhunter.		
				Octaviana	Octavian—Dau. of Shuttle—Zara by Delpini—Flora by King Fergus—Atalanta by Matchem—Lass of the Mill by Oroonoko.		
		Diversion	Folly	Whalebone	Waxy—Penelope by Trumpator—Prunella by Highflyer—Promise by Snap—Julia by Blank—Spectator's dam.		
				Defiance	Rubens—Little Folly by Highland Fling—Harriet by Volunteer—Dau. of Alfred—Magnolia by Marske.		
				Middleton	Phantom—Web by Waxy—Penelope by Trumpator—Prunella by Highflyer—Promise by Snap—Julia by Blank.		
				Little Folly	Highland Fling—Harriet by Volunteer—Dau. of Alfred—Magnolia by Marske—Dau. of Babraham—Dau. of Sedbury.		
FENELLA	Cambuscan	Newminster	Touchstone	Camel	Whalebone—Dau. of Selim—Maiden by Sir Peter—Dau. of Phoenomenon—Matron by Florizel—Maiden by Matchem.		
				Banter	Master Henry—Boadicea by Alexander—Brunette by Amaranthus—Mayfly by Matchem—Dau. of An. Starling.		
			Beeswing	Dr. Syntax	Paynator (Trumpator)—Dau. of Beningbrough—Jenny Mole by Carbuncle (Babraham)—Dau. of Prince T'Qassaw (Snip)—Dau. of Regulus.		
				Daughter of	Ardrossan—Lady Eliza by Whitesworth—Dau. of Spadille—Sylvia by Y. Marske—Ferret by Bro. to Silvio—Dau. of Regulus.		
		The Arrow	Slane	Royal Oak	Catton—Dau. of Smolensko—Lady Mary by Beningbrough—Dau. of Highflyer—Dau. of Marske—A la Grecque by Regulus.		
				Daughter of	Orville—Epsom Lass by Sir Peter—Alexina by King Fergus—Lardella by Y. Marske—Dau. of Cade—Beaufremont's dam.		
	Monarque	The Ba.St. of Th.Emp.*	South down	Defence	Whalebone—Defiance by Rubens—Little Folly by Highland Fling—Harriet by Volunteer—Dau. of Alfred—Magnolia.		
				Feltona	X Y Z (Haphazard)—Jahetta by Beningbrough—Dau. of Drone (Herod)—Contessina by Y. Marske—Tuberose by Herod.		
				Defence	Whalebone—Defiance by Rubens—Little Folly by Highland Fling—Harriet by Volunteer (Eclipse)—Dau. of Alfred.		
				Sis. to Dangerous	Reveller—Design by Tramp—Defiance by Rubens—Little Folly by Highland Fling—Harriet by Volunteer (Eclipse).		
	La Favorita	The Arrow		Royal Oak	Catton—Dau. of Smolensko—Lady Mary by Beningbrough—Dau. of Highflyer—Dau. of Marske—A la Grecque by Regulus.		
				Ada	Whisker—Anna Bella by Shuttle—Dau. of Drone (Herod)—Contessina by Y. Marske—Tuberose by Herod—Grey Starling.		
	Constance	Poetess		Partisan	Walton—Parasol by Pot-8-os—Prunella by Highflyer—Promise by Snap—Julia by Blank—Spectator's dam by Partner.		
				Pauline	Moses—Quadrille by Selim—Canary Bird by Whiskey or Sorcerer—Canary by Coriander—Miss Green by Highflyer.		
		Gladiator		Hercule	Rainbow—Amable by Election—Aladdin's dam by Walnut—Dau. of Javelin—Sis. to Spadille by Highflyer—Flora by Squirrel.		
		Lanterne		Elvira	Eryx (Milo)—Sis. to Bos by Buzzard (Woodpecker)—Bennington's dam by Percy Arabian—Dau. of Herod (Tartar)—Dau. of Snap (Snip)—Chalkstone's dam by Shepherd's Crab—Miss Meredith by Cade (Godol.)—Little Hartley Mare by Bart. Childers (Darley Arabian)—Flying Whig by Wm's Woodstock Arabian—Dau. of St. Victor Barb—Dau. of Why-not, son of Fenwick Barb—Royal Mare.		

* The Emperor given.

ROYALTY (Imp.)

Royalty will be located at the Lakewood Stud, near Lexington, Ky., at $25 the season, dams of winners free. Application to C. M. Corbin, agent, Lexington, Ky.

ROYALTY by Kingcraft, son of King Tom, bred by Mr. Barne, foaled 1878, dam Rose, dam of Gaston by Oulston, son of Melbourne and the great Alice Hawthorn, out of Anemone by Tadmor, winner of the Column Stakes, Rowley mile at Newmarket Craven Meeting; the Gratwicke Produce Stakes, 1¼ miles, at Goodwood, and third to Flying Dutchman in the Derby, son of Ion, winner of the Clearwell and other Stakes, and second in the Derby to Amato, beating Grey Momus, and second in the Doncaster St. Leger to Don John, beating Lanercost and others, he was also sire of Wild Dayrell, winner of the Derby. Kingcraft, his sire, is a son of King Tom, and is own brother to Great Tom; Kingcraft won the Derby and is now coming prominently to the front as a sire, the best of his get so far are Strathblane, Leap Year, Royal, Apollo, Cabul and King Shepherd; Oulston, the sire of his dam, and son of Melbourne, was a capital good horse, and would have shown much better but for distemper at the critical moment, so highly was he esteemed, that he sold for $30,000. Royalty never run in public, but he is a highly bred horse, full of racing strains, and traces to Eclipse, through his most famous descendants Whisker, Whalebone, King Fergus, Orville, Blacklock, Joe Andrews, Mercury, &c., to Herod through Highflyer, Woodpecker and Walton, and thence through Oriental sources to the famous old Vintner Mare. He ought to make a good sire.

PEDIGREE OF ROYALTY (Imp.)

ROYALTY (Imp.)	KINGCRAFT.	Voltigeur.	Martha Lynn.	Whisker.		Waxy—Penelope by Trumpator—Prunella by Highflyer—Promise by Snap Julia by Blank—Spectator's dam by Partner—Bonny Lass.
				Florantbe.		Octavian—Caprice by Anvil—Madcap by Eclipse—Dau. of Blank—Dau. of Blaze—Dau. of Y. Greyhound—Dau. of Cur. Bay Barb.
		King Tom.	Pocahontas.	Nabocklish.		Rugantino—Butterfly by Master Bagot—Dau. of Bagot (Herod)—Mother Brown by Trunnion (Cade)—Dau. of Old Eng.—Dau. of Bol Starling.
				Miss Tooley.		Teddy the Grinder—Lady Jane by Sir Peter—Paulina by Florizel—Captive by Matchem—Calliope by Slouch—Lass of the Mill by Oroonoko.
			Harkaway.	Sultan.		Selim—Bacchante by Williamson's Ditto—Sis. to Calomel by Mercury—Dau. of Herod—Folly by Marske—Vixen by Regulus—Dau. of Hut. Spot.
				Trampoline.		Tramp—Web by Waxy—Penelope by Trumpator—Prunella by Highflyer—Promise by Snap—Julia by Blank—Spectator's dam by Partner.
			Fanny Dawson.	Muley.		Orville—Eleanor by Whiskey—Y. Giantess by Diomed—Giantess by Matchem—Molly Longlegs by Babraham—Dau. of Cole's Foxhunter.
				Clare.		Marmion—Harpalice by Gohanna—Amazon by Driver—Fractious by Mercury—Dau. of Woodpecker—Everlasting by Eclipse—Hyaena by Snap.
		Woodcraft.	Marpessa.	Blacklock.		Whitelock—Dau. of Coriander—Wildgoose by Highflyer—Coheiress by Pot-8-os—Manilla by Goldfinder—Dau. of Old Eng.
				Daughter of.		Phantom—Dau. of Overton—Gratitude's dam by Walnut—Dau. of Ruler—Piracantha by Matchem—Prophetess by Regulus.
			Glencoe.	Mulatto.		Catton—Desdemona by Orville—Fanny by Sir Peter—Dau. of Diomed—Desdemona by Marske—Y. Hag by Skim—Hag by Crab.
				Leda.		Filho-da-Puta—Treasure by Camillus—Dau. of Hyacinthus—Flora by King Fergus—Atalanta by Matchem—Lass of the Mill by Oroonoko.
		Daughter of.	Wedding day.	Partisan.		Walton—Parasol by Pot-8-os—Prunella by Highflyer—Promise by Snap—Julia by Blank—Spectator's dam by Partner—Bonny Lass by B. Bolton.
				Fawn.		Smolensko—Jerboa by Gohanna—Camilla by Trentham—Coquette by Compton Barb—Sis. to Regulus by Godol. Arabian—Grey Robinson.
			Venison.	Camel.		Whalebone—Dau. of Selim—Maiden by Sir Peter—Dau. of Phoenomenon—Matron by Florizel—Maiden by Matchem—Dau. of Squirt—Lot's dam.
				Margellina.		Whisker—Manuella by Dick Andrews—Mandane by Pot-8-os—Young Camilla by Woodpecker—Coquette by Compton Barb—Sis. to Regulus.
	ROSE.	Ouiston.	Melbourne.	Comus.		Sorcerer—Houghton Lass by Sir Peter—Alexina by King Fergus—Lardella by Y. Marske—Dau. of Cade—Beaufremont's dam by Bro. to Fearnought.
				Clinkerina.		Clinker—Pewet by Tandem—Termagant by Tantrum—Cantatrice by Sampson—Dau. of Regulus—Marske's dam by Blacklegs (Bay Turk.)
			Humphrey Clinker.	Cervantes.		Don Quixote—Evelina by Highflyer—Termagant by Tantrum—Cantatrice by Sampson—Dau. of Regulus—Marske's dam by Blacklegs.
				Daughter of.		Golumpus—Dau. of Paynator—Sis. to Zodiac by St. George—Abigail by Woodpecker—Firetail by Eclipse—Dau. of Blank—Naylor by Cade.
		Alice Hawthorn.	Muley Moloch.	Muley.		Orville—Eleanor by Whiskey—Y. Giantess by Diomed—Giantess by Matchem—Molly Longlegs by Babraham—Dau. of Cole's Foxhunter.
				Nancy.		Dick Andrews—Spitfire by Beningbrough—Dau. of Y. Sir Peter (Doge)—Dau. of Engineer—Dau. of Wil. Arabian—Dau. of Hutton's Spot.
			Rebecca.	Lottery.		Tramp—Mandane by Pot-8-os—Y. Camilla by Woodpecker—Camilla by Trentham—Coquette by Compton Barb—Sis. to Regulus by Go. Arabian.
				Daughter of.		Cervantes—Anticipation by Beningbrough—Expectation by Herod—Dau. of Skim—Dau. of Janus (Godol.)—Spinster by Crab.
		Tadmor.	Ion.	Cain.		Paulowitz (Sir Paul)—Dau. of Paynator—Dau. of Delpini—Dau. of Y. Marske—Gentle Kitty by Silvio (Cade)—Dau. of Dorimond.
				Margaret.		Edmund (Orville)—Medora by Selim—Dau. of Sir Harry (Sir Peter)—Dau. of Volunteer—Dau. of Herod—Golden Grove by Blank.
			Palmyra.	Sultan.		Selim—Bacchante by Williamson's Ditto—Sis. to Calomel by Mercury—Dau. of Herod—Folly by Marske—Vixen by Regulus.
				Hester.		Camel—Monimia by Muley—Sis. to Petworth by Precipitate—Dau. of Woodpecker—Sis. to Juniper by Snap—Dau. of Blank.
		Anemone.	Taurus.	Ardrossan.		John Bull—Miss Whip by Volunteer (Eclipse)—Wimbleton by Evergreen (Herod)—Sis. to Calash by Herod—Teresa by Matchem.
				The Smolt.		Viscount or Stamford—Penelope by Shuttle—Lady Sarah by Fidget (Florizel)—Dau. of Alfred (Matchem)—Magnolia by Marske.
		Monoeda.	Mona.	Partisan.		Walton—Parasol by Pot-8-os—Prunella by Highflyer—Promise by Snap—Julia by Blank—Spectator's dam by Partner.
				Miltonia.		Patriot—Miss Muston by King Fergus (Eclipse)—Columbine by Espensykes (Matchem)—Dau. of Babraham Blank (Babraham)—Dau. of Lonsdale Arabian—Dau. of Cyprus Arabian—Crab's dam by Basto (Byerly Turk)—Sis. to Mixbury Galloway by Curwen Bay Barb—Dau. of Curwen's Spot (Selaby Turk)—Dau. of White-legged Lowther Barb—Old Vintner Mare.

SAXON (Imp.)

(WINNER OF THE BELMONT STAKES AT JEROME PARK, 1874.)

Saxon will be located as private stallion at the Rancocas Stud, near Jobstown, Burlington Co., N. J., Mr. P. Lorillard, proprietor. There will be annual sales of his surplus.

SAXON by Beadsman, son of Weatherbit, by Sheet Anchor, bred by Sir Joseph Hawley, foaled 1871, dam Girasol by Asteroid, son of Stockwell, out of Gillyflower, by Venison, son of Partisan. Beadsman, the sire of Saxon, won the Derby and was sire of Blue Gown, winner of the Derby, and Pero Gomes, winner of the St. Leger. Mendicant, the dam of Beadsman won the Oaks, and Miss Letty, the dam of Weatherbit, was an Oaks winner. Asteroid, the sire of Saxon's dam, won the Hester Cup and the Ascot Gold Cup, and is highly esteemed as a sire in France. Venison, the sire of his great grandam, was one of the best horses of his day. The Ugly Buck, a 2,000 guineas winner, was by him, also Kingston and Miami, an Oaks winner. The blood is highly esteemed for stoutness. Imp. Saxon made his first appearance on the turf as a three-year-old, when he started four times, won one race, was second once, and unplaced twice. He won the Belmont Stakes, at Jerome Park, 1¼ miles in 2:39¼, beating Grinstead, Aaron Pennington, and six others. At Long Branch was second to Brigand in the Jersey Derby, beating Aaron Pennington, Rutherford, imp. Macaroon, and four others. This closed the turf career of imp. Saxon; since his retirement he has sired some very promising colts. The following are the best, all bred in the Rancocas Stud: In America, Gerald started six times, won two races, was second in three; won dash of one-half mile with 110 lbs., in :50¼, and the Foam Stakes, five furlongs, in 1:02¼. After reaching England he had a walk over in the Subscription Stakes at Newmarket, was third in the Rous Memmorial Stakes, won by Dutch Oven, and was second in the Middle Park Plate, Nereid, Boreas and Geraldine, winners in England, Delaware, Edith, Geranium, Godiva, Itaska, Quoque, Rocco, Cedric, Hiawasse, winner of the Ladies' Stake at Jerome Park, Mermaid Stakes at Sheepshead Bay and Monmouth Oaks at Long Branch, proving herself one of if not the best filly of the year 1882, Lytton, Montauk and a few others. Saxon is a brown horse, 15¾ hands, with a plain head, good well placed shoulders, strong back, broad hip and large muscular thighs and stifles, with good legs and feet. He has a double cross of Touchstone and traces through Whalebone and Pot-8-os, several times to Eclipse and through Orville to Beningbrough, by King Fergus, son of Eclipse. The blood is both speedy and stout, and his descendents must be valuable to the thoroughbred horse of this country. Saxon's pedigree has not been given in full until in this volume, where it can be found fully extended, through the noted Coffin Mare.

PEDIGREE OF SAXON.

SAXON.	BEADSMAN.	Weatherbit.	Sheet Anchor.	Priam.	Morgiana.	Lottery.	Tramp.	Dick Andrews—Dau. of Gohanna—Fraxinella by Trentham—Dau. o Woodpecker—Everlasting by Eclipse—Hyaena by Snap.
							Mandane.	Pot-8-os—Y Camilla by Woodpecker—Camilla by Trentham—Coquette by Compton Barb—Sis. to Regulus by Godol. Arabian.
			Miss Letty.				Muley.	Orville—Eleanor by Whiskey—Y Giantess by Diomed—Giantess by Matchem—Molly Longlegs by Babraham—Dau. of Cole's Foxhunter.
							Miss Stephenson	Scud or Sorcerer—Sis. to Petworth by Precipitate—Dau. of Woodpecker—Sis. to Juniper by Snap—Y Marske's dam by Blank.
		Mendicant.		Fanny's dam.			Emilius.	Orville—Emily by Stamford—Dau. of Whiskey—Gr. Dorimant by Dorimant—Dizzy by Blank—Dizzy by Driver—Dau. of Smiling Tom.
							Cressida.	Whiskey—Y Giantess by Diomed—Giantess by Matchem—Molly Longlegs by Babraham—Dau. of Cole's Foxhunter—Dau. of Partner (Jigg).
							Orville.	Beningbrough—Evelina by Highflyer—Termagant by Tantrum—Cantatrice by Sampson—Dau. of Regulus—Marske's dam.
							Daughter.	Buzzard—Hornpipe by Trumpator—Luna by Herod—Proserpine, sis. to Eclipse by Marske—Spiletta by Regulus—Mother Western.
			Touchstone.	Banter.	Camel.		Whalebone.	Waxy—Penelope by Trumpator—Prunella by Highflyer—Promise by Snap—Julia by Blank—Spectator's dam by Partner—Bonny Lass.
							Daughter of.	Selim—Maiden by Sir Peter—Dau. of Phoenomenon—Matron by Florizel—Maiden by Matchem—Dau. of Squirt—Lot's dam.
							Master Henry.	Orville—Miss Sophia by Stamford—Sophia by Buzzard—Huncamunca by Highflyer—Cypher by Squirrel—Dau. of Regulus.
							Boadicea.	Alexander—Brunette by Amaranthus—Mayfly by Matchem—Dau. of An. Starling—Dau. of Grasshopper—Dau. of Newton Arabian.
				Lady Moore Carew.	Tramp.	Kite.	Dick Andrews.	Joe Andrews—Dau. of Highflyer—Dau. of Cardinal Puff—Dau. of Tatler—Dau. of Snip—Dau. of Framp. Whiteneck—Dau. of Pel Barb.
							Daughter of.	Gohanna—Fraxinella by Trentham—Dau. of Woodpecker—Everlasting by Eclipse—Hyaena by Snap—Miss Belsea by Regulus.
							Bustard.	Castrel—Miss Hap by Shuttle—Sis. to Haphazard by Sir Peter—Miss Hervey by Eclipse—Clio by Y Cade—Dau. of Starling.
							Olympia.	Sir Oliver—Scotilla by Anvil—Scota by Eclipse—Harmony by Herod—Rutilia by Blank—Dau. of Regulus—Dau. of Soreheels.
	GIRASOL.	Asteroid.	Stockwell.	Pocahontas.	The Baron.		Irish Birdcatcher	Sir Hercules—Guiccioli by Bob Booty—Flight by I. Escape—Y. Heroine by Bagot—Heroine by Hero—Dau. of Snap—Sis. to Regulus.
							Echidna.	Economist—Miss Pratt by Blacklock—Gadabout by Orville—Minstrel by Sir Peter—Matron by Florizel—Maiden by Matchem.
							Glencoe.	Sultan—Trampoline by Tramp—Web by Waxy—Penelope by Trumpator—Prunella by Highflyer—Promise by Snap—Julia.
							Marpessa.	Muley—Clare by Marmion—Harpalice by Gohanna—Amazon by Driver—Fractious by Mercury—Dau. of Woodpecker.
			Teetotum.	Touchstone.			Camel.	Whalebone—Dau. of Selim—Maiden by Sir Peter—Dau. of Phoenomenon—Matron by Florizel—Maiden by Matchem.
							Banter.	Master Henry—Boadicea by Alexander—Brunette by Amaranthus—Mayfly by Matchem—Dau. of An. Starling—Dau. of Grasshopper.
				Versatility.			Blacklock.	Whitelock—Dau. of Coriander—Wildgoose by Highflyer—Coheiress by Pot-8-os—Manilla by Goldfinder—Dau. of Old Eng.
							Arabella.	Williamson's Ditto—Esther by Shuttle—Dau. of Drone—Dau. of Matchem—Jocasta by Cornforth's Forester—Sis. to Y Cade.
		Venison.	Partisan.				Walton.	Sir Peter—Arethusa by Dungannon—Dau. of Prophet—Virago by Snap—Dau. of Regulus—Sis. to Othello by Crab—Miss Slamerkin.
							Parasol.	Pot-8-os—Prunella by Highflyer—Promise by Snap—Julia by Blank—Spectator's dam by Partner—Bonny Lass by Bay Bolton.
			Fawn.				Smolensko.	Sorcerer—Wowski by Mentor—Waxy's dam by Herod—Lisette by Snap—Miss Windsor by Godol. Arabian—Sis. to Volunteer.
							Jerboa.	Gohanna—Camilla by Trentham—Coquette by Comp. Barb—Sis. to Regulus by Godol. Arabian—Gr. Robinson by Bald Galloway.
		Gillifower.	King of Clubs.				Muley.	Orville—Eleanor by Whiskey—Y Giantess by Diomed—Giantess by Matchem—Molly Longlegs by Babraham—Dau. of Cole's Foxhunter.
							Y. Mignonette.	Bustard (Castrel)—Mignonette by Sorcerer—Symmetry by Sir Peter—Phantasmagoria by Precipitate—Dau. of Herod.
		Temerity.	Dau. of				Blucher.	Waxy—Pantina by Buzzard—Dau. of Trentham—Sis. to Drone by Herod—Lilly by Blank—Peggy by Cade—Sis. to Wid. Mare.
							Spell.	Sorcerer (Trumpator)—Dau. of Mark Anthony (Spectator)—Noisette by Squirrel (Traveler)—Carina by Marske (Squirt)—Thunder's dam by Blank (Godol.)—Dizzy by Driver (Wynn Arabian)—Dau. of Smiling Tom (Conyer's Arabian)—Dau. of Oysterfoot—Dau. of Merlin (Bustler)—Dau. of Commoner (Place's White Turk)—Coffin Mare by Selaby Turk—Dau. of Place's White Turk.

SENSATION,

(WINNER OF JUVENILE AND NURSERY STAKES AT JEROME PARK, JULY, CRITERION AND AUGUST STAKES AT MONMOUTH PARK, SARATOGA AND FLASH STAKES AT SARATOGA, AND CENTRAL STAKES AT BALTIMORE, 1879.)

Sensation will stand the season of 1883 at the Bolingbrooke Stud, near Middleburg, Md., at $100 the season. Application to R. W. Walden, Middleburg, Md.

SENSATION by imp. Leamington, son of Faugh-a-Ballagh, bred by Mr. A. Welch, Erdenheim Stud, Pa., foaled, 1877, dam Susan Beane, dam of Stratford, Susquehanna, Onondaga, etc., by Lexington, son of Boston, out of Sally Lewis, dam of John Morgan, Hunter's Lexington Acrobat, etc., by imp. Glencoe. Sensation was truly the sensation of his two-year old year. Started eight times and won all of his races. Jerome Park, May 31, won the Juvenile Stakes, half-mile, defeating Ethel and nine others ; time, :50. Monmouth Park, July 8, won the July Stakes, five furlongs, defeating his stable companions, Grenada and Rosalie, who finished, respectively, second and third, and ten others ; time, 1:07. Saratoga, July 22, won the Flash Stakes, half-mile, Grenada and Rosalie again finishing second and third, five others came in behind them ; time, :49¼. Same meeting, July 29, won the Saratoga Stakes, three-quarter mile, defeating Grenada, who finished second, Beata, Glidelia, Giroflé and By-and By ; time, 1:18. Monmouth Park, Aug. 23, won the August Stakes, three-quarter mile, defeating Grenada, who ran second, and seven others ; time, 1:18¼. Same meeting, Aug. 26, won the Criterion Stakes, three-quarter mile, carrying 5 lbs. penalty, and defeated Grenada, second, and five others ; time, 1:22 ; track slow and heavy. Jerome Park, Oc. 2, won the Nursery Stakes, three-quarter mile, defeating Ferncliff, Grenada and four others ; time, 1:18. Baltimore, Oct. 23, won the Central Stakes, one mile, defeating Grenada and Oden ; time, 1:50¼. Total winnings, for the year, $20,250. He met and defeated all the best two-year olds of his year, winning from a half to one mile. He bursted his foot in the spring of 1880, which compelled his retirement. He is from one of the great racing families of the country. Acrobat and Hunter's Lexington, full brothers to his dam, were fine race-horses and could stay a distance. John Morgan, a half brother, was also a superior race-horse, and for his chances a very successful stallion, Motto, Nannie Lewis, Aldebaran were all good ones. Glenmore is also from the same family, and his dam traces back to the dam of the great race-horse Medoc, who was the most successful sire in any day on all sorts of mares. Sensation is a brown, full 16 hands high, with a white stripe down his face and a little white on the pastern of his left fore leg. He has a fine well placed shoulder and is symmetrically formed all over with faultless action and good temper. From being a son of Leamington, and tracing to a racing family and being an uncommon fine race-horse, he should get race-horses. He has the Pantaloon and Whalebone crosses on the sire's side, and the Glencoe on the dam's with the blood of Sir Archy and Diomed through its best sources.

PEDIGREE OF SENSATION.

SENSATION.	Daughter of.	IMP. LEAMINGTON.	Daphne.	Maid of Honor.	Laurel.	Idalia.	Castrel.	Pantaloon.

Waxy. / Penelope.	Pot-8-os (Eclipse)—Maria by Herod (Tartar)—Lisette by Snap (Snip)—Miss Windsor by Godol. Arabian—Sis. to Volunteer by Y. Belgrade. Trumpator—(Conductor)—Prunella by Highflyer—Promise by Snap—Julia by Blank (Godol.)—Spectator's dam by Partner (Jigg).		Feugh-a-Ballagh. / Guleedoli. / Flight. / Bob Booty. / Sir Hercules. / Peri. / Whalebone.
Wanderer. / Thalestris.	Gohanna (Mercury)—Catherine by Woodpecker (Herod)—Camilla by Trentham (Sweepstakes)—Coquette by Compton Barb—Sis. to Regulus. Alexander (Eclipse)—Rival by Sir Peter (Highflyer)—Hornet by Drone (Herod)—Manilla by Goldfinder (Snap).		
Chanticleer. / Ierne.	Woodpecker—Dau. of Eclipse (Marske)—Rosebud by Snap—Miss Belsea—Regulus (Godol.)—Dau. of Bart. Childers (Darley Arabian). Bagot (Herod)—Dau. of Gamahoe (Bustard by Crab)—Patty by Tim (Squirt)—Miss Patch by Justice (Litton Arabian)—The Ringtail Galloway.		
Irish Escape. / Young Heroine.	Commodore—Buffer's dam by Highflyer (Herod)—Shift by Sweetbriar (Syphon)—Black Susan by Snap—Ld. Bruce's Cade Mare. Bagot (Herod)—Heroine by Hero (Cade)—Dau. of Snap—Sis. to Regulus by Godol. Arabian—Grey Robinson by the Bald Galloway.		
Buzzard. / Daughter of.	Woodpecker—Misfortune by Dux (Matchem)—Curiosity by Snap—Dau. of Regulus—Dau. of Bartlet's Childers—Dau. of Honeywood Arabian. Alexander, Dau. of Highflyer—Dau. of Alfred (Matchem)—Dau. of Engineer (Sampson)—Bay Malton's dam by Cade (Godol.)—Lass of the Mill.		
Peruvian. / Musidora.	Sir Peter—Dau. of Budrow (Eclipse)—Escape's dam by Squirrel—Dau. of Babraham (Godol.)—Dau. of Golden Ball (Partner)—Bushy Molly. Meteor (Eclipse)—Maid of All Work by Highflyer—Sis. to Tandem by Syphon (Squirt)—Dau. of Regulus (Godol.)—Dau. of Snip.		
Blacklock. / Wagtail.	Whitelock (Hambletonian)—Dau. of Coriander (Pot-8-os)—Wildgoose by Highflyer—Coheirers by Pot-8-os (Eclipse)—Manilla by Goldfinder. Prime Minister (Sancho)—Dau. of Orville—Miss Grimstone by Weasel (Herod)—Dau. of Ancaster (Blank)—Dau. of Damascus Arabian.		
Champion. / Etiquette.	Selim (Buzzard)—Podagra by Gouty (Sir Peter)—Jet by Magnet (Herod)—Jewel by Squirrel—Sophia by Blank (Godol.). Orville (Beningbrough)—Boadicea by Alexander—Brunette by Amaranthus (Old Eng.)—Mayfly by Matchem—Dau. of An. Starling.		
Sir Archy. / Daughter of.	Imp. Diomed—Castianira by Rockingham (Highflyer)—Tabitha by Trentham—Dau. of Bosphorus—Dau. of Wm.'s Forester—Dau. of Coalition Colt. Imp. Saltram (Eclipse)—Dau. of Symme's Wildair—Dau. of Driver (Imp. Othello)—Dau. of Imp. Fallower (Blank)—Dau. of Imp. Vampire.		SUSAN BEANE. / Sally Lewis. / Motto. / Imp. Glencoe. / Lady Imp. Tompkins. / Barefoot. / Alice Carneal. / Imp. Sarpedon. / Lexington. / Sultan. / Rowena. / Sister to Tuckahoe. / Boston. / Timoleon. / Trampoline.
Ball's Florizel. / Daughter of.	Imp. Diomed—Dau. of Imp. Shark—Dau. of Harris' Eclipse—Dau. of Imp. Fearnought—Dau. of Imp. Jolly Roger—Dau. of Imp. Sober John (Rib). Imp. Alderman (Pot-8-os)—Dau. of Imp. Clockfast (Gimcrack)—Dau. of Symme's Wildair—Kitty Fisher by Imp. Fearnought.		
Emilius. / Icaria.	Orville—Emily by Stamford—Dau. of Whiskey—Gr. Dorimant by Dorimant—Dizzy by Blank—Dizzy by Driver, dau. of Smiling Tom. The Flyer—Parma by Dick Andrews—May by Beningbrough—Primrose by Mambrino—Cricket by Herod—Sophia by Blank—Lord Leigh's Diana.		
Sumpter. / Lady Grey.	Sir Archy—Flirtilla's dam by Imp. Robin Redbreast (Sir Peter)—Dau. of Imp. Obscurity (Eclipse)—Slamerkin by Imp. Wildair (Cade). Robin Grey (Imp. Royalist)—Maria by Melzar (Imp. Medley)—Dau. of Imp. Highflyer—Dau. of Imp. Fearnought (Regulus)—Dau. of Ariel.		
Selim. / Bacchante.	Buzzard—Castrel's dam by Alexander (Eclipse)—Dau. of Highflyer—Dau. of Alfred (Matchem)—Dau. of Engineer (Sampson)—Bay Malton's dam. Williamson's Ditto (Sir Peter)—Sis. to Calomel by Mercury—Dau. of Herod—Folly by Marske—Vixen by Regulus—Dau. of Spot.		
Tramp. / Web.	Dick Andrews (Joe Andrews)—Dau. of Gohanna (Mercury)—Fraxinella by Trentham (Sweepstakes)—Dau. of Woodpecker (Herod). Waxy—Penelope by Trumpator—Prunella by Highflyer—Promise by Snap—Julia by Blank—Spectator's dam by Partner—Dau. of Bay Bolton.		
Tramp. / Rosamond.	Dick Andrews—Dau. of Gohanna—Fraxinella by Trentham—Dau. of Woodpecker—Everlasting by Eclipse—Hyaena by Snap—Miss Belsea. Buzzard (Woodpecker)—Roseberry by Phoenomenon (Herod)—Miss West by Matchem (Cade)—Dau. of Regulus—Dau. of Crab—Dau. of Childers.		
Am. Eclipse. / Katy Ann.	Duroc (Diomed)—Miller's Damsel by Imp. Messenger (Mambrino)—Dau. of Pot-8-os—Dau. of Gimcrack (Cripple)—Snap-Dragon by Snap. Ogle's Oscar (Imp. Gabriel)—Modoc's dam by Imp. Expedition (Pegasus)—Maid of the Oaks by Imp. Spread Eagle (Volunteer)—Annette by Imp. Shark (Marske)—Dau. of Rockingham (Partner)—Dau. of Gallant (Imp. Fearnought)—Dau. of True Whig (Fitzbugh's Regulus)—Dau. of Imp. Regulus (Regulus by Godol.)—Imp. Diamond by Cullen Arabian—Lady Thigh by Croft's Partner—Dau. of Greyhound (White Barb Chillaby—Dau. of Cur. Bay Barb—Dau. of D'Arcy Chestnut Arabian—Old Montague Mare.		

SPENDTHRIFT,

(WINNER OF THE SANFORD STAKE FOR TWO-YEAR OLDS AT LOUISVILLE, YOUNG AMERICA STAKE, No. 1, AT NASHVILLE, BELMONT, LORILLARD STAKES AT JEROME PARK, CHAMPION STAKES AND JERSEY DERBY AT MONMOUTH PARK.)

Will stand the season of 1883 *at the farm of Wm. M. Kenney, Lexington, Ky., at* $50 *the season. Application to Wm. M. Kenney, Lexington, Ky.*

SPENDTHRIFT by imp. Australian son of West Australian, bred in the Woodburn Stud, Ky., foaled 1876, dam Aerolite, dam of Mozart, Rutherford Fellowcraft, etc., by Lexington out of Florine, dam of Idlewild, by imp. Glencoe. Aerolite, Spendthrift's dam is one of the great brood mares of the Woodburn Stud as her produce shows, her full sister Idlewild was the best mare of her day, ran 4 miles when five years old, 117 lbs., in 7:26½, and is the dam of Wildidle that ran 4 miles, in 7:25½. Spendthrift was the Phoenominal two-year old of 1878, won all his races five in number, at Lexington, Ky., won Sweepstakes for two-year olds, one mile, in 1:58½, beating Montreal, Scully and three others. At Louisville, Ky., won the Sanford Stakes for two-year olds, one mile, in 1:46½, beating Montreal, Trinidad and five others, among which was Goodnight and Strathmore. Same place won a Sweepstake for two-year olds, one mile, in 1:45. At Nashville, Tennessee, won the Young America Stakes, No 1, for two-year olds, three-quarters of a mile, in 1:16½, beating Lord Murphy, Charlemagne and Cal. Morgan. At same place, won a Sweepstake for two-year olds, one mile, in 1:44½, beating Lord Murphy, the only other starter.

Season of 1879 he started eight times, won five races, and was second in three. Spendthrift made his first appearance at Jerome Park, May 31. He ran second in the Withers Stakes, one mile, won by his stable companion, Dan Sparling, Report was third, Harold, Plevna and Mulrooney unplaced. Time, 1:48. Spendthrift is really entitled to the credit of this valuable stake, as he was almost pulled to a standstill to allow his companion, Sparling, to win. Same meeting, June 5, won the Belmont Stakes, 1½ miles, defeating Monitor, Jericho, Pawnee, Rochester and Harold; time, 2:42¾. Same meeting, June 10, won the rich Lorillard Stakes, 1⅝ miles, defeating Harold, Magnetism, Report, Dan Sparling, Monitor, Rochester, Jericho, Boardman, Plevna and Eunice. This race was the grandest achievement ever accomplished by a three-year old in America. Spendthrift, who carried 5 lbs. penalty for winning the Belmont Stakes, making his weight 123 lbs. and was almost left at the post. Harold delayed the start by his ugly temper, and gave Spendthrift a vicious kick just as the signal for the start was given. Harold bolted off in the lead, and Spendthrift was the last to leave the starting point, fully 50 yards in his rear. Harold never ran so well before, and led all through the first mile. Spendthrift began to creep up, but made no perceptible gain until a mile had been run, he then began to pass his horses, but had to take the extreme outside of the track to get around them. The excitement was intense when Harold turned into the stretch with fully 30 yards lead on Spendthrift. Coming down the straight Spendthrift gradually gained on Harold and collared him at the seven-eighth pole. The race was then over as the game son of Australian came on and won easily by two lengths, Harold second, Magnetism third; time, 2:25¾. Monmouth Park, July 8, won the Jersey Derby, 1½ miles, defeating his only competitor, Wilful, with ease; time, 2:53. Saratoga, N. Y., July 9, Spendthrift met the son of Enquirer, Falsetto, for the first time. The two colts were bred and raised within a few miles of one another, but the former having changed hands, represented the East, and the latter the South. The race was for the Travers Stakes, 1¾ miles, Falsetto won, Spendthrift was a good second, Harold third, Jericho and Dan Sparling unplaced; time, 3:09½. The report was current, just before this race, that Spendthrift had been complaining in his feet, and was also muscle sore. Spendthrift had undoubtedly lost the form that he displayed when he won the Lorillard Stakes, which was the best and fastest race ever run in America by a three-year old. Same Meeting, Aug. 12, Falsetto again defeated Spendthrift, who finished second, in the Kenner Stakes, 2 miles; Jericho was third, Monitor and Harold unplaced; time, 3:35½. Monmouth Park, Aug. 23, Spendthrift won the Champion Stakes for all ages, 1½ miles, defeating Report, Bramble, Volturno, Harold and Bonnie Oaks; time, 2:41½. The track was heavy and slow. Jerome Park, N. Y., Oct. 2, Spendthrift, although unfit to run, started in the Jerome Stakes, 1¾ miles; Monitor won; Spendthrift second, Report third, Jericho fourth; time, 3:12. The performances of Spendthrift, in or out of condition, were all creditable as the time and weights will show. Spendthrift did not start as four-year old, ran two races at Jerome Park when unfit at 5 years old, was second to Barrett, one mile, in 1:44½, and was unplaced in the other race. Spendthrift has the Touchstone, Whisker and Whalebone blood on the sire's side, the Glencoe on the dam's side, and is much inbred to Sir Archy and Diomed, with the Gimcrack blood through imp. Medley. As Fellowcraft is a success, Spendthrift must be.

PEDIGREE OF SPENDTHRIFT.

SPENDTHRIFT	**IMP. AUSTRALIAN** (West Australian)	Emilia (Young Emilius — Emilius — Persian) / Mowerina (Touchstone — Emma — Whisker — Shoveler) / Melbourne (Dau. of Humphrey Clinker) / Variety	Comus.	Sorcerer (Trumpator) Houghton Lass by Sir Peter (Highflyer)—Alexina by King Fergus (Eclipse)—Lardella by Y. Marske—Dau. of Cade (Godol.)
			Clinkerina.	Clinker (Sir Peter)—Pewet by Tandem (Syphon)—Termagant by Tantrum (Cripple by Godol.)—Cantatrice by Sampson—Dau. of Regulus.
			Cervantes.	Don Quixote (Eclipse)—Evelina by Highflyer—Termagant by Tantrum—Cantatrice by Sampson (Blaze)—Dau. of Regulus—Marske's dam.
			Daughter of.	Golumpus (Gohanna)—Dau. of Paynator (Trumpator)—Sis. to Zodiac by St. George (Auvil)—Abigail by Woodpecker (Herod)—Firetail by Eclipse.
			Camel.	Whalebone (Waxy)—Dau. of Selim (Buzzard)—Maiden by Sir Peter—Dau. of Phoenomenon (Herod)—Matron by Florizel (Herod).
			Banter.	Master Henry (Orville)—Boadicea by Alexander (Eclipse)—Brunette by Amaranthus (OldEng.)—Mayfly by Matchem (Cade)—Dau. of An.Starling.
			Whisker.	Waxy (Pot-8-os)—Penelope by Trumpator (Conductor)—Prunella by Highflyer—Promise by Snap (Snip)—Julia by Blank—Spectator's dam.
			Gibside Fairy.	Hermes (Mercury)—Vicissitude by Pipator (Trumpator)—Beatrice by Sir Peter—Pyrrha by Matchem—Duchess by Whitenose—Miss Slamerkin.
			Orville.	Beningbrough (King Fergus)—Evelina by Highflyer—Termagant by Tantrum—Cantatrice by Sampson—Dau. of Regulus—Marske's dam.
			Emily.	Stamford (Sir Peter)—Dau. of Whiskey (Saltram)—Gr. Dorimant by Dorimant—Dizzy by Blank—Dizzy by Driver—Dau. of Smiling Tom.
			Scud.	Beningbrough—Eliza by Highflyer—Augusta by Eclipse—Hardwick's dam by Herod (Tartar)—Dau. of Bajazet (Godol.)—Dau. of Regulus.
			Goosander.	Hambletonian (King Fergus)—Rally by Trumpator—Fancy, Sis. to Diomed by Florizel—Dau. of Spectator (Crab)—Horatia by Blank.
			Waxy.	Pot-8-os (Eclipse)—Maria by Herod—Lisette by Snap—Miss Windsor by Godol. Arabian—Dau. of Y. Belgrade—Dau. of Bartlet's Childers.
			Penelope.	Trumpator—Prunella by Highflyer—Promise by Snap—Julia by Blank—Spectator's dam by Partner—Dau.of Bay Bolton—Dau. of Darley Arabian.
			Selim, or *Soothsayer.	Sorcerer—Golden Locks by Delpini (Highflyer)—Violet by Imp. Shark—Dau. of Syphon (Squirt)—Quick's Charlotte by Blank.
			Sprite.	Bobtail (Precipitate)—Catharine by Woodpecker—Camilla by Trentham—Coquette by the Compton Barb—Sis. to Regulus by Godol.
	AEROLITE	Lexington (Boston — Alice Carneal — Imp. Glencoe — Sultan — Trampoline) / Sar-petion (Sister to Tuckahoe) / Timoleon / Rowena / Florine / Melody / Rodolph's dam / Imp. Medoc	Sir Archy.	Imp.Diomed—Castianira by Rockingham (Highflyer)—Tabitha byTrentham—Dau. of Bosphorus—Dau. of Wm.'s Forester—Dau. of Coalition Colt.
			Daughter of.	Imp. Saltram (Eclipse)—Dau. of Symme's Wildair—Dau. of Driver (Imp. Othello)—Dau. of Imp. Fallower (Blank)—Dau. of Imp. Vampire.
			Ball's Florizel.	Imp. Diomed—Dau. of Imp. Shark—Dau. of Harris' Imp. Eclipse—Dau. of Imp. Fearnought—Dau. of Imp. Jolly Roger—Dau. of Imp. Sober John.
			Daughter of.	Imp. Alderman (Pot-8-os)—Dau. of Imp. Clockfast (Gimcrack)—Dau. of Symme's Wildair—Kitty Fisher by Imp. Fearnought—Imp. Kitty Fisher.
			Emilius.	Orville—Emily by Stamford—Dau. of Whiskey—Gr. Dorimant by Dorimant—Dizzy by Blank—Dizzy by Driver (Snake).
			Icaria.	The Flyer (Vandyke, Jr.)—Parma by Dick Andrews—May by Beningbrough—Primrose by Mambrino—Cricket by Herod—Sophia.
			Sumpter.	Sir Archy—Flirtilla's dam by Imp. Robin Redbreast (Sir Peter)—Dau. of Imp. Obscurity (Eclipse)—Slamerkin by Imp. Wildair—Imp. Cub Mare.
			Lady Grey.	Robin Grey (Royalist)—Maria by Melzar (Imp. Medley)—Dau. of Imp. Highflyer—Dau. of Imp. Fearnougbt—Dau. of Ariel (Imp. Traveler).
			Selim.	Buzzard—Dau. of Alexander (Eclipse)—Dau. of Highflyer—Dau. of Alfred (Matchem)—Dau. of Engineer (Sampson)—Bay Malton's dam by Cade.
			Bacchante.	Williamson's Ditto (Sir Peter)—Sis. to Calomel by Mercury (Eclipse)—Dau. of Herod—Folly by Marske—Vixen by Regulus—Dau. of Hutton's Spot.
			Tramp.	Dick Andrews—Dau. of Gohanna—Fraxinella by Trentham—Dau.of Woodpecker—Everlasting by Eclipse—Hyaena by Snap—Miss Belsea.
			Web.	Waxy—Penelope by Trumpator—Prunella by Highflyer—Promise by Snap—Julia by Blank—Spectator's dam by Partner (Jigg).
			Am. Eclipse.	Duroc (Diomed) Millers Damsel by Imp. Messenger—Dau. of Pot-8-o's—Dau. of Gimcrack—Snap-Dragon by Snap—Fribble's dam by Regulus.
			Young Maid of the Oaks.	Imp. Expedition (Pegasus)—Maid of the Oaks by Imp. Spread Eagle—Annette by Imp. Shark—Dau. of Rockingham—Dau. of Gallant.
			Haxall's Moses.	Imp. Sir Harry (Sir Peter)—Mermaid by Waxy—Promise by Buzzard—Dau. of Precipitate (Mercury)—Lady Harriet by Mark Anthony (Spectator).
			Daughter of.	Blackburn's Whip (Imp. Whip by Saltram)—Maria by Craig's Alfred (Imp. Medley by Gimcrack)—Dau. of Tayloe's Bellair (Imp. Medley)—Dau. of Imp. Medley—The Bellair Mare was brought from Virginia to Kentucky and certified to be thoroughbred.

*Soothsayer given.

SPRINGBOK,

(WINNER OF THE BELMONT STAKES AT JEROME PARK, SARATOGA CUP AT SARATOGA, AND MANY OTHER RACES,)

Will stand the season of 1883, *at the Edgewater Stud, Harrison County, Ky., at* $100 *the season. Application to Hon. T. J. Megibben, Lairs Station, Ky.*

SPRINGBOK by imp. Australian, son of West Australian, bred in the Woodburn Stud, Ky., foaled 1870; dam, Hester by Lexington, 2d dam, Heads I Say, dam of Maggie Hunter, Hazard, etc., by imp. Glencoe out of imp. Heads or Tails, by Lottery. Springbok came out as a two-year old, started in two races. Jerome Park won a dash of five furlongs for two-year olds in 1:05¼, beating Minnie Mac, Katy Pease and others, and was unplaced in the Saratoga Stakes, at Saratoga, three-quarters of a mile, won by Catesby in 1:17½. As a three-year old started in seven races, of which he won three. At Jerome Park won the Belmont Stakes for three-year olds, one mile, 5 furlongs, beating Count D'Orsay, imp. Strachino, Waverley and six others, among which were Fellowcraft and imp. Ill-Used. Same place won a race of mile heats in 1:45½, 1:44½, beating imp. Buckden and two others; won mile heats in 1:46½, 1:48, 1:48½, Minnie Mac won the first heat. At Monmouth Park was second in the Jersey Derby for three-year olds, 1½ miles, won by Tom Bowling in 2:45¾; at Jerome Park was second in the Jerome Stakes for three-year olds, 2 miles, won by Tom Bowling, no official time given; at Saratoga, was unplaced in the Travers Stakes, for three-year olds, 1¾ miles, won by Tom Bowling in 3:00¾, and was third in the Kenner Stakes for three-year olds, 2 miles, won by imp. Il-Used in 3:39. As a four-year old, started in nine races of which he won eight. Jerome Park, won a selling race, 1⅝ miles, in 3:14¼, carrying 115 lbs., and beating Mate, Fellowcraft and others; won a handicap sweepstakes one mile and 5 furlongs, in 2:53; at Utica, N. Y., won the Citizens' Handicap Stakes, for all ages, 2 miles, in 3:36¾, beating Artist and Katy Pease; same place won the Hotel Purse, mile heats, in 1:45, 1:42¾; at Saratoga won a dash of 1¼ miles, in 2:09¾, beating Mate, Survivor, and Dublin; won the Saratoga Cup, 2¼ miles, in 4:11¾, beating Preakness, Katy Pease and Wanderer; won a dash of 2 miles and a furlong in 3:56, won a dash of 3 miles in 5:42¼, beating Preakness and Fellowcraft; Jerome Park, was second in the Jockey Club Handicap, 2 miles, won by Preakness in 3:42. As a five-year old, he started in six races, winning four and running dead heat in one. At Jerome Park, won a dash of 1½ miles, in 2:43½, beating Mate, the only other starter; won a race of mile heats in 1:44¾, 1:46¼, beating Spendrift, Big Fellow, and Bill Bruce; won a dash of one mile and a furlong in 1:58½, beating Bob Woolley, Mate and four others; at Saratoga, ran dead heat with Preakness in the Saratoga Cup, 2¼ miles, in 3:56¼, the fastest race ever ran at the distance; at Jerome Park won a dash of 1¾ miles in 3:12, beating Milner, Big Fellow and two others; at Saratoga was second in a Sweepstakes, 1¼ miles, won by Grinstead in 2:08¾. As a six-year old, started once in a race of mile heats and was distanced in the first heat. In this race Freebooter was the winner, with 101 lbs., while Springbok carried 124 lbs. Springbok was a first class race-horse, and is descended from a racing family on both sides; he is much inbred to Waxy through Whisker, Whalebone, and Web, and traces on his dam's side to Eleanor by Whiskey, the first mare to win both the Derby and Oaks. In addition to his Diomed blood through Lexington, his dam traces to Diomed's best daughter in England, Young Giantess, the dam of Sorceror, and a sister to Roxana, who first brought the great Godolphin Arabian into notice to a daughter of Spanker. Only a few of his get have been trained. Clipsetta was one of the best two-year olds of the past year. Won the Ladies' Stake at Louisville, Ky., five furlongs, in 1:03½, and Tennessee Stake, three-quarters of a mile, defeating such ones Ella, Vera, Bondholder, Ascender, etc. She unfortunately died early in the season. Springbok is a bright chestnut, 16 hands high, with star and snip over his left nostril, and white spot between the nostrils, and black spot over his right eye, left fore leg white over the ankle, both hind feet white nearly to the hocks. He is a horse of great substance and power, highly finished all over without a particle of lumber, and will make his mark in the stud.

PEDIGREE OF SPRINGBOK.

SPRINGBOK.								
IMP. AUSTRALIAN.	West Australian.	Melbourne.	Touch-stone.	Humphrey Clinker.	Dau. of Clinker.	Comus.	Sorcerer—Houghton Lass by Sir Peter—Alexina by King Fergus—Lardella by Y. Marske—Dau. of Cade—Beaufremout's dam.	
						Clinkerina.	Clinker—Pewet by Tandem—Termagant by Tantrum—Cantatrice by Sampson—Dau. of Regulus—Marske's dam by Blacklegs.	
			Mowerina.	Emma.		Cervantes.	Don Quixote—Evelina by Highflyer—Termagant by Tantrum—Cantatrice by Sampson—Dau. of Regulus—Marske's dam by Blacklegs.	
						Daughter of.	Golumpus—Dau. of Paynator—Sis. to Zodiac by St. George—Abigail by Woodpecker—Firetail by Eclipse—Dau. of Blank—Dau. of Cade.	
		Emilius.	Young Emilius.	Whisker.	Shoveler.	Camel.	Whalebone—Dau. of Selim—Maiden by St. Peter—Dau. of Phoenomenon—Matron by Florizel—Maiden by Matchem—Dau. of Squirt.	
						Banter.	Master Henry—Boadicea by Alexander—Brunette by Amaranthus—Mayfly by Matchem—Dau. of Au. Starling—Dau. of Grasshopper.	
						Whisker.	Waxy—Penelope by Trumpator—Prunella by Highflyer—Promise by Snap—Julia by Blank—Spectator's dam by Partner—Bonny Lass.	
						Gibside Fairy.	Hermes—Vicissitude by Pipator—Beatrice by Sir Peter—Pyrrha by Matchem—Duchess by Whitenose—Miss Slamerkin by Y. True Blue.	
						Orville.	Beningbrough—Evelina by Highflyer—Termagant by Tantrum—Cantatrice by Sampson—Dau. of Regulus—Marske's dam by Blacklegs.	
						Emily.	Stamford—Dau. of Whiskey—Gr. Dorimant by Dorimant—Dizzy by Blank—Dizzy by Driver—Dau. of Smiling Tom—Dau. of Oysterfoot.	
						Scud.	Beningbrough—Eliza by Highflyer—Augusta by Eclipse—Hardwiek's dam by Herod—Dau. of Bajazet—Dau. of Regulus—Dau. of Lon's Bay Arabian.	
						Goosander.	Hambletonian—Rally by Trumpator—Fancy, Sis. to Diomed by Florizel—Sis. to Juno by Spectator—Horatia by Blank—Dau. of F. Childers.	
			Emilia.	Persian.	Variety.	Waxy.	Pot-8-os—Maria by Herod—Lisette by Snap—Miss Windsor by Godol. Arabian—Sis. to Volunteer by Y. Belgrade—Dau. of Bart. Childers.	
						Penelope.	Trumpator—Prunella by Highflyer—Promise by Snap—Julia by Blank—Spectator's dam by Partner—Bonny Lass by Bay Bolton.	
						Selim, or Soothsayer.*	Sorcerer—Golden Locks by Delpini—Violet by Shark—Dau. of Syphon—Charlotte by Blank—Dau. of Crab—Dau. of Dy. Dimple.	
						Sprite.	Bobtail—Catbarine by Woodpecker—Camilla by Trentham—Coquette by Compton's Barb—Sis. to Regulus by Godol. Arabian—Grey Robinson.	
HESTER.	Lexington.	Boston.	Sister to Tuckahoe.	Timoleon.		Sir Archy.	Diomed—Castianira by Rockingham—Tabitha by Trentham—Dau. of Bosphorus—Dau. of Wm.'s Forester—Dau. of Coalition Colt—Dau. of Bustard.	
						Daughter of	Imp. Saltram—Dau. of Symme's Wildair—Dau. of Driver (Imp. Othello)—Dau. of Fallower (Blank)—Dau. of Imp. Vampire (Regulus).	
						Ball's Florizel.	Diomed—Dau. of Imp. Shark—Dau. of Harris' Eclipse—Dau. of Fearnought—Dau. of Jolly Roger—Dau. of Sober John—Dau. of Imp. Shark.	
				Sarpedon.		Daughter of.	Alderman—Dau. of Clockfast—Dau. of Symme's Wildair—Y. Kitty Fisher by Fearnought—Imp. Kitty Fisher by Cade—Dau. of Som. Arabian.	
		Alice Carneal.				Emilius	Orville—Emily by Stamford—Dau. of Whiskey—Gr. Dorimant by Dorimant—Dizzy by Blank—Dizzy by Driver—Dau. of Smiling Tom.	
				Rowena.		Icaria.	The Flyer—Parma by Dick Andrews—May by Beningbrough—Primrose by Mambrino—Cricket by Herod—Sophia by Blank.	
						Sumpter.	Sir Archy—Flirtilla's dam by Robin Redbreast—Dau. of Obscurity—Old Slamerkin by Imp. Wildair—Imp. Cub Mare by Cub—Amaranthus' dam.	
						Lady Grey.	Robin Grey—Maria by Melzar—Dau. of Highflyer—Dau. of Fearnought—Dau. of Ariel—Dau. of Jack of Diamonds—Imp. Diamond by Cul. Arabian.	
		Glencoe.	Sultan.			Selim.	Buzzard—Castrel's dam by Alexander—Dau. of Highflyer—Dau. of Alfred—Dau. of Engineer—Bay Malton's dam by Cade—Lass of the Mill.	
						Bacchante.	Williamson's Ditto—Sis. to Calomel by Mercury—Dau. of Herod—Folly by Marske—Vixen by Regulus—Dau. of Hut's Spot—Dau. of Bay Bolton.	
			Trampoline.			Tramp.	Dick Andrews—Dau. of Gohanna—Fraxinella by Trentham—Dau. of Woodpecker—Everlasting by Eclipse—Hyaena by Snap.	
	Heads-I-Say.					Web.	Waxy—Penelope by Trumpator—Prunella by Highflyer—Promise by Snap—Julia by Blank—Spectator's dam by Partner—Bonny Lass.	
	Heads or Tails.		Lottery.			Tramp.	Dick Andrews—Dau. of Gohanna—Fraxinella by Trentham—Dau. of Woodpecker—Everlasting by Eclipse—Hyaena by Snap.	
						Mandane.	Pot-8-os—Y. Camilla by Woodpecker—Camilla by Trentham—Coquette by Compton's Barb—Sis. to Regulus by Godol. Arabian—Gr. Robinson.	
			Active.			Partisan.	Walton—Parasol by Pot-8-o's—Prunella by Highflyer—Promise by Snap—Julia by Blank—Spectator's dam by Partner—Bonny Lass.	
						Eleanor.	Whiskey—Y. Giantess, Sorcerer's dam, by Diomed—Giantess by Matchem (Cade)—Molly Longlegs by Babraham (Godol.)—Dau. of Cole's Foxhunter (Brisk by Dar. Arabian)—Dau. of Partner (Jigg)—Sis. to Roxana by the Bald Galloway (St. Victor Barb)—Sis. to Chanter by the Akaster Turk—Dau. of Leede's Arabian—Dau. of Spanker (D'Arcy Yellow Turk).	

*Soothsayer given.

STONEHENGE (Imp.)

(WINNER OF THE COTTAGERS' CUP AT LONG BRANCH, 1873,)

Will be located during the season at the Brookdale Stud, Mr. D. D. Withers, proprietor, near Holmdel, N. J., and used as a private stallion.

STONEHENGE, by Blair Athol, best son of Stockwell, bred by Mr. W. Blenkiron, foaled 1870, dam Coimbra, dam of Light Wine, etc., by Kingston, son of Venison, out of Calcavella, dam of Queen Bee, etc., by Irish Birdcatcher. His sire, Blair Athol, won the double events, Derby and St. Leger, and his sire, Stockwell, was the greatest and grandest of all the English stallions. Kingston, the sire of his dam, traveled all over England, and was winner in the best of company. Irish Birdcatcher, by Sir Hercules, son of Whalebone, was not only a good race-horse, but he got The Baron, winner of the St. Leger, and he got Stockwell and Rataplan. Birdcatcher was also Sire of Daniel O'Rourke, a Derby winner, Songstress, winner of the Oaks, Knight of St. George and Warlock, winners of the St. Leger. Faugh-a-Ballagh, the sire of Leamington, was own brother to Birdcatcher. Stonehenge made his *debut* as a two-year-old in the Nursery Stakes at Jerome Park, but was unplaced. This was his only start in his two-year-old form. When three years old, he started six times, won one race, the Cotagers' Cup, at Long Branch, 1¼ miles, in 2:44½. He was third to Tom Bowling in the Robins Stake, with Lizzie Lucas and The Minstrel behind him. Was third to Survivor and Fellowcraft in a race of 1¼ miles, with four others behind. He was unplaced in his other races. The Julietta colt showed himself a good two-year-old. He won the Surf Stakes at Sheepshead Bay, 5 furlongs, in 1:03¼, beating Onondaga and Memento ; won August Stakes at Long Branch, three-quarters of a mile, in 1:16, with 115 lbs., beating Wyoming, Onondaga and Memento. Was second in 1882 to Forester, in the Withers Stakes, second to Runnymede, in the Tidal Stakes at Sheepshead Bay, one mile, in 1:43¾. Won Club Purse, one mile in 1:43½, beating Barrett and Fellowplay. Buckstone (2) won the Moet and Chandon Stakes, three-quarters of a mile in 1:21, track heavy, defeating a field of five. Won the Homebred Produce Stakes, three-quarters of a mile in 1:18¼, both at Long Branch. Very few mares were ever bred to Stonehenge. He is a blood bay, with blaze face and snip, near hind leg roan and white to the hock, is fifteen hands, 2½ inches high, and weighs 1,140 lbs. With a Glencoe cross, through Stockwell, and a double cross of Whalebone, through Irish Birdcatcher, fortified by the blood of Eclipse and Herod, he only needs a chance to distinguish himself as a sire.

PEDIGREE OF STONEHENGE.

STONEHENGE								
BLAIR ATHOL	Stockwell	The Baron	Birdcatcher	Sir Hercules	Whalebone—Peri by Wanderer—Thalestris by Alexander—Rival by Sir Peter—Hornet by Drone—Manilla by Goldfinder—Dau. of Old Eng.			
			Echidna	Guiccioli	Bob Booty—Flight by I. Escape—Y. Heroine by Bagot—Heroine by Hero—Dau. of Snap—Sis. to Regulus by Godol. Arabian.			
		Pocahontas	Glencoe	Economist	Whisker—Floranthe by Octaviau—Caprice by Anvil—Madcap by Eclipse—Dau. of Blank—Dau. of Blaze—Dau. of Y. Greyhound.			
			Marpessa	Miss Pratt	Blacklock—Gadabout by Orville—Minstrel by Sir Peter—Matron by Florizel—Maiden by Matchem—Dau. of Squirt—Lot's dam.			
	Blink Bonny	Melbourne	Humphrey Clinker	Sultan	Selim—Bacchante by Williamson's Ditto—Sis. to Calomel by Mercury—Dau. of Herod—Folly by Marske—Vixen by Regulus.			
				Trampoline	Tramp—Web by Waxy—Penelope by Trumpator—Prunella by Highflyer—Promise by Snap—Julia by Blank—Spectator's dam by Partner.			
			Dau. of Clinker	Muley	Orville—Eleanor by Whiskey—Y. Giantess by Diomed—Giantess by Matchem—Molly Longlegs by Babraham—Dau. of Cole's Foxhunter.			
				Clare	Marmion—Harpalice by Gohanna—Amazon by Driver—Fractious by Mercury—Dau. of Woodpecker—Everlasting by Eclipse—Hyaena.			
		Queen Mary	Gladiator	Comus	Sorcerer—Houghton Lass by Sir Peter—Alexina by King Fergus—Lardella by Y. Marske—Dau. of Cade.			
				Clinkerina	Clinker—Pewet by Tandem—Termagant by Tantrum—Cantatrice by Sampson—Dau. of Regulus—Marske's dam by Blacklegs.			
			Dau. of	Cervantes	Don Quixote—Evelina by Highflyer—Termagant by Tantrum—Cantatrice by Sampson—Dau. of Regulus—Marske's dam by Blacklegs.			
				Daughter of	Golumpus—Dau. of Paynator—Sis. to Zodiac by St. George—Abigail by Woodpecker—Firetail by Eclipse—Dau. of Blank—Naylor by Cade.			
			Partisan	Partisan	Walton—Parasol by Pot-8-os—Prunella by Highflyer—Promise by Snap—Julia by Blank—Spectator's dam by Partner—Bonny Lass.			
				Pauline	Moses—Quadrille by Selim—Canary Bird by Whiskey or Sorcerer—Canary by Coriander—Miss Green by Highflyer—Harriet by Matchem.			
			Venison	Plenipotentiary	Emilius—Harriet by Pericles—Dau. of Selim—Pipylina by Sir Peter—Rally by Trumpator—Fancy, Sis. to Diomed by Florizel.			
				Myrrha	Whalebone—Gift by Y. Gohanna—Sis. to Grazier by Sir Peter—Dau. of Trumpator—Sis. to Postmaster by Herod—Dau. of Snap.			
COIMBRA	Caroline	Irish Birdcatcher	Sir Hercules	Walton	Sir Peter—Arethusa by Dungannon—Dau. of Prophet—Virago by Snap—Dau. of Regulus—Sis. to Othello by Crab—Miss Slamerkin.			
				Parasol	Pot-8-os—Prunella by Highflyer—Promise by Snap—Julia by Blank—Spectator's dam by Partner—Bonny Lass by Bay Bolton.			
			Guiccioli	Smolensko	Sorcerer—Wowski by Mentor—Waxy's dam by Herod—Lisette by Snap—Miss Windsor by Godol. Arabian—Sis. to Volunteer.			
				Jerboa	Gohanna—Camilla by Trentham—Coquette by Compton Barb—Sis. to Regulus by Godol. Arabian—Gr. Robinson by Bald Galloway.			
		Kingston	The Fawn	Royal Oak	Catton—Dau. of Smolensko—Lady Mary by Beningbrough—Dau. of Highflyer—Dau. of Marske—A la Grecque by Regulus.			
				Daughter of	Orville—Epsom Lass by Sir Peter—Alexina by King Fergus—Lardella by Y. Marske—Dau. of Cade—Beaufremont's dam by Bro. to Fearnought.			
			Partisan	Octavian	Stripling (Phœnomenon)—Dau. of Oberon—Sis. to Sharper by Ranthos (Matchem)—Dau. of Sweepstakes—Sis. to Careless by Regulus.			
		Queen Ann		Daughter of	Shuttle—Katharine by Delphi—Dau. of Paymaster (Herod)—Dau. of Le Sang—Dau. of Rib (Crab)—Graudam of Eclipse Mother Western.			
	Potentate's Irish dam	Gnicci-oli	Garcia	Whalebone	Waxy—Penelope by Trumpator—Prunella by Highflyer—Promise by Snap—Julia by Blank—Spectator's dam by Partner.			
				Peri	Wanderer—Thalestris by Alexander—Rival by Sir Peter—Hornet by Drone—Manilla by Goldfinder—Dau. of Old Eng. (Godol.).			
			Slane	Bob Booty	Chanticleer—Ierne by Bagot—Dau. of Gamahoe—Patty by Tim—Misa by Justice—Ringtail Galloway by Cur. Bay Barb.			
		Calcavella		Flight	I. Escape—Y. Heroine by Bagot—Heroine by Hero—Dau. of Snap—Sis. to Regulus by Godol. Arabian—Gr. Robinson by Bald Galloway.			
			Irish Drone	Master Robert	Buffer—Spinster by Shuttle—Dau. of Sir Peter—Bab. by Bordeaux-Speranza by Eclipse—Virago by Snap—Sis. to Othello by Crab.			
				Daughter of	Sir Walter Raleigh (Waxy)—Miss Tooley by Teddy the Grinder—Lady Jane by Sir Peter—Paulina by Florizel—Captive by Matchem.			
				Don Juan	Orville—Peterea by Sir Peter—Mary Gr. by Friar (South)—Timante by Tim (Squirt)—Sis. to Noble by Gamahoe (Bustard).			
				Moll-in-the-Wad	Hambletonian (King Fergus)—Spitfire by Pipator (Imperator)—Farewell by Slope (Highflyer)—Dau. of Y. Marske—Dau. of Bro. to Silvio (Cade)—Sis. to Stripling by Hutton's Spot.			

STRACHINO (Imp.)

(STRACHINO, WINNER OF THE SUMMER HANDICAP AT SARATOGA, 1873, AND SECOND TO ILL-USED IN THE KENNER, SAME YEAR.)

Strachino will stand the season of 1883, at the Lakewood Stud, near Lexington, Ky., at $25 the season. Application to C. M. Corbin, Agent, Lexington, Ky.

STRACHINO, by Parmesan, son of Sweetmeat, bred by Lord Bradford, foaled 1870, dam May Belle, dam of Waterwitch, Rosabel, etc., by Hetman Platoff, son of Brutandorf, out of a daughter of Sultan, sire of imp. Glencoe. As a two-year-old, Strachino started three times; was second to Count D'Orsay, in a Sweepstakes for two-year-olds, three-quarters of a mile, in 1,19¼, and unplaced in the other two races. When three year old he started five times and won two races. At Saratoga, won dash of 1¼ miles, in 2:11¼, beating Joe Daniels, Ortolan and Wizard. Same place, August 5, won the Summer Handicap, 2 miles, in 3:36¾; was second to imp. Ill-Used in the Kenner Stakes, 2 miles, in 3:39. He was then retired from the turf and placed in the stud. Parmesan, his sire, was a good horse, and sired Cremorne, who won the Derby and Grand Prix-de-Paris, in 1872, and Ascot Gold Cup in 1873, and also Favonius, winner of the Derby and the Goodwood Cup. Hetman Platoff, the sire of his dam, was a superior race-horse; sire of Cossack, winner of the Derby, and the dam of Daniel O'Rourke, winner of the Derby, and Knight of St. George, winner of the St. Leger. Sultan, the sire of his grandam, was the sire of imp. Glencoe, Ibrahim, Bay Middleton and Achmet, winners of the 2,000 guineas in 1834-35-36 and '37. Bay Middleton, also won the Derby. Muley, the sire of his great grandam, was the sire of imp. Margrave, Leviathan, and Little Wonder, a Derby winner. The most creditable of Strachino's get, are, Strychnine, and Neufchatel, both showed themselves good horses. Strychnine's races were principally over the timber. He won 1½ miles, over six hurdles, in 2:50¾; won 1¼ miles, over five hurdles, in 2:19¼, and several other good races. Neufchatel won Rancocas Handicap, one mile and a furlong, in 1:57, and purse at Saratoga, same distance, in 1:55½. Other winners by him are, Baby, Ersilia, Hope (Sphinx), Peytona Barry and Sinbad. He has only covered a very few mares. Strachino is a black, 15¼ hands high, well and truly shaped, but a little light in bone. He is a finely bred horse, and much inbred to the famous Pot-8-os, son of Eclipse on both sides, with a large infusion of Herod blood, through his best sons, and traces through the famous Lady High to the old Montague Mare.

PEDIGREE OF STRACHINO (Imp.)

STRACHINO (Imp.)								
PARMESAN.	Sweetmeat.	Gladiator.	Pauline.	Partisan.		Waltou.		Sir Peter—Arethusa by Dungannon—Dau. of Prophet—Virago by Snap—Dau. of Regulus—Sis. to Othello by Crab—Miss Slamerkin.
						Parasol.		Pot-8-os—Prunella by Highflyer—Promise by Snap—Julia by Blank—Spectator's dam by Partner—Bonny Lass by Bay Bolton.
			Lollypop.	Starch or Voltaire.*		Moses.		Whalebone or Seymour—Dau. of Gohanna—Grey Skim by Woodpecker—Silver's dam by Herod—Y. Hag by Skim—Hag by Crab.
						Quadrille.		Selim—Canary Bird by Whiskey or Sorcerer—Canary by Coriander—Miss Green by Highflyer—Harriet by Matchem—Flora by Reg.
				Belinda.		Blacklock.		Whitelock—Dau. of Coriander—Wildgoose by Highflyer—Coheiress by Pot-8-os—Manilla by Goldfinder—Dau. of Old Eng.
						Daughter of.		Phantom—Dau. of Overton—Gratitude's dam by Walnut—Dau. of Ruler—Piracantha by Matchem—Prophetess by Regulus.
		Gruyère.	Verulam.	Lottery.		Blacklock.		Whitelock—Dau. of Coriander—Wildgoose by Highflyer—Coheiress by Pot-8-os—Manilla by Goldfinder—Dau. of Old Eng.—Dau. of Cul. Arabian
						Wagtail.		Prime Minister—Dau. of Orville—Miss Grimstone by Weasel—Dau. of Ancaster—Dau. of Dam Arabian—Dau. of Sampson.
				Wire.		Tramp.		Dick Andrews—Dau. of Gohanna—Fraxinella by Trentham—Dau. of Woodpecker—Everlasting by Eclipse—Hyaena by Snap.
						Mandane.		Pot-8-os—Y. Camilla by Woodpecker—Camilla by Trentham—Coquette by Comp. Barb—Sis. to Regulus by Godol. Arabian—Gr. Robinson.
			Touchstone.			Waxy.		Pot-8-os—Maria by Herod—Lisette by Snap—Miss Windsor by Godol. Arabian—Sis. to Volunteer by Y. Belgrade—Dau. of Bart. Childers.
		Jennala.				Penelope.		Trumpator—Prunella by Highflyer—Promise by Snap—Julia by Blank—Spectator's dam by Partner—Bonny Lass by Bay Bolton.
						Camel.		Whalebone—Dau. of Selim—Maiden by Sir Peter—Dau. of Phoenomenon—Matron by Florizel—Maiden by Matchem—Dau. of Squirt.
				Emma.		Banter.		Master Henry—Boadicea by Alexander—Brunette by Amaranthus—Mayfly by Matchem—Dau. of An. Starling—Dau. of Grasshopper.
						Whisker.		Waxy—Penelope by Trumpator—Prunella by Highflyer—Promise by Snap—Julia by Blank—Spectator's dam by Partner—Bonny Lass.
						Gibside Fairy.		Hermes—Vicissitude by Pipator—Beatrice by Sir Peter—Pyrrha by Matchem—Duchess by Whitenose—Miss Slamerkiu.
MAY BELLE.	Daughter of.	Hetman Platoff.	Brutandorf.	Blacklock.		Whitelock.		Hambletonian—Rosalind by Phoenomenon—Atalanta by Matchem—Lass of the Mill by Oroonoko—Dau. of Traveler.
						Daughter of.		Coriander—Wildgoose by Highflyer—Coheiress by Pot-8-os—Manilla by Goldfinder—Dau. of Old Eng.—Dau. of Cul. Arabian.
				Mandane.		Pot-8-o's.		Eclipse—Sportsmistress by War Sportsman—Golden Locks by Oroonoko—Valiant's dam by Crab—Dau. of Partner.
						Y. Camilla.		Woodpecker—Camilla by Trentham—Coquette by the Compton Barb—Sis. to Regulus by Godol. Arabian—Gr. Robinson.
			Daughter of.	Comus.		Sorcerer.		Trumpator—Y. Giantess by Diomed—Giantess by Matchem—Molly Longlegs by Babraham—Dau. of Cole's Foxhunter.
						Houghton Lass.		Sir Peter—Alexina by King Fergus—Lardella by Y. Marske—Dau. of Cade—Beaufremont's dam by Bro. to Fearnought.
				Marciana.		Stamford.		Sir Peter—Horatia by Eclipse—Countess, Delpini's dam by Blank—Dau. of Rib (Crab)—Dau. of Wynn Arabian.
						Marcia.		Coriander—Faith by Pacolet—Atalanta by Matchem—Lass of the Mill by Oroonoko—Dau. of Old Traveler—Miss Makeless.
		Sultan.	Selim.			Buzzard.		Woodpecker—Misfortune by Dux—Curiosity by Snap—Dau. of Regulus—Dau. of Bart. Childers—Dau. of Honeywood Arabian.
						Selim's Dam.		Alexander—Dau. of Highflyer—Dau. of Alfred—Dau. of Engineer—Bay Malton's dam by Cade—Lass of the Mill by Traveler.
			Bacchante.			Williamson's Ditto.		Sir Peter—Arethusa by Dungannon—Dau. of Prophet—Virago by Snap—Dau. of Regulus—Sis. to Othello by Crab.
						Sis. to Calomel.		Mercury—Dau. of Herod—Folly by Marske—Vixen by Regulus—Dau. of Hutton's Spot—Dau. of Bay Bolton.
		Salute.	Muley.			Orville.		Beningbrough—Evelina by Highflyer—Termagant by Tautrum—Cantatrice by Sampson—Dau. of Regulus—Marske's dam.
						Eleanor.		Whiskey—Y. Giantess by Diomed—Giantess by Matchem—Molly Longlegs by Babraham—Dau. of Cole's Foxhunter.
			Dolcamara.			Waxy.		Pot-8-os—Maria by Herod—Lisette by Snap—Miss Windsor by Godol. Arabian—Sis. to Volunteer by Y. Belgrade—Dau. of Bart. Childers.
						Witchery.		Sorcerer—Cobbea by Skyscraper (Highflyer)—Dau. of Woodpecker (Herod)—Heinel by Squirrel (Traveler)—Principessa by Blank (Godol.)—Dau. of Cullen Arabian—Grieswood's Lady Thigh by Partner (Jigg)—Dau. of Greyhound (White Barb Chillaby)—Sophonisba's dam by Curwen Bay Barb—Dau. of D'Arcy Chestnut Arabian—Dau. of Whiteshirt—Old Montague Mare.

*Voltaire given.

STRATFORD

Will be used as private stallion in the Chester Valley Stud, Chester Valley, Pa., the property of A. J. Cassatt, Esq.

STRATFORD (Leamington 2d), by imp. Leamington, son of Faugh-a-Ballagh, bred by A Welch, Erdenheim Stud, Pa., foaled 1873, dam Susan Beane, dam of Sensation, by Lexington, son of Boston, out of Sally Lewis, dam of Hunter's Lexington, John Morgan Acrobat, etc., by imp. Glencoe. Stratford was an exceedingly promising horse as a two-year old, but having been taken with a severe attack of distemper, was totally unable to start and the disease left him in such a poor plight, having injured his lungs, so that whilst he had speed, he was unable to stay a distance. At three years old he started in fifteen races, winning two, running second in five, third in one, and unplaced in the others. Point Breeze Park, Pa., won purse three-quarters of mile a in 1:17¼, beating Durango, Paladin, and four others ; same place won purse heats of half a mile in :49¾, :49¼, :49¾, beating First Chance, who won first heat, Hobkirk and Grey Lag, the fastest three heats ever run. Jerome Park, ran second to Ambush, one mile in 1:48, beating Woodlands. Long Branch, ran second to Romney, three quarters of a mile in 1:18. Faithless Hattie F, and three others behind him. Point Breeze Park ran second to First Chance, three quarters of a mile in 1:15, beating Culpepper and two others. Ran second to Waco, one mile in 1:44, beating Hobkirk, Emma G and another. Washington, D.C., ran second to Burgoo, 1¼ miles in 2:14, beating First Chance, Fadladeen and one other. As a four year ran unplaced in three races. Stratford is a highly bred horse, own brother to the great Sensation, and is bred from one of the great racing families of America, a family which were almost uniformly large and profitable winners on the turf, and very successful as stallions and brood mares, the family which produced Sensation, John Morgan, Acrobat, Hunter's Lexington, Motto, Nannie Lewis, Glenmore, and a host of others, possessing speed, conformation, racing lineage and blood he cannot fail as a sire. Stratford is a brown, 15¾ hands, with a Leamington blaze in his face and black legs, he has magnificient shoulders, good middle piece, good back hip and loin, and excellent legs and feet. He much resembles his sire in general conformation and appearance.

PEDIGREE OF STRATFORD.

STRATFORD.	**IMP. LEAMINGTON.**	Daughter of.	Daphne.	Maid of Honor.	Pantaloon. Laurel.	Guiccioli. Idalia. Castrel.	Faugh-a-Ballagh. Sir Hercules. Bob Flight. Booty. Peri. Whalebone.	Waxy. Penelope.	Pot-8-os—Maria by Herod—Lisette by Snap—Miss Windsor by Godol. Arabian—Sis. to Volunteer by Y. Belgrade—Dau. of Bart. Childers. Trumpator—Prunella by Highflyer—Promise by Snap—Julia by Blank—Spectator's dam by Partner—Bonny Lass by Bay Bolton.
								Wanderer. Thalestris.	Gohanna—Catharine by Woodpecker—Camilla by Trentham—Coquette by Compton Barb—Sis. to Regulus by Godol. Arabian. Alexander—Rival by Sir Peter—Hornet by Drone—Manilla by Goldfinder—Dau. of Old Eng.—Dau. of Cullen Arabian.
								Chanticleer. Ierne.	Woodpecker—Dau. of Eclipse—Rosebud by Snap—Miss Belsea by Regulus—Dau. of Bart. Childers—Dau. of Honeywood Arabian. Bagot—Dau. of Gamahoe—Patty by Tim—Miss Patch by Justice—Ringtall Galloway by Cur. Bay Barb—Sis. to Witty Mare.
								Irish Escape. Young Heroine.	Commodore—Buffer's dam by Highflyer—Shift by Sweetbriar—Bl. Susan by Snap—Lord Bruce's Dau. of Cade—Dau. of Belgrade. Bagot—Heroine by Hero—Dau. of Snap—Sis. to Regulus by Godol. Arabian Gr. Robinson by Bald Galloway—Dau. of Snake.
								Buzzard. Selim's dam.	Woodpecker—Misfortune by Dux—Curiosity by Snap—Dau. of Regulus—Dau. of Bart. Childers—Dau. of Hon. Arabian. Alexander—Dau. of Highflyer—Dau. of Alfred—Dau. of Engineer—Bay Malton's dam by Cade—Lass of the Mill.
								Peruvian. Musidora.	Sir Peter—Dau. of Budrow—Escape's dam by Squirrel—Dau. of Babraham—Dau. of Golden Ball—Busby Molly by Ham. Ct. Childers. Meteor—Maid of all Work by Highflyer—Sis. to Tandem by Syphon—Dau. of Regulus—Dau. of Snip—Dau. of Cottingham.
								Blacklock. Wagtail.	Whitelock—Dau. of Coriander—Wildgoose by Highflyer—Coheiress by Pot-8-os—Manilla by Goldfinder—Dau. of Old Eng. Prime Minister—Dau. of Orville—Miss Grimstone by Weasel—Dau. of Ancaster—Dau. of Dam Arabian—Dau. of Sampson.
								Champion. Etiquette.	Selim—Podagra by Gouty—Jet by Magnet—Jewel by Squirrel—Sophia by Blank—Diana by Second—Dau. of Stan. Arabian. Orville—Boadicea by Alexander—Brunette by Amaranthus—Mayfly by Matchem—Dau. of An. Starling—Dau. of Grasshopper.
	SUSAN BEANE.	Lexington. Boston.	Alice Carneal. Sister to Tuckahoe.	Rowena. Sarpedon.	Sultan. Trump-oline. Bare-foot.	Glencoe. Lady Thompktus.	Motto. Timoleon.	Sir Archy. Daughter of.	Diomed—Castianira by Bockingham—Tabitha by Trentham—Dau. of Bosphorus—Dau. of Wm's Forester—Dau. of Coalition Colt. Imp. Saltram—Dau. of Symme's Wildair—Dau. of Driver (Imp. Othello)—Dau. of Fallower (Blank)—Dau. of Vampire.
								Ball's Florizel. Daughter of.	Diomed—Dau. of Imp. Shark—Dau. of Harris' Eclipse—Dau. of Imp. Fearnought—Dau. of Jolly Roger—Dau. of Sober John—Dau. of Shock. Alderman—Dau. of Clockfast—Dau. of Symme's Wildair—Y. Kitty Fisher by Imp. Fearnought—Imp. Kitty Fisher by Cade—Dau. of Som. Arabian.
								Emilius. Icaria.	Orville—Emily by Stamford—Dau. of Whiskey—Gr. Dorimant by Dorimant—Dizzy by Blank—Dizzy by Driver—Dau. of Smiling Tom. The Flyer—Parma by Dick Andrews—May by Beningbrough—Primrose by Mambrino—Cricket by Herod—Sophia by Blank—Diana.
								Sumpter. Lady Gray.	Sir Archy—Flirtilla's dam by Robin Redbreast—Dau. of Obscurity—Slamerkin by Wildair—Imp. Cub Mare by Cub—Amaranthus' dam. Robin Grey—Maria by Melzar—Dau. of Highflyer—Dau. of Fearnought—Dau. of Ariel—Dau. of Jack of Diamonds—Imp. Diamond.
								Selim. Bacchante.	Buzzard—Castrel's dam by Alexander—Dau. of Highflyer—Dau. of Alfred—Dau. of Engineer—Bay Malton's dam by Cade—Lass of the Mill. Williamson's Ditto—Sis. to Calomel by Mercury—Dau. of Herod—Folly by Marske—Vixen by Regulus—Dau. of Hutton's Spot.
								Tramp. Web.	Dick Andrews—Dau. of Gohanna—Fraxinella by Trentham—Dau. of Woodpecker—Everlasting by Eclipse—Hyaena by Snap. Waxy—Penelope by Trumpator—Prunella by Highflyer—Promise by Snap—Julia by Blank—Spectator's dam by Partner—Bonny Lass.
								Tramp. Rosamond.	Dick Andrews—Dau. of Gohanna—Fraxinella by Trentham—Dau. of Woodpecker—Everlasting by Eclipse—Hyaena by Snap. Buzzard—Roseberry by Phoenomenon—Miss West by Matchem—Dau. of Regulus—Dau. of Crab—Dau. of Bart. Childers—Dau. of Basto.
								Am. Eclipse.	Duroc—Millers Damsel by Messenger—Dau. of Pot-8-os—Dau. of Gimcrack—Snap-Dragon by Snap—Fribble's dam by Regulus.
								Katy Ann.	Ogle's Oscar (Imp. Gabriel)—Y. Maid of the Oaks, Medoc's dam by Imp. Expedition (Pegasus by Eclipse)—Maid of the Oaks by Imp. Spread Eagle (Volunteer)—Annette by Imp. Shark (Marske)—Dau. of Rockingham (Partner)—Dau. of Gallant (Imp. Fearnought)—Dau. of True Whig (Fitzbugh's Regulus)—Dau. of Imp. Regulus (Regulus by Godol.)—Imp. Diamond by Cullen Arabian—Lady Thigh by Croft's Partner—Dau. of Greyhound (White Barb Chillaby)—Dau. of Curwen Bay Barb—Dau. of D'Arcy Ch. Arabian—Dau. of Whiteshirt—Old Montague Mare.

TEN BROECK,

WINNER OF PHOENIX HOTEL STAKE AT LEXINGTON, MERCHANTS POST STAKE, MAXWELL HOUSE STAKE AT NASHVILLE, LOUISVILLE CUP, GALT HOUSE PLATE AT LOUISVILLE, AND THE BOWIE STAKE AT BALTIMORE, MD.,)

Will stand the season of 1883 *at Nantura Stud, at* $100 *the season. Application to F. B. Harper, Midway, Ky.*

TEN BROECK, by imp. Phaeton, son of King Tom, bred by John Harper foaled 1872, dam Fanny Holton, by Lexington, out of Nantura dam of Longfellow, by Brawner's Eclipse. Ten Broeck made his bow to the public as a three-year-old, by winning the Phoenix Hotel Stake, one mile and a furlong in 2:11¾, track deep in mud, beating Bill Bruce, Goldmine and three others, among which was Aristides. The track was muddy and very heavy. Won Post Stakes for all ages, 3 miles in 5:31, beating Stampede Vandalite and two others. At Nashville, Tenn., won the Merchants Post Stake in 3:36½, 3:40¼, Bob Woolley the only other starter. Won the Maxwell House Stakes for three-year-olds, mile heats, in 1:44, 1:45, beating Damon and Bob Woolley. At Lexington, Ky., Fall Meeting, won a sweepstake for three-year-olds, one mile and five furlongs, in 2:49¼, beating Bob Woolley, Elemi, King Alfonso and Emma C. This race stood as the fastest on record until beaten by Bend Or, in 1882. Was second in the Kentucky St. Leger, for three-year-olds, 2 miles, won by King Alfonso in 3:34½. Was unplaced in his other three races. As a four-year-old he started in eight races, winning seven and was second in the other. At Louisville, Ky., won a race of two mile heats in 3:38¾, 3:38. Same place won the Louisville Cup, 2¼ miles in 4:03¾. Monmouth, the only other starter, won the Galt House Plate for four-year-olds, 2½ miles, in 4:35¾, beating Steinbok, Damon and Cruisan. At Lexington Fall Meeting won a dash of one mile and five furlongs in 2:51¾. Same place won a dash of 2 miles and five furlongs in 4:58½. Louisville, Ky., won Post Stake, 3 miles, in 5:26½, beating Add, the only other starter. Won dash of four miles against time of Fellowcraft, 7:19½, in 7:15¾, which stands as the fastest four miles ever run. As a five-year-old started ten times and won nine races. Lexington, Ky., walked over for a purse, 1¼ miles. Same place won a dash of 2 miles and a furlong in 3:53¼, beating Katrine and Chestnut Oaks. Louisville, Ky., won a dash of one mile against time in 1:39¾, the fastest mile ever run. Won a dash of 2 miles against time True Blue's, time 3:32½, in 3:27½. Lexington, Ky., won a dash of 2 miles and a furlong in 3:56½, Fairplay the only other starter. Won a dash of 3 miles in 5:34¼, beating Heretog, Bill Dillon and Katrine. Won a dash of 1¼ mile in 2:11¼, beating Courier. Won a dash of 2 miles in 3:36, beating Tolona and Whisper. At Baltimore won the Bowie Stakes, four mile heats, in 7:42½, 7:40. Was second in a dash of 2 miles, won by Parole in 4:37¾. As a six-year-old started twice and won both races. Lexington. Ky., won a dash of 1¼ miles in 2:48¼, beating Leonard, Vera Cruz, Bill Bass and Aristides. Louisville, Ky., won a match race against Mollie McCarty, four mile heats, in 8:19¾, Mollie was distanced first heat. This closed his turf career. Ten Broeck was a first-class race-horse, but ran in and out on account of condition. The family is a racing one, possessing both speed and bottom. His two-year-olds made their appearance last season and ran creditably. Lord Ragland won the Equity Stakes at Saratoga, three-quarters of a mile, in 1:19, defeating Baron Faverot, Barnes, and others. He also won a mile dash at Louisville with 113 lbs. in 1:46¾, defeating a field of seven, Cardinal McCloskey won 5 furlongs in 1:04, and Maiden Stakes at Louisville, three-quarters of a mile in 1:22, track muddy, beating a field of twelve. Same place won Belle Meade Stakes, three-quarters of a mile, in 1:16, beating Ascender and three others. Ten Broeck is a blood bay, with small star and little white on his hind feet; stands about 16½ hands high; has rather a plain head and ear; large jaw, and immense throttle; good strong neck, well set on broad, oblique shoulders, with an abundance of muscle over the shoulder-blade; great depth of girth; large, roomy barrel; strong, muscular back; arched loin, with broad, strong hips; great length from the point of the hip to the whirlbone; immense muscular thigh and stifles, with broad, good hocks, and sound, good legs and feet; he weighs about 1,250 lbs. He is almost a perfect model of a race-horse. In addition to his Glencoe cross, he has the Whisker, Whalebone, Pantaloon and Orville blood, and is much inbred to Sir Archy and Diomed on the dam's side, having seven crosses of that blood, he will be a success.

PEDIGREE OF TEN BROECK.

TEN BROECK.	FANNY HOLTON.	Nantura.	Queen Mary.	Lady Bertrand.	Brawner's Eclipse. Dau. of Am. Eclipse.	Lexington. Alice Carneal.	Boston. Sarpedon. Rowena. Sister to Tuckahoe. Timoleon.	Sir Archy. Daughter of.	Diomed—Castianira by Rockingbam—Tabitha by Trentbam—Dau. of Bosphorus—Dau. of Wm's Forester—Dau. of Coalition Colt—Dau. of Bustard. Imp. Saltram—Dau. of Symme's Wildair—Dau. of Driver (Imp. Othello)—Dau. of Fallower (Blank)—Dau. of Vampire (Regulus).
								Ball's Florizel. Daughter of.	Diomed—Dau. of Imp. Shark—Dau. of Harris' Eclipse—Dau. of Fearnought—Dau. of Jolly Roger—Dau. of Sober John—Dau. of Shock. Alderman—Dau. of Clockfast—Dau. of Symmes' Wildair—Y. Kitty Fisher by Fearnought—Imp. Kitty Fisher by Cade—Dau. of Som. Arabian.
								Emilius. Icaria.	Orville—Emily by Stamford—Dau. of Whiskey—Gr. Dorimant by Dorimant—Dizzy by Blank—Dizzy by Driver—Dau. of Smiling Tom. The Flyer—Parma by Dick Andrews—May by Beningbrough—Primrose by Mambrino—Cricket by Herod—Sophia by Blank—Diana.
								Sumpter. Lady Grey.	Sir Archy—Flirtilla's dam by Robin Redbreast—Dau. of Obscurity—Slamerkin by Wildair—Imp. Cub Mare by Cub—Amaranthus' dam. Robin Grey—Maria by Melzar—Dau. of Highflyer—Dau. of Fearnought—Dau. of Ariel—Dau. of Jack of Diamonds—Imp. Diamond.
								Duroc. Miller's Damsel.	Diomed—Amanda by Grey Diomed—Dau. of Va. Cade—Dau. of Hickman's Independence—Dolly Fine by Silvereye—Dau. of Badger. Messenger—Dau. of Pot-8-os—Dau. of Gimcrack—Snap-Dragon by Suap—Dau. of Regulus—Dau. of Bart Childers—Dau. of Honeywood's Arabian.
								Henry. Young Romp.	Sir Archy—Dau. of Diomed—Bellona by Bellair—Indian Queen by Meades Pilgrim—Dau. of Imp. Janus (Janus.) Duroc—Romp by Messenger—Dau. of Pot-8-os—Dau. of Gimcrack—Snap-Dragon by Snap—Dau. of Regulus—Dau of Bart Childers.
								Sir Archy. Eliza.	Diomed—Castianira by Rockingbam—Tabitha by Trentham—Dau. of Bosphorus—Dau. of Wm's Forester—Dau. of Coalition Colt—Dau of Bustard. Bedford—Imp. Mambrina by Mambrino—Sis. to Naylor's Sally by Blank—Dau. of Ward—Dau. of Merlin—Dau. of Pert—Dau. of St. Martin.
								† Brimmer, or Blue Beard.*	Brimmer (Blue Beard)—Dau. of Lamplighter (Imp. Medley)—Dau. of Medley (Gimcrack)—Dau. of Fearnought (Regulus)—Dau. of Janus.
								Woodpecker's dam.	Imp. Buzzard (Woodpecker)—The Faun by Craig's Alfred (Imp. Medley)—Shepherdess by King Herod (Fearnought)—Dau. of Moreton's Imp. Traveler (Partner)—Dau. of Imp. Whittington (Whitenose)—Dau. of Imp. Childers (Blaze)—Dau. of Babraham (Godol.)—Dau. of Bethel's Arabian—Dau. of Graham's Champion—Dau. of Darley Arabian—Dau. of Old Merlin.
	IMP. PHAETON.	King Tom. Pocahontas. Merry Sunshine. Daughter of. Sis. to Pompey.	Harkaway. Fanny Dawson. Glencoe. Marpessa. Storm. Falstaff. Ghuznee.	Economist.		Whisker. Floranthe.			Waxy—Penelope by Trumpator—Prunella by Highflyer—Promise by Snap—Julia by Blank—Spectator's dam by Partner—Bonny Lass. Octavian—Caprice by Anvil—Madcap by Eclipse—Dau. of Blank—Dau. of Blaze—Dau. of Y. Greyhound—Dau. of Curwen Bay Barb.
						Nabocklish. Miss Tooley.			Rugantino—Butterfly by Master Bagot—Dau. of Bagot (Herod)—Mother Brown by Trunnion (Cade)—Dau. of Old Eog.—Dau. of Bolton Starling. Teddy the Grinder—Lady Jane by Sir Peter—Paulina by Florizel—Captive by Matchem—Calliope by Slouch—Lass of the Mill by Oroonoko.
						Sultan. Trampoline.			Selim—Bacchante by Williamson's Ditto—Sis. to Calomel by Mercury—Dau. of Herod—Folly by Marske—Vixen by Regulus—Dau. of Spot. Tramp—Web by Waxy—Penelope by Trumpator—Prunella by Highflyer—Promise by Snap—Julia by Blank—Spectator's dam by Partner.
						Muley. Clare.			Orville—Eleanor by Whiskey—Y. Giantess by Diomed—Giantess by Matchem—Molly Longlegs by Babraham—Dau. of Cole's Foxhunter. Marmion—Harpalice by Gohanna—Amazon by Driver—Fractious by Mercury—Dau. of Woodpecker—Everlasting by Eclipse—Hyaena by Snap.
						Camel. Banter.			Whalebone—Dau. of Selim—Maiden by Sir Peter—Dau. of Phoenomenon—Matron by Florizel—Maiden by Matchem—Dau. of Squirt—Lot's dam. Master Henry—Boadicea by Alexander—Brunette by Amaranthus—Mayfly by Matchem—Dau. of An. Starling—Dau. of Grasshopper.
						Pantaloon. Languish.			Castrel—Idalia by Peruvian—Musidora by Meteor—Maid of all Work by Highflyer—Sis. to Tandem by Syphon—Dau. of Regulus—Dau. of Snip. Cain—Lydia by Poulton—Variety by Hyacinthus—Sis. to Swordsman by Weasel—Dau. of Turk—Dau. of Locust—Dau. of Changeling.
				Touchstone.		Touchstone. Decoy.			Camel—Banter by Master Henry—Boadicea by Alexander—Brunette by Amaranthus—Mayfly by Matchem—Dau. of Ancaster Starling. Filho-da-Puta—Finesse by Peruvian—Violante by John Bull—Dau. of Highflyer—Everlasting by Eclipse—Hyaena by Snap—Miss Belsea.
						Emilius. Variation.			Orville—Emily by Stamford—Dau. of Whiskey—Gr. Dorimant by Dorimant—Dizzy by Blank—Dizzy by Driver—Dau. of Smiling Tom. Bustard (Castrel)—Johanna Southcote by Beningbrough—Lavinia by Pipator—Dick Andrews' dam by Highflyer—Dau. of Cardinal Puff.

*Blue Beard by Imp. Sterlingdam. Brilliant by Imp. Matchem 2d dam, Imp. by Brilliant, as the author believes.
† Brimmer given.

TOM OCHILTREE

Will be located the season of 1883, *at the Bolingbrooke Stud, near Middleburg, Md., and will be permitted to serve mares at $25 the season. Application to R. W. Walden, Middleburg, Md.*

Tom Ochiltree by Lexington, son of Boston, bred by A. J. Alexander, Woodburn Stud, near Spring Station, Ky., foaled 1872, dam Katona, the dam of Metarie and Sanford, by Voucher, son of Wagner, out of Countess by imp. Margrave, winner of the St. Leger in 1832; Lexington will be found in this book; Wagner, the sire of Voucher he the sire of Katona, was closely inbred to Sir Archy; he defeated the great Grey Eagle in the two memorable contests, four mile heats at Louisville, Kentucky, in 1839; Voucher was a fine race-horse and was held in high esteem in his day; Margrave, the sire of his grandam, was a large, fine horse and a very successful sire; sired Brown Dick, whose three miles in 5:30, 5:28¾ has not often been excelled; he was also sire of Blue Dick, a famous horse, and of Molly Jackson, whose famous third heat of three miles in 5:28¾, has never been equalled. Tom Ochiltree did not run in his two-year old form, but scored his first victory at Baltimore, and won four out of the nine races in which he started in his three-year old form; Baltimore, won dash of three-quarters of a mile in 1:24¾, beating Audubon and seven others; won the Preakness Stakes a Sweepstakes for three-year olds, 1½ miles in 2:43½, beating Viator and seven others; Jerome Park, won the Annual Sweepstakes for three-year olds, 2 miles and a furlong in 4:09½, beating Chesapeake and Ascension; Baltimore, Md., won the Dixie Stakes for three-year olds, 2 miles in 3:42½, beating Viator, Aristides, Rhadamanthus and other good horses; was third in the Breckenridge Stakes for three-year olds, 2 miles, won by Aristides, Viator second in 3:36¼, he carrying a penalty of five pounds, and was unplaced in his other races; four-years old, started in ten races and won eight; Baltimore, Md., won the Baltimore Cup, 2¼ miles in 4:09, beating Stampede, Viator and four others; Jerome Park, won the Jockey Club Handicap, two miles in 3:41¾, beating Kildare, Chesapeake and five others; won the Centennial Stakes for all-ages, 2¾ miles in 5:09½, beating Acrobat and Olitipa; Monmouth Park, won the Monmouth Cup, 2½ miles in 4:48½, Stampede the only other starter; won the Capital Stakes for four-year olds, three miles in 5:35¾, beating Chesapeake and Ascension; at Saratoga, won the Saratoga Cup, 2¼ miles in 4:06½, beating Parole, Big Sandy and Madge; Jerome Park, won the Maturity Stakes for four-year olds, three miles in 5:43½, beating Chesapeake, Mattie A, and Grey Nun; won the Centennial Cup, four miles in 7:36, beating Acrobat, Big Sandy and D'Artagnan; at Saratoga, was second in the All-aged Sweepstakes, 1¼ miles, won by Parole in 2:12¾; was unplaced in race of two mile heats, won by Add in 3:47½, 3:48¾; Ochiltree won first heat, but was distanced in the second; five years old, started fourteen times and was first in nine races; Baltimore, Md., won the Baltimore Cup, 2¼ miles in 4:14; won race of two mile heats in 3:43, distanced the field first heat; Jerome Park, won the Westchester Cup, 2¼ miles in 4:09¾, beating Athlene and Fellowcraft; won a dash of 2½ miles in 4:36½, Athlene the only other starter; Saratoga, won a dash of 2 miles in 3:39½, beating Athlene and Aunt Betsey; won a handicap dash of 2 miles in 3:42½, beating Cloverbrook, Oriole and two others; Ochiltree carried 120 lbs.; Jerome Park, won the Grand National Handicap, 2¼ miles in 4:18½, carrying 124 lbs., beating Parole, Inspiration and Galway; won dash of 1¾ miles in 3:14, beating Virginius and Warlock, track heavy; Saratoga was second in the All-aged Stakes, 1¼ miles, won by Vera Cruz (3), Ochiltree carried 124 lbs.; was second in the Saratoga Cup, 2¼ miles, won by Parole in 4:04¼; was second in a dash of 2¼ miles, won by Whisper in 4:02; was second in a dash of 1¾ miles, won by Vera Cruz in 3:17; at Baltimore, was third in a dash of 2¼ miles, won by Parole in 4:37¾, track very heavy. Tom Ochiltree is one of Lexington's best sons, he could run fast and stay under heavy weights, his great size, coupled with symmetry of form, should commend him to breeders. He is deeply inbred to Diomed through his many Archy crosses, and the Eclipse cross is an addition through a staying family, fortified with a triple cross of Orville, through his sons, Muley and Emilius. Ochiltree is a bay, 16 hands 2½ inches high, no white except a small star. He is one of the truest and best shaped big horses in the world, all bone and muscle without a particle of lumber.

PEDIGREE OF TOM OCHILTREE.

TOM OCHILTREE.	LEXINGTON.	Boston.	Timoleon.	Sir Archy.
				Dau. of Florizel.
			Robin Brown's dam.	Ball's Dau. of Florizel.
		Alice Carneal.	Sarpedon.	
			Rowena.	Lady Grey. Sumpter. Icaria. Emilius.
	KATONA.	Voucher.	Wagner.	Sir Charles.
				Maria West.
		Imp. Britannia.	Muley.	Nancy.
		Countess.	Imp. Margrave.	Chatham's dam. Am. Eclipse. Muley.
		Daughter of.	Dau. of	

Detailed pedigree:

Diomed.	Florizel—Sis. to Juno by Spectator—Horatia by Blank—Dau. of F. Childers—Miss Belvoir by Gr. Grantham—Dau. of Paget Turk.
Castianira.	Rockingham—Tabitha by Trentham—Dau. of Bosphorus—Dau. of Wm.'s Forester—Dau. of Con. Colt—Dau. of Bustard (Crab)—Charming Molly.
Saltram.	Eclipse—Virago by Snap—Dau. of Regulus—Sis. to Othello by Crab—Miss Slamerkin by Y. True Blue—Dau. of Ox. Dun. Arabian—Royal Mare.
Daughter of.	Symme's Wildair (Imp. Fearnought)—Dau. of Driver (Imp. Othello)—Dau. of Imp. Fallower (Blank)—Dau. of Imp. Vampire (Regulus.)
Diomed.	Florizel—Sis. to Juno by Spectator—Horatia by Blank—Dau. of F. Childers—Miss Belvoir by Gr. Grantham—Dau. of Paget Turk—Betty Percival.
Daughter of.	Imp. Shark—Dau. of Harris' Eclipse—Dau. of Fearnought—Dau. of Jolly Roger—Dau. of Sober John (Rib by Crab)—Dau. of Shock.
Alderman.	Pot-8-os—Lady Bolingbroke by Squirrel—Cypron, Herod's dam by Blaze—Selima by Bethel's Arabian—Dau. of Graham's Champion.
Daughter of.	Clockfast—Dau. of Symme's Wildair—Y. Kitty Fisher by Fearnought—Imp. Kitty Fisher by Cade—Da. of Som. Arabian—Bald Charlotte by Old Royal.
Orville.	Beningbrough—Evelina by Highflyer—Termagant by Tantrum—Cantatrice by Sampson—Dau. of Regulus—Marske's dam by Blacklegs.
Emily.	Stamford—Dau. of Whiskey—Gr. Dorimant by Dorimant—Dizzy by Blank—Dizzy by Driver—Dau. of Smiling Tom—Dau. of Oysterfoot.
The Flyer.	Vandyke, Jr.—Azalia by Beningbrough—Gillyflower by Highflyer—Dau. of Goldfinder—Sis. to Grasshopper by Marske—Dau. of Cullen Arabian.
Parma.	Dick Andrews—May by Beningbrough—Primrose by Mambrino—Cricket by Herod—Sophia by Blank—Diana by Second—Dau. of Stan. Arabian.
Sir Archy.	Diomed—Castianira by Rockingham—Tabitha by Trentham—Dau. of Bosphorus—Dau. of Wm.'s Forester—Dau. of Con. Colt—Dau. of Bustard.
Flirtilla's dam.	Robin Redbreast—Dau. of Obscurity—Slamerkin by Wildair—Imp. Cub Mare by Cub—Amaranthus' dam by Second—Dau. of Starling.
Robin Grey.	Royalist—Belle Mariah by Grey Diomed—Queen by Imp. St. George—Dau. of Cassius—Primrose by Imp. Dove—Stella by Othello.
Maria.	Melzar—Dau. of Highflyer—Dau. of Fearnought—Dau. of Ariel—Dau. of Jack of Diamonds—Imp. Diamond by Cul. Arabian—Lady Thigh.
Sir Archy.	Diomed—Castianira by Rockingham—Tabitha by Trentham—Dau. of Bosphorus—Dau. of Wm.'s Forester—Dau. of Coalition Colt.
Daughter of.	Imp. Citizen—Dau. of Commutation—Dau. of Dare Devil—Sally Shark by Imp. Shark—Betsey Pringle by Fearnought—Imp. Jenny Dismal.
Marion.	Sir Archy—Dau. of Imp. Citizen—Dau. of Imp. Alderman—Dau. of Asche's Roebuck—Dau. of King Herod (Imp. Fearnought)—Dau. of Imp. Partner.
Ella Crump.	Imp. Citizen—Dau. of Huntsman (Mousetrap by Y. Marske)—Dau. of Symme's Wildair—Dau. of Fearnought (Regulus)—Dau. of Imp. Janus.
Orville.	Beningbrough—Evelina by Highflyer—Termagant by Tantrum—Cantatrice by Sampson—Dau. of Regulus—Marske's dam by Blacklegs.
Eleanor.	Whiskey—Y. Giantess by Diomed—Giantess by Matchem—Molly Longlegs by Babraham—Dau. of Cole's Foxhunter—Dau. of Partner.
Dick Andrews.	Joe Andrews—Dau. of Highflyer—Dau. of Cardinal Puff—Dau. of Tatler—Dau. of Snip—Dau. of Godol. Arabian—Dau. of Framp. Whiteneck.
Spitfire.	Beningbrough—Dau. of Y. Sir Peter (Doge)—Dau. of Engineer—Dau. of Wilson's Arabian—Dau. of Hutton's Spot—Dau. of Mogul—Dau. of Crab.
Orville.	Beningbrough—Evelina by Highflyer—Termagant by Tantrum—Cantatrice by Sampson—Dau. of Regulus—Marske's dam by Blacklegs.
Eleanor.	Whiskey—Y. Giantess by Diomed—Giantess by Matchem—Molly Longlegs by Babraham—Dau. of Cole's Foxhunter—Dau. of Partner.
Election.	Gohanna—Chestnut Skim by Woodpecker—Silver's dam by Herod—Y. Hag by Skim—Hag by Crab—Ebony by F. Childers—Ebony by Basto.
Fair Helen.	Hambletonian—Helen by Delpini—Rosalind by Phoenomenon—Atalanta by Matchem—Lass of the Mill by Oroonoko—Dau. of Traveler.
Duroc.	Diomed—Amanda by Grey Diomed—Dau. of Va. Cade—Dau. of Hickman's Independence—Dolly Fine by Imp. Silvereye (Cul. Arabian).
Millers Damsel.	Messenger—Dau. of Pot-8-os—Dau. of Gimcrack—Snap-Dragon by Snap—Dau. of Regulus—Dau. of Bart Childers—Dau. of Hon. Arabian.
Rattler.	Sir Archy—Sumpter's dam by Robin Redbreast—Dau. of Obscurity—Imp. Cub Mare by Cub—Amaranthus' dam by Second.
Daughter of.	Thornton's Diomed (Imp. Diomed)—Dau. of Tiger (Cook's Whip)—Dau. of Imp. Shark (Marske)—Dau. of Imp. Fearnought (Regulus).

UNCAS,

(WINNER OF THE KENTUCKY STAKES AT SARATOGA AND WEST-CHESTER CUP AT JEROME PARK, N. Y.)

Uncas will be used as private stallion in the Brookdale Stud, Monmouth County, near Holmdel, N. J., Mr. D. D. Withers, proprietor.

UNCAS by Lexington, son of Boston, bred in Woodburn Stud, Kentucky, foaled 1876, dam Coral, dam of Wanderer by Vandal, son of Glencoe, out of Cairn Gorme, by Cotherstone, winner of the 2,000 guineas and Derby, son of Touchstone, winner of the St. Leger, Doncaster Cups in 1835 and 1836, and Ascot Gold Cups in 1836 and 1837. Uncas only started three times at two-years old; won the Kentucky Stakes at Saratoga, three-quarters of a mile in 1:20½, beating Harold, Idler, Dan Sparling, &c.; he ran second for the Saratoga Stakes to Harold, and second in the Nursery at Jerome Park to the King Ernest gelding. Uncas was then shipped to England, and in 1879 ran unplaced in the 2,000 guineas, won by Charibert; he behaved very badly at the post and delayed the start. He was then returned to America, and at four years old started fifteen times; won five races, was second in six, third in three and unplaced in one; Jerome Park, June 5, won the Westchester Cup, 2¼ miles, in 4:09½, beating Ferida, Monitor and Franklin; a most capital race; Gravesend, June 23, ran second to Monitor in Coney Island Cup, 2¼ miles, 4:36½, beating Ferida and Danicheff; June 26, ran second to Glenmore in Stirrup Cup, two miles and a furlong, in 3:48½, beating Jim Beck; an excellent race; Long Branch, July 5, ran second to Report (4), 108 lbs.; Uncas (4), 114 lbs.; in Shrewsberry Handicap, 1¾ miles, in 3:12¼, beating Ferida (4), 105 lbs., and Danicheff (5), 100 lbs.; was third to Report, 115 lbs., and Monitor, 120 lbs.; Uncas, 121 lbs., in Monmouth Cup, 2¼ miles, in 4:07; ran third to Luke Blackburn and Monitor in Champion Stakes, 1½ miles, in 2:34; the fastest race ever run at the distance, Grenada and Report behind him; August 21, won Handicap Sweepstake, 1¼ miles, in 2:16¼, Uncas, 112 lbs., beating One Dime (4), 115 lbs.; Gravesend, September 4, ran third to Luke Blackburn and Monitor in Great Challenge Stakes, 1½ miles, in 2:38, beating One Dime; September 7, ran second to Glenmore (5), 107 lb.; Uncas, 107 lbs., 1⅝ miles, in 3:07, beating Monitor, 109 lbs., Krupp Gun and Mintzer, September 14, was beaten by Luke Blackburn a match, each carrying 108 lbs., 1½ miles, in 2:42½; September 23, won handicap sweepstakes, one mile and three furlongs, 107 lbs. up, in 2:21¾, beating Mary Anderson (3), 78 lbs., and Checkmate (5), 114 lbs. This is the fastest and best race ever run at the distance. Jerome Park, October 7, won Grand National Handicap, 2¼ miles, carrying 113 lbs., in 4:05½, beating Monitor, 116 lbs.; Ferida, 114 lbs., and Franklin (5), 102 lbs.; Baltimore, October 20, was beaten by Monitor in Pimlico Stakes, 2 miles and a furlong, in 3:44½, the fastest race ever run at the distance; Jerome Park, November 2, won handicap sweepstakes, 1¾ miles, in 3:16½, 119 lbs., beating Harlequin (4), 89 lbs., and Krupp Gun (5), 100 lbs.; at five-years old, started five times, was unplaced in the Jockey Club Handicap at Jerome, 2 miles, won by Grenada, in 3:43; was beaten mile heats by Sir Hugh, 103 lbs., Uncas, 129 lbs., in 1:48, 1:50, track deep in mud; was unplaced in Coney Island Cup, 2¼ miles, won by Glenmore, in 3:58¾; was unplaced in handicap sweepstakes, 1¼ miles, won by Krupp Gun, in 2:11¼; was third to Greenland and Ferida in Handicap Sweepstakes at Monmouth Park, 1½ miles, in 2:39½. Uncas is a blood bay; stands 15½ hands high, with his right fore foot white, and a small star in his forehead. He is quite a compact, well and evenly-formed horse all over, having a neat head and neck, with good shoulders and depth of girth, with extra good body, hips, stifles, and excellent legs and feet. The pedigree is one of the best in the Stud Book, and from a distinguished racing family. His dam is by Glencoe's best son, and he traces back through an own sister to Glencoe, to a Natural Barb Mare. If the blood of Lexington and Glencoe is to be preserved to the country, it is through just such pure channels as Uncas presents.

PEDIGREE OF UNCAS.

UNCAS.		LEXINGTON.	Boston.	Timoleon.	Sir Archy.	Diomed.		Florizel—Sis. to Juno by Spectator—Horatia by Blank—Dau. of F. Childers—Miss Belvoir by Gr. Grantham—Dau. of Paget Turk.
						Castianira.		Rockingham—Tabitha by Trentham—Dau. of Bosphorus—Dau. of Wm's Forester—Dau. of Coalition Colt—Dau. of Bustard (Crab).
				Robin Brown's dam.	Dau. of Ball's Florizet.	Imp. Saltram.		Eclipse—Virago by Snap—Dau. of Regulus—Sis. to Othello by Crab—Miss Slamerkin by Y. True Blue—Dau. of Ox. Dun. Arabian.
						Daughter of.		Symme's Wildair (Fearnought)—Dau. of Driver (Imp. Othello)—Dau. of Fallower (Blank)—Dau. of Imp. Vampire (Regulus).
						Diomed.		Florizel—Sis. to Juno by Spectator—Horatia by Blank—Dau. of F. Childers—Miss Belvoir by Gr. Grantham—Dau. of Paget Turk.
						Daughter of.		Imp. Shark—Dau. of Harris' Eclipse—Dau. of Fearnought—Dau. of Jolly Roger—Dau. of Sober John (Rib)—Dau. of Imp. Shock.
				Sarpedon.	Dau. of Emilius.	Alderman.		Pot-8-os—Lady Bolingbroke by Squirrel—Cypron, Herod's dam by Blaze—Selima by Bethel's Arabian—Dau. of Graham's Champion.
						Daughter of.		Clockfast—Dau. of Symme's Wildair—Y. Kitty Fisher by Fearnought—Imp. Kitty Fisher by Cade—Dau. of Somerset Arabian.
						Orville.		Beningbrough—Evelina by Highflyer—Termagant by Tantrum—Cantatrice by Sampson—Dau. of Regulus—Marske's dam by Blacklegs.
		Alice Carneal.				Emily.		Stamford—Dau. of Whiskey—Gr. Dorimant by Dorimant—Dizzy by Blank—Dizzy by Driver—Dau. of Smiling Tom—Dau. of Oysterfoot.
				Sumpter.	Icaria.	The Flyer.		Vandyke, Jr.—Azalia by Beningbrough—Gillyflower by Highflyer—Dau. of Goldfinder—Sis. to Grasshopper by Marske.
						Parma.		Dick Andrews—May by Beningbrough—Primrose by Mambrino—Cricket by Herod—Sophia by Blank—Diana by Second.
			Rowena.			Sir Archy.		Diomed—Castianira by Rockingham—Tabitha by Trentham—Dau. of Bosphorus—Dau. of Coalition Colt—Dau. of Bustard (Crab).
						Flirtilla's dam.		Robin Redbreast—Dau. of Obscurity—Slamerkin by Wildair—Imp. Cub Mare by Cub—Amaranthus' dam by Second.
				Lady Grey.		Robin Grey.		Royalist—Belle Mariah by Gr. Diomed—Queen by Imp. St. George—Dau. of Cassius—Primrose by Imp. Dove—Stella by Othello.
						Maria.		Melzar—Dau. of Highflyer—Dau. of Fearnought—Dau. of Ariel—Dau. of Jack of Diamonds—Imp. Diamond by Cul. Arabian.
	CORAL.	Vandal.	Glencoe.	Sultan.		Selim.		Buzzard—Castrel's dam by Alexander—Dau. of Highflyer—Dau. of Alfred—Dau. of Engineer—Bay Maltou's dam by Cade (Godol.)
						Bacchante.		Williamson's Ditto—Sis. to Calomel by Mercury—Dau. of Herod—Folly by Marske—Vixen by Regulus—Dau. of Hut. Spot—Dau. of Bay Bolton.
				Trampoline.		Tramp.		Dick Andrews—Dau. of Gobanna—Fraxinella by Trentham—Dau. of Woodpecker—Everlasting by Eclipse—Hyaena by Snap—Miss Belsea.
						Web.		Waxy—Penelope by Trumpator—Pruella by Highflyer—Promise by Snap—Julia by Blank—Spectator's dam by Partner—Bonny Lass.
			Alaric's dam.	Tranby.		Blacklock.		Whitelock—Dau. of Coriander—Wildgoose by Highflyer—Coheiress by Pot-8-os—Manilla by Goldfinder—Dau. of Old Eng.
						Daughter of.		Orville—Miss Grimstone by Weasel—Dau. of Ancaster—Dau. of Dam Arabian—Dau. of Sampson—Dau. of Oroonoko—Sis. to Mirza.
		Cairn-gorme.		Lucilla.		Trumpator.		Sir Solomon—Dau. of Hickory (Imp. Whip)—Imp. Trumpetta by Trumpator—Sis. to Lambinos by Highflyer—Dau. of Eclipse.
						Lucy.		Orphan—Lady Grey by Robin Grey—Maria by Melzar—Dau. of Highflyer—Dau. of Fearnougbt—Dau. of Ariel—Dau. of Jack of Diamonds.
			Cotherstone.	Touchstone.		Camel.		Whalebone—Dau. of Selim—Maiden by Sir Peter—Dau. of Phoenomenon—Matron by Florizel—Maiden by Matchem—Dau. of Squirt—Lot's dam.
						Banter.		Master Henry—Boadicea by Alexander—Bruuette by Amaranthus—Mayfly by Matchem—Dau. of An. Starling—Dau. of Grasshopper (Crab).
				Emma.		Whisker.		Waxy—Penelope by Trumpator—Prunella by Highflyer—Promise by Snap—Julia by Blank—Spectator's dam by Partner—Bonny Lass.
						Gibside Fairy.		Hermes—Vicissitude by Pipator—Beatrice by Sir Peter—Pyrrha by Matchem—Duchess by Whitenose—Miss Slamerkin by Y. True Blue.
		Glenluce.	Slane.			Royal Oak.		Catton—Dau. of Smolensko—Lady Mary by Beningbrough—Dau. of Highflyer—Dau. of Marske—A la Grecque by Regulus.
						Daughter of.		Orville—Epsom Lass by Sir Peter—Alexina by King Fergus—Lardella by Y. Marske—Dau. of Cade—Beaufremont's dam.
			Glencairne.			Sultan.		Selim—Bacchante by Williamson's Ditto—Sis. to Calomel by Mercury—Dau. of Herod—Folly by Marske—Vixen by Regulus.
						Trampoline.		Tramp—Web by Waxy—Penelope by Trumpator (Conductor)—Prunella by Highflyer (Herod)—Promise by Snap (Snip)—Julia by Blank (Godol.)—Spectator's dam by Partner (Jigg)—Bonny Lass by Bay Bolton (Grey Hautboy)—Dau. of Darley Arabian—Dau. of Byerly Turk—Dau. of Taffolet Barb—Dau. of Place's White Turk—Natural Barb Mare.

VENTILATOR

Will be located for the season of 1883, as private stallion, in the Brookdale Stud, near Holmdel, Monmouth Co., N. Y., Mr. D. D. Withers, proprietor.

VENTILATOR, by Vandal, best son of imp. Glencoe, bred by Gen. W. G. Harding, Belle Meade Stud, near Nashville, Tenn., foaled, 1872, dam Carolin, the dam of Bounce, By-the-Way, Ella, etc., by imp. Scythian, son of Orlando, by Touchstone, 2d dam Rosette, dam of Quartermaster, by imp. Yorkshire, out of Picayune, the dam of Doubloon, Florin, Louis d'Or, etc., by Medoc, son of American Eclipse. Ventilator made his first appearance as a two-year-old in the Young America Stakes, No. 1, one mile, at Nashville, Tenn., running second to Katie Pearce in 1:45½, with Elemi, Leona, Bob Woolley, and six others behind him. Ran dead beat with Elemi, for the Young America Stakes, No. 2, one mile, in 1:46¾; Elemi beat him the deciding heat in 1:49¾. Behind him in this were Katie Pearce, Bob Woolley, and five others. At three years old was unplaced in the Clark Stakes at Louisville, won by his stable companion, Volt: geur. In 1876 and '77, he was in retirement. In 1878, he came out in poor hands, ran second in one race and unplaced in seven. In 1879, started in 21 races, all over timber, won four, was second in three, third in five, and unplaced in the others. He ran 2¼ miles over the Steeple Chase Course, at Sheepshead Bay, in 4:27¼, and won the second heat in a hurdle race of heats, 1¼ miles in 2:23. In 1880, started in 14 races, won seven, was second in five, and unplaced in two. His races were all over timber, and some of them fast ones, beating such horses as Judith, Bertha, Pomeroy, Chimney-sweep, etc. During his retirement he covered three mares, and got Mary Anderson, Bagdad, and Ventriloquist, all of them winners in good company. The family is a famous racing one on both sides. On the sire's side belong Lexington, Vandal, Monarchist, Volturno, Ruric, Alaric, Luke Blackburn, Hindoo, Monitor, and others of the best horses of the American turf. On the side of his dam the family is perhaps equally famous, such horses as Doubloon, Florin, Louis d'Or, the best horses of their day, as also Quartermaster, Vagrant and Bounce. Ventilator is a dark chestnut, with a small leaf-shaped star in the forehead, 15¼ hands high, but very stout, well shaped and muscular. He weighs 1,055 lbs. He will get race-horses with a fair chance.

PEDIGREE OF VENTILATOR.

VENTILATOR.	**VANDAL.**	**Glencoe.**	**Sultan.**		Buzzard.	Woodpecker—Misfortune by Dux—Curiosity by Snap—Dau. of Regulus—Dau. of Bart. Childers—Dau. of Hon. Arabian—Dam of True Blues.
					Castrel's dam.	Alexander—Dau. of Highflyer—Dau. of Alfred—Dau. of Engineer—Bay Malton's dam by Cade—Lass of the Mill by Traveler.
			Bacchante.		Williamson's Ditto.	Sir Peter—Arethusa by Duugannon—Dau. of Prophet—Virago by Snap—Dau. of Regulus—Sis. to Othello by Crab—Miss Slamerkin.
					Sis. to Calomel.	Mercury—Dau. of Herod—Folly by Marske—Vixen by Regulus—Dau. of Hutton's Spot—Dau. of Bay Bolton—Dau. of Fox Cub.
		Trampoline.	Tramp.		Dick Andrews.	Joe Andrews—Dau. of Highflyer—Dau. of Cardinal Puff—Dau. of Tatler—Dau. of Snip—Dau. of Godolphin Arabian.
					Daughter of.	Gohanna—Fraxinella by Trentham—Dau. of Woodpecker—Everlasting by Eclipse—Hyaena by Snap—Miss Belsea by Regulus.
			Web.		Waxy.	Pot-8-os—Maria by Herod—Lisette by Snap—Miss Windsor by Godol. Arabian—Sis. to Volunteer by Y. Belgrade—Dau. of Bart. Childers.
					Penelope.	Trumpator—Prunella by Highflyer—Promise by Snap—Julia by Blank—Spectator's dam by Partner—Bonny Lass by Bay Bolton.
		Alaric's dam.	Tranby.	Black-lock.	Whitelock.	Hambletonian—Rosalind by Phoenomenon—Atalanta by Matchem—Lass of the Mill by Oroonoko—Dau. of Traveler—Miss Makeless.
					Daughter of.	Coriander—Wildgoose by Highflyer—Coheiress by Pot 8-os—Manilla by Goldfinder—Dau. of Old Eng.—Dau. of Cul. Arabian—Miss Cade.
				Dau. of	Orville.	Beningbrongh—Evelina by Highflyer—Termagant by Tantrum—Cantatrice by Sampson—Dau. of Regulus—Marske's dam.
					Miss Grimstone.	Weasel—Dau. of Ancaster—Dau. of Dam Arabian—Dau. of Sampson—Dau. of Oroonoko—Sis. to Mirza by Godol. Arabian.
		Lucilla.	Trumpator.		Sir Solomon.	Imp. Tickle Toby (Alfred)—Vesta by Dreadnought (Celer)—Bandy by Clockfast—Dau. of Americus (Imp. Shark)—Dau. of Imp. Fearnought.
					Dauphter of.	Hickory (Imp. Whip)—Imp. Trumpetta by Trumpator—Sis. to Lambinos by Highflyer—Dau. of Eclipse—Vauxhall Snap's dam, by Cade.
			Lucy.		Orphan.	Ball's Florizel (Diomed)—Fair Rachel by Diomed—Susan Jones by Imp. Shark (Marske)—Dau. of Thornton's Wildair (Symme's Wildair).
					Lady Grey.	Robin Gray—Maria by Melzar—Dau. of Highflyer—Dau. of Fearnought—Dau. of Ariel—Dau. of Jack of Diamonds.
	CAROLIN.	Orlando.	Touch-stone.		Camel.	Whalebone—Dau. of Selim—Maiden by Sir Peter—Dau. of Phoenomenon Matron by Florizel—Maiden by Matchem—Dau. of Squirt.
					Banter.	Master Henry—Boadicea by Alexander—Brunette by Amaranthus—Mayfly by Matchem—Dau. of An. Starling—Dau. of Grasshopper (Crab).
			Vulture.		Langar.	Selim—Dau. of Walton—Y. Giantess by Diomed—Giantess by Matchem—Molly Longlegs by Babraham—Dau. of Cole's Foxhunter.
					Kite.	Bustard (Castrel)—Olympia by Sir Oliver—Scotilla by Anvil—Scota by Eclipse—Harmony by Herod—Rutilia by Blank.
		Scythian.	Hetman Platoff.		Brutandorf.	Blacklock—Mandane by Pot-8-os—Y. Camilla by Woodpecker—Camilla by Trentham—Coquette by Comp. Barb—Sis. to Regulus.
					Daughter of.	Comus—Marciana by Stamford—Marcia by Coriander—Faith by Pacolet—Atalanta by Matchem—Lass of the Mill by Oroonoko.
			Scythia. Princess.		Slane.	Royal Oak—Dau. of Orville—Epsom Lass by Sir Peter—Alexina by King Fergus—Lardella by Y. Marske—Dau. of Cade—Beaufremont's dam.
					Sis. to Cobweb.	Phantom—Filagree by Soothsayer—Web by Waxy—Penelope by Trumpator—Prunella by Highflyer—Promise by Snap—Julia.
		Yorkshire.	St. Nicholas.		Emilius.	Orville—Emily by Stamford—Dau. of Whiskey—Gr. Dorimant by Dormant—Dizzy by Blank—Dizzy by Driver—Dau. of Smiling Tom.
					Sea-Mew.	Scud—Goosander by Hambletonian—Rally by Trumpator—Fancy, Sis. to Diomed by Florizel—Dau. of Spectator—Horatia.
			Miss Rose.		Tramp.	Dick Andrews—Dau. of Gohanna—Fraxinella by Trentham—Dau. of Woodpecker—Everlasting by Eclipse—Hyaena by Snap.
					Daughter of.	Sancho—Blacklock's dam by Coriander—Wildgoose by Highflyer—Coheiress by Pot-8-os—Manilla by Goldfinder—Dau. of Old England.
		Picayune.	Medoc.		Am. Eclipse.	Duroc—Millers Damsel by Messenger—Dau. of Pot-8-os—Dau. of Gimcrack—Snap-Dragon by Snap—Dau. of Regulus—Dau. of B. Childers.
					Y. Maid of the Oaks.	Expedition—Maid of the Oaks by Spread Eagle—Annette by Imp. Shark—Dau. of Rockingham—Dau. of Gallant—Dau. of True Whig.
		Rosette.	Sally Howe.		Tiger.	Cook's Whip—Jane Hunt by Hampton's Paragon—Moll by Imp. Figure—Slamerkin by Wildair—Imp. Cub Mare by Cub—Amaranthus' dam.
					Lady Robin.	Robin Gray (Royalist)—Dau. of Quicksilver (Imp. Medley)—Dau. of Meade's Celer (Janus by Janus, Son of Go. Arabian).

VIATOR,

(WINNER OF THE SEQUEL STAKES AT SARATOGA, WESTCHESTER CUP AT JEROME PARK, AND PHILADELPHIA CUP AT PHILADELPHIA, PA.),

Will stand at the Cloverbrook Stud. Property of Mr. Usher Clabaugh, near Middleburg, Md., at $25 the season, dams of winners free.

VIATOR by Vauxhall. son of Lexington, bred by E. A. Clabaugh, foaled 1872, dam Heatherbelle by imp. Balrownie, son of Annandale, out of L'Anglaise by Hobbie Noble. Viator made his appearance as a three-year old, started eight times and won two races. Saratoga, won the Sequel Stakes for three-year olds, 2 miles, in 3:43¼, beating Gen. Harvey, Vagabond, and Paul Pry ; won the Three-year old Stakes, 1¼ miles, in 2:48¼. Baltimore, was second in the Preakness Stakes, 1½ miles, won by Tom Ochiltree in 2:43½ ; was second in the Dixie Stakes for three-year olds, 2 miles, won by Tom Ochiltree in 3:42¼ ; was second in the Breckenbridge Stakes for three-year olds, 2 miles, won by Aristides in 3:36¼. At Monmouth Park was third in the Jersey Derby for three-year olds, 1½ miles, won by Calvin in 2:43½ ; was unplaced in his other races. As a four-year old started in eight races, of which he won four. Baltimore, won a race of 2 mile heats in 3:41, 3:43, beating Joe Cerns and three others. Jerome Park, won the Westchester Cup, 2¼ miles, in 4:10¼, beating St. Martin, Joe Cerns and Lelaps. Point Breeze Park, Pa., won the Philadelphia Club Cup, 2¼ miles, in 4:37¼, beating Chesapeake, Shirley, and Madge. Saratoga, won a dash of 2 miles in 3:37, beating Preston and Brother to Bassett (Charley Howard). Saratoga, was second in a dash of 4 miles won by St. Martin in 7:44¾, only two starters. Baltimore, was third in the Baltimore Cup, 2¼ miles, won by Tom Ochiltree in 4:09. and was unplaced in his other races. Viator is a highly bred horse, his sire, Vauxhall, was one of Lexington's best sons, and traces back to an own sister of Muley Molock. Viator has the Diomed and Orville blood on the side of his sire, and the blood of Old Queen Mary, coup'ed with that of Whalebone through Touchstone and Sir Hercules, with the Herod and Eclipse through reputable sources. Viator is a bright chestnut, 16 hands high, with star in his forehead and one hind foot white. He measures 74 inches around the girth, and is finely and well developed.

PEDIGREE OF VIATOR.

VIATOR						
VAUXHALL	Lexington	Boston	Sir Archy	Sir Archy.	Diomed—Castianira by Rockingbam—Tabitha by Trentham—Dau. of Bosphorus—Dau. of Wm's Forester—Dau. of Coalition Colt.
				Daughter of.	Saltram—Dau. of Symme's Wildair—Dau. of Driver (Imp. Othello)—Dau. of Fallower (Blank)—Dau. of Vampire.
			Sister to Tuckahoe.	Ball's Florizel.	Diomed—Dau. of Imp. Shark—Dau. of Harris' Eclipse—Dau. of Fearnought—Dau. of Jolly Roger—Dau. of Sober John—Dau. of Shock.
				Daughter of.	Alderman—Dau. of Clockfast—Dau. of Symme's Wildair—Y. Kitty Fisher by Fearnought—Imp. Kitty Fisher by Cade.
		Alice Carneal.	Sarpedon.	Emilius.	Orville—Emily by Stamford—Dau. of Whiskey—Gr. Dorimant by Dorimant—Dizzy by Blank—Dizzy by Driver—Dau. of Smiling Tom.
				Icaria.	The Flyer—Parma by Dick Andrews—May by Beningbrough—Primrose by Mambrino—Cricket by Herod—Sophia by Blank—Diana.
			Rowena.	Sumpter.	Sir Archy—Flirtilla's dam by Robin Redbreast—Dau. of Obscurity—Slamerkin by Wildair—Imp. Cub Mare by Cub—Amaranthus' dam.
				Lady Grey.	Robin Gray—Maria by Melzar—Dau. of Highflyer—Dau. of Fearnought—Dau. of Ariel—Dau. of Jack of Diamonds—Imp. Diamond.
	Verona.	Yorkshire.	St. Nicholas.	Emilius.	Orville—Emily by Stamford—Dau. of Whiskey—Gr. Dorimant by Dorimant—Dizzy by Blank—Dizzy by Driver—Dau. of Smiling Tom.
				Sea-Mew.	Scud—Goosander by Hambletonian—Rally by Trumpator—Fancy, Sis. to Diomed by Florizel—Dau. of Spectator—Horatia by Blank.
			Miss Rose.	Tramp.	Dick Andrews—Dau. of Gohanna—Fraxinella by Trentham—Dau. of Woodpecker—Everlasting by Eclipse—Hyaena by Snap—Miss Belsea.
				Daughter of.	Sancho—Blacklock's dam by Coriander—Wildgoose by Highflyer—Coheiress by Pot-8-os—Manilla by Goldfinder—Dau. of Old Eng.
		Britannia.	Muley.	Orville.	Beningbrough—Evelina by Highflyer—Termagant by Tantrum—Cantatrice by Sampson—Dau. of Regulus—Marske's dam by Blacklegs.
				Eleanor.	Whiskey—Y. Giantess by Diomed—Giantess by Matchem—Molly Longlegs by Babraham—Dau. of Cole's Foxhunter—Dau. of Partner.
			Nancy.	Dick Andrews.	Joe Andrews (Eclipse)—Dau. of Highflyer—Dau. of Car. Puff—Dau. of Tatler—Dau. of Snip—Dau. of Go. Arabian—Dau. of Framp. Whiteneck.
				Spitfire.	Beningbrough—Dau. of Y. Sir Peter (Doge)—Dau. of Engineer—Dau. of Wil. Arabian—Dau. of Hut. Spot—Dau. of Mogul.
HEATHERBELLE	L'Anglaise.	Hobbie Noble.	Annandale.	Touchstone.	Camel.	Whalebone—Dau. of Selim—Maiden by Sir Peter—Dau. of Phoenomenon Matron by Florizel—Maiden by Matchem—Dau. of Squirt.
					Banter.	Master Henry—Boadicea by Alexander—Brunette by Amaranthus—Mayfly by Matchem—Dau. of An. Starling—Dau. of Grasshopper (Crab).
			Balrownie.	Lottery.	Tramp—Mandane by Pot-8-os—Y. Camilla by Woodpecker—Camilla by Trentham—Coquette by Comp. Barb—Sis. to Regulus by Go. Arabian.
				Daughter of.	Cervantes—Anticipation by Beningbrough—Expectation by Herod—Dau. of Skim—Dau. of Janus (Godol.)—Spinster by Crab.
		Peri.	Phyrne.	Partisan.	Walton—Parasol by Pot-8-os—Prunella by Highflyer—Promise by Snap—Julia by Blank—Spectator's dam by Partner—Bonny Lass.
				Pauline.	Moses—Quadrille by Selim—Canary Bird by Whiskey or Sorcerer—Canary by Coriander—Miss Green by Highflyer—Harriet by Matchem.
	Queen Mary.	Irish Birdcatcher.	Pantaloon.	Plenipotentiary.	Emilius—Harriet by Pericles—Dau. of Selim—Pipylina by Sir Peter—Rally by Trumpator—Fancy, Sis. to Diomed by Florizel—Dau. of Spectator.
				Myrrha.	Whalebone—Gift by Y. Gohanna—Sis. to Grazier by Sir Peter—Sis. to Amaitor by Trumpator—Dau. of Herod—Dau. of Snap.
			Dau. of Gladiator.	Castrel.	Buzzard—Selim's dam by Alexander—Dau. of Highflyer—Dau. of Alfred—Dau. of Engineer—Bay Malton's dam by Cade—Lass of the Mill.
				Idalia.	Peruvian—Musidora by Meteor—Maid of All Work by Highflyer—Sis. to Tandem by Syphon—Dau. of Regulus—Dau. of Snip.
	Perdita.		Rebecca.	Touchstone.	Camel—Banter by Master Henry—Boadicea by Alexander—Brunette by Amaranthus—Mayfly by Matchem—Dau. of An. Starling.
				Decoy.	Filho-da-Puta—Finesse by Peruvian—Violante by John Bull—Dau. of Highflyer—Everlasting by Eclipse—Hyaena by Snap.
				Sir Hercules.	Whalebone—Peri by Wanderer—Thalestris by Alexander—Rival by Sir Peter—Hornet by Drone—Manilla by Goldfinder.
				Guicciolli.	Bob Booty—Flight by I. Escape—Y. Heroine by Bagot—Heroine by Hero—Dau. of Snap—Sis. to Regulus by Godol. Arabian—Gr. Robinson.
				Langar.	Selim—Dau. of Walton—Y. Giantess by Diomed—Giantess by Matchem—Molly Longlegs by Babraham—Dau. of Cole's Foxhunter.
				Delenda.	Gohanna (Mercury)—Carthage, Sis. to Hannibal by Driver (Trentham)—Fractious by Mercury (Eclipse)—Dau. of Woodpecker (Herod)—Everlasting by Eclipse (Marske)—Hyaena by Snap (Snip)—Miss Belsea by Regulus (Godol.)—Dau. of Bartlet's Childers (Dar. Arabian)—Dau. of Honeywood's Arabian—Byerly Mare dam of the Two True Blues.

VIRGIL,

(WINNER OF THE SEQUEL STAKES, TWO MILES, AT PATERSON, N. J., IN 1867,)

Will stand the season of 1883 at the Elmendorf Stud, Fayette County, Ky., at the season. Application to D. Swigert, Muir's P. O. Ky. Annual sales of yearlings in May.

VIRGIL by Vandal, son of Glencoe, bred by Hymen C. Gratz, Woodford County, Kentucky, was foaled spring of 1864, dam Hymenia, dam of Ansel, Mollie Wood, etc., by imp. Yorkshire, son of St. Nicholas by Emilius. Virgil was a good race-horse, he won at Paterson, N. J., in 1867, mile heats, in 1:51½, 1:51, beating Dot, Mittie and Metarie, track heavy; Jerome Park, won mile heats, in 1:48, 1:50½, 1:49, beating Morrissey, No. 3, and others; at Saratoga, won three-quarters of a mile in 1:18¼, beating Annie Workman, Luther and others; was second to Ruthless in Sequel Stakes, 2 miles, in 3:37½; at Paterson Fall Meeting, won mile dash, beating the noted James A. Connolly, Redwing, etc., in 1:48¼; same place, won Sequel Stakes, 2 miles, in 3:48¾, beating Morrissey. After the death of Mr. R. A. Alexander, in 1867, he passed into the hands of Mr. Swigert, and ran a few races; was then sold and put at work over timber. In 1871, won 1½ miles, over six hurdles, in 2:48¾, and two mile heats, over eight hurdles, in 4:08, 3:58; ran a dead heat in one with Blind Tom; was second in two others, and third in one; in 1872, ran second in one race. Vandal, the sire of Virgil, was the best son of Glencoe, not only as a race-horse, but as a sire; his turf career was short but brilliant; he won three mile heats, in 5:36, 5:33. Imp. Yorkshire, the sire of his dam, was a very successful stallion, being the sire of Zampa, Magic, Modonna, Princeton, Wagram, Waterloo, Lodi and a host of others. Virgil's first foals came out in 1875; as two-year olds, he had only nine living; Vagrant won nearly all the two-year old stakes at Lexington and Louisville, and the following year, won the Phœnix Hotel Stake at Lexington, 1¼ miles, in 1:56¾; the Kentucky Derby at Louisville, 1½ miles, in 2:38¼, beating Creedmore, Parole and others; he also won the Grand Exposition Stakes at Philadelphia, 1½ miles, in 2:42¼. Vigil, another son, in 1876, then three years old, won the Summer Handicap at Saratoga, 1¼ miles, in 3:07¼; the Grand National Handicap at Jerome Park, 2½ miles, in 4:11; won Dixie Stakes at Baltimore, 2 miles, in 3:41½, beating Parole, Heretog and Algerine, track heavy, and taking up a penalty of five pounds; won the Breckenridge Stakes, 2 miles, in 3:37½, beating Parole and Virginius, he also won other good races. Vera Cruz, another of the same year, was a first-class horse, won the Sweepstakes for all-ages at Saratoga, 1877, 1¼ miles, defeating Ochiltree and Parole; won the Breckenridge Stake at Baltimore same year, 2 miles, in 3:40¼, and the Kentucky St. Leger, 2 miles, at Louisville, in 3:35; other good ones by him are Virginius, Virgilian, Vermont, Fairplay, Blossom, Santa Anita, Valparaiso, Pride, Virginia, Valleria, Vinita, Frank McLaughling, Vici, Joe Rodes, Mamore, Vanguard, Uberto, Carley B, a winner of the Travers Stakes, 1882; the Relief Stakes, and a mile and a furlong in 1:55. Anglia, Clarence, Cliquot, Mistral, Mamie O, Harry Hill, a real good horse, Nana, Little Katie, Kite, and last, though not least, Hindoo, the best horse which has appeared in this country for more than twenty years, for his brilliant performances. I must refer you to his card in this book. Virgil is a dark brown, standing full 16 hands, with a bright star in his forehead. He has quite a neat head and ear; fine, good neck; well placed, oblique shoulders; good depth of girth; well-shaped body, ribbed home to broad, strong hips, with good sweep in his quarters. He was roughly used toward the end of his racing career, and, in consequence, his legs show the effects of his knocks over the timber. He is yet vigorous and in fine health, and was at the head of the list of winning sires in 1881, and bids fair to earn greater laurels as a sire. He has crosses of Diomed and American Eclipse, and is very much inbred to the famous English Eclipse on both sides, and to the Godolphin Barb.

PEDIGREE OF VIRGIL.

						Ancestor	Details
VIRGIL.	VANDAL.	Imp. Glencoe.	Imp. Trampoline.	Sultan.	Bacchante.		
					Web.	Tramp.	
						Buzzard.	Woodpecker—Misfortune by Dux—Curiosity by Snap—Dau. of Regulus—Dau. of Bart. Childers—Dau. of Hon. Arabian—Dau. of True Blues.
						Castrel's dam.	Alexander—Dau. of Highflyer—Dau. of Alfred—Dau. of Engineer—Bay Malton's dam by Cade—Lass of the Mill by Traveler—Miss Makeless.
					Selim.	Williamson's Ditto.	Sir Peter—Arethusa by Dungannon—Dau. of Prophet—Virago by Snap—Dau. of Regulus—Sis. to Othello by Crab—Miss Slamerkin.
						Sis. to Calomel.	Mercury—Dau. of Herod—Folly by Marske—Vixen by Regulus—Dau. of Hutton's Spot—Dau. of Bay Bolton—Dau. of Fox Cub.
						Dick Andrews.	Joe Andrews—Dau. of Highflyer—Dau. of Cardinal Puff—Dau. of Tatler—Dau. of Snip—Dau. of Godol. Arabian—Dau of Frampton's Whiteneck.
						Daughter of.	Gohanna—Fraxinella by Trentham—Dau. of Woodpecker—Everlasting by Eclipse—Hyaena by Snap—Miss Belsea by Regulus.
						Waxy.	Pot-8-os—Maria by Herod—Lisette by Snap—Miss Windsor by Godol. Arabian—Sis. to Volunteer by Y. Belgrade—Dau. of Bart. Childers.
						Penelope.	Trumpator—Prunella by Highflyer—Promise by Snap—Julia by Blank—Spectator's dam by Partner—Bonny Lass by Bay Bolton.
		Alaric's dam.	Imp. Tranby.	Black-lock.		Whitelock.	Hambletonian—Rosalind by Phoenomenon—Atalanta by Matchem—Lass of the Mill by Oroonoko—Dau. of Traveler—Miss Makeless.
						Daughter of.	Coriander—Wildgoose by Highflyer—Coheiress by Pot-8-os—Manilla by Goldfinder—Dau. of Old Eng.—Dau. of Cullen Arabian—Miss Cade.
				Dau. of		Orville.	Beningbrough—Evelina by Highflyer—Termagant by Tantrum—Cantatrice by Sampson—Dau. of Regulus—Marsk's dam by Blacklegs.
						Miss Grimstone.	Weasel—Dau. of Ancaster—Dau. of Dam Arabian—Dau. of Sampson—Dau. of Oroonoko—Sis. to Mirza by Godol. Arabian.
		Lucilla.	Trump-ator.			Sir Solomon.	Tickle Toby (Alfred)—Vesta by Dreadnought (Celer)—Bandy by Clockfast—Dau. of Americus (Imp. Shark)—Dau. of Imp. Fearnought (Regulus).
						Daughter of.	Hickory (Imp. Whip)—Imp. Trumpetta by Trumpator—Sis. to Lambinos by Highflyer—Dau. of Eclipse—Vauxhall, Snap's dam by Cade.
			Lucy.			Orphan.	Ball's Florizel (Diomed)—Fair Rachel by Diomed—Susan Jones by Imp. Shark (Marske)—Dau. of Thornton's Wildair (Symme's Wildair).
						Lady Grey.	Robin Grey—Maria by Melzar—Dau. of Highflyer—Dau. of Fearnought—Dau. of Ariel—Dau. of Jack of Diamonds—Imp. Diamond.
	HYMENIA.	Imp. Yorkshire.	Miss Rose.	St. Nicholas.	Tramp.	Orville.	Beningbrough—Evelina by Highflyer—Termagant by Tantrum—Cantatrice by Sampson—Dau. of Regulus—Marske's dam by Blacklegs.
						Emily.	Stamford—Dau. of Whiskey—Gr. Dorimant by Dorimant—Dizzy by Blank—Dizzy by Driver—Dau. of Smiling Tom—Dau. of Oysterfoot.
					Seamew.	Scud.	Beningbrough—Eliza by Highflyer—Augusta by Eclipse—Hardwick's dam by Herod—Dau. of Bajazet—Dau. of Regulus.
						Goosander.	Hambletouian—Rally by Trumpator—Fancy, Sis. to Diomed by Florizel—Dau. of Spectator—Horatia by Blank—Dau. of F. Childers.
				Emilius.	Dau. of	Dick Andrews.	Joe Andrews (Eclipse)—Dau. of Highflyer—Dau. of Cardinal Puff—Dau. of Tatler—Dau. of Snip—Dau. of Godol. Arabian.
						Daughter of.	Gohanna—Fraxinella by Trentham— Dau. of Woodpecker— Everlasting by Eclipse—Hyaena by Snap—Miss Belsea by Regulus.
			Cripple.	Medoc.		Sancho.	Don Quixote—Dau. of Highflyer—Sis. to Tandem by Syphon—Dau. of Regulus—Dau. of Snip—Dau. of Cottingham—Warlock Galloway.
						Blacklock's dam	Coriander—Wildgoose by Highflyer—Coheiress by Pot-8-os—Manilla by Goldfinder—Dau. of Old Eng.—Dau. of Cul. Arabian—Miss Cade.
				Y. Maid of the Oaks.		Am. Eclipse.	Duroc—Millers Damsel by Messenger—Dau. of Pot-8-os—Dau. of Gimcrack—Snap-Dragon by Snap—Dau. of Regulus.
						Expedition—Maid of the Oaks by Spread Eagle—Annette by Imp. Shark—Dau. of Rockingham—Dau. of Gallant—Dau. of True Whig.
		Little Peggy.	Cook's Princess.	Grecian		Cook's Whip.*	Imp. Whip (Saltram)—Speckleback by Randolph's Celer (Meade's Celer dam by Sloe)—Speckleback by Meade's Celer—Dau. of Sober John.
						Jane Hunt.	Hampton's Paragon (Flimnap)—Moll by Imp. Figure—Slamerkin by Imp. Wildair—Imp. Cub Mare by Cub—Amaranthus' dam by Second.
			Mary Bedford.	Cook's Whip.		Imp. Whip.	Saltram—Dau. of Herod (Tartar)—Dau. of Oroonoko (Crab)—Creampot's dam by Cartouche—(Bald Galloway)—Seabright Arabian Mare.
						Speckleback.	Randolph's Celer (Meade's Celer dam by Sloe)—D. Speckleback by Meade's Celer (Janus by Janus by Godol.)—Dau. of Sober John (Rib).
		Peggy Stewart.				Duke of Bedford	Imp. Bedford (Dungannon)—Dau. of Voltaire by Imp. Janus by Godol.)—Nancy Washington by Imp. Master Stephen (Son of Regulus.)
						Daughter of.	Imp. Speculator (Dragon)—Dau. of Dare Devil (Magnet)—Imp. Trumpetta by Trumpator (Conductor)—Sis. to Lambinos by Highflyer (Herod)—Dau. of Eclipse (Marske)—Vauxhall, Snap's dam by Cade (Godol.)—Dau. of Bolton Littlejohn (Partoer)—Durham's Favorite by Son of the Bald Galloway—Daffodil's dam by Sir T. Gascoigne's Foreign Horse.

*Same as Blackburn's Whip.

VIRGILIAN

Will stand the season of* 1883, *at the Bolingbrooke Stud, near Middleburg, Md., at* $25 *for the season. Application to R. W. Walden, Middleburg, Md.

VIRGILIAN, by Virgil, son of Vandal, bred by Mr. M. H. Sanford, foaled, 1874, dam La Henderson, dam of Ferida, by Lexington, out of Kitty Clark, dam of Maiden by Glencoe. Virgilian, at three years old, started eight times. Galveston, Texas, was second in the Gulf City Stakes for three-year-olds, 1½ miles, won by Ella Rowett, in 2:42½. Houston, Texas, was second in a race of mile heats, won by Belle Barclay, in 1:46¾, 1:46½, 1:51. Virgilian won the first heat. Won race of mile heats in 1:52, 1:53. Austin, Texas, was second in a race of mile heats, won by Ella Rowett, in 1:51½, 1:54. Was second in a dash of 1¼ miles, won by Ella Rowett, in 2.13½. Was second in a race of mile heats for beaten horses, won by Belle Barkley, in 1:45, 1:44½, 1:48½., Virgilian won the first heat. Galveston, Texas, was second in a dash of 1¼ miles, won by Ella Rowett, in 2.13½ ; was second in a race of mile heats, won by Ella Rowett in 1:51½, 1:54. At (4) started three times. At New Orleans, was third in a dash of 1⅛ miles, won by Conrad in 1:56½. Cincinnati, was unplaced in a race of mile heats, won Tolono in 1:47½, 1:47½. Won a dash of one mile in 1:44½. Was second in a race of mile heats, three in five, won by Shortline in 1:47¾, 1:46, 1:47. At (5) started in 33 races. At Savannah, Ga., was second in a dash of one mile and a furlong, won by Egypt in 1:59½; unplaced in a dash of one mile, won by Essillah, in 1:47. Charleston, was third in a race of mile heats won by Essillah in 1:45¾, 1:47. New Orleans, was second in mile heats, three in five, won by Verdigris in 1:57¾, 1:58¾, 2:05¼, track muddy ; was second in a dash of 1¼ miles, won by Kingsland, in 2:17 ; won handicap mile heats in 1:46, 1:46½, 1:48½. Blue Gown won the first heat. Won a dash of one mile in 1:46¼. Louisville, Ky., was unplaced in a race of mile heats, won by King Faro, in 1:44, 1:42¼, 1:45 ; was second in a selling race, one mile and a furlong, won by Egypt in 1:57¼; was third in a selling race, one mile and a furlong, won by Egypt in 1:56¾ ; was third in a dash of one mile, won by Bill Bass in 1:44½. Cincinnati, Ohio, was unplaced in a dash of one mile, won by Claudia in 2:17½; won race of mile heats, three in five, in 1:45½, 1:45¼, 1:46¼. Chicago, was second in a dash of 1¼ miles, won by Mintzer in 2:16½ ; unplaced in a race of mile heats, three in five, won by Janet in 1:48¾, 1:46, 1:54¾, 1:59. Detroit, Mich., won race of mile heats in 1:45¾, 1:44½; was second in a mile dash, won by Glenmore, in 1:42¾. Sheepshead Bay, was third in a race of heats of three-quarters of a mile, won by Janet Murray, in 1:19, 1:19½; was second in a dash of 1¼ miles, won by Shylock in 2:18 ; won race of heats of three-quarters of a mile, in 1:22½, 1:23 ; was second in a race of mile heats, won by Baton Rouge in 1:46½, 1:46¾ ; won a race of three-quarters of a mile heats, in 1:20½, 1:21½, 1:23¼. Monmouth Park, unplaced in a dash of 1¼ miles, won by Invermoor, in 2:15; was second in a dash of one mile and a furlong, gentlemen riders, won by Erastus Corning (aged), with 145 lbs., in 2:18¼. Virgilian carried 160 lbs.; Was second in a Handicap sweepstakes, 1¼ miles, won by Checkmate in 2:13¾ Prospect Park, was third in a Handicap sweepstakes heats of one mile and a furlong, won by Glenmore in 1:58¾, 2:00, 2:02¾, Chiquita won the first heat and Virgilian was ruled out in the third; was unplaced in a race of mile heats, won by Edwin A, in 1:45, 1:44¾, 1:47 ; was unplaced in a dash of one mile, won by Egypt in 1:45 ; was unplaced in a race of mile heats, won by Mollie McGinley, in 1:44, 1:45, 1:46¼, 1:49¼, 1:51, Virgilian won the first heat; was unplaced in a race of mile heats, won by Warfield in 1:44½, 1:45. Baltimore, was unplaced in a dash of 1¼ miles, won by Juanita, in 2:19½. Washington, D. C., was second in a dash of one mile and a furlong, won by Serge in 2:05 ; was third in a dash of 2 miles, over eight hurdles, won by Lizzie D in 3:57. Virgilian is descended from a racing family ; he is by Virgil, sire of the great Hindoo, and his dam is dam of Ferida, and his grandam the grandam of the popular favorite, Parole. Many other distinguished race-horses have descended from the family. In addition to a double cross of Glencoe, he is much inbred to Sir Archy and Diomed, and traces through the imported Cub Mare to the Layton Barb. Mare. Virgilian is a blood b y with black points, stands full 15¾ hands high, with great substance and power and an excellent temper.

PEDIGREE OF VIRGILIAN.

VIRGILIAN.							
Kitty Clark.	LA HENDERSON.	Glencoe.	Sultan.	Tramp-oline.	Vandal.	VIRGIL.	Selim.	Buzzard—Dau. of Alexander—Dau. of Highflyer—Dau. of Alfred—Dau. of Engineer—Bay Malton's dam by Cade—Lass of the Mill.
							Bacchante.	Williamson's Ditto—Sis. to Calomel by Mercury—Dau. of Herod—Folly by Marske—Vixen by Regulus—Dau. of Hutton's Spot—Dau. of B. Bolton.
			Imp. Glencoe.		Alaric's dam.	Tramp.	Dick Andrews — Dau. of Gohanna—Fraxinella by Trentham—Dau. of Woodpecker—Everlasting by Eclipse—Hyaena by Snap—Miss Belsea.
						Web.	Waxy — Penelope by Trumpator — Prunella by Highflyer —Promise by Snap—Julia by Blank—Spectator's dam by Partner—Bonny Lass.
					Luella.	Blacklock.	Whitelock—Dau. of Coriander—Wildgoose by Highflyer—Coheiress by Pot-8-os—Manilla by Goldfinder—Dau. of Old Eng.—Dau. of Cul. Arab'n.
					Tranby.	Daughter of.	Orville—Miss Grimstone by Weasel—Dau. of Ancaster—Dau. of Dam Arabian—Dau. of Sampson—Dau. of Oroonoko.
						Trumpator.	Sir Solomon—Dau. of Hickory—Imp. Trumpetta by Trumpator—Sis. to Lambinos by Highflyer—Dau. of Eclipse.
						Lucy.	Orpban—Lady Grey by Robin Grey—Maria by Melzar—Dau. of Highflyer —Dau. of Fearnought—Dau. of Ariel—Dau. of Jack of Diamonds.
				Hymenia.	Yorkshire.	Emilius.	Orville—Emily by Stamford—Dau. of Whiskey—Gr. Dorimant by Dorimant—Dizzy by Blank—Dizzy by Driver—Dau. of Smiling Tom.
					St. Nicholas.	Sea-Mew.	Scud—Gousander by Hambletonian—Rally by Trumpator—Fancy, Sis. to Diomed by Florizel—Dau. of Spectator—Horatia by Blank.
					Miss Rose.	Tramp.	Dick Andrews— Dau. of Gohanna—Fraxinella by Trentham — Dau. of Woodpecker—Everlasting by Eclipse—Hyaena by Snap—Miss Belsea.
						Daughter of.	Sancho—Blacklock's dam by Coriander—Wildgoose by Highflyer—Coheiress by Pot-8-os—Manilla by Goldfinder—Dau. of Old Eng.
				Little Peggy.	Cripple.	Medoc.	Am. Eclipse—Y. Maid of the Oaks by Expedition—Maid of the Oaks by Spread Eagle—Annette by Imp. Shark—Dau. of Rockingham.
						Grecian Princess	Cook's Whip—Jane Hunt by Hampton's Paragon—Moll by Figure—Slamerkin by Imp. Wildair—Imp. Cub Mare by Cub—Amaranthus' dam.
					Peggy Stewart.	Cook's Whip.*	Imp. Whip—Speeklebaek by Randolph's Celer (Meade's Celer dam by Sloe)—Speckleback by Meade's Celer (Janus)—Dau. of Sober John.
						Mary Bedford.	Duke of Bedford — Dau. of Speculator (Dragon) —Dau. of Dare Devil (Magnet)—Imp. Trumpetta by Trumpator.
		Lexington.	Boston.	Sister of Tuckahoe.	Timoleon.	Sir Archy.	Diomed—Castianira by Rockingham—Tabitha by Trentham—Dau. of Bosphorus—Dau. of Wm.'s Forester—Dau. of Coalition Colt.
						Daughter of.	Saltram—Dau. of Symme's Wildair—Dau. of Driver (Imp. Othello)—Dau. of Fallower (Blank)—Dau. of Vampire (Regulus).
						Ball's Florizel.	Diomed—Dau. of Imp. Shark—Dau. of Harris' Eclipse—Dau. of Fearnought—Dau. of Jolly Roger—Dau. of Sober John—Dau. of Shock (Jigg).
						Daughter of.	Alderman—Dau. of Clockfast—Dau. of Symme's Wildair—Y. Kitty Fisher by Fearnought—Imp. Kitty Fisher by Cade—Dau. of Som. Arabian.
			Alice Carneal.	Sarpedon.	Rowena.	Emilius.	Orville—Emily by Stamford—Dau. of Whiskey—Gr. Dorimant by Dorimant—Dizzy by Blank—Dizzy by Driver—Dau. of Smiling Tom.
						Icaria.	The Flyer—Parma by Dick Andrews—May by Beningbrough—Primrose by Mambrino—Cricket by Herod—Sophia by Blank.
						Sumpter.	Sir Archy—Flirtilla's dam by Robin Redbreast—Dau. of Obscurity—Slamerkin by Wildair—Imp. Cub Mare by Cub—Amaranthus's dam.
						Lady Grey.	Robin Grey—Maria by Melzar—Dau. of Highflyer—Dau. of Fearnought—Dau. of Ariel—Dau. of Jack of Diamonds—Imp. Diamond.
	Miss Obstinate.	Glencoe.	Sultan.	Tramp-oline.		Selim.	Buzzard—Castrel's dam by Alexander—Dau. of Highflyer—Dau. of Alfred —Dau. of Engineer—Bay Malton's dam by Cade—Lass of the Mill.
						Bacchante.	Williamson's Ditto—Sis. to Calomel by Mercury—Dau. of Herod — Folly by Marske—Vixen by Regulus—Dau. of Hutton's Spot.
						Tramp.	Dick Andrews—Dau. of Gohanna— Fraxinella by Trentham—Dau. of Woodpecker—Everlasting by Eclipse—Hyaena by Snap.
						Web.	Waxy—Penelope by Trumpator—Prunella by Highflyer—Promise by Snap —Julia by Blank—Spectators's dam by Partner.
	Jenny Slamerkin.	Sump-ter.				Sir Archy.	Diomed—Castianira by Rockingham—Tabitha by Trentham—Dau. of Bosphorus—Dau. of Wm.'s Forester—Dau. of Coalition Colt.
						Flirtilla's dam.	Robin Redbreast—Dau. of Obscurity—Slamerkin by Wildair—Imp. Cub Mare by Cub—Amaranthus' dam by Second—Dau. of Starling.
						Tiger.	Cook's Whip—Jane Hunt by Hampton's Paragon—Moll by Figure—Slamerkin by Wildair—Cub Mare by Cub—Amaranthus' dam.
						Paragon.	Imp. Buzzard—Indiana by Columbus (Imp. Pantaloon)—Jane Hunt by Paragon (Imp. Flimnap—Moll by Imp. Figure (Grey Figure)—Slamerkin by Imp. Wildair (Cade)—Cub Mare by Cub (Fox)—Amaranthus' dam by Second (F. Childers)—Leede's dam by Starling (Bay Bolton)—Sis. to Vane's Partner by Partner (Jigg)—Sis. to Guy by Greyhound (White Barb Chillaby)—Brown's Farewell by Makeless (Oglethorpe Arabian)—Dau. of Brimmer—Dau. of Place's White Turk—Dau. of Dodsworth—Layton Barb Mare.

* Same as Blackburn's.

VOLTURNO,

(WINNER OF THE PLANTERS' HOUSE STAKE AT ST. LOUIS, 1878; UNITED STATES HOTEL STAKE AT SARATOGA; BRECKENRIDGE STAKE AT BALTIMORE, 1879, AND LOUISVILLE CUP IN 1880,)

Will stand the season of 1883 *at the Stud Farm of his owner, Mr. Samuel Powers, near Decatur, Ill., by private contract.*

VOLTURNO by imp. Billet, son of Voltigeur, bred by Samuel Powers, Decatur, Ill., foaled 1876, dam Sprightly own sister to Nevada, dam of Luke Blackburn, Salina and Crucifix by Lexington out of Lightsome by imp. Glencoe. Volturno at two years old started in five events; won four, and ran third in one. St. Louis, Mo., June 5, won Planters' House Stakes, three-quarters of a mile, in 1:18, defeating Goodnight, Athelstane and two others. Same meeting, June 8, ran third in the Lucas and Hunt Stakes, one mile, won by Lah-tu nah, in 1:45¼, Goodnight second; four others were behind him, including La Favorita, who, as well as Volturno, carried 5 lbs. penalty. Saratoga, Aug. 21, won 5-furlong dash in 1:04¾, defeating Boardman, good second, and three others. Saratoga, Aug. 28, won three-quarters of a mile handicap, for all ages, in 1:17, beating Alleveur, Janet Murray, Franklin, Fusillade, and St. James. Boston, Mass., Sept. 6; won Revere House Stakes, one mile, defeating Scotilla (late Jessie Donaldson) easily in 1:54¼. Three years old started ten times; won six races, was second in two, third in one and unplaced in one. Volturno, who gave unmistakable evidence of great promise in his two-year-old form, unfortunately went amiss early in the season, and had to forego his Spring engagements. His first appearance in 1879 was at Saratoga, July 25; ran second to Franklin in dash of one mile; time, 1:46½; Enterprise and Bennett also ran. Same place, July 30, finished third in a field of ten to Dan Sparling and Jennie B, one mile; time, 1:44¾. Same place, Aug. 5, won the United States Hotel Stakes, 1½ miles, defeating Harold, Bulwark, Rochester and Audax; time, 2:41½. Same place, Aug. 15, won handicap sweepstakes, 1¼ miles, defeating Gov. Hampton and Mary Ann; time, 2:10¾. Monmouth Park, N. J., Aug. 23, finished fourth in the Champion Stakes, 1½ miles, won by Spendthrift; Report second, Bramble third, Harold fifth, Bonnie Oaks last; time, 2:41½. Same place, Aug. 30, won the Atlantic Handicap, 1½ miles, defeating Bonnie Carrie, Monitor, Dan Sparling, Claudia and Farley; time, 2:43. Brighton Beach, N. Y., Sept. 10, won handicap, 1¾ miles, defeating Enterprise, Gov. Hampton, Peter Hynes, The Nipper, Lizzie D, and Le Roi; time, 3:08½. Same place, Sept. 25, won the Sequel Handicap, 1¾ miles, defeating Gen. Philips and Lady Middleton; time, 3:08½. Jerome Park, Oct. 9, ran unplaced in Handicap Sweepstakes, 1¾ miles, won by Lou Lanier; time, 3:10; ten started. Ended a brief and brilliant season by winning the Breckenridge Stakes, at Baltimore, Oct. 25, distance 2 miles, defeating Harold, Aureolus and Monitor; time, 3:35½; Monitor carried 112 lbs., which included 5 lbs. penalty for winning the Dixie Stakes; the rest, 110 lbs. each. Four years old started six times, won four races and was unplaced in two. Lexington, May 14, won Club Purse, 2 miles and a furlong, in 3:51, beating Jils Johnson and two others. Louisville, May 18, won Club Purse, 1¼ miles, in 2:12¾, beating One Dime and Bucktie. May 21, won Louisville Cup, 2¼ miles, in 4:20½, beating Blue Eyes, Cammie F., Himyar and two others; track very muddy. St. Louis, June 10, beat Turin for Club Purse, 2½ miles, in 5:01½; he afterwards complained in his near fore leg and has not run since. If high breeding and racing lineage is worth anything in breeding race-horses, Volturno should make his mark. His dam Sprightly, is own sister of Nevada, dam of Luke Blackburn, Crucifix, dam of Fairplay and Quito and Salina a famous race-mare. Volturno is a blood bay, highly finished, of great substance and power, with the best of temper. He was a fine feeder and was both a speedy and a game horse. He should succeed in the stud.

PEDIGREE OF VOLTURNO.

VOLTURNO.	IMP. BILLET.	Voltigeur.	Martha Lynn.	Mulatto. Dau. of Blacklock.	Whitelock. Daughter of.	Hambletonian—Rosalind by Phœnomenon—Atalanta by Matchem—Lass of the Mill by Oroonoko—Dau. of Old Traveler. Coriander—Wildgoose by Highflyer—Coheiress by Pot-8-os—Manilla by Goldfinder—Dau. of Old Eng.—Dau. of Cul. Arabian.
					Phantom. Daughter of.	Walton—Julia by Whiskey—Y. Giantess by Diomed—Giantess by Matchem —Molly Longlegs by Babraham—Dau. of C. Foxhunter. Overton—Gratitude's dam by Walnut—Dau. of Ruler—Piracantha by Matchem—Dau. of Regulus—Jenny Spinner.
			Leda.		Catton. Desdemona.	Golumpus—Lucy Grey by Timothy—Lucy by Florizel—Frenzy by Eclipse —Dau. of Engineer—Dau. of Blank—Lass of the Mill by Old Traveler. Orville—Fanny by Sir Peter—Dau. of Diomed—Desdemona by Marske—Y. Hag by Skim—Hag by Crab—Ebony by F. Childers—Ebony by Basto.
					Filho-da-Puta. Treasure.	Haphazard—Mrs. Barnet by Waxy—Dau. of Woodpecker—Heinel by Squirrel—Principessa by Blank—Dau. of Cul. Arabian—Lady Thigh. Camillus—Dau. of Hyacinthus—Flora by King Fergus—Atalanta by Matchem—Lass of the Mill by Oroonoko—Dau. of Old Traveler.
		Calcutta.	Flatcatcher.	Touchstone.	Camel. Banter.	Whalebone—Dau. of Selim—Maiden by Sir Peter—Dau. of Phœnomenon —Matron by Florizel—Maiden by Matchem—Dau. of Squirt. Master Henry—Boadicea by Alexander—Brunette by Amaranthus—Mayfly by Matchem—Dau. of An. Starling—Dau. of Grasshopper.
				Decoy.	Filho-da-Puta. Finesse.	Haphazard—Mrs. Barnet by Waxy—Dau. of Woodpecker—Heinel by by Squirrel—Principessa by Blank—Dau. of Cul. Arabian. Peruvian—Violante by John Bull—Dau. of Highflyer—Everlasting by Eclipse —Hyæna by Snap—Miss Belsea by Regulus—Dau. of Bart. Childers.
			Miss Martin.	St. Martin.	Actæon. Galena.	Scud—Diana by Stamford—Dau. of Whiskey—Gr. Dorimant by Dorimant —Dizzy by Blank—Dizzy by Driver—Dau. of Smiling Tom. Walton—Comedy by Comus—Dau. of Star—Dau. of Y. Marske—Emma by Telemachus—A-la-Grecque by Regulus—Dau. of Allworthy.
				Wagtail.	Whisker. Daughter of.	Waxy—Penelope by Trumpator—Prunella by Highflyer—Promise by Snap —Julia by Blank—Spectator's dam by Partner. Sorcerer—Dau. of Sir Solomon—Dau. of Y. Marske—Dau. of Phœnomenon —Calliope by Slouch—Lass of the Mill by Oroonoko.
	SPRIGHTLY.	Lexington.	Boston.	Timoleon.	Sir Archy. Daughter of.	Diomed—Castianira by Rockingham—Tabitha by Trentham—Dau. of Bosphorus—Dau. of William's Forrester—Dau. of Coalition Colt. Saltram—Dau. of Symme's Wildair—Dau. of Driver (Imp Othello)—Dau. of Fallower (Blank)—Dau. of Vampire (Regulus).
				Sister to Tuckahoe.	Ball's Florizel. Daughter of.	Diomed—Dau. of Imp Shark—Dau. of Harris' Eclipse—Dau. of Fearnought—Dau. of Jolly Roger—Dau. of Sober John—Dau. of Shock. Alderman—Dau. of Clockfast—Dau. of Symme's Wildair—Y. Kitty Fisher by Fearnought—Imp. Kitty Fisher by Cade (Godol).
		Alice Carneal.	Sarpedon.		Emilius. Icaria.	Orville—Emily by Stamford—Dau. of Whiskey—Gr. Dorimant by Dorimant —Dizzy by Blank—Dizzy by Driver—Dau. of Smiling Tom. The Flyer—Parma by Dick Andrews—May by Beningbrough—Primrose by Mambrino—Cricket by Herod—Sophia by Blank—Diana.
			Rowena.		Sumpter. Lady Grey.	Sir Archy—Flirtilla's dam by Robin Redbreast—Dau. of Obscurity—Slamerkin by Wildair—Imp. Cub Mare by Cub—Amaranthus' dam. Robin Grey—Maria by Melzar—Dau. of Highflyer—Dau. of Fearnought— Dau. of Ariel—Dau. of Jack of Diamonds—Imp. Diamond by Cul. Arabian.
		Glencoe.	Sultan.		Selim. Bacchante.	Buzzard—Castrel's dam by Alexander—Dau. of Highflyer—Dau. of Alfred —Dau. of Engineer—Bay Malton's dam by Cade. Williamson's Ditto—Sis. to Calomel by Mercury—Dau. of Herod—Folly by Marske—Vixen by Regulus—Dau. of Hut's Spot—Dau. of Bay Bolton.
			Trampoline.		Tramp. Web.	Dick Andrews—Dau. of Gohanna—Fraxinella by Trentham—Dau. of Woodpecker—Everlasting by Eclipse—Hyænea by Snap—Miss Belsea. Waxy—Penelope by Trumpator—Prunella by Highflyer—Promise by Snap —Julia by Blank—Spectator's dam by Partner—Bonny Lass.
		Trustee.			Catton. Emma.	Golumpus—Lucy Grey by Timothy—Lucy by Florizel—Frenzy by Eclipse —Dau. of Engineer—Dau. of Blank—Lass of the Mill by Old Traveler. Whisker—Gibside Fairy by Hermes—Vicissitude by Pipator—Beatrice by Sir Peter—Pyrrha by Matchem—Duchess by Whitenose—Miss Slamerkin.
	Lightsome. Levity. Vandal's Dam.				Tranby. Lucilla.	Blacklock—Dau. of Orville—Miss Grimstone by Weasel—Dau. of Ancaster —Dau. of Dam Arabian—Dau. of Sampson—Dau. of Oroonoko. Trumpator (Sir Solomon)—Lucy by Orphan (Ball's Florizel)—Lady Grey by Robin Grey (Royalist)—Maria by Melzar—Dau. of Highflyer—Dau. of Fearnought—Dau. of Ariel—Dau. of Jack of Diamonds—Imp.Diamond by Cullen Arabian—Lady Thigh by Croft's Partner—Dau. of Greyhound —Dau. of Curwen Bay Barb—Dau. of D'Arcy Ch. Arabian—Dau. of Whiteshirt—Old Montague Mare.

WANDERER,

(WINNER OF THE RAILROAD STAKES AT NASHVILLE, 1872; THE MONMOUTH CUP AT LONG BRANCH, AND WESTCHESTER CUP AT JEROME PARK, 1873.)

Will stand the season of 1883 *at the farm of Mr. T. J. Nichols, Bourbon Co., Ky., at* $100 *the season. Application to Thos. J. Nichols, Paris, Ky.*

WANDERER by Lexington, son of Boston, bred in the Woodburn Stud, Ky., foaled 1868, dam Coral, dam of Uncas by Vandal, son of Glencoe out of imp. Cairngorme by Cotherstone, winner of the 2,000 guineas and Derby, son of Touchstone, winner of the St. Leger.

Wanderer is descended from one of the most noted racing families of England, tracing back through an own sister to imp. Glencoe to the famous Web by Waxy. The family has furnished some of the most noted race-horses and successful sires of the English turf. From it came Whalebone, winner of the Derby in 1810; Whisker, winner of the same event in 1815; Cobweb, winner of the Oaks and 1,000 guineas in 1824; Riddlesworth, winner of the 2,000 guineas and Derby in 1836; Glencoe, winner of the 2,000 guineas in 1831; Bay Middleton, winner of the 2,000 guineas and Goodwood Cup in 1834; Blue Gown, winner of the Derby in 1868; Silvio, winner of both Derby and St. Leger in 1877, and a host of others.

Wanderer made his first appearance as a three-year-old and was unplaced in the Belmont Stakes at Jerome Park, and the Jersey Derby at Long Branch, both events having been won by his half brother, Harry Bassett. At Long Branch he won a club purse, mile heats, in 1:48¾, 1:48¼, defeating a field of seven. In his four-year-old form, at New Orleans, he won a race of mile heats in 1:51, 1:47½, 1:47½, beating Frank Ross, winner of the first heat; Niagara and Glenrose; won the Railroad Stakes at Nashville, Tenn., two-mile heats, in 3:41¼, 3:38½, beating Hollywood, Frogtown, etc., and walked over for club purse, two-mile heats. As a five-year-old he won the Monmouth Cup at Long Branch, 2½ miles, in 4:31½, beating Preakness, Hubbard and others; won the Westchester Cup at Jerome Park, 2¼ miles, in 4:04, beating True Blue, Eolus and others. At Saratoga ran second to Hubbard, 3 miles in 5:34, beating Harry Bassett and King Henry. Same meeting, ran second to Arizona, 1½ miles, in 2:38, beating Boss Tweed and Eolus. As a six-year-old won club purse at Savannah, Ga., 2 miles, in 3:43½, beating Granger and four others, and also same meeting, a club purse, 1¼ miles, in 2:18¾, beating Ortolan and Tabitha. Nashville, Tenn., won the Johnson Stakes, 2¼ miles, in 4:06½, beating Planchette, St. George, and two others. At Jerome Park ran second to Shylock, son of Lexington, in the Westchester Cup, 2¼ miles, in 4:13, beating Lizzie Lucas, Abd-el-Koree and two others, track heavy. Saratoga, won club purse, 2¼ miles, in 4:00½, beating Fellowcraft, Jack Frost, Galway and Katie Pease. Same place, ran second to Fellowcraft, 4 miles, in 7:19½, the fastest race at the distance ever run up to that date. In this race Wanderer beat Katie Pease and was timed the distance in 7:20.

Wanderer has been quite a success in the stud, having only a few mares he sired One Dime a winner 1⅛ miles in 1:55½, 1¼ miles in 2:09¾, mile heats in 1:44½, 1:44½. Elkhorn Stakes 1⅝ miles in 3:05¾. Minnie C. (Mrs. Chubbs), winner of the filly stakes at Lexington. Juanita 1¼ miles in 2:10. Lizzie S filly stakes at Lexington half-mile in 0:49. Coquette Stakes at St. Louis, three-quarters of a mile in 1:18½; five furlongs in 1:02; three-quarters of a mile in 1:16½; one mile in 1:43. Mary Lamphier, Farragut, Nomad, Wakefield, Cash Clay, Waterford, Prophet, Rambler, Wandering winner one mile in 1:45¼, and Capital Stakes one mile in 1:44¾, and others all winners. His colts are the best the dams have produced. He is a rich golden chestnut, with the marks of his sire; is handsomely shaped and of very blood like appearance, muscular and highly finished. His sire was the best race-horse and stallion this country has produced; his dam is by the best son of imp. Glencoe and traces through an own sister to Glencoe and Web by Waxy to a natural Barb Mare. This is one of the pure sources through which the blood of Lexington and Glencoe should be preserved.

PEDIGREE OF WANDERER.

WANDERER.		**LEXINGTON.**	Boston.	Robin Brown's dam.	Daughter of Ball's Florizel.	Timoleon.	Sir Archy. Daughter of.	Diomed.	Florizel—Sis. to Juno by Spectator—Horatia by Blank—Dau. of F. Childers—Miss Belvoir by Gr. Grantham.
								Castianira.	Rockingham—Tabitha by Trentham—Dau. of Bosphorus—Dau. of Wm's Forester—Dau. of Coalition Colt—Dau. of Bustard.
								Imp. Saltram.	Eclipse—Virago by Snap—Dau. of Regulus—Sis. to Othello by Crab—Miss Slamerkin by Y. True Blue—Dau. of Ox. Dun. Arabian.
								Daughter of.	Symme's Wildair (Fearnought)—Dau. of Driver (Imp. Othello)—Dau. of Fallower (Blank)—Dau. of Vampire (Regulus).
								Diomed.	Florizel—Sis. to Juno by Spectator—Horatia by Blank—Dau. of F. Childers—Miss Belvoir by Gr. Grantham—Dau. of Paget Turk.
								Daughter of.	Imp. Shark—Dau. of Harris' Eclipse—Dau. of Fearnought—Dau. of Jolly Roger—Dau. of Sober John—Dau. of Shock (Old Shock).
								Imp. Alderman.	Pot-8-os—Lady Bolingbroke by Squirrel—Cypron, Herod's dam by Blaze—Selima by Beth. Arabian—Dau. of Graham's Champion.
								Daughter of.	Clockfast—Dau. of Symme's Wildair—Y. Kitty Fisher by Fearnought—Imp. Kitty Fisher by Cade—Dau. of Som. Arabian.
		Alice Carneal.		Sarpedon.	Emilius.			Orville.	Beningbrough—Evelina by Highflyer—Termagant by Tantrum—Cantatrice by Sampson—Dau. of Regulus—Marske's dam.
								Emily.	Stamford—Dau. of Whiskey—Gr. Dorimant by Dorimant—Dizzy by Blank—Dizzy by Driver—Dau. of Smiling Tom—Dau. of Oysterfoot.
			Rowena.		Icaria.			The Flyer.	Vandyke, Jr.—Azalia by Beningbrough—Gillyflower by Highflyer—Dau. of Goldfinder—Sis. to Grasshopper by Marske—Dau. of Cul. Arabian.
								Parma.	Dick Andrews—May by Beningbrough—Primrose by Mambrino—Cricket by Herod—Sophia by Blank—Diana by Second—Dau. of Stan. Arabian.
					Sumpter.	Lady Grey.		Sir Archy.	Diomed—Castianira by Rockingham—Tabitha by Trentham—Dau. of Bosphorus—Dau. of Wm's Forester—Dau. of Coalition Colt (Godol.)
								Flirtilla's dam.	Robin Redbreast—Dau. of Obscurity—Slamerkin by Wildair—Imp. Cub Mare by Cub—Amaranthus' dam by Second—Dau. of Starling.
								Robin Grey.	Royalist—Belle Mariah by Grey Diomed—Queen by Imp. St. George—Dau. of Cassius—Primrose by Imp. Dove—Stella by Othello.
								Maria.	Melzar—Dau. of Highflyer—Dau. of Fearnought—Dau. of Ariel—Dau. of Jack of Diamonds—Imp. Diamond by Cullen Arabian.
	CORAL.	Vandal.	Alaric's dam.	Glencoe.	Tranby.	Trampoline.	Sultan.	Selim.	Buzzard—Castrel's dam by Alexander—Dau. of Highflyer—Dau. of Alfred—Dau. of Engineer—Bay Malton's dam by Cade.
								Bacchante.	Williamson's Ditto—Sis. to Calomel by Mercury—Dau. of Herod—Folly by Marske—Vixen by Regulus—Dau. of Hut. Spot.
								Tramp.	Dick Andrews—Dau. of Gohanna—Fraxinella by Trentham—Dau. of Woodpecker—Everlasting by Eclipse—Hyaena by Snap).
								Web.	Waxy—Penelope by Trumpator—Prunella by Highflyer—Promise by Snap—Julia by Blank—Spectator's dam by Partner.
								Blacklock.	Whitelock—Dau. of Coriander—Wildgoose by Highflyer—Coheiress by Pot-8-os—Manilla by Goldfinder—Dau. of Old Eng. (Godol.)
								Daughter of.	Orville—Miss Grimstone by Weasel—Dau. of Arcaste—Dau. of Dam Arabian—Dau. of Sampson—Dau. of Oroonoko—Sis. to Mirza.
					Lucilla.			Trumpator.	Sir Solomon—Dau. of Hickory—Imp. Trumpetta by Trumpator—Sis. to Lambinos by Highflyer—Dau. of Eclipse—Vauxhall, Snap's dam.
								Lucy.	Orphan—Lady Grey by Robin Grey—Maria by Melzar—Dau. of Highflyer—Dau. of Fearnought—Dau. of Ariel—Dau. of Jack of Diamond.
		Cotherstone.		Touchstone.				Camel.	Whalebone—Dau. of Selim—Maiden by Sir Peter—Dau. of Phoenomenon—Matron by Florizel—Maiden by Matchem—Dau. of Squirt—Lot's dam.
								Banter.	Master Henry—Boadicea by Alexander—Bruette by Amaranthus—Mayfly by Matchem—Dau. of An. Starling—Dau. of Grasshopper (Crab).
			Emma.					Whisker.	Waxy—Penelope by Trumpator—Prunella by Highflyer—Promise by Snap—Julia by Blank—Spectator's dam by Partner—Bonny Lass.
								Gibside Fairy.	Hermes—Vicissitude by Pipator—Beatrice by Sir Peter—Pyrrha by Matchem—Duchess by Whitenose—Miss Slamerkin by Y. True Blue.
		Cairngorm.	Slane.					Royal Oak.	Catton—Dau. of Smolenski—Lady Mary by Beningbrough—Dau. of Highflyer—Dau. of Marske—A-la-Grecque by Regulus—Dau. of Allworthy.
								Daughter of.	Orville—Epsom Lass by Sir Peter—Alexina by King Fergus—Lardella by Y. Marsk—Dau. of Cade—Beaufremont's dam by Bro. to Fearnought.
		Glenluce.	Glencairne.					Sultan.	Selim—Bacchante by Williamson's Ditto—Sis. to Calomel by Mercury—Dau. of Herod—Folly by Marske—Vixen by Regulus—Dau. of Spot.
								Trampoline.	Tramp—Web by Waxy—Penelope by Trumpator (Conductor)—Prunella by Highflyer (Herod)—Promise by Snap (Snip)—Julia by Blank (Godol.)—Spectator's dam by Partner (Jigg)—Bonny Lass by Bay Bolton (Grey Hautboy)—Dau. of Darley Arabian—Dau. of Byerly Turk—Dau. of Taffolet Barb—Dau. of Place's White Turk—Natural Barb Mare.

WHISPER,

(WINNER OF NASHVILLE CUP, LOUISVILLE CUP AT LOUISVILLE, KY., AND OTHER GOOD RACES.)

Will stan the season of 1883 at the Fleetwood Stud, near Frankfort, Franklin Co., Ky., at $50 the season. Application to Agent, Fleetwood Stud, Frankfort, Ky.

WHISPER by Planet, son of Revenue, bred in the Woodburn Stud, Ky., foaled 1870, dam Mattie Gross, dam of Mate, Grenada, etc., by Lexington, out of Dick Doty's dam, by Am. Eclipse. Whisper did not run as a two-year old. At three years old was unplaced in the Phoenix Hotel Stakes, 1¼ miles won by Artist, in 2:12½. Monmouth Park, unplaced in the Jersey Derby, 1½ miles, won by Tom Bowling, in 2:45¾; was second in the Jersey Jockey Club Purse, mile heats, best three in five, won by Arizona, in 1:46, 1:48¾, 1:47¾, 1:53½, 1:55, Whisper won the first two heats; was third in the Cottagers Cup, 1½ miles, won by imp. Stonehenge, in 2:44½; unplaced in a Consolation Purse, 1⅛ miles, won by Shylock in 2:44½. Saratoga, unplaced in the Kenner Stakes, 2 miles, won by imp. Ill-Used, in 3:39. At (4) Jerome Park, walked over for purse of $700, 1¾ miles. Monmouth Park, was second in the Monmouth Cup, 2½ miles, won by Tom Bowling in 4:42½; was second in a dash of 4 miles, won by Fellowcraft, in 7:43. Jerome Park, was unplaced in a dash of 1⅛ miles, won by Grinstead, in 2:40¾; was third in a dash of 2½ miles, won by Acrobat, in 4:33¾. Baltimore, distanced first heat of the Bowie Stakes, 4 mile heats, won by Jack Frost in 7:33, 7:41, 8:11; Bessie Lee won the first heat. At (5) Louisville, Ky., unplaced in a dash of one mile and a furlong, won by Calvin, in 1:56½; unplaced in Louisville Club Stakes, 2¼ miles, won by Ballinkeel, in 4:01½; won a handicap, mile heats, in 1:52¾, 1:53¾. At (6) Louisville, Ky, was third in a dash of 1¼ miles, won by Brakesman in 2:11; was third in a dash of 2 miles and a furlong won by Elemi in 3:49½; was second in a race of mile heats, won by Kilburn in 1:45¾; 144¼, 148¼; Whisper won the first heat. Lexington, Ky., Fall Meeting, was third in a dash of 1½ miles, won by Phillis, in 2:37¼; won a selling race, one mile and a furlong in 1:58. Louisville, Ky., won a handicap sweepstakes, 1⅝ miles, in 3:09 Nashville, Tennessee, won dash of 1½ miles for all ages in 2:44½. At (7) Nashville, Tenn., won the Nashville Cup, 2¼ miles, in 4:08; was second in a dash of 1⅜ miles, won by McWhirter, in 2:38½. Louisville, Ky., won a dash of 2 miles, in 3:36¾; won the Louisville Cup, 2¼ miles, in 3:59¼. Saratoga, won handicap for all ages, 1¾ miles, in 3:12¾; was third in a dash of one mile and a furlong, won by Vera Cruz, in 1:57½; won a dash of 2¼ miles in 4:02. Louisville Fall Meeting unplaced in a handicap, 1⅝ miles, won by Longbow, in 3:07¾; Whisper was third in a dash of 2 miles, won by Ten Broeck, in 3:36. At (8) Louisville, Ky., was second in the Louisville Cup, 2¼ miles, won by Mahlstick, in 4:07½; won a handicap dash of 4 miles in 7:36. St. Louis, Mo., won the Blow Stakes, 3 mile heats, in 5:39, 5;35½. Whisper is by the best son of Revenue, Planet, a winner at all distances over the best horses of his day. Whisper's dam, Mattie Gross, is the dam of Mate and Granada, and his grandam was the dam of Dick Doty, the famous four miler, whilst his great grandam was the dam of Eliza Jenkins and the Big Archy Mare, which produced the great race-horse Creath, who beat Alice Carneal and won a second heat of 3 miles, in 5:43, in 1841. Whisper is a bay, full 16 hands high, with a star and right hind leg white above the hoof. He is one of the finest and best shaped horses in America and could not only run fast but stay a distance. In addition to being a grandson of imp. Trustee, he is much inbred to Sir Archy and Diomed, having ten crosses of that most desirable blood. He has also a double cross of Whisker. His colts, now coming two years old, are very promising.

PEDIGREE OF WHISPER.

WHISPER							
PLANET.	Revenue.	Rosalie Somers.	Trustee.	Golumpus.	Gohanna—Catharine by Woodpecker—Camilla by Trentham—Coquette by Comp. Barb—Sis. to Regulus by Godol. Arabian—Gr. Robinson.
				Lucy Grey.	Timothy—Lucy by Florizel—Frenzy by Eclipse—Dau. of Engineer—Dau. of Blank—Lass of the Mill by Traveler—Miss Makeless.
			Emma Catton.	Whisker,	Waxy—Penelope by Trumpator—Pruuella by Highflyer—Promise by Snap—Julia by Blank—Spectator's dam by Partner—Bonny Lass.
				Gibside Fairy.	Hermes—Vicissitude by Pipator—Beatrice by Sir Peter—Pyrrha by Matchem—Duchess by Whitenose—Miss Slamerkin by Y. True Blue.
		Sir Mischief.	Charles.	Sir Archy.	Diomed—Castianira by Rockingham—Tabitha by Trentham—Dau. of Bosphorus—Dau. of Wm.'s Forester—Dau. of Coalition Colt.
				Daughter of.	Imp. Citizen—Dau. of Commutation—Dau. of Dare Devil—Sally Shark by Imp. Shark—Betsey Pringle by Fearnought—Imp. Jenny Dismal.
				Virginian.	Sir Archy—Meretrix by Magog—Narcissa by Imp. Shark—Rosetta by Imp. Centinel—Diana by Clodius—Sally Painter by Imp. Sterling.
				Daughter of.	Imp. Bedford—Dau. of Bellair—Dau. of Imp. Shark—Dau. of Symme's Wildair—Dau. of Lexington (Wildair)—Dau. of Spanking Roger.
	Nina.	Boston.	Timoleon.	Sir Archy.	Diomed—Castianira by Rockingham—Tabitha by Trentham—Dau. of Bosphorus—Dau. of Wm.'s Forester—Dau. of Coalition Colt.
				Daughter of.	Saltram—Dau. of Symme's Wildair—Dau. of Driver (Imp. Othello)—Dau. of Fallower (Blank)—Dau. of Vampire.
			Sis. to Tuckahoe.	Ball's Florizel.	Diomed—Dau. of Shark—Dau. of Harris' Eclipse—Dau. of Fearnought—Dau. of Jolly Roger—Dau. of Sober John—Dau. of Shock.
				Daughter of.	Alderman—Dau. of Clockfast—Dau. of Symme's Wildair—Y. Kitty Fisher by Fearnought—Imp. Kitty Fisher by Cade.
		Frolicksome Fanny.	Lottery.	Tramp.	Dick Andrews—Dau. of Gohanna—Fraxinella by Trentham—Dau. of Woodpecker—Everlasting by Eclipse—Hyaena by Snap.
				Mandane.	Pot-8-os—Y. Camilla by Woodpecker—Camilla by Trentham—Coquette by Comp. Barb—Sis. to Regulus by Godol. Arabian—Gr. Robinson.
			Sis. to Catterick.	Whisker.	Waxy—Penelope by Trumpator—Prunella by Highflyer—Promise by Snap—Julia by Blank—Spectator's dam by Partner.
				Daughter of.	Bay Trophonius—Dau. of Slope—Lardella by Y. Marske—Dau. of Cade—Beaufremont's dam by Bro. to Fearnought.
	MATTIE GROSS.	Lexington.	Boston.	Sir Archy.	Diomed—Castianira by Rockingham—Tabitha by Trentham—Dau. of Bosphorus—Dau. of Wm.'s Forester—Dau. of Coalition Colt.
			Timoleon.	Daughter of.	Saltram—Dau. of Symme's Wildair—Dau. of Driver (Imp. Othello)—Dau. of Fallower (Blank)—Dau. of Vampire (Regulus).
			Sis. to Tuckahoe.	Ball's Florizel.	Diomed—Dau. of Imp. Shark—Dau. of Harris' Eclipse—Dau. of Fearnought—Dau. of Jolly Roger—Dau. of Sober John—Dau. of Shock.
				Daughter of.	Alderman—Dau. of Clockfast—Dau. of Symme's Wildair—Y. Kitty Fisher by Fearnought—Imp. Kitty Fisher by Cade (Godol.)
		Alice Carneal.	Sarpedon.	Emilius.	Orville—Emily by Stamford—Dau. of Whiskey—Gr. Dorimant by Dorimant—Dizzy by Blank—Dizzy by Driver—Dau. of Smiling Tom.
				Icaria.	The Flyer—Parma by Dick Andrews—May by Beningbrough—Primrose by Mambrino—Cricket by Herod—Sophia by Blank.
			Rowena.	Sumpter.	Sir Archy—Flirtilla's dam by Robin Redbreast—Dau. of Obscurity—Slamerkin by Wildair—Imp. Cub Mare by Cub—Amaranthus' dam.
				Lady Grey.	Robin Grey—Maria by Melzar—Dau. of Highflyer—Dau. of Fearnought—Dau. of Ariel—Dau. of Jack of Diamonds.
Dick-Doty's dam.	Am. Eclipse.	Miller's Damsel.	Duroc.	Diomed.	Florizel—Sis. to Juno by Spectator—Horatia by Blank—Dau. of F. Childers—Miss Belvoir by Gr. Grantham—Dau. of Paget Turk.
				Amanda.	Grey Diomed—Cade—Dau. of Hick's Independence—Dolly Fine by Silvereye—Dau. of Badger—Dau. of Forester.
				Messenger.	Mambrino—Dau. of Turf—Sis. to Figurante by Regulus—Dau. of Starling Snap's dam by Fox—Gipsy by Bay Bolton.
				Daughter of.	Pot-8-os—Dau. of Gimcrack—Snap-Dragon by Snap—Dau. of Regulus—Dau. of Bart. Childers—Dau. of Honeywood Arabian.
Nell.	Dau. of Orphan.			Ball's Florizel.	Diomed—Dau. of Imp. Shark—Dau. of Harris' Eclipse—Dau. of Fearnought—Dau. of Jolly Roger—Dau. of Sober John—Dau. of Shock.
				Fair Rachel.	Diomed—Susan Jones by Imp. Shark (Marske)—Dau. of Thornton's Wildair, Son of Symme's Wildair by Fearnought.
				Imp. Buzzard.	Woodpecker—Misfortune by Dux—Curiosity by Snap—Dau. of Regulus—Dau. of Bart. Childers—Dau. of Hon. Arabian—Dam of True Blues.
				Daughter.	Silvertail (Imp. Fearnought by Regulus)—Dau. of Imp. Dove, Son of Y. Cade by Cade by Godolphin Arabian.

WILFUL,

(WINNER OF THE JOCKEY CLUB HANDICAP AT JEROME PARK, SEASIDE HANDICAP AT PROSPECT PARK, AND HANDICAP SWEEPSTAKES AT MONMOUTH PARK IN 1879),

Will stand the season of 1883 at the Bullfield Stud, near Hanover Junction, Va., at $25 the season. Application to Major Thomas W. Doswell, Hanover Junction, Va.

WILFUL by imp. Australian, son of West Australian, bred by John Hunter, N. Y., foaled 1876, dam, imp. Pussy, dam of Bangweola, and Lelaps by Diophantus out of Agapemone by Bay Middleton, son of Sultan. Wilful ran unplaced in Champagne Stake at Jerome Park when two years old, As a three-year old started eleven times ; won three races, was second in four, third in one, and unplaced in three. Jerome Park, June 7, made in his maiden effort in the Jockey Club Handicap, 2 miles, defeating his stable companion, Lou Lanier, who finished second, Gen. Philips, Bonnie Wood, Warfield, and Bertha ; time, 3:42¾. Prospect Park, L. I., Inauguration Meeting, Coney Island Jockey Club, June 24, won the Seaside Handicap, 2 miles, defeating Gen. Philips. Gov. Hampton and Bramble ; time, 3:34¾ ; this was one of the best contested races of the year. Same meeting, June 26, ran second to Kenney in the Brighton Hotel Purse, 1¼ miles ; time, 3:07½ ; Gov. Hampton and Gen. Philips also ran. Monmouth Park, July 5, won handicap sweepstakes, 1½ miles, defeating Kenney, Pilot, Lou Lanier and Belle ; time, 2:41. Same place, July 8, ran second to Spendthrift in the Jersey Derby, 1½ miles ; time, 2:53. Same place, July 10, finished second in the Shrewsbury Handicap, 1¾ miles, won by his stable companion, Lou Lanier; time, 3:11¾ ; Warfield, Terror and Zoo-Zoo also ran. Saratoga, July 24, ran second to Bramble in the Saratoga Cup, 2¼ miles, Lou Lanier third, Belle and Denicheff unplaced ; time, 4:11¾ ; this closed his racing career. Wilful is a very finely bred horse, having a double cross of Touchstone and is much inbred to Waxy through his best sons, Whisker and Whalebone, and to Godolphin Arabian through Regulus and Matchem. Lelaps, his half-brother, has done well in the stud, and Wilful should succeed. He is a dark chestnut without white, except a small star in his forehead, is 16 hands high, and highly finished all over. His colts, from what we hear, are very promising and fine.

PEDIGREE OF WILFUL.

WILFUL.								
IMP. AUSTRALIAN.	West Australia.	Melbourne.	Mowerina.	Touchstone.	Dau. Humphrey of Clinker.	Emma.	Comus. Clinkerina.	Sorcerer—Houghton Lass by Sir Peter—Alexina by King Fergus—Lardella by Y. Marske—Dau. of Cade—Beaufremont's dam. Clinker—Pewet by Tandem—Termagant by Tantrum—Cantatrice by Sampson—Dau. of Regulus—Marske's dam by Blacklegs.
							Cervantes. Daughter of.	Don Quixote—Evelina by Highflyer—Termagant by Tantrum—Cantatrice by Sampson—Dau. of Regulus—Marske's dam by Blacklegs. Golumpus—Dau. of Paynator—Sis. to Zodiac by St. George—Abigail by Woodpecker—Firetail by Eclipse—Dau. of Blank—Dau. of Cade.
							Camel. Banter.	Whalebone—Dau. of Selim—Maiden by Sir Peter—Dau. of Phoenomenon—Matron by Florizel—Maiden by Matchem—Dau. of Squirt. Master Henry—Boadicea by Alexander—Brunette by Amaranthus—Mayfly by Matchem—Dau. of An. Starling—Dau. of Grasshopper (Crab).
			Emilia.	Young Emilius.	Whisker. Shoveler.	Emilius.	Whisker. Gibside Fairy.	Waxy—Penelope by Trumpator—Prunella by Highflyer—Promise by Snap—Julia by Blank—Spectator's dam by Partner. Hermes—Vicissitude by Pipator—Beatrice by Sir Peter—Pyrrha by Matchem—Duchess by Whitenose—Miss Slamerkin by Y. True Blue.
							Orville. Emily.	Beningbrough—Evelina by Highflyer—Termagant by Tantrum—Cantatrice by Sampson—Dau. of Regulus—Marske's dam by Blacklegs. Stamford—Dau. of Whiskey—Gr. Dorimant by Dorimant—Dizzy by Blank—Dizzy by Driver—Dau. of Smiling Tom—Dau. of Oysterfoot.
							Scud. Goosander.	Beningbrough—Eliza by Highflyer—Augusta by Eclipse—Hardwick's dam by Herod—Dau. of Bajazet—Dau. of Regulus. Hambletonian—Rally by Trumpator—Fancy, sis. to Diomed by Florizel—Sis. to Juno by Spectator—Horatia by Blank (Godol.)
				Persian.	Variety.		Waxy. Penelope.	Pot-8-os—Maria by Herod—Lisette by Snap—Miss Windsor by Godol. Arabian—Sis. to Volunteer by Y. Belgrade—Dau. of Bart. Childers. Trumpator—Prunella by Highflyer—Promise by Snap—Julia by Blank—Spectator's dam by Partner—Bonny Lass by Bay Bolton.
							Selim or *Soothsayer. Sprite.	Sorcerer—Goldenlocks by Delpini—Violet by Shark—Dau. of Syphon—Quick's Charlotte by Blank—Dau. of Crab—Dau. of Dyer's Dimple. Bobtail—Catharine by Woodpecker—Camilla by Trentham—Coquette by Compton Barb—Sis. to Regulus by Godol. Arabian—Gr. Robinson.
		IMP. PUSSY.	Agapemone.	Diophantus.	Orlando.	Touchstone.	Camel. Banter.	Whalebone—Dau. of Selim—Maiden by Sir Peter—Dau. of Phoenomenon—Matron by Florizel—Maiden by Matchem—Dau. of Squirt. Master Henry—Boadicea by Alexander—Brunette by Amaranthus—Mayfly by Matchem—Dau. of An. Starling—Dau. of Grasshopper.
						Vulture.	Langar. Kite.	Selim—Dau. of Walton—Y. Giantess by Diomed—Giantess by Matchem—Molly Longlegs by Babraham—Dau. of Cole's Foxhunter. Bustard (Castrel)—Olympia by Sir Oliver—Scotilla by Anvil—Scota by Eclipse—Harmony by Herod—Rutilia by Blank.
				Equation.	Emilius.		Orville. Emily.	Beningbrough—Evelina by Highflyer—Termagant by Tantrum—Cantatrice by Sampson—Dau. of Regulus—Marske's dam by Blacklegs. Stamford—Dau. of Whiskey—Gr. Dorimant by Dorimant—Dizzy by Blank—Dizzy by Driver—Dau. of Smiling Tom—Dau. of Oysterfoot.
					Maria.		Whisker. Gibside Fairy.	Waxy—Penelope by Trumpator—Prunella by Highflyer—Promise by Snap—Julia by Blank—Spectator's dam by Partner. Hermes—Vicissitude by Pipator—Beatrice by Sir Peter—Pyrrha by Matchem—Duchess by Whitenose—Miss Slamerkin by Y. True Blue.
			Venus.	Bay Middleton.	Sultan.	Cobweb.	Selim. Bacchante.	Buzzard—Castrel's dam by Alexander—Dau. of Highflyer—Dau. of Alfred—Dau. of Engineer—Bay Malton's dam by Cade—Lass of the Mill. Williamson's Ditto—Sis. to Calomel by Mercury—Dau. of Herod—Folly by Marske—Vixen by Regulus—Dau. of Hutton's Spot.
							Phantom. Filagree.	Walton—Julia by Whiskey—Y. Giantess by Diomed—Giantess by Matchem—Molly Longlegs by Babraham—Dau. of Cole's Foxhunter. Soothsayer—Web by Waxy—Penelope by Trumpator—Prunella by Highflyer—Promise by Snap—Julia by Blank—Spectator's dam.
			Echo.	Sir Hercules.			Whalebone. Peri.	Waxy—Penelope by Trumpator—Prunella by Highflyer—Promise by Snap—Julia by Blank—Spectator's dam by Partner. Wanderer—Thalestris by Alexander—Rival by Sir Peter—Hornet by Drone—Manilla by Goldfinder—Dau. of Old Eng.—Dau. of Cul. Arabian.
							Emilius. Daughter of.	Orville—Emily by Stamford—Dau. of Whiskey—Gr. Dorimant by Dorimant—Dizzy by Blank—Dizzy by Driver—Dau. of Smiling Tom. Scud or Pioneer—Canary Bird by Whiskey or Sorcerer—Canary by Coriander (Pot-8-os)—Miss Green by Highflyer—Harriet by Matchem (Cade)—Flora by Regulus (Godol.)—Dau. of Bartlet's Childers (Darley Arabian)—Dau. of Bay Bolton—Dau. of Belgrade Turk.

* Soothsayer given.

WILDIDLE,

(WINNER OF THE NURSERY STAKES, FORDHAM AND JOCKEY CLUB HANDICAPS AT JEROME PARK,)

Will stand the season of 1883 *at the Stud Farm of J. C. Judson, Santa Clara, Cal., at* $100 *the season. Application to J. C. Judson, Santa Clara, Cal.*

WILDIDLE, by imp. Australian, son of West Australian, bred in the Woodburn Stud, Ky, foaled 1870, dam Idlewild, by Lexington out of Florine by imp· Glencoe. Wildidle made his bow to the public by winning the Nursery Stakes, one mile, at Jerome Park, in 1:48¾, defeating Long Branch, Catesby, and eleven others. He was out of condition, and ran unplaced in one race as a three year old. At four years old, was second to Catesby, in Maturity Stakes, 3 miles, in 5,36, beating Carver and Ransom ; was unplaced in purse 1¾ miles, won by Grinstead in 3:10 ; was second to Acrobat in purse, 2¼ miles, in 4:38¾, beating Whisper—all run at Jerome Park. At five years old, 104 lbs. Jerome Park, won the Fordham Handicap, 1¼ miles in 2:12, beating Spindrift, aged, 118 lbs, Preakness, aged, 131, and nine others ; won the Jockey Club Handicap, 111 lbs., two miles in 3:38½, beating Preakness, 130 lbs.,Grinstead (4), 110 lbs., and Tubman (aged), 115 lbs. Monmouth Park, was beaten by Aaron Pennington and Ballenkeel in Monmouth Cup, 2½ miles, in 4 34; was second to Rutherford, in 4 mile dash, run in 7:34¾, Big Fellow and Bessie Lee behind him ; won Club Purse, 2-mile heats, 3:40¾. 3:47¼, beating Dublin. Saratoga, was unplaced in Saratoga Cup, 2¼ miles, in 3:56¼, dead heat, and stakes divided between Preakness and Springbok—this is the fastest race ever run at the distance ; was second to Rutherford in Club Purse, 3 miles, in 5:38, beating Madge ; was second to Grinstead (4), 110 lbs, in the Summer Handicap, 2 miles, in 3:37¼, Wildidle (5), 114, beating Mattie W (8), 98 lbs.; won the Club Purse, 4 miles, in 7:39, beating Rutherford. San Francisco, Cal., won the Wise Plate, 4 miles in 7:25½, beating Grinstead, Sherman and Revenue, Jr. Wildidle comes honestly by his racing qualities. His dam was second to no mare ever raised in America. She ran 4 miles over the Centreville Course, L. I., 1863, when 5 years old, with 117 lbs, in 7:26¼, and this was the best time ever made by a mare, until beaten by Ferida, in 1880, when she ran a first heat in 7:23½. Wildidle, for his chances, has been a successful sire ; the best of his get are, Tillie C, May D, Record, Jack Douglass, Ellen Douglass, Belshaw, Jim Douglas, winner of ten out of fourteen races in 1881, Wildidler, Lottie J, and some others. Wildidle is inbred to Waxy on the sire's side, and has much of the blood of Sir Archy and Diomed, in addition to a cross of Eclipse, through his famous son, Medoc, and three crosses of imp. Medley, son of Gimcrack, by Cripple, son of the Godolphin Arabian.

PEDIGREE OF WILDIDLE.

WILDIDLE.					
IMP. AUSTRALIAN.	West Australian.	Melbourne.	Dau. of Humphrey Clinker.	Comus.	Sorcerer—Houghton Lass by Sir Peter—Alexina by King Fergus—Lardella by Y. Marske—Dau. of Cade (Godol.)
				Clinkerina.	Clinker—Pewet by Tandem—Termagant by Tantrum—Cantatrice by Sampson—Dau. of Regulus—Marske's dam.
		Mowerina.	Emma.	Cervantes.	Don Quixote—Evelina by Highflyer—Termagant by Tantrum—Cantatrice by Sampson—Dau of Regulus—Marske's dam.
				Daughter of.	Golumpus—Dau. of Paynator—Sis. to Zodiac by St. George—Abigall by Woodpecker—Firetail by Eclipse—Sis. to Contest by Blank.
		Touchstone.		Camel.	Whalebone—Dau. of Selim—Maiden by Sir Peter—Dau. of Phoenomenon—Matron by Florizel—Maiden by Matchem.
				Banter.	Master Henry—Boadicea by Alexander—Brunette by Amarauthus—Mayfly by Matchem—Dau. of An. Starling—Dau. of Grasshopper.
	Emilia.	Young Emilius.	Emilius.	Whisker.	Waxy—Penelope by Trumpator—Prunella by Highflyer—Promise by Snap Julia by Blank—Spectator's dam by Partner—Bonny Lass.
				Gibside Fairy.	Hermes—Vicissitude by Pipator—Beatrice by Sir Peter—Pyrrha by Matchem—Duchess by Whitenose—Miss Slamerkin by Y. True Blue.
			Shoveler.	Orville.	Beningbrough—Evelina by Highflyer—Termagant by Tantrum—Cantatrice by Sampson—Dau. of Regulus—Marske's dam by Blacklegs.
				Emily.	Stamford—Dau. of Whiskey—Gr. Doriman by Dorimant—Dizzy by Blank—Dizzy by Driver—Dau. of Smiling Tom.
		Persian.	Whisker.	Scud.	Beningbrough—Eliza by Highflyer—Augusta by Eclipse—Hardwick's dam by Herod—Dau. of Bajazet—Dau. of Regulus.
				Goosander.	Hambletonian—Rally by Trumpator—Fancy, Sis. to Diomed by Florizel—Dau. of Spectator—Horatia by Blank—Dau. of F. Childers.
			Variety.	Waxy.	Pot-8-os—Maria by Herod—Lisette by Snap—Miss Windsor by Godol. Arabian—Sis. to Volunteer by Y. Belgrade—Dau. of Bart. Childers.
				Penelope.	Trumpator—Prunella by Highflyer—Promise by Snap—Julia by Blank—Spectator's dam by Partner—Bonny Lass by Bay Bolton.
				Selim or Soothsayer.*	Sorcerer—Golden Locks by Delpini—Violet by Shark—Dau. of Syphon—Quick's Charlotte by Blank—Dau. of Crab—Dau. of Dyer's Dimple.
				Sprite.	Bobtail—Catherine by Woodpecker—Camilla by Trentham—Coquette by Comp. Barb—Sis. to Regulus by Godol. Arabian—Gr. Robinson.
IDLEWILD.	Florine.	Lexington.	Boston.	Sir Archy.	Diomed—Castianira by Rockingham—Tabitha by Trentham—Dau. of Bosphorus—Dau. of Wm's Forester—Dau. of Coalition Colt.
			Sister to Timoleon.	Daughter of.	Saltram—Dau. of Symme's Wildair—Dau. of Driver (Imp. Othello)—Dau. of Fallower (Blank)—Dau. of Vampire—(Regulus.)
		Alice Carneal.	Tuckahoe.	Ball's Florizel.	Diomed—Dau. of Imp. Shark—Dau. of Harris' Eclipse—Dau. of Fearnought (Regulus)—Dau. of Jolly Roger—Dau. of Sober John.
				Daughter of.	Alderman—Dau. of Clockfast—Dau. of Symme's Wildair—Y. Kitty Fisher by Fearnought—Imp. Kitty Fisher by Cade—Dau. of Som. Arabian.
			Rowena. Sarpedon	Emilius.	Orville—Emily by Stamford—Dau. of Whiskey—Gr. Dorimant—Dizzy by Blank—Dizzy by Driver—Dau. of Smiling Tom.
				Icaria.	The Flyer—Parma by Dick Andrews—May by Beningbrough—Primrose by Mambrino—Cricket by Herod—Sophia by Blank—Diana by Second.
	Glencoe.	Sultan.		Sumpter.	Sir Archy—Flirtilla's dam by Robin Redbreast—Dau. of Obscurity—Slamerkin by Wildair—Cub Mare by Cub—Amaranthus' dam.
				Lady Grey.	Robin Grey—Maria by Melzar—Dau. of Highflyer—Dau. of Fearnought—Dau. of Ariel—Dau. of Jack of Diamonds.
		Trampoline.		Selim.	Buzzard—Castrel's dam by Alexander—Dau. of Highflyer—Dau. of Alfred—Dau. of Engineer—Bay Malton's dam by Cade (Godol.)
				Bacchante.	Williamson's Ditto—Sis. to Calomel by Mercury—Dau. of Herod—Folly by Marske—Vixen by Regulus—Dau. of Hutton's Spot.
	Melody.			Tramp.	Dick Andrews—Dau. of Gohanna—Fraxinella by Trentham—Dau. of Woodpecker—Everlasting by Eclipse—Hyaena by Snap (Snip).
				Web.	Waxy—Penelope by Trumpator—Prunella by Highflyer—Promise by Snap—Julia by Blank—Spectator's dam by Partner—Bonny Lass.
	Rodolph's dam.	Medoc.		Am. Eclipse.	Duroc—Millers Damsel by Messenger—Dau. of Pot-8-os—Dau. of Gimcrack—Suap-Dragon by Snap—Dau. of Regulus—Dau. of Bart. Childers.
				Y. Maid of the Oaks.	Expedition—Maid of Oaks by Spread Eagle—Annette by Imp. Shark—Dau. of Rockingham—Dau. of Gallant—Dau. of True Whig.
				Haxall's Moses.	Sir Harry (Sir Peter)—Mermaid by Waxy—Promise by Buzzard—Dau. of Precipitate—Lady Harriet by Mark Anthony—Georgiana by Matchem.
				Daughter of.	Blackburn's Whip (Imp. Whip)—Maria by Craig's Alfred (Imp. Medley)—Dau. of Tayloe's Bellair (Imp. Medley)—Dau. of Imp. Medley—The Bellair Mare was brought from Virginia to Kentucky and certified as thoroughbred.

*Soothsayer given.

WOODLANDS (Imp.)

(WOODLANDS, WINNER OF THE FINDON STAKES, AT GOODWOOD, AND THE CORPORATION STAKES, AT BRIGHTON, IN 1874,)

Will be located for the season of 1888, *at the Erdenheim Stud, Chestnut Hill, Pa. He will be allowed to serve mares at* $50 *the season each, and* $5 *to the groom. Application to be made to Major J. R. Hubbard, Chestnut Hill, Philadelphia, Pa.*

WOODLANDS, by Nutbourne son of the Nabob, bred by Mr. James Terry, foaled 1872, dam Whiteface dam of Miss Needle Hermitage, Review etc., by Turnus, out of Nan Darrell by Inheritor. Woodlands made his *debut* as a two-year old at Goodwood in the Findon Stakes, three-quarters of a mile, which he won defeating Galba, Stray Shot, Prince Arthur and Caledon. At Brighton he won the Corporation Stakes, half a mile, beating Galba and Zanzozee ; at Newmarket was unplaced in the Middle Park Plate, won by Plebian by Joskin ; at Newmarket Houghton Meeting, was unplaced in the old Nursery Stakes, Rowley mile, won by Trojan by Adamas ; at three-years old started four times, was unplaced in the City and Suburban Handicap, won by Dalham, a four-year old carrying 99 lbs ; was unplaced in the Derby, won by Galopin by Vidette ; was unplaced in the Royal Hunt Cup (Handicap) at Ascot, won by Thuringian Prince ; Newmarket Houghton Meeting, was unplaced in the Cambridgeshire Stakes (handicap), won by Sutton, a four-year old carrying 83 lbs ; at four years old, started six times, ran second in two races, and unplaced in four ; was unplaced in the Lincolnshire Handicap, one mile, won by Controversey with Brigg Boy second, thirty-two started ; was unplaced in the City and Surburban at Epsom, won by Thunder, twenty-three started ; was unplaced in the Chesterfield Cup (handicap) at Londonderry, won by Coomassie by King Tom, twenty three started ; at Newmarket second October Meeting, ran second to Rosebery by Speculum (4) 101 lbs ; Woodland (4) 99 lbs ; in Cesarewitch Stakes, (handicap) with Merry Duchess, Hampton, Coomassie and twenty-four others behind him ; Newmarket Houghton Meeting, was unplaced in the Cambridgeshire Stakes (handicap) won by Rosebery, the only time the Cesarewitch and this race was ever won by the same horse except when won by Foxhall ; Liverpool Autumn Meeting, ran second to Footstep (3) 83 lbs ; Woodlands (4) 99 lbs., in the Liverpool Autumn Cup (handicap) with Lord Gowran, Thorn and twenty others behind him ; as a five-year old ran only one race, was second to Harbinger (3) 89 lbs. by Pero Gomez in the Brighton Stakes (handicap) at Brighton, Woodlands (5) 118 lbs., with Peterboro, Dalham, American Mate and three others behind him ; at six years old started five times, won two races, was second in one and unplaced in two. At Epsom Spring Meeting was unplaced in the Great Metropolitan Stakes (handicap) won by Mida, by Parmesan (3) 77 lbs., thirteen started, seven finished behind Woodlands ; at Chester ran second to Pageant by Elland (aged), 124 lbs. ; Woodlands (6) 114 lbs., for the Chester Trades Cup (handicap), Jester, Hopbloom, Ridotto and five others behind him. The next day he won the Great Cheshire Handicap Stakes, carrying 113 lbs., defeating Antient Pistol, Footstep and Avontes ; at seven years old ran unplaced in the Epsom Summer Handicap Plate, won by Chippendale, this was his last race. Woodlands served no mares in England, and has no foals in this country old enough to race, but he is strongly inbred to Herod and Eclipse through popular and successful sources, and should get race horses.

PEDIGREE OF WOODLANDS (Imp.)

Partisan. Nanine.	Walton—Parasol by Pot-8-os (Eellpse)—Prunella by Highflyer—Promise by Snap—Julia by Blank—Spectator's dam by Partner. Selim (Buzzard)—Bizarre by Peruvian (Sir Peter)—Violante by John Bull (Fortitude)—Dau. of Highflyer—Everlasting by Eclipse.
Emilius. Whizgig.	Orville—Emily by Stamford—Dau. of Whiskey—Gr. Dorimaut by Dorimant Dizzy by Blank (Godol.)—Dizzy by Driver (Snake)—Dau. of Sm. Tom. Rubens—Penelope by Trumpator—Prunella by Highflyer—Promise by Snap—Julia by Blauk—Spectator's dam by Partner—Bonny Lass.
Whalebone. Daughter of.	Waxy—Penelope by Trumpator—Prunella by Highflyer—Promise by Snap—Julia by Blank—Spectator's dam by Partner—Bouny Lass. Selim—Maiden by Sir Peter—Dau. of Phoeuomenon—Matron by Florizel—Maiden by Matchem—Dau. of Squirt—Lot's dam by Mogul.
Muley. Sis. to Petworth.	Orville—Eleanor by Whiskey (Saltram)—Y. Giantess by Diomed—Giantess by Matchem (Cade)—Molly Longlegs by Babraham. Precipitate (Mercury)—Dau. of Woodpecker—Sis. to Juniper by Snap—Y. Marske's dam by Blank—Bay Starling by Bolton Starling.
Royal Oak. Daughter of.	Catton—Dau. of Smolensko—Lady Mary by Beningbrough—Dau. of Highflyer—Dau. of Marske—A la Grecque by Regulus—Dau. of Allworthy. Orville—Dau. of Buzzard (Woodpecker)—Hornpipe by Trumpator—Luna by Herod (Tartar)—Proserpine, Sis. to Eclipse by Marske.
Little John. Daughter of.	Octavius (Orville)—Gr. Skim by Woodpecker—Silver's dam by Herod—Y. Hag by Skim—Hag by Crab—Ebony by Childers—Ebony by Basto. Phantom—Sis. to Election by Gohanna—Ch. Skim by Woodpecker—Silver's dam by Herod—Y. Hag by Skim (Starling) Hag by Crab—Ebony.
Langar. Olympia.	Selim—Dau. of Walton—Y. Giantess by Diomed—Giantess by Matchem—Molly Longlegs by Babraham—Dau. of Cole's Foxhunter—Sis. to Cato. Sir Oliver (Sir Peter)—Scotilla by Anvil (Herod)—Scota by Eclipse—Harmony by Herod—Rutilia by Blank—Dau. of Regulus (Godol.)
Tramp. Filagree.	Dick Andrews—Dau. of Gobanna—Fraxinella by Trentham—Dau. of Woodpecker—Everlasting by Eclipse—Hyaena by Snap—Miss Belsea. Soothsayer (Sorcerer)—Web by Waxy—Penelope by Trumpator—Prunella by Highflyer—Promise by Suap—Julia by Blank (Godol.)
Muley. Aquelina.	Orville—Eleanor by Whiskey—Y. Giantess by Diomed—Giantess by Matchem—Molly Longlegs by Babraham—Dau. of Cole's Foxhunter. Eagle (Volunteer)—Sis. to Petworth by Precipitate—Dau. of Woodpecker Sis. to Juniper by Snap—Y. Marske's dam by Blank—Bay Starling.
Soothsayer. Quadrille.	Sorcerer—Goldenlocks by Delpini—Violet by Shark—Dau. of Syphon—Quick's Charlotte by Blank—Dau. of Crah. Selim—Canary Bird by Whiskey or Sorcerer—Canary by Coriander (Pot-8-os)—Miss Green by Highflyer—Harriet by Matchem.
Whalebone. Defiance.	Waxy—Penelope by Trumpator—Prunella by Highflyer—Promise by Snap—Julia by Blank—Spectator's dam by Partner. Rubens (Buzzard)—Little Polly by Highland Fling—Harriet by Volunteer—Dau. of Alfred—Magnolia by Marske—Dau. of Babraham.
Marmion. Harpalice.	Whiskey—Y. Noisette by Diomed—Noisette by Squirrel—Carina by Marske—Thunder's dam by Blank—Dizzy by Driver. Gohanna—Amazon by Driver—Fractious by Mercury—Dau. of Woodpecker—Everlasting by Eclipse—Hyaena by Snap.
Tramp. Mandane.	Dick Andrews—Dau. of Gobanna—Fraxinella by Trentham—Dau. of Woodpecker—Everlasting by Eclipse—Hyaena by Snap. Pot-8-os—Y. Camilla by Woodpecker—Camilla by Trentham—Coquette by the Compton Barb—Sis. to Regulus by Godol. Arabian.
Walton. Anticipation.	Sir Peter—Arethusa by Dungannon—Dau. of Prophet (Regulus)—Virago by Snap—Dau. of Regulus—Sis. to Othello by Crab. Beningbrough (King Fergus)—Expectation by Herod—Dau. of Skim—Dau. of Janus (Godol.)—Spinster by Crab—Spinster.
Whitelock. Daughter of.	Hambletonian (King Fergus)—Rosalind by Phoenomenon—Atalanta by Matchem—Lass of the Mill by Oroonoko—Dau. of Traveler. Coriander—Wildgoose by Highflyer—Coheiress by Pot-8-os—Manilla by Goldfinder—Dau. of Old Eng.—Dau. of Cullen Arabian.
Comus. Lisette.	Sorcerer—Houghton Lass by Sir Peter—Alexina by King Fergus (Eclipse)—Lardella by Y. Marske—Dau. of Cade—Beaufremont's dam. Hambletonian — Constantia by Walnut (Highflyer)—Contessina by Y. Marske (Marske)—Tuberose by Herod (Tartar)—Gray Starling by Starling (Bay Bolton)—Coughing Polly by Bartlet's Childers (Darley Arabian)—Dau. of Counsellor (Shaftsbury Turk)—Dau. of Snake (Lister Turk)— Dau. of Luggs (D'Arcy White Turk) — Dau. of Woodcock (Merlin).

* Morisco given.

THE HORSE-BREEDERS' GUIDE

AND

HAND BOOK.

PART II.

DEAD SIRES.

AMERICAN ECLIPSE,

(WINNER OF THE GREAT SECTIONAL MATCH BETWEEN THE NORTH AND SOUTH, RUN OVER THE UNION COURSE, L. I., MAY 27TH, 1823, BEATING HENRY.)

ECLIPSE, by Duroc, son of imp. Diomed, bred by Gen. Nathaniel Coles, Desoris, Queens Co., L. I., foaled May 25th, 1814, dam Miller's Damsel, by imp. Messenger, son of Membrino, out of imp. mare by Pot-8-os, son of the great English Eclipse. Eclipse was trained at three years old, and tried; and again at four years old ; but ran his first race at five years old, at Newmarket, Long Island, 2-mile heats, which he won, beating Black-eyed Susan, by Sir Archy, and Sea Gull. March 15th, 1819, Eclipse was sold to Mr. Van Ranst, and in June, 1819 won Club Purse, at Bath L. I., defeating Little John, by Potomac, Bond's Eclipse, and James Fitz James. October, same year, won Club Purse at Bath, 4-mile heats, beating Little John, Fearnought, and one other, in 8:13, 8:08. In 1820 and '21 he covered mares on Long Island. October 15th, 1821, won the Club Purse, Jamaica, L. I., 4-mile heats, defeating the noted Lady Lightfoot, then nine years old, Flag of Truce and Heart of Oak, in 8:04, 8:02. Lady Lightfoot was distanced in the second heat. In May, 1822, won Club Purse over the Union Course, L. I,, beating Sir Walter, by Hickory, in 7:54, 8:00. October, 1822, won Club Purse, 4-mile heats, over Union Course, beating Sir Walter, Duchess of Marlborough, and Slow and Easy, in 7:58, second heat no time. A challenge having appeared in a New York paper in which Jas. J. Harrison, of Virginia, proposed to run Sir Charles by Sir Archy, against Eclipse, 4-mile heats, for $5,000 or $10,000, the race to be run over the Washington Course, the challenge was accepted by Mr. Van Ranst, and $5,000 forfeit put up on each side, the race to be run November 20th. Both horses came to the post and the riders were mounted, when Mr. Harrison announced that in consequence of an accident to Sir Charles, he would pay forfeit, but proposed to run a dash of 4 miles, for $1,500 a side. This was accepted, and the horses started. The first two miles were run in 3:50, when Sir Charles broke down, and Eclipse galloped the balance of the distance. Sir Charles carried 120, and Eclipse 126 lbs. On the evening of the same day, Col. Wm. R. Johnson, of Virginia, proposed to produce a horse on the last Tuesday in May, 1823, to run 4-mile heats against Eclipse, over the Union Course, for $20,000 a side. The challenge was immediately accepted by John C. Stephens, Esq. John Richards, intended for the match, broke down, and Henry, by Sir Archy was substituted. The race was run May 27th, 1823. Henry won the first heat, 7:37½, Eclipse the second and third in 7:49, 8:24, Eclipse carried 126 lbs., Henry (4) 108 lbs. Col. Johnson again challenged to run Henry against Eclipse, the same race, for $20,000, or $50,000, but the challenge was declined.

Eclipse was as famous in the stud as on the turf. He stood in New York, Virginia, and Kentucky. The most famous of his get were, Ariel, Lance, Lady Jackson, Black Maria, Shark, Goliah, O'Kelly, Godolphin, Maryland Eclipse, Rocker, Medoc, Midas, Mingo, Ten Broeck, Monmouth Eclipse, Bay Maria, Tom Kimball, Gano, and many others. Ariel was the great mare of her day. She ran fifty-seven races and won forty-two, seventeen of which were 4-mile heats. Black Maria also ran a large number eleven winning ones, at 3 and 4-mile heats. Eclipse was a chestnut horse, 15¼ hands high, with a star in his forehead and near hind foot white; was heavy set, and full of bone and muscle. The following were some of his measurements : head 23¾ in.; neck 25 in.; from point of shoulder to point of buttocks 65¾ in.; girth 74 in.; around the arm, 21¼ in.; below the knee, 7¾ in.; around the tibia 18¾ in.; the hock 16¾ in.; from hip to point of hock 37¼ in.; he measured the same around the flank as girth 74 in., and the same height at hip as withers, 61 in. An examination of his pedigree will show that he was very much inbred to the Darley Arabian, through Childers, and to the Godolphin Arabian through Blank, Cade, Regulus and Cripple. Eclipse died the property of Jilson Yates, in Shelby County, Ky., in Aug, 1847, then in the 34th year of his age.

PEDIGREE OF AMERICAN ECLIPSE.

AMERICAN ECLIPSE.	DUROC.	Diomed.	Florizel. Dau. of Herod.	Tartar.	Partner—Meliora by Fox (Clumsy)—Milkmaid by Sir Wm. Blacket's Snail (Partner)—Dam the Shield's Galloway.	
				Cypron.	Blaze (F.Childers)—Selima by Bethel's Arabian—Dau. of Graham's Champion—Dau. of Darley Arabian—Dau. of Merlin.	
			Sister to Juno. Horatia. Spectator. Dau. of	Cygnet.	Godol. Arabian—Blossom by Crab—Dau. of F. Childers—Miss Belvoir by Grey Granthem—Dau. of Paget Turk—Betty Percival.	
				Daughter of.	Cartouche (Bald Galloway)—Ebony by F. Childers (Dar. Arabian)—Ebony by Basto (Byerly Turk)—Massey Mare by His. Black Barb.	
				Crab.	Alcock Arabian—Sis. to Soreheels by Basto—Sis. to Mixbury by Cur. Bay Barb—Dau. of Spot—Dau. of Whitelegged Lowther Barb.	
				Daughter of.	Partner—Bonny Lass by Bay Bolton—Dau. of Dar. Arabian—Dau. of Byerly Turk—Dau. of Taffolet Barb—Dau. of Place's White Turk.	
				Blank.	Godol. Arabian—Lit. Hartley Mare by Bart. Childers—Flying Whig by Wm's Woodstock Arabian—Dau. of St. Victor Barb—Dau. of Whynot.	
				Daughter of.	F. Childers—Miss Belvoir by Gr. Granthani—Dau. of Paget Turk—Betty Percival by Leede's Arabian—Dau. of Spanker.	
		Amanda.	Grey Diomed. Dau. of Medley.	Gimcrack.	Crippple (Godol.)—Miss Elliott by Grisewood's Partner (Partner)—Caelia by Partner—Dau. of Bloody Buttocks—Dau. of Greyhound.	
				Arminda.	Snap—Miss Cleveland by Regulus—Midge by a son of Bay Bolton—Dau. of Bart. Childers—Dau. of Hon. Arabian.	
				Sloe.	Partner (Moreton's Imp. Traveler)—Imp. Blossom by Sloe (Crab)—Dau. of Regulus (Godolphin Arabian).	
				Daughter of.	Imp. Vampire (Regulus) Imp. Calista by Forester—Dau. of Crab—Dau. of Hobgoblin—Bajazet's dam by Whitefoot.	
			Dolly Va Cade. Fine.	Fearnought.	Regulus—Silvertail by Henage's Whitenose (Hall's Arabian)—Dau. of Rattle—Dau. of Dar. Arabian—Old Child Mare.	
				Daughter of.	Jolly Roger—Imp. Kitty Fisher by Cade—Dau. of Som. Arabian—Bald Charlotte by Old Royal—Dau. of Beth. Castaway—Dau. of Brimmer.	
		Daughter of.		Silvereye.	Cul. Arabian—Dau. of Cur. Bay Barb—Dau. of Byerly Turk—Dau. of Curwen's Spot—Dau. of Whitelegged Lowther Barb—Vintner Mare.	
				Daughter of.	Imp. Badger (Bosphorus)—Dau. of Forester—Dau. of Imp. Silvereye—Dau. of Imp. Monkey (Lonsdale Bay Arabian).	
	MILLER'S DAMSEL.	Messenger.	Mambrino. Vauxhall Eug'n'r. Snaps dam.	Sampson.	Blaze (F. Childers)—Dau. of Hip (Cur. Bay Barb)—Dau. of Spark (Honeycomb Punch)—Dau. of Snake (Lister Turk)—Lord D'Arcy's Queen.	
				Daughter of.	Young Greyhound (Greyhound by White Barb Chillaby)—Dau. of Curwen's Bay Barb.	
				Cade.	Godol. Arabian—Roxanna by the Bald Galloway—Sis. to Chanter by the Akaster Turk—Dau. of Leede's Arabian—Dau. of Spanker.	
				Daughter of.	Bolton Little John (Partner)—Durham's Favorite by a son of the Bald Galloway—Daffodil's dam by Sir T. Gascoigus Foreign Horse.	
		Daughter of.	Turf.	Matchem.	Cade—Dau. of Partner—Dau. of Makeless—Dau. of Brimmer—Dau. of Place's White Turk—Dau. of Dodsworth—Layton Barb Mare.	
				Daughter of.	An. Starling—Dau. of Orford Turk—Dau. of Merlin (Bustler)—Dau. of Pert (Ely Turk)—Dau. of Commoner—Coppin Mare.	
		Pot-8-o's.	Sis. to Figurante.	Regulus.	Godol. Arabian—Grey Robinson by the Bald Galloway—Dau. of Snake—Gr. Wilkes by Hautboy—Miss D'Arcy's Pet Mare.	
				Snap's dam.	Fox—Gipsy by Bay Bolton—Dau. of Newcastle Turk—Dau. of By. Turk—Dau. of Taffolet's Barb—Dau. of Place's White Turk—Nat. Barb Mare.	
				Marske.	Squirt—Dau. of Blacklegs—Dau. of Bay Bolton—Dau. of Fox Cub—Dau. of Coneyskins—Dau. of Hut. Grey Barb—Dau. of Hut. Royal Colt.	
				Spiletta.	Regulus—Mother Western by Smith's Son of Snake—Dau. of Ld. D'Arcy's Old Montague—Dau. of Hautboy—Dau. of Brimmer.	
		Sportsmistress. Eclipse.		Warren's Sportsman.	Cade—Silvertail by Henage's Whitenose—Dau. of Rattle—Dau. of Dar. Arabian—Old Child Mare by Gres. Bay Arabian—Vixen.	
				Golden Locks.	Oroonoko (Crab)—Valiant's dam by Crab—Dau. of Partner—Thwait's Dun Mare by the Akaster Turk.	
		Gimcrack.		Cripple.	Godol. Arabian—Blossom by Crab—Dau. of F. Childers—Miss Belvoir by Gr. Granthem—Dau. of Paget Turk—Betty Percival.	
				Miss Elliott.	Grisewood's Partner—Caelia by Partner—Dau. of Bloody Buttocks—Dau. of Greyhound—Brocklesby Betty.	
	Daughter of. Snap-Dragon.			Snap.	Snip—Dau. of Fox—Dau. of Newcastle Turk—Dau. of Byerly Turk—Dau. of Taffolet Barb—Dau. of Place's White Turk—Barb Mare.	
				Daughter of.	Regulus (Godo.l)—Dau. of Bartlet's Childers (Darley Arabian)—Dau. of Honeywood's Arabian—Byerly Mare, dam of the Two True Blues.	

AUSTRALIAN (Imp.)

(WINNER OF THE DOSWELL STAKE AT NEW ORLEANS AND PRODUCE STAKES AT LEXINGTON, KY., 1861.)

AUSTRALIAN by West Australian, son of Melbourne, bred by Mr. W. E. Duncombe, imported by the late A. Keene Richards, along with his dam in 1858, then a suckling, dam Emilia by Young Emilius, son of Emilius by Orville. West Australian, his sire, won the three great events—the 2,000 guineas, Derby and St. Leger in 1853. Emilius, his grandsire, through his dam, won the Derby in 1823, and Whisker, his great grandsire, the Derby in 1815, and his sire, Waxy, won it in 1793. Australian was a fine race-horse, running under the silver and gray of Richard in the name of Millington. He made his *début* in the Doswell Stakes at New Orleans, April 1, 1861, mile heats. This he won handily, with 5 lbs. overweight, in 1:49¼, 1:48½, beating Regret, Tom Reddy, Uncle True and Ninette; Louisville, May 20, ran third and fifth in the Association Stake, mile heats, in 1:48¾, 1:48, won by Lillie Ward, Myrtle second, Nannie Craddock third, Rubicon fourth; same place, May 24, ran third in the Galt House Stake, 2 mile heats, won by Lillie Ward, in 3:38¾, 3:40; Rubicon second; Lexington, Ky., June 3d, ran second to Lillie Ward in the Association Stake, mile heats, in 1:52¼, 1:51½, track muddy, beating Rubicon, John Morgan, Crichton, Wells, &c.; same place, ran second to Kansas in the Citizens' Stake, 2 mile heats, in 3:44, 3:46, 3:45, track muddy; Millington won first heat and was second in the last, beating Rubicon, Myrtle, Nannie Craddock, &c.; Lexington, Ky., September 23, 1861, Produce Stakes, for three-year olds, mile heats, 12 starters; John Morgan won, Myrtle second, imp. Millington third; Myrtle won the first heat in 1:46¾, Millington second; Millington won second in 1:46¾; John Morgan won the last two in 1:47½, 1:49; September 27, Produce Stakes, for three-year olds, two mile heats, 9 starters, imp. Millington won in 3:43½, 3:40¾. John Morgan second, Myrtle third and distanced. In the Fall of 1861, Millington was purchased by the late R. A. Alexander, and his name was changed to Australian. He ran one race under his colors. Lexington, June 7, 1862, 3 mile heats, for all-ages, 6 starters; John Morgan was third, first and first; Idlewild won the first heat, in 5:43¾, and was drawn after the second; Ella D, by Vandal, was fifth, second and second; Australian fourth, fifth and third; John Morgan won second and third heats in 5:41, 5:45¼. As a stallion, Australian ranks second to none ever imported. The best of his get were Fellowcraft, 4 miles, in 7:19½, the first horse to beat Lexington's time, 7:19¾; Abd-el-Kader, 4 miles, 7:31¾; Abd-el-Koree, 4 miles, when three years old, 7:33; Wildidle, 4 miles, 7:25½; Rutherford, Spendthrift, Mozart, Springlet, Zoo Zoo, Lizzie, Lucas, Trinidad, Baden Baden, Albert, Nellie Booker, Silent Friend, 4 miles, 7:30¼; Helmbold, Wilful, Atilla, Mate, Leinster, Pride of the Village, Madge, Maggie B B, dam of Iroquois, Farfaletta, dam of Falsetto, Ivy Leaf, dam of Bramble, Brambaletta, &c.; Hilarite, Springbok, 2¼ miles, 3:56¼; fastest on record; Hazem, Queen's Own, Sunlight, Blanche J. Baronet, N. Y. Weekly, and many others. Australian was a dark chestnut without white, and measured 15¾ hands in height, had neat head and neck, broad forehead, great breadth between the jaws; oblique shoulders, with great depth of girth; round, good barrel; good flank, good hip and arched loin; good length from the point of hip to whirlbone, and thence to the hock, which was bony and strong; sound legs and feet and good length of pasterns. He combined the Eclipse blood through Whalebone, Whisker, Don Quixote and Mercury, and Herod and Matchem through the best sources and traces, through a sister of the great Regulus by the Godolphin Arabian to the Sedbury Royal Mare. Australian died at Woodburn Stud, the property of A. J. Alexander, October 15th, 1879. His descendents will keep his memory green.

PEDIGREE OF AUSTRALIAN (Imp.)

AUSTRALIAN (Imp.)					Melbourne.	Humphrey Clinker.	Clinkerina.	Sorcerer.	Trumpator (Conductor)—Y. Giantess by Diomed—Giantess by Matchem—Molly Longlegs by Babraham—Dau. of Cole's Foxhunter.
								Houghton Lass.	Sir Peter—Alexina by King Fergus (Eclipse)—Lardella by Young Marske—Dau. of Cade—Beaufremont's dam by Bro. to Fearnought.
							Comus.	Clinker.	Sir Peter—Hyale by Phoenomenon (Herod)—Rally by Trumpator—Fancy, Sis. to Diomed by Florizel—Dau. of Spectator—Horatia by Blank.
								Pewet.	Tandem (Syphon)—Termagant by Tantrum (Cripple by Godol.)—Cantatrice by Sampson (Blaze)—Dau. of Regulus—Marske's dam by Blacklegs.
					Daughter of.	Cervantes.		Don Quixote.	Eclipse—Grecian Princess by Wm's Forester—Dau. of Coalition Colt (Godol.)—Dau. of Bustard (Crab)—Charming Molly by Second.
				WEST AUSTRALIAN.				Evelina.	Highflyer—Termagant by Tantrum—Cantatrice by Sampson—Dau. of Regulus—Marske's dam by Blacklegs (Bay Turk)—Dau of Bay Bolton.
			Dau. of.					Golumpus.	Gohanna—Catherine by Woodpecker (Herod)—Camilla by Trentham (Sweepstakes)—Coquette by Compton Barb.—Sister to Regulus.
								Daughter of.	Paynator (Trumpator)—Sis. to Zodiac by St. George (Anvil)—Abigail by Woodpecker—Firetail by Eclipse—Dau. of Blank—Dau. of Cade.
					Touchstone.	Camel.		Whalebone.	Waxy—Penelope by Trumpator—Prunella by Highflyer—Promise by Snap—Julia by Blank—Spectator's dam by Partner—Bonny Lass.
								Daughter of.	Selim (Buzzard)—Maiden by Sir Peter—Dau. of Phoenomenon—Matron by Florizel—Maiden by Matchem—Dau. of Squirt—Lot's dam.
				Mowerina.		Banter.		Master Henry.	Orville—Miss Sophia by Stamford (Sir Peter)—Sophia by Buzzard—Huncamunca by Highflyer—Cypher by Squirrel—Fribble's dam by Regulus.
								Boadicea.	Alexander (Eclipse)—Brunette by Aramanthus (Old Eng.)—Mayfly by Matchem (Cade)—Dau. of An. Starling—Dau. of Grasshopper (Crab).
					Emma.	Whisker.		Waxy.	Pot-8-os—Maria by Herod (Tartar)—Lisette by Snap (Snip)—Miss Windsor by Godol. Arabian—Sister to Volunteer by Y Belgrade.
								Penelope.	Trumpator—Prunella by Highflyer—Promise by Snap—Julia by Blank—Spectator's dam by Partner—Bouny Lass by Bay Bolton.
						Gibside Fairy.		Hermes.	Mercury (Eclipse)—Rosina by Woodpecker—Petworth by Herod—Golden Grove by Blank—Spinster by Partner—Dau. of Bloody Buttocks.
								Vicissitude.	Pipator (Conductor)—Beatrice by Sir Peter—Pyrrha by Matchem—Duchess by Whitenose (Godol.)—Miss Slamerkin by Y. True Blue.
	EMILIA.	Young Emilius.	Emilius.	Orville.				Beningbrough.	King Fergus (Eclipse)—Dau. of Herod—Pyrrha by Matchem—Duchess by Whitenose—Miss Slamerkin by Y. True Blue—Dau. of Ox Dun. Arabian.
								Evelina.	Highflyer—Termagant by Tantrum—Cantatrice by Sampson—Dau. of Regulus—Marske's dam by Blacklegs—Dau. of Bay Bolton—Dau. of Fox Cub
				Emily.				Stamford.	Sir Peter—Horatia by Eclipse—Countess by Blank—Dau. of Rib (Crab)—Dau. of Wynn. Arabian.—Dau. of Governor—Dau. of Al. Arabian.
								Daughter of.	Whiskey—Gr. Dorimant by Dorimant—Dizzy by Blank—Dizzy by Driver—Dau. of Smiling Tom—Dau. of Oysterfoot—Dau. of Old Merlin.
			Shoveler.	Scud.				Beningbrough.	King Fergus—Dau. of Herod—Pyrrha by Matchem—Duchess by Whitenose—Miss Slamerkin by Y. True Blue—Dau. of Ox. Dun. Arabian.
								Eliza.	Highflyer—Augusta by Eclipse—Hardwicke's dam by Herod—Dau. of Bajazet—Dau. of Regulus—Dau. of Lon's Bay Arabian.
				Goosander.				Hambletonian.	King Fergus—Dau. of Highflyer—Monimia by Matchem—Dau. of Alcides (Babraham)—Dau of Crab (Alcock Arabian)—Snap's dam.
								Rally.	Trumpator—Fancy, Sis. to Diomed by Florizel—Dau. of Spectator—Horatia by Blank—Dau. of F, Childers—Miss Belvoir by Gr. Grantham.
		Whisker.	Waxy.					Pot-8-o's.	Eclipse—Sportsmistress by Warren's Sportsman—Golden Locks by Oroonoko—Valiant's dam by Crab—Dau. of Partner.
								Maria.	Herod—Lisette by Snap—Miss Windsor by Godol. Arabian—Sis. to Volunteer by Y. Belgrade—Dau. of Bartlet's Childers (Dar. Arabian).
			Penelope.					Trumpator.	Conductor—Brunette by Squirrel—Dove by Matchless (Godol.)—Dau. of An. Starling—Dau. of Grasshopper—Dau. of Newton Arabian.
								Prunella.	Highflyer—Promise by Snap—Julia by Blank—Spectator's dam by Partner—Bonny Lass by Bay Bolton—Dau. of Darley Arabian.
		Persian.	Selim or *Soothsr.					Sorcerer.	Trumpator—Y. Giantess by Diomed—Giantess by Matchem—Molly Longlegs by Babraham—Dau. of Cole's Foxhunter.
								Golden Locks.	Delpini—Violet by Shark (Marske)—Dau. of Syphon—Charlotte by Blank—Dau. of Crab—Dau. of Dyer's Dimple.
		Variety.	Sprite.					Bobtail.	Precipitate (Mercury)—Bobtail by Eclipse—Faith by Herod—Curiosity by Snap—Dau. of Regulus—Dau. of Bart. Childers.
								Catharine.	Woodpecker—Camilla by Trentham—Coquette by the Comp. Barb.—Sis. to Regulus by Godol. Arabian—Gray Robinson by the Bald Galloway (St. Victor Barb.)—Sis. to Country Wench by Snake (Lister Turk)—Grey Wilkes by Old Hauthoy (White D'Arcy Turk)—Miss D'Arcy's Pet Mare out of a Sedbury Royal Mare.

* Soothsayer given.

BONNIE SCOTLAND (Imp.)

(WINNER OF THE LIVERPOOL ST. LEGER AND DONCASTER STAKES IN 1856.)

Bonnie Scotland, by Iago, son of Don John, winner of the St. Leger in 1838, bred by Mr. W. I'Anson, foaled 1853, imported by Capt. Cornish into Boston in 1857, dam Queen Mary, dam of Balrownie; Haricot, dam of Caller Ou and Blink Bonny, dam of Blair Athol by Gladiator. Bonnie Scotland was badly hurt at two years old, but he came out when three years old and started in four races, winning two, running second in one and unplaced in the other. He won the Liverpool St. Leger, twenty-three subscribers, 1¾ miles, beating Omar Pacha, Tom Thumb, and two others; was fourth in the Great Yorkshire Stakes at York, 176 subscribers, won by Fazzoletto, with Brother to Bird on the Wing second, Stork third. He ran second to Warlock for the Doncaster St. Leger, 133 subscribers, twenty-five starters, St. Leger course. In this race he beat Ellington (winner of the Derby), Artillery, Rogerthorpe and others. He won the Doncaster Stakes, 1¼ miles, ninety-three subscribers, beating Ellington (the Derby winner), Brother to Bird on the Wing, Manganese, Alleppo, California and others. This was his last race. After his importation he was purchased by Messrs. Reber and Kutz and taken to Ohio. There being few thoroughbred mares in that State he made no reputation, sired Malcolm, Dangerous and Ontario; he passed into the hands of E. A. Smith, when he got Frogtown, a capital good horse. Smith sold him to Messrs. Parks, of Illinois, where he got Experience Oaks and Nathan Oaks. From Parks he passed to the hands of Gen. W. G. Harding in 1872, and commenced his brilliant career as a sire of winners; the first of his get were Belle of the Meade, an excellent two-year-old, and Bushwhacker, winner of the Bowie Stakes and the Great Long Island Stakes, both 4 mile heats. Although dead, he stands, in 1882, at the head of winning sires, and his winning sons and daughters are a legion. The following, the most noted, will show his quality as a sire: Aranza, Brambaletta, 5 furlongs, in 1:02¼; 7 furlongs, 1:30; one mile and a furlong in 1:54, the fastest on record. Bye the Way, Bonnie Wood Bramble, mile heats in 1:43, 1:44; 1⅛ miles, 118 lbs., 1:58; 2¼ miles, 4:01¾. Boardman, mile in 1:40½. Boatman, 115 lbs., 2 miles, 3:34. Barret, three-quarters in 1:14, the fastest on record; 1⅛ miles, 118 lbs., in 1:56½. Ben Hill, Bonnie Carie, Baton Rouge, Belle of the Highlands, 1⅛ miles in 1:55½. Bye and Bye, Bushwhacker, 2 miles in 3:30; 4 miles, 7:31; 2 mile heats, 3:36, 3:36½, 3:38½. Balance All, Beatitude, Boulevard, Bayard, Bounce, mile heats in 1:42, 1:41½; mile and 3 furlongs in 2:23¼. Bride Cake, Boswell, Bingin, Bathgate, Bombast, Bonnie Castle, Brooklyn, Bliss, Big Medicine, Bootjack, mile in 1:42; 1 1/16 miles in 1:49¾; Baltic, Bosworth, Bancroft, Duke of Kent, Joe Howell, three-quarter heats in 1:14½, 1:14½, 1:15, fastest on record; Julia Bruce, Maggie Ayr, Luke Blackburn, 1½ miles in 2:34, fastest ever run; 1¾ miles, 3:04; 2 miles, 3:35¼; Glidelia, 1¾ miles in 3:01, the fastest in the world; J. W. Norton and a host of others. His daughter, Kelpie, produced Janet, 4 miles in 7:23. Ontario produced McWhirter, 2 miles in 3:30½, the fastest ever run by a three-year old. Being a half brother to Blink Bonny, the dam of Blair Athol, and from a family which has produced the greatest number of noted horses, his descendants should be valuable in the stud. The long list named speaks volumes for the Belle Meade Stud, as nearly every animal named was bred there. Two sons of the old hero are located there and the blood should be preserved to the country, and there is no better opportunity than to cross his sons on the Lexington and Glencoe blood, and it will prove our theory that in breeding is the surest and best mode to rear the race horse and the only way to preserve and perpetuate pure blood and racing strains. His stock are all remarkable for soundness, symmetry, muscular power, good action, with the best of feet. He died at Belle Meade, Feb. 1st, 1880, in the twenty-seventh year of his age, game to the last moment.

PEDIGREE OF BONNIE SCOTLAND.

BONNIE SCOTLAND.	IAGO.	Don John.	Waxy. Penelope.	Pot-8-os—Maria by Herod—Lisette by Snap—Miss Windsor by Godol. Arabian—Sis. to Volunteer by Y. Belgrade (Belgrade Turk). Trumpator—Prunella by Highflyer—Promise by Snap—Julia by Blank—Spectator's dam by Partner—Dau. of Bay Bolton.
		Hetman Platoff's dam. Tramp or Wvly.* Margaretta. Whalebone.	Sir Peter. Sis. to Cracker.	Highflyer—Papillon by Snap—Miss Cleveland by Regulus—Midge by Son of Bay Bolton—Dau. of Bartlet's Childers—Dau. of Hon. Arabian. Highflyer—Nutcracker by Matchem—Miss Starling by Starling—Dau. of Partner—Dau. of Croft's Bay Barb—Dau. of Makeless.
		Marciana. Comus.	Sorcerer. Houghton Lass.	Trumpator—Y. Giantess by Diomed—Giantess by Matchem—Molly Longlegs by Babraham—Dau. of Cole's Foxhunter—Dau. of Partner. Sir Peter—Alexina by King Fergus—Lardella by Y. Marske—Dau. of Cade—Beaufremont's dam by Bro. to Fearnought—Miss Windham.
			Stamford. Marcia.	Sir Peter—Horatia by Eclipse—Countess by Blank—Dau. of Rib (Crab)—Dau. of Wynn Arabian—Dau. of Governor—Dau. of Alcock's Arabian. Coriander—Faith by Pacolet—Atalanta by Matchem—Lass of the Mill by Oroonoko—Dau. of Old Traveler.
	Scandal. Selim. Castrel's Buzzard. dam.		Woodpecker. Misfortune.	Herod—Miss Ramsden by Cade—Dau. of Lonsdale Bay Arabian—Dau. of Bay Bolton—Dau. of Dar. Arabian—Dau. of Byerly Turk. Dux (Matchem)—Curiosity by Snap—Dau. of Regulus—Dau. of Bartlet's Childers—Dau. of Honeywood's Arabian.
			Alexander. Daughter of.	Eclipse—Grecian Princess by Wm's Forester—Dau. of Coalition Colt (Godol.)—Dau. of Bustard (Crab)—Charming Molly by Second. Highflyer—Dau. of Alfred—Dau. of Engineer—Bay Malton's dam by Cade—Lass of the Mill by Old Traveler—Miss Makeless.
		Daughter of. Hap-hazard. Dau. of.	Sir Peter. Miss Hervey.	Highflyer—Papillon by Snap—Miss Cleveland by Regulus—Midge by Son of Bay Bolton—Dau. of Bartlet's Childers. Eclipse—Clio by Y. Cade—Dau. of Old Starling—Dau. of Bart. Childers—Dau. of Bay Bolton—Dau. of Byerly Turk—Dau. of Bustler.
			Precipitate. Colibri.	Mercury (Eclipse)—Dau. of Herod—Maiden by Matchem—Dau. of Squirt—Dau. of Mogul—Dau. of Bay Bolton—Dau. of Pul. Ch. Arabian. Woodpecker—Camilla by Trentham—Coquette by Compton Barb—Sis. to Regulus by Godol. Arabian—Gr. Robinson by Bald Galloway.
	QUEEN MARY. Gladiator. Partisan. Parasol. Moses.	Pauline. Quadrille.	Sir Peter. Arethusa.	Highflyer—Papillon by Snap—Miss Cleveland by Regulus—Midge by Son of Bay Bolton—Dau. of Barlet's Childers. Dungannon (Eclipse)—Dau. of Prophet (Regulus)—Virago by Snap—Dau. of Regulus—Sis. to Othello by Crab.
			Pot-8-o's. Prunella.	Eclipse—Sportsmistress by Warren's Sportsman (Cade)—Golden Locks by Oroonoko—Valiante's dam by Crab—Dau. of Partner. Highflyer—Promise by Snap—Spectator's dam by Partner—Bonny Lass by Bay Bolton—Dau. of Darley Arabian—Dau. of Byerly Turk.
			Whalebone or Seymour.† Daughter of.	Delpini (Highflyer)—Bay Javelin by Javelin (Eclipse)—Y. Flora by Highflyer—Flora by Squirrel—Angelica by Snap—Dau. of Regulus. Gohanna—Gr. Skim by Woodpecker—Silver's dam by Herod—Y. Hag by Skim (Starling)—Hag by Crab—Ebony by Childers—Ebony.
	Daughter of. Plenipotentiary. Harriet. Emilius.	Myrrha. Whalebone. Gift.	Selim. Canary Bird.	Buzzard—Castrel's dam by Alexander—Dau. of Highflyer—Dau. of Alfred (Matchem)—Dau. of Engineer—Bay Malton's dam by Cade. Whiskey or Sorcerer—Canary by Coriander—Miss Green by Highflyer—Harriet by Matchem—Flora by Regulus—Dau. of Bart. Childers.
			Orville. Emily.	Beningbrough—Evelina by Highflyer—Termagant by Tantrum—Cantatrice by Sampson—Dau. of Regulus—Marske's dam. Stamford—Dau. of Whiskey—Gr. Dorimant by Dorimant—Dizzy by Blank—Dizzy by Driver—Dau. of Smiling Tom (Con. Arabian).
			Pericles. Daughter of.	Evander (Delpini)—Dau. of Precipitate—Sis. to Ospray by Highflyer—Dau. of Snap—Dau. of Orford Barb—Dau. of Bart. Childers. Selim—Pipylina by Sir Peter—Rally by Trumpator—Fancy, Sis. to Diomed by Florizel—Dau. of Spectator—Dau. of Blank (Godol.)
			Waxy. Penelope.	Pot-8-os—Maria by Herod—Lisette by Snap—Miss Windsor by Godol. Arabian—Sis. to Volunteer by Y. Belgrade—Dau. of Childers. Trumpator—Prunella by Highflyer—Promise by Snap—Julia by Blank—Spectator's dam by Partner—Bonny Lass.
			Y. Gohanna. Sis. to Grazier.	Gohanna—Gr. Skim by Woodpecker—Silver's dam by Herod—Y. Hag by Skim—Hag by Crab—Ebony by Childers—Ebony. Sir Peter—Sis. to Amaltor by Trumpator—Dau. of Herod—Dau. of Snap—(Snip)—Dau. of Gower Stallion (Godolphin)—Dau. of Flying Childers (Darley Arabian).

* Waverly given.
† Seymour given.

BOSTON,

(WINNER OF THIRTY-FOUR MILE HEAT AND NINE THREE MILE HEAT RACES.)

BOSTON by Timoleon, son of Sir Archy, bred by John Wickham, Va., foaled in 1833, dam sister to Tuckahoe, by Ball's Florizel, son of imp. Diomed, out of a daughter of imp. Alderman, by Pot-8-os, son of English Eclipse. Timoleon, the sire of Boston, was the best race-horse of his day, started in seventeen races, won nine, walked over for four, and lost two. Florizel, the sire of his dam, had no equal in his day, he never lost a heat or paid a forfeit, "never knew the touch of a spur or heard the flourish of a whip." Boston made his debut as a three-year old at Broadrock, Va., mile heats, but was beaten by an indifferent colt, by bolting. Petersburg, Va., won purse 2 mile heats in 4:01, 4:00, track muddy, defeating a field of five. Hanover Court House, won Club Purse, 3 mile heat in 6:25, 6:19, track deep in mud, defeating Betsey Minge and five others. This was the first race in which he started under the name of Boston, derived from a popular game of cards. National Course, Washington, May 4th, 1837, won Club Purse, 3 mile heats, in 6:04, 6:10, track heavy, defeating a field of five. Same Course, October 5th, won Club Purse, 3 mile heats, in 5:55, 5:53, beating Prince George, Mary Selden, and five others. Baltimore, Md., won purse, 3 mile heats, in 5:51, 6:08, defeating Camsidel and Cippus. 1838, Camden, N. J., won Club Purse, 3 mile heats, in 5:51, 6:02, beating Betsey Andrew. Union Course, L. I., walked over for purse, 3 mile heats. Beacon Course, N. J., won purse, 4 mile heats, beating Dosoris, in 8:04, 8:01. Camden, N. J., won purse, 4 mile heats, beating Decatur, in 8:36, 8:41, track very heavy. Union Course, L. I., won Club Purse, 4 mile heats, beating Charles Carter, in 7:40; Carter was withdrawn after the first heat; $15,000 was refused for Boston that day. Beacon Course, N. J., won Club Purse, 4 mile heats, beating Duane, who won first heat, in 7:52, 7:54, 8:30, track muddy. Petersburg, Va., won Club Purse, 4 mile heats, in 9:25, beating Polly Green. Baltimore Central Course, won purse, 4 mile heats, beating Balie Payton, in 8:05, track muddy; Payton withdrew after the first heat. Kendal Course, received half purse to withdraw. Camden, N. J., received half the purse, 4 mile heats, to withdraw. Union Course, L. I., won purse, 4 mile heats, beating Decatur, in 8:00, 7:57½, track muddy. Beacon Course, N. J., won purse, 4 mile heats, beating Decatur, in 8:12, 8:26, track very heavy. 1839, Petersburg, Va., was beaten by Portsmouth, in match $10,000 a side, 2 mile heats, in 3:50, 3:48. Broadrock, Va., won purse, 3 mile heats, in 5:46, Lady Clifden and Brocklesby withdrawn after first heat. Washington, D. C., won purse, 4 mile heats, in 7:53, 8:06, beating Tom Walker and three others. Camden, N. J., walked over for purse, 4 mile heats. Trenton, N. J., won purse, 4 mile heats, in 7:57, 8:24, beating Decatur and Vashti. Union Course, L. I., won purse, 4 mile heats, beating Decatur and Balie Peyton, in 7:47, 8:02. Petersburg, Va., won purse, 4 mile heats, beating The Queen and Omega, in 8:02, 7:52. Camden, N. J., won purse, 4 mile heats, in 7:49; Omega second, and withdrawn. Trenton, N. J., won purse, 4 mile heats, beating Decatur, in 7:57, 7:56. 1840, Petersburg, Va., won purse, 4 mile heats, in 7:50, 8:04, beating Andrewetta, who won first heat and was drawn after the second. Washington, D. C., won purse, 4 mile heats, in 8:02, 8:06, beating Reliance, and Cippus, track muddy. Petersburg, Va., won purse, 4 mile heats, in 7:57, beating Bandit, drawn after the first heat. Broadrock, Va., won purse, 3 mile heats, in 5:56, 5:49, beating Texas and two others. Augusta, Ga., defeated Gano in match for $10,000 a side, 4 mile heats, in 7:57, Gano drawn after first heat, track muddy. Same place, won purse, 4 mile heats, beating Santa Anna, and Omega, in 7:52, 7:49. The owners of Boston then challenged Wagner, fresh from his victories over Grey Eagle and the whole United States, but no one accepted. Two English gentlemen challenged to run against Boston or the best American horse, 4 miles; the owner of Boston at once accepted, and offered to run Boston against any horse they could produce, for $50,000 a side, one race to be run in the United States and the other in England; this was declined. The owner of Boston then offered to bet $50,000 to $40,000 and run Boston 4 mile heats against any number of horses they might import, allowing them to name their horse at the post; this was also declined. 1841, Boston then went to the stud in Virginia, and covered 42 mares at $100 each; in the fall he was trained again, and at Washington, D. C., won purse, 4 mile heats, in 7:59, 8:24, beating Accident and two others. Baltimore, won purse, 4 mile heats, beating Mariner, who won first heat, in 8:00½, 8:05, 8:10, track very muddy. Camden, N. J., was distanced the first heat in the 4 mile heat race, won by Fashion, in 7:42, 7:48; John Blout won first heat and broke down in the second. The result of this race led to a challenge to run Boston against Fashion, 4 mile heats, over the Union Course, L. I., for $20,000 a side, half forfeit; the race was run May 10th, 1842, and resulted in the defeat of Boston, in

Continued on page 192.

PEDIGREE OF BOSTON.

BOSTON.	TIMOLEON.	Sir Archy.	Imp. Diomed.	Florizel.	Herod.	Tartar—Cypron by Blaze (Childers)—Selima by Bethell's Arabian—Dau. of Graham's Champion—Dau. of Darley Arabian.
					Daughter of.	Cygnet (Godol.)—Dau. of Cartouche (Bald Galloway)—Ebony by Childers—Ebony by Basto—Massey Mare by His. Black Barb.
				Sis. to Juno.	Spectator.	Crab (Alcock's Arabian)—Dau. of Partner (Jigg)—Bonny Lass by Bay Boltou—Dau. of Darley Arabian—Dau. of Byerly Turk.
					Horatia.	Blank (Godol.)—Dau. of Childers (Darley Arabian)—Miss Belvoir by Gr. Grantham (Brownlow Turk)—Dau. of Paget Turk.
			Imp. Castianira.	Rockingham.	Highflyer.	Herod—Rachel by Blank—Dau. of Regulus—Dau. of Soreheels (Basto)—Dau. of Makeless (Oglethorpe Arabian)—Royal Mare.
					Purity.	Matchem (Cade)—Dau. of Squirt (Bartlet's Childers)—Lot's dam by Mogul (Godol.)—Camilla by Bay Bolton—Old Lady by Pullein's Ch. Arabian.
				Tabitha.	Trentham.	Sweepstakes (Gower Stallion)—Miss South by South (Regulus)—Dau. of Cartouche—Ebony by Childers—Ebony by Basto.
					Daughter of.	Bosphorus (Babraham)—Dau. of Wm's Forester—Dau. of Coalition Colt (Godol.)—Dau. of Bustard (Crab)—Charming Molly by Second.
		Daughter of.	Imp. Saltram.	Eclipse.	Marske.	Squirt (Bartlet's Childers)—Dau. of Blacklegs (Hutton's Bay Barb)—Dau. of Bay Bolton (Gr. Hautboy)—Dau. of Fox Cub (Clumsy).
					Spiletta.	Regulus (Godol.)—Mother Western by Smith's Son of Suake—Dau. of Old Montague—Dau. of Hautboy—Dau. of Brimmer.
				Virago.	Snap.	Snip (Childers)—Sis. to Slipby by Fox (Clumsy)—Gipsy by Bay Bolton—Dau. of Newcastle Turk—Dau. of Byerly Turk—Dau. of Taffolet Barb.
					Daughter of.	Regulus—Sis. to Othello by Crab—Miss Slamerkin by Y. True Blue—(Wm's Turk)—Dau. of Oxford Dun Arabian.
			Dau. of Symme's Wildair.		Imp. Fearnought.	Regulus—Silvertail by Henage's Whitenose (Hall Arabian)—Dau. of Rattle (Son of Harpur's Barb)—Dau. of Darley Arabian—Old Child Mare.
					Daughter of.	Imp. Jolly Roger (Roundhead)—Imp. Kitty Fisher by Cade (Godol.)—Dau.of Som. Arabian—Bald Charlotte by Old Royal (Holderness Turk).
					Driver.	Imp.Othello (Crab)—Millia by Imp.Spark (Honeycomb Punch—Queen Mab by Musgrove Grey Arabian—Dau. of Hampton Court Childers.
					Daughter of.	Imp. Fallower by Blank by Godolphin Arabian—Dau. of Imp. Vampire by Regulus by Godolphin Arabian.
	ROBIN BROWN'S DAM.	Daughter of.	Imp. Alderman.	Ball's Florizel.	Herod.	Tartar—Cypron by Blaze—Selima by Bethell's Arabian—Dau. of Graham's Champion—Dau. of Darley Arabian—Dau. of Merlin.
				Imp. Diomed.	Daughter of.	Cygnet—Dau. of Cartouche—Ebony by Childers—Ebony by Basto (Byerly Turk)—Massey Mare by His. Black Barb.
				Sis. to Juno.	Spectator.	Crab—Dau. of Partner—Bonny Lass by Bay Bolton—Dau. of Darley Arabian—Dau. of Byerly Turk—Dau. of Taffolet Barb.
					Horatia.	Blank—Dau. of Childers—Miss Belvoir by Gr. Grantham—Dau. of Paget Turk—Betty Percival by Leede's Arabian—Dau. of Spanker.
			Lady Bolingbroke.	Imp. Shark.	Marske.	Squirt—Dau. of Blacklegs—Dau. of Bay Bolton—Dau. of Fox Cub—Dau. of Coneyskins (Lister Turk)—Dau. of Hutton's Gr. Barb.
					Daughter of.	Snap—Warwickshire Wag's dam by Marlborough (Godolphin Arabian)—Natural Barb Mare grandam of Tiney.
				Pot-8-o's.	Harris' Eclipse.	Partner (Jigg)—Bay Bloody Buttocks by Bloody Buttocks—Dau. of Greyhound (White Barb Chillaby)—Dau. of Makeless—Dau. of Brimmer.
					Daughter of.	Imp. Fearnought—Dau. of Imp. Jolly Roger—Dau. of Imp. Sober John (Rib)—Dau. of Imp. Shock by Shock Son of Jigg by Byerly Turk.
		Dau. of Clockfast.	Daughter of.	Dau. of.	Eclipse.	Marske—Spiletta by Regulus—Mother Western by Smith's Son of Snake—Dau. of Old Montague—Dau. of Hautboy—Dau. of Brimmer.
					Sportsmistress.	Warren's Sportsman (Cade)—Golden Locks by Oroonoko (Crab)—Valiant's dam by Crab—Dau. of Partner—Thwait's Dun Mare.
					Squirrel.	Traveler (Partner)—Gr. Bloody Buttocks by Bloody Buttocks—Dau. of Greyhound—Dau. of Makeless (Oglethorpe Arabian)—Dau. of Brimmer
			Imp. Clockfast.		Cypron.	Blaze—Selima by Bethell's Arabian—Dau. of Graham's Champion—Dau. of Darley Arabian—Dau. of Old Merlin (Bustler).
					Gimcrack.	Cripple (Godol.)—Miss Elliott by Grisewood's Partner—Caelia by Partner—Gr. Brocklesby by Bloody Buttocks—Brocklesby by Greyhound.
					Miss Ingram.	Regulus—Miss Doe by Sedbury (Partner)—Miss Mayes by Bartlet's Childers—Dau. of Counsellor (Shaftesbury Turk)—Dau. of Snake.
					Symme's Wildair.	Imp. Fearnought—Dau. of Imp. Jolly Roger—Imp. Kitty Fisher by Cade—Dau. of Somerset Arabian—Bald Charlotte by Old Royal.
					Y. Kitty Fisher.	Imp. Fearnought—Imp. Kitty Fisher by Cade—Dau. of Somerset Arabian—Bald Charlotte by Old Royal—Dau. of Bethell's Castaway (Merlin)—Dau. of Brimmer (D'Arcy Yellow Turk).

BOSTON—Continued.

7:32¼, 7:45, the fastest race run to that date. Same course, May 13. Boston won purse, 4 mile heats, defeating Mariner, who won first heat, in 8:13, 7:46, 7:58¼. Camden, N. J., Boston won 4 mile beat purse, defeating Treasurer, in 8:00¼, 8:05. Alexandria, D. C., was beaten by Wilton Brown, 4 mile heats, in 8:09, 7:55, 7:49 ; Boston won second heat, beating Reliance. Baltimore, Md., won purse, 4 mile heats, beating Wilton Brown and two others, in 8:09, 7:57. Petersburg, Va., closed his turf career by winning Club Purse, 3 mile heats, in 6:10, 6:21, beating Black Dick, track very heavy. He started in 45 races, won 40, 30 of which were 4 mile heats, nine 3 mile heats, and one 2 mile heats.

The best of his get were Lexington, Arrow, Atilla, Big Boston, Bob Johnson, Big Indian, Bostona, Clara Minter, Commodore, Cracker, Die Clapperton, Dick Doty, Financier, Goldpin, John Hopkins, Inspector, Jenny Lind, Madeline (grandam of Iroquois), Midway, Nat Blick, Orator, Nina dam of Planet, Exchecquer, etc., Red Eye, Ringgold, Rosalie, Tally-ho, Wade Hampton, White-Eye, Betty King, Lecompte, winner of the first heat of 4 miles better than 7:30 and the only horse which ever defeated Lexington, who won the time match in 7:19¾, and beat Lecompte in 7:23¼. Boston was a chestnut, with white blaze down his face extending over his muzzle, hence he was called "Old Whitenose ;" he had a plain head, very fine shoulders, with great length, and was wonderfully fine through the heart and chest, with powerful loin, thighs and hocks, and long springy pasterns and good sound legs and feet. Boston was very much inbred to Eclipse and Herod, and through the best sources to the Darley and Godolphin Arabians. His memory will always be green through the turf exploits of his sons and daughters, and the name of Boston and Lexington will be spoken of and referred to as long as racing is known.

DIOMED (Imp.)

WINNER OF THE FIRST DERBY EVER RUN, IN 1780, THE CLARET STAKES AND HIS MAJESTY'S PLATE.

DIOMED, by Florizel, son of Herod, bred by Sir Chas. Bunbury, foaled 1777, dam Sister to Juno, by Spectator, son of Crab, out of Horatia, by Blank. 1780 Newmarket Second Spring Meeting, won a sweepstake, Ditch-in beating Antagonist, Diadem and Savannah ; Epsom, won the Derby Stakes, last mile of the course, defeating Budrow, Spitfire and six others ; Newmarket July Meeting, walked over for sweepstakes across the flat ; Tuesday, First October Meeting, received forfeit from four others ; Ditch-in, next day, won the Perram Plate, Ditch-in, beating Rover, Marygold and eight others ; Friday, received forfeit from Catalpa, Rowley mile ; Second October Meeting, won a subscription of 20 guineas each, 8 subscribers, B. M., beating Teetotum, Duchess and two others. 1781—Newmarket Craven Meeting, Diomed received 250 guineas forfeit from Savannah in match over the Beacon course ; First Spring Meeting, won the Fortesque Stakes, Ditch-in, beating Spitfire, King William and three others ; Second Spring Meeting, won Claret Stakes, Beacon course, beating Antagonist, Arske and four others ; Nottingham, met his first defeat, running second to Fortitude, by Herod, in the Nottingham Stakes, twice around the course, Bay Bolton, by Matchem, and one other behind him; Newmarket First October Meeting, was beaten by Budrow, by Eclipse, Beacon course. 1782—Newmarket First October Meeting, paid forfeit to Crop, in sweepstakes, D. C. 1783—Newmarket, was unplaced in the Craven Stakes, from the ditch to the turn of the lands, won by Alaric ; Newmarket First Spring Meeting, was third to Laburnam and Drone, over the R. C. course, six others behind him ; same meeting, ran second to Drone for the King's Plate, R. C. course, Grasshopper, Buccaneer and Nottingham behind him ; Ascot Heath, was third to Soldier and Oliver Cromwell, four miles, beating Truth and Guilford ; won Her Majesty's Plate, four-mile heats, beating Lottery, who won the first heat ; Winchester, was second to Anvil in Her Majesty's Plate, four-mile heats, beating Mercury ; Lewes, was beaten by Mercury and Diadem for Her Majesty's Plate, four-mile heats ; Diomed fell lame in the race and was retired from the turf. After the season of 1798 Diomed, then in his twenty-second year, was sold for 50 guineas, and afterwards resold to Col. John Hoomes, of Virginia, for 1,000 guineas. He was a successful sire in England : the most noted of his get were Glaucus, Lais, Playfellow, Robin Grey, Grayhound, Wrangler Cedar, Victor, Valiant, Montezuma, Sir Cecil, Anthony, Whisker, Champion, Little Pickle, Fanny, Laurentina, Egham, Agamemnon, Frolic, Lord Fitzwilliam's mare the dam of Wonder, Miracle, Caleb Quotem, Cossack, etc., Young Noisette, the dam of Navigator, Clermont, Marmion, etc., Young Giantess, the dam of Sorcerer, and Eleanor, the first mare which ever won the Oaks and Derby, and the dam of Muley, sire of imp. Leviathan; Margrave, etc., Julia, the dam of Phantom, Lydia, dam of

Continued on page 194.

PEDIGREE OF DIOMED.

DIOMED	SISTER TO JUNO.									
	FLORIZEL.	Daughter of Cygnet.	Cygnet.	Herod.	Tartar.	Jigg.	Byerly Turk—Dau. of Spanker, son of D'Arcy Yellow Turk, out of Old Morocco Mare by Morocco Barb.
						Sis. to Mixbury.	Curwen Bay Barb—Dau. of Spot (Selaby Turk)—Dau. of Whitelegged Lowther Barb—Old Vintner Mare.
				Cypron.	Blaze.	Fox.	Clumsy (Hautboy)—Bay Peg by Leede's Arabian—Y. Bald Peg by Leede's Arabian—Old Morocco Mare.
						Milkmaid.	Sir W. Blacket's Snail (Partner)—Dam the Shield's Galloway.
					Meliora. Partner.	Childers.	Darley Arabian—Betty Leedes by Careless (Spanker)—Sis. to Leedes by Leede's Arabian—Dau. of Spanker—Barb Mare.
						Confederate filly.	Grey Grantham (Brownlow Turk)—Dau. of Duke of Rutland's Black Barb—Dau. of Bright's Roan.
				Godol. Arabian.	Selima.	Bethell's Arabian.	Was sire of Selima, the grandam of Herod, who was the sire of a larger number of race horses, stallions and mares than any horse that ever lived.
						Daughter of.	Graham's Champion—Harpur's Arabian—Dau. of Darley Arabian—Dau. of Merlin (Bustler).
					Blossom.		The most noted of all the Eastern sires about whom opinions are divided as to whether he was an Arab or Barb, the best judges inclining to the opinion that he was a Barb. He was purchased in Paris by Mr. Coke in 1728, who gave him to Mr. R. Williams, by whom he was presented to Earl Godolphin. He was a brown bay, 15 hands high, with some white on the off hind heel. Died 1753.
		Daughter of.	Cartouch.			Crab.	Alcock Arabian—Sis. to Sorebeels by Basto—Dau. of Cur. Bay Barb—Dau. of Curwen's Spot—Dau. of Whitelegged Lowther Barb.
						Daughter of.	Childers—Miss Belvoir by Gr. Grantham—Dau. of Paget Turk—Betty Percival by Leede's Arabian—Dau. of Spanker.
			Ebony.			The Bald Galloway.	St. Victor Barb—Dau. of Whynot (Fenwick Barb)—Royal Mare.
						Daughter of.	Hampton Court Cripple Barb—Dau. of Makeless (Ogle Arabian)—Dau. of Brimmer—Dau. of Place's White Turk—Dau. of Dodsworth.
						Childers.	Darley Arabian—Betty Leedes by Careless—Sis. to Leedes by Leede's Arabian—Dau. of Spanker—Barb Mare.
						Ebony.	Basto (Byerly Turk)—Massey Mare by His. Black Barb.
	Horatia.	Daughter of.	Spectator.	Crab.	Sis. to Sorebeels. Alcock Arabian.		Was the sire of Crab, Spot and Gentleman, and of the dams of Dismal and Trifle. He covered only a few mares. Crab was a fine race-horse, and was sire of many eminent horses.
						Basto.	Byerly Turk—Bay Peg by Leede's Arabian—Dau. of Spanker—Bald Peg by Lord Fairfax's Morocco Barb.
						Sis. to Mixbury.	Curwen Bay Barb—Dau. of Spot—Dau. of Whitelegged Lowther Barb—Old Vintner Mare.
				Daughter of.	Bonny Lass. Partner.	Jigg.	Byerly Turk—Dau. of Spanker by D'Arcy Yellow Turk, out of Morocco Mare by Morocco Barb.
						Sis. to Mixbury.	Curwen Bay Barb—Dau. of Spot—Dau. of Whitelegged Lowther Barb—Old Vintner Mare.
						Bay Bolton.	Grey Hautboy (Hautboy)—Dau. of Makeless—Dau. of Brimmer (Yellow Turk)—Dau. of Diamond (Jew's Trump).
						Daughter of.	Darley's Arabian—Dau. of Byerly Turk—Dau. of Taffolet Barb—Dau. of Place's White Turk—Natural Barb Mare.
		Daughter of.	Blank.	Lit. Hart-ley Mare.	Godol. Arabian.		The most noted of all the Eastern sires about whom opinions are divided whether he was an Arab or Barb. The best judges inclined to the opinion that he was a Barb. He was purchased in Paris by Mr. Coke in 1728, who gave him to Mr. R. Williams, by whom he was presented to Earl Godolphin. He was a brown bay, 15 hands high, with some white on off hind heel. He died in 1753.
						Bartlet's Childers.	Darley Arabian—Betty Leedes by Careless—Sis. to Leedes by Leede's Arabian—Dau. of Spanker—Barb Mare.
						Large Hartley Mare.	His Blind Horse (Holderness Turk)—Flying Whig by Wm's Woodstock Arabian—Dau. of St. Victor Barb.
				Miss Belvoir.	Childers.	Darley Arabian.	Was purchased by Mr. Darley, a merchant abroad, who presented him to his brother, Mr. J. Brewster Darley, of Buttercramb, now Aldby Park—He covered but few mares besides Mr. Darley's.
						Betty Leedes.	Careless—Sis. to Leedes by Leede's Arabian—Dau. of Spanker—Barb Mare.
						Grey Grantham.	Brownlow Turk, brought into England by Lord Brownlow in 1770. The Stud Book does not give Grey Grantham's dam.
						Daughter of.	Paget Turk—Betty Percival by Leede's Arabian—Dau. of Spanker—Barb Mare.

DIOMED (Imp.)—Continued.

Corporal ; Cressida, the dam of imp. Priam. There is scarcely a good horse in England of this day but what has some of his blood. In America, he sired Sir Archy, called the Godolphin Arabian of America ; Ball's Florizel, Duroc, sire of Am. Eclipse; Top-Gallant, Potomac, Stump the Dealer, Vingt'un, the dams of Henry, Shylock, Cicero, Lady of the Lake, Richmond, Diomed Eagle, Duchess of Marlborough, Maria Archy, Fanny Hill. He also sired Lady Chesterfield, Wringjaw, Miss Jefferson, Peacemaker, Hamiltonian, Hanie's Maria, the best mare of her day ; Wonder, Virginius, St. Tammany, Truxton, Herod, Madison, Sting and a host of others. Diomed was a solid chestnut, without white except on the heel of his right hind foot ; 15¾ hands high, with great substance and muscular power, which he transmitted to his stock. He died in Virginia in 1808, aged thirty-one years. He left behind him a name and fame which will endure to the end of all time, and crowned with laurels of the two great racing countries of the world, England and America.

GLENCOE,

(WINNER OF THE TWO THOUSAND GUINEAS AT THE NEWMARKET FIRST SPRING MEETING, 1834, AND THIRD FOR THE DERBY AT EPSOM TO PLENIPOTENTIARY ; AND WINNER OF THE GOODWOOD CUP SAME YEAR ; ALSO WINNER OF THE GOLD CUP AT ASCOT IN 1835.)

GLENCOE, by Sultan, was bred by Lord Jersey in 1831. He was a beautiful golden chestnut, with both hind legs white half way to the hocks, and a large star in his forehead. His head was a little Roman, very expressive in character, with fine thin muzzle, well set on a stout neck, which ran into well-shaped shoulders, being oblique and rather light in the blades. He had good length, with round barrel, well ribbed to strong broad hips, a little swayed in the back, with heavy muscular quarters, big stifles, and sound legs and rather flat feet. Glencoe commenced his racing career by winning the Riddlesworth Stakes at the Newmarket Craven Meeting in 1834, and ran second to Plenipotentiary in a sweepstakes over the Rowley Mile at the Newmarket First Spring Meeting, and defeated Ganges for the Desert Stakes across the Flat. Same meeting won the 2,000 Guineas Stakes, Rowley Mile, beating Flatterer, Bentley and four others. He ran third to the great Plenipotentiary for the Derby Stakes at Epsom, Shilelagh second; nineteen others started. At Ascot Heath he saved his stake from Plenipotentiary in a walk over for the St. James' Palace Stakes. Won the Goodwood cup at Goodwood, defeating Colwick, Famine, St. Giles, Marpessa, and five others. Same meeting won the Racing Stakes, Drawing Room Stake Course. At Newmarket Second October Meeting won the Garden Stakes, two middle miles, beating Glaucus and Colwick. At Ascot Heath, 1835, won the Ascot Gold Cup, 2½ miles, defeating Bran, Nonsense and six others. At the Newmarket Second October Meeting Lord Jersey challenged for the whip and named Glencoe; the challenge was not accepted. James Jackson, of Alabama, sent an order to England to purchase the best horse in the market, and named Plenipotentiary, Priam and Glencoe. Glencoe was purchased at a round sum and made the season of 1836 in England as the property of Mr. Jackson. He sired that year Pocahontas, Darkness, Glimpse, Malaga, Ruthless, Vapor and Wardan. Pocahontas, his daughter, in England, has placed his name imperishably upon the scroll of honor through her three great sons, Stockwell, Rataplan and King Tom. Stockwell sired Lady Augusta, Repulse and Achievement, winners of the 1,000 guineas; The Marquis, Lord Lyon, Bothwell and Gang Forward, winners of the 2,000 guineas; Blair Athol, Lord Lyon and Doncaster, winners of the Derby; Regalia, winner of the Oaks; St. Albans, Caller Ou, The Marquis, Blair Athol, Lord Lyon and Achievement, winners of the St. Leger; King Tom sired Tomato, winner of 1,000 guineas; Hannah, winner of 1,000 guineas, Oaks and St. Leger; Tormentor and Hippia, Oaks winners; Kingcraft, a Derby winner; Imp. Great Tom, sire of Tennyson, Tocsin and Ella; Imp. Phaeton, sire of King Alfonso and Ten Broeck, Imp. King Ban, sire of Punster, Queen Bau, and King Ernest, sire of Report; Marathon, Kingcraft, &c. There is scarcely a good stallion in England to-day that does not possess a strain of the blood of this great horse, viz.: Blair Athol, Bertram, Controversy, Cremorne, Cornelion, Cardinal York, Chevron, Craig Millar, Clanronald, Doncaster, Forerunner, Geo. Frederick, Hollywood, Hopbloom, Isonomy, Julius, Kaiser, Kingcraft, King Lud, Kisber, Lord Roland, Mask, Maximilian, Martyrdom, Master Kildare, Nunebam, New Holland, Prince Charlie, Petrarch, Statesman; Straun, Sir Bevys, Silvio, Skylark, Springfield, Uncas, Wenlock, Winslow, etc. The most distinguished of his get in America were Adelgasia, Aduella, Budelight,

Continued on page 196.

PEDIGREE OF GLENCOE.

GLENCOE.						
SULTAN.	Bacchante.	Sister to Calomel.	Dau. of Mercury.	Williamson's Ditto.	Castrel's dam.	Selim.
					Alexander.	Buzzard.
				Arethusa. Sir Peter.		Woodpecker.
					Dau. of.	Misfortune.

		Herod.	Tartar—Cypron by Blaze (Childers)—Selima by Bethell's Arabian—Dau. of Graham's Champion—Dau. of Darley Arabian.
		Miss Ramsden.	Cade (Godol.)—Dau. of Lonsdale Bay Arabian—Dau. of Bay Bolton—Dau. of Darley Arabian—Dau. of Byerly Turk.
		Dux.	Matchem (Cade)—Duchess by Whitenose (Godol.)—Miss Slamerkin by Y. True Blue (Wm.'s Turk)—Dau. of Oxford Dun Arabian.
		Curiosity.	Snap (Snip)—Dau. of Regulus (Godol.)—Dau. of Bartlet's Childers (Darley Arabian)—Dau. of Honeywood Arabian.
		Eclipse.	Marske (Squirt)—Spiletta by Regulus (Godol.)—Mother Western by Smith's Son of Snake—Dau. of Montague—Dau. of Hautboy.
		Grecian Princess.	Wm.'s Forester (Forester)—Dau. of Coalition Colt (Godol.)—Dau. of Bustard (Crab)—Charming Molly by Second.
		Highflyer.	Herod—Rachel by Blank (Godol.)—Dau. of Regulus (Godol.)—Dau. of Soreheels (Basto)—Dau. of Makeless—Royal Mare.
		Sister to Doctor.	Alfred (Matchem)—Dau. of Herod—Dau. of Engineer (Sampson)—Bay Malton's dam by Cade (Godol.)—Lass of the Mill.
		Highflyer.	Herod—Rachel by Blank—Dau. of Regulus—Dau. of Soreheels—Dau. of Makeless (Oglethorpe Arabian.)—D'Arcy's Royal Mare.
		Papillon.	Snap—Miss Cleveland by Regulus—Midge by Son of Bay Bolton—Dau. of Bartlet's Childers—Dau. of Hon. Arabian.
		Dungannon.	Eclipse—Aspasia by Herod—Doris by Blank—Helen by Spectator (Crab)—Daphne by Godol. Arabian.
		Daughter of.	Prophet (Regulus)—Virago by Snap—Dau. of Regulus—Sis. to Othello by Crab—Miss Slamerkin by Y. True Blue.
		Eclipse.	Marske—Spiletta by Regulus—Mother Western by Smith's Son of Snake—Dau. of Montague—Dau. of Hautboy.
		Daughter of.	Tartar (Partner)—Dau. of Mogul (Godol.)—Dau. of Sweepstakes (Oxford Arabian)—Sis. to Sloven by Bay Bolton.
		Herod.	Tartar—Cypron by Blaze—Selima by Bethell's Arabian—Dau. of Graham's Champion (Harpur's Arabian).
		Folly.	Marske—Vixen by Regulus—Dau. of Hutton's Spot—Dau. of Bay Bolton (Gr. Hautboy)—Dau. of Fox Cub (Clumsy).

TRAMPOLINE.	Tramp.	Daughter of.	Gohanna. Dau. of.	Pot-8-o's.	Waxy.	Web.
		Dick Andrews.	Joe Andrews.	Maria.	Fraxinella.	
	Trumpator.				Prunella.	Penelope.

		Eclipse.	Marske—Spiletta by Regulus—Mother Western by Smith's Son of Snake—Dau. of Montague—Dau. of Hautboy—Dau. of Brimmer.
		Amaranda.	Omnium (Snap)—Cloudy by Blank—Fancy by Crab (Alcock Arabian) Widdington Mare by Partner.
		Highflyer.	Herod—Rachel by Blank—Dau. of Regulus—Dau. of Soreheels—Dau. of Makeless—C. D'Arcy's Royal Mare.
		Daughter of.	Cardinal Puff (Babraham)—Dau. of Tatler (Blank)—Dau. of Snip (Alcock Arabian)—Dau. of Godol. Arabian.
		Mercury.	Eclipse—Dau. of Tartar—Dau. of Mogul—Dau. of Sweepstakes—Dau. of Bay Bolton—Dau. of Curwen Bay Barb.
		Precipitate's dam.	Herod—Maiden by Matchem (Cade)—Dau. of Squirt (Bartlet's Childers)—Dau. of Mogul—Dau. of Bay Bolton.
		Trentham.	Sweepstakes—Miss South by South (Regulus)—Dau. of Cartouche (Bald Galloway)—Ebony by Childers—Ebouy by Basto.
		Fractious' dam.	Woodpecker—Everlasting by Eclipse—Hyæna by Snap—Miss Belsea by Regulus—Dau. of Bartlet's Childers.
		Eclipse.	Marske—Spiletta by Regulus—Mother Western by Smith's Son of Snake—Dau. of Montague—Dau. of Hautboy.
		Sportsmistress.	Warren's Sportsman (Cade)—Golden Locks by Oroonoko (Crab)—Valiant's dam by Crab—Dau. of Partner.
		Herod.	Tartar—Cypron by Blaze—Selima by Bethell's Arabian—Dau. of Graham's Champion—Dau. of Darley Arabian.
		Lisette.	Snap—Miss Windsor by Godol. Arabian—Sis. to Volunteer by Y. Belgrade—Dau. of Bartlet's Childers.
		Conductor.	Matchem—Dau. of Snap—Dau. of Cullen Arabian—Lady Thigh by Partner—Dau. of Greyhound (Wh. Barb Chillaby).
		Brunette.	Squirrel (Traveler)—Dove by Matchless (Godol.)—Dau. of Ancaster Starling—Dau. of Grasshopper (Crab).
		Highflyer.	Herod—Rachel by Blank—Dau. of Regulus—Dau. of Soreheels—Dau. of Makeless—C. D'Arcy's Royal Mare.
		Promise.	Snap—Julia by Blank—Spectator's dam by Partner—Bonny Lass by Bay Bolton—Dau. of Darley Arabian—Dau. of Byerly Turk—Dau. of Taffolet Barb—Dau. of Place's White Turk—Natural Barb Mare.

GLENCOE—Continued.

Bonnie Lassie, Bonnie Laddie, Blonde, Compromise, Charmer (the best mare of her day), Don Juan, Fanny King, Frankfort, Harper, Highlander, Hugh L. French, Magnolia, Moth, Nannie Lewis, Novice, Nicholas 1st, Sully Lewis, Sallie Waters, Panic, Pryor, Peytona, Rigadoon. Reel, Star Davis, Torchlight, Topaz, Vandal, Wild Irishman. Reel produced Lecompte, Starke, Prioress, War Dance, etc. Fanny King, Brown Dick. Topaz, dam of Austerlitz, Wagram, Waterloo, Colton and Lodi. Magnolia, Princeton, Skedaddle, Daniel Boone, Kentucky, Gilroy and Madeline, the latter the grandam of Iroquois, winner of the Derby and St. Leger; Rhoda Fleetwing. Nebula, Asteroid and Asterisk, Novice, Norfolk, Kitty Clark, Maiden, the dam of Parole, and La Henderson, dam of Felida; Florine Idlewild, the dam of Wildidle, and Aerolite, dam of Fellowcraft, Spendthrift, etc.; Mildred, Monarchist and Minx, the dam of Monitor. Sally Lewis, Acrobat and Susan Beane, the dam of Sensation. Sister to Pryor. Colossus and Glycera; Lightsome Sprightly, the dam of Volturno, and Nevada, the dam of Luke Blackburn. Glencoe was much inbred to Herod, Eclipse and Matchem. Few of his sons were ever in the stud, as he was notorious as a getter of fillies. Vandal sired Mollie Jackson, Alta Vela, Vandalite. Virgil, sire of Hindoo; Coral, the dam of Wanderer and Uncas, and other noted ones; Star Davis, sire of Matt Davis, Day Star and others. It is safe to say that few or none of the most famous horses now on the turf but have a cross of Glencoe. Glencoe stood in Alabama and Tennessee from 1837 to 1848; he was then purchased by W. F. Harper and taken to Kentucky, where he stood to the day of his death. He was purchased by the late A. Keene Richards in the summer of 1857 and died at his farm in August of that year, aged 26 years. Such was his indomitable courage that he literally died standing upon his feet. His name and fame is as enduring as time.

LEAMINGTON (Imp.)

(WINNER OF WOODCOTE STAKES AT WARWICK, CHESTERFIELD STAKES AT DERBY, STEWARDS CUP AT SHREWSBURY, CHESTER CUP AT CHESTER, AND GOODWOOD STAKES.)

LEAMINGTON, by Faugh-a-Ballagh, son of Sir Hercules, bred by Mr. Halford, foaled 1853, dam by Pantaloon, son of Castrel; Faugh-a-Ballagh was own brother to Irish Birdcatcher, and won the St. Leger in 1844; Pantaloon, sire of Leamington's dam, was a superior race-horse; started seven times as a three-year-old; won six races, and was first in the seventh, but disqualified for loss of weight. He was a valuable stallion, sire of Ghuznee, winner of the Oaks in 1841; Satirist, winner of the St. Leger, in 1851; Jocose, dam of Macaroni; Pantolonade, dam of the Prime Minister, sire of Knight of the Garter, and Fair Helen, the dam of Lord of the Isles, winner of the Two Thousand Guineas in 1855, and sire of Dundee, &c. Leamington was considered a first-class race-horse, especially with heavy weights. When two years old he started five times, lost three, and won two races—the Woodcote Stakes at Warwick, defeating Ceres and Mavourneen, and the Chesterfield Stakes at Derby, beating Stork and four others. As a three-year-old, started ten times; lost seven, won three—the Wrotterby Stakes at Wolverhampton, beating Harrie and two others, the Town Plate at Warwick, beating Elfrida, Octavin, and three others, and the Steward's Cup at Shrewsbury, beating Octavia, Agra, and eight others. At four years old, started five times; lost three and won two—the Tradesman's Plate at Chester, beating Dramour, Dulcamara, and thirty-two others, and the Goodwood Stakes at Goodwood. In this race, 2¼ miles, he carried 118 pounds, and beat eighteen horses. Gunboat, three years old, 91 pounds, was second, Somerset (3), 88 pounds, third, and Fisherman, 4 years old, with 124 pounds up, was not placed. The odds were 100 to 3 against Leamington. In his five year old year he only started once and was beaten. In his six year old year he started three times; was beaten once, paid forfeit to Saunterer, and won the Chester Cup, course 2¼ miles, in which he beat a field of thirty-two horses, including the American mare Prioress and the great Fisherman. This ended his turf career. Leamington made six seasons in England, but was not regarded as a success in the stud. The best of his get in England were Procella, Catalogue, Coup d' Etat, Lady Warwick, Lemonade, Queen of Crystal, Lady of Coverdale, Bella, Boleno, Cheltenham, Fitzroy, Fortunatus, Warwick, Variation, Ruppera, Cora, Catiline, Haymaker and others. He was a success in America from the start, he made his first season in America at the Bosque Bonita Stud in Kentucky, and the fruits of that season were Enquirer, a first-class race-horse, and one of the most successful stallions in the country; Longfellow, a superior race-horse and successful sire. Lyttleton, Lynchburg, Miss Alice, Anna Mace, then followed Eolus, a fine race-horse and one of the most promising sires in the country, Ida Wells. Nettie

Continned on page 198.

PEDIGREE OF LEAMINGTON (Imp.)

LEAMINGTON (Imp.)	**FAUGH-A-BALLAH**	Sir Hercules	Whalebone	Pot-8-o's	Eclipse (Marske)—Sportmistress by Sportsman (Cade)—Golden Locks by Oroonoko (Crab)—Valiaut's dam by Crab (Alcock Arabian).
			Penelope	Maria	Herod (Tartar)—Lisette by Snap (Snip)—Miss Windsor by Godol. Arabian—Sis. to Volunteer by Y. Belgrade—Dau. of Bartlet's Childers.
		Peri	Wanderer	Trumpator	Conductor (Matchem)—Brunette by Squirrel (Traveler)—Dove by Matchless (Godol.)—Dau. of An. Starling—Dau. of Grasshopper (Crab).
			Thalestris	Prunella	Highflyer (Herod)—Promise by Snap (Snip)—Julia by Blank (Godol.)—Spectator's dam by Partner (Jigg)—Bonny Lass by Bay Bolton.
		Bob Booty	Chanticleer	Gohanna	Mercury (Eclipse)—Dau. of Herod—Maiden by Matchem—Dau. of Squirt—Dau. of Mogul (Godol.)—Dau. of Bay Bolton (Gr. Hautboy).
			Ierne	Catharine	Woodpecker (Herod)—Camilla by Treutham (Sweepstakes)—Coquette by the Compton Barb—Sis. to Regulus by Godol. Arabian.
	Guiccioli	Flight	Y. Heroine	Alexander	Eclipse—Grecian Princess by Wm's Forester—Dau. of Coalition Colt (Godol.)—Dau. of Bustard (Crab)—Charming Molly by Second.
				Rival	Sir Peter (Highflyer)—Hornet by Drone (Herod)—Manilla by Goldfinder (Snap)—Dau. of Old Eng. (Godol.)—Dau. of Cul. Arabian.
			Irish Escape	Woodpecker	Herod—Miss Ramsden by Cade—Dau. of Lonsdale's Bay Arabian—Dau. of Bay Bolton—Dau. of Darley Arabian—Dau. of Byerly Turk.
				Daughter of	Eclipse—Rosebud by Snap—Miss Belsea by Regulus—Dau. of Bartlet's Childers (Darly Arabian)—Dau. of Honeywood's Arabian.
				Bagot	Herod—Marotte by Matchem (Cade)—Dau. of Traveler (Partner)—Dau. of Hartley's Bl. Horse (Holderness Turk)—Dau. of Grasshopper (Crab).
				Daughter of	Gamahoe (Bustard by Crab)—Patty by Tim (Squirt)—Miss Patch by Justice (Litton Arabian)—Ringtail Galloway by Cur. Bay Barb.
				Commodore	Highflyer—Dau. of Matchem—Dau. of Dainty Davy (Traveler)—Dau. of Son of Mogul—Dau. of Crab—Dau. of Bay Bolton—Dau. of Cur. Bay Barb.
				Buffer's dam	Highflyer—Shift by Sweetbriar (Syphon)—Bl. Susan by Snap—Lord Bruce's Cade Mare by Cade—Dau. of Belgrade—Dau. of Clif. Arabian.
				Bagot	Herod—Marotte by Matchem—Dau. of Traveler (Partner)—Dau. of Hartley's Blind Horse (Holderness Turk)—Dau. of Grasshopper.
				Heroine	Hero (Cade)—Dau. of Snap—Sis. to Regulus by Godol. Barb—Gr. Robinson by Bald Galloway (St. Victor Barb)—Dau. of Snake (Lister Turk).
DAUGHTER OF	Daphne	Laurel	Blacklock	Woodpecker	Herod—Miss Ramsden by Cade—Dau. of Lon's Bay Arabian—Dau. of Bay Bolton—Dau. of Darley Arabian—Dau. of Byerly Turk.
				Misfortune	Dux (Matchem)—Curiosity by Snap—Dau. of Regulus (Godol.)—Dau. of Bartlet's Childer's (Darley Arabian)—Dau. of Hon. Arabian.
			Wagtail	Alexander	Eclipse—Grecian Princess by Wm's Forester—Dau. of Coalition Colt—Dau. of Bustard—Charming Molly by Second—Dau. of Stanyan Arabian.
				Daughter of	Highflyer—Dau. of Alfred—Dau. of Engineer—Bay Malton's dam by Cade—Lass of the Mill by Traveler—Miss Makeless by Y. Greyhound.
		Pantaloon	Castrel	Sir Peter	Highflyer—Papillon by Snap—Miss Cleveland by Regulus—Midge by Son of Bay Bolton—Dau. of Bartlet's Childers—Dau. of Honeywood Arabian.
				Daughter of	Budrow (Eclipse)—Escape's dam by Squirrel—Dau. of Babrabam—Dau. of Golden Ball (Partner)—Bushy Molly by Hamp. Ct. Childers—Bushy Molly.
			Idalia	Meteor	Eclipse—Dau. of Merlin (Second)—Mother Pratt by Marksman (Godol.)—Dau. of Mixbury (Spot)—Dau. of Bald Galloway.
				Maid of all Work	Highflyer—Sis. to Tandem by Syphon—Dau. of Regulus—Dau. of Snip (Childers)—Dau. of Cottingham (Har. Bl. Horse).
	Maid of Honor	Champion	MusidoraPeruvian	Whitelock	Hambletonian (King Fergus)—Rosalind by Phœnomenon (Herod)—Atalanta by (Matchem—Lass of the Mill by Oroonoko—Dau. of Traveler.
				Daughter of	Coriander (Pot-8-os)—Wildgoose by Highflyer—Coheiress by Pot-8-os—Manilla by Goldfinder (Snap)—Dau. of Old Eng.—Dau. of Cullen Arabian.
			Dau. of Buzzard	Prime Minister	Sancho (Don Quixote)—Miss Hornpipe Teazle by Sir Peter—Hornpipe by Trumpator—Luna by Herod—Proserpine by Marske—Spiletta by Regulus.
				Daughter of	Orville—Miss Grimstone by Weasel (Herod)—Dau. of Ancaster—Dau. of Dam. Arabian—Dau. of Sampson—Dau. of Oroonoko—Sis. to Mirza.
	Etiquette			Selim	Buzzard—Castrel's dam by Alexander—Dau. of Highflyer—Dau. of Alfred (Matchem)—Dau. of Engineer—Bay Malton's dam by Cade.
				Podagra	Gouty (Sir Peter)—Jet by Magnet (Herod)—Jewel by Squirrel—Sophia by Blank—Diana by Second—Dau. of Stan. Arabian.
				Orville	Beningbrough (King Fergus)—Evelina by Highflyer—Termagant by Tantrum—Cantatrice by Sampson—Dau. of Regulus.
				Boadicea	Alexander (Eclipse)—Brunette by Amaranthus (Old Eng. by Godol.)—Mayfly by Matchem (Cade by Godol.)—Dau. of Ancaster—Starling (Starling by Bay Bolton)—Dau. of Grasshopper (Crab)—Dau. of Sir M. Newton's Arabian—Dau. of Pert (Ely Turk)—Dau. of St. Martins (Spanker)—Dau. of Sir E. Hale's Arabian—The Oldfield Mare.

LEAMINGTON (Imp.)—Continued.

Norton, Reform, a promising stallion and good race-horse, Hyder Ali, James A, Radamanthus, Olitipa, Golden Gate, Janet Norton, Bob Woolley, Katie Pearce, Aristides, a first-class race-horse and sire of Henlopen, Pera, Hattie F, Fugitive, Parole, who not only defeated the best in America, but went to England and defeated good horses on their own chosen ground, Harold, Idler, Loiterer, Perfection, Ferncliff, Lucifer, Susquehanna, Verdict, Pique, Maritana, Annie Augusta, Faithless, Spinaway, Girofle, Spark, Gossip, Rosalie, Democrat, Outcast, Sioux, Blazes, Sunbeam, Kate Clark, Pawnee, Bounce. Onondaga, Girofla, Wyandotte, Francesca, Iroquois, who crossed the Atlantic and placed the great events, the Derby and St. Leger, to the credit of America, the unbeaten and unfortunate Sensation, and many others, all winners. He was exiled and condemned in the land of his birth, but was appreciated and will be remembered in the land of his adoption. His sons are proving successful stallions and his daughters producing winners. Leamington was a brown, 16½ hands high, with a beautiful head and neck, good shoulders, great depth of chest, good back, great length, but light body and flank, good length of hip, and as fine hind legs and hock as were ever placed under a horse. He died the property of Mr. A. Welch, in the Erdenheim Stud, Chestnut Hill, Pa., Monday, May 6th, 1878. Let his blood be preserved by crossing some son of Lexington with his daughters from Lexington mares.

LEXINGTON,

(WINNER OF THE ASSOCIATION AND CITIZENS' STAKES AT LEXINGTON, KY., IN 1853, AND THE GREAT STATE STAKE OF NEW ORLEANS, 1854.)

LEXINGTON by Boston, bred by Dr. E. Warfield, The Meadows near Lexington, Ky., foaled 1850, dam Alice Carneal, dam of Waxy, Umpire, Release, etc., by imp. Sarpedon, son of Emilius. Lexington, during his turf career, met with only one defeat. He made his *debut* at Lexington, Ky., Spring meeting, of 1853, in the Association Stake for three-year olds ; mile heats, 20 subscribers, 12 starters. The track was almost knee deep in mud, and raining. In a false start, Lexington, then called Darley by Dr. Warfield, from his resemblance to the Darley Arabian, ran away, in company with Madonna and Garret Davis, and ran two miles and three quarters before they could be stopped. Garret Davis was then withdrawn, and Lexington was led to the post at once and the word given. He distanced all but three of the colts the first heat, including Vandal, Blonde, Hebron and Big Boston. Vandal, Blonde and Hebron were all famous on the turf. Wild Irishman was second in both heats, Fanny Fern fourth and third, and Madonna third and distanced. The time of the race was 1:55½, 1:57. The same week he won the Citizens' Stakes, two-mile heats, beating Midway, who won the first heat, Garret Davis, who was third, and distanced Margaret West, Hebron, Blonde and Eva ; time 3:42½, 3:41½, 3:49. Darley was then sold to Captain Willa Viley and Richard Ten Broeck, and his name was changed to Lexington. He was then matched against Sally Waters, three-mile heats, the owners of the mare betting $5,000 against $3,500 on the horse. The race was run at New Orleans, over the Metairie Course, Dec. 2, 1853, the track being deep in mud. Lexington won in 6:23½, 6:24½, distancing the mare in the second heat. His next appearance was for the great State Stake, $5,000 each, play or pay, four-mile heats; Kentucky entered Lexington; Alabama, Highlander; Louisiana, Arrow, and Mississippi Lecompte. Lexington won in 8:08¾, 8:04, track muddy, distancing Arrow in the first heat, and Highlander in the second. Highlander was the favorite. A week after he met Lecompte and Rheube for the Jockey Club Purse, four-mile heats. In this he was defeated, in 7:26, 7:38½, the best race to that day ever run in America. It was and is still claimed that his defeat was caused by his jockey, Henry Meichon, pulling him up at the end of the third mile, in second heat, thinking the race was ended. Richard Ten Broeck, who had now become the sole owner of Lexington, feeling that his horse could beat the best time made, 7:26, challenged Lecompte, or any other horse, to run Lexington four-mile heats for $25,000, or run him against the time, 7:26. The latter proposition was accepted, and the race was run over the Metairie Course, New Orleans, April 2, 1855. Lexington won in 7:19¾, running first mile in 1:47¼; second, 1:52¼; third, 1:51¼; fourth, 1:48½; thus beating the best time on record 6¼ seconds. On the 14th of April he met his great rival, Lecompte, for the Jockey Club Purse, $1,000, and an inside stake of $2,500, each four-mile heats. Lexington won the first heat in 7:23¾, and Lecompte was withdrawn. This ended the turf career of Lexington. In 1856, while in England, Mr. R. A. Alexander purchased Lexington from Mr. Ten Broeck, paying $7,500 cash and $7,500 more upon his return home to America,

Continued on page 200.

PEDIGREE OF LEXINGTON.

LEXINGTON.	**BOSTON.**	Robin Brown's dam.	Sir Archy.	Timoleon.	Florizel.	Herod—Dau of Cygnet—Dau. of Curtouche—Ebony by Flying Childers—Old Ebony by Basto—Massy Mare by His. Barb.
					Sis. to Juno.	Spectator—Horatia by Blank—Dau. of F. Childers—Miss Belvoir by Gr. Grantham—Dau. of Paget Turk—Betty Percival.
				Saltram.	Rockingham.	Highflyer—Purity, Sis. to Pumpkin, by Matchem——Dau. of Squirt—Lot's dam by Mogul—Camilla by Bay Bolton—Old Lady.
					Tabitha.	Trentham—Dau. of Bosphorus (Babraham)—Dau. of Wm's. Forester—Dau. of Coalition Colt (Godol.)—Dau. of Bustard (Crab)—Char. Molly.
				Castianira.	Eclipse.	Marske (Squirt)—Spiletta by Regulus—Mother Western by Smith's Son of Snake—Dau. of Montague—Dau. of Hautboy—Dau.of Brimmer.
					Virago.	Snap—Sis. to Othello by Crab(Alcock Arabian)—Miss Slamerkin by Y. True Blue—Dau. of Oxford Dun Arabian—Blacklegged Royal Mare.
			Daughter of.	Diomed.	Symme's Wildair.	Imp. Fearnought (Regulus)—Dau. of Jolly Roger—Imp. Kitty Fisher by Cade—Dau. of Som. Arabian—Bald Charlotte by Old Royal.
					Daughter of.	Driver (Imp. Othello by Crab, Dau. of Fallower (Blank by Godol.)—Dau. of Imp. Vampire (Regulus by Godol.)
			Ball's Florizel.	Dau. of Alderman.	Florizel.	Herod—Dau of Cygnet—Dau. of Cartouche—Ebony by Flying Childers—Ebony by Basto (By. Turk)—Massey Mare by His. Bl. Barb.
					Sis. to Juno.	Spectator—Horatia by Blank—Dau. of Fl. Childers—Miss Belvoir by Gr. Grantham—Dau. of Paget Turk—Betty Percival by Leede's Arabian.
				Dau. of Diomed.	Imp. Shark.	Marske (Squirt by Syphon)—Dau. of Snap (Snip)—Warwickshire's Wag's dam by Marlborough (Godol.)—Natural Barb Mare.
					Daughter of.	Harris' Eclipse (Partner)—Dau. of Fearnought—Dau. of Jolly Roger (Roundhead)—Dau of Sober John (Rib)—Dau. of Imp. Sbock.
		Daughter of.			Pot-8-o's.	Eclipse—Sportsmistress by War Sportsman (Cade)—Goldenlocks by Oroonoko—Valiant's dam by Crab—Thwart's Dun Mare.
					Lady Bolingbroke.	Squirrel—Cypron by Blaze—Selima by Bethell's Arabian—Dau. of Graham's Champion—Dau. of Dar. Arabian—Dau. of Merlio.
					Clockfast.	Gimcrack—Miss Ingram by Regulus—Miss Doe by Sedbury—Miss Mayes by Bart. Childers—Dau. of Counsellor—Dau. of Snake.
					Daughter of.	Symme's Wildair—Y. Kitty Fisher by Fearnought—Imp. Kitty Fisher by Cade—Dau. of Som. Arabian—Bald Charlotte by Old Royal.
	ALICE CARNEAL.	Rowena.	Sumpter.	Emillus.	Beningbrough.	King Fergus—Dau. of Herod—Pyrrha by Matchem—Duchess by Whitenose—Miss Slamerkin by Y. True Blue—Dau. of Ox Dun Arabian.
					Evelina.	Highflyer—Termagant by Tantrum—Cantatrice by Sampson—Dau. of Regulus—Marske's dam by Blacklegs.
				Orville.	Stamford.	Sir Peter—Horatia by Eclipse—Countess, Delpini's dam by Blank—Dau. of Rib—Dau. of Wynn Arabian.
					Daughter of.	Whiskey—Gr. Dorimant by Dorimant—Dizzy by Blank—Dizzy by Driver—Dau. of Smiling Tom—Dau. of Oysterfoot.
			Lady Grey.	Emily.	Vandyke, Jr.	Walton—Dabchick by Pot-8-os—Drab by Highflyer—Hebe by Chrysolite—Prosepine, Sis. to Eclipse by Marske.
					Azalia.	Beningbrough—Gillyflower by Highflyer—Dau. of Goldfinder—Sis. to Grasshopper by Marske—Dau. by Cullen Arabian.
				The Flyer.	Dick Andrews.	Joe Andrews—Dau. of Highflyer—Dau. of Car. Puff (Babraham)—Dau. of Tatler—Dau. of Snip—Dau. of Godol. Arabian—Dau. of Whiteneck.
					May.	Beningbrough—Primrose by Mambrino—Cricket by Herod—Sophia by Blank—Diana by Second—Dau. of Stan. Arabian.
		Flirtilla's dam.	Sir Archy.	Sarpedon.	Diomed.	Florizel—Sis. to Juno by Spectator—Horatia by Blank—Dau. of F. Childers—Miss Belvoir by Grantham—Dau. of Paget Turk.
					Castianira.	Rockingham—Tabitha by Trentham—Dau. of Bosphorus—Dau. of Wm.'s Forester—Dau. of Coalition Colt.—Dau. of Bustard.
				Icaria.	Robin Redbreast.	Sir Peter—Wren by Woodpecker—Papillon, Sir Peter's dam by Highflyer—Miss Cleveland by Regulus—Midge by Son of Bay Bolton.
					Daughter of.	Obscurity (Eclipse)—Slamerkin by Wildair (Cade)—Cub Mare by Cub—Amarauthus' dam by Second—Flash's dam by Starling.
		Robin Maria.	Robin Grey.	Parma.	Royalist.	Saltram—Dau. of Herod—Carina by Marske—Dau. of Blank—Dizzy by Driver—Dau. of Smiling Tom—Dau. of Oysterfoot.
					Belle Mariah.	Grey Diomed (Imp. Medley)—Queen by Imp. St. George (Dragon)—Dau. of Cassius—Primrose by Imp. Dove—Stella.
					Melzar.	Imp. Medley—Kitty Fisher by Symme's Wildair—Kitty Fisher by Imp. Vampire (Regulus)—Imp. Kitty Fisher by Cade—Dau. of Som. Arabian.
					Daughter of.	Highflyer (Highflyer)—Dau. of Fearnought (Regulus)—Dau. of Ariel (Imp. Traveler)—Dau. of Jack of Diamonds (Cul. Arabian)—Imp. Diamond by Cullen Arabian—Lady Thigh by Croft's Partner (Jigg)—Dau. of Greyhound (Wh. Barb Chillaby)—Sophonisba's dam by Curwen's Bay Barb—Dau. of D'Arcy's Ch. Arabian—Dau. of Whiteshirt—Old Montague Mare.

LEXINGTON—Continued.

if the horse was then alive. Lexington was not only the best race-horse America ever produced, but was the king of stallions. He sired Norfolk, Asteroid, Idlewild, dam of Wildidle, Kentucky, Daniel Boone, Goodwood, Bay Flower, Ansel, Lightning, Laura Farris, Thunder, Lancaster, Beacon, Bayswater, Bayonet, Preakness, Colton, Harry of the West, King Lear, Lilly Ward, Arcola, Optimist, who made a reputation in England and France, Maiden, dam of Parole, Merrill, Marion, Hollywood, Ulrica, Spartan, Wanderer, Uncas, Garrick, Chesapeake, Kadi, Harry Bassett, Charley Howard, Monarchist, the coming sire, Jack Malone, to whose daughter's Bonnie Scotland is indebted in a great measure for his success, Minx, dam of Monitor, Nevada, dam of Luke Blackburn, Salina, Crucifix, Sprightly, dam of Volturno, Woodbine, dam of Belle of the Meade, Bonnie Wood, etc., Susan Beane, dam of Sensation, Acrobat, Hunter's Lexington, Vauxhall, sire of Viator, Cloverbrook, etc., Lever, Pat Malloy, sire of Ozark, Duke of Magenta, Spartan, Jamaica, dam of Foxhall, Aerolite, dam of Fellowcraft, Spendthrift and Rutherford, Hester, dam of Springbok, Fanny Holton, dam of Ten Broeck, Kingfisher, Stamps, The Nun, Annie Bush, dam of Bushwhacker, Madame Dudley, Squeeze'em, dam of Day Star, Florence, dam of Hindoo, Betty Ward, Echo, dam of Report, Millie J, Finesse, La Polka, Arizona, dam of Aranza, Kathleen, dam of Geo. Kinney, Regan, dam of Vigil and Vera Cruz, Ratan, dam of Girofle, Susan Ann, dam of Thora, La Henderson, dam of Ferida, Lemonade, dam of Saunterer, Lady Motley, dam of Blazes, Lark, dam of Harry Hill, Mattie Gross, dam of Grenada and Mate, Veritas, Waltz, dam of Glidelia, Item, dam of Sparling, Ada Cheatham, dam of Lida Stanhope, Hira, dam of Himyar, Lady Wallenstein, dam of Wallenstein, Mollie Wood, dam of Sagamore, Georgia Bowman, dam of Lucy May, Paris Belle, Mazurka, dam of Zoo Zoo, Skylight, Mollie Cad, La Rose, Mundane, The Banshee, Springbrook, grandam of Checkmate, Sarong, dam of Aristides, Cordelia, Blunder, Edeny, Nannie Butler, Jury, dam of Passaic, Kentucky Belle, Lute, dam of Virginius, Fanny Cheatham, Bonnet, Minnie Minor, dam of Warwick, Morlachi, Carrie Atherton, and others too numerous to mention. His daughters have made the reputation of nearly all the stallions in the country and his sons are not failures as evidenced by the breeding of the daughters of Jack Malone, Asteroid and Kingfisher. The difficulty is that they have not had access to the blood and could not with the views of breeders get the best mares. Lexington was a blood bay, standing 15¾ hands high, with four white feet above the ankles, a large star and white strip down the face, extending over the upper lip. He was not only the best race-horse America has ever produced, but the emperor of stallions. He died July 1st, 1875, in the Woodburn stud, having lived until two of his sons sold for more than was given for him, $15,000, Norfolk $15,001, Duke of Magenta $20,000. The blood is worthy of preservation, and this can only be done by some in breeding.

PHAETON (Imp.)

PHAETON, by King Tom, son of Harkaway, bred by Mr. J. Johnstone, foaled 1865, dam Merry Sunshine, by Storm, son of Touchstone. As a race-horse Phaeton from some unknown cause was a failure. Started once as a two-year old, ran third in the Findon Stakes, three-quarters of a mile, at Goodwood, to Rabican and Vale Royal, beating Ajax, Tibicen, False Alarm, Elmira and Madrid. At three years old, started once in plate for three-year olds, Rowley mile (one mile 17 yards), at Newmarket First Spring Meeting; was unplaced, Vale Royal winning, with Hipp a second. This ended his turf career. His success in the stud was phœnominal, he got race-horses from all kinds of mares and every variety of blood, but those from the daughters of Lexington and Vandal were his best. The first, two, or three years he covered but few mares, but in 1872 he sired King Alfonso, Ten Broeck, Katie, Phœbe Mayflower, Phyllis, St. Martin, Tolona and Aramis. King Alfonso won the Tobacco Stakes at Louisville, mile heats 1:44½, 1:45½. The Kentucky St. Leger, 2 miles in 3:34½, beating Ten Broeck, Geo. Graham and others; and The Galt House Stake, 2 mile heats in 3:34, 3:40½, 3:49, beating Geo. Graham, who won the first heat by a head from King Alfonso, Emma C and three others. Ten Broeck ran and won in and out of condition, he won many of the prominent stakes, and has the fastest mile on record 1:39¾, the fastest two miles 3:27½, three miles in 5:31 and 5:26½, the third best on record, and the fastest four miles in the world, 7:15¾. Tolona won 1½ miles in 2:38¾, 2 miles in 3:36½, and 2¼ miles in 4:35½. Phyllis won 1½ miles in 2:37½, and 1¼ miles with 151 lbs. in 2:01. St. Martin won 2 miles in 3:37¾, and was winner at four miles. Aramis, Phœbe Mayflower and Katie were all winners in fast time. He also sired Jack Hardy, Belle Barclay, King Faro, winner of the Dixie stake, Lisbon, Felicia, winner of the Kentucky Oaks and Woodburn stakes, Patriot, Kinlock, Harry Peyton, Wheeler, Emma G, The Nipper, Carrie Anderson and other good winners. Phaeton stood full 16 hands high, and

Continued on page 202.

The Horse-Breeders' Guide and Hand Book.

PEDIGREE OF PHAETON (Imp.)

							Name	Description
PHAETON (Imp.)	KING TOM.	Harkaway.	Economist.	Florantie Whisker			Waxy.	Pot-8-os—Maria by Herod—Lisette by Snap—Miss Windsor by Godol. Arabian—Sis. to Volunteer by Y. Belgrade—Dau. of Bart. Childers.
							Penelope.	Trumpator—Prunella by Highflyer—Promise by Snap—Julia by Blank—Spectator's dam by Partner—Bonny Lass by Bay Bolton.
			Fanny Dawson.	Miss Tooley.	Nabocklish.		Octavian.	Stripling—Dau. of Oberon (Highflyer)—Sis. to Sharper by Ranthos—Dau. of Sweepstakes—Sis. to Careless by Spanker—Barb. Mare.
							Caprice.	Anvil (Herod)—Madcap by Eclipse—Dau. of Blank—Dau. of Blaze (F. Childers)—Dau. of Y. Greyhound—Dau. of Bartlet's Childers.
		Pocahontas.	Glencoe.	Sultan.			Rugantino.	Commodore (Tug) (Rover by Herod)—Smallhopes by Scaramouch (Snap)—Dau. of Blank—Dau of Traveler—Dau. of Ancaster Starling.
							Butterfly.	Master Bagot—Dau. of Bagot (Herod)—Mother Brown by Trunnion—Dau. of Old England—Dau. of Bolton Starling.
							Teddy the Grinder.	Asparagus (Pot-8-os)—Stargazer by Highflyer—Miss West by Matchem—Dau. of Regulus—Dau. of Crab—Dau. of F. Childers.
							Lady Jane.	Sir Peter—Paulina by Florizel—Captive by Matchem—Calliope by Slouch Lass of the Mill by Oroonoko—Dau of Traveler.
							Selim.	Buzzard—Castrel's dam by Alexander (Eclipse)—Dau. of Highflyer—Dau. of Alfred (Bro. to Conductor)—Dau. of Engineer.
							Bacchante.	Williamson's Ditto—Sis. to Calomel by Mercury—Dau. of Herod—Folly by Marske—Vixen by Regulus—Dau. of Hutton's Spot.
			Marpessa.	Muley.	Tramp-oline.		Tramp.	Dick Andrews—Dau. of Gohanna—Fraxinella by Trentham—Dau. of Woodpecker—Everlasting by Eclipse—Hyaena.
							Web.	Waxy—Penelope by Trumpator—Prunella by Highflyer—Promise by Snap—Julia by Blank—Spectator's dam.
				Clare.			Orville.	Beningbrough—Evelina by Highflyer—Termagant by Tantrum—Cantatrice by Sampson—Dau. of Regulus.
							Eleanor.	Whiskey—Y. Giantess by Diomed—Giantess by Matchem—Molly Longlegs by Babraham—Dau. of Cole's Foxhunter (Brisk).
							Marmion.	Whiskey—Y. Noisette by Diomed—Noisette by Squirrel—Carina by Marske—Dau. of Blank—An. Dizzy by Driver.
							Harpalice.	Gohanna—Amazon by Driver—Fractious by Mercury—Dau. of Woodpecker Everlasting by Eclipse—Hyaena by Snap.
	MERRY SUNSHINE.	Storm.	Touchstone.	Bauter.	Camel.		Whalebone.	Waxy—Penelope by Trumpator—Prunella by Highflyer—Promise by Snap—Julia by Blank—Spectator's dam.
							Daughter of.	Selim—Maiden by Sir Peter—Dau. of Phoenomenon—Matron by Florizel—Maiden by Matchem—Dau. of Squirt.
							Master Henry.	Orville—Miss Sophia by Stamford—Sophia by Buzzard—Huncamunca by Highflyer—Cypher by Squirrel—Dau. of Regulus.
							Boadicea.	Alexander—Brunette by Amaranthus—Mayfly by Matchem—Dau. of An. Starling—Dau. of Grasshopper (Crab).
			Ghuznee.	Panta-loon.			Castrel.	Buzzard—Selim's dam by Alexander—Dau. of Highflyer—Dau. of Alfred—Dau. of Engineer—Bay Malton's dam.
							Idalia.	Peruvian—Musidora by Meteor—Maid of All Work by Highflyer—Sis. to Tandem by Syphon—Dau. of Regulus (Godol.)
				Lan-guish.			Cain.	Paulowitz (Sir Paul)—Dau. of Paynator (Trumpator)—Dau. of Delpini—Dau. of Marske—Gentle Kitty by Silvio (Cade).
							Lydia.	Poultou (Sir Peter)—Variety by Hyacinthus (Coriander)—Dau. of Weasel (Herod)—Dau. of Turk (Reg.)—Dau. of Locust.
		Falstaff.	Touch-stone.	Decoy.			Camel.	Whalebone—Dau. of Selim—Maiden by Sir Peter—Dau. of Phoenomenon—Matron by Florizel—Maiden by Matchem (Cade).
							Banter.	Master Henry—Boadicea by Alexander—Brunette by Amaranthus—Mayfly by Matchem—Dau. of An. Starling—Dau. of Grasshopper.
							Filho-da-Puta.	Haphazard—Mrs. Barnet by Waxy—Dau. of Woodpecker—Heinel by Squirrel—Principessa by Blank—Dau. of Cul. Arabian.
							Finesse.	Peruvian (Sir Peter)—Violante by John Bull—Dau. of Highflyer—Everlasting by Eclipse—Hyaena by Snap—Miss Belsea by Regulus.
		Daughter of.	Emilius.				Orville.	Beningbrough—Evelina by Highflyer—Termagant by Tantrum—Cantatrice by Sampson—Dau. of Regulus—Marske's dam by Blacklegs.
							Emily.	Stamford—Dau. of Whiskey—Gr. Dorimant by Dorimant—Dizzy by Blank—Dizzy by Driver—Dau. of Smiling Tom—Dau. of Oysterfoot.
		Sister to Pompey.	Vari-ation.				Bustard.	Castrel—Miss Hap by Shuttle—Sis. to Haphazard by Sir Peter—Dau. of Eclipse—Clio by Y. Cade—Dau. of Starling—Dau. of Bart. Childers.
							Johannah Southcote.	Beningbrough (King Fergus)—Lavinia by Pipator (Imperator)—Dick Andrew's dam by Highflyer—Dau. of Cardinal Puff (Babraham by Godol.) Dau. of Tatler (Blank)—Dau. of Snip (Flying Childers)—Dau. of Godol. Arabian—Dau. of Frampton's Whiteneck—Dau. of Pelham Barb.

PHAETON Imp.—Continued.

weighed, when in condition, over 1,300 lbs. He had a remarkably neat head, ear and good, strong, well-shaped neck, great breadth of forehead and width of jaw. His shoulders were oblique and well placed, with muscle well distributed over a broad shoulder-blade, great depth of girth; well shaped, round barrel, ribbed home to strong, broad, muscular hips; his back and loin a model of strength; great length from the point of the hip to the whirlbone, and thence to stifle and hocks. Cut him off at his knees, and it would have been difficult to find a more perfect model of shape, strength and muscular development. But his legs were very defective, and particularly light below the knee for such an immense carcass. None of his descendants have had legs. He was a handsomely bred horses. In addition to his double cross of Touchstone, he had the Glencoe, Whalebone and Whisker blood upon the foundation of Herod, Eclipse and Matchem. He died the property of Richard Ten Broeck in the spring of 1874, just as his value as a stallion was established, and in the zenith of his fame; the blood, conformation and constitution of this great horse should be preserved.

SIR ARCHY.

SIR ARCHY, by imp. Diomed, son of Florizel by Herod, bred by Col. John Tayloe, Mt. Acry, Va., foaled 1805, dam imp. Castianira, by Rockingham, son of Highflyer, by Herod. Sir Archy, although bred in Virginia, was from imported English sources on both sides. Castianira, his dam, was imported when three year old by Col. Tayloe, in 1799, and ran successfully in Virginia. Sir Archy was her second foal, and made his first appearance on the turf over the Fairfield Course, Va., in the sweepstakes, two mile heats; seven started; the race was won by True Blue, defeating Sir Archy, Wrangler, Virginius and others; no time. At Washington, D. C., he was distanced in a sweepstake by Bright Phoebus, own brother to Miller's Damsel, the dam of Am. Eclipse; no time. He was laboring under an attack of distemper in both of these races. Col. W. R. Johnson now purchased him, and the following spring, 1809, won the Post Stake at Fairfield, Va., distance and time not given. The following week he was defeated at Newmarket, Va., for the Club purse, four miles heats, by Wrangler, after a desperate struggle; no time given. In the fall of the same year he won the Jockey Club purse at Richmond, Va., four miles heats, defeating Wrangler, Ratray, Tom Tough and Minerva. Sir Archy took the lead and ran the first two miles in 3:46, very fast at that date, when the race was over, he almost walking over the score. The following week he distanced the field in the first heat of a four mile heat race at Newmarket, Va.; no time. In a fortnight he defeated Blank for the Jockey Club purse, four miles heats, at Scotland Neck, N. C., in 7:52—8:00. The following day he was purchased by A. J. Davie, the owner of Blank, for $5,000, and relegated to the Stud. As a sire he had no equal in his day. The most renowned of his get are Lady Lightfoot, Vanity, Reality, Timoleon, Sire of Boston, Virginian, Director, Sir Charles, Sir William, Muckle John, Henry, Kosciusco, Crusader, Rattler, Childers, Sumpter, Flirtilla, Flirtilla Jr., Janet, Contention, Carolinean, Napoleon, Tecumseh, Bertrand, Pacific, Saxe Weimer, Stockholder, Gohanna, Betsey and John Richards, Marion, Cherokee, Arab, Coquette, Tariff, Isabella, Phillis, Charlotte Temple, Virginia Taylor, Jemima Wilkerson, Sir Arthur, Lady Lagrange, Sally Hope, Industry, Merling, Sea Gull, Sir Archy of Transport, Sir Archy Montorio, Sir William of Transport, Giles Scroggins, Pilot (Wild Will of the Woods), Chas. Kemble, Herr and Fanny Cline, Cicero, sire of Trifle's dam, Garrison's Zinganee, Gabriella, Phoenomena, Sir Richard, Pandora, Lady Burton, Lawrence, Napoleon, Roanoke, Mark Anthony and many others. Sir Archy was inbred to Herod; Diomed, his sire, was by Florizel, son of Herod, and Rockingham, the sire of his dam, was by Highflyer, the best son of Herod, and he traces on both sides many times to the Godolphin and Darley Arabians through their best sons, Cade, Babraham, Blank, Gower Stallion, Regulus, Blaze, Flying and Bartlet's Childers. Sir Archy was a blood bay with no white except the heel of his right hind foot, full 16 hands high, his shoulders were unexceptional, very deep in his girth, back short and strong, arms and thighs long and muscular and bone large. He possessed both speed and bottom and remarkable constitution which he imparted to all his stock. The more of this blood we can get into our race-horses of the present day the better. He died on June 7th, 1833, full of honors and years, meriting the sobriquet of the "Godolphin Arabian of America."

PEDIGREE OF SIR ARCHY.

							Ancestor	Description
SIR ARCHY.	IMP. DIOMED.	Florizel.	Sister to Juno.	Spectator.	Daughter of.	Dau. of Cygnet.	Herod.	Partner.	Jigg—Sis. to Mixbury by Cur. Bay Barb—Dau. of Spot (Selaby Turk)—Dau. of Wh. Legged Lowther Barb—Old Vintner Mare.
							Cypron.	Meliora.	Fox (Clumsy)—Milkmaid by Sir Wm. Blacbet's Snail (Croft's Partner)—Dam the Shield's Galloway.
						Tartar.	Blaze.	Fly. Childers—Contederate Filly by Grey Grantham—Dau. of Duke of Rutland's Black Barb—Dau. of Bright's Roan.
							Selima.	Bethel's Arabian—Dau. of Graham's Champion (Harpur's Arabian)—Dau. of Darley Arabian—Dau. of Old Merlin (Bustler).
				Horatia.	Dau. of Crab.		Godol. Arabian.	The most famous of all the Eastern sires—Purchased in Paris by Mr. Coke. Died property of Earl Godolphin in 1753.
							Blossom.	Crab—Dau. of Fl. Childers—Miss Belvoir by Gr. Grantham—Dau. of Paget Turk—Betty Leedes by Leedes' Arabian—Dau. of Spanker.
							Cartouch.	The Bald Galloway—Dau. of Hampt. Ct. Crippled Barb—Dau. of Makeless—Dau. of Brimmer—Dau. of Place's Wh. Turk—Dau. of Dodsworth.
							Ebony.	Flying Childers (Dar. Arabian)—Ebony by Basto (Byerly Turk)—Massey Mare by Mr. Massy's Black Barb.
					Dau. of Blank.		Alcock Arabian.	Was the sire of Crab, Spot and Gentleman, and the dam of Dismal and Trifle. He covered but few mares.
							Sis. to Sorebeels.	Basto—Sis. to Mixbury by Cur. Bay Barb—Dau. of Spot—Dau. of Wh. legged Lowther Barb—Old Vintner Mare.
							Partner.	Jigg—Sis. to Mixbury by Cur. Bay Barb—Dau. of Spot—Dau. of White-legged Lowther Barb—Old Vintner Mare.
							Bonny Lass.	Bay Bolton—Dau. of Dar. Arabian—Dau. of Byerly Turk—Dau. of Taffolet Barb—Dau. of Place's White Turk—Natural Barb Mare.
							Godol. Arabian.	The most famous of all the Eastern sires. Purchased in Paris by Mr. Coke. Died the property of Earl Godolphin in 1753.
							Little Hartley Mare.	Bart. Childers—Large Hartley Mare by His. Blind Horse—Flying Whig by Wm.'s Woodstock Arabian—Dau. of St. Victor Barb.
							Flying Childers.	Darley Arabian—Betty Leedes by Careless—Sis. to Leedes by Leedes' Arabian—Dau. of Spanker—Barb Mare dam of Spanker.
							Miss Belvoir.	Grey Grantham—Dau. of Paget Turk—Betty Percival by Leedes' Arabian Dau. of Spanker (Yellow Turk.)
	CASTIANIRA.	Rockingham.	Tabitha.	Trentham.	Sweepstakes.	Dau. of Matchem.	Rachel.	Herod.	Tartar.	Partner—Meliora by Fox—Milkmaid by Sir Wm. Blacket's Snail (Croft's Partner)—Dam the Shield's Galloway.
							Cypron.	Blaze—Selima by Bethell's Arabian—Dau. of Gra. Champion—Dau. of Darley Arabian—Dau. of Old Merlin (Bustler.)
		Illichfiyer.					Blank.	Godol. Arabian—Little Hartley Mare by Bartjet's Childers—Flying Whig by Woodstock Arabian—Dau. of St. Victor Barb—Dau. of Whyuot.
							Daughter of.	Regulus (Godol.)—Dau. of Sorebeels (Basto)—Dau. of Makeless (Oglethorpe Arabian)—C. D'Arcy's Royal Mare.
			Purity.				Cade.	Godol. Arabian—Roxana by the Bald Galloway—Sis. to Chanter by Akaster Turk—Dau. of Leede's Arabian—Dau. of Spanker.
							Daughter of.	Partuer—Dau. of Makeless—Dau. of Brimmer—Dau. of Place's White Turk—Dau. of Dodsworth—Layton Barb Mare.
				Miss South.			Squirt.	Bart. Childers—Sis. to Country Wench by Snake—Grey Wilkes by Hautboy—Miss D'Arcy's Pet Mare—Dau. of Sed. Royal Mare.
							Lot's dam.	Mogul—Camilla by Bay Bolton—Old Lady by Pullen's Ches. Arabian—Dau. of Rockwood—Dau. of Bustler.
							Gower Stallion.	Godol. Arabian—Dau. of Whitefoot—Lit. Hartley's Mare by Bartlet's Childers—Flying Whig by Wm.'s Woodstock Arabian.
							Daughter of.	Partner—Dau. of Makeless—Dau. of Brimmer (Yellow Turk)—Dau. of Place's White Turk—Dau. of Dodsworth—Layton Barb Mare.
							South.	Regulus (Godolphin)—Dau. of Sorebeels (Basto)—Dau. of Makeless (Oglethorpe Arabian)—D'Arcy Royal Mare.
							Daughter of.	Cartouche (Bald Galloway)—Ebony by Fly. Childers—Ebony by Basto (Byerly Turk)—Massey Mare by His. Black Barb.
		Daughter of.	Dau. of Bosphorus.				Babraham.	Godol. Arabian—Large Hartley Mare by Hartley's Blind Horse—Flying Whig by Wm'a Woodstock Arabian—Dau. of St. Victor Barb.
							Daughter of.	Hamp. Ct. Childers (Flying Childers)—Dau. of Leedes by Leed'es Arabian) Moonah Barb Mare.
							Wm.'s Forester.	Forester (Hartley's Blind Horse)—Dau. of Looby (Bay Bolton)—Margery by Partner—Dau. of Woodcock—Dau. of Makeless.
							Daughter of.	Coalition Colt (Godol.)—Dau. of Bustard (Crab)—Ld. Leigh's Charming Molly by Second (F. Childers)—Hanger's Brown Mare by Stanyan Arabian—Gipsey by King William's No-tongued Barb—Dau. of Makeless—Royal Mare.

VANDAL.

VANDAL by Glencoe, son of Sultan, bred by Dr. B. W. Dudley, Lexington, Ky., foaled 1850, dam Alario's dam by imp. Tranby, son of Blacklock. Vandal was a first-class race-horse, did not start as a two-year old, but came out the spring he was three years old, and was distanced the first heat, in the Association Stake, mile heats, won by Darley (Lexington), in 1:55¼, 1:57, the track was fetlock deep in mud, and the rain pouring down in sheets ; Louisville, Ky., won the Galt House Stake, mile heats, in 1:53, 1:53, 1:56, track very heavy, beating Ellen Bateman, Madonna, winner of the first heat, distanced in the third, and Campbell's bay colt by Altorf ; same meeting, ran second to Fanny Fern in sweepstake, mile heats, in 1:52¾, 1:53, track heavy ; Garret Davis, Wild Irishman, and Madonna behind him ; Mobile, Ala., won sweepstake for three-year olds, mile heats, beating Midway in 1:56¼, 1:57, track heavy ; New Orleans, ran second to Maid of Orleans in Club Purse, 2 miles, in 3:56, beating Betty King ; Lexington, Ky., Spring Meeting, 1854, won Club Purse, 3 mile heats, beating Mary Taylor, Lewis Wetzel and two others, in 5:42¼, 6:36¼ ; Louisville Ky., won Club Purse, 3 miles, in 5:46, beating Mary Taylor ; Lexington, Ky., Fall Meeting, ran third in fist heat for the Club Purse, 4 mile heats, won by Frankfort, in 7:41 ; Vandal was withdrawn. The spring of 1855 he came out and easily defeated Frankfort and Henry Perritt for the Club Purse, 3 mile heats, in 5:36½, 5:33, an excellent race. This closed his turf career. The first of his get which appeared were Ella D, Mollie Jackson and Jack the Barber, all were creditable performers ; Ella D won at 1, 2 and 3 mile heats ; Mollie Jackson was the best mare of any day, she won 4 miles, in 7:34, and 3 mile heats, in 5:35¼, 5:34¼, 5:28¾, this third heat is the fastest and best third heat ever run. Jack the Barber was also a creditable performer, as was also Seven Oaks, which won seven out of eight races. He covered very few mares, and for some five or six years none, and it was not until he passed into the hands of Gen. W. G. Harding, of the Belle Meade Stud, was he regularly used for stud purposes. He sired Versailles, a fine race-horse, Vergo, and Capitola, the dam of King Alfonso, Coral, the dam of Wanderer and Uncas, Virgil, the sire of Vigil, Vera Cruz and the great Hindoo. In the Belle Meade Stud he made his great reputation ; those by him in this stud were Vicksburg, Vanderbilt, Vassal, Nettie B, Ventilator, sire of Mary Anderson, Vaultress, Vagabond, Valentine, Van Leer, Van Dorn, Vindicator, Vortex, Volcano, Valerian, dam of Boatman ; Voltigeur, winner of the Clark Stake at Louisville, defeating Calvin and ten others ; Vinaigrette, winner of the Kentucky Oaks, Vidette, dam of Camargo, winner of the Fall's City Stake, mile heats, in 1:42½, 1:43¼, and Vandalite, one of the best race-mares which ever faced the starter, winner of the Dixie Stakes at Baltimore, 2 miles in 3:35½, beating Madge, Brigand and twelve others, and taking up the penalty of 5 lbs.; won the Breckenridge Stakes, 2 miles in 3:35 ; the best time in which the two races were ever run ; Newburn, (Council Bluffs), Survivor, Highland Vintage, Grey Steel (Grey Friar), Sallie Gardner, Vocalist, and many others. Vandal was a blood bay, with little or no white, 15¾ hands high, and was the best son of the great Glencoe, and has proved himself a worthy son of a worthy sire. He died at Belle Meade early in the spring of 1872, just as his reputation had been established, and shown to the world that he had not disgraced his high racing lineage, from which the great Lexington had descended. The Glencoe blood has done wonders in England through old Pocahontas, and it should be preserved and perpetuated through his best son and daughters in America.

The Horse Breeders' Guide and Hand Book.

PEDIGREE OF VANDAL.

VANDAL.	IMP. GLENCOE.	Sultan.	Bacchante.	Selim.	Castrel's dam.	Woodpecker.	Herod (Tartar)—Miss Ramsden by Lonsdale Bay Arabian—Dau. of Bay Bolton—Dau. of Darley Arabian—Dau. of Byerly Turk.
						Misfortune.	Dux (Matchem)—Curiosity by Snap (Snip)—Dau. of Regulus (Godol.)—Dau. of Bartlet's Childers (Darley Arabian)—Dau. of Hon. Arabian.
				William son's Ditto	Dick Andrews.	Alexander.	Eclipse (Marske)—Grecian Princess by Wm's Forester—Dau. of Coalition Colt (Godol.)—Dau. of Bustard (Crab)—Charming Molly.
				Sister to Calomel.		Daughter of.	Highflyer (Herod)—Dau. of Alfred (Matchem)—Dau of Engineer (Sampson)—Bay Malton's dam by Cade (Godol.)—Lass of the Mill.
		Trampoline.	Tramp.			Sir Peter.	Highflyer—Papillon by Snap—Miss Cleveland by Regulus—Midge by Son of Bay Bolton—Dau. of Bartlet's Childers.
						Arethusa.	Dungannon (Eclipse)—Dau. of Prophet (Regulus)—Virago by Snap—Dau. of Regulus—Sis. to Othello by Crab—Miss Slamerkin by Y. True Blue.
					Dau. of	Mercury.	Eclipse—Dau of Tartar (Partner)—Dau. of Mogul (Godol.)—Dau. of Sweepstakes (Oxford Arabian)—Dau. of Bay Bolton—Dau. of Cur. Bay Barb.
					Wary.	Daughter of.	Herod—Folly by Marske—Vixen by Regulus—Dau. of Hutton's Spot—(Hartley's Blind Horse)—Dau. of Bay Bolton.
			Web.	Penelope.		Joe Andrews.	Eclipse—Amaranda by Omnium (Snap)—Cloudy by Blank (Godol.)—Dau. of Crab (Alcock Arabian)—Widdrington Mare by Partner.
						Daughter of.	Highflyer—Dau. of Cardinal Puff (Babraham)—Dau. of Tatler (Blank)—Dau. of Snip (Childers)—Dau. of Godol. Arabian.
						Gohanna.	Mercury—Dau. of Herod—Maiden by Matchem—Dau. of Squirt (Bartlet's Childers—Dau. of Mogul—Dau of Bay Bolton.
						Fraxinella.	Trentham (Sweepstakes)—Dau. of Woodpecker—Everlasting by Eclipse—Hyaena by Snap—Miss Belsea by Regulus.
						Pot-8-o's.	Eclipse—Sportsmistress by Warren's Sportsman (Cade)—Golden Locks by Oroonoko (Crab)—Valiant's dam by Crab.
						Maria.	Herod—Lisette by Snap—Miss Windsor by Godol. Arabian—Sis. to Volunteer by Y. Belgrade (Belgrade Turk)—Dau. of Bartlet's Childers.
						Trumpator.	Conductor (Matchem)—Brunette by Squirrel (Traveler)—Dove by Matchless (Godol.)—Dau. of Ancaster Starling).
						Prunella.	Highflyer—Promise by Snap—Julia by Blank—Spectator's dam by Partner (Jigg)—Dau. of Bay Bolton—Dau. of Darley Arabian.
	ALARIC'S DAM.	Lucilla.	Trumpator.	Blacklock.	White-lock.	Hambletonian.	King Fergus (Eclipse)—Moumia by Matchem—Dau. of Alcides (Babraham)—Dau. of Crab—Snap's dam by Fox.
						Rosalind.	Phoenomenon (Herod)—Atalanta by Matchem (Cade)—Lass of the Mill by Oroonoko—Dau. of Traveler (Partner)—Miss Makeless by Y. Greyound.
				Imp. Tranby.	Dau. of Orville.	Coriander.	Pot-8-os—Lavender by Herod—Dau. of Snap—Miss Roan by Cade—Madame by Bloody Buttocks—Dau. of Partner.
						Wild-Goose.	Highflyer—Coheiress by Pot-8-os—Mauilla by Goldfinder (Snap)—Dau. of Old England (Godol.)—Dau. of Cullen Arabian.
				Daughter of.		Beningbrough.	King Fergus—Dau. of Herod—Pyrrha by Matchem—Duchess by Whitenose (Hall Arabian)—Miss Slamerkin by Y. True Blue.
						Evelina.	Highflyer—Termagant by Tantrum (Cripple)—Dau. of Sampson (Greyhound)—Dau. of Regulus—Marske's dam by Blacklegs.
				Miss Grimstone.		Weasel.	Herod—Dau. of Eclipse—Dau. of Brilliant (Florizel)—Dau. of Shepherd's Crab (Crab)—Dau. of Godol. Arabian.
						Daughter of.	Ancaster (Blank)—Dau. of Damascus Arabian—Dau. of Sampson—Dau. of Oroonoko—Sophia by Godol. Arabian.
		Lucy.	Sir Solomon.			Imp. Tickle Toby	Alfred (Matchem)—Caclia by Herod—Proserpine, Sis. to Eclipse by Marske (Squirt)—Spiletta by Regulus—Mother Western.
						Vesta.	Dreadnought (Meade's Celer)—Bandy by Imp. Clockfast (Gimcrack)—Dau. of Americus (Imp. Shark)—Dau. of Imp. Fearnought.
			Dau. of			Hickory.	Imp. Whip (Saltram)—Dido by Imp. Dare Devil (Magnet)—Dau. of Symme's Wildair (Imp. Fearnought)—Dau. of Imp. Clockfast.
						Imp. Trumpetta.	Trumpator (Conductor)—Sis. to Lambinos by Highflyer—Dau. of Eclipse—Vauxhall, Snap's dam by Cade—Dau. of Bolton Littlejohn.
		Orphan.				Ball's Florizel.	Imp. Diomed—Dau. of Imp. Shark (Marske)—Dau. of Harris' Eclipse Partner)—Dau. of Imp. Fearnought (Regulus)—Dau. of Sober John.
						Fair Rachel.	Imp. Diomed (Florizel)—Susan Jones by Imp. Shark (Marske)—Dau. of Thornton's Wildair (Symme's Wildair).
		Lady Grey.	Dau. of Grey.			Robin Grey.	Imp. Royalist (Saltram)—Belle Mariab by Grey Diomed (Imp. Medley)—Queen by Imp. St. George (Dragon)—Dau. of Cassius—Primrose.
						Maria.	Melzar (Imp. Medley)—Dau. of Imp. Highflyer—Dau. of Imp. Fearnought—Dau. of Ariel (Imp. Traveler)—Dau. of Imp. Jack of Diamonds (Cullen Arabian)—Imp. Diamond by Cullen Arabian—Lady Thigh by Croft's Partner (Jigg)—Dau. of Greyhound (White Barb Chillaby)—Sophonisba's dam by Curwen Bay Barb—Dan. of D'Arcy's Chestnut Arabian—Dau of Whitesbirt—Old Montague Mare

www.ingramcontent.com/pod-product-compliance
Lightning Source LLC
Chambersburg PA
CBHW031831230426
43669CB00009B/1305